Professional SQL Server 2000 DTS

Mark Chaffin
Brian Knight
Todd Robinson

with

Cary Beuershausen
Robin Dewson
Trey Johnson

Wrox Press Ltd. ®

Professional SQL Server 2000 DTS

wrox

Published by Wrox Press Ltd,
Arden House, 1102 Warwick Road, Acocks Green,
Birmingham, B27 6BH, UK
Printed in the United States
ISBN 1-861004-41-9

Trademark Acknowledgements

Credits

Authors
Mark Chaffin
Brian Knight
Todd Robinson

Additional Material
Cary Beuershausen
Robin Dewson
Trey Johnson

Technical Reviewers
Terry Allen
Robin Dewson
Derek Fisher
Damien Foggon
Scott Hanselman
Hope Hatfield
Trey Johnson
Frank Miller
Paul Morris
Upen Patel
David Schultz

Category Manager
Bruce Lawson

Development Editor
Dominic Lowe

Technical Architect
Tony Davis

Technical Editors
Catherine Alexander
Claire Brittle
Peter Morgan
Lisa Stephenson

Author Agent
Tony Berry

Project Administrators
Cilmara Lion
Chandima Nethisinghe

Production Coordinator
Tom Bartlett

Figures
Shabnam Hussain

Cover
Shelley Frazier

Proof Reader
Christopher Smith

About the Authors

Mark Chaffin

Mark Chaffin is Data Warehouse Architect for Encore Development (http://www.encoredev.com) and has developed numerous decision support systems for clients in such industries as technology, mortgage banking, retail, sports statistics, financial services, and insurance. He also has experience in clickstream analytics, data mining, transactional application architecture, Internet application architecture, database administration, and database design.

I'd like to thank my wife, Carol, who's been incredibly supportive during this process, and to my son Ben, who's smile and laughter always puts things in perspective.

I'd also like to thank my friends and associates at Encore Development for their willingness to always lend an ear, especially Rob Dumoulin and Trey Johnson. Without their help, this would not have been possible.

Brian Knight

Brian Knight (MCSE, MCDBA) is a Senior Database Administrator at Alltel in Jacksonville, Florida, where he manages the mortgage enterprise database system. Brian focuses his developmental time on merging database technologies such as Oracle and DB2 into SQL Server, using DTS and OLAP. He also writes several weekly columns and co-runs the SQL Server area of Swynk.com (a BackOffice-focused Internet site) and writes columns for SQL Magazine.

Quite a few thanks are in order. First and foremost thanks needs to go to my wife for putting up with me disappearing for night after night when deadlines got tight. Thanks Jenn for also reading my chapters even though you didn't understand a word of what you were reading. This book is dedicated to you, who were the real reason my part was done on time. A huge 'thanks!' needs to go to my boss at Alltel, David Page, for putting up with a tired and uncoordinated employee during the writing of this book. The development editor, Dominic, deserves special thanks for giving this book idea a chance and breaking the mold. Finally, thanks go to the Tonys (Tony Berry and Tony Davis) and the other editors for pulling all this together into something that has cohesion. Finally, I would like to thank the Pepsi Cola Company for providing me with enough Mountain Dew to make it through the late nights of writing this book. I alone have caused a severe shortage of caffeine drinks in Jacksonville and sincerely apologize.

Todd Robinson

Todd Robinson (MCP, MCP+I, MCP+SB, MCSE, MCSE+I, MCSD, MCDBA, MCT, CCNA) lives in Atlanta, Georgia, where he is an Internet application developer and data-warehousing guru for MetLife. He specializes in COM+, ASP, XML, SQL Server, and related Microsoft .net technologies. In addition to his normal job duties at MetLife, he is President of GradesNow.com, an Internet application service provider for the education community. GradesNow.com allows teachers, students and parents to communicate with one another and show grades online via a web browser.

I have to thank my wife Eileen for enduring all the late nights I worked on this book, especially those days that I would go to bed the same time you would wake to go teach. Without your support, this book would not be possible. I would also like to thank the wonderful people at Wrox, especially Dominic for giving me this opportunity to help write this book. It is really a thrill to be writing a book for a company that puts out the best programmer reference books in the world. In addition, the editors of this book, especially Peter Morgan and Lisa Stephenson, are to be commended for their hard work in getting this book to press.

I would also like to thank my friend David Sandor, who instilled in me all the knowledge I seldom use, and for picking up the slack when I was mired in writing. Also thanks go to Mark Cochran for supplying me all the hardware to run seven different versions of Windows and SQL all at once. I would like to thank Randy Rhude and Karen Olson at MetLife, who gave me the opportunity to learn and develop my skills with DTS enough to write a book about it. Finally I wish to thank Sergey Dvinin, the object master, for the VB help in the final chapter.

This book is dedicated to my wife Eileen, my cat Nikki, and my dog Sidney, who took shifts staying up with me while writing this book. After thousands of cups of caffeinated beverages and three lint brushes, its finally finished.

Cary Beuershausen

Cary Beuershausen is a Client/Server Programming Consultant in the Internet Solutions group at Alltel (http://www.alltelmd.com) in Jacksonville, Florida. He has developed and implemented document management and workflow solutions in the education, legal, finance, and government sectors. His most recent work has been related to mortgage servicing and Electronic Bill Presentment and he's looking forward to providing B2B solutions in the mortgage industry with ASP, XML, and just about any other acronym he can find.

Cary's tools of choice are Borland Delphi and Microsoft Visual Basic with a dose of SQL Server thrown in for good measure. In addition to being a full-time programmer, he has also found himself in the classroom teaching VBScript training classes that he developed. He has been pounding out code since his dad brought home a Timex Sinclair ZX-81 many, many years ago and he felt the rush of getting the computer to do what he told it to. Now he gets pumped up trying to figure out how to use the word "polymorphism" in every conversation.

I especially want to thank God for blessing me with the ability He has, my wife Jennifer for putting up with my exceedingly long hours at the computer, our wonderful dog Sandy for staying up with me, and my family for always supporting me.

Robin Dewson

Robin started out on the Sinclair ZX80 (but failing to run a power station, as they claimed), then worked his way through the ZX81 and Spectrum to studying computers at the Scottish College of Textiles, where he was instilled with the belief that mainframes were the future. After many years, he eventually saw the error of his ways and started using Clipper, FoxPro, and Visual Basic. Robin is currently working on a trading system called "Kojak" in a large US investment bank in London, and it was here that he owes a massive debt to Annette Kelly, Daniel Tarbotton, and Andy "I don't really know, I've only been here a week" Sykes for giving him his "big break".

I would like to thank all at Wrox for putting up with me over the years, especially to Tony Berry for sticking with me, Cilmara Lion for being so nice and supportive, and the DTS team for their faith. I would like to dedicate this to my family, who as usual has been very supportive in all my work. To Scott, a future International rugby star, Cameron a future Olympic Equestrian Gold Medallist, little Ellen "catch that kiss daddy?", who keeps her two big brothers in their place, but especially to my long-suffering wife, Julie. The most perfect mother I could ever have married.

"Up the Blues"

Trey Johnson

Trey Johnson is an international data-warehousing speaker and data-warehousing consultant employed by Encore Development, a provider of web-powered business solutions for Fortune 1000 and mid-market organizations.

Trey has been delivering technology solutions with Microsoft SQL Server since version 4.x. Since this start, Trey's love of data and databases has grown and led him to enterprise multi-terrabyte databases on the Microsoft SQL Server 2000 platform, leveraging the power of technologies like DTS. During the course of his career, Trey has utilized SQL Server and transformation technologies, like DTS, in the delivery of comprehensive Decision Support Solutions for diverse industries such as Health Care, Industrial Warehousing, Financial organizations, Retail, and other service firms.

Thanks to the Wrox team of editors and authors who gave me an opportunity to contribute and share what I know. A special thanks to Mom, Dad, Tori, KayBeth, and Alyssa who have always shown support me in anything I do. Thanks are surely not enough for the joys of my life, Andrea and Preston (growing up way too quick by the way), who undoubtedly make my life complete!

Table of Contents

Introduction   **1**

  Who Should Read this Book   **1**

  How to Get the Most from this Book   **2**

  What's Covered in this Book   **2**

  Conventions Used   **3**

  Customer Support   **4**
    Source Code   4
    Errata   4
    p2p.wrox.com   4

Chapter 1: Welcome to DTS   **7**

  The Next Generation in Database Solutions   **8**
    What is OLE DB?   9

  The DTS Package   **10**
    Connections   11
    Tasks   12
    Steps   12
    Global Variables   13
    A Simple Package   13

  What's New in 2000?   **14**

  The DTS Toolbox   **15**
    Using the Wizards   16
    Transferring Data Using the Import/Export Wizard   16
      Accessing the Wizard   16
      Choosing the Destination Database   19
      Copy Tables and Views Option   20
      Saving and Scheduling the Package   24
      Naming and Executing the Package   26
      Using Queries to Transfer Data   27
      Query Builder   29
      Transferring SQL Objects   32
      Transferring SQL Objects Continued   34
    The Copy Database Wizard (CDW)   36
      Accessing the Copy Database Wizard   36
      Specifying Items and Executing the Package   38
    The DTS Designer   41
      Accessing the DTS Designer   41
      Viewing DTS Packages   42

A Note About NT Authentication Security   **43**

Summary   **44**

Chapter 2: DTS Fundamentals   47

DTS Designer   **47**

Tasks Available in SQL Server 2000   **49**

ActiveX Script Task	49
Transform Data Task	50
Execute Process Task	51
Execute SQL Task	51
Copy SQL Server Objects Task	51
Send Mail Task	51
Bulk Insert Task	51
Data Driven Query Task	52
Execute Package Task	52
Transfer Error Messages Task	52
Transfer Master Stored Procedures Task	53
Transfer Jobs Task	53
Transfer Logins Task	53
Transfer Databases Task	53
Dynamic Properties Task	53
File Transfer Protocol Task	53
Message Queue Task	54
Custom Tasks	54

Creating a DTS Package   **54**
  Making the Connections   54
  Inserting the Data Pump Task   56
  Precedence Constraints   62
  Saving Packages   65
    Where to Save your Package?   66
    Loading a Package   67
    Version Control   67
  Executing Packages   68
    The Dtsrun Utility   69
    The Dtsrunui Utility   71
    Scheduling a Package Using SQL Server Agent   72

Logging DTS Activity   **75**

Global Variables   **77**
  Scope of Global Variables   77
    Creating a Global Variable using the DTS Designer   78

The Bulk Insert Task   **79**

The Execute Process Task   **85**

The Execute SQL Task   **86**

The Copy SQL Server Objects Task   **90**

The Send Mail Task   **92**

The Transfer Error Messages Task   **93**

The Transfer Databases Task   **94**

The Transfer Master Stored Procedures Task   **94**

The Transfer Jobs Task   **95**

The Transfer Logins Task   **95**
    Disconnected Edit   96

DTS Interoperability   **96**

Developer Samples   **97**

Summary   **98**

Chapter 3: Advanced Tasks   **101**

The Multiphase Data Pump   **102**
  Multiphase Data Pump Example   105
    Pre Source Example   113
    Row Transform Example   115
    Post Row Transform Example   116
    On Batch Complete Example   118
    Post Source Data Example   118
    On Pump Complete Example   119

Table of Contents

Data Driven Query (DDQ)   **120**
    Data Driven Query Example   120

Dynamic Properties Task   **127**

File Transfer Protocol Task   **128**
    Configuring the FTP Task   129
    Dynamic Properties Task   131
    Dynamic Properties Task Example   132

Execute Package Task   **140**
    Execute Package Task Example   141
        Setting Global Variables   142
        Executing and Debugging the Task   144

Message Queue Task   **145**
    Receiving Messages   148

Summary   **151**

Chapter 4: Advanced Settings in DTS   **153**

Advanced Package Options   **154**
    Lineage   155
        Saving Data to Meta Data Services   156
    Scanning Options   158
    Transactions   161
        ACID Properties   161
        Setting Up a New Package Transaction   162
        Inherited Transactions   165
        Transaction Isolation Levels   166
    OLE DB   168

General Package Properties   **169**
    Parallelism   169
    Assigning Priorities to Tasks   171

Transform Data Task Options   **173**
    Exception File   174
    Data Movement Options   176
        Max Error Count   176
        First and Last Row Setting   177
        Fetch Buffer Size   177
        Data Movement Options Example   177
    SQL Server Options   186
        Use Fast Load   186

Data Scrubbing   **188**

DTS Lookup   **191**
    Setting Up a Data Lookup   192

Common Errors   **201**

Date Time Conversion   201

Importing from Excel   202

Target Table Has an Identity   203

Error Handling   203

Choosing an Error File   203

Fail Package on First Error   204

Summary   **204**

Chapter 5: Querying Heterogeneous Data   **207**

Heterogeneous Data   **207**

What are Linked Servers?   208

Remote Servers   209

Putting it All Together   210

Adding a Linked Server   **212**

Creating a Linked Server   212

Adding a Linked Server in Enterprise Manager   212

Creating a Linked Server in Transact-SQL   214

Creating a Linked Server on a Single Server   216

Linked Server Security   216

Linked Server Security in Enterprise Manager   217

Linked Server Security in Transact-SQL   218

Other Linked Server Options   219

Data Access   219

Allowing Stored Procedures on a Linked Server   220

Collation   220

Setting Options in Enterprise Manager   221

Using Linked Servers   **221**

Querying a Linked Server   221

Executing a Stored Procedure   222

Viewing Servers and Tables   223

Gathering Meta Data Using Transact-SQL   224

Using sp_linkedservers   225

Gathering Remote Database Information   225

Gathering Remote Table Information   225

Gathering Remote Column Information   226

Gathering Remote Security Information   227

Gathering Remote Key and Index Information   228

Pass-Through Queries   230

Linked Servers at Run Time   231

Deleting a Linked Server   232

Linked Server Limitations   **233**

Summary   **233**

Table of Contents

Chapter 10: Security and DTS   367

Locking Down the msdb Database   368
Windows Authentication   368
SQL Server Authentication   369
    SQL Server Out-Of-The-Box Security   369
Scheduled Package Security   371

DTS Password Protection   373
Owner Password   374
User Password   375

Meta Data Services   375
Meta Data Is Abstract   375
Meta Data Has Context   375

Auditing with the Microsoft Meta Data Services   376

Backing Up Your Databases   382
Backing Up the msdb Database   383
    Using Enterprise Manager   384
    Using Transact-SQL   388
    Using a Backup Maintenance Plan   389

Summary   399

Chapter 11: Error Handling   401

DTS Errors   401
DTS Designer Error Handling   402

Package-Level Auditing and Error Handling   403
Package Auditing   403
    Viewing Logs   404
    Programmatic Logging   407
Package Error Handling   409
    Error File   409
    Event Log   410

Task Object Error Handling   410
Scripting Error Handling   411
    DTSStepScriptResult   412
    Restart/Retry a Workflow   414
    Programmatically Choose to Execute a Step   415
    Set Task Properties   415
    Implement Loops   415
    Initialize Global Variables   416
    DTSTaskExecResult   416
    DTSTransformStatus   417

Error Handling from External Applications   420
dtsrun – Command Line Execution   421
Executing from Visual Basic   421

Design Considerations for Optimal Error Handling   **423**

Multiple Precedence Constraints   424
GetExecutionErrorInfo   425
Putting It All Together   426

Summary   **429**

Chapter 12: Writing Your Own Custom Tasks   **431**

What is a Custom Task?   **432**

Why Use a Custom Task?   **432**

Functionality Not Possible from an ActiveX Script   432
Code Maintenance/Reuse   432
Ease of Use for Non-Programmers   433
Encapsulation of Business Logic   433
Security   433
Performance   433
Profit   433

The Task Object Model   **433**

The CustomTask Interface   434

Building Your First Custom Task   **437**

Registering and Using a Custom Task   439
Building the DLL   439
Registering the Task in DTS   440
Running the Task   441
Unregistering a Task   441

More About Custom Tasks   **442**

The CustomTaskUI Interface   442

How DTS Uses a Custom Task   **445**

Design Time   445
Run Time   445
Design vs. Run Time   445
Common Situations   445

Building a Complex Custom Task   **447**

Steps to Build   448
CustomTaskUI Interface   449
CustomTask Interface   452
Adding the User Interface   460
Adding the Final Touch   468
The End Result   469
Execute on Main Thread   471

Debugging a Custom Task   **472**

Summary   **473**

Table of Contents

Chapter 13: Data Warehouse Loading   475

Data Warehousing Basics and Terminology   476
What is a Data Warehouse?   476
Dimensional Modeling   477
     Star Schemas   477
     Snowflake   478
     Star versus Snowflake   479
     Hybrid Star/Snowflake Designs   479
     OLTP versus OLAP   480
     Data Warehouses versus Data Marts   482

Creating a Dimensional Data Model   483
Issues to Consider   484
     Identify Clear Subject Areas   484
     Choose the Grain of Facts   484
     Identify Dimensions   484
     Choose the Time Context of Facts   484
     Surrogate Keys   485
     Suggested Reading   485

Creating a Solid ETL Design   486
Purpose of the ETL   486
Extract   486
Transform   486
     Formatting   486
     Surrogate Key Lookup   487
Load   487
     Bulk Mode   487
     Batch Mode   487
     Single Row Mode   487
Incremental versus Full Reloads   488
Data Transformation Document   488

From Source to Stage   489
Data Acquisition   490
     Linked Servers   490
Staging Area Physical Design   490
     Get In and Get Out   490
     Using File Groups in Staging   491
     Drop Indexes Before Loading   491
     Stage Definition – Extraction   491
     Stage Definition – Transformation   492
     Row-by-Row   492
     Set-Based Processing   493

From Stage to Warehouse   **496**
  Stored Procedures versus DTS Tasks   496
    Reusability   496
    Performance   496
    Suitability   496
  Indexing   497
    Stage   497
    Dimensions   497
    Facts   497
  Referential Integrity   497

Integrating Analysis Services   **497**
  Analysis Services Overview   498
  Incremental Processing   499

Summary   **501**

Chapter 14: Using DTS from Other Applications   **503**

Application Overview   **504**
  What Technologies Will We Be Using?   504
    SQL-DMO   504
    COM+   505
    ASP   505
    CDO   506
  What Tools Do You Need?   507
  Designing the Solution   508

Data Services   **509**
  Creating the Package List Table   510
  Creating the Package   510
  Populating the Table   512

Business Services   **512**
  Creating the DLL   513
    Coding the Package Class   514
    Compiling the Component   523
  Installing the Component in Component Services   523
    Creating the COM+ Application   523
    Adding the Component   526

User Services   **529**
  General Declarations   529
  Checking the QueryString   530
  Displaying the Packages   531
    The ShowPackages Subroutine   531
  Displaying the Properties   534

Putting It All Together   **535**
  Troubleshooting   538
  Taking Things Further   539

Summary   **539**

Table of Contents

Chapter 15: Warehouse Data Load — 541

Extract, Transformation and Load — 542

The Northwind Dimensional Data Model — 545

Some Terms You'll Need — 545
Orders Dimensional Model — 545
Order Items Dimensional Model — 547
Creating the Northwind_DW Database — 548
DDL — 549
  DIM_CALENDAR — 549
  DIM_CUSTOMER — 550
  DIM_EMPLOYEE — 551
  DIM_GEOGRAPHY — 552
  DIM_PRODUCT — 553
  DIM_SHIPPER — 553
  DIM_SUPPLIER — 554
  FACT_ORDER_ITEMS — 555
  FACT_ORDERS — 557
  Foreign Key Constraints — 558

The Northwind Staging Area Data Model — 561

DDL — 562
  STAGE_CUSTOMER — 562
  STAGE_EMPLOYEE — 563
  STAGE_GEOGRAPHY — 564
  STAGE_ORDER_ITEMS — 564
  STAGE_ORDERS — 565
  STAGE_PRODUCT — 566
  STAGE_SHIPPER — 567
  STAGE_SUPPLIER — 567

The Northwind ETL Auditing Data Model — 568

Jobs and Tasks — 568
DDL — 569
  AUDIT_JOB — 569
  AUDIT_TASK — 570
  Foreign Key Constraint — 570

Populating Default Values — 571

Time Dimension — 571
The Calendar Dimension — 572
All Other Dimensions — 573
  DIM_GEOGRAPHY — 573
  DIM_CUSTOMER — 574
  DIM_EMPLOYEE — 574
  DIM_SHIPPER — 574
  DIM_SUPPLIER — 574
  DIM_PRODUCT — 575

Microsoft Analysis Services — 575

Designing the ETL Workflow — **578**

ETL 1 (the Master Workflow Package) — 579
    Global Variables — 580
    Connections — 581
    Set Connection Values Task — 585
    Audit Information — 586
    Auditing/Error Handling — 589
    Executing Lower-Tier Packages — 599
    Write Job Completion Info — 599

ETL 2 — 601
    Creating the Package — 602
    Package Properties — 602
    Global Variables — 603
    Connections — 604
    Set Connection Values — 604
    Drop Stage Indexes — 606
    Extracting Dimension Information — 608
    Extracting Fact Information — 618
    Set Connection Values...Part 2 — 623
    Auditing and Error Handling — 625

ETL 3 — 626
    Creating the Package — 627
    Package Properties — 628
    Global Variables — 628
    Connections — 629
    Set Connection Values — 629
    Create Stage Indexes — 630
    Transforming and Loading Dimensions — 633
    Fact Cleansing — 646
    Auditing and Error Handling — 650

ETL 4 — 650
    Creating the Package — 651
    Package Properties — 651
    Global Variables — 651
    Connections — 652
    Set Connection Values — 653
    Fact Table Loads — 653
    Process Cubes — 669
    Auditing and Error Handling — 671

ETL 1 Revisited — 672

Answering Northwind's Business Questions — **673**

Northwind Analysis Services Database — 674
    Shared Dimensions — 674
    Orders Cube — 675
    Order Items Cube — 676

Analytical Questions — 677
    Who Are Northwind's Most Profitable Customers? — 681
    Which Regions Are Selling the Most Products? — 681

Summary — **683**

Table of Contents

TransferObjectsTask2   **732**

Transformation   **733**

Transformation2   **734**

TransformationInfo   **734**

TransformationInfos   **735**

Transformations   **735**

TransformationSet   **736**

TransformationSets   **737**

Global Constants   **738**

Appendix B: ADO Object Summary   741

Microsoft ActiveX Data Objects 2.6 Library Reference   **741**

The Objects   741
The Command Object   743
The Connection Object   744
The Error Object   746
The Errors Collection   746
The Field Object   747
The Fields Collection   748
The Parameter Object   748
The Parameters Collection   749
The Properties Collection   750
The Property Object   750
The Record Object   750
The Recordset Object   751
The Stream Object   755
ADO Method Calls – Quick Reference   757
    Command Object Methods   757
    Connection Object Methods   757
    Errors Collection Methods   757
    Field Object Methods   757
    Fields Collection Methods   757
    Parameter Object Methods   757
    Parameters Collection Methods   757
    Properties Collection Methods   758
    Record Object Methods   758
    Recordset Object Methods   758
    Stream Object Methods   759

Appendix C: Visual Basic Functions and Keywords — 761

Operators — 761

Assignment Operator — 762
Arithmetic Operators — 762
Concatenation Operators — 764
Comparison Operators — 765
Logical Operators — 767
Bitwise Operators — 768
Operator Precedence — 769
Math Functions — 770
Date and Time Functions and Statements — 773
Array Functions and Statements — 782
String Functions and Statements — 785
String Constants — 800
Conversion Functions — 801
Miscellaneous Functions, Statements, and Keywords — 805

Appendix D: Variable Naming and Other Code Conventions — 819

Variable Naming Conventions — 819
Hungarian Notation — 820
Procedure Naming — 820
Indentation — 820
Commenting — 821

Appendix E: Microsoft Scripting Run Time Reference — 823

Objects — 823
The Dictionary Object — 824
The Drive Object — 824
The Drives Collection — 825
The File Object — 825
The Files Collection — 826
The FileSystemObject Object — 826
The Folder Object — 827
The Folders Collection — 828
The TextStream Object — 829
Constants — 829
Method Calls Quick Reference — 831

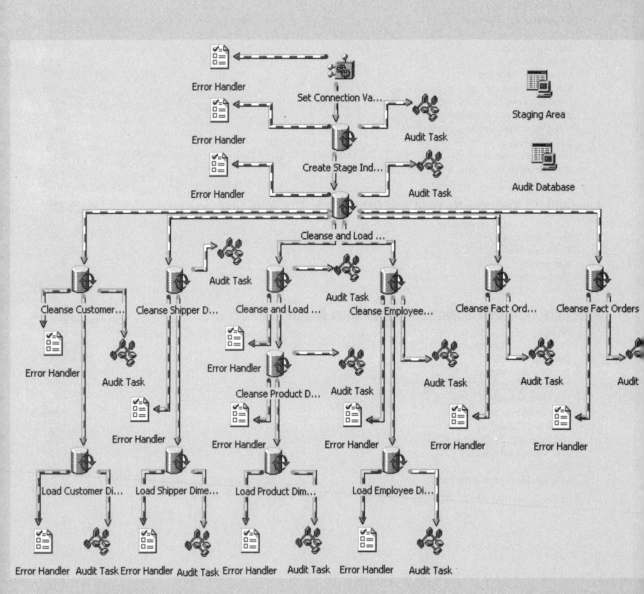

Error Handler

Set Connection Va...

Audit Task

Staging Area

Error Handler

Audit Task

Error Handler

Create Stage Ind...

Audit Task

Audit Database

Cleanse and Load ...

Audit Task

Cleanse Customer...

Cleanse Shipper D...

Cleanse and Load ...

Audit Task

Cleanse Employee...

Cleanse Fact Ord...

Cleanse Fact Orders

Error Handler

Audit Task

Error Handler

Error Handler

Cleanse Product D...

Audit Task

Audit Task

Audit Task

Audit

Error Handler

Error Handler

Error Handler

Error Handler

Error Handler

Load Customer Di...

Load Shipper Dime...

Load Product Dim...

Load Employee Di...

Error Handler   Audit Task Error Handler   Audit Task Error Handler   Audit Task   Error Handler   Audit Task

Introduction

DTS – not just another pretty acronym. Microsoft introduced Data Transformation Services (DTS) in SQL Server 7.0 and it was hailed as an integrated way of loading data. Programmers quickly found its limitations however. In SQL Server 2000, DTS grew up to be a powerhouse in data loading and other workflow systems. However, DTS isn't just for loading data: you can also FTP files, send messages to a message queue, or run any executable or ActiveX script.

Who Should Read this Book

A common misconception is that DTS is a database administration tool and only handles data. Well, nothing could be farther from the truth! DTS also is a great tool for developers and data warehouse engineers.

This book is in the *Professional* series and is targeted at intermediate to advanced SQL Server users, developers and administrators who have a firm knowledge of basic client-server architecture. This book assumes that you have a working knowledge of SQL Server. The first few chapters are written for those who are just learning DTS and the later chapters are geared for those who have been using it for years.

Transformation projects for companies can take up to half of the total project timeline. This, of course, depends on the number of sources and the complexity of the transformation. This book is also for managers who are coordinating one of these projects and need to know the terms their programmers are using.

The case study in this book requires some knowledge of Analysis Services (previously OLAP Services). You will need to know for that section how to create OLAP cubes and dimensions, but don't worry – we do provide the code in case you don't know how to do these tasks!

How to Get the Most from this Book

The software requirements for this book are as follows:

❑ Either Windows NT 4.0 (SP 4 or greater) with the Windows NT 4.0 Option Pack, or Windows 2000. You can use Windows 98 but you may not be able to test some sections in the book.

❑ Microsoft Visual Basic 6.0

❑ Microsoft SQL Server 2000

❑ Analysis Services 2000

The Windows NT 4 Option Pack can be ordered (or downloaded free) from Microsoft's web site at http://www.microsoft.com/ntserver/nts/downloads/recommended/NT4OptPk/default.asp.

A downloadable evaluation version of SQL Server is available at http://www.microsoft.com/sql/productinfo/evaluate.htm

What's Covered in this Book

This book consists of 14 chapters and a case study, all combining to give you a thorough introduction to SQL Server DTS.

Chapter 1 introduces us to the whole area of DTS. We explain what it entails, and exactly what functionality it has for us to manipulate. The chapter also goes into detail on a number of Wizards that DTS makes available to help us in our many duties. These Wizards make life easier and introduce us to a little of what using DTS means.

Chapter 2 goes into more depth on exactly what tasks are available in DTS. There are seventeen in total, and each one is briefly introduced before the chapter moves on to creating your first DTS package and using some of the tasks in it. These tasks are the ones that you would be most likely to use over and over again in your own packages.

Chapter 3 goes into more detail on some of the DTS tasks that contain more complex steps within them, and are probably going to be the most useful tasks that you will find within DTS. Full working examples are included to give you a better handle on what to expect from DTS.

Chapter 4 is where we turn our attention to packages as a whole, rather than the tasks within them. We look at the many options available to us when setting up, saving and loading a package.

Chapter 5 looks at using linked servers. We create one of our own, with which we perform some of the examples in this chapter. We look at many issues relating to linked servers, such as querying them, and gathering meta data, especially when the two (or more) servers involved are not of the same type. **Chapter 6** builds on this by looking at the issues involved in converting data from different types of sources to use in a real-world situation.

Chapter 7 looks at the role of ActiveX technology in DTS. This chapter concerns itself with the basics of programming terminology in DTS. To really appreciate what ActiveX can allows us to do we need to understand what DTS contains; this is so that we know what we have to work with and how to manipulate it to best suit our needs. To this end, **Chapter 8** looks at the DTS Object Model. Once we have examined this, we return to some more advanced ActiveX scripting in **Chapter 9** that will allow us to do more with DTS.

At this point we must consider how to make the packages we created secure if we do not want our information to be compromised. **Chapter 10** focuses on security issues, such as making sure that only the right people have access to our packages, and making sure that if security is breached, we can recover effectively.

In the same respect, we must also make sure that the people who are allowed to see our information can access what they need. **Chapter 11** concerns itself with error handling, and how we can ensure that if something does go wrong, we can not only recover, but also make sure that we learn from it. There are a number of ways to handle errors, which are looked at in this chapter.

Chapter 12 recognizes that sometimes DTS just isn't enough, and teaches us how to write our own custom tasks to make the functionality that we need if DTS does not already provide it. This chapter looks at the reasons why we would want to write our own tasks, and also provides an example to show us exactly what is involved in extending the functionality of DTS ourselves.

Chapter 13 then looks at the concept of data warehousing. It considers the issues involved in getting the data ready for a warehouse, and also looks at the different ways our data can be constructed to be most efficient, quick and timely. It looks at the theoretical side of the stages involved in preparing for a data warehouse.

Chapter 14 looks at how we can use DTS from other applications than the DTS Designer and SQL Server. It goes through a number of methods whereby we can use other applications to get to our packages and tasks.

Chapter 15 is actually a case study that takes everything we have learned and places it into a comprehensive example of how to set up and build our own complex package, teaching us that it can be done, and giving us the confidence to use our knowledge in the real world.

Conventions Used

You are going to encounter different styles as you are reading through this book. This has been done to help you easily identify different types of information and to help you keep from missing any key points. These styles are:

> **Important information, key points, and additional explanations are displayed like this to make them stand out. Be sure to pay attention to these when you find them.**

General notes, background information, and brief asides look like this.

❑ Keys that you press on the keyboard, like *Ctrl* and *Delete*, are displayed in italics

❑ If you see something like, `BackupDB`, you'll know that it is a filename, object name or function name

❑ The first time you encounter an **important word**, it is displayed in bold text

❑ Words that appear on the screen, such as menu options, are in a similar font to the one used on screen, for example, the File menu

This is how code samples look the first time they are introduced:

```
Private Sub Command_Click
    MsgBox "Don't touch me"
End Sub
```

Whereas code that you've already seen, or that doesn't relate directly to the point being made, looks like this:

```
Private Sub Command_Click
    MsgBox "Don't touch me"
End Sub
```

Customer Support

We want to know what you think about this book: what you liked, what you didn't like, and what you think we can do better next time. You can send your comments, either by returning the reply card in the back of the book, or by e-mail (to feedback@wrox.com). Please be sure to mention the book title in your message.

Source Code

Full source code for the case study and the examples used in this book, can be downloaded from the Wrox web site at: http://www.wrox.com.

Errata

We've made every effort to make sure that there are no errors in the text or the code. However, to err is human, and as such we recognize the need to keep you informed of any mistakes as they're spotted and corrected. Errata sheets are available for all our books at www.wrox.com. If you find an error that hasn't already been reported, please let us know.

p2p.wrox.com

For author and peer support join the Visual Basic mailing lists. Our unique system provides **programmer to programmer™ support** on mailing lists, forums and newsgroups, all *in addition* to our one-to-one e-mail system. Be confident that your query is not just being examined by a support professional, but by the many Wrox authors and other industry experts present on our mailing lists. At p2p.wrox.com you'll find a list specifically aimed at SQL Server developers that will support you, not only while you read this book, but also as you start to develop your own applications.

To enroll for support just follow this four-step system:

1. Go to http://p2p.wrox.com.

2. Click on the **SQL** button.

3. Click on sql_server as the type of mailing list you wish to join.

4. Fill in your e-mail address and password (of at least 4 digits) and e-mail it to us.

Why this System Offers the Best Support

You can choose to join the mailing lists or you can receive them as a weekly digest. If you don't have the time, or facility, to receive the mailing list, then you can search our online archives. Junk and spam mails are deleted, and your own e-mail address is protected by the unique Lyris system. Any queries about joining or leaving lists, or any other queries about the list, should be sent to listsupport@p2p.wrox.com.

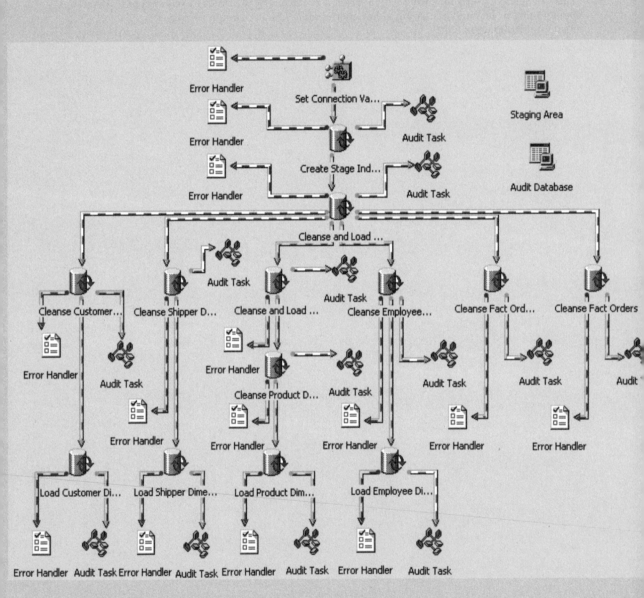

Error Handler

Set Connection Va...

Audit Task

Staging Area

Error Handler

Create Stage Ind...

Audit Task

Audit Database

Error Handler

Cleanse and Load ...

Audit Task

Audit Task

Cleanse Customer...

Cleanse Shipper D...

Cleanse and Load ...

Cleanse Employee...

Cleanse Fact Ord...

Cleanse Fact Orders

Error Handler

Audit Task

Error Handler

Audit Task

Audit Task

Audit Task

Audit

Error Handler

Cleanse Product D...

Audit Task

Error Handler

Error Handler

Error Handler

Load Customer Di...

Load Shipper Dime...

Load Product Dim...

Load Employee Di...

Error Handler   Audit Task   Error Handler   Audit Task   Error Handler   Audit Task   Error Handler   Audit Task

1

Welcome to DTS

A company's data is its life. Since the evolution of the mainframe and relational databases, companies have been evolving and increasing their productivity through database products like SQL Server and Oracle. The problem with evolution, however, is that some database systems are left behind. They are just too expensive to convert to the newer systems.

In the past, as a company upgraded its database system, a programmer would have to reprogram the communication layer through complex code. To remedy the time-to-market problem this created, Microsoft invented different ways to communicate with legacy and modern relational databases via an open standard layer called OLE DB. This breakthrough allowed programmers to communicate with IBM's DB2 database using code similar to that used to communicate to a Microsoft's SQL Server database. Suddenly portability became much easier.

This solved the problem of a program's portability, but what happens when you have a DB2 database that you need to convert to a SQL Server database? For example, your company purchases another company that still uses a legacy VSAM (mainframe driven) system. Your company, however, has its corporate database infrastructure in SQL Server. Converting the VSAM system may be too expensive and time consuming. In the meantime, you need the data that a sales representative is entering into a dumb terminal (DT) from the company you bought to flow to your SQL Server system in the shipping department. In the past, this process would have taken quite a while to program and employee turnover would be so bad from the merger that by the time you finished the development of a workflow system, you would have no one to support it.

This scenario is being repeated throughout the data processing industry daily. As companies merge, they need a way to rapidly develop an application to transition data from any source to any destination. Doing this on the mainframe is expensive and the human resources to do this are dwindling.

In this package, data is transformed from SQL Server 1 to SQL Server 2. The execution of this task is considered a step. This is shown as a solid line with an arrowhead pointing at the destination. If that step fails, then the operator (system administrator) is e-mailed – the failure line (the one between **SQL Server 2** and the **Email Operator**) is displayed in red in the Designer. If the transfer succeeds – the lower horizontal line, displayed in green in the Designer – then an ActiveX script is fired off to move the log files into an archive directory. Once the move is complete, a batch file is executed to send a broadcast message (using net send) to all network administrators of the package's completion.

This just displays the steps in the package – the result of the package execution is not displayed in the Designer. In the above example, the network administrators are informed of the package's completion, not its success or failure. The administrator would then have to go to the log files and determine if it was properly executed. You can also program more complex logic in ActiveX to send a message regarding the package's success or failure.

What's New in 2000?

SQL Server 2000 has expanded the power of DTS substantially. The DTS engine improvements that are discussed in Chapter 2 and 3 include:

- ❏ Ability to save packages to Visual Basic files. You can then place the .BAS file into your VB program.

- ❏ Integration with Windows 2000 security (Kerberos) and the ability for Windows 2000 users to cache packages.

- ❏ Ability to execute individual steps. In SQL Server 7.0, you had to disable all other steps to debug problems in one step. In SQL Server 2000, that's no longer necessary.

- ❏ Ability to run packages asynchronously.

- ❏ Support for Microsoft data link files (.udl). This allows you to create a .udl file that expresses the connection strings (the ones you define in your package to point to the source and destination) and to use it for your connection. In SQL Server 7.0, the .udl file was compiled at design time, now it's not compiled until runtime. This allows you to dynamically configure the .udl at run time.

- ❏ Addition of an HTML Web page source.

- ❏ Multi-phase data pump, which allows a failed insertion attempt to not fail the entire package, as well as giving you the ability to break a transformation into a number of stages, which are completely customizable. This is discussed in great detail in Chapter 3.

- ❏ Ability to edit a package disconnected from the network.

- ❏ Ability to save your DTS files as template (.DTT) files.

The most exciting addition to DTS in SQL Server 2000 is the new tasks. The complete list of tasks is discussed in Chapter 2. The added tasks are:

- ❏ File transfer protocol (FTP) transformation

- ❏ Microsoft Message Queue

- ❏ Dynamic Properties

- ❏ Execute Package

- ❑ Move Database
- ❑ Move Users
- ❑ Move Messages
- ❑ Move Jobs
- ❑ Move Master Stored Procedures

There are also some added tasks once you install Analysis Services. These include one to reprocess an OLAP cube and one to train a data mining model. Although the DTS user interface (the DTS Designer) has not had a major facelift, it does have some added functionality.

The DTS Toolbox

Microsoft has given us several tools to create our packages. A DTS programmer can create a package with:

- ❑ **Import and Export Wizards** – which automatically create the package for you after asking a series of questions.
- ❑ **DTS Designer** – a graphical user interface (GUI) that allows you to design and execute packages.
- ❑ **DTS Programming Interfaces** – series of APIs that are accessible through COM interfaces and any COM compliant programming language such as Visual Basic or C++ and scripting languages. Built into DTS is the ability to program in VBScript and JavaScript. We'll look at this much more in the Chapter 8. This can be expanded to any installed script, however, such as PerlScript.

As you might expect, the simplest way to create a package is through the wizards. As the wizards are also the easiest way to get a little hands-on experience of DTS, we'll take a look at these wizards here. However, as we'll see later, this method is also the weakest in terms of functionality. That's why, in the remainder of the book, we'll be using the wizards as little as possible and be exploring the alternatives.

In DTS, the easiest way to move data is through the built-in wizards. The wizards allow you to quickly create DTS packages or not even see the packages at all, and just execute them without saving them. They give you the basics you need to create a package to transform data, but lack depth. Most of what we discuss in the further chapters can't be done with the wizards. The wizards are only meant to transform data; any other functionality you might want is missing.

The wizards do provide a great way to create a basic package. The last step the wizard provides is the ability to save the package for later execution, and at that point, you can modify the package to add your own logic and the features that are missing. For example, you may know a flat file named transform.txt is going to be in a certain location daily for transformation. However, you'll need to fetch the file using the FTP task. You can use the wizard to create the transformation part of the package and then save it. After you save it, you can edit the package in the DTS Designer and add the FTP functionality.

Using the Wizards

SQL Server provides an array of wizards to guide us through exporting and importing data. There are two core wizards that help you move or copy data: The **Import/Export Wizard** and the **Copy Database Wizard (CDW)**. The wizards are an ideal way to migrate data from development to production or to create the root of a package to add logic to later. In this section, we will work our way through examples that will teach us how to:

❑ Export and import data from a database with DTS Wizards (we only go through the export wizard – although the import wizard is almost identical).

❑ Export and import database objects such as stored procedures and triggers.

❑ Create packages through the wizards that you can later edit in Designer.

❑ Save and schedule packages for later execution.

In the examples, we will provide sections that are hands-on, so that you can begin to get a feel for DTS. Interspersed between these are sections describing the functionality of the other options available, to provide a comprehensive overview of what we can achieve with the wizards.

In SQL Server 6.5, we were able to transfer database objects using Transfer Manager. Transfer Manager is a distant relative to DTS, but it lacks some of the functionality that DTS provides. This functionality has carried over into SQL Server 2000 with the Copy objects and data between SQL Server databases option that we will discuss in a moment. Some of the differences include:

❑ A direct way to save jobs to add custom components into them

❑ Access to OLE DB compliant data sources other than SQL Server

❑ Customization with ActiveX scripts

❑ A workflow type system

Transferring Data Using the Import/Export Wizard

Accessing the Wizard

In this example, we'll import data from the SQL Northwind database into a database called Wrox. To create the empty Wrox database, click your right mouse button in Enterprise Manager under the database tree node and select New Database. It will not matter where your database is located.

You can also transform your data in this example into the TempDB database. The next time your SQL Server stops and starts, the tables you create in this example will be purged. The TempDB database is a nice way to test transformations before you move them over to the live database, and it automatically cleans itself out after the server cycles. Never use the TempDB database for this purpose in production, however, since you could slow the performance of some queries by doing this.

As with most wizards, there are many ways of accessing them. You can access the wizards (as long as you have highlighted **Databases**) through the **Tools** menu, **Wizards**, then **Data Transformation Services** (or **Management** for the **Copy Database Wizard**); or **Tools**, then **Data Transformation Services**. However, the primary way to access the DTS **Import** and **Export Wizards** is to open **SQL Server Enterprise Manager**, and click with your right mouse button on the database you want to import/export from – in this case, the **Northwind** database. Then select **All Tasks**, and **Export Data**:

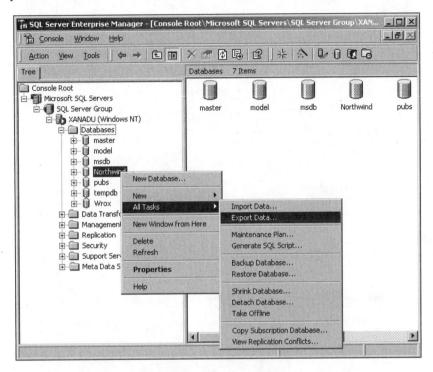

Once you're in the wizard, make sure you read each question very carefully. The wrong answer could result in you purging records from your tables unintentionally. If you're transforming into a production database or any database that contains data you care about, make sure you backup the database before running the wizard. Note also that entries are added into the log, so that we can recover the data, if necessary.

The reason we choose to access the **Import/Export Wizard** by clicking our right mouse button on the database is it takes a step out of the process. Since we did this, the first screen overleaf is already fully completed for us. If you came into the wizard another way, and had not highlighted the **Northwind** database first, you would need to select **Northwind** as the source connection database in the drop down box at the bottom of the screen. You will need to enter the necessary security information (username and password). As in ODBC data sources, the OLE DB provider for SQL Server supports either using standard **SQL Server** or **Windows Authentication**. Those using Windows 98 on their machines will have to click the **Refresh** button to see the database listings populate.

The first screen you see prompts you for your Data Source, defaulting to the OLE DB Provider for SQL Server:

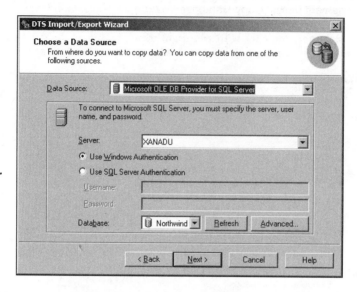

Advanced Options

If you need more advanced OLE DB connection options in your transformation procedure, click the Advanced... button to reveal the screen below:

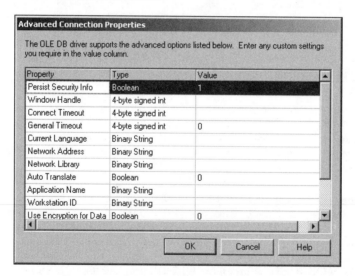

The dialog box that will appear will present you with a number of OLE DB connection options that are specific to the provider. In the OLE DB provider for SQL Server you will see options such as increasing the connection timeout, or specifying an IP address for the source server. Note that if you need to specify any Boolean values, they must be represented with a 0 (False) or 1 (True).

The Application Name and Workstation ID options are nice for auditing purposes. Each database management system (DBMS) has its own way of auditing who is connected, but in SQL Server if you adjust these two options, you can run a stored procedure named SP_WHO2 from the server, and detect which application and server name is connecting.

Note that you can also view connection information in Enterprise Manager. If you open Enterprise Manager and drill down into the Management node, you can select Current Activity, then Process Info to see the current connections. The Process Info item, as shown below, is the only item that contains the level of granularity to let you see with which applications users are connecting. This is a handy tool to debug connectivity problems and to determine if your connection request is even making it to the server. Active connections performing a query are lit, while sleeping connections are gray.

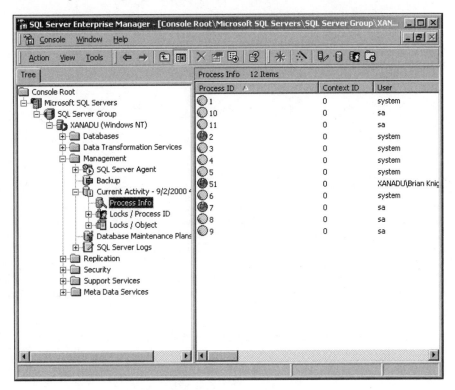

Choosing the Destination Database

Once you've set all the options in the Choose a Data Source page, click Next. The Wizard will then prompt you to select the destination database. Repeat the above steps for the destination database, this time selecting Wrox as the database. Again, you may have to click Refresh to see the Wrox database in the drop-down box.

On clicking Next, you'll be presented with the following options:

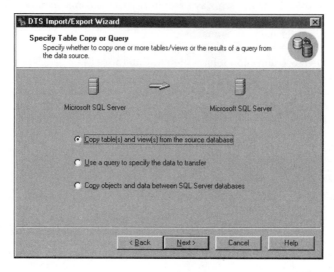

We'll look at what each of these does in turn. For the purposes of the current example, choose the Copy table(s) and view(s) from the source database option.

Copy Tables and Views Option

The easiest of the three options is to select Copy table(s) and view(s) from the source database. This option transfers data from the source database, but it does lack in selectivity. In other words, this option will select all data from any given table. If you wish to selectively transfer data, use the next option (Use a query to specify the data to transfer), which we will examine later in the chapter.

The first dialog box in this section of the wizard will ask you which tables and views you'd like to transfer into the Wrox database. For the purpose of our example, select only the Suppliers table from the source column:

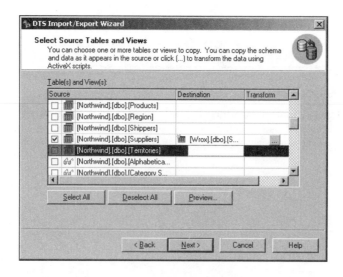

The destination column will automatically be filled after you check the source. This does not mean that the table exists in the destination database. By default, if the table does not exist in the destination database, then the DTS engine will create it for you. If the table does already exist, then DTS will by default append the new data to the existing data. The destination column will also allow you to select another table from a drop-down list if you've already created one that's more suitable.

Advanced Options – Column Mappings Tab

In the Transform column, you can click on the three dots to select some more advanced options. If your destination table does not have the same schema as the source table or view, then you could specify which columns to transfer and their mapping here. You can ignore certain columns by clicking on them, then selecting the <ignore> option from the Source drop-down box. The reason you'll see a drop-down box for only the Source column is that if you adjusted the Destination, you would receive an error. The error would be generated by DTS sending data to a column that's being ignored. A typical reason you'd ignore columns is if you only wanted a subset of the data vertically, or if you wanted the destination table to assign the identity column and not take on the identity from the source.

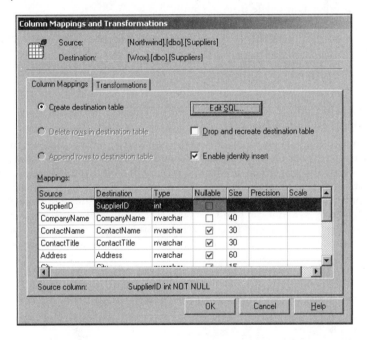

The options that are not needed are grayed out. For example, you can't append data to a table that doesn't exist. Let's have a look at options provided by the Column Mappings tab (although we will not apply any of them in this example):

❑ **Create destination table.** This will also allow you to customize the transformation into that table. If the table already exists, you are still given the option; however, you would need to select the option to **Drop and recreate the destination table**. Otherwise you would receive an error on execution complaining about a name conflict in creating the table.

❑ **Append rows to destination table.** If you were receiving incremental updates from a source, you would use this option.

❑ **Delete rows in destination table.** Use this if you want to complete a data refresh without dropping and recreating the table.

❑ **Enable identity insert.** This option will turn off identity fields temporarily during the insert. This is only needed if you're inserting into a table that has an identity column (or a column that's auto numbering a column). You would receive an error upon inserting data into a table that has an identity column unless you have this checked. This is because the system wants to auto assign the new data a number. This option is automatically checked if there is a column on the destination with an identity column in it.

❑ **Drop and recreate the destination table.** Use this option if you want to delete the table and recreate it with a different schema.

As you can see, the append rows and delete rows options are not available when you have the **Create Destination Table** radio box selected. The **Create destination table** radio box is automatically selected when the table does not exist on the destination. This is because the table doesn't exist. If you select the box **Drop and recreate the destination table** and the table has not been created, you'll receive an error when executing the package as shown below. This is due to DTS issuing a drop command of a table that doesn't exist yet. The DTS engine will detect that the table does not exist on the destination and not allow you to select, append, or delete from the table.

You can also click the **Edit SQL** button to modify the script used to create the table by hand. For example, you could add statements to this to add the necessary primary and foreign keys. You will also need to add any constraints or identity column information in here as shown below. The dialog box does not support GO statements, which you will receive by default if you generate a script from Enterprise Manager. There is an unusual workaround that you must do to create primary keys in this fashion. After you try to exit this dialog box and go back to the transformation screen, DTS performs a check on your SQL code. When it can't find the table, DTS will return an error since you can't issue an ALTER TABLE statement (which is used to create constraints and primary keys) on a table that doesn't exist yet. The workaround is to create a shell of the table on the destination with one column:

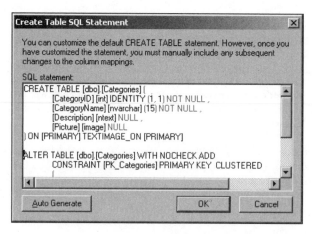

It is because of this workaround that I would recommend that you just create tables that need Primary Keys and constraints on the destination before you try to transform the data into them. You can also run through the wizard and then add the constraints afterwards. You can also select the Copy objects and data between SQL Server databases branch of the wizard, which we will cover shortly in this chapter. This feature is still nice if you'd like to modify the schema slightly on the destination. Those who participated in the Beta program will remember that this wizard had the Foreign and Primary key capabilities in it during the beta phases. It was pulled in the production, but Microsoft has promised to revisit this ability in a later release of SQL Server.

Advanced Options – Transformations Tab

You can also perform more customized transformations. By going to the Transformations tab, as shown in the following screenshot, you can write ActiveX logic to transform the data before it is committed to the destination. For more complex logic, use DTS Designer. It offers more flexibility than the wizard's transformation tab will offer. To enable this option, select the option to Transform information as it is copied to the destination.

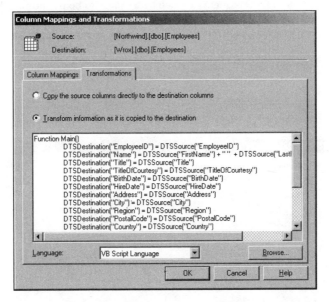

As we will discuss in a later chapter, after you select this option, your transformation of data will slow considerably because records must pass through logic in a script versus the built-in COM object that DTS provides. You can write your script in any scripting language that is installed on the client running the package. The only exception is if you want to schedule the package. In that case, you can only use scripting languages that are installed on the server, since SQL Server Agent is actually executing the package. To change the scripting language, select the new language from the drop-down box seen above. The fastest of the scripting methods is VBScript followed by JavaScript. If you chose a language other than those two, REXX for example, you take on a slight risk because DTS may have not been tested in the scripting language.

Why would you use this feature then if it is considerably slower? You can use this to perform a number of functions that you couldn't perform with a straight copy. For example, if you received two fields on the source, FirstName and LastName, and wanted to merge the fields onto the destination as just Name, you could do so with a transformation script shown overleaf. Make sure you add a space between the two fields with an empty string " ". You can separate fields with the plus sign (+).

```
DTSDestination("Name") = DTSSource("FirstName") + " " + DTSSource("LastName")
```

You can also use this feature to make fields upper case or to convert a zip code to the proper format. For example, the Customers table in the Northwind database has a number of postal codes from around the world, some alphanumeric, some numeric. With VBScript, you could determine if the postal code met a certain requirement, like length, and then transform it. Other fields would be copied straight through. The code below shows you an example on how to do perform such logic. Don't worry about the code quite yet. Several chapters are dedicated to how to do this in more detail.

```
If LEN(DTSSource("PostalCode")) = 9 Then
DTSDestination("PostalCode") = Left(DTSSource("PostalCode"),5) + "-" +
Right(DTSSource("PostalCode"),4)
Else
DTSDestination("PostalCode") =DTSSource("PostalCode")
```

As we mentioned earlier, the DTS Designer is a much better place to be performing this type of transformation. Quite a few pre-defined transformations have already been set up for you in the Designer. For example, you can easily make a field upper case in Designer with one click and no programming.

Saving and Scheduling the Package

After clicking OK and Next, you will be prompted to save, schedule, and execute the package. For the purpose of this example, check the box that causes the package to Run immediately, and save the package onto the local SQL Server by selecting the following options:

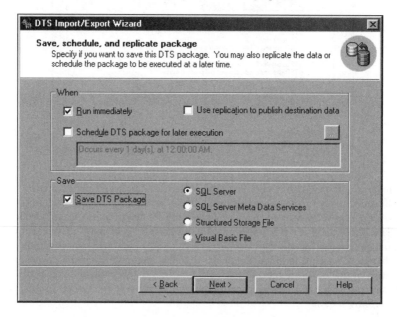

We'll go into details about the various places to save your package in Chapter 2.

Advanced Options

If you check Use replication to publish destination data, the Create Publication Wizard will begin after the data Import/Export Wizard finishes transforming the data. You can then set up you destination database to replicate to other sources, or schedule a package for later execution. This option will only work if SQL Server Agent is running. If it is not running, the wizard will insert the record into the MSDB database, which holds job information, and schedule the job, but the job will not be executed. You will have to start it manually from Enterprise Manager or wait until the next scheduled cycle arrives. A scheduled job can be manually executed by drilling down to the Jobs node under SQL Server Agent (which is under Management).

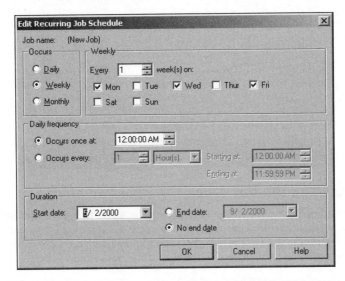

You will have to save the package before it can be scheduled. If you do not save the package, you will receive the below error:

If you schedule a package for later execution, SQL Server Agent will execute the package as a `CmdExec` job using a utility called `DTSRUN`, which we will discuss later in the book. If your source and destination connections use Windows Authentication, then you will need to ensure that the account that starts the SQLServerAgent service has permissions to the destination and source database, and is started. You can change the permission for SQL Server Agent by drilling down under the Management group and clicking on SQL Server Agent with your right mouse button, then selecting Properties, to reveal the screen shown overleaf:

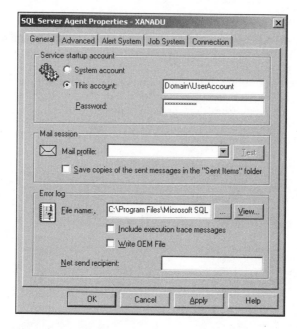

Naming and Executing the Package

When you have completed the information required on the save, schedule and replicate package dialog, and clicked Next, you will be prompted to name the DTS package that you have just created. Name this example package Ch1_CopyData. You can also specify an owner and user password here. We will discuss this in the next chapter; so in the meantime, leave this blank.

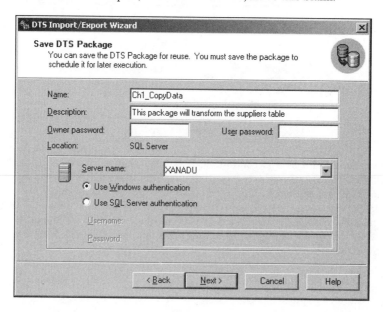

Make sure that you also add a meaningful description in the appropriate box. As you add more and more packages to your server, naming conventions and descriptions become increasingly important. The descriptions and names you type in these examples can later be loaded into the Microsoft Meta Data Services as meta data (data about your data). This meta data will allow you to view details about your package, the connections that it has and other descriptive data.

Click Next, and you will be presented with a summary screen. Clicking on Finish will cause the package to execute, first saving the package in the event that an error occurs. If an error occurs, you will be given an opportunity to go back and correct the problem. Data that has already been transformed will stay committed on the destination database.

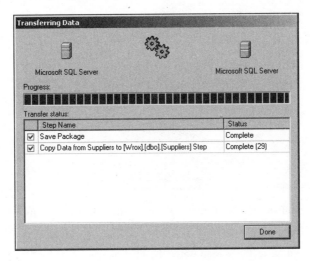

You should find that the Suppliers table has been added to your Wrox database.

The Import/Export Wizard is really designed to transfer data rapidly from source to destination. It does not provide much room for customization. Once your data has been transferred, if you didn't alter the SQL statement used to create the table, you will have to create the primary key and foreign key relationships. Also any type of other information, like identity fields, will need to be created. You will not have to worry about this if you're transferring into a table that already exists.

If you recall, Copy table(s) and view(s) was only one option that our Wizard offered us for transferring our data. What about the other options?

Using Queries to Transfer Data

Follow the steps above to get back to the Specify Table Copy or Query screen. This time we'll export only a select set of records into the Wrox database from Northwind.

In this example, we'll create a table that will be used for bulk faxing. Some of our data in the source table is useless for this purpose and needs to be excluded.

Select Use a query to specify the data to transfer. You can transfer data from one or more views or tables with this option. You are then given the option to type a query into the dialog box (Query statement) or use Query Builder to help you create the query. We will go into more detail on the Query Builder in a few moments. Since our query is simple, just type the following query in the Query statement. This query will select all the suppliers that have entered a fax number:

```
select supplierid, country, companyname, contactname, fax
from suppliers where fax is not null
order by supplierid
```

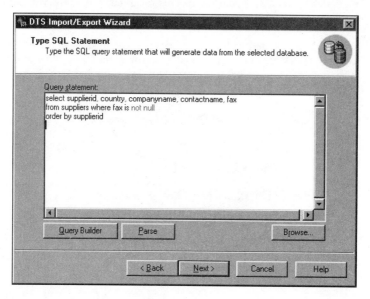

The **Parse** button will confirm that your query is a valid one. The **Parse** button checks all object names to makes sure that everything exists. The **Browse** button will allow you to find a prewritten script.

After you have continued on to the screen below by clicking the **Next** button, you may want to click on the "..." button under the **Transform** column to adjust the destination table schema, as shown earlier. The default table name that the data will be transferred into is **Results**, as shown below. You can only do one query at a time with the **Import/Export Wizard**.

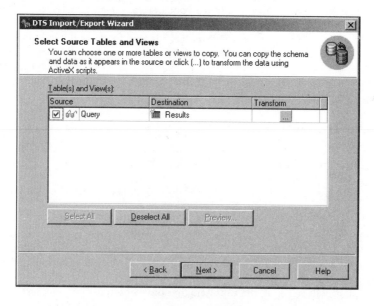

Execute your package as you did in the previous example (chose to run it immediately and save it the local SQL Server), but this time save it as Ch1_QueryResult. Again, you will see the same screen as you did before as it executes step after step. First the package will save as previously, then transform your new table named Results.

Query Builder

We briefly touched on the Query Builder in the last example. The Query Builder allows you to easily build queries that can include multiple tables from the same source database. You cannot go outside the source database or select views in the Query Builder. It is a superb way to build quick queries for those who are do not like the rigors of programming a nasty inner join in T-SQL. You will see Query Builder is available in a number of DTS tasks.

Once again, repeat the steps to get back to the Query statement screen seen previously. This time open Query Builder, chose the columns you want in your query and double-click on them. The interface will only allow you to select one column at a time.

In this example, we are de-normalizing the database slightly. This means that we're translating all the foreign keys into their real data. We've taken CustomerID in the Order table and joined it with the Customers table to find out the customer's CompanyName.

Begin by selecting the columns shown in the next screenshot:

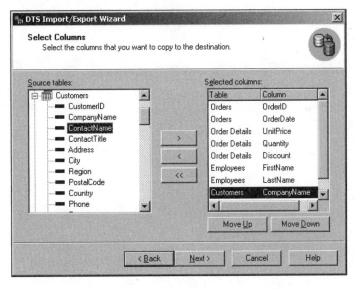

Next, select the column(s) on which you want your query to be ordered. Unless you change this later in the Query statement screen, the query will be sorted in ascending order. In our example, the CompanyName column will be ordered first, beginning with the 'A's, followed by the OrderID. This performs the same action as an ORDER BY clause. Query Builder does not have the ability to do GROUP BY clauses. GROUP BY clauses allow you to see the combined orders that each customer made. If you want to do a GROUP BY, then you will have to make the adjustments in the Query statement screen we saw earlier.

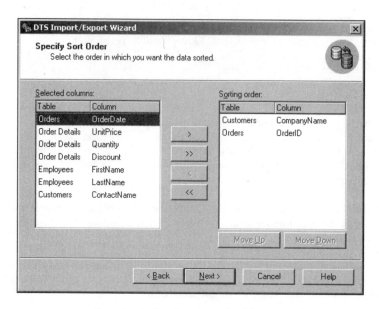

In the next screen, you can set the criteria for the query, by filtering your query horizontally based on another column, or data in the column. This screen performs the same action as the WHERE clause. The first Column: drop-down box will set the column you want to filter. Then, the Oper: drop-down box sets the operator that will be used (=, <, >, <>). Finally, setting the Value/Column: drop-down box makes the comparison.

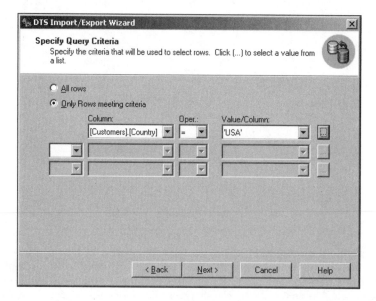

To select an actual value, you can select the browse button ("...") next to the Value/Column: drop-down box. To select a value, double-click on the value and it will populate the drop-down box.

You are then returned to the **Query statement** screen where you can then modify any part of the query by hand, now that the hard part of your query is written:

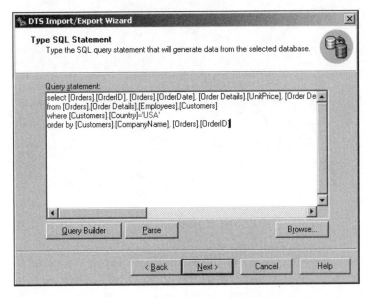

Some of the limitations of Query Builder stop most programmers from using it. The inability to perform a GROUP BY clause or sort in a descending manner is a big restriction. Most programmers find themselves writing their query in Enterprise Manager then copying and pasting the query into the **Query statement** screen. By right-clicking on any table in Enterprise Manager and selecting **Query** from the **Open Table** option, you can write a very effective query without any of the restrictions.

Transferring SQL Objects

We will now look at the final option on the Specify Table Copy or Query screen. The Copy objects and data between SQL Server databases option is a close relative to Transfer Manager in SQL Server 6.5 and gives you the ability to transfer SQL Server objects between databases. You can transfer any SQL Server object from any SQL Server 2000 instance to any SQL Server 2000 instance. You can also go from any SQL Server 7.0 instance to 7.0 instance or upgrade to 2000 with this branch of the wizard. To demonstrate how it works, we're going to copy selected objects from the Orders table into Northwind.

Again, follow the steps to get back to the Specify Table Copy or Query screen, and select Copy objects and data between SQL Server databases. You should see the screen below as the first screen. This screen is similar to Transfer Manager.

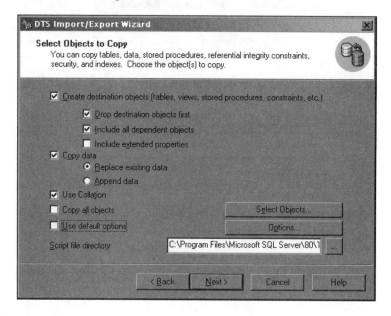

Advanced Options

You can configure this branch of the wizard to perform the following functions:

❑ The Create destination objects option will create the objects you wish to transfer on the destination server. Uncheck this option if you wish to only transfer data.

❑ The Drop destination objects first will drop all the objects on the destination SQL Server before it issues the commands to create them again. Check this option if you think that the objects you're trying to transfer may already be on the destination server, and you'd like to re-create them. If you run through the wizard and experience errors, you may want to check this option as well. Otherwise, you may see the error shown above opposite which states that the object already exists on the destination server. This is because you went part way through the transfer and there is no rollback performed.

- The **Include all dependent objects** option will transfer objects that depend on the table you're trying to transfer. For example, any views that depend on the table will be transferred if you select this option.

- The **Include extended properties** option will transfer all extended properties on SQL Server 2000 databases. This option does not apply if you're transferring objects from a SQL Server 7.0 database.

- The **Copy data** option will enable you to transfer the data from the source to the destination server.

- The **Replace existing data** will purge the source tables before it transfers the new data into it.

- The **Append data** option will add the new data from the source at the end of the table on the destination server.

- The **Use collation** option will enable you to transfer data between servers of different collations.

- The **Copy all objects** option will transfer all objects in the database and not allow you to select certain objects to transfer. This includes all tables, views, stored procedures, functions, defaults, rules, and user-defined data types. If you uncheck this option, you are given the option to select which objects you would like to transfer. The **Select Objects** button allows you to check the objects you'd like to transfer from the source SQL Server, as shown below:

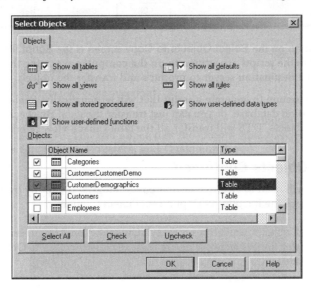

- The **Use default options** checkbox will transfer the other SQL Server objects like indexes, users, and primary and foreign keys. If you wish to specify other attributes to transfer, such as logins, you must uncheck this option and select the **Options** button. This will open the screen overleaf, which will allow you to specify more advanced options.

The More Info >>> button will show you the step details. For example, in the following screenshot you can see that we received an error from a user being connected to the source database:

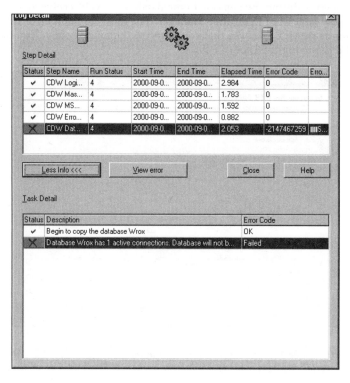

If you select more than one database to move, only one database is moved at a time. Again, once you have validated the move, you can delete the physical files from the source, if they're no longer needed:

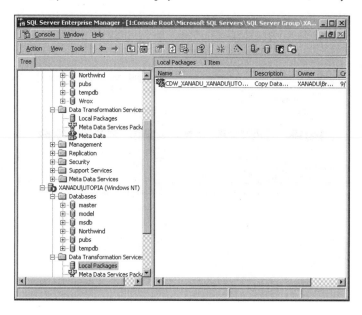

Because CDW uses detach and attach processes, it can move a database much faster than the DTS Import/Export Wizard. CDW also physically creates the database. The advantage to the Import/Export Wizard is that it can handle heterogeneous data and can import into databases that already exist.

The DTS Designer

We said earlier that the DTS Designer is a GUI that allows us to design and execute packages. We will examine it in much more detail in the next chapter, but before we take a preliminary look here, you need to realize that this is a very powerful utility. Not only can you use the DTS Designer to create new packages, but you can also edit existing packages, including those created with the wizards. Let's begin by seeing how we access this Designer.

Accessing the DTS Designer

To access the DTS Designer, open SQL Server Enterprise Manager, then click your right mouse button on the Data Transformation Services group and click New Package or you can click Action from the Enterprise Manager menu and select New Package.

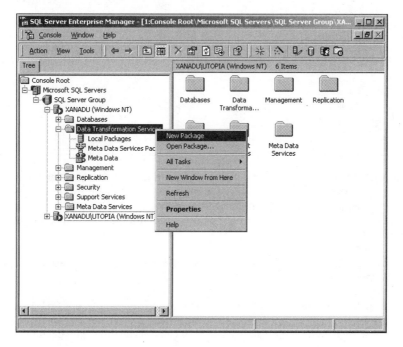

Viewing DTS Packages

In the examples in this chapter, we've saved our packages locally onto our SQL Server. To view a package after you've saved with the Wizard, select Local Packages under the Data Transformation Services group in Enterprise Manager. In the right pane, you will the packages that you have saved:

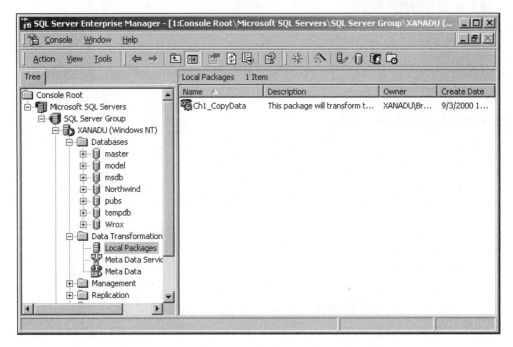

We will cover the advantages of saving packages in the various formats in the next chapter. If you have saved a package as a Meta Data Services package, you can open it again by clicking Meta Data Services Packages under the Data Transformation Services group in Enterprise Manager. To open COM-structured file packages, click your right mouse button on the Data Transformation Services group, then select Open Package.

You can execute a package in Enterprise Manager by clicking your right mouse button on the package, then selecting Execute Package.

Double-clicking on any package opens it in the DTS Designer. For example, our Ch1_CopyData package looks like the screenshot above opposite. In the below package, you can see that the first step to the right is to create the table needed, then we transform the data from Connection1 to Connection2 in the second step.

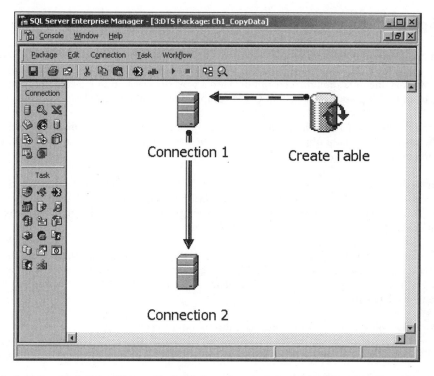

Although the wizards do not offer much flexibility, they are a good building block if you wish to edit them in DTS Designer later. We'll go into more detail about the various options and DTS Designer in the next chapter.

A Note About NT Authentication Security

SQL Servers running Windows 98 will not be able to use Windows Authentication. However, if you're signing into a domain and try to access a SQL Server on the network running Windows NT or 2000, then this option is available. It is important to note that Windows Authentication is the preferred method to access SQL Server since no passwords are passed over the network or saved. A majority of the SQL Server security bugs that Microsoft has announced were based on standard SQL Server security. For example, many SQL Server bugs are announced where SQL Server saves the sa password as clear text in the registry.

Summary

DTS is a collection of objects and tools that allow you to transform data easily, and is an integral part of SQL Server. In the past, you would have had to buy expensive programs to do such a task. DTS is not just for transforming data though. You can develop a workflow system to execute programs or scripts. You can even develop your own custom COM components to plug into DTS.

We've seen that the package is the primary component of DTS and is what you create and execute. Inside the package is a set of objects called tasks, which are a set of instructions, and steps, which tell DTS which order to execute the tasks in.

After our basic introduction to DTS, we moved on to look at the Wizards that DTS provides to help simplify some of the most fundamental tasks. They also provide us with the essentials to create a package. You can create a package in the wizards, then go back into it in Enterprise Manager (after saving the package in the wizard) to add your own logic into the package.

One of the most efficient ways to move data is through the **Copy Database Wizard**, which will move the database and all related items. The **DTS Import/Export Wizard** also provides an easy way to convert data quickly from other sources such as Excel or DB2. We have an entire chapter dedicated to heterogeneous data conversion.

There are three ways of transforming our data through the wizard:

❑ The copying data option is the fastest way to transfer your data but lacks in selectivity.

❑ Using a query to select data to be transferred allows you to copy select data. In this chapter, we had an example where we filtered the **Suppliers** table to only return suppliers in the USA.

❑ The transfer of SQL Server objects allows you to transfer objects like tables, stored procedures, and views.

In the next chapter we will discuss more advanced ways of manually creating a package through the DTS Designer.

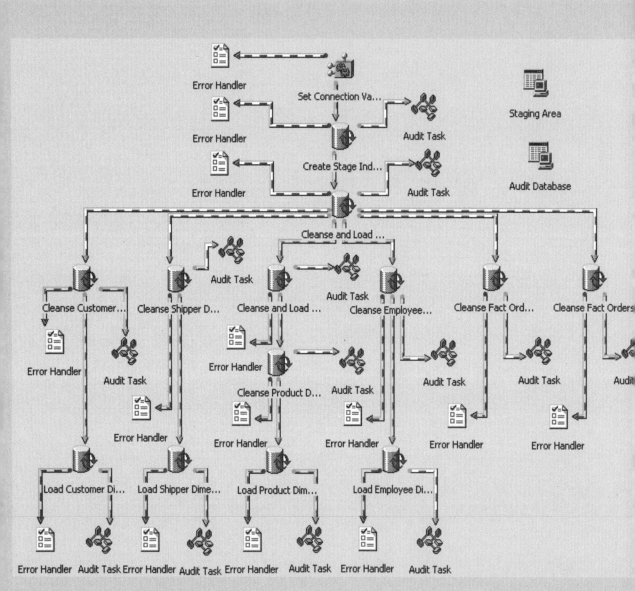

Error Handler

Set Connection Va...

Audit Task

Staging Area

Error Handler

Create Stage Ind...

Audit Task

Audit Database

Error Handler

Cleanse and Load ...

Audit Task

Cleanse Customer...   Cleanse Shipper D...   Cleanse and Load ...   Cleanse Employee...   Cleanse Fact Ord...   Cleanse Fact Orders

Error Handler

Audit Task

Error Handler

Audit Task

Audit Task

Audit Task

Audit Task

Audit

Error Handler

Cleanse Product D...

Audit Task

Error Handler

Error Handler

Error Handler

Error Handler

Error Handler

Load Customer Di...   Load Shipper Dime...   Load Product Dim...   Load Employee Di...

Error Handler   Audit Task   Error Handler   Audit Task   Error Handler   Audit Task   Error Handler   Audit Task

2

DTS Fundamentals

It is now time to leave the world of SQL Server wizards far behind and graduate to the DTS Designer and other tools that DTS has to offer. After all, the wizards can only get you so far.

In this chapter we will:

❑ Explain the different types of tasks and connections

❑ Create a package with DTS Designer

❑ Find other ways of transforming your data

❑ Explain the options you have available for where you can save your packages, and how they are relevant

❑ Find out how to schedule your package and alternative ways to execute it

DTS Designer

One of the tools in your DTS arsenal is the **DTS Designer**. DTS Designer is the graphical tool that allows you to create packages and workflow processes quickly and easily. As we mentioned in the previous chapter, DTS is a collection of objects that allow you to quickly create transformation processes and workflow systems. The Designer gives you the ability to piece together the object model puzzle visually, leaving the heavy DTS programming to the power users. This is where DTS programmers spend most of their time in developing DTS packages. The GUI tool offers you flexibility and light error handling when designing your packages. Although it is a very powerful tool, at times it can be clunky and awkward: some common functions that you can do in other Microsoft visual development environments, such as Visual Basic, can't be done in Designer. For example, you can't copy and paste multiple tasks at one time: instead, you have to copy and paste each individual task. We'll point out other items of awkward Designer behavior as the book goes on.

The Designer will allow you to:

❑ Easily create, save, and manage packages

❑ Register and manage custom tasks

.❑ Create a flow of data to be transformed

❑ Integrate seamlessly with the Microsoft Meta Data Services (called Microsoft Repository in SQL Server 7.0), where you can share meta data and lineage information (we'll talk about this more in the section about saving packages)

❑ With SQL Server 2000, you also have the ability to execute individual steps

To open the DTS Designer window, open Enterprise Manager, right-click on the Data Transformation Services folder as shown below, and then select New Package.

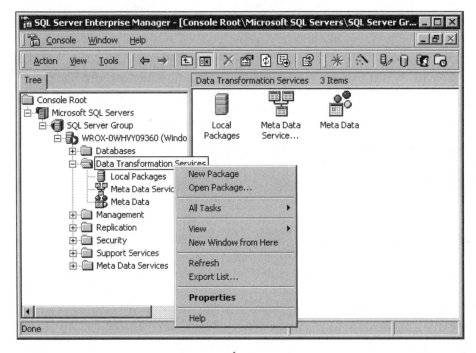

You can also access it by clicking on the Data Transformation Services folder and then selecting New Package under the Action menu. You will then be presented with the Design Sheet. The Design Sheet looks like the following screen:

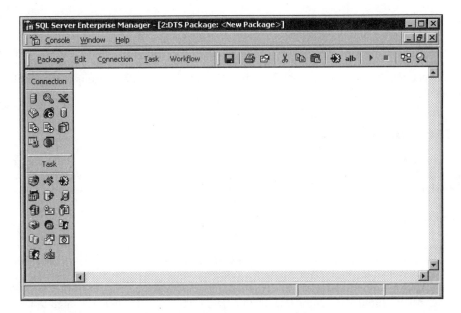

Take some time to navigate through the menus. Most of the items in the menus are very self-explanatory; those bits that aren't obvious will be covered in detail later in the book. We are spending most of this chapter on the pieces that aren't. Note that the icons on the left of the window are docked versions of the Connection and Task menus, and that the icons along the top essentially form the Package menu.

If you open the Designer in SQL Server 7.0, you may notice that your icons are out of alignment. For example, you may see the data connection section on the left pane hidden below your screen. This bug was fixed in Service Pack 1 for SQL Server 7.0. If this occurs with you, make sure that you adjust the icons to where you can see all the options by clicking and dragging their groups.

Tasks Available in SQL Server 2000

In this section, we will briefly touch on the 17 built-in tasks that you have available to you in SQL Server 2000's DTS. We will cover these in much greater detail in future chapters. We will also explain some of the new tasks that have been added into SQL Server 2000, as well as the feature enhancements to the old SQL Server 7.0 tasks.

ActiveX Script Task

The **ActiveX Script Task** gives a DTS programmer the ability to run ActiveX scripts inside a DTS package. By default, scripts can be written in either JScript or VBScript. However, you can also add any Windows Scripting Host compliant language, such as PerlScript if needed. This task gives you more flexibility with the package by allowing you to expand the normal scope of what a DTS package can do. For example, you can set an ActiveX task to loop through an ADO recordset and send mail with your custom COM component to everyone in the list. The task also allows you to dynamically change parameters as well as gives you full programming functionality in a package. We dedicate the chapters '*ActiveX Script Task Fundamentals*' and '*Advanced ActiveX Scripting*' in this book to how to take full advantage of this task.

It is important to note that ActiveX scripts are executed on whichever system executes the package. For example, if you have a quad-processor server and execute a script from a DTS package from your workstation, which is only a single processor machine, the package will execute poorly because all the records are going to execute locally on your machine. You can avoid this by scheduling the package to run, then executing the SQL Server job. By doing that, DTS will use the permissions setup for the SQL Server Agent as well as take advantage of the larger machine.

Transform Data Task

The **Transform Data Task** allows you to transform data from any OLE DB compliant data source to any compliant data source. You will also see this task called the **Data Pump Task**; we will use both names interchangeably throughout this book (you'll also see both terms in Microsoft documentation).

The Data Pump task makes cleaning your data easy as well. It has the ability to:

❑ Automatically try to map columns between the source and destination data sources. This feature saves programmers hours of trying to figure out which columns on the source correspond with columns on the destination data source. The DTS logic for this automated mapping of columns first weighs column name then ordinal column location to decide how the column should be mapped. Unfortunately, DTS is not intelligent enough to know that if you have a column with an character value, it can't be mapped to a column with a integer value. This test is performed by SQL Server, not DTS, at the task's run time.

❑ Narrow the source rowset by running a query. For example, you can select a piece of the data rather than transform every record in the table. We will outline this in our later example.

Each column mapping can use a variety of scripting languages or transformation methods. The default transformation is Copy Column. This is the fastest and most limited of the transformations. Using ActiveX in your transformation gives you added function, but also slows your transformation considerably. The Copy Column transformation copies the data without changing it. When transforming data, ActiveX Scripts can be used to manipulate the data before it is copied to the destination. For example, with an ActiveX script you can take a substring of the data and format a phone number property, adding dashes where necessary. We did something similar to this with the postal code in the last chapter where we detected if the postal code was nine digits long and then performed an action based on this. If an ActiveX script is not powerful enough, you can use a custom transformation. A custom transformation is written in C++ and can transform data that has special rules, performing much faster than ActiveX scripts. SQL Server 2000 has a number of these built into DTS; for instance, DTS is now equipped with custom transformations to take the source data and write it to the destination in upper case, or trim the white spaces from the end of the string (custom transformations are, however, beyond the scope of this book).

SQL Server 2000 has also added several new features to this task. The most important of these new features is the multiphase data pump. This feature allows you to:

❑ Set up row-level restartability that will not allow the entire step to fail due to one failed insertion.

❑ Customize the data pump procedure to allow for events to execute before and after the transformation.

❑ Row-by-row level handling of data that allows you to execute customized procedures if a constraint is broken, for example.

We will go into much more detail about the advanced multiphase data pump settings in the next chapter. Lastly, you can pass parameters into your Transform Data task. This means you can have a query that says:

```
SELECT * FROM Customers WHERE CustomerID = ?
```

The question mark (?) is a placeholder for a value that you will pass in. This uses global variables to pass variables. We will go into global variables in great detail in the next chapter.

> *In SQL Server 7.0's DTS Designer, it is not located under the Task menu with the other tasks but rather under the Workflow menu, called Add Transform. In SQL Server 2000's Designer, the task can be found under the Task menu with the rest of the tasks.*

 # Execute Process Task

The **Execute Process Task** allows you to execute any Windows compatible program or batch file. The boundaries of this task are endless because of how open ended it is. One use for the Execute Process task is to have an executable program called by this task that breaks one flat file into many flat files for import. After the program has run, and the flat file has been broken up, you can proceed to transform the individual files.

 # Execute SQL Task

With the **Execute SQL Task**, you can execute any SQL statement that you could from the tools your target database system uses. This is commonly used to run maintenance procedures after a data import, such as rebuilding an index. Now in SQL Server 2000, you can output the results of this task to a global variable and use those variables in another task easily. You can also pass global variables into the task.

 # Copy SQL Server Objects Task

The **Copy SQL Server Objects Task** can copy objects such as stored procedures or triggers. Any SQL Server object can be transferred by this task. As you may expect, with this functionality comes a performance hit. The transferring of SQL Server objects can run quite slow. If you are only copying data, it is not recommended that you use this task. Instead use the Transfer Data task.

 # Send Mail Task

The **Send Mail Task** allows you to send e-mail to a recipient. This is commonly used to alert an operator of the success or failure of a task. This task will also allow you to send attached files. For the Send Mail task to work you will need to configure the instance of SQL Server that's running the task with MAPI. This can be done in the Control Panel and we will discuss this later in this chapter.

 # Bulk Insert Task

The **Bulk Insert Task** is the least flexible, but fastest task that DTS has to offer. This task has the same speed benefits and problems that running Bulk Copy Program (BCP) from a command prompt has. The Bulk Insert task uses a SQL Server T-SQL command, BULK INSERT, which was introduced in SQL Server 7.0, to perform its operations. The main difference between BULK INSERT and BCP is that BULK INSERT cannot export data whereas BCP can. Some of the rules that apply are as follow:

- ❏ SQL Server must be the destination.

- ❏ Data column mapping in the source file must be identical to the destination table or file.

- ❏ The number of columns in the source file must be the same as the number of columns in the destination table or file.

- ❏ The columns are copied to the SQL Server destination table exactly as it appears in the source file.

Data Driven Query Task

The **Data Driven Query (DDQ) task** is one of the slower transform data tasks but ranks as one of the most powerful. This task allows you to scan through the source rowset record by record and perform a query automatically based on the data that is retrieved. For example, you could create a DDQ to perform the following functions based on the data:

- ❏ Insert new customers that don't exist in the destination database but are in the source.

- ❏ Update a customer's record with a priority flag where the customer has spent more than $1000 a month.

- ❏ Delete any customers from the destination database where the customer has a canceled service flag.

- ❏ Execute a stored procedure.

A DDQ is best used when there is a need for a record-by-record action. If there is not a need for this type of flexibility, then, due to performance, use either a Data Pump or a Bulk Insert task. This is because DDQs go through a recordset row-by-row, whereas with the Data Pump task, you can change the sizes of batches to commit records at any given rate. This task, like the Data Pump task, can now accept parameters. We show you how to use this task in the next chapter.

Execute Package Task

This task is new to SQL Server 2000. The Execute Package task gives you the ability to easily separate your package into individual components. You would want to use this task if you have a piece of the package, like an auditing procedure, that you continuously use. Rather than have that slice of the package in each one of your packages, you can separate it into its own package and call it from other packages easily. This task also allows you to send global variables to the package being executed. We will show you how to use this task in great detail in the next chapter.

Transfer Error Messages Task

This task is new to SQL Server 2000. You can use this task to transfer user-specified error messages, which are created by the sp_addmessage stored procedure or in Enterprise Manager under **Manage SQL Server Messages** under the **Tools** menu. Some applications create customized error messages that reside in the sysmessages table in the Master database. A reason to use this task would be to transfer the customized user-defined error messages from a SQL Server 7.0 machine to a SQL Server 2000 machine. The Copy Database wizard relies heavily on this task. The destination must be a SQL Server 2000 instance.

Transfer Master Stored Procedures Task

This task is new to SQL Server 2000. The Transfer Master Stored Procedures task will transfer stored procedures from the `Master` database from any SQL Server 7.0 or 2000 instance to a SQL Server 2000 instance. The Copy Database wizard relies heavily on this task. The destination must be a SQL Server 2000 instance.

 # Transfer Jobs Task

This task is new to SQL Server 2000. The Transfer Jobs task will transfer all SQL Server jobs, which are stored in the MSDB database, to the destination server, which must be SQL Server 2000. The Copy Database wizard relies heavily on this task.

 # Transfer Logins Task

This task is new to SQL Server 2000. The Copy Database wizard relies heavily on this task. The destination must be a SQL Server 2000 instance.

 # Transfer Databases Task

This task is new to SQL Server 2000. This task will transfer a database from a SQL Server 7.0 or 2000 instance to a SQL Server 2000 database. The Copy Database wizard relies heavily on this task to transfer databases.

 # Dynamic Properties Task

This task is new to SQL Server 2000. The Dynamic Properties task allows you to dynamically set DTS objects to a value that can be received from an INI file, environment or global variable, query, constants or data file. This is the ideal way to make your package more dynamic and act more like a program. Rather than recreating a package over and over again for each server and manually setting connection settings, you can use this package to read the environment variable and dynamically set the connection server, allowing you to distribute the same package for each server. This type of process was previously done with complex ActiveX scripts, using the DTS object model. We show you how to use this in the next chapter.

 # File Transfer Protocol Task

This task is new to SQL Server 2000. The FTP task will allow you to receive files from internal or external servers using FTP. This task was previously done with either custom components or the command line FTP program provided with Windows. This task is explained in the next chapter.

Message Queue Task

This task is new to SQL Server 2000. The Message Queue task is commonly referred to as the MSMQ task. It allows your packages to communicate with any other application through the Microsoft Message Queue service. This will allow you to send or receive messages or distribute files to any other application or package using the MSMQ service. This task is handy to use to pause a package until other subsidiary packages check-in. This task is explained in the next chapter.

Custom Tasks

Custom tasks allow you to expand the functionality of DTS. They can be written in any COM-compliant programming language such as Visual Basic or C++. You can add these tasks under the task menu and register custom task. We create a custom task in the *Writing Your Own Custom Tasks* chapter. There are also two tasks that are added when you install Analysis Services: one for reprocessing an OLAP cube and another for training a data mining model.

Creating a DTS Package

Now it's time to create your first package from DTS Designer. In this example, we will create a new database on the Wrox development server we created in the previous chapter. We will then create a new package that will transfer two tables from the Northwind database to the Wrox database using the proper **precedence constraints** (which we will explain shortly). This will ensure that we keep the database referential integrity. The table we are transferring from the Northwind database contains a list of categories of products; however, in our destination database, we only need to transfer the vegetarian products. Most of this work can be accomplished with the Data Pump task.

Making the Connections

The first thing we need to do is to open DTS Designer. To do this, right-click on the Data Transformation Services folder, then select New Package. At this point, we are ready to define our connections. We will be defining a connection to our source server and to our destination server. Once these have been established, we can then add the task that will connect them.

❑ From the Connection menu, select Microsoft OLE DB Provider for SQL Server.

❑ Name the connection "Source Server". Under server, choose the server you'd wish to connect to. If you are on a Windows 95 or 98 machine, choose SQL Server authentication, unless you're authenticating to a domain where you have an NT account established in SQL Server. On Windows NT or 2000, you can choose any authentication method. Finally, select the Northwind database for the database option. You will have to click the Refresh button to see the full list of databases if you have Windows 95 or 98. With Windows 2000 and NT, the list will already be populated.

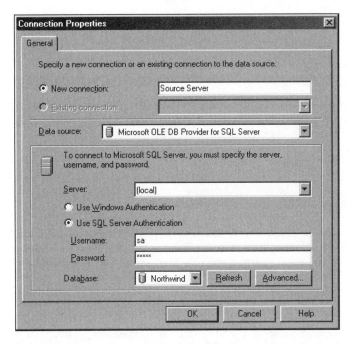

❑ Select a SQL Server connection again, but this time name it **Destination Database** and choose **Wrox** as the database. If the `Wrox` database has not been created, then select <New> from the database drop-down box and it will allow you to create it here.

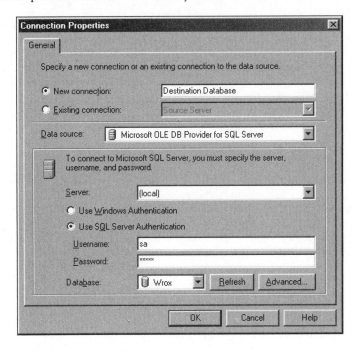

We have purposely selected two options above to discuss two more important points. DTS is a very "localized" environment. When we select "local" as the server name, this can cause some problems in a multi-server environment. If you execute this package from a remote workstation, the DTS engine in SQL Server will look for the Northwind database on the computer executing the package, not on the server in where the package resides.

This also applies when you are defining text files for import. When defining a source as a file (Excel, Text, or Access for example), the package will look at the person's computer who is either executing the package or designing the package. If you are designing a package at your workstation for a server in the production server room, you could very well have a package that works during design time but fails during run time in the production environment. This is because when you design the package, you may have a C:\Wrox\ConvertFlat.txt on your machine, but it will not exist on the server. It is recommended that you use the full UNC path, (\\MACHINENAME\SHARE\FOLDER\FILENAME.TXT) to avoid ever having this problem or any confusion.

An exception to this is the Bulk Insert task because it uses the same rules that apply to the BULK INSERT command, which we will cover in this chapter. If you select c:\wrox\sourceflat.bcp as your source BCP file, DTS will interpret this as sourceflat.bcp on the remote server that stores the package. A package executed remotely will pass because it will always be looking at the same drive on the same server.

If you are executing the package from the server where the package is saved however, then you will experience no problems. The advantage of storing the server name as "local" is that it allows you to transport the package fairly easily. You will be able to move the package to a different server without having to rename the server name in possibly dozens of locations. If you use physical names of servers, and migrate a package to production from development, it makes for many trips to the server room.

> *There is another minor point that needs to be made in the above scenario. If you are running SQL Server Personal Edition under a stand-alone Windows 95 or 98, you do not have the ability to select Windows authentication but the option still exists. You will have to select SQL Server authentication. This is because Windows Authentication doesn't exist for SQL Servers running on Windows 95 or 98 not participating in a domain. Keep in mind that when you select SQL Server authentication, you may have to change the password and possibly the username when you transport the package to a different server.*

Inserting the Data Pump Task

Now that you have the connections established, you can move forward with the transformation. You can now add the Data Pump task into the package. You can use this task by clicking on the source data connection and, while holding down the *Ctrl* key, clicking on the destination data source; then click on the Transform Data Task under the Task docked menu. You can also select the task under the Tasks menu. If you do this, Designer will prompt you to click on the source and destination connections. After either method, an arrow will then appear connecting the two data connections.

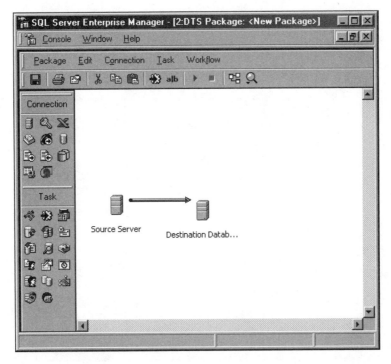

Unlike other tasks, no GUI will open automatically to let you configure the task. You will have to double-click on the arrow as shown above to see the properties. A few rules apply to using this task:

❑   You must have a source connection defined. This is usually a table but can also be a flat file or any OLE DB compliant provider.

❑   A destination must also be defined. This is also usually a table but can be a flat file or any OLE DB compliant provider.

❑   Columns must be mapped for the transformation. This mapping can be one-to-one, one-to-many or many-to-one. For example, if you have customer name broken into two separate fields on the mainframe, but you'd like it combined in SQL Server as one field, you can do that with a many to one mapping. We will cover this in this chapter.

Next double-click on the arrow between the two connections to open up the transformation task. You are first presented with a list of tables and views. You can either select a table or view or write a manual query to narrow down the results. If you'd like to transfer the entire contents of the `Categories` table, then you can select the **Categories** table from the drop-down box and proceed to the next tab.

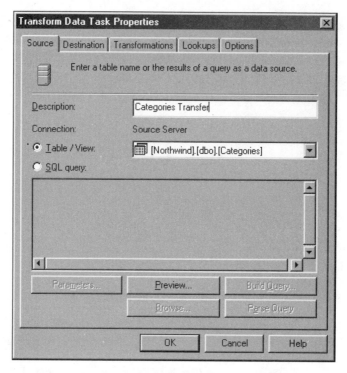

You can also preview the data by selecting a table such as Categories and selecting **Preview**:

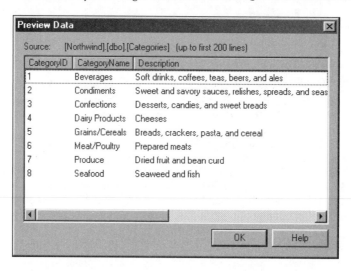

Since we want only vegetarian meals, we are going to want to narrow the results by excluding seafood and meat products. To narrow the results vertically so that we only transfer vegetarian products, select the SQL query option and exclude **CategoryID 6** and **8**. You can do this by using the following query:

```
Select * from Categories where CategoryID not in (6,8)
```

Click on the **Destination** tab. If you currently do not have any tables in your `Wrox` database, the task will prompt you to create one at this time as shown below. You can modify the scripts that create the table here as well. If you are not prompted to create the `Categories` table, this means you have at least one user-defined table in the database and will need to click the **Create New** button at this time. Make sure that you change the name of the table to `Categories` in this **Create Table** screen, otherwise, DTS will create a table on the destination called `New Table`.

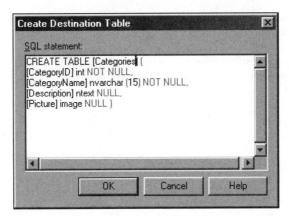

Next, click on the **Transformation** tab as shown in the following screenshot. DTS will automatically map the columns by name for you. You can map each column and choose a transformation method individually under this tab. The default transformation method is **Copy Column**. You can go to the **Options** tab if you do not want to customize the transformation.

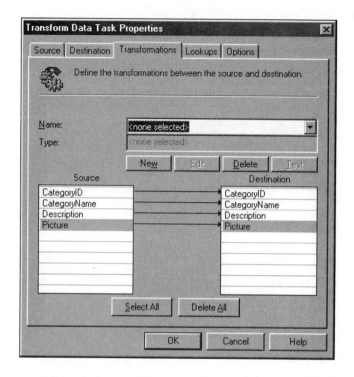

Each arrow you see above represents a COM object that must be called to transform the data. When you have identical meta data on both the source and destination database, it makes sense to "piggyback" all the transformations on one COM object. In our particular example, you will not see a huge performance boost since it is very straightforward, but when transforming 20 or more columns you will begin to see a steady improvement up to 15 percent.

To share the one transformation object, you will first delete the current transformations by clicking Delete All. Then, click Select All and click New. Select Copy Column as the transformation method. Rename the method Copy All Columns; select all columns as the source and destination and confirm that they display in the same order on both tabs by clicking the Properties button on the follow on screen (not shown here). When you click OK you should see the transformation tab look like the first screenshot on the following page:

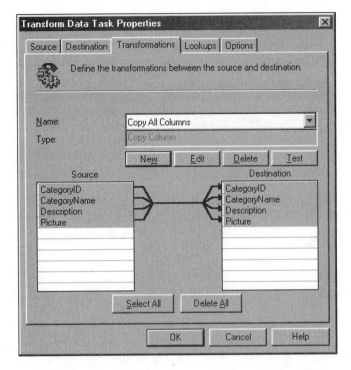

You can also test each transformation to make sure your script validates. When you do this, records are copied to a temporary text file as shown below and no data is actually committed to your database. The temporary file will be placed in the temp directory of the workstation designing the package, so if hard drive space is an issue and you're transferring a large amount of data, do not use this option. DTS will clean up the temporary files after you click Done.

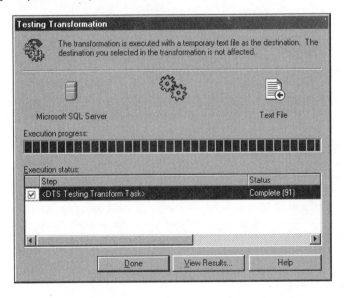

If you happen to receive an error, you can double-click on the step and you will receive the error's details. With the `Categories` table however, this option will not work because of the column `Picture`, which is a image data type. Large BLOB type files can not be transported into a text file. If you try this with the `Categories` table, you'll receive the following error:

> **Your first Data Pump task is now complete. It is crucial to note the importance of naming your tasks with a recognizable name.**

Naming your tasks properly is important because:

- ❑ When executing your package, you will recognize which task fails or succeeds.

- ❑ The DTS object model uses the task's description to call it.

- ❑ When you dynamically change task properties, it makes it much simpler to remember a name like "Category Transfer" rather than "Data Pump Task: undefined".

- ❑ As your package gets larger, you can move your mouse over the task and see the name of it without having to open each task.

You now need to add another Data Pump task to load the `Products` table. This time use the query:

```
select * from Products where CategoryId not in (6, 8)
```

and call the Data Pump task Products Transfer. When clicking on the Destination tab, you will have to click Create New to add the new table into the source table. Make sure you change the name of the table to `Products` from `New Table` in the DDL scripts.

When executing a DTS package, by default, you have no control of which task will be executed first. You can gain control of the task sequence by using **precedence constraints**. So what are they?

Precedence Constraints

Precedence constraints link two steps in a sequential order. In Designer, it will visually look like the lines representing precedence constraints are connecting tasks, but in actuality, they are connecting steps. For example, if you have to load a database in sequential order to protect referential integrity you could use precedence constraints to do so. To create a precedence constraint, you can click the first task, then, while holding the *Ctrl* key, click on which task you'd like to constrain. All the precedence constraints are under the workflow menu in the Designer. There are three different types of constraints:

❑ Completion – The completion constraint will cause Task B to wait for Task A to complete before beginning.

❑ Success – The success constraint will allow Task B to execute only when Task A completes and succeeds.

❑ Failure – This allows you to handle basic rudimentary error control in your package. The on failure constraint will only execute Task C if Task A fails. This is ideal for e-mailing an operator if a data load fails.

You can also set constraints by right-clicking on the task and, under Workflow, going to Workflow Properties. This advanced method of setting constraints is ideal for when you have a complex hierarchy of steps or strong referential integrity.

In our example, the Category table should be loaded before the Products table because of the referential integrity (**RI**). To add a constraint:

❑ Right-click on the Products Data Pump step, then select Workflow Properties.

❑ Click New, then select Category Transfer as the source step, Success as the constraint, and Products Transfer as the destination step.

❑ If you have more complex RI, you can add additional constraints by clicking New again.

Your package should now look like the example below. You can adjust the arrows to make the package more presentable. You can also clean the package up by right-clicking in the Designer Sheet and selecting Auto Layout. Cleaning the package up manually usually yields a better result than using the DTS Auto Layout feature. A good DTS programmer will also add annotation to make the package easier to read by using the Add Text Annotation option under the Package menu.

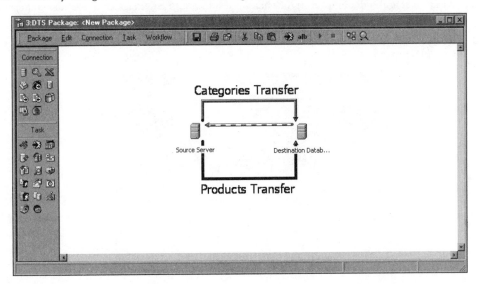

Now you will need to add a task that will check the database for corrupt tables after the transformation completes. In actuality, SQL Server 2000 databases are very good about not becoming corrupt unless there is a power shortage or hardware failure.

❑ Under the Task menu add an Execute SQL task and name it "Maintenance On Wrox Database".

❑ Select Destination Database as the connection.

❑ Under the SQL Statement type DBCC CHECKDB.

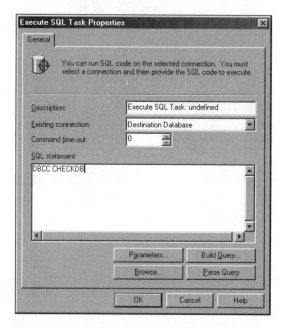

❑ After closing the dialog box, right-click on the Execute SQL task that you just created and under Workflow, select Workflow Properties.

❑ Create a success constraint between the Products Transfer step and the Maintenance On Wrox Database step:

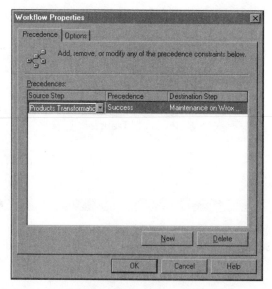

Your first package is now complete. It is a good idea to save it before you execute it to ensure your work doesn't go to waste – however, we will go on to the different options for saving our package in a moment. To execute your package you can click **Execute** under the **Package** menu. If everything goes as planned, you should see the screenshot below. If the package did fail, you would see a red mark next to the step that failed. You can double-click on the failed step to see the detailed error. Chapter 4, *Advanced Settings in DTS* covers common mistakes made in transformations and how to avoid them.

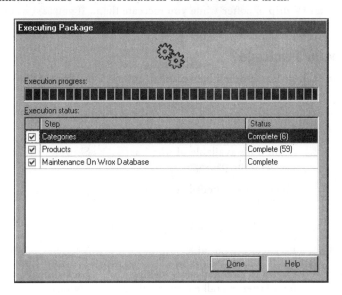

Saving Packages

Where do you save the package that you just created? In DTS you have four options:

❑ Meta Data Services (Repository) – This is the most powerful location in which to save your DTS packages. These packages are saved into the MSDB database. It gives you the flexibility to save package meta data and execution information (**lineage**). Meta data is essentially data that describes data; for instance, you can see data about what type of connections your package is making and details about each task.

❑ COM-Structured Storage File – This is the fastest method of saving and loading your package. This will save your package with a .DTS extension.

❑ SQL Server – This is the default location to save your packages. Packages that are saved here are saved in a BLOB field in the sysdtspackages table. The sysdtspackages table is located in the MSDB database.

❑ Visual Basic File – Saves the package as a .BAS file. This is one of the best ways to learn the DTS object model. Once you save a file into a Visual Basic file, it becomes much harder to open and edit graphically. Native version control is also lost. If you want to save your DTS files in this format, save them also in another format for editing.

To execute a package using its GUID use the following syntax:

```
DTSRun /G "{A02EF403-8806-11D4-8DF1-000094B63497}" /F "C:\Test.dts"
```

Don't worry too much about learning these switches – we're about to show you a much easier way to generate this long command line in a GUI.

Arguments provided to this command are listed below:

Argument	Description
/?	Provides a list of commands.
~	Specifies that the parameter to follow is encrypted and its value is represented in a hexadecimal text format. Can be used with the /S, /U, /P, /F, /R, /N, /M, /G, and /V options.
/S server_name	Represents the NetBios name of the server that the package resides on.
/U user_name	Login ID of a SQL Server user that has permissions to execute the package.
/P password	Password for the user_name login account.
/E	Uses a Windows Authentication trusted connection rather than a standard SQL Server authentication. Will not work with SQL Server Desktop Edition on a Windows 95/98 machine.
/N package_name	Is the name of a DTS package to execute.
/M package_password	Is an optional password assigned to the DTS package when it was created.
/G package_guid_string	The GUID for the package ID.
/V package_version_guid_string	The GUID that is assigned to the version you'd like to execute.
/F filename	The name of the COM-structured file. This normally has a .DTS extension.
/R repository_database_name	The name of the Microsoft Repository where the package is saved. If no repository name is given, then the default name is assumed.
/!X	Retrieves the package from SQL Server and then writes the package contents to the DTS file specified in the filename argument, rather than updating the package in SQL Server from a file. This package will not be executed with this argument.

Argument	Description
/!D	Deletes the DTS package from SQL Server or the Repository. In this case the file will not be executed, only deleted.
/!Y	Will display the encryption command used to execute the package. Best used accompanied by the ~ argument.

The Dtsrunui Utility

Located in the depths of your tools directory, dtsrunui.exe is a hidden treasure. This small application, which is only available to SQL Server 2000 users, allows you to quickly write a DTSRUN statement, which can execute a package from the command line. DTSRunUI can also automate the process of passing parameters to the package.

The tool is located in the tools directory of your C drive. By default, the file is located in the C:\Program Files\Microsoft SQL Servers\80\Tools\Binn folder. When opening, simply enter the server and login information and then click the ellipsis, "...", to find the packages on that server. You can execute packages stored as a COM-structured file (.DTS). VB stored files cannot be executed. On this screen you can also schedule your package for later execution.

After you've identified your package, click **Advanced**. This section will allow you to pass the values of global variables to the package. As you saw in the last section on the DTSRun program, the command line parameters can be quite long and complex. You can click **Generate** to generate the command line execution command.

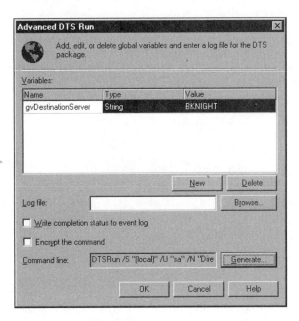

The complete final command line looks like this:

```
DTSRun /S "(local)" /U "sa" /N "DirectLoad" /G "{E8312068-2BA9-1RD4-A0EB-
402310020838}" /V "{82D7C034-2CH3-11D4-A0DD-40033020828}" /A
"gvDestinationServer":"8"="BKNIGHT" /W "0"
```

Scheduling a Package Using SQL Server Agent

The easiest way to schedule a package is to right-click on the package then select Schedule Package. A dialog box will prompt you on the frequency with which you'd like the package to execute.

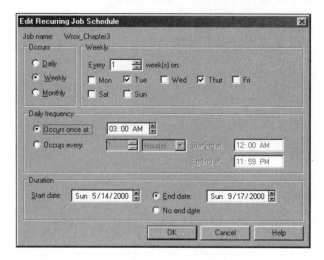

SQL Server schedules packages by using its internal job system. The job system uses SQL Server Agent to execute events on a timer. For the scheduler to work, you will need to have SQL Server Agent running. If you created a job without scheduler on, the job will not fail; it will wait in queue until the SQL Server Agent has started and it has reached the next point in the schedule where it is allowed to execute. For example, if a job is scheduled to execute Monday and Wednesday at midnight and you forget to start SQL Server Agent until Monday at 1 a.m., the job will execute on Wednesday at midnight.

Across all platforms, you can start the SQL Server Agent service by using the SQL Server Service Manager that is located in the SQL Server program files group. You can also set the service to start automatically here when the server reboots.

The procedure for scheduling tasks outlined above will create a job that the SQL Server Agent service executes. It also provides the base functionality behind the job system in SQL Server. The advantage to scheduling a job in this manner is that it uses the DTS command with an encrypted flag (~), which makes the password used to execute the package unreadable. These jobs are stored in the MSDB database in the sysjobs, sysjobschedules, and sysjobsteps tables. You can see the list of other jobs by opening Enterprise Manager and by expanding the Management folder. Under the SQL Server Agent group, click the Jobs icon.

You can also create a job manually by right-clicking the Jobs icon, which is under the Management group, then SQL Server Agent and selecting New Job. This allows you to take advantage of a few more options and take full control of the scheduling system. You can also edit jobs after they've been scheduled through this method. The first dialog box you will see will prompt you for general descriptive data:

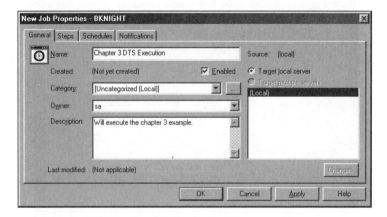

Once you have typed the descriptive information, then you can move to the Steps tab. The Steps tab is where the functionality resides in a job; it acts as a traffic light, directing which step will execute first and what will happen if a step fails. The Steps tab, in reality, is a lighter version of DTS. To add a new step in this job, click the New button.

The step name is only used as a description of the task and has no programmatic use. The type option allows you to execute the following types of commands:

❑ ActiveX scripts.

❑ Operating system commands. If you use this option make sure you fully qualify any path that is outside the C:\Program Files\Microsoft SQL Server\MSSQL\Binn directory (this directory will vary depending on where you installed the Program Files).

❑ Replication commands.

❑ T-SQL queries.

❑ For the purpose of DTS, we will use an operating system command to execute our package:

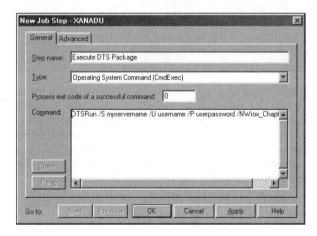

Each time the package is executed, the success or failure of each step is logged once enabled. To open a log in Enterprise Manager, right-click on a package and select **Package Logs**. Drill down to the log and version you care about and select **Open Log**. You can also receive more details about the steps that failed by double-clicking on an individual step. The log's information is stored in the `sysdtspackagelog` table in the MSDB database.

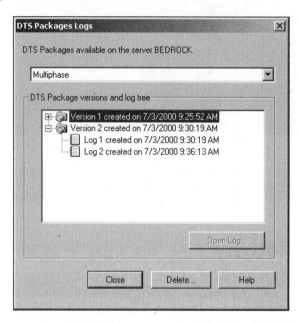

After you open a log, you can view more information, to a more granular detail, by clicking **More Info**. Information displaying in the top scope is from the `sysdtssteplog` table and the detailed information in the bottom pane is from the `sysdtstasklog` table. Again, both tables are in the MSDB database.

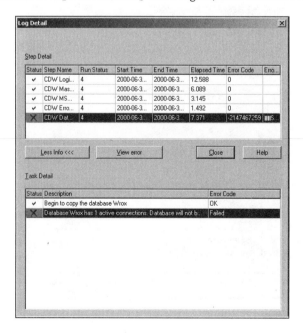

Global Variables

Global Variables provide an internal storage area where you can store data and share it across functions in an Active Script task or steps within a package; you can also use global variables to pass parameters to other packages. Typical use of a global variable would be to set a parameter in a query so that the package execution can have built-in selection criteria. For instance, if you had a package which built report data for a particular date, it would be better to specify that date via a Global Variable than to have to edit the package and replace the instance of that date in every query.

Scope of Global Variables

Scope refers to the lifetime of the variable reference in memory. The scope depends on where the variables are declared or initialized. Whether a global variable is still accessible after a package has executed depends on how the global variable was created.

A global variable created during design time, as in the DTS Designer, continues to retain the value it had when the package finished execution, but only if the package is saved. Let's say that we create a global variable called gvDate in a package and set it to the value of "09/01/2000". During the package execution, an ActiveX script changes the value of "09/01/2000" to the next month, "10/01/2000". The next time you execute the package, the global variable will contain "10/01/2000", not "09/01/2000".

However, global variables created dynamically in an ActiveX script have two scopes. If they are created before the Function Main() declaration, they are available to all functions in the script (don't worry, you will see this in the next chapter). This is the equivalent to module-level scope. If they are declared within a function, they are available only inside that function. This is equivalent to procedure-level scope.

Finally if you specify a variable using the dtsrun command or using the dtsrunui utility, the global variable can be set, but since the package does not save itself after execution, the changes to the variable will be lost. It will retain the original value stored in the package when it was last saved.

Creating a Global Variable using the DTS Designer

Global Variables can be set in a variety of ways, but most often are set using the DTS Designer when designing a package. To create a global variable for your package, go to Package | Properties and select the Global Variables tab. The following dialog appears:

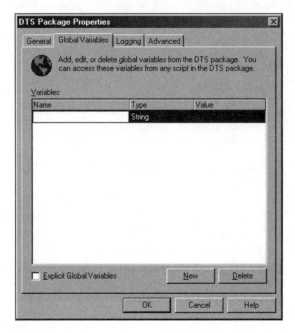

Here you can specify the global variables for your package. You can add variables as well as remove them. Remember to use proper notation when naming the variable to help you remember what information is contained in it.

The valid options for the type are:

<other>	LPSTR
Boolean	LPWSTR
Currency	Pointer
Date	Real (4 byte)
Decimal	Real (8 byte)
HResult	String
Int	Unsigned Int
Integer	Unsigned Int (1 byte)
Integer (1 byte)	Unsigned Int (2 byte)
Integer (small)	Unsigned Int (4 byte)

If you wish to, you can enter a value for the global variable. Once the package is saved, this value will be the default value for that particular variable.

The option **Explicit Global Variables** requires you to define the variable prior to referencing it in an assignment. In other words, you must declare the global variable before trying to set it to a particular value. For those of you who are familiar with VB and VBScript, this is similar to using `Option Explicit`. You can even use global variables to pass objects for you – you will see examples of this later in the book. In addition to creating a variable using the designer, you can also create and set a global variable by using an ActiveX Script task, which, again, will be covered in more detail in later chapters.

Global variables are everywhere in DTS as the examples in later chapters will show. They can be referenced from inside and outside the package, and you can set them from numerous places, including the DTS package designer, by an ActiveX Script Task, via a Message Queue, and even using an Execute SQL task. We will now look in more detail at some of the tasks we briefly touched upon earlier – these are the tasks that will best prepare you to build packages of your own. Some of the more complex, or less common, tasks, however, are covered in the next chapter.

The Bulk Insert Task

The Bulk Insert task is the fastest way to import data from a flat file. As we mentioned earlier, the Bulk Insert task uses a similar engine to BCP, but it only allows you to import data. BCP allows you also to export data to a flat file. This task is also the least powerful. The source data you transfer in this task must align perfectly to the destination table. If it does not align, then you must use the Data Pump task for the transformation.

First, you will need to create a table in the `Wrox` database with the following script:

```
CREATE TABLE [BulkInsert] (
    [Column1] [varchar] (15) NULL ,
    [Column2] [varchar] (15) NULL ,
    [Column3] [varchar] (15) NULL
) ON [PRIMARY]
```

The source flat file can be found on the Wrox web site or you can create one like the semi-colon delimited file below. Name the file `convertflat.txt` and place it in a directory called `Wrox` on your C drive.

```
Column1;Column2;Column3
datacolumn1;datacolumn2;datacolumn3
datacolumn1;datacolumn2;datacolumn3
```

If you try to add the Bulk Insert task before you have a SQL Server connection established, you will receive the following error message:

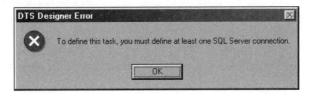

Create a new package and establish a SQL Server connection to the `Wrox` database as you did in the previous example. For the existing connection option, use the Destination Database that we created earlier. You can add a Bulk Insert task from the **Task** menu. If you are on a Windows 95 or 98 machine, you will have to click on the refresh button to see a list of tables. The destination table will be the `BulkInsert` table we created earlier. The source data file will be the above flat file. The example overleaf calls the file `convertflat.txt` in the `C:\Wrox` directory. The column delimiter should be a semicolon, since each column is separated by a semicolon in our example. This will tell the Bulk Insert task that every time it finds a semicolon, to move to the next column. Other options also exist that we will discuss in a moment. You can also add customized column delimiters here as well.

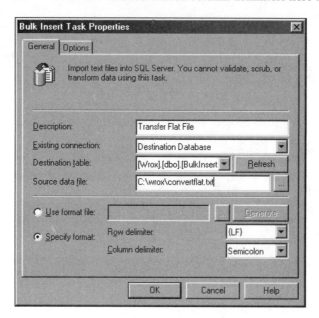

By clicking on the **Options** tab, you can set more advanced settings for this task as shown opposite. We will go into some of the more advanced settings in the next chapter. At this time, you can set several optional settings:

- ❑ The **Check constraints** option ensures that the BULK COPY process passes through constraints during the load. By default BULK COPY ignores constraints.

- ❑ The **Enable identity insert** setting turns on the identity insert option that we mentioned in the last chapter. With this option on, you are allowed to insert into a column with identities.

- ❑ With the **Sorted data** option checked, you can supply the task with a column name in the destination table by which to sort the data.

- ❑ The **Table Lock** setting will create an exclusive table lock on the destination table, preventing any other user from accessing the data until the task completes. This is normally unnecessary; however, if you are doing your inserts on a heavily used table, it may be needed. This option will also speed up your load slightly since SQL Server will not have to escalate the locks to a table lock.

- ❑ The **Data file type** option allows you to specify different types of source flat files. For example, this option allows you to load data that was outputted in BCP native format.

❑ The Insert batch size option allows you to specify how many records to commit to the destination at a time. A setting of 0 means that the records will all be committed at once. If an error occurs during the transfer, then all records are rolled back. A batch size of 1 means that each record is committed individually.

❑ The First row option is needed when your source flat file has column headers. The first row in the source data file consists of a header column so we will start at row two. If you specify the last row as 0, it will continue to bulk copy the data until it reaches the end of the file.

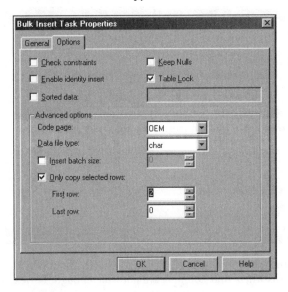

The final package should look like the following screenshot. Notice that there is no arrow connecting the connection and the task in this instance: you'll only see the arrow connecting connections and tasks in the Transform Data task.

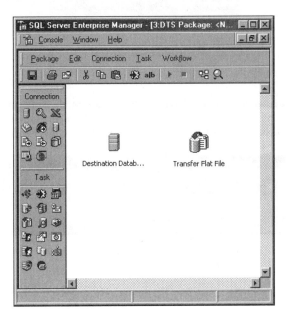

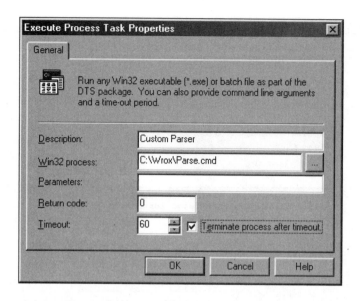

The Execute SQL Task

The Execute SQL task is one of the handiest tasks provided in SQL Server 7.0 but has improved dramatically in SQL Server 2000. SQL Server 2000 has added the ability to pass parameters in and receive rowsets or single values as output. The task uses Global Variables heavily internally, which we went over briefly earlier in this chapter. Global Variables are an essential part of DTS, which allow you to pass data in and out of packages and steps. It is how DTS breaks out of its typical mode where Step1 can't communicate to Step2.

In this example, we're going to perform a very typical exercise in a data load procedure. Packages can sometimes take a long time to develop and you only want to develop a package once and make it reusable. Wouldn't it be nice to be able to add a record into a table when you bring a new customer into your project and have your DTS package work for them automatically? The Execute SQL Task could handle part of that process. The task could go out to the table that you created, and lookup the path for the client that you pass it, then transform the data from that path after it's created using a variety of other tasks. You'd first have to create a table in the Wrox database to hold your meta data, as shown below:

```
CREATE TABLE [dbo].[Client_MetaData] (
    [Client_ID] [int] NOT NULL ,
    [Client_Path] [varchar] (50) NOT NULL
) ON [PRIMARY]
```

Then populate the table with a few records, as shown below:

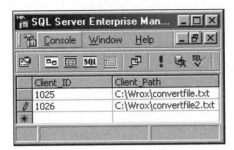

Next we'll have to create a new package and create a few global variables. One global variable will store the client number that we're going to query against and another will store the path to the extract file for the client. The extract path will be found dynamically based on the first global variable. Name the global variables as shown below and assign the first global variable the value of 1025. You can assign these under the Global Variables tab in Package Properties:

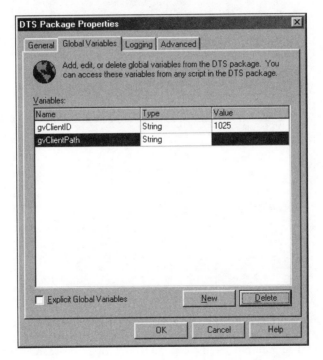

You will then want to create a connection, as you did in the previous examples, to the Wrox database. You must create a connection before you can use the Execute SQL task. The Execute SQL task only has a few parameters:

❑   The Description option is a user-defined descriptive name for your task.

❑   The Existing Connection option defines what connection you will execute the command against. This can be heterogeneous as we will discuss in the two heterogeneous data chapters.

❑   The **Command time-out** option is the amount of time that DTS will wait for the command to finish. The step fails if the time-out expires. A setting of 0 is an unlimited amount of time. If you set this option, make sure you leave a large window for your command to finish. We will set this to 60 seconds as shown below because the query in actuality should only take a second. If the query takes any more than a minute, then something has gone wrong and you will want your package to terminate. Not setting this option could cause your package to hang indefinitely while DTS waits for this step to finish.

❑   The **SQL statement** is a valid SQL command for the connection. This could be any SQL statement that is supported by your target connection. In our case, we're querying the client meta data table to find out what the file's path should be. You represent input parameters with a question mark. Input parameters allow you to create one SQL statement that you can reuse in your package. For example, in our case we want to find out what the path is, based on the client number.

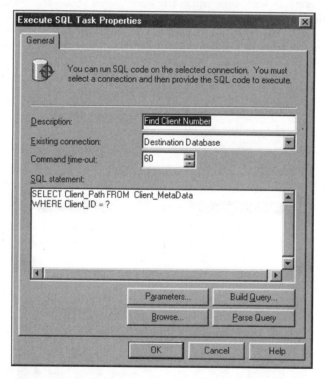

You can then click on the **Parameters** button to set what global variable the question mark is mapped to. We need to map ours to the `gvClientID` global variable as shown below under the **Input Parameters** tab. If you had multiple parameters you were trying to pass in, you could assign them based on their ordinal position. So if you have:

```
SELECT Path FROM Client_MetaData
WHERE Client_ID = ? and NextDate = ?
```

Parameter1 would be `Client_ID` and Parameter2 would be `NextDate` in the above query.

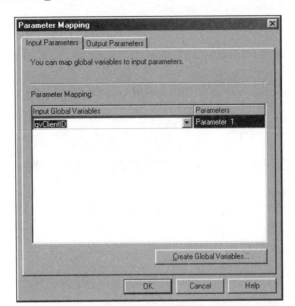

The final step is to define what, if any, output parameters you'd like to define. In our case, we would want the value from the query to be saved as the global variable `gvClientPath`. If you were selecting more than one column, then multiple columns would appear in the parameters column and you would have the opportunity to assign them to global variables too. You can also save the entire rowset if you're retrieving more than one record. The rowset can later be used in proceeding steps as a disconnected ADO recordset. This is useful if you'd like to list all the clients to perform an action on and then loop through the list of clients in a later task.

After executing the package, you will be able to go back to the global variable list and see that it is now set to the proper value. If you don't save the package, then the global variable is set back to Null. Global variables are only alive for the life of package, whether in run time or design time.

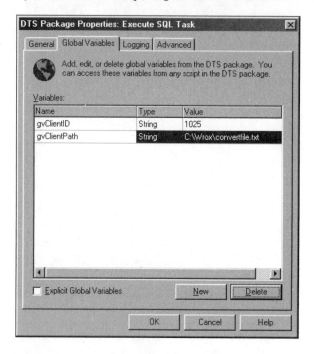

The Copy SQL Server Objects Task

The Copy SQL Server Objects task is a useful way of copying SQL Server objects and their dependencies from one SQL Server instance to another. It is similar to the SQL Server 6.5 Transfer Manager as it only can transfer SQL Server objects. The main difference between this task and the Copy Database task is that this task does not utilize detaching and attaching databases. With this in mind, this task may take longer to execute since it does have to physically copy data, whereas the Copy Database Wizard (CDW) or Copy Database task copies the entire database then attaches it. With this task, you can transfer objects from:

❑ SQL Server 7.0 to SQL Server 7.0

❑ SQL Server 7.0 to SQL Server 2000

❑ SQL Server 2000 to SQL Server 2000

You cannot downgrade your database from SQL Server 2000 to 7.0. The fact that you can transfer 7.0 databases to 7.0 is a key difference between this and CDW. Valid objects are the same as for the Copy Database Wizard. Since the options are almost exactly the same, we won't spend too much time on the task. As in CDW, you must only specify a SQL Server as your source and destination as shown below. Unlike CDW, the Transfer SQL Server Objects task can only copy one database at a time, which is selected from the Database drop-down box. As always, users of Windows 95 and 98 machines will have to click refresh to see a list of the databases. For the Destination, you will have to specify a database for the SQL Server objects to be transferred to.

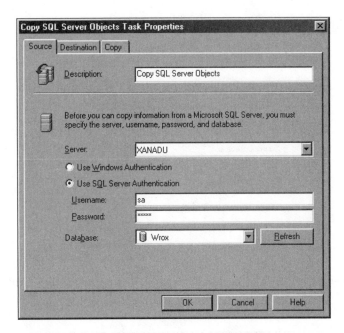

Under the **Copy** tab, you are presented with the familiar items that we explored in the last chapter in the CDW section:

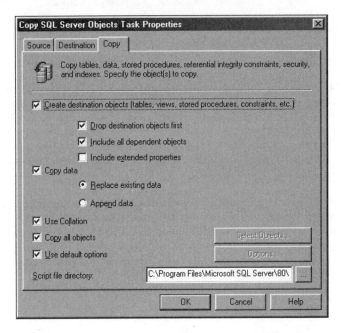

The main thing to remember is that CDW is faster, but you are not allowed to have any connections to the source database at the time of transfer. The Copy SQL Server Objects task allows you to execute the task while your database is online. Your database will of course slow down during the process, but to a minor degree. Another key difference is that this task will not create the database for you as CDW does; you must already have your database created before you can proceed in configuring the task.

The Send Mail Task

The Send Mail task is a simple task that you can use to send e-mail messages to anyone with e-mail access.

The most challenging part in the deployment of this task is cutting through your own internal red tape.

Source Database   Destination Datab...

Send Mail to Oper...

Most of the configuring is done by your MAPI client. You can configure the MAPI client in the Control Panel under **Mail and Fax**. If you haven't configured the MAPI client you will receive the following error when you try to add the Send Mail Task.

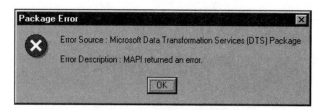

Package Error

Error Source : Microsoft Data Transformation Services (DTS) Package

Error Description : MAPI returned an error.

OK

To configure the task, select the profile name from the drop-down box, keeping in mind that the drop-down box will display the locally defined profile names. If you're designing a package from a workstation that has MAPI installed properly and then execute the package as a job, the package may fail unless MAPI is configured the same way on the server. This will be the same name as appears in your Control Panel when you click **Show Profiles**. The message will be sent using the account that you have configured in MAPI. The password option will pass the appropriate password to sign into the mail account used by the profile.

Lastly, you can attach files by typing the full path to the file. Semicolons can separate multiple files. Again, attached files will be pulled from the machine executing the package. If you're developing a package from your workstation and have a file called C:\Wrox\file.txt, then the make sure it also exists on the server when it executes as a job.

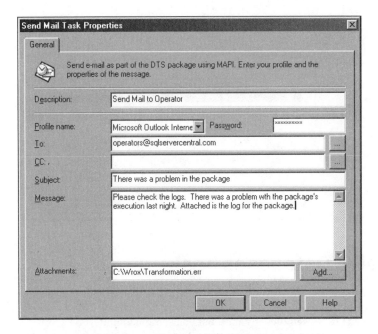

If the file attachment does not exist, you will get the following error:

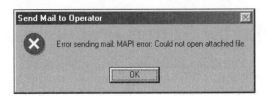

We will also cover how to use CDO to send mail as well as through the ActiveX Script task later in the book. CDO provides you with a way of sending the message completely through SMTP and so you don't have to have a MAPI clien installed.

The Transfer Error Messages Task

The Transfer Error Message task transfers all user-defined error messages that you may have added onto a server. A custom error message can be added in T-SQL with the sp_addmessage stored procedure. It can also be created in Enterprise Manager under the Tools menu and Manage SQL Server Messages. These user-defined messages may be needed for your application to work and previously, you would have to recreate the error messages on each server you wished to install your application on.

This task is used heavily in CDW and, like the other CDW tasks, the destination must be a SQL Server 2000 instance. The source can be a SQL Server 7.0 or 2000 instance. To configure the task, simply define your source and destination connections inside the task as you did in CDW. Under the Error Messages tab, you can either transfer all the user-defined errors detected at the package's run time or you can specify the errors you'd like to transfer as shown below. The task will search the destination server to make sure there are no conflicts in the errors. As you can see in the following screenshot there is an error 50001 on the destination and that error will not be transferred.

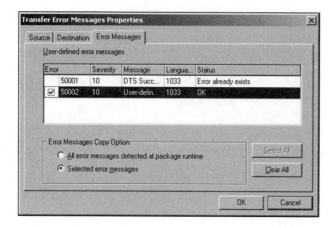

The Transfer Databases Task

The Transfer Database task allows you to move or copy a database. This task uses the same screens that CDW does. It is also the task that CDW uses to move or copy your databases. Again, your source can be a SQL Server 7.0 or SQL Server 2000 instance, but your destination must be a SQL Server 2000 instance. You can transfer one or more databases at a time. The same rules apply to this task that apply to CDW.

The Transfer Master Stored Procedures Task

The Transfer Master Stored Procedures task copies user-defined stored procedures that may be stored in your SQL Server 7.0 or 2000 Master database. The destination must be a SQL Server 2000 instance. This task is configured in exactly the same way as the Transfer Error Messages task we mentioned earlier. After establishing your connections inside the task, go to the Stored Procedures tab, where you can either transfer all the stored procedures or a select number. You cannot transfer a stored procedure that has a duplicate name on the destination, as you can see below:

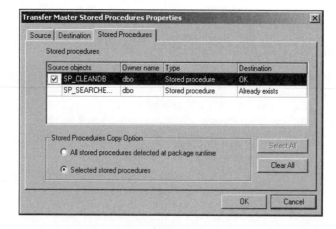

The Transfer Jobs Task

The Transfer Jobs task gives you the ability to quickly transfer SQL Server Agent jobs from any SQL Server 7.0 or 2000 instance to any SQL Server 2000 instance. You configure this task as you configure the other CDW tasks. After specifying a source and destination server inside the task, you can specify to transfer all the jobs at run time or just a select few as shown below. The task will not allow you to transfer a task with an identical name on the destination.

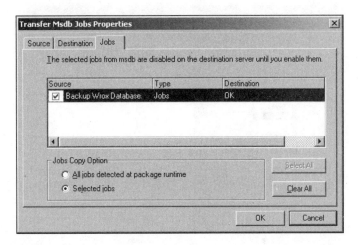

The Transfer Logins Task

The Transfer Logins task allows you to transfer all the logins for a particular database or all the databases on a given SQL Server. Your source can be a SQL Server 7.0 or 2000 instance and your destination must always be a SQL Server 2000 instance. Again, the configuration of the task is duplicated from CDW where you must specify a source and destination inside the task. Then, you can either transfer all the logins for the server or specify certain databases for which you'd like to transfer the logins, as you can see below:

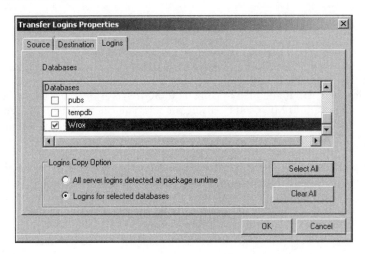

Disconnected Edit

The disconnected edit feature in SQL Server 2000's DTS Designer can be accessed under the **Package** menu. This option allows you to edit any DTS connection, step, task, or global variable. The disconnected edit mode is a convenient way to edit all the package's properties in one screen. To edit a property, simply drill down the left pane until to you find a property you'd like to edit. At that point, double-click the property on the right to open it.

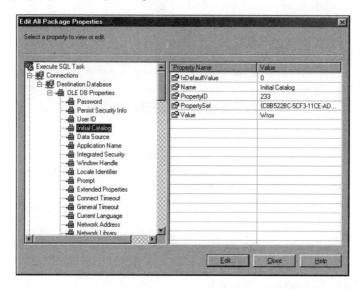

This mode should only be used by advanced users. This is because each DTS task provides error checking and validation to prevent you from connecting to a bad FTP site, for example. This is ignored when in Disconnected Edit Mode. The main reason for using this mode is if you don't have direct access to a system that the package needs to see. For example, if the staging server isn't yet equipped with network access. The problem with this is that the disconnected edit mode does not provide any type of validation. If you happen to mistype a FTP site, then the edit screen will allow you to do this.

DTS Interoperability

This section is best begun by overturning a widely misconceived notion – you do not need SQL Server to run DTS. You do need SQL Server to use the DTS Designer but the DTS engine is currently freely re-distributable. This is true as long as you save your packages as COM-structured files. You will need a **Client Access License** (**CAL**) if you plan to connect to SQL Server in your package. For more information about the various Microsoft licensing models, you can visit the SQL Server homepage (http://www.microsoft.com/sql). If you built a DTS application that moved data from Sybase to Oracle however, you would only need a license for Sybase and Oracle.

With all the functionality of DTS, you can make a package standalone with only eight DLL files, five RLL files (resource files) and one executable. All these files can be found in the \x86\binn directory of your SQL Server CD-ROM. On the server, these executable and DLL files can be found in the MSSQL\Binn directory and the English resource (.RLL) file can be found in the MSSQL\Binn\Resources\1033 directory. You will need the following files:

File	Purpose
Axscphst.dll Axscphst.rll	Manages the ActiveX scripting.
Dtsffile.dll Dtsffile.rll	OLE DB flat file provider used in the DTS Package Designer and Wizards.
Dtspkg.dll Dtspkg.rll	Manages the package.
Dtspump.dll Dtspump.rll	Holds the ActiveX constants for the DTS Pump task.
Sqlresld.dll	Required for loading satellite resource files.
Dtsrun.exe Dtsrun.rll	Command file that will execute a DTS package.
Custtask.dll	Handles any custom task, such as the File Transfer Protocol task.
Sqlwoa.dll Sqlwid.dll	Unicode and ANSI translation for SQL Server.

If you plan to make any database connections, you'll also need the connectivity files (MDAC 2.6), which can be found on the SQL Server CD as well. You can also use the SQLREDIS.EXE file that is found on your SQL Server CD and is included in every service pack release. SQLREDIS.EXE includes all the client components you'll need to run a DTS package and connect.

Developer Samples

Packaged with every SQL Server CD are several developer samples, including:

- ❑   DTS packages
- ❑   DTS custom applications
- ❑   ActiveX scripts

The sample packages and programs can be found and uncompressed from a file on the SQL Server CD in the \DevTools\Samples\DTS\Unzip_DTS.exe file. Once uncompressed, you can walk through some of the examples, which are written in Visual Basic and C++. This allows you to preview some of the code that DTS uses and the processes to load data from a relational OLTP database to a data warehouse. All of these types of processes will be discussed in this book.

Summary

This chapter provides you with the basics as to how you can navigate around DTS Designer and transform your first data, whether relational or flat. In this chapter we discussed the different types of tasks and how to use the Data Pump and the Bulk Insert tasks. We also explored where to save your packages and the various ways to execute them. You can execute your package from Enterprise Manager, DTSRUNUI, DTSRun, or as a job in SQL Server Agent. A key point in executing your packages utilizes the system from where you're executing the package. For example, if you're executing the package from your workstation, but the package is stored on the server, then your machine will take the performance hit of running the package.

Some important points that you will need to remember are:

❑ The Bulk Insert task is the fastest task to transfer data, but the least robust.

❑ The ActiveX script task is the most versatile but lacks speed.

❑ The fastest way to save and load a file is as a COM-structured storage file. The slowest is saving your package into the Microsoft Meta Data Services.

❑ How to execute a package with the dtsrun utility.

❑ We can schedule a package to be executed at a point in time with Microsoft SQL Server Agent or to be executed immediately.

❑ The DTS run-time requirements are independent from SQL Server and with a few files can be run on any machine.

In the next chapter we will cover some more DTS tasks and explore the Transform Data Task more deeply.

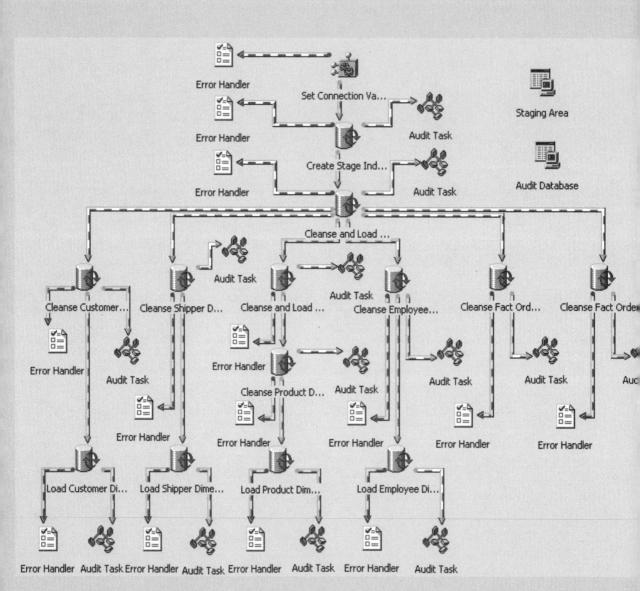

Error Handler

Set Connection Va...

Audit Task

Staging Area

Error Handler

Error Handler

Create Stage Ind...

Audit Task

Audit Database

Error Handler

Cleanse and Load ...

Cleanse Customer...

Cleanse Shipper D...

Audit Task

Cleanse and Load ...

Audit Task

Cleanse Employee...

Cleanse Fact Ord...

Cleanse Fact Order

Error Handler

Audit Task

Error Handler

Audit Task

Cleanse Product D...

Audit Task

Audit Task

Audit Task

Aud

Error Handler

Error Handler

Error Handler

Error Handler

Error Handler

Error Handler

Load Customer Di...

Load Shipper Dime...

Load Product Dim...

Load Employee Di...

Error Handler   Audit Task   Error Handler   Audit Task   Error Handler   Audit Task   Error Handler   Audit Task

3

Advanced Tasks

Commonly in using DTS we don't break out of the box of thinking that DTS is only for transforming data. DTS also offers a number of options for those who are trying to add functionality to their programs. In SQL Server 2000, Microsoft has added a number of new features that enhance the transformation process, but also give added ability for DTS to act as a collaborative tool. In the previous chapter, we met the tasks available in SQL Server 2000. In this chapter, we're going to look at what we can do with these tasks in more detail.

In SQL Server 7.0, to make a package dynamic or communicate with other packages, you had to use complex ActiveX tasks and programs to do this with brute force. Now in SQL Server 2000, much of the need to program your own solutions has been replaced by new tasks. Don't worry though, we're still going to discuss how to perform these functions in ActiveX later in the book.

In this chapter we will:

- ❑ Explore the new functionality of the Multiphase Data Pump
- ❑ Use more advanced tasks such as Data Driven Queries
- ❑ Explain how to receive files through FTP and Message Queuing through DTS
- ❑ Make your code modular with the Execute Package task
- ❑ Dynamically set the parameters for tasks, connections, or global variables
- ❑ Use Message Queing to communicate with other applications or DTS Packages

We'll start with one of the most significant improvements incorporated into SQL Server 2000: the multiphase data pump.

The Multiphase Data Pump

In SQL Server 7.0, we only had one phase to the Transform Data task – the Row Transform phase. Now the Row Transform phase has been broken into six functionally different phases to give us more flexibility.

Some of the added abilities given through the data pump additions are:

❑ Transformation Extensibility – the ability to add logic for your own custom error handling, initialize/free your own COM components, use other script-enabled technologies like ADO (ActiveX Data Objects) programming or perform disparate transformation steps, such as writing header records, rows, and footer records.

❑ Transformation Restartability – the ability to maintain "success points" in your transformations to restart from later should a complete failure occur.

❑ Data Cleansing and Data Awareness – provide mechanisms for us to deal with known errors and resubmit data; allow for us to keep accurate counters of the good and bad data and the types of errors that occur.

Let's first take a look at a diagram of the new phases in SQL Server 2000:

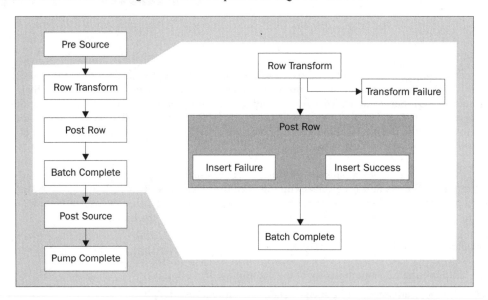

As mentioned, there are six phases that comprise the multiphase data pump. The phases are:

❑ **Pre Source Data** – Phase executes once at the beginning of the transformation. Functions scripted for execution within this phase are run before the first record is fetched from the source. In general, the functions you will write for this are initialization or start-up functions. Some examples would be initializing counter variables, performing preliminary SQL against your target (for example, truncate tables or drop indexes), initializing a COM object for later use, initializing ADO Connections, writing HEADER data to a table or file, and countless others. We will explore these concepts more in our examples later in the chapter.

❑ **Row Transform** – Phase was the only transformation phase in 7.0. Now recognized as the default phase in SQL Server 2000; DTS users who don't use the multiphase functionality will still utilize this phase of the data pump. As a whole, all transformations will use the row transform phase to move data on a column per row level between source and destination data sources.

❑ **Post Row Transform** – Phase is executed for each row that is transformed. This phase is divided into three sub-phases: Transform Failure, Insert Success, and Insert Failure. Within these three sub-phases, we have the opportunity to address the quality of the data (data type integrity), correct data issues for the transform, maintain counters and respond to the state of the individual row. Utilizing this phase and its sub-phases will be explored in our examples.

❑ **On Batch Complete** – Phase executes for each batch; by default, there is only one batch per data pump. The Insert Batch Size, and thus the number of batches, can be changed on the Options tab under the Transform Data Task Properties, shown below.

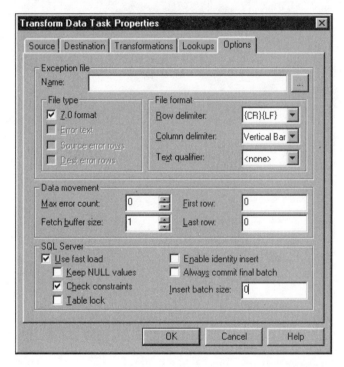

One example use of this phase would be for auditing the state of a larger, multi-batch table load.

❑ **On Pump Complete** – Phase executes after all rows have been transformed. During this phase, we can perform non data-dependent tasks, like finalizing counter variables, capturing the final status of the pump, freeing memory associated with COM objects, or other script-enabled technologies.

❑ **Post Source Data** – Phase also executes after all rows are transformed but, unlike the On Pump Complete phase, the Post Source Data phase can access data. This data access can be used to write footer rows to the target of your transformation.

Now that we understand the basic plumbing of the multiphase data pump, we need to ensure that, as an option, it has been enabled. By default, the multiphase data pump is not exposed to the DTS Designer User Interface. At this point it suffices to say that the data pump task becomes slightly more complex once this option is enabled. To enable the multiphase data pump within the DTS UI, you will need to launch SQL Server 2000 Enterprise Manager. If you already have both the Enterprise Manager and the DTS Designer UI, you will need to close the DTS Designer. Within the Enterprise manager, right-click on the **Data Transformation Services** menu under one of your registered servers, then select **Properties**. At this point you will be presented with the **Package Properties** dialog, as shown below. To show the multiphase data pump elements in the DTS Designer, you should select the **Show multi-phase pump in DTS Designer**. This option only deals with whether or not the multiphase options are shown in the Designer. The SQL Server 2000 DTS run-time will always support multiphase transforms in packages regardless of whether this options is enabled.

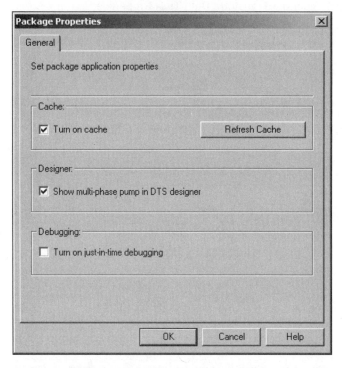

The astute observer will also note that this dialog provides for a few other options new to DTS in SQL Server 2000: DTS introduces caching and control over the debugging of ActiveX Scripting.

DTS was notoriously slow when opening an existing or a new package in the Designer. A reason for this poor performance is that when the Designer opens it interrogates the registry to determine what DTS Tasks, Transforms, and OLEDB Providers are registered on the machine. This results in a significant amount of preliminary work each time an instance of the designer is opened. To overcome this, Caching was made available. When enabled, through the **Turn on cache** option, all DTS Tasks, Transforms, and OLEDB Providers information is placed into the Cache. This cache is used when starting up the Designer. To keep the cache current, you should click the **Refresh Cache** button which will add any new Tasks, Transforms, and OLEDB Providers and their interface information to the DTS Cache.

You may have stumbled upon script debugging in prior DTS versions if you had the Microsoft Script Debugger and other development tools installed. Unfortunately, you had no control over whether you were going to use the debugger from within the DTS environment. The Turn on just-in-time debugging option provides you with the control to turn on and off the debugging of ActiveX Scripts. When this option is turned on, DTS gives this information to the Microsoft Scripting Engines which in turn will call upon one of the debuggers installed with Windows 2000, NT 4.0 Option Pack, or Visual Interdev 6.0, if an error arises.

Although debugging is beyond the scope of this chapter, it is important to note that this level of control exists. Debugging will allow us access to the functions and variables hosted in the ActiveX scripting environment and give us the ability to understand issues within the multiphase data pump and other areas with a lesser amount of work.

Multiphase Data Pump Example

You've been presented with quite a bit of information about the multiphase data pump. Let's explore some common examples of how we can leverage this very powerful functionality.

We'll start by opening the DTS Designer (by selecting Data Transformation Services | New Package) and configure two data source connections. The graphic below shows that we have established a SQL Server connection, named Northwind, to our relational data source, which happens to be the Northwind database and a second connection, named Northwind Output, to the SQL Server tempdb database as our target data source. For the purposes of our example, we will be transforming data from the Northwind Orders table into a table named Orders in the tempdb database. You may want to transform the data into another database, rather than tempdb, to retain your example.

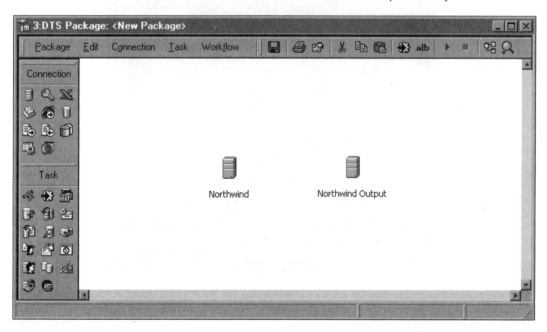

Let's begin to explore the other phases of the multiphase data pump. While on the Transformations tab, select Pre source data from the Phases filter group and select New:

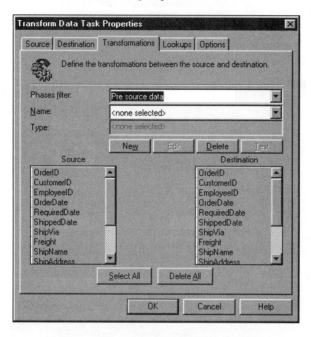

When the dialog box appears asking what type of transformation you would like to create, select ActiveX Script:

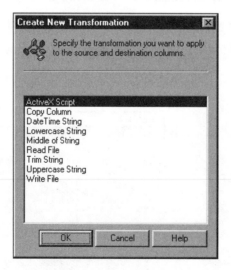

Once you click OK, you will be taken to the Tranformation Options Dialog. On the General tab, select Properties. This will take you to the DTS ActiveX Scripting editor, like the one shown below, where we can add our ActiveX code for the remainder of our example.

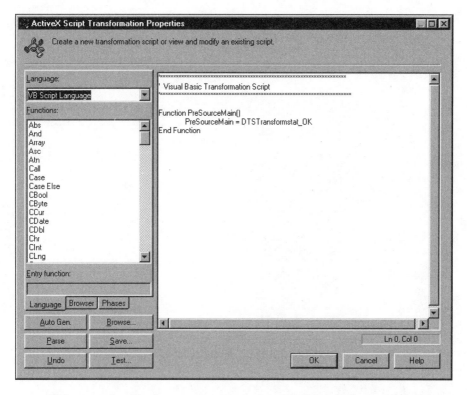

Before we go further, we should take a moment to explore the ActiveX Script editor. There are three tabs on the left hand side of the editor. These tabs are:

❑ **Language** – the area of the editor where the registered scripting language is selected, its supported internal functions are listed, and an entry function (not applicable to multiphase functions) is defined (as shown above).

❑ **Browser** – provides the collection of constant values returned by tasks, steps, and tranform phase functions. It also provides access to variables within the Source Columns collection, Destination Columns collection and the DTS Package Global Variables collection (set within the DTS Package Properties). Properly formed text can be added to your script editor for any individual item in this browser by double-clicking upon it. Your **Browser** tab will look similar to the one here:

❑　　**Phases** – the core area of the scripting editor for defining ActiveX Script Transformation functions for all phases of the multiphase datapump. The **Phases** tab is shown below:

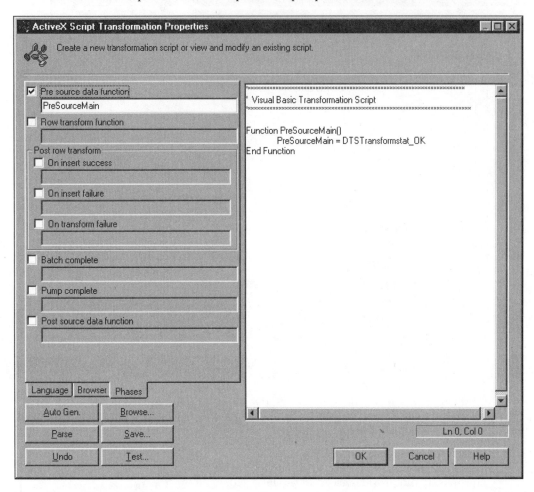

Our editor at this point looks a little sparse. In order to explore all of the phases of the multiphase data pump, check all of the phase options. Click the **Auto Gen**. button, which, as its name implies, will generate a stubbed-in function for each phase.

At this point your code should resemble the code below:

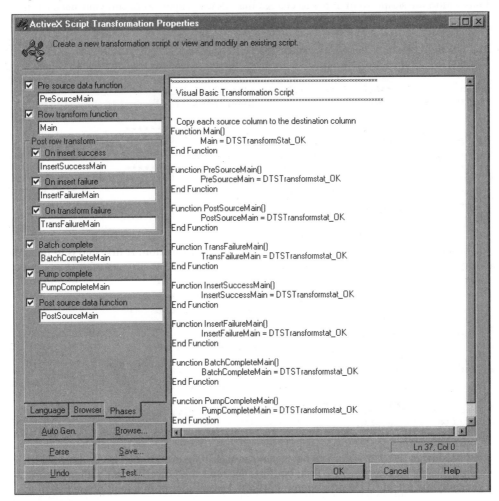

We have devoted a section to each phase of the data pump in their order of execution.

Pre Source Example

You may recall that the PreSourceMain phase is executed prior to the starting of any transformation, making this a perfect stage to initialize variables and startup functions. Here is our example PreSourceMain function:

```
Dim oConn  'A global object that we will use for an ADO Connection
```

On Batch Complete Example

You may recall that we changed our batch size in the Transform Data Task Properties on the Options tab to 100. This setting provides that the On Batch Complete phase will be called every 100 records.

```
Function BatchCompleteMain()
'*******
'    Account for Each Completed Batch
'*******
    DTSGlobalVariables("gnBatchesCompleted").Value = _
        DTSGlobalVariables("gnBatchesCompleted").Value + 1

    BatchCompleteMain = DTSTransformstat_OK
End Function
```

Post Source Data Example

The Post Source Data phase is called upon the final read of data from the data source. Our example below uses this phase to finalize counter values and reuse the COM Object, oConn, which is our persistent ADO Connection, to write an event to our SQL Server's event log using the stored procedure xp_logevent.

```
Function PostSourceMain()
Dim sMsg
Dim sSQL

'***********************************************************
'    Build a message from the global variables and
'    display it and write it to the SQL Server Event Log
'***********************************************************

sMsg = "The Example Transform Completed as follows:" & chr(13) & _
    DTSGlobalVariables("gnRowsSucceeded").Value & _
    " rows succeeded" & chr(13) & _
    DTSGlobalVariables("gnRowsFailed").Value & _
    " rows failed" & chr(13) & _
    DTSGlobalVariables("gnRowsCleansed").Value & _
    " rows were cleansed" & chr(13) & _
    "within a total of " & _
    DTSGlobalVariables("gnBatchesCompleted").Value  & _
    " batches"


Msgbox sMsg

sSQL = "execute master..xp_logevent 60000,'" & sMsg & "',informational"

oConn.Execute sSQL

    PostSourceMain = DTSTransformstat_OK
End Function
```

The above code should generate a message box like the one shown below:

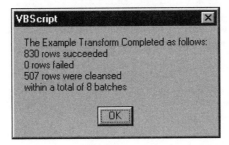

You may recall that we set our batch size to 100 and therefore we should have 9 batches not 8, as has been reported. This shows that we have placed this logic in the wrong phase as there is still one outstanding batch to be committed. We should have placed our logic in the On Pump Complete phase.

On Pump Complete Example

Remember that the On Pump Complete phase is called when all data has been written to the destination. We should have better luck with the following example if we reuse our `PostSourceMain` logic from within this phase.

```
Function PumpCompleteMain()

'*******
'    Re-use the logic from PostSourceMain
'*******

PumpCompleteMain = PostSourceMain

'*******
'    Do Some Cleanup of the globally allocated resources
'*******

oConn.Close
Set oConn = nothing

End Function
```

Notice that we are also using this phase to clean up our global ADO connection; something you should do with any global COM objects. Upon execution of this phase, you should see a message box which correctly reflects our batch count as 9 batches.

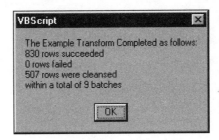

There is a great deal that can be done with the Multiphase Data Pump to address virtually any transformation need. Some ways in which you could explore this further might include:

❑ Aggregating data as you move data in and in; the On Batch Complete or On Pump Complete phases putting those aggregations into a table

❑ Using the error handling methods presented later in the book to fully audit and respond to fatal data issues

❑ Performing additional cleansing, such as data type checking in the On Row Transform and On Transform Failure phases

Data Driven Query (DDQ)

The **Data Driven Query** (**DDQ**) is a close relative to the Transform Data task. It gives you some of the best functionality of any of the data loading tasks. The Data Pump task supports only the insertion of records directly, whereas the Data Driven Query can flexibly support the insertion, updating, and deletion of records in response to data being transformed. In addition to these capabilities, the DDQ can also handle user commands, such as stored procedures. The DDQ's architecture provides for the scanning of source data rowsets record-by-record and performing one of the supported actions against a target connection.

As you can imagine, this approach of transforming data on a record-by-record basis can impede the performance of tranformation operations compared to the limited, albeit faster functionality of the Data Pump task. The Data Pump task with a SQL Server target supports the Fast Load option, which in itself is a key reason for the performance difference between the two task types. Other contributing factors include the ability to set a batch size on the data pump versus the single record DDQ transactions.

The distinguishing feature of the DDQ is its flexibility. We'll attempt to explore these aspects of the DDQ task within our example. As you work through the example, you will most likely think of many practical applications for the DDQ task.

Data Driven Query Example

We'll start by creating a new DTS package. As you can see below, we have created a package with a **Source** connection and **Destination** connection, which both map to our SQL Server and the `tempdb` database. We have also created a Data Driven Query named **DDQ Example**.

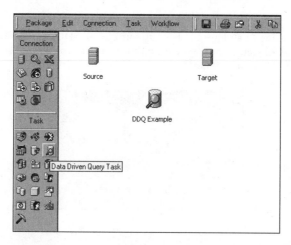

In order to get to this point, we need to first create a couple of tables in tempdb that we need for our example. Here is the DDL for our tables:

```
CREATE TABLE [Transactions] (
    [CUSTID] [int] NOT NULL ,
    [BALANCE] [int] NOT NULL ,
    [CODE] [char] (10))
```

The table above, Transactions, represents an extract of transactions from an OLTP production system. CUSTID is our customer identifier and BALANCE represents a financial measure of the customer's transaction. The CODE column indicates the status of the record as NEW (and should be added) and UPDATE (and should be updated).

```
CREATE TABLE [Customers] (
    [CUSTID] [int] NOT NULL ,
    [BALANCE] [int] NULL )
```

Our target table, or in the DDQ our **Bound Table,** for transformation is the Customers table above. We'll be transforming data from the Transactions table to the Customers table.

At this point, you can add the connections following your creation of the tables in tempdb. After adding of your Source and Target connections, you should add a DDQ resembling that which follows.

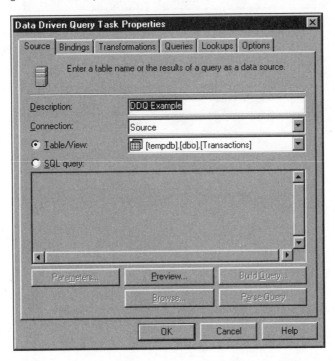

Here we are defining the Source information; you can preview your table by selecting the Preview button.

The next tab of your DDQ, the Bindings tab, should resemble the image shown below:

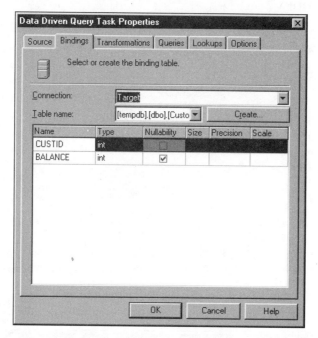

Here we are defining the target table as our newly created Customers table. Now that the **Source** and **Bindings** information has been set we need to take a close look at the **Transformations** tab, as this is a key part of the decision logic and the link to the DDQ's functionality.

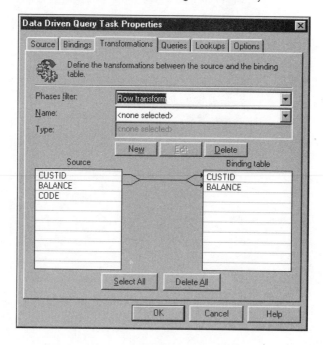

Your **Transformations** tab will resemble the above. We'll expand the logic of our transform by editing the ActiveX transformation between the **Source** and **Binding** table. Let's delve deeper into our example by exploring our ActiveX transform in detail.

The default ActiveX Script transformation created by DTS is:

```
' Copy each source column to the destination column
Function Main()
   DTSDestination("CUSTID") = DTSSource("CUSTID")
   DTSDestination("BALANCE") = DTSSource("BALANCE")
   Main = DTSTransformstat_InsertQuery
End Function
```

The transformation above will copy the column values from the source to the destination columns collection and then perform an insert based upon the DTS internal constant, DTSTransformstat_InsertQuery. While straightforward, this transform is not nearly robust enough to touch upon all of the DDQ features and our example's flexible transformation logic.

Transformation Logic

For our example, the decision tree will consist of two branches. Our extract identifies, through the Code column, if the customer record already exists. Existing customers are flagged with an UPDATE value in the Code column. These customers' balances are adjusted for the new purchase. Conversely, new customers are flagged with a NEW value in the Code column. These customer transactions will result in a record being added with a base balance of $1000.

In order to achieve this logic, we'll need to eliminate our existing tranformation from the **Transformations** tab. This is done by selecting the transformation and selecting the **Delete** button. We'll then create a transform that resembles the following:

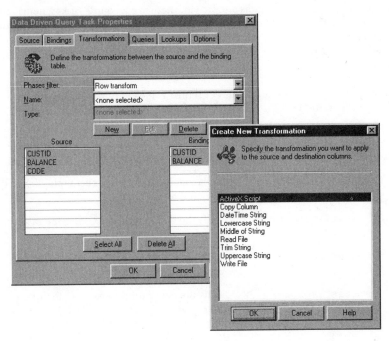

123

You should select the three columns from the Source table and the two columns from the Bindings table and click the New button. The Create New Transformation dialog will appear and you should select the ActiveX Script transform.

As we alluded to earlier, our logic is to process the Transactions table record-by-record and determine if the Code column contains an UPDATE or NEW value. If the record is NEW, then a row is added to the Customers table and the balance is set. If the record is UPDATE, then the customer's balance is updated. Here is the logic in our ActiveX Script transform:

```
Function Main()

  Select Case Ucase(Trim(DTSSource("Code")))

    Case "UPDATE"
      DTSDestination("Balance").Value = DTSSource("Balance").Value
      DTSDestination("CustID") = DTSSource("CustID")
      Main = DTSTransformStat_UpdateQuery

    Case "NEW"
      DTSDestination("CustID") = DTSSource("CustID")
      DTSDestination("Balance") = (1000 - DTSSource("Balance"))
      Main = DTSTransformStat_InsertQuery

    Case Else
      Main = DTSTransformStat_SkipRow

  End Select

End Function
```

While we haven't developed VBScript as a topic yet, there are a couple of key items to know when looking at our transformation. The Select Case statement evaluates an expression. In our case, this expression is an all upper case (Ucase) version of the data found in the Code source column. Based upon the value of this expression, we evaluate to one of three conditions for either an UPDATE, NEW, or an Else condition.

You might notice that we are assigning different return values to our function. These return values determine what query in the DDQ is to be run. Our options for the DDQ, available in our editor on the Browse tab, are:

Constant	Description
DTSTransformStat_DeleteQuery	Tells the data pump to execute the delete query assigned to the DDQ.
DTSTransformStat_InsertQuery	Tells the data pump to execute the insert query assigned to the DDQ.
DTSTransformStat_UpdateQuery	Tells the data pump to execute the update query assigned to the DDQ.
DTSTransformStat_UserQuery	Tells the data pump to execute the query defined in the user query property of the DDQ.

In addition to the above, all of the `DTSTransformStat_*` constants defined in the Multiphase section are also capable of being used. Note we are using the `DTSTransformStat_SkipRow` constant for the `Else` condition in our transformation.

In order to use the various query options, we'll need to define our queries on the **Queries** tab. We can define up to four queries, under the query type option. It is important to note that the queries defined in each of these types do not have to match the query type. For instance, should you need four `Insert` queries to go to destinations, you could define one in each of the four query types. However, we'll focus more on our traditional example supporting a single `Insert` query and a single `Update`.

At this point, you will need to create the two queries: one for inserting and one for updating. The question marks within our queries represent parameter placeholders that DTS will use to map the data from the destination columns in the ActiveX Transformation when executing.

```
INSERT
INTO Customers
(CUSTID, BALANCE)
VALUES (?, ?)
```

To create this query on the **Queries** tab, select **Insert** from the **Query type** drop-down and then enter the `INSERT` query from above. You will also want to ensure that the parameters are mapped correctly, which can be managed by clicking the **Parse/Show Parameters** button and then selecting the appropriate value from the **Destination** column for each parameter.

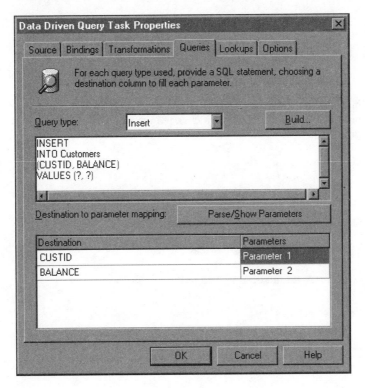

```
UPDATE Customers
SET BALANCE = (BALANCE - ?)
Where CustID = ?
```

You should add the Update query above and configure the DDQ Queries tab as shown below:

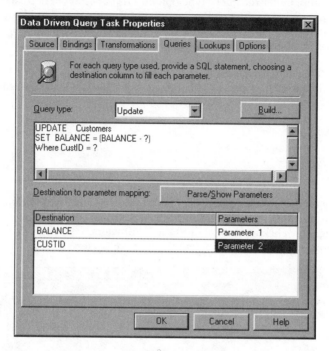

It is especially important to check the order of the parameters to make sure they are in the same order as the question marks. You will notice that we changed the order above to insure that CUSTID was our second parameter and the BALANCE column was the first parameter.

After clicking OK, the task is complete.

However, before we can run our new DDQ task, we'll need to insert some records:

```
INSERT into Transactions values(1, 100, 'UPDATE')
INSERT into Transactions values(2, 90, 'NEW')
INSERT into Transactions values(3, 120, 'NEW')
```

Next, insert one customer into the Customers table:

```
INSERT into Customers values(1, 4000)
```

As you can see, we have two customers above that have transactions, but don't have records in the Customers table – these are customers 2 and 3.

Once run, your final results, as taken from the `Customers` table, should be:

CUSTID	BALANCE
1	3900
2	910
3	880

Realistically, there is a great deal more that can be done with the DDQ as we have barely tapped its potential. Remember, the DDQ is your best and exclusive solution when performing complex insert and update transformations between disparate source systems. Due to the performance implications, you should consider your alternatives wisely and weigh approaches using the DDQ against set-based transformations with technologies like Transact SQL and batch-oriented transactions in stored procedures. If you are moving data and only inserting, then the Data Pump Transform task is a more appropriate alternative. The DDQ rightfully has its place and you are likely to see and find many uses for it as you explore this very powerful complement to the DTS feature set.

Beyond transformations are a whole host of other tasks in DTS; let's take a closer look at the remainder of the tasks.

Dynamic Properties Task

The key component that DTS helps you perform is data extraction, transforming, and loading (ETL). ETL is the process where you extract data from an OLTP or legacy system, scrub the data, then load it into a data warehouse. We have several chapters and case studies dedicated to this later in the book. Very rarely in any ETL process can you create a load procedure and have it work for every client. You normally resort to creating a customized ETL process for each client you would like to load or customer you'd like to service.

A typical ETL scenario would be where a file is FTPed to a server at night. Meanwhile, you have a SQL Server job that scans the directory every 15 minutes between midnight and noon to see if the file has been deposited. Once the job detects a file that ends with a `.TXT` extension, it moves it to the appropriate client directory. Files that are named `088031500.txt` would be moved to the `088` subdirectory for client directory `088`. Then the ETL process would begin. The process would clean the data where necessary and insert it into client 088's database. Finally, the process would archive the `088031500.txt` file into a subdirectory under the `088` directory called `031500` (March 15th's file). The directory that is two weeks old is then purged.

In most instances, you would have to create a program to do the ETL process and then customize it for each client. Could this be a case for DTS? The nice thing about DTS is that its entire object model is exposed. Anything you can spend 10 minutes to create in Designer, can easily be created and duplicated in the object model and then made to be dynamic based on a set of information like client number. This was previously done with the ActiveX Script task or by writing the code completely in another programming language like Visual Basic. The problem with this is that most DBAs do not know how to program.

Another important point that needs to be discussed is the use of UNC paths. Whether you use a mapped drive or a fully qualified UNC path, security becomes an issue with the File Transfer Protocol task. This task has no support for share-level security: you must already have logged onto the share either at boot time or interactively. If you try to go to a share \\ComputerName\Extract that happens to be secured by NT security, the task will not prompt you for a Username and Password to sign in with. Instead, you will receive the following error when you try to close the task or move to the next tab.

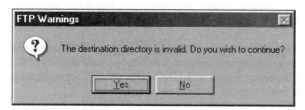

The only workaround for this behavior is to logon to the share either before you execute the package or at boot up of Windows. This security behavior will carry over to the next connection type we will discuss.

In the next tab, select the files you'd like to transfer and click the arrow or double-click on the file. You can click the double-arrow (>>) to move over all the files in a given directory. To navigate to subdirectories, double-click on the directory name.

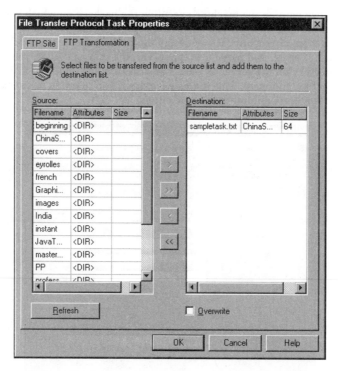

In some cases, the file you're going to receive already exists in the destination path or you're going to pull the file several times. In these instances, make sure you check the **Overwrite** box. Otherwise, your package will fail the second time you run it with the following error:

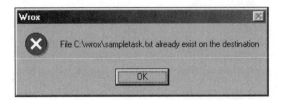

The other type of connection source that can be used with this task is a directory. With this type of connection, you can connect to any UNC path, share, or local directory. The same rules, however, apply to this that apply to the destination directory that we mentioned earlier. This is an easy way of moving a file from one directory to another. You can also use it to move a file from one computer on the network to another if you have a drive mapped or UNC specified with a connection already established. You can configure the task as you did with the Internet site connection. The only change is that now, you will specify a source directory, not an FTP site as shown below:

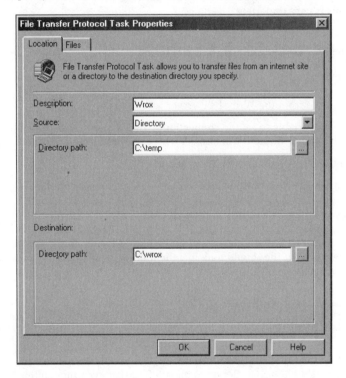

Dynamic Properties Task

One of the most powerful additions to DTS in SQL Server 2000 was the Dynamic Properties Task. Previously, in SQL Server 7.0, you had to write complex ActiveX scripts to perform something like this. One look at the code needed to change a property for an object and you can truly appreciate this gem of a task. In SQL Server 7.0, the cleanest way to make a package dynamic was to have an ActiveX Script task before each item you wanted to make dynamic or each call you wanted to make to the object model. This became quite cumbersome when you wanted to change your code, because you had to do it in every instance where it occurred. In the below example, which was ported over from SQL Server 7.0, you have a simple purge of a table then load. The way we made the package dynamic was to create a ActiveX Script task before each item to especially rename the connection.

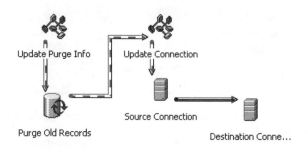

The Dynamic Properties task allows you to set any property of a DTS package at run time to a number of things, such as a global variable or INI file. This task puts a graphical interface in front of the DTS object model and allows you to take control of your package without having to know how to program. For most DBAs, this is very important.

Dynamic Properties Task Example

In this example, we are going to set up a data load procedure and make it dynamic. The package will:

❑   Download a file from the Wrox FTP server as we did before.

❑   Read a global variable to set the connection strings and determine whether a table needs to be created. The global variable will also set where the flat file will be transferred.

❑   Purge the table we're going to be inserting into.

❑   Bulk insert the file to a dynamic location based on a global variable.

Start the project by creating an FTP task that downloads `ftp.wrox.co.uk/ChinaShop/sampletask.txt` from the Wrox web site. No login credentials will be needed to login to the FTP site. This file should be placed locally in the `C:\Wrox` directory as in the last example. The simple flat file should look like the following (delimited by tabs and by carriage returns at the end of each line):

```
datacol1   datacol2   datacol3
dataa   datab   datac
datad   datae   dataf
```

Next, create a connection to the SQL Server database that you'd like the data to be transferred to and call the connection **Destination SQL Server**. You will find that even though this is a dynamic package, we'll still have to "fake" quite a few items. For example, even though you set the connection up here, we're going to dynamically change it later. DTS validates every connection before you close the configuration screen. The only way around this is to go to **Disconnected Edit** under the package menu.

The nice thing about the Bulk Insert task is that the `sampletask.txt` file doesn't actually have to exist to configure the task. Since you're going to dynamically set the properties later, you can pick any table or view as the destination as shown below. Our delimiter for the flat file is a **Tab** and a {LF} signifies a new row.

As you may remember, the flat file's first row held the column names. To make sure that we only load data into the table, set the starting row at 2. The last row of 0 tells DTS to continue loading data until the end of file.

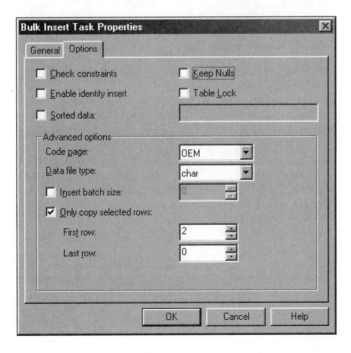

The next task we're going to have to establish is one to determine if a table named `sampletask` is already created. If it isn't, then this task will create it. We can do this with a Execute SQL task. One of the ways of detecting if a table exists is to look in the `SysObjects` table and see if there's a record with a name of `sampletask`. Here's some code to perform this function:

```
If (SELECT Count(*) from SysObjects WHERE Name = 'sampletask') = 0
BEGIN
CREATE TABLE [sampletask] (
    [Datacol1] varchar(50) NULL,
    [Datacol2] varchar(50) NULL,
    [Datacol3] varchar(50) NULL )
END
```

You now have the flexibility to insert your data anywhere, even if the table doesn't exist yet. The task will look like this:

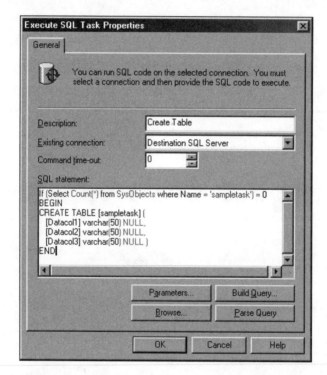

In this example, we're also assuming that we're going to completely flush any old data that may exist in the table and reload it. To do this, we're going to need another Execute SQL task that is configured like the following:

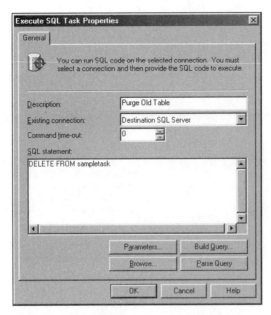

Now the fun part begins. As you can see, all the tasks are dependent on a connection named **Destination SQL Server**. It is due to this type of relational system that we can change the connection in one location and all the tasks will follow suit. The first step to make this package dynamic is to create a global variable for each setting we're going to make dynamic. You can use other items to make tasks dynamic that we'll discuss shortly.

To create global variables, go to **Properties** under the **Package** menu. Then go to the **Global Variables** tab and create two global variables: **gvDestinationDB** and **gvDestinationTable**. For more information on global variables, you can refer back to the chapter on *DTS Fundamentals*. The two global variables should point to the Northwind database, and the table Northwind.dbo.sampletask:

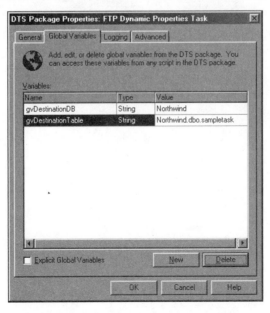

These two global variables will be used to dynamically change the task's properties. We'll also use them in the next example.

Add the Dynamic Properties task, found under the Tasks menu. The first screen you should see will display the current list of properties that are being set by the task. As you can see below, we have not set anything yet:

Click Add to begin creating dynamic properties. You can then drill down through the objects in your package and set the properties dynamically. The first property we will set is for our SQL Server connection. Drill down the Connections tree until you find the Initial Catalog of the Destination SQL Server setting: you can also check the Leave this dialog box open after adding a setting option to add multiple settings and not be taken back to the main screen again.

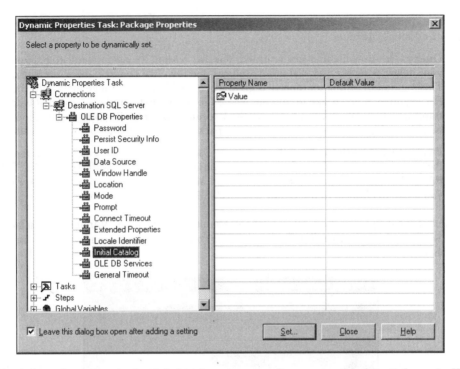

Double-click on this setting in the right-hand pane to start the process of making it dynamic. You can also select the property in the right-hand pane and select the **Set** button.

This screen is the core of this task. You can choose to set your connection to a:

❑ **Global variable**. The most common way of settings properties dynamically, this method is easy to create and allows you to pass in parameters from outside the package. In a later example, we'll use this method of setting properties to pass in parameters using the Execute Package task.

❑ **Constant**. This is typically used to assign the default value of an item, such as DTSStepExecStat_Completed. This is one way of resetting a value back to the default settings after changing it in another task. The full range of constants and what they mean are shown in the following table:

Constant	Value	Description
DTSStepExecStat_Completed	4	Step execution completed
DTSStepExecStat_Inactive	3	Step execution inactive
DTSStepExecStat_InProgress	2	Step execution in progress
DTSStepExecStat_Waiting	1	Step is waiting to execute

❑ **INI file**. This supports a single line property value. This is ideal if you have a program that already uses an INI file to set the program's values (like ClientID). This way your package can share the same settings as the program.

137

The last step is to create a Success precedence constraint between the various tasks. As we discussed in the previous chapter, you can create a precedence constraint by clicking on the first task, then while holding the *Ctrl* key click on the dependent task. Finally, select On Success from the Workflow menu. You will need to create On Success precedence constraints between all of your tasks, as shown below. These constraints will determine the order in which the package will execute. If the steps execute in the wrong order, then you will potentially be inserting into a table that doesn't exist yet.

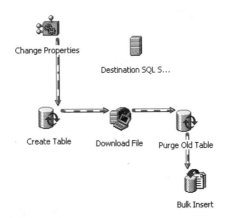

At this point, execute the package task. After it succeeds, change the global variables under the Package Properties screen to point to any other database and execute it again. One database that you can easily point to is the pubs database, since it's a sample database that is automatically installed with SQL Server. Save this package to the local SQL Server as Dynamic Properties Task. We'll use this package in the next example.

Execute Package Task

The package we just created wasn't too complex, but say we wanted to use the functionality of this task in several other places – if we had to go through creating it each time, it could get kind of tedious. Wouldn't it be great if we only had to do that once, and we could then call it from other packages?

The **Execute Package task** is an excellent way to make your package more modular. We can call the package we just created in the last example using this task, and since we used the Dynamic Properties task, we can bulk insert the flat file into any database just by passing it the two global variables it needs. This is advantageous for a number of reasons. For instance, if you have a standard set of tasks that you use for transforming data, like that we created in the Dynamic Properties task example, you don't want to have to modify each occurrence in every package any time you want to make a minor change. Instead, you want to be able to modify it once and have it work globally across all of your other packages automatically.

We're going to cheat a little bit and show you the end result of a package we're going to create in the next example. This example is going to make two calls to the package you just created in the Dynamic Properties task example. Imagine doing this all in one package. It would be an enormous burden to edit the package because of the double-maintenance. The alternative is to use the Execute Package task to call the child package we created earlier twice. The resulting package will look like this in Designer:

This task also makes things simpler when coding. If your code is modular, there's no need to modify the same piece of code in 30 packages. All you would have to do is modify the source package, and every package that calls it will follow suit.

The other benefit is security. There may also be instances where you need to access sensitive financial data, like employee salaries, but you don't want other programmers to have access to the data. In this scenario, you can break that process out of your main package and call the salary package from the main package using the Execute Package task. When you break your packages apart, more sensitive parts can be kept inaccessible to the public. We'll talk more about package security in the *DTS Security* chapter.

Execute Package Task Example

Let's start by creating a new package and adding our first Execute Package task from the Tasks menu. This task will Bulk Insert the text file into the pubs database. This task is especially easy to configure. First, enter your login credentials for the server that holds the package. At that point you can simply define the package name and version under the Package Name text box. The simplest way of finding the package name and version is to click on the (...) next to the package name option. If there is only one package and one version on the server, the text box will be filled automatically. Otherwise, as in our case, a selection box will appear that will allow you to drill down to the version level of any package on the server. If you select the top-level package, then DTS will interpret this to mean that you'd like to run the latest version of the package.

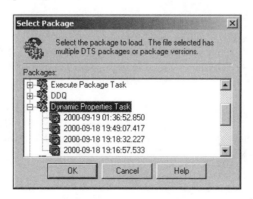

A common DTS mistake is to specify a version of the package you'd like to execute, then save a new version. At that point, DTS will continue to execute your old DTS package and not the newly modified package. That's why, if you always intend to execute the latest version of your package, you should select the package here and not specify the version. You can execute any packages except for those stored in VB format (at present, this functionality is not supported).

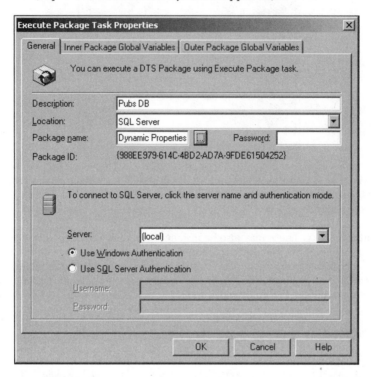

Note: you also do not want to execute the same package you're in. This could create an endless loop and crash your SQL Server unless done correctly by setting breakpoints. If you want to call the same package that you're already in, it's a good idea to create a copy of the package and execute the copy.

Setting Global Variables

The Execute Package task makes heavy use of DTS Global Variables. DTS uses these only if you'd like the packages to communicate to each other. There are two types of global variables that can be sent to your DTS package: inner and outer. The idea of having two types of global variables is relatively confusing and causes a glazed-over look in most programmer's eyes until they use them for the first time.

You can use **inner** global variables to set the child package's global variables inside the Execute Package task. The key thing to remember with inner global variables is that they don't pass a global variable from the package, but instead set the other package's global variable from the Execute Package task.

The **outer** global variables will pass to the child package the global variables from the parent package. If the global variables do not exist on the child package, they are created temporarily. The reason we bring this up is because global variables are case sensitive. If your parent package uses a global variable called gvDestinationDB and your child package uses gvdestinationDB, then the package will fail if you use outer global variables. The Execute Package Task will actually create a second global variable with the parent's information. If they do exist, they are changed to the global variables sent to them.

> **The outer global variables can only be set at the parent package level, not the task level. The inner global variables are set at the task level.**

In our example, the child package requires that we set two global variables using the inner global variable feature in the Execute Package task. These two global variables – named gvDestinationDB and gvDestinationTable – are used to dynamically determine where the table will be transformed.

We could also send outer global variables to the package for this but that would require that we have the two global variables defined in the parent package. Sending outer global variables wouldn't give us the flexibility to run the Execute Package task twice and send two different sets of values.

Inner global variables do not require us to have the global variables set up locally, which has the benefit of allowing your package to become completely modular. Under the Inner Package Global Variables tab, set your inner global variables by selecting the drop down box in the Name column and then assigning a value to it as shown below. You will have to click New to pass additional values or click on the next line down.

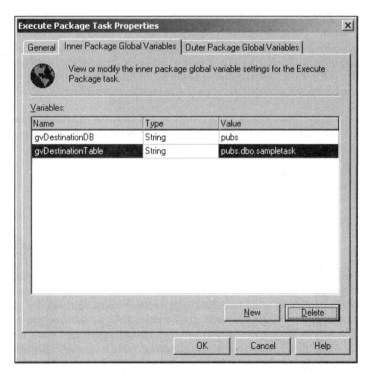

Although Message Queuing is shipped with Windows 2000, it does not install by default. You must go into **Add/Remove Programs** in the Control Panel to install it. There are two components to the program: a client program and a server. For the Message Queuing task to function, you must have both components. The server software can be installed anywhere on your network; the client software must be installed on the database server. You can have both the server and the client on the same machine; however, if you were using Message Queuing in large volume, it would be advantageous to scale the system out to another server. The last requirement to use the task is to set up a queue to send the messages to.

In DTS, the Message Queuing task allows you to:

❑ Send messages between different packages, even if the packages are on different servers

❑ Communicate with other applications that utilize Message Queuing

❑ Wait for other packages to check-in before proceeding

❑ Divide your package into smaller components on separate servers and utilize the other server's processors as well

❑ Distribute files, such as DTS packages

You can add this task from the **Tasks** menu. From the Message drop-down box, you can configure the task to either receive or send multiple messages. If you select receive a message, then the screen changes. We'll discuss receiving message shortly. For sending messages, you will have to specify a destination queue to send the messages to.

There are two main types of queues that Message Queuing supports: public and private queues. **Public queues** publish their properties and description to an Active Directory; the actual contents of the queue do not publish to the active directory. Public queues are not supported in a workgroup environment. A **private queue** does not broadcast itself to the Active Directory, but instead keeps itself local to the computer that holds the queue. There are a few other types of queues that we will not discuss in this book but more information about them can be found in Books Online.

In this example, we're going to be sending a message to the package we created earlier in the *Dynamic Properties Task* section. We'll create the same two global variables (gvDestinationDB and gvDestinationTable) in a new package. Then we're going to send global variables to that Dynamic Properties package.

The screenshot below shows that we're going to send our messages to BEDROCK\private$\SQLServer. Broken apart, this means that we're going to send our messages to the server named BEDROCK and to a private queue named SQLServer.

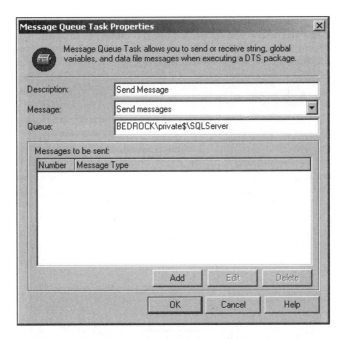

After selecting **Send Messages** from the **Message** drop-down box, you can create a new message to send, by clicking **Add**. The next dialog box that appears allows you to select what type of message you'd like to send. Messages can be data files, global variables, or strings. In our case, we're going to pass a global variable to the package that we created in the Dynamic Properties task example. Select **Global Variables Message** from the **Message type** drop-down box and then select **New**. A drop-down-box will populate with every global variable in the current package. If you have not created the two global variables we'll need, then do so now by clicking **Create Global Variables**. After you select your first global variable, click **New** to add the other.

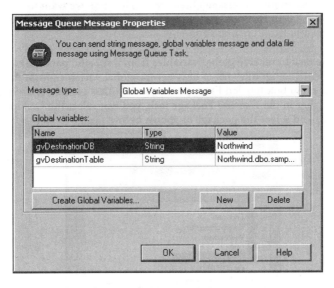

You are now ready to save your package once again under the same name. Then, execute the package named **Message Queuing Task**, which will send the global variables to the destination package. Next execute the **Dynamic Properties Task** package that we just saved. The child package will then transform based on the global variables it reads from the queue. You can also execute the **Dynamic Properties Task** first, as long as you send the message within the 2 minute window we specified earlier. Otherwise, you'll receive the following error:

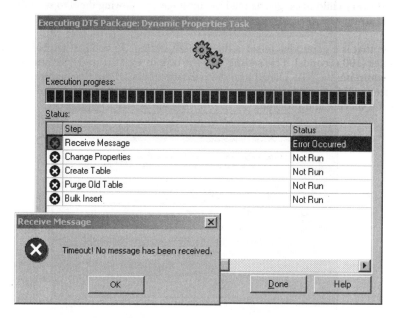

Message Queuing is a great way to communicate with applications that would normally not communicate as well as legacy applications. It is also a fantastic way of keeping your sales people up to date with the latest information, since they're not always hooked into the network. You can have messages and files for the sales people sitting in a queue and wait for them to dial into the network to receive them.

Summary

In this chapter we learned how to leverage some of the new SQL Server 2000 tasks to speed up the programming process. Many custom ActiveX programmed tasks can be replaced with one of the better performing SQL Server 2000 tasks, such as the Dynamic Properties task. These not only save time, but also keep you from mistyping a property name and debugging your typo for hours. We also learned about some new tasks that have been added in SQL Server 2000. Some of the major tasks that are new include:

- ❑ File Transfer Protocol Task – Allows you to receive files from other directories in a UNC path or from an Internet FTP site. Typically developers would use a VB component or `ftp.exe` in 7.0.

- ❑ Dynamic Properties Task – Allows you to dynamically set any of your package's objects. Previously you would have to call the DTS object model from an ActiveX task. This is all done now through a graphical interface. Due to this, your time to market on a product is shortened.

- ❑ Execute Package Task – Gives you the ability to execute a package inside a package. We also used to do these in ActiveX Script. Now you can execute a package from within a package through a graphical interface.

- ❑ Message Queue Task – Allows you to send messages or files to a temporary queue and pick them up once another package or client connects.

In some cases, these new tasks alone shorten the time to market on a package by a week or more. This alone can be a compelling reason to upgrade to SQL Server 2000 for some customers. In the next chapter, we're going to cover some of the more advanced topics for these tasks, including transactions, which are a way of guaranteeing the integrity of your data.

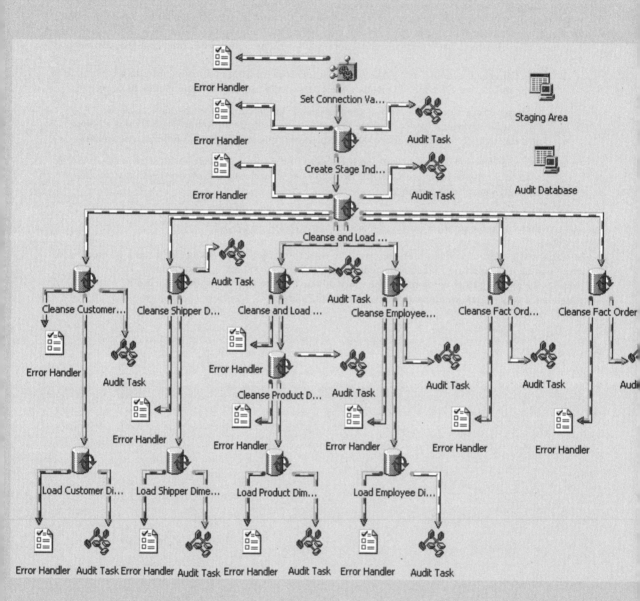

Error Handler

Set Connection Va...

Audit Task

Staging Area

Error Handler

Create Stage Ind...

Audit Task

Audit Database

Error Handler

Cleanse and Load ...

Audit Task

Cleanse Customer...

Cleanse Shipper D...

Audit Task

Cleanse and Load ...

Audit Task

Cleanse Employee...

Cleanse Fact Ord...

Cleanse Fact Order

Error Handler

Audit Task

Error Handler

Audit Task

Cleanse Product D...

Audit Task

Audit Task

Audit Task

Aud

Error Handler

Error Handler

Error Handler

Error Handler

Error Handler

Error Handler

Error Handler

Load Customer Di...

Load Shipper Dime...

Load Product Dim...

Load Employee Di...

Error Handler   Audit Task Error Handler   Audit Task Error Handler   Audit Task   Error Handler   Audit Task

Advanced Settings in DTS

In the previous chapter, we saw how we can utilize the basic tasks available in DTS to transform our data. Typically in a DTS package, we don't have just one task; we have quite a few built into a workflow to accomplish our needs. There are some advanced package and task options in DTS that allow us to manipulate how the package is handled as a whole, as well as the individual tasks. These allow you to perform a variety of enhancements, such as tune packages and tasks for performance, and log error information to help you debug. That's what we'll be looking at in this chapter.

In SQL Server 2000, these options are available via the DTS Designer, as well as programmatically via the various DTS objects. We will be using the DTS Designer for these examples, but we will discuss how to set these options via code later in the book.

In this chapter, we'll go over the options that can help you set up your package better, and take advantage of some of the ways that DTS processes information. In particular, we will see:

- ❑ Advanced package options
- ❑ Options specific to the Transform Data task
- ❑ What DTS lookup is
- ❑ How to deal with some common errors

Let's start by looking at what options are available to us with the advanced options we can set for DTS packages.

Advanced Package Options

Once a package is complete – or we at least know exactly what the package will have in it when it is complete – we can start to consider what advanced options will be necessary to create the final solution. There are several advanced options that we can set for our packages via the **DTS Package Properties** dialog, some of which we've already seen something of in the previous chapters.

You can display this dialog by opening the relevant package in DTS Designer, and selecting **Package | Properties** from the drop-down list. To start with, we'll take a look at the **Advanced** tab:

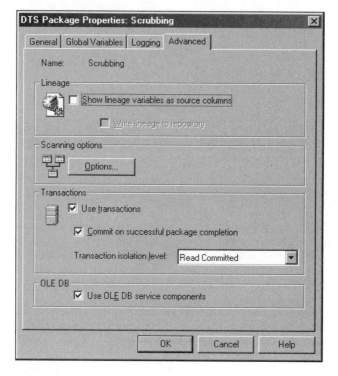

The options that we can set here concern:

- ❑ Data lineage
- ❑ Scanning database schema information into the Repository (Meta Data Services)
- ❑ Controlling transactions
- ❑ OLE DB service components

Some of the advanced options we can set for a package are very important – for instance, the ability to set a transaction for the entire package (we'll cover transactions in a little while). The data lineage portion can also be useful, to allow us to quickly determine where the data came from, as well as what transformations we've applied to it.

Let's take a look at each of these four areas in more detail.

Lineage

This section is all about how to achieve an audit on tasks within DTS packages, how and where to store that audit information, and what the options actually mean.

Data lineage is a feature that gives the package the ability to take any piece of data, and determine the source of that data and what transformations have then been applied to it.

> **This option is only available when a DTS package has been saved to Meta Data Services. If you select this feature on the Advanced tab, anywhere other than Meta Data Services, you are prompted to alter your decision back to Meta Data Services. If you need to do this, chose Save As from the Package menu in the DTS Designer. In the Location: list, choose Meta Data Services.**

As you can see from the screenshot above, there are two options shown for data lineage in the Lineage section of the Advanced tab:

❑   Show lineage variables as source columns

❑   Write lineage to repository

Before describing a bit more about these two options, it's worthwhile taking a moment out to describe in detail what a repository is. A repository is simply a place where data is stored. In many people's eyes, a repository is seen as a database, although in fact any place that information is stored can be seen as a repository. SQL Server is a repository for information about its databases, from table and column information, to the actual contents of the data. Microsoft Access is another repository, as is a plain text file. The latest repository to find favor within the computing industry at present is an XML file. There is nothing magical about using the repository as a technical term.

By selecting the Show lineage variables as source columns, you are informing DTS that you wish to switch data auditing on – in other words, that you wish to store information about the data that passes in and out of your package. This option is used in most cases to figure out which rows were imported or modified by a package.

Once you have done this, then the next thing to consider is how to store that auditing information. Access to the second option, which lets you Write lineage to repository – that is, to Meta Data Services, is only available when you select the first option.

However, before selecting the Show lineage option, you really must be sure that auditing the data and what is being modified is something that you wish to log. Having this option selected will slow down your package, and depending on what the package is doing, this could end up being quite a considerable overhead.

You may find that you only need use this option for testing, or when there is a problem with the package in production and you need to track what changes are happening to the data. This option is also used when external data sources are being imported, and you don't have control over these sources: for example, if the data source is an outside company, and there is some problem with their data.

Saving Data to Meta Data Services

If you chose this option, you have two different ways to use Data Lineage: either column based or row based. We will first of all describe what these options are, and then discuss how to implement them.

Row-Level Data Lineage

Row-level data lineage stores the source of the data and the transformations applied to it. It does this by storing a unique value – either an integer or a GUID (Global Unique Identifier, in other words, no two GUIDs will be the same) – in a lineage column in your destination. While each auditing action is being performed at row level, the information is stored in the lineage column. This allows the data lineage to be tracked at the package and row levels of a table. This in turn provides a complete audit trail of data transformation and DTS package execution information, which can later be retrieved and inspected.

In Meta Data Services, an object associated with this type of lineage contains lineage values (package execution Globally Unique Identifiers), the user name, the name of the server that is executing the package (or (local) for locally based SQL Servers), and the time of execution.

To demonstrate lineage in action involves a number of complex operations which have not been covered in this book at this point, but we find ourselves in a Catch 22 situation. To wait until later in the book to cover these important options means that you may not be thinking of the full picture, but to go through these options now involves several learning curves. So don't worry if you feel you're short of knowledge in certain areas – our aim here is just to walk through the requirements to ensure lineage works.

First of all, we have to import the meta data about a database into Meta Data Services. You complete this by navigating to the Data Transformation Services node in Enterprise Manager, selecting Meta Data Services, right-clicking, and then selecting Import Metadata:

Which brings up the following screen for your details:

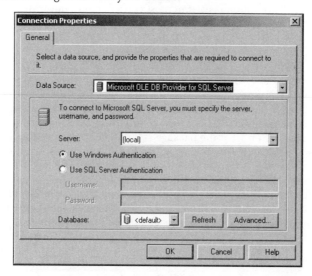

Once this is complete, auditing through lineage is possible.

To record the audit GUID information in a column within the destination table, you need to create a column large enough, within the destination table, to hold a numeric of type `bigint`. It is this column that will hold the necessary GUID.

When you come to move the data from the source table to the destination table within your DTS package, and your data transformation is that of a row level transformation, DTS automatically supplies a column identifier within the source table called `DTSLineage_Full` (it also supplies a column called `DTSLineage_Short`, but you're better off not using this, as it doesn't give a unique enough identifier). Don't worry, DTS doesn't actually physically alter your table: the new GUID column only exists during the DTS package run time. As each row is moved to the destination table, each row will have this DTS GUID in place.

Column-Level Data Lineage

Column-level data lineage only stores information about a column, and not every row in the repository. It allows you to see if a specific column is being used to import data from (as a source) or to put data into (being used as the destination) when looking at the package attributes in the repository. It does not, however, allow you to determine which rows were affected by a package execution.

However, it does give a greater level of granularity than row level data lineage, as you can track at a column level, which can make it easier to track audit information. All that is required to use this type of lineage is to save the package into the repository and turn the scanning options on (which we will show you how to do next). After you've executed the package, right-click on the relevant Transform Data task, and select Properties. Click on the Transformation tab as shown in the next screenshot.

In both row- and column-level data lineage, the following screenshot demonstrates the two new columns that DTS provides for the GUID's in the transformation:

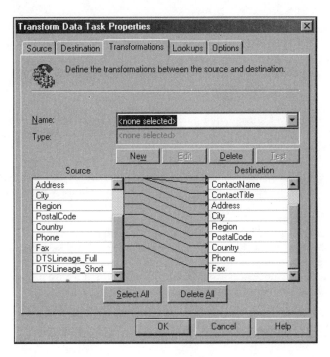

On the left you can see the source columns for a Transform Data task. The last two columns, DTSLineage_Full and DTSLineage_Short, provide the GUID audit information. The destination table though, does not have a column to place these values into, and no mapping is shown. This proves that it is not mandatory to map these new columns to the destination table. You may have several Transform Data tasks within your package, but only one that you wish to monitor. In that case, you would only map the lineage information when required.

> **REMEMBER: in order for either column- or row-lineage to work, the package must be saved in the Meta Data Services.**

If you do not save the packages in the Meta Data Services and try to use lineage, you will receive an error message like this:

Lineage gives a very valuable and powerful method of automating auditing of data manipulation.

That's all we've got time for on lineage. If you want to know more, take a look at SQL Server Books Online.

Now let's get back to the Advanced option tab, and take a look at the second available option: Scanning options.

Scanning Options

No, we're not talking about half tone or color correction, but the ability of the Meta Data Services to capture information about the schema of your database. In conjunction with the lineage options, it allows you to track either row- or column-level lineage.

In order to track column-level lineage on a package, all that's required is to save the package into the Repository, and set the Scanning options Resolve package references to scanned catalog meta data box, which we will see in a minute.

Now we're not going to go over the lineage and auditing of packages here in depth - we're saving that for later. While we're on these screens, however, we want you to know what the options are.

This whole section is to allow us to bring in catalog information about a data source which is outside SQL Server. For example, if you were trying to import information from a Microsoft Visual FoxPro database in to SQL Server, you would create a package in Meta Data Services, use OLE DB as the data source of the existing data to import, in this case Visual FoxPro, and the package would then scan the data to import and place the necessary catalog information, which would be tables, columns, and so on, into the DTS Meta Data Services information model.

The DTS scanner, which is used to scan the source data to import, is passed an OLE DB provider. It then examines the schema using the inbuilt functionality within OLE DB, which provides this information The scanner creates a set of corresponding instance objects in Meta Data Services, using the SQL Servers Database Model and DTS Meta Data Services information models.

To get into the options for scanning, you'll need to click the Options button in the Scanning options section below Lineage in the Properties dialog:

You should find yourself in the Scanning Options dialog:

You'll notice that there is a great deal of use of the word "catalog" on all of these options. Don't be put off – a catalog is simply another name for a data structure. Every database, from Oracle through to SQL Server, has a data structure. You could quite easily call this its catalog. The reason the term catalog is used in this context, is that DTS actually performs, through OLE DB, catalog function calls to retrieve this information.

The options on this dialog let us specify:

❑ Whether the package should use existing catalogs, or always scan through the data source and return a new instance of the catalog

❑ Whether it should gather only the pertinent columns or all of them

By returning the whole catalog, any layout or data changes since the last time the catalog was created will be retrieved. Let's look at each option in detail, so that you can determine which options may suit you in your situation.

The Resolve package references to scanned catalog meta data checkbox enables all the other scanning options, which link the package to Meta Data Services meta data. If this box is checked, the following two subsets of options become available:

- ❑ Which catalogs should be scanned?

  - ❑ Use scanned catalogs if already present in repository is in essence informing you as a developer, that if a catalog exists, there will be no refresh of the Meta Data for the catalog you wish to use. The catalog that has already been saved will be the catalog that is used in the DTS package. This is perfect for when the catalog won't change, however, if there is a change to the catalog, then problems may arise. This is obviously a faster option when running the package, as there is no rechecking. However, you are opening yourself up to potential failure. This is the default.

  - ❑ Scan all referenced catalogs into repository is exactly the opposite to the above option. Every time the package is executed, DTS will scan everything about a catalog (all table, column, and meta data information) into Meta Data Services, even if the information is not used, and refresh the Meta Data Services data model. Obviously, this is safer than the previous option, but more costly in terms of time, resources, and performance. This option will probably be used in development, testing, and after an initial installation. However, each scenario is different. The number of external catalogs that are used will determine how slow this process becomes. Do use with thought.

- ❑ Select a scanning option

  - ❑ Scan catalog if not already present in repository will add the catalog of the data source, if there is not a catalog present in Meta Data Services. (This is the default selection if scanning options are enabled.) This option would potentially be used in development when creating a new package, or if the package is looking for a new data source each time it is run. For example, if you receive a file each day that has the date as part of the file name, then this option should be selected.

  - ❑ Scan catalog always will scan a catalog for a data source into Meta Data Services, whether it is present already or not. Perhaps the most essential time that this option will be used will be when the whole catalog is in flux. For example, say the catalog for your data source has differing numbers of columns of information: perhaps there is one record per customer, and there is a column for each order that customer placed. Obviously this is the slower option of the two, as the catalog is always scanned.

You should now feel comfortable with how to ensure that catalog information – in other words, the schema or layout of data source information – can be kept up to date. This should ensure that your package is working with the correct information at all times. Also remember the performance implications that the choice you make will have on your package – from this you should be able to weigh up the pros and cons of each choice, and the risks involved.

Transactions

In order to discuss what transactions are, we must define what a transaction actually is.

> **A transaction is an atomic unit of work that either succeeds or fails as a whole.**

There is no such thing as a partial completion of a transaction. Since a transaction can be made up of multiple tasks, and with SQL 2000, multiple packages, each task or package must succeed for the transaction as a *whole* to be successful. If any one part of a transaction fails, then the entire transaction fails.

When a transaction fails, the system returns everything back to the state it was in before the transaction was started. This process of undoing the changes is known as a **rollback**. For example, if a task in a DTS package joined the current transaction, and it fails during its process, the system needs to "roll back" the previous tasks and return itself into its original state.

A critical part of any database is to ensure that any operations it performs are performed correctly. If a database were to partially complete an operation, then the data in the database would be *inconsistent*. SQL Server has its own built-in transaction processing system whose sole purpose is to ensure that a transaction completes in its entirety or not at all. If all of the tasks are completed successfully, then the changes to the database are *committed*, and the database can proceed to the next transaction or task. If any part of the operation does not complete successfully, which would leave the database in an invalid state, the database will rollback the changes and put itself back to its original state.

ACID Properties

When SQL Server creates a transaction, it will ensure the transaction will have certain characteristics. These characteristics are known as the **ACID properties**.

ACID is an acronym for:

- **A**tomicity
- **C**onsistency
- **I**solation
- **D**urability

Let's look at each of these in more detail:

Atomicity

The **atomicity** property identifies that the transaction is either fully completed, or not at all. Any updates a transaction might perform in the database are completed in their entirety. If for any reason an error occurs and the transaction is unable to complete all its tasks, the database is returned to the state it was in before the transaction even started. SQL Server uses a write-ahead transaction log where changes are written to the log before they are applied or committed to the actual data pages. As long as the data source is able to undo any uncommitted changes if a transaction is rolled back, the technique used by a data source for managing its transactions isn't important.

Consistency

A transaction enforces consistency in the database's data by ensuring that at the end of any transaction the database is in a valid state. If the transaction completes successfully, then all the changes to the database will have been properly made, and the database will be in a valid state. If any error occurs in a transaction, then any changes already made will be automatically rolled back and the database will be returned to its original state. Since the database is assumed to be in a consistent state when the transaction was started, it will once again be in a consistent state. In SQL Server, this includes all internal data structures, such as B-tree indexes or doubly linked lists.

Transactions must also maintain data consistency and integrity when multiple concurrent users are accessing and modifying the same data, a concept that goes hand-in-hand with the next ACID property, isolation.

Isolation

Transactions are performed in isolation, which makes them appear to be the only action that the database is executing at a given time. If there are two transactions, both of which perform the same function, running at the same time, transaction isolation will ensure that each transaction thinks it has exclusive use of the database.

This property is sometimes called serializability, because in order to prevent one transaction's operations from interfering with another's, requests must be serialized or sequenced so that only one request for the same data can be serviced at a time.

Isolation not only guarantees that multiple transactions cannot modify the same data at the same time, but also guarantees that changes caused by one transaction's operations will not be seen by another transaction until the changes are either committed or aborted. Concurrent transactions will be unaware of each other's partial and inconsistent changes. This means that all requests to modify or read data already involved in a transaction are blocked until the transaction completes. Most data sources, such as SQL Server and other RDBMS, implement isolation through the use of locks. Individual data items or sets of data are locked from concurrent access if they are involved in a transaction.

Durability

Durability means that once a transaction has been successfully completed, all of the changes it made to the database are permanent. There are checkpoints that prevent the database from losing information, even if the database fails. By logging the tasks a transaction performs, the state of the system can be recreated even if the hardware itself has failed. The concept of durability allows the database administrator know that a completed transaction is a permanent part of the database, regardless of what happens to the database later on.

Setting Up a New Package Transaction

A package transaction does not exist until a step attempts to join it. At this point, a new transaction is created for the package, and the step proceeds with its attempt. If other steps attempt to join the package transaction before the first transaction has committed or rolled back, they are enlisted in the first transaction. Although a package may initiate several transactions, only one package transaction can be active at a time.

Joining the Package Transaction

The attempt to join the package transaction takes place only after any workflow script has been processed. If a step joins the package transaction, any updates made by the step accumulate in the package transaction. If a step does not join the package transaction, database changes are committed in autocommit mode: one at a time, as they are requested.

In order to join a transaction successfully, the package step must:

❑ Be one of several supported task types. For example, the Execute SQL task is supported, but the Send Mail task is not.

Tasks that cannot take part in a transaction are:

❑ The FTP Task

❑ The Dynamic Properties task

❑ The Send Mail task

❑ The Copy SQL Server Objects task

Some tasks allow the user to create their own scripts or programs and run them from DTS. Although these tasks can create and independently manage their own local or distributed transactions, they have no access to the DTS package transaction. These tasks are:

❑ The ActiveX Script task

❑ The Execute Process task

Some supported tasks can join the package transaction if the right connections are supported. These tasks are:

❑ The Bulk Insert task

❑ The Data Driven Query task

❑ The Transform Data task

❑ The Execute Package task

❑ The Execute SQL task

❑ The Message Queue task

> **NOTE: If the package includes Execute Package tasks, transaction behavior can differ from that described above. For more information about transactions and the Execute Package task, see Inherited Transactions below.**

All of the above three groups of tasks may commit or roll back the current transaction.

❑ Use destination connections that support transactions. For example, an instance of SQL Server is supported, but a connection to Microsoft Access 2000 is not.

Supported Connection Types are:

❑ Microsoft OLE DB Provider for SQL Server.

❑ ODBC data source. The ODBC driver must support the connection attribute SQL_ATT_ENLIST_IN_DTC and this attribute must be set. For more information, see the ODBC documentation.

❑ Microsoft Data Link. Microsoft Data Link is used to access any installed OLE DB provider. An OLE DB provider must implement the ITransactionJoin interface if it is to join a distributed transaction. For more information, see the OLE DB documentation.

If the preceding conditions are not met, the attempt to join the package transaction fails, and the package halts at run time.

In DTS Designer, a step attempts to join the package transaction if you:

❑ Select the Use transactions check box in the DTS Package Properties dialog box:

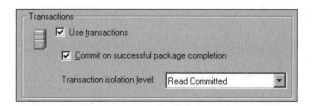

❑ Select the Join transaction if present check box in the Workflow Properties dialog box of a step (to open this dialog, right-click and select Workflow | Workflow Properties, and choose the Options tab):

> Note: When a step joins the package transaction, each connection used by the step is enlisted in the distributed transaction. All updates for such a connection accumulate in the package transaction, even if they originate in a step that did not explicitly join the package transaction. Therefore, to make transactional and non-transactional updates to the same database from one package, you must use two connections.

A package transaction is committed when either of the following events occurs:

❏ A step completes successfully and the Commit transaction on successful completion of this step check box is selected.

❏ The package completes successfully and the Commit on successful package completion check box is selected.

The current package transaction is rolled back when any of the following events occurs:

❏ The package fails.

❏ The package finishes and the Commit on successful package completion check box is cleared for the package.

❏ A step fails and the Rollback transaction on failure check box is selected for the step.

> Note: Some operations can leave the current transaction in an invalid state (for example, failure during a commit or rollback, or a rollback in a subpackage). Attempts to join or commit an invalid transaction fail the package. To terminate the invalid transaction, and so allow a new package transaction to start, trigger a rollback in the controlling package.

Inherited Transactions

The Execute Package task allows you to execute a Data Transformation Services (DTS) package as one step of a parent package. This subpackage may create its own package transactions, or it may inherit the parent package transaction.

A package inherits the parent package transaction if both of the following are true:

❏ The package is invoked by an Execute Package task

❏ The Execute Package task that invoked the package also joined the parent package transaction.

In the following diagram, there are six packages that all use transactions. Each package contains numerous tasks. Only the Execute Package tasks are shown. Package A executes packages B and C, which in turn execute packages D, E, and F. The Execute Package tasks that join the package transactions are indicated with an underline.

The other settings are:

❑ Chaos – This selection is only relevant when you are using DTS for a non-SQL Server data source. This is also perhaps the most dangerous selection that can be made. If your DTS package writes any data, then if anything goes wrong, you cannot roll back the changes – once created, they cannot be reversed. Therefore, a DTS task transaction operating at the Chaos level offers no isolation whatsoever to any other units of work that are using the data source. If your package is running when updates are being performed by other units of work, then your transaction within the package will see any uncommitted changes made by other transactions. If they then rolled back their changes, your DTS package would not be affected and would run as if the data was committed. In addition, any update locks by your package aren't held to the end of the transaction. **SQL Server uses SQL-92 which does not allow the Chaos isolation level. Other RDBMS do.**

❑ Read Committed – This is probably the selection that you will make the most. This option will provide your package with the greatest level of data integrity. A package that operates at this level cannot see modifications made by other transactions within other units of work, until those units of work that have outstanding transactions are committed. At this level of isolation, dirty reads – where you are wanting to read data which has been altered, but not yet committed – are not possible, but nonrepeatable reads and phantoms are possible.

❑ Read Uncommitted – This option is similar to the Chaos option. However this option is available to SQL Server, and transactions are supported for your package. If you create a package which operates at the Read Uncommitted level it can see uncommitted changes made by other transactions. At this level of isolation, dirty reads, nonrepeatable reads, and phantoms are all possible.

❑ Repeatable Read – A DTS package operating at the Repeatable Read level is guaranteed that each transaction within the package will not see any changes made by other transactions to values the package transaction has already read. Therefore, if a transaction reads the same data twice, it will always see the original data. At this level of isolation, dirty reads and nonrepeatable reads are not possible, but phantoms are.

❑ Serializable – A transaction operating at the Serializable level guarantees that all concurrent transactions interact only in ways that produce the same effect as if each transaction were entirely executed one after the other. At this isolation level, dirty reads, nonrepeatable reads, and phantoms are not possible.

We have now covered lineage, scanning, and transactions. We now come to the last option on the Advanced options tab, which is the OLE DB option.

OLE DB

You can select this option to instantiate the OLE DB provider data source objects using the OLE DB service components, or clear it to instantiate the data source objects directly with CoCreateInstance. Using the default True option offers session pooling and IRowsetChange, which may not be supported by some OLE DB providers. This setting is ignored by the DTS providers (PackageDSO, RowQueue, FlatFile) and by the Microsoft OLE DB Provider for SQL Server.

That covers all the options we can set under the Advanced tab. Now let's move on and take a look at the General tab of the package properties dialog.

General Package Properties

There are a couple of advanced options that can also be set on the General tab within the package properties dialog. These options look at the package as whole, where one option will allow you to determine how many tasks can run at any one time, with the second option determining how to prioritize tasks while a package is running. We're going to look at options on the General tab in the DTS Package Properties dialog, concerning the following:

❑ Parallelism

❑ Task priorities

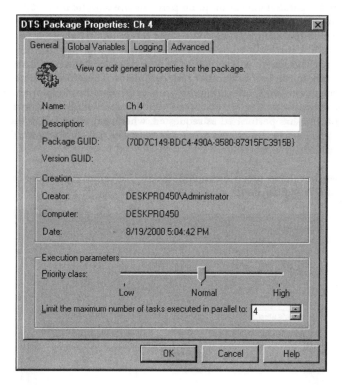

As you can see from the above screenshot, both of these options are in the Execution Parameters section. Let's now discuss them in more detail.

Parallelism

Parallelism in DTS deals with concurrency of data flow from the source to destination. For safety, only one task can use a connection at a time. Thus, to achieve parallel execution, we must set up different connections for each task.

Then you can set the individual **Task Priority** relative to the package itself:

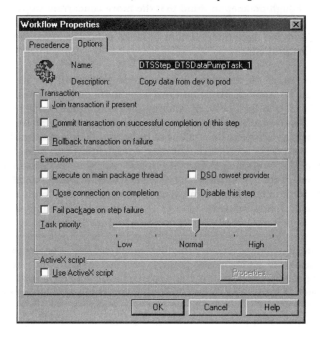

The higher the value, the faster the task will execute in relation to other tasks with a lower thread priority in this package. The available options are as follows, where the defaults for the task priority in the package are all 3, or **Normal**.

Constant	Value	Description
DTSStepRelativePriority_Lowest	1	Lowest thread priority
DTSStepRelativePriority_BelowNormal	2	Below normal thread priority
DTSStepRelativePriority_Normal	3	Normal thread priority
DTSStepRelativePriority_AboveNormal	4	Above normal thread priority
DTSStepRelativePriority_Highest	5	Highest thread priority

So far, we've looked at the options available for any package and also how to alter settings for specific tasks. In addition to what we have covered above, there are several options we can set that are specific to the Transform Data task. We'll look at these next.

Transform Data Task Options

We've already seen the Transform Data task in quite some detail in the last few chapters. This task is specifically designed to cover scenarios where you wish to move data from one data source to another, and while doing this, also transform some of that data.

Just to see these properties, create or open a package, and place two Microsoft OLE DB providers within the package. Point both of them to the `Northwind` database for the moment:

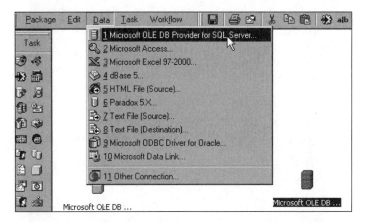

Once these two connections have been created in the package, select Transform Data Task, from the Task menu:

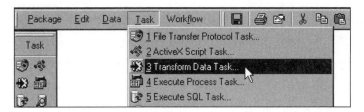

Then select the two data sources one at a time, which will then insert a Transform Data task (the black arrowed line) between the two data sources.

We can configure the properties associated with this task by right-clicking on the relevant Transform Data task and selecting Properties. The advanced options are on the Options tab:

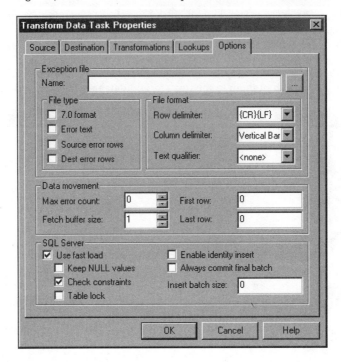

In this dialog we can specify:

❑ An Exception file along with its type and format

❑ Data Movement options, such as the Max error count, along with Fetch buffer size and First and Last row

❑ SQL Server options such as Use fast load, Enable identity insert, and Always commit final batch

We'll look at what each of these does in turn.

Exception File

Oftentimes we will want to see if anything goes wrong during the execution of a particular Data Pump task. An **exception file** logs the bad rows at the expense of a small bit of overhead. If there are no errors to report, then there is no degradation in speed. We will look at the different options here and what you would use them for. We'll see more on exception files in Chapter 11.

The exception file will contain any SQL exception errors that are created during the package execution. Even though we may loose a tiny bit of speed, it can give us valuable information on where to look for the source of a problem. The description and number of the error raised will be identical to the message you would receive if you executed the script in a T-SQL window, or via a scheduled job.

We can configure an Exception file in the Options tab of the Properties dialog:

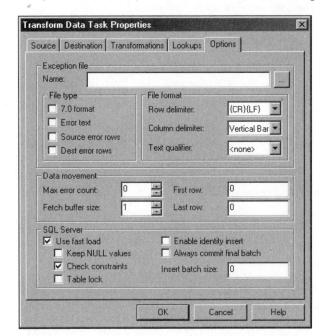

Either type in the file name you want, or use the ... to select an existing file. You need to make sure that the file path information is the same on the local machine as it is on the server. Using a relative path (using a UNC) typically works best. If the file does not exist, DTS will create it – as long as the path is valid. And if the file does exist, it will append to it.

New to the SQL Server 2000 Transform Data task is the ability to save not only the step execution and error information, but also the source and destination rows that cause the errors. With this information, you can easily fix the problem, then either manually add the rows, or create a new source file to input the rows into the destination. In order to save this information, you will need to uncheck the 7.0 format box under File Type, and check the Error text, Source error rows, and Dest error rows options. If the 7.0 format box is checked, the other three options are disabled:

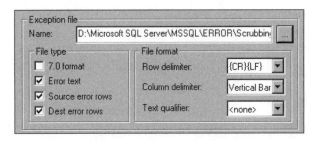

Also related to the file type properties are the File format properties. These properties specify how the error rows are written into the exception file. The possible row delimiters, which separate one error from another, are as follows:

- ❑ {CR}{LF}
- ❑ {CR}
- ❑ {LF}
- ❑ Semicolon
- ❑ Comma
- ❑ Tab
- ❑ Vertical Bar
- ❑ <none>

The column delimiter separates each column in the row. The possible column delimiters are as follows:

- ❑ Semicolon
- ❑ Comma
- ❑ Tab
- ❑ Vertical Bar

Finally the text qualifier specifies if any characters should enclose a string value. The reason this may be necessary is if you have a possibility of the column delimiter appearing naturally in the data. For example, if you had a comma as the comma delimiter and had a value of Arron, Hank it would appear as two distinct values. Using a text qualifier of Double Quote (") would make the value "Arron, Hank" which would be interpreted as a single value. The possible values for the text qualifier are:

- ❑ Double Quote (")
- ❑ Single Quote (')
- ❑ <none>

Data Movement Options

There are four options that come under the Data movement category.

Max Error Count

The MaximumErrorCount property in code or the Max error count box in the Transform Data task specifies the maximum number of error rows before the data pump terminates. The default of this property is 0, which means that it will continue until it reaches the end of the source. If it's possible that your data could come in dirty, without much validation, you may want to set this number to a small value so you don't have to wait long before you're informed that there's a problem. Your package execution will still fail, but it will stop processing source rows once it reaches this maximum. It will generate an error similar to this:

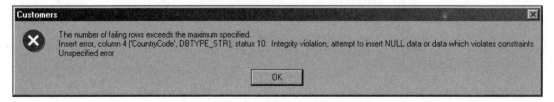

First and Last Row Setting

The First row and Last row checkboxes allow you to specify the first and last row of a dataset from the source. By default, the First row is set to 0, and the Last row is also set to 0 (which means until there are no more rows).

Now, depending on the setting of the insert commit size (which we'll look at shortly), the entire set of rows or a section would be committed depending on your settings. How are you ever going to fix this mistake? Well, once you fix the error you could truncate the table and start over, but if it's a large load with many fields, why waste the effort already done? Simply set the First row to the next record you need to restart on, and set the Last row to a value greater than the First row and let it rip.

The First row and Last row settings allow you to easily select a subset of a file to process, giving you finite control over your load process. It can even be used to load a single row if needed.

Fetch Buffer Size

The Fetch buffer size property specifies the number of rows to fetch in a single operation from the OLE DB source. If you are retrieving data sequentially, in the primary key/clustered index order, then the larger the chunk, the less disk I/O operations are required to get the information off the drive. In addition, since more data will be in the buffer, presumably in faster memory, doing the transformation will subsequently be faster as well, at the expense of eating up more memory. Once the transformation has finished with the buffer, the whole buffer is cleared out, and then the next set of rows are fetched and loaded in to the buffer.

You can adjust the Fetch buffer size property to achieve the best balance between memory usage and reduced overhead. However, you'll find that you'll rarely adjust this unless you know exactly what you are doing. There are no tools within DTS to aid you in your calculations, and you will need to sit down and figure out whether returning a different number of rows will aid your transformation. If you wish to alter this value, the optimum from an I/O view point would be to create a buffer size the same as the page size within the database. A value greater than 1 is ignored if the data source uses BLOB storage objects. The default is 100.

Now let's put what we've learned about these options to good use in an example.

Data Movement Options Example

Let's imagine that we have a text file containing historical sales data for the last ten years – from 1990 to the end of 1999. We have a file called `Sales.txt` that starts something like this:

```
SalesDate,SalesAmt
1/1/1990,273088.39
1/2/1990,24450.1
1/3/1990,186413.11
1/4/1990,327640.37
1/5/1990,68342.6
.........
```

You can download a copy of this file from the Wrox web site at http://www.wrox.com.

We want to load this into the **Sales** table in our **Wrox** database on SQL Server. However, there's an error on the row that contains July 4 1995 (the 1981st row in the file):

```
7/4/1995,24713>58
```

Let's see how we'd work around this.

First, in order to load this file we need to create a table in the **Wrox** database to load it into. Run the following to create this table:

```
CREATE TABLE [Sales] (
[SalesDate] smalldatetime NOT NULL,
[SalesAmt] money NOT NULL )
```

Next, we're going to set up a package that looks like the following:

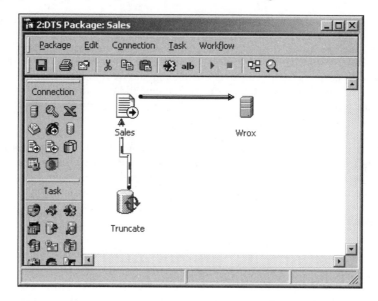

Start by creating a Microsoft OLE DB Provider for SQL Server connection to the Wrox database, calling the connection Wrox:

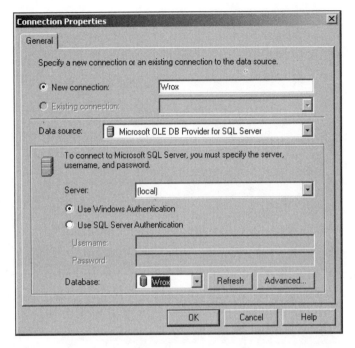

Next we need a connection to our sources file, Sales.txt. Select Connection | Text File (Source), rename the connection as Sales and click the ... to browse to your copy of Sales.txt:

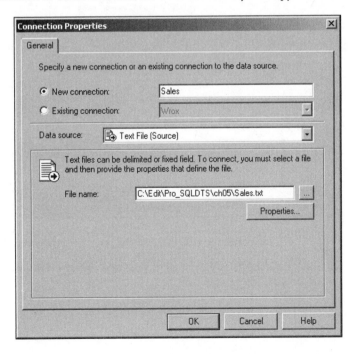

Click **OK**, and you're taken to the properties of the file. We let DTS know that the First row has column names by selecting the option as shown below – all the other values are already specified correctly:

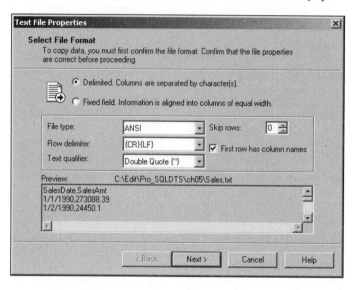

Click **Next** to move to the next screen where we need to specify the column delimiter. In this case, it is a comma delimited file, so we don't need to change anything:

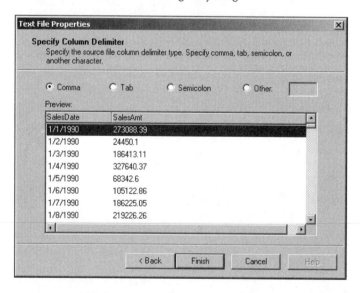

Click **Finish**. Now we have the source and destination defined, so we can add our task.

Add an **Execute SQL Task** from the Task menu, call it **Truncate**, specify Wrox as the connection and add the following line to the SQL statement box:

```
TRUNCATE TABLE Sales
```

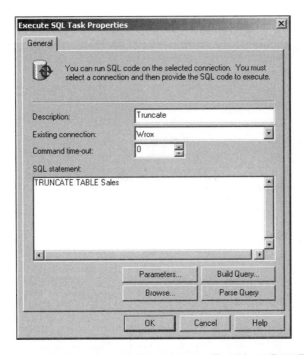

Now that both the source and destination are defined, select Transform Data Task from the Task menu and set up the transformation between the two. Call up the Properties dialog, and name the it Sales Load. The Source tab of the transformation properties page should look like the picture below (except, of course, the file location will differ):

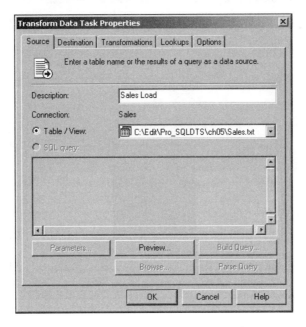

Here is the output from the Exception file:

```
DATA TRANSFORMATION SERVICES: Data Pump Exception Log


Package Name: Sales
Package Description: (null)
Package ID: {E072A1F3-96C3-4C41-95CF-F7722E7FEB15}
Package Version: {A3533791-0EFB-4CF9-A8DF-A65228019898}
Step Name: DTSStep_DTSDataPumpTask_1

@@ExecutionStarted

Execution Started: 28/09/2000 14:22:23

@@LogSourceRows: C:\Program Files\Microsoft SQL
Server\MSSQL\SalesErrors.txt.Source
@@LogDestRows: C:\Program Files\Microsoft SQL Server\MSSQL\SalesErrors.txt.Dest

@@ErrorRow:  2011
Error during Transformation 'DTSTransformation__2' for Row number 2011. Errors
encountered so far in this task: 1.

Error Source: Microsoft Data Transformation Services (DTS) Data Pump
Error Description:TransformCopy 'DTSTransformation__2' conversion error:
Conversion invalid for datatypes on column pair 1 (source column 'SalesAmt'
(DBTYPE_STR), destination column 'SalesAmt' (DBTYPE_CY)).
Error Help File:sqldts80.hlp
Error Help Context ID:30501
@@SourceRow:  Logged
@@DestRow:  Not Available

@@ExecutionCompleted

Execution Completed: 28/09/2000 14:22:26

**********************************************************************
```

The transformation task created a file called Sales.txt.Source which contains the row which caused the fatal error:

```
7/4/1995,24713>58
```

Now we have several options about how to deal with this bad row. OK, the obvious choice would be to fix the Sales Amount and re-run the package – but what fun would that be? Let's play with some of the options and see how we can work around this problem.

The first thing we should try is to set the First row to 2012, to skip over the first part of the file to see if we can load the latter half. Remember, we can set this in the Options tab in the Transform Data Task Properties:

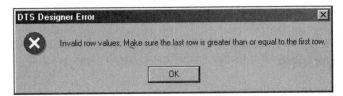

Now if we click OK when we set these values we get the following message:

Now this is contrary to what Books Online says about the Last Row property. It says that 0 means it will run to there are no more rows. Oh well, they can't be 100% right all of the time. Lets choose an arbitrary value outside of the range we're loading, say 999999 for the Last row. It should now look like this:

Now let's run the package to see what happens:

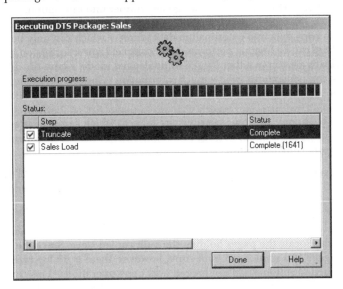

Insert Batch Size

The Insert batch size option (or the `InsertCommitSize` property if you're setting it in any coded solution) specifies the number of successful rows inserted between commit operations, if supported by the OLE-DB provider (the specific option is, `IRowsetFastLoad`).

If the provider does not support this method – and at present, only SQL Server does support it – it will commit after every insertion. The default value is 0, which means the inserts are batched in a single transaction, and completed in one hit. SQL Server will follow the normal rules for committing the data to the database using this option, which means that at the end of the transaction, the information is written to disk.

Always Commit Final Batch

This is related to the insert batch size. If this option is checked it will commit the last batch prior to moving to the next step. So if we have a source containing 2634 rows, and the insert batch size is the default 1000, then the first 1000 records would be committed, then the next 1000, and the final 634 rows will be committed if this option is checked prior to executing any other steps. If the option is not checked, then the commit will occur upon the completion of the package.

Personally, I really do recommend that this option is set to `True`, otherwise you may find inconsistent results with later steps within your package if you are reusing the data. The default for this option is `False` (unchecked).

Well that completes our look at the Transform Data task advanced options. Now for something completely different ....

Data Scrubbing

We've all heard of the phrase "garbage in, garbage out". If you're building a data warehouse with data that is incorrect, or has some data inconsistencies in it, there is no reason to build one at all.

> **Data scrubbing is the art of removing and cleaning data from your various sources.**

When users are relying on this information as a basis for critical business decisions, it is necessary to make sure the quality of the data is the very best.

For instance, it's very unlikely that your company will have only one source for most pieces of information. Let's take for example a list of countries. Over time, as countries are formed and some are dissolved, the list changes on some servers, and not on others. Some may use a three-character code to represent the country code, some may use four, some simply use a numeric identity field. In any case, to make sure all of your USAs stay as USA when put in the warehouse, you will need to carefully look at the data.

One way of scrubbing data is to create a bunch of "lookup" tables in the warehouse, or in another database located on the warehouse server. One of those tables would be the list of countries you are going to use – hopefully one based on some standard like ANSI.

Let's go ahead and demonstrate this by creating a table in the Wrox database called Country. Use the following SQL to do this:

```
CREATE TABLE [dbo].[COUNTRY] (
    [COUNTRYCODE] [char] (2) NOT NULL ,
    [COUNTRY] [varchar] (70) NOT NULL
)
```

Populate it with the country list countrycode.txt: you can find this file in the code download for the book available from the Wrox web site, or downloaded it from http://www.dts2000.com/countrylist.txt.

You can either insert the countries one at a time, or better still, use your skills to create a simple Transform Data task to transfer the data from the text file to the new table (just follow the steps in our example earlier in the chapter). The data is simple and straight forward and should pose no problems whichever method you chose.

Now that we have a lookup table for country, we can look at our "source" table, the Customers table in Northwind to see if there are going to be any problems when we actually do the data load. What we're going to do to check for errors is to simply left join the Customer table against this new Country table by the country, and look for NULLs. Whatever falls out will be the rows for which we don't have a country defined in our "lookup" table. To demonstrate the idea, lets look at the following tables below.

These are the distinct countries from Customers in the Northwind database:

- Argentina
- Austria
- Belgium
- Brazil
- Canada
- Denmark
- Finland
- France
- Germany
- Ireland
- Italy
- Mexico
- Norway
- Poland
- Portugal
- Spain
- Sweden
- Switzerland
- UK
- USA
- Venezuela

And in our list of countries (Country in the Wrox database), we happen to have all the countries spelled out. So UK would be United Kingdom, and USA would be United States.

Join the Customers table from NorthWind to our Country table in the Wrox database via the following query:

```
SELECT Northwind.dbo.Customers.CustomerID,
    Northwind.dbo.Customers.CompanyName,
    Northwind.dbo.Customers.Country
FROM Northwind.dbo.Customers LEFT OUTER JOIN
    COUNTRY ON
    Northwind.dbo.Customers.Country = COUNTRY.COUNTRY
WHERE (COUNTRY.COUNTRY IS NULL)
```

We get the following rows that "fall out", meaning that these countries do not exist in our lookup table in the warehouse:

WHITC	White Clover Markets	USA
THEBI	The Big Cheese	USA
THECR	The Cracker Box	USA
TRAIH	Trail's Head Gourmet Provisioners	USA
RATTC	Rattlesnake Canyon Grocery	USA
SAVEA	Save-a-lot Markets	USA
SPLIR	Split Rail Beer & Ale	USA
LETSS	Let's Stop N Shop	USA
LONEP	Lonesome Pine Restaurant	USA
OLDWO	Old World Delicatessen	USA
GREAL	Great Lakes Food Market	USA
HUNGC	Hungry Coyote Import Store	USA
LAZYK	Lazy K Kountry Store	USA
SEVES	Seven Seas Imports	UK
EASTC	Eastern Connection	UK
ISLAT	Island Trading	UK
NORTS	North/South	UK
AROUT	Around the Horn	UK
BSBEV	B's Beverages	UK
CONSH	Consolidated Holdings	UK

Now we have the fun task of determining what that data actually means. In this case it's a simple difference in spelling, but it might not always be that obvious.

In some cases it is simply a matter of changing the data. For instance, let's say the country name changed and you are a geography scholar and realize it. Or it could be that someone fat-fingered it into the original database, which did not have any constraints. Now do you simply make a change in your load process to fix these errors, or is this something that should be fixed in the source system? Either way, scrubbing the data can take days if not weeks if the systems you are getting the data from were poorly designed.

Modern database design tools and methodologies typically prevent these mistakes from occurring in new environments. You will most likely encounter these issues with older database designs, or designs by people who think third normal form is a type of opening in chess.

> *If you want to become more involved with SQL Server and data design, and how to avoid pitfalls with this, try* Professional SQL Server 7.0 Programming, *ISBN 1-861002-31-9, or* Professional SQL Server 2000 Programming, *ISBN 1-861004-48-6, both from Wrox Press.*

So how do you deal with these problems? Most scrubbing occurs typically in the Transform Data task, when you are supplying the transformation information. If you wanted to trap a predictable error from the source data, you could use an Active X script transformation to check the source value, and dynamically set the destination value. We'll look at an example in the next section when we discuss lookups.

So we've gone over the scrubbing of the data, but there will be instances where you will want to do a substitution. However, doing this using `Case` statements gets to be impractical. This is why DTS provides us with lookups.

DTS Lookup

The lookup feature of DTS allows you to make another, new connection utilizing an existing connection already defined in the package during the execution of the DTS task, and include data from that connection in the destination table as part of a lookup. It is similar to doing a join to an existing table to get additional information, but this can be done across other databases and other servers. A join would be typically limited to the current source database.

For example, say you have a destination table that must include the postal abbreviation for a customer's state, for example, ME for Maine. However, the data for state in the source table contains the full name (Maine). A lookup table in another database, possibly on a different server, contains the name of each state and its postal abbreviation. You can write a transformation such that when the source data for the state column is read, as part of the query you connect to the lookup table, query it for the postal abbreviation, and write the results to the appropriate column in the destination table.

Lookups are used frequently to validate data against information stored in other tables. The feature is particularly useful when it is not practical to perform a join operation on another table using a distributed query.

One advantage of the lookup feature is that it can be invoked from inside the transformation function. We associate a query and a connection with the lookup. Although we can achieve similar functionality using COM objects and global variables, the advantage of a lookup is that it uses an established connection, optimized for quick data retrieval. However, if you can do a join to get the data, it is faster than a similar lookup query.

Setting Up a Data Lookup

You can use lookups as part of a Transform Data task or a Data Driven Query task. Lookup definitions are made on the Lookups tab of each of the tasks. In the following screenshot, you will notice that we are using the connection created in the package named Wrox, and will be connecting to an external lookup table, CountryCode:

In just a few moments we'll go through an example of using a lookup query. The steps we need to perform are:

❑ Set the connections. You need to create connections for the source table, destination table, and lookup table.

❑ Create a Transform Data or Data Driven Query task, and specify the source and destination tables.

❑ Add a lookup definition, including the lookup query.

❑ Map the source and destination columns involved in the lookup with an ActiveX script. The ActiveX script calls the lookup query each time data in the column of interest must be moved, for every row in the source table.

> **Because using ActiveX scripts affects execution speed, use lookups carefully when moving large sets of data.**

Let's create a package that demonstrates a few of these scrubbing techniques. The first thing we need to do is create a new package. Then we need to create two connections, one to the Northwind database, and the other to our Wrox database. Save the package as Scrubbing.

Now we need to prepare for the data we are going to load from Northwind into the Wrox database by creating a table in the Wrox database. Do this using the following SQL:

```
CREATE TABLE [dbo].[CUSTOMER_COUNTRY] (
    [CustomerID] [nchar] (5) NOT NULL ,
    [CompanyName] [nvarchar] (40) NOT NULL ,
    [Country] [nvarchar] (70) NOT NULL ,
    [CountryCode] [char] (2) NOT NULL
)
```

Now that we have the table, let's build the rest of the package. Insert an Execute SQL task, whose responsibility it will be to truncate the CUSTOMER_COUNTRY table in the Wrox database each execution. Call it **Truncate**, select **Wrox**, and enter the following SQL statement:

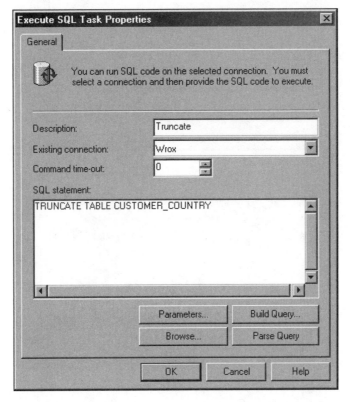

Now we need to set up the transformation between the two databases. Create a Data Transformation task selecting the **Northwind** connection as the source and **Wrox** as the destination.

Now open up the properties dialog for the Transform Data task. On the **Source**, we are going to specify the query to supply the data:

```
SELECT CustomerID, CompanyName, Country
FROM   Customers
```

as follows:

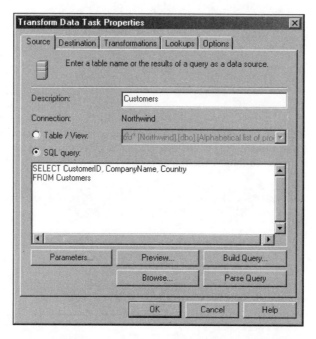

On the Destination tab, we need to select the CUSTOMER_COUNTRY table:

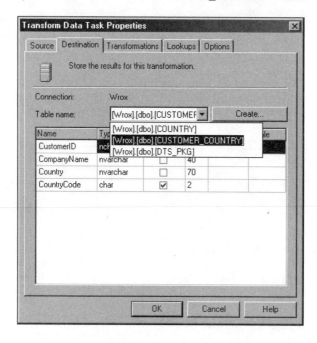

Now the default transformations should appear when we select the **Transformations** tab:

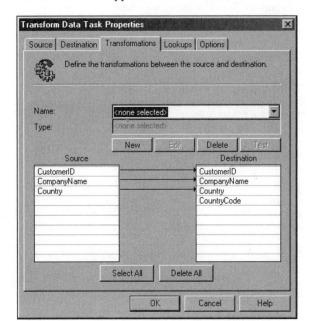

Next, we need to set up the lookup to populate the `CountryCode` field.

Click on the **Lookups** tab. Let's specify this lookup name as **CountryCode** and select the **Wrox** connection as the source. Click on the ... button in the **Query** column to set up the query:

We're going to set up a parameterized query to select the CountryCode based upon the Country provided by the source database. Type the following code:

```
SELECT      COUNTRYCODE
FROM        COUNTRY
WHERE       (COUNTRY = ?)
```

into the window that appears:

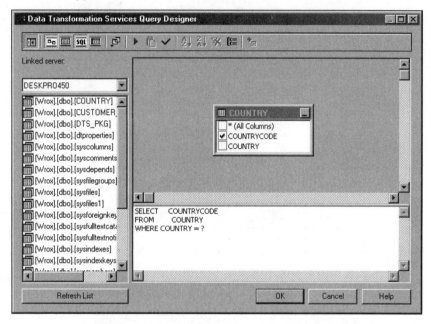

The ? will be replaced by the Country provided by the source database. Click OK to close down the Query Designer.

Now we need to set up the ActiveX Script task to populate the CountryCode:

Go back to the Transformations tab and select Country from the Source and CountryCode from the Destination. Click New:

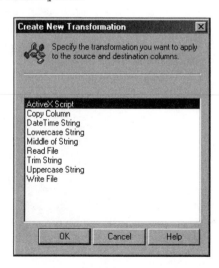

Select **ActiveX Script** if it's not already selected, and click **OK**. Then click **Properties**, and modify the code in the window that appears to the following:

```
Function Main()
    DTSDestination("CountryCode") = _
            DTSLookups("CountryCode").Execute(DTSSource("Country").Value)
    Main = DTSTransformStat_OK
End Function
```

> **Don't worry if you don't understand this code – we'll be devoting the whole of Chapter 7 to introducing you to using VBScript in an ActiveX Script task.**

We are assigning `CountryCode` to the value returned from the lookup `CountryCode` by the `Country` value supplied it.

Parse the ActiveX script to make sure it is fine, and then click **OK**. Click **OK** again.

Your transformation task should look like this:

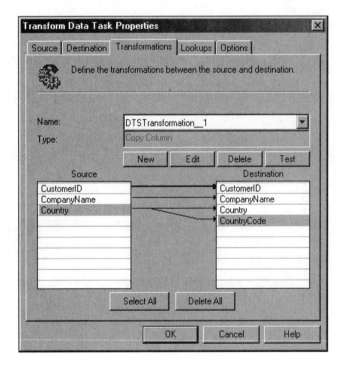

Click OK to save the changes. Finally, we need a Workflow step On completion from our Truncate task to the Northwind connection. Let's see what the package looks like now:

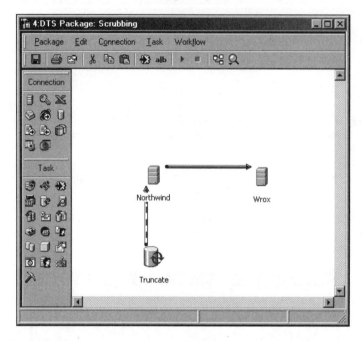

If your package looks like this, you're ready to execute it. Let's run the package and see what happens.

Uh oh, looks like we got an error:

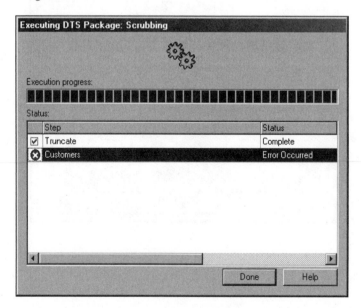

Double-click on the red circle to get detailed information about the step failure:

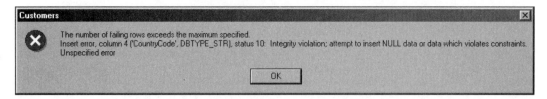

Looks like we ended up with NULL values trying to be inserted into CUSTOMER_COUNTRY. This occurred because there are countries in the Northwind Customer table which do not exist in our Country table. Now how can we change the source so that it has the appropriate country prior to the lookup occurring?

The easiest way is to change the SQL in the SELECT statement for the Transform Data task **Source** via some decision type function like Case. Using this query, we can eliminate the error:

```
SELECT CustomerID, CompanyName,
   Case Country
      WHEN 'USA' Then 'United States'
      WHEN 'UK' Then 'United Kingdom'
      ELSE Country
   End as Country
FROM Customers
```

The added benefit is that this is faster than the Active X script. However, this method relies on the decision function being supported by the database you are connecting to as the source.

We could also effectively change the data further along in the transformation using an ActiveX Script task. We will be using the source column Country to now populate both the Country and CountryCode column in the destination.

The first thing we need to do is remove the existing transformations of the source Country and create a new one. Select the **Source Country** and the **Destination Country and CountryCode** as shown below:

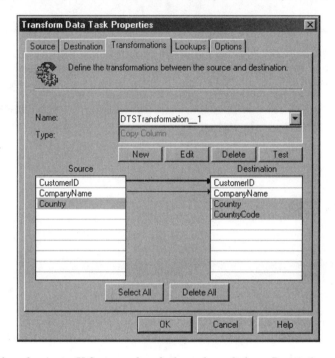

Click **New** and select the ActiveX Script task as before, then click on **Properties**.

The following code inserted into the ActiveX Script task changes the Country information to the correct value. We first fix the Country, then use the new value to do the lookup.

```
Function Main()

Dim Country

    Select Case DTSSource("Country")
        Case "USA"
            Country = "United States"
        Case "UK"
            Country = "United Kingdom"
        Case Else
            Country = DTSSource("Country")
    End Select

    DTSDestination("Country") = Country

    DTSDestination("CountryCode") = _
            DTSLookups("CountryCode").Execute(Country)
    Main = DTSTransformStat_OK
End Function
```

Click **OK** three times to get back to the Designer window and execute the package.

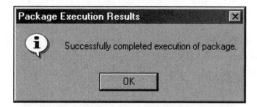

Perfect!

So now we've seen how to perform a lookup, as well as carry out some data scrubbing along the way.

Common Errors

Before we leave this chapter, we're going to discover how to avoid perhaps some of the more common errors which could arise in importing data from different data sources.

First of all, let's take a look at date and time conversions.

Date Time Conversion

This is perhaps the most contentious issue for the introduction of errors within packages – importing date and time information.

In most systems that you are importing date or time information from, you cannot be certain what format the date and time information is in – it could be a string, or a data-specific data type, or even a non-conforming format where the data will not be in the correct format for SQL.

One way to ensure that you don't receive an error when attempting to populate a date time field is setting up an Active Script task between the date source and destination columns:

```
'****************************************************************
'   Visual Basic Transformation Script
'   Copy each source column to the
'   destination column
'****************************************************************

Function Main()
    DTSDestination("ACCTG_DATE")     = CDate(DTSSource("Col002"))
    DTSDestination("LOAN_ORIG_DATE") = CDate(DTSSource("Col028"))
    DTSDestination("MTG_MAT_DATE")   = CDate(DTSSource("Col030"))
    Main = DTSTransformStat_OK
End Function
```

Once all the source and destination columns have been selected and the task created, all that's left to do is add `CDate` to the source to prepare it for the destination.

However, as we've said before, ActiveX is a slow method of processing information. Another method – new to SQL 2000 – is to use the Transformation tab in the Transform Data task properties. This gives us the ability to select which type of transformation we would like to occur.

Remember the Create New Transformation dialog we saw earlier, from the Transformation tab on the task's properties dialog? We selected the ActiveX Script option here. However, one of the choices is a DateTime string transformation:

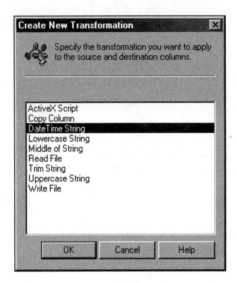

This will convert the date to a standard format, and will also run a great deal faster and safer than the ActiveX script example. If at all possible, you should use this option of date and time transformation whenever dealing with dates and times.

Importing from Excel

Another vexing problem that most of us will encounter is importing data from an Excel spreadsheet. The two most common problems here are:

- The source field coming in as NULL when the destination field is set to not NULL
- Source fields being the wrong data type

There is no elegant solution for fixing these issues – you'll have to use an intermediate task to scrub the values for you. Typically, this is done using an ActiveX Script task, which gives you the greatest flexibility in checking for possible problems in the source file. In rare cases, you'll need to open the spreadsheet and make some modifications to it in order to prepare it for DTS.

To remove the NULL fields, you simply input a single quote (') and a space. This effectively creates a non-NULL field that will import as a blank. You could set up an Excel macro to replace all the empty fields, create an ActiveX Script task to complete the transformation, or even create an option on the Transformations tab of the task's properties to alter the data. A cell of data in an Excel spreadsheet is no different to data from any other data source, and so transforming the column data is just as easy to do here as it is for any other data source.

The other issue is with a destination column that is text, say char(2), but the source appears to be a numeric field. Typically it is a field that contains values like 01, 02, 03, AA, BB, CC, etc. Excel treats the first value as a number, so DTS will import it as 1, not 01. Once again, to touch up this field, you need to add the single quote in front of the number. This will make it a text field.

Target Table Has an Identity

There will be times when you need to load a table, identity values and all. If you try to do it in DTS without setting the options correctly (which we saw earlier) you're likely to receive this message:

Error at Destination for Row number 1. Errors encountered so far in this task: 1.
Insert error, column 1 ('ColumnName', DBTYPE_I4), status 9: Permission denied.

This problem can be avoided by selecting both Use fast load and Enable identity insert during DTS operations. Both options are found on the Advanced tab of the Data Transformation Properties window.

If you have triggers defined with your destination table, the triggers will be ignored when Use fast load is enabled.

Error Handling

No matter how hard you try, no one is infallible, just as the data that you will be importing will never be perfect 100% of the time. Therefore, in this section we'll summarize how to deal with errors, and how to log those errors so that you can find out what went wrong and then correct it.

Advanced error handling techniques will be covered in Chapter 11.

Choosing an Error File

In order to better troubleshoot problems with your DTS package, it is always a good idea to set up an error file. Much like a log, information regarding any errors that occur is appended to the file each time a package executes, regardless of success or failure. If a package fails, it will give you detailed information as to which step failed and what error occurred while executing that step.

For example, if we tried to insert a duplicate value into a primary key, we would get an error message something like:

```
Error at Destination for Row number 146. Errors encountered so far in this task:
1.
The statement has been terminated.
Violation of primary key constraint 'PK_CountryCode__090A5324'. Cannot insert
duplicate key in object 'Country_Code'.
```

If you want to log more errors to the exception file, either do not use the fast load option, or set the insert commit size to another value, such as 1.

Fail Package on First Error

The **FailOnError** property specifies whether package execution stops when there is an error in any step. This option is different from any precedence constraints you may have set inside your package. If this option is set, no more tasks are executed once an error occurs, even those with a precedence of OnFailure.

Probably the most common occasion when this property is set is when the package is small and straightforward, with perhaps a handful of steps. These steps are all dependant on the previous step being a success, and so it is quicker to stop the package immediately, rather than let each step run and fail and give multiple failures to investigate. Also, the last step might be a step that indicates that the package has run successfully, in which case you would not want this to run.

This option is purely a fast way of stopping a package.

Summary

In this chapter we discussed the advanced DTS options. Having learned how to audit the data coming into the package, and how to scan the data, we then moved on and learned how transactional processing can fit into a developed and final packaged solution that you wish to create.

There are many and varied aspects to transactional processing within DTS, and there is a vast amount to think about and consider when setting up your package. It is usually this area that determines the strength of a package when moving into a productive environment. With the incorrect transactional options set, you can make a poor package not only in performance, but also in reliability, a very professional solution.

We've also seen how to take complex packages, and determine whether to run several tasks simultaneously or not, and whether to prioritize one task over another.

One major task that will be performed in a number of packages is when you need to pull information into the package without actually performing any DTS work on that data. We discussed lookups, and how to bring information from these into the package, and then pass this into the destination data source.

Finally, no-one is perfect. Errors will inevitably occur, and the last section was used to overview a few common errors that may occur, and how to then cope with these within your package.

With all of this knowledge you should be able to set up a complex and powerful package with transactions and error handling correctly created. In the next chapter, we are going to look at linked servers.

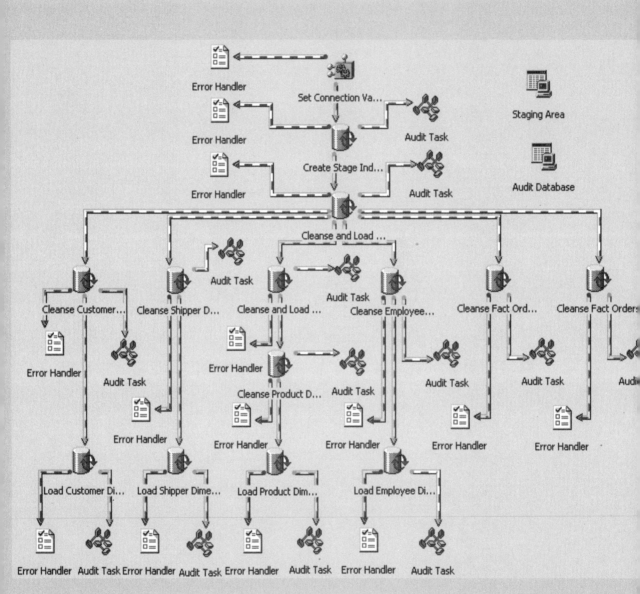

Error Handler

Set Connection Va...

Audit Task

Staging Area

Error Handler

Create Stage Ind...

Audit Task

Audit Database

Error Handler

Audit Task

Cleanse and Load ...

Audit Task

Cleanse Customer...   Cleanse Shipper D...   Cleanse and Load ...   Cleanse Employee...   Cleanse Fact Ord...   Cleanse Fact Orders

Audit Task

Error Handler   Audit Task

Error Handler

Cleanse Product D...

Audit Task   Audit Task   Audit Task   Audi

Error Handler   Audit Task

Error Handler

Error Handler   Error Handler   Error Handler   Error Handler

Load Customer Di...   Load Shipper Dime...   Load Product Dim...   Load Employee Di...

Error Handler   Audit Task   Error Handler   Audit Task   Error Handler   Audit Task   Error Handler   Audit Task

5

Querying Heterogeneous Data

In an enterprise environment, you will experience all types of database systems, and integrating all of these could prove quite challenging. This chapter will explain how to access data from various different sources using something called **linked servers**.

In this chapter we will explain:

- ❑ How to create a linked server
- ❑ How to query a linked server
- ❑ Some common conversion problems and pitfalls
- ❑ The limitations of linked servers
- ❑ The OPENQUERY and OPENROWSET commands

However, we'll start by defining exactly what we mean by heterogeneous data.

Heterogeneous Data

Applications are becoming increasingly more distributed in nature. In addition, programmers are now required to develop applications that seamlessly merge data from legacy systems with relational databases. The term legacy is a relatively open term that we'll use to describe flat database systems. This data from other database management systems is called **heterogeneous data**. For example, companies often have their inventory data in a mainframe type environment, while their marketing system is in a relational database like SQL Server.

One solution to this perplexing problem is to merge all of your databases. This method is often very expensive due to the resources and time needed to perform such a task. That's not to mention that some DBMSs could not handle all the data traffic. You will also find that the different databases systems, like inventory and marketing, have different owners, and merging the two could prove to be a political nightmare.

A less expensive approach to a heterogeneous environment is to write **distributed queries**. With the arrival of OLE DB, we can now access data from almost any data source directly using distributed queries. Distributed queries allow you to write a query that gathers part of the information from, for example, a DB2 source and the other part of the information from, say, a SQL Server source. We can also write these queries against other SQL Server databases, called **homogeneous** databases, depending on the version of SQL Server. Writing distributed queries has the following advantages:

❑ Less expensive than transferring or replicating the data

❑ Works against any DBMS or anything that has an OLE DB provider, including Index and Directory Services

❑ Allows us to use SQL against any provider

We can run distributed queries against multiple servers using **linked servers**.

What are Linked Servers?

The ability to write distributed queries using linked servers was introduced with SQL Server 7.0. Linked servers are similar to linked tables in Access. A linked server will allow you to execute a command against any data source that you have defined as a linked server. Since distributed queries use OLE DB, we can not only access relational databases, but also legacy database systems. Linked servers can also use ODBC through the OLE DB provider for ODBC.

Previously, in data processing, accessing heterogeneous data meant that you would have to install expensive and complex gateways. Sybase, for example, had Direct Connect that would have to be installed separately. With SQL Server's linked server feature, SQL Server acts as the middle-tier. As far as the client knows, they only connect to SQL Server, while the linked server manages the connections for them, as shown in the following diagram. This is an inexpensive solution that Microsoft provides wrapped into SQL Server.

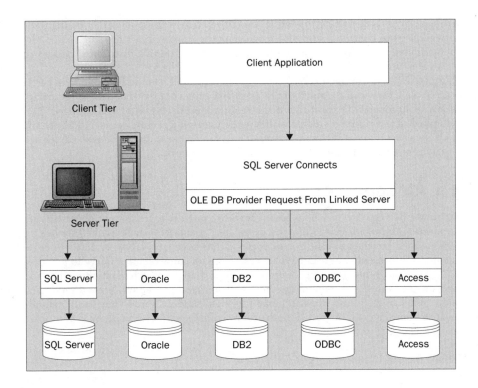

Remote Servers

In past releases of SQL Server, you could use **remote servers** to access homogeneous data. This has been preserved in SQL Server 7.0 and 2000 for backward compatibility and is still used in replication. As it is used in replication, it'll probably be preserved in future releases.

For example, the diagram below shows the use of a remote server. The client connects to a SQL Server (in this case, SQL Server 1), which, in turn, passes a request to the remote SQL Server (SQL Server 2). The remote SQL Server (2) will then execute the request on behalf of the client. The actual processing occurs on the destination machine (2), which then sends the results back to the requesting server (1). Finally, the remote server (2) sends the results to the SQL Server (1), which then sends the results back to the client.

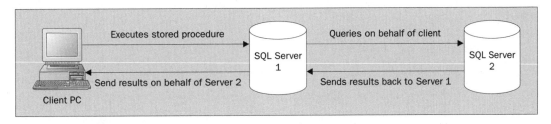

Remote servers were also the primary way for SQL Server to handle replication. Since the source server the client was connecting to (**SQL Server 1** in the above diagram) was executing the query on behalf of the client, only one connection was required.

Since the release of SQL Server 7.0, linked servers have replaced remote server configurations. Remote servers only allow us to execute a stored procedure on the remote machine, and do not allow us to run an ad hoc distributed query. Linked servers are optimized for running distributed queries against their OLE DB provider and use as much as possible the benefits of the OLE DB provider you're connecting to. For example, if you're connecting to Access, then you would use the Jet driver and the linked server would let the Access database do much of the work and only act as a organizer of the data, joining it if needed. If you want to execute a stored procedure on a remote system in a SQL Server 7.0 or later, you should use linked servers (unless you have already configured a remote server). If Microsoft follows the same pattern for phasing out a technology, remote servers will eventually be phased out in a later release. Today remote servers are still being used for replication.

Putting it All Together

You might be wondering why, in a book about DTS, we need to learn about distributed queries. Well, DTS can interact with linked servers directly using the Execute SQL task. Linked servers can also join against data in any other data source. For example, if you have a SQL Server data source and an Oracle data source that is represented as a Linked Server, then you can execute a query to join these tables in a simple SQL statement. When merging systems, we often load records from multiple heterogeneous data sources into staging tables, and then merge them with a stored procedure. Linked servers can sometimes enable you to skip some of these steps and load more polished data into your staging environment, mainly because your data can be joined on the fly in your Execute SQL task or stored procedure before it even reaches a staging environment.

Using DTS we can use linked servers to:

❑   Purge the data staging area

❑   Run incremental updates on remote systems

❑   Run dynamic queries in ActiveX scripts using ADO to connect to your linked server

For example, you can purge records from a linked server simply by qualifying the object name with the linked server and database name, as you do with SELECT statements. It is convenient to use this method because you can create a linked server in one location and call it from any query. For OLE DB providers that may be a little more difficult to configure, such as DB2, this can save some time in your package creation since you won't have to create an OLE DB connection for each package. Instead, you can call it using a four-part qualifier from any query task as shown below.

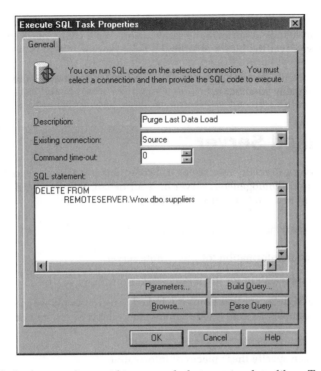

You can also use a linked server from within any task that queries data, like a Transform Data task. This allows you to capture part of your data from one database system, while the other part of your data comes from another database system. The task below queries the Orders table from the remote Northwind database while the Customers are pulled from the local Northwind database.

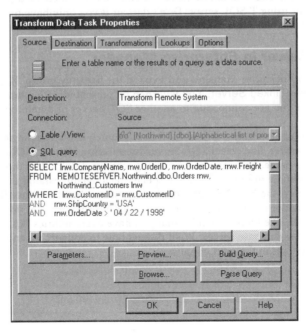

Option	Required?	Description
Provider string	No	Any connection string required by the OLE DB provider. This is not required for SQL Server connections. Some OLE DB connections like DB2 however, will require this option. For DB2, you could use the OLE DB Provider for DB2 to connect to the DB2 system. You would have to install the Windows 9.x or NT Client for Host Integration Services to do this. Then you could build a Data Link file to obtain this provider string easily.
Location	No	The location of the data source translated by the provider. This option is not required when connecting to SQL Servers or most database servers. Providers like the OLE DB Provider for Indexing Service use this property. The location is passed to the OLE DB provider as the DBPROP_INIT_LOCATION property to initialize the provider.
Catalog	No	For most providers, this option will change the database that the user is connecting to from their default database to what is specified here. If nothing is specified, then the user's default database is used.

Creating a Linked Server in Transact-SQL

You can't script a linked server through Enterprise Manager as you can with scripting databases with the Generate SQL option. This will be especially important when you are trying to build backup and restore strategies or installation scripts for a new server. If a server crashes, you want to be able to run scripts quickly to rebuild your linked servers without having to walk through the GUI again. You can easily build a script manually to add a linked server and assign it the proper security.

You can create a linked server in T-SQL using the following syntax:

```
sp_addlinkedserver [@server =] 'server'
                   [, [@srvproduct =] 'product_name']
                   [, [@provider =] 'provider_name']
                   [, [@datasrc =] 'data_source']
                   [, [@location =] 'location']
                   [, [@provstr =] 'provider_string']
                   [, [@catalog =] 'catalog']
```

Keep in mind that even though some of the options may not be required, your linked server may not work without them. As we mentioned earlier, if you use the OLE DB Provider for DB2, you must use the provider string, even though it's an optional setting. When creating a linked server through T-SQL, the provider name becomes extremely important and required. The @provider option in the definition above will designate which OLE DB provider to use. The table opposite shows the mapping between the data source and provider name:

Remote OLE DB data source	OLE DB provider	Provider Name	Data Source	Provider String
SQL Server	Microsoft OLE DB Provider for SQL Server	SQLOLEDB	SQL Server Name	–
Oracle	Microsoft OLE DB Provider for Oracle	MSDAORA	SQL*Net alias for the Oracle database	–
IBM DB2 Database	Microsoft OLE DB Provider for DB2	DB2OLEDB	Specified in the provider string	Can be found by creating a Data Link
ODBC data sources	Microsoft OLE DB Provider for ODBC	MSDASQL	Data source name (DSN) of an ODBC data source	Connection string if needed
File System	Microsoft OLE DB Provider for Indexing Service	MSIDXS	Indexing service catalog name	–
Microsoft Excel Spreadsheet	Microsoft OLE DB Provider for Jet	Microsoft.Jet.OLEDB.4.0	Full path to the Excel file	–
Microsoft Access/Jet	Microsoft OLE DB Provider for Jet	Microsoft.Jet.OLEDB.4.0	Full path to the Access file	–

The following example will add a linked server to an Access database called `Northwind.mdb` in the `C:\Wrox` folder:

```
EXEC sp_addlinkedserver
    @server='REMOTEACCESSDB',
    @srvproduct='Jet 4.0',
    @provider='Microsoft.Jet.OLEDB.4.0',
    @datasrc='C:\Wrox\Northwind.mdb'
```

As we discussed earlier, the product name is not required in our example above; however, it makes our meta data a little more readable for non-programmers. We'll discuss meta data with linked servers in a moment. Another important note is that the linked server stored procedures and GUI will not check the source to confirm that the file or database exists. If you mistype the path or IP address, you will not know until you try to query the source that is provider specific.

Creating a Linked Server on a Single Server

If you're reading this book at home, and don't have the luxury of another SQL Server to query against, you will need to create a linked server that loops back to your local server in order to test out what we're discussing in this chapter.

You can execute the following query to create a linked server that loops back to your local server:

```
EXEC sp_addlinkedserver
    @server=remoteserver,
    @srvproduct = 'SQLServer OLEDB Provider',
    @provider = 'SQLOLEDB',
    @datasrc = '<Your Local Server Name>'
```

Remember two things about the above query:

❏ The @datasrc parameter is the name of your local server or the server you wish to connect to. This works the same way for Windows 95 or 98 machines running Desktop Edition.

❏ If no security information is gathered, the linked server will assume that the user connecting to it has an exact duplicate account on the remote server.

Since we're looping back to our local server, you will have an account and don't have to worry about security. If, on the other hand, your linked server connects to a remote machine, security is of great importance.

Linked Server Security

In order for SQL Server to act as a client on the remote server, you'll have to assign it the proper security so SQL Server can login.

This is where SQL Server's integration with NT security really is helpful. Imagine we have a database server farm of 10 servers in the same domain. Each server has 1000 users that query it on a regular basis. If these servers were running standard SQL Server security across the 10 servers, then we would need a few DBAs just to administrate the passwords and user names. They would be administrating 10,000 user names and trying to keep the passwords all in sync. With Windows Authentication Mode, we can use one NT login, administrated by the NT network administrator, to login to all 10 servers.

We would also have a security problem when using SQL Server standard security. With Windows Authentication Mode, we can force the user to change their NT network login every 30 days, and lock them out after a certain amount of failed attempts.

Windows Authentication Mode security can be fully utilized when using a linked server environment in SQL Server 2000 and Windows 2000. The default option when linking servers is for the SQL Server to sign into the linked server using the password and username of whoever is making the request, whether the user is using standard SQL Server security or an NT account.

Linked Server Security in Enterprise Manager

We can set the security for our linked server in Enterprise Manager by clicking the Security tab when viewing the linked server properties:

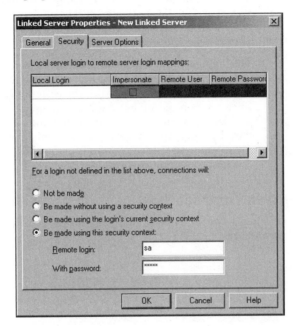

The options we can set on this screen are:

Option	Description
Local server login to remote server login mappings	This option allows you to set up a mapping between users on the local system and logins on the remote server. In other words, the linked server will see that you're connecting with the login of MyUserName then map that to DB2MyUserName on the remote server. To set this option, select the local login from the drop-down box. If you check the impersonate box, then the login credentials must exactly match on the remote system and the local system. Otherwise, you can uncheck this and manually type the login ID and password that will be used on the remote system.
Not be made	Typically, the Not be made option goes hand in hand with the mapping of individual users. When you map a local individual user to a remote individual user, you can use this option to set the rules for anyone else trying to use the linked server. When this option is set in parallel with the mappings of individual users, any user in the mapping list will be allowed a connection to the remote server and anyone else will be denied access.
Be made without using a security context	Some database systems, such as Access or an Excel spreadsheet, may not require that you set any security context. If this is the case, then use this option.

Table continued on following page

Option	Description
Be made using the login's current security context	This is the default option when setting up a linked server. If you are linking to another SQL Server, and the user has an account on that system as well, this option is ideal when used in conjunction with NT Integrated security. Otherwise, you will have to manage security on both systems.
Be made using this security context	This option will hard code the remote login ID and password. It will not give you any control over what access rights individual users can have on the remote system. It is the easiest way of setting the security since everyone is authenticated with the same login. The only problem is that if anyone is doing auditing on the source system, they'll see numerous logins with the same ID on the source system. There's no way to identify who is performing an action if you have this security option enabled.

Linked Server Security in Transact-SQL

Assigning security to your linked server through T-SQL is slightly more complex. You'll need to use the following stored procedure to set the security:

```
sp_addlinkedsrvlogin [@rmtsrvname =] 'rmtsrvname'
                     [,[@useself =] 'useself']
                     [,[@locallogin =] 'locallogin']
                     [,[@rmtuser =] 'rmtuser']
                     [,[@rmtpassword =] 'rmtpassword']
```

The parameters for this query are as follows:

Parameter	Required?	Description
@rmtsrvname	Yes	The name of your linked server.
@useself	No	Boolean. Will pass the remote server the security context for the user that you are currently logged in as. This is the equivalent of the **Be made using the login's current security context** option. The @useself parameter with a value of true is the default security option if no others have been set. A value of false will force the linked server to use the @rmtuser and @rmtpassword.
@locallogin	No	Required for mapping a local user to a remote account. This option is the equivalent of the local logins to remote server logins mapping option.
@rmtuser	No	Is used when the @useself is set to false. This option, in conjunction with the @rmtpassword parameter, is the equivalent to the **Be made using this security context** option in Enterprise Manager.
@rmtpassword	No	Is used to designate the password that will be passed to the remote server when the @useself parameter is set to false. This option is associated with the @rmtuser parameter.

The example code below will set the security for an Access database set up as a remote server called REMOTEACCESSDB. In this example, we're allowing only the sa account to use the remote login Admin with a NULL password. All other users will be denied access.

```
EXEC sp_addlinkedsrvlogin
    @rmtsrvname='REMOTEACCESSDB',
    @useself='false',
    @locallogin='sa',
    @rmtuser='Admin',
    @rmtpassword=NULL
```

You can also set the security context to pass the logged in user's credentials to the source system using the following syntax:

```
EXEC sp_addlinkedsrvlogin 'REMOTEACCESSDB', 'true'
```

Other Linked Server Options

The last step we have to do before we can use our linked server is establish the rules that our linked server will use. The server options we can set here concern:

- ❏ Collation
- ❏ Data access
- ❏ Remote procedure calls
- ❏ Command and connection timeout settings

Enterprise Manager can't set some of the options that you can set in T-SQL, such as the lazy schema validation option, which we will cover in a moment. You may find yourself using T-SQL much more than the GUI.

The most basic of these rules is the data access option.

Data Access

The Data Access option will turn on access to distributed queries:

You can uncheck this option when viewing the properties of a linked server to temporarily disable the main functionality of linked servers until you're ready to take the linked server back online. This option is by default set to True, which allows access to the linked server's data.

You can also disable data access in T-SQL use the following syntax:

```
EXEC sp_serveroption '<linked server name>', 'data access', 'false'
```

To allow access to the data, you can use the following syntax:

```
EXEC sp_serveroption '<linked server name>', 'data access', 'true'
```

Allowing Stored Procedures on a Linked Server

The RPC and RPC Out options enable support for **remote procedure calls**. Remote procedure calls (RPCs) in SQL Server are generally stored procedures on a remote server. The RPC option enables RPC calls for the local server, while the RPC Out option allows an RPC call for a remote server.

```
EXEC sp_serveroption '<linked server name>', 'rpc', 'true'
EXEC sp_serveroption '<linked server name>', 'rpc out', 'true'
```

We will cover how to execute stored procedures on a remote system in a moment.

Collation

The Collation Compatible option is checked when you are linking to a database server that operates with the same sort order and character set. Checking this option, or setting it to `true`, will tell SQL Server that the source and destination servers both have the same case and accent sensitivity. If a server has accent sensitivity turned on, this would mean that the character value of José would not be the same as the value of Jose. If this option is set to `false`, or is unchecked, then SQL Server will always examine comparisons on character columns locally.

If this option is checked, these comparisons are done on the source server, not the linked server. This option not being set could slow down your queries considerably. If you turn on this option and you have different character sets, then you risk receiving bad data from the server. By default, Collation Compatible is turned off.

To set the collation compatible option in T-SQL use the below stored procedure:

```
EXEC sp_serveroption '<linked server name>', 'collation compatible', 'true'
```

Two other collation options need special attention. The first option is Use Remote Collation. When this option is set, SQL Server will query the remote SQL Server for its collation, or for non-SQL Server systems, you must provide a Collation Name. The collation name must be a valid collation supported by SQL Server, and to use this option, the remote database must use the same collation throughout its entire database. You cannot have column-level collation with this option set.

Another option along the collation line is the lazy schema validation option. This option can only be set in T-SQL. This helps you when running a new SQL Server feature called Distributed Partitioned Views (DPVs) and allows SQL Server to not check the meta data for schema validation. DPVs allow you to partition your SQL Server data vertically and scale-out to multiple servers. If this option is set to `false`, which is the default, SQL Server will perform a validation on the meta data before it compiles the query plan. Otherwise, it will wait until query execution to check the meta data. If the schema on the remote system has changed, it will return an error. For that reason, only use this option when you are programming Distributed Partitioned Views and need the extra performance boost this options offers.

Setting Options in Enterprise Manager

You can also set the same options in Enterprise Manager under the **Server Options** tab as shown below.

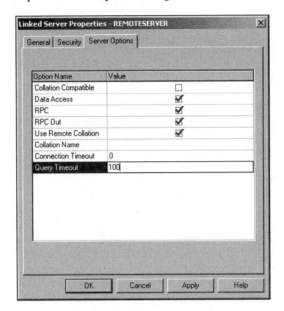

Two other options that we have not discussed yet are the **Connection Timeout** and **Query Timeout**. The **Connection Timeout** is the amount of time that SQL Server will allow you to successfully connect to the linked server before failing. The **Query Timeout** setting specifies how long the linked server will allow you to spend running a query before it times out. It is generally a good idea to set this just in case the remote system doesn't have this configured. If it doesn't, then a query that did not complete would run until it was interactively stopped. If the remote system has a timeout setting and it is set to a lower timeout setting, then the remote system's setting would overrule the settings of the client.

Using Linked Servers

Finally, you should have all the steps completed to begin using your linked server. Now let's see how we can use linked servers.

Querying a Linked Server

First, we'll take a look at how to run a query against a linked server, specifically, the linked server that loops back to our local server that we created earlier.

One of the methods of querying a linked server is to use the four-part qualifier as shown in the query below. Run the query to conditionally select records from the `Suppliers` table in the `Northwind` database where the suppliers are in the USA:

```
SELECT SupplierID,CompanyName
FROM REMOTESERVER.Northwind.dbo.Suppliers WHERE Country = 'USA'
```

As you can see above, we have fully qualified not only the database but also the linked server name before the database and table.

The result of this query is:

	SupplierID	CompanyName
1	2	New Orleans Cajun Delights
2	3	Grandma Kelly's Homestead
3	16	Bigfoot Breweries
4	19	New England Seafood Cannery

A key point to remember here is that collation compatible is set to `false` by default, therefore the entire recordset is moved to the local server first from the linked server, and then processed on the local server. This is a waste of processing power, and goes against all the principals of distributed queries. Since we know that both the linked server and the local server are using the same character set and sort order, we will want to turn on collation compatible:

```
EXEC sp_serveroption 'REMOTESERVER', 'collation compatible', 'true'
```

Suppose you have a customer database in one location, and your orders database in another. Wouldn't it be great if you could pull orders from one database and customers from another, without having to migrate the data? Well, linked servers will also allow you to join queries together from two different servers. This can also be done even if both servers are linked. The following query will pull the customers from one server and the orders from the remote server that we've established:

```
SELECT  lnw.CompanyName, rnw.OrderID, rnw.OrderDate, rnw.Freight
FROM    REMOTESERVER.Northwind.dbo.Orders rnw, Northwind..Customers lnw
WHERE   lnw.CustomerID = rnw.CustomerID
AND     rnw.ShipCountry = 'USA'
AND     rnw.OrderDate > ' 04 / 22 / 1998'
```

This will return:

	CompanyName	OrderID	OrderDate	Freight
1	Great Lakes Food Market	11061	1998-04-30 00:00:00.000	14.0100
2	Save-a-lot Markets	11064	1998-05-01 00:00:00.000	30.0900
3	White Clover Markets	11066	1998-05-01 00:00:00.000	44.7200
4	Rattlesnake Canyon Grocery	11077	1998-05-06 00:00:00.000	8.5300

Make sure you use these queries sparingly. This query will not perform especially robustly in SQL Server. The reason for the slow nature of this query is because all the joins are being done on the local server, causing more data to be transmitted over the network than is needed.

Executing a Stored Procedure

You can also execute a stored procedure on your remote server, if the RPC options are both set to True. If these options were set to False, however, and you were to execute a stored procedure, you would receive the following error message:

```
Server: Msg 7411, Level 16, State 1, Line 1
Server 'remoteserver' is not configured for RPC.
```

You can set these two options to `True` by using the following query:

```
EXEC sp_serveroption 'remoteserver', 'rpc', 'true'
EXEC sp_serveroption 'remoteserver', 'rpc out', 'true'
```

Once these are set to `True`, you are free to run any stored procedures on either server. Try the following:

```
EXEC remoteserver.Northwind.dbo.CustOrderHist @CustomerID='ANTON'
```

This will return the following results:

	ProductName	Total
1	Alice Mutton	18
2	Boston Crab Meat	10
3	Chang	20
4	Chocolade	15
5	Geitost	38
6	Gumbär Gummibärchen	30
7	Ipoh Coffee	15
8	Louisiana Hot Spiced Okra	4
9	Perth Pasties	25
10	Queso Cabrales	74
11	Raclette Courdavault	15
12	Ravioli Angelo	5
13	Rhönbräu Klosterbier	30
14	Sasquatch Ale	40
15	Singaporean Hokkien Fried Mee	20

Viewing Servers and Tables

So we've added a linked server and set the security. Now, how do you view its meta data? To see this information about your linked server, simply expand the server name and click on Tables. You will see the tables in the default catalog in the right pane. Unfortunately, Enterprise Manager is limited in what you can see after you create a linked server. You are limited to only seeing the table or view names in the catalog, as shown in the screenshot overleaf. We'll use T-SQL in a moment to extract more quality data about the linked server.

Parameter	Description
@table_server	Name of the linked server you would like information about.
@table_catalog	Changes the default catalog for your query. If this option is not set, the default database for the user setup in the linked server is used.
@table_schema	Narrows the object owners you'd like to query. For example, dbo would be a table_schema. This is especially useful in other DBMSs.
@table_name	Find out information about a specific table.
@table_type	Will narrow your query down to a specific table type such as TABLE, SYSTEM TABLE, or VIEW.

Let's try a more enhanced query:

```
EXEC sp_tables_ex
    @table_server = 'remoteserver',
    @table_catalog='Northwind',
    @table_schema='dbo',
    @table_name='Suppliers'
```

This time we'll see a narrower result set:

	TABLE_CAT	TABLE_SCHEM	TABLE_NAME	TABLE_TYPE	REMARKS
1	Northwind	dbo	Suppliers	TABLE	NULL

Gathering Remote Column Information

We can gather information about columns by using sp_columns_ex. This stored procedure will provide information such as column names, nullability, and data types for an individual column, or list all the column information for every column in a table. The same basic rules apply to sp_columns_ex that apply to sp_tables_ex. Again, the only required parameter is @table_server, but running the stored procedure with only this parameter is unpractical. The query would run endlessly, like if you executed sp_columns_ex without narrowing your criteria.

Here are the variables you can use:

Parameter	Description
@table_server	Name of the linked server you would like information about.
@table_catalog	Changes the default catalog for your query. If this option is not set, the default database for the user setup in the linked server is used.
@table_schema	Narrows the object owners you'd like to query. For example, dbo would be a table_schema. This is especially useful in other DBMSs.
@table_name	Find out information about a specific table.
@table_type	Will narrow your query down to a specific table type such as TABLE, SYSTEM TABLE, or VIEW.
@column_name	Name of the column you want information on.

Here's a sample of how to use `sp_columns_ex`:

```
EXEC sp_columns_ex
    @table_server = 'remoteserver',
    @table_catalog = 'Northwind',
    @table_name   = 'Suppliers',
    @table_schema = 'dbo',
    @column_name='CompanyName'
```

This returns a lot of details for a single record (which will appear all on one line after running the query, but has been reformatted for the purposes of this page!):

	TABLE_CAT	TABLE_SCHEM	TABLE_NAME	COLUMN_NAME	DATA_TYPE	TYPE_NAME
1	Northwind	dbo	Suppliers	CompanyName	-9	nvarchar

	COLUMN_SIZE	BUFFER_LENGTH	DECIMAL_DIGITS	NUM_PREC_RADIX	NULLABLE
1	40	80	NULL	NULL	0

	REMARKS	COLUMN_DEF	SQL_DATA_TYPE	SQL_DATETIME_SUB	CHAR_OCTET_LENGTH
1	NULL	NULL	-9	NULL	80

	ORDINAL_POSITION	IS_NULLABLE	SS_DATA_TYPE
1	2	NO	39

As you can see, this includes:

❑ Column names

❑ Column nullability

❑ Precision and scale

❑ Data type and length

Gathering Remote Security Information

To diagnose a security error, you will need the stored procedure `sp_table_privileges_ex`. This stored procedure will return the table and which rights each user has to the table. You run `sp_table_privileges_ex` the same way you run the other meta data stored procedures, by using the required parameter of `@table_server` to declare the linked server name. Again, do not run this stored procedure without accompanying the `@table_server` with a `@table_catalog` parameter.

For example, to find out the permissions for the `Suppliers` table in the `Northwind` database, execute the following:

```
EXEC sp_table_privileges_ex
    @table_server = 'remoteserver',
    @table_catalog = 'Northwind',
    @table_name   = 'Suppliers',
    @table_schema = 'dbo'
```

This produces a result something like this, depending on the permissions for your database:

	TABLE_CAT	TABLE_SCHEM	TABLE_NAME	GRANTOR	GRANTEE	PRIVILEGE	IS_GRANTABLE
1	Northwind	dbo	Suppliers	dbo	dbo	DELETE	YES
2	Northwind	dbo	Suppliers	dbo	dbo	INSERT	YES
3	Northwind	dbo	Suppliers	dbo	dbo	REFERENCES	YES
4	Northwind	dbo	Suppliers	dbo	dbo	SELECT	YES
5	Northwind	dbo	Suppliers	dbo	dbo	UPDATE	YES

Gathering Remote Key and Index Information

When you're inserting or updating data on a remote server, you'll commonly need key information such as foreign key and indexing information. Without this information, you could spend hour upon hour researching the order to load the data by trial-and-error.

Primary Keys

The main concern when inserting into an unknown table is the primary keys. You can derive primary key information about the remote server, if any exists, by using the sp_primarykeys stored procedure as shown below:

```
EXEC sp_primarykeys
    @table_server = 'remoteserver',
    @table_catalog = 'Northwind',
    @table_name  = 'Suppliers',
    @table_schema = 'dbo'
```

Again, we've used the same parameters that we've been using for meta data information. This stored procedure will report which column is the primary key in a given table, for example:

	TABLE_CAT	TABLE_SCHEM	TABLE_NAME	COLUMN_NAME	KEY_SEQ	PK_NAME
1	Northwind	dbo	Suppliers	SupplierID	1	NULL

Foreign Keys

One of the most frustrating problems you might encounter when inserting or updating data is foreign key surprises. The stored procedure sp_foreignkeys was written to take the guesswork out of foreign keys on a remote system.

We can use the following parameters to execute this stored procedure:

Parameter	Description
@table_server	Name of the linked server you want to query.
@pktab_name	Name of the table that holds the primary key.
@pktab_schema	Name of the owner who owns the primary key table.
@pktab_catalog	Name of the database or catalog where the primary keys exist.
@fktab_name	Name of the table where the foreign keys exist.
@fktab_schema	Name of the owner of the foreign key table.
@fktab_catalog	Name of the database or catalog that holds the foreign key.

In the following stored procedure example, we are trying to find out which foreign keys exist in the `Orders` table, and where they link to:

```
EXEC  sp_foreignkeys
    @table_server = 'remoteserver',
    @pktab_catalog = 'Northwind',
    @pktab_schema = 'dbo',
    @pktab_name='Orders'
```

As you can see when you execute the above, the `Orders` table is linked to the `Order Details` table by the `OrderID` column:

	PKTABLE_CAT	PKTABLE_SCHEM	PKTABLE_NAME	PKCOLUMN_NAME	
1	Northwind	dbo	Orders	OrderID	
	FKTABLE_CAT	FKTABLE_SCHEM	FKTABLE_NAME	FKCOLUMN_NAME	KEY_SEQ
1	Northwind	dbo	Order Details	OrderID	1
	UPDATE_RULE	DELETE_RULE	FK_NAME	PK_NAME	DEFERRABILITY
1	1	1	NULL	NULL	NULL

Indexes

There is one additional stored procedure that comes in handy when querying your linked servers. We can find out what indexes are on a table by using `sp_indexes`. You can use this stored procedure with the same base parameters that we've been using throughout this section, but this stored procedure also offers two additional parameters to narrow the results:

❑   The `@index_name` parameter is, as its name suggests, the name of the index

❑   The `@is_unique` parameter, which is a bit (0 is false, 1 is true), designates the index as a unique index

The following example will return all indexes in the `Suppliers` table:

```
EXEC sp_indexes
    @table_server = 'remoteserver',
    @table_catalog = 'Northwind',
    @table_name  = 'Suppliers',
    @table_schema = 'dbo'
```

When executing the stored procedure, you can see three indexes. Other information that `sp_indexes` provides is:

❑   Index name

❑   Uniqueness of index

❑   Type of index (clustered, non-clustered)

❑   Columns that make up the index

	TABLE_CAT	TABLE_SCHEM	TABLE_NAME	NON_UNIQUE	INDEX_QUALIFIER	INDEX_NAME
1	Northwind	dbo	Suppliers	0	Suppliers	PK_Suppliers
2	Northwind	dbo	Suppliers	1	Suppliers	CompanyName
3	Northwind	dbo	Suppliers	1	Suppliers	PostalCode

	TYPE	ORDINAL_POSITION	COLUMN_NAME	ASC_OR_DESC	CARDINALITY	PAGES	FILTER_CONDITION
1	1	1	SupplierID	A	29	1	NULL
2	3	1	CompanyName	A	NULL	NULL	NULL
3	3	1	PostalCode	A	NULL	NULL	NULL

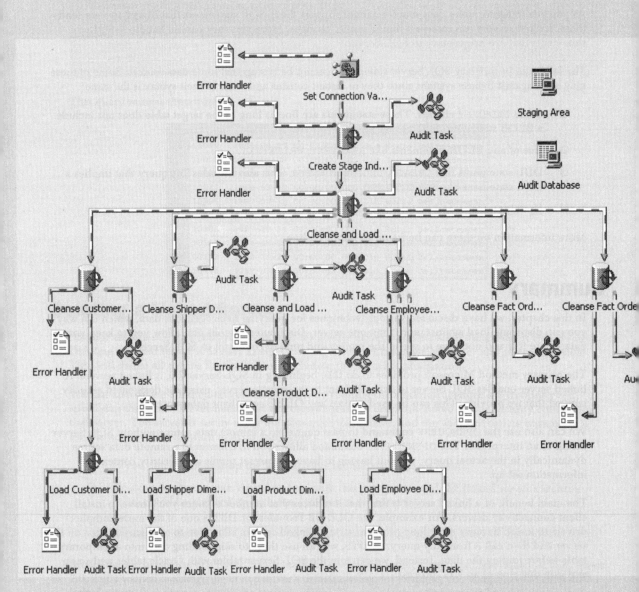

6

Converting Heterogeneous Data

In the previous chapter, we saw how we can deal with heterogeneous data using distributed queries. But suppose that rather than do a distributed query, you have decided to convert your data to SQL Server. Microsoft provides you with a number of tools, including DTS and Upsize Wizards for Access, to convert your heterogeneous data to SQL Server. You can also use DTS to convert your data to another heterogeneous database. For example, if you needed, for whatever reason, to convert your data to DB2 on the host, then you could use DTS to specify DB2 as the destination.

In this chapter, we're going to discuss a few these heterogeneous data sources using DTS, and some issues behind converting to SQL Server using DTS. We'll discuss converting data from the Microsoft Office database Access and from an Excel spreadsheet. We'll also discuss DB2, which is a database system that uses a slightly more unconventional method to convert data.

We unfortunately couldn't cover all of the database systems in the chapter, but this should give you a good sampling of some of the issues you'll face in your conversion. If you'd like more information about these, you can visit: http://www.microsoft.com/data for all the OLE DB provider information you need.

Let's start by looking at what we need to consider before launching into an upgrade.

Pre-Conversion Checklist

Your SQL Server upgrade can be as simple as upgrading from SQL Server 6.5 to 2000, or as difficult as upgrading an Access application with its queries to SQL Server. In each scenario, you will need to follow your own rigorous guidelines before upgrading. If these guidelines are not met, you risk your queries not working, or even worse, losing data.

Upgrading consist of the following high level steps:

❑ **Feasibility** – Determine if SQL Server can handle the load of your data, or if using SQL Server is overkill. Is the target database an overkill for your application? For example, if you're building an application to be used by only three users, then you may want to consider SQL Server Desktop Engine, which is optimized for five users or less. SQL Server Desktop Engine also has no licensing cost associated with it. Also, determine if you meet the minimum hardware requirements for an upgrade to the target DBMS and for other specialized needs like clustering.

❑ **Planning** – Map out the steps to performing the upgrade. For some legacy systems or relational database systems that weren't planned well, it may take months to map out on paper how the data will be converted. This may be because proper constraints weren't or couldn't be used in the older system. Don't forget that this step also includes application planning. For example, if you are moving from Oracle to SQL Server, you will need to convert your PL/SQL queries and stored procedures. The process of upgrading your queries generally will take longer than the actual transfer of data. Make sure all this is accounted for here.

❑ **Testing** – Create a test environment to perform an upgrade. You will make your manager and the end customers much more comfortable if they know that the upgrade has been fully tested. This is when SQL Server 2000 becomes especially useful. With SQL Server 2000, you can have multiple isolated instances of SQL Server. This allows you to have several levels of testing. For example, you can have testing of the integration with your other applications on one server while another SQL Server instance holds new development testing.

❑ **Execution** – The planning and testing is now over, and it's time to implement your solution. If it all paid off, you will reap the rewards during this step.

❑ **Lesson's Learned** – No process is perfect. There are bound to be flaws in your solution that will need to be addressed here. Make sure to document them all fully for the next time you need to perform this process. It's fine to make mistakes, just don't make them twice.

Migrating Access Data Using DTS

In SQL Server, upgrading from Access is as easy as running through the Import/Export Wizard. DTS provides a method to convert your Access database to SQL Server quickly. There are other methods that Access 2000 includes, like the Upsizing Wizard. The Upsizing Wizard provides an easy way to convert your data, relationships, and primary keys to SQL Server, but it is not nearly as fast as DTS. First, it is important to note what DTS will not convert:

❑ Primary keys and relationships will not convert to their SQL Server counterparts

❑ Rules or defaults

❑ Queries

These items must be upgraded after the data conversion manually. DTS will handle generating the schema, but it will stop at that point.

So let's jump into it shall we? In this example, we are going to convert data from the sample database Northwind.mdb, which is installed with Access. To upgrade your Access database to SQL Server 2000, first go to the DTS Import Wizard, select Microsoft Access for your source, and click on the ... to choose the Northwind.mdb database. There will be no need to type a username and password unless you have a secured Access database.

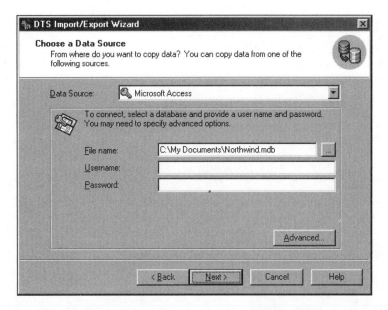

You'll then be asked to choose your destination. Select Microsoft OLE DB Provider for SQL Server. Create a new database for the purpose of this example called Northwind2, as we did in the first chapter, by selecting <new> from the database drop-down box. Enter the appropriate login credentials and click Next.

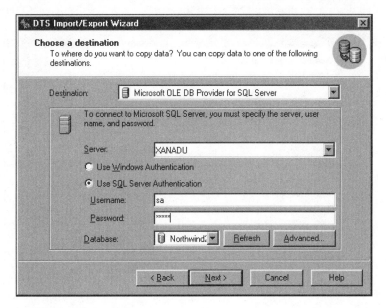

As you may recall from the last chapter, you will now have the option to either select the tables to upgrade as a whole or create a query to upgrade tables. We're going to select Copy table(s) or view(s) from source database.

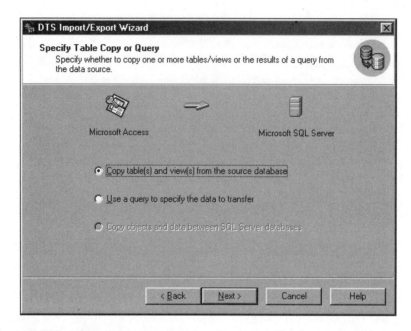

You can now select the tables that you wish to transfer. Access also has a type of query called a Select Query. These are represented in the screen below with glasses. These are close relatives to SQL Server views, which we'll discuss in a moment. Select all the tables, but leave the Select Queries unchecked.

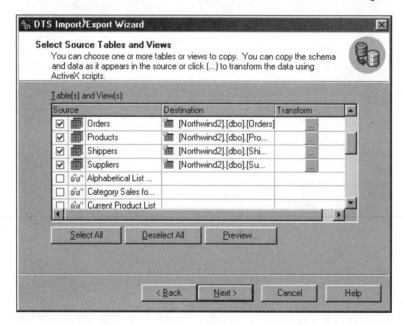

Click the ... by the **Orders** table to enter the transformation properties for that table, if any of the table's properties needs adjusting.

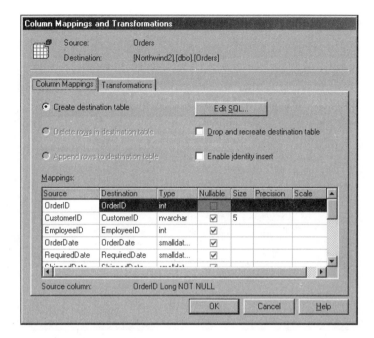

One of the primary things to watch in the **Column Mappings** tab is the use of the nvarchar or other Unicode data type. When the DTS engine sees a column using a character data type, it assumes you would like to upgrade the column to nvarchar. Nvarchar fields, which hold Unicode data, perform less efficiently than varchar fields, and use twice as much space as their varchar brother data type.

It doesn't stop there though. DTS also uses the nvarchar data type for smaller character fields as well. Make sure if you are not planning to use Unicode that you do not waste processing power and storage space on unneeded nvarchar fields.

If this is a new table on the destination, you can modify the column data type information. A few other general rules of thumb apply as you select your data type:

❑ Only use the varchar data type for character fields over 8 bytes in length. For anything below, you should use char fields. The reason being is there is a slight overhead charge for using a varchar field and the benefits that you would receive from a storage perspective are overshadowed by the performance hit from trimming the data.

❑ The int data type performs more efficiently than smallint or tinyint (4 byte blocks that the int data type uses are ideal for Intel processors). The other smaller versions of the data type do save data storage if it is at a premium.

If needed, you can change the data type in the column mapping tab as well as any other column properties as we did in Chapter 1.

If you want more information on the DTS Import Wizard, you might want to refer back to where we covered this wizard in Chapter1.

Then, you could select from the view named vw_orders by using the following syntax:

```
SELECT * FROM vw_orders
```

❑ **Transact-SQL scripts** – Using T-SQL statements is the most flexible of the three options. It is ad-hoc SQL – in other words, almost anything you could do in an Access Query, you could perform in a T-SQL script. They are not compiled onto the SQL Server, which makes them run slower than stored procedures. However, they can be executed directly in the program or manually.

To upgrade an Access query, open the query in Access in Design View, then select SQL View under the View menu (or click on the SQL button). In the screenshot below, you can see the Quarterly Orders query in the Northwind database that ships with Access:

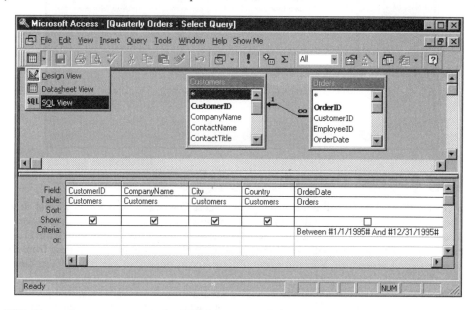

The SQL View allows you to view the SQL syntax involved in making the query:

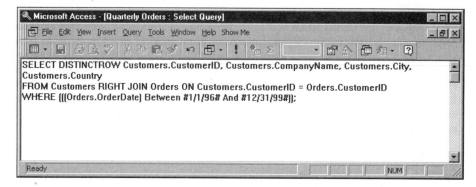

To convert the above query to SQL Server standards, copy and paste the query from the SQL View window into Query Analyzer, and change the database to the Northwind2 database that you transferred earlier by selecting Northwind2 from the drop-down box as shown below.

It's important to remember that some of the syntax shown here is proprietary to Access. You will have to change the **DISTINCTROW** keyword to **DISTINCT**. You will also have to change the pound signs (#) to single quotes ('). Finally, take out the semicolon at the end of the query.

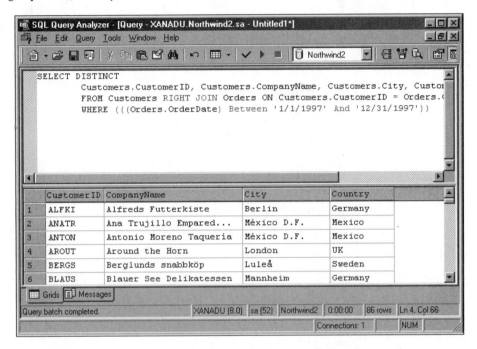

It's that simple. The main issue that you will experience is the sheer number of queries that you will need to convert. Another problem you will experience is with queries using parameters. Access has the functionality to present a interactive dialog box to ask the user what parameters they would like to send the query. SQL Server does not offer this functionality and only accepts parameters in stored procedures. For more information on this topic, you can look at *Professional Access 2000 Programming* from Wrox Press, *ISBN 1-861004-08-7*.

Converting Data From Excel

Often times you can't predict how you're going to receive data. At most companies, you have many departments all tracking their budgets, sales figures, and expense reports in a variety of systems that are completely incompatible with each other. It becomes your job often to merge these systems into one seamless system so they could be accessed from the web; or the finance department wants to know how much promotions spent last month without receiving a propriety spreadsheet that only the promotion people can read. This can become quite dizzying and it is normally the job of the person who handles the data conversion to find a solution to merging the systems' data.

Converting data from an Excel spreadsheet is not as easy as an Access migration. Since Excel is a closer relative to a flat file, we must treat it as such. It's because of this that the DTS Import Wizard rarely works as it should. You will have to create a custom DTS Package to perform this type of conversion.

In this example, we'll be transferring an Excel spreadsheet named Sales.xls to a SQL Server database called Sales. We first created an Excel spreadsheet, as shown below, with four columns. One column holds miscellaneous product names, the second holds the quantity in stock of those products, then the price, and finally the gross assets based on quantity multiplied by price. We also have a header on the top that reads January Sales. Change the sheet's name to JanSales from Sheet1 by clicking on your right mouse button on Sheet1 and selecting rename. Finally, format the Price and Total columns to use currency data types by highlighting the data, then selecting Format cells with your right mouse button. Below is an Excel spreadsheet that we will be transferring:

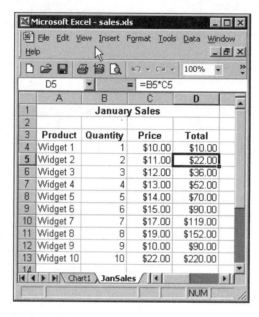

First create a new DTS package in DTS Designer. Establish a SQL Server connection to your local server and make the default database a new database called Sales. Call the connection SQL Server Sales Database.

Next, create a connection to an Excel document:

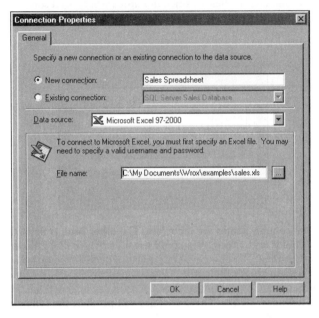

Create a Transform Data task connecting the Excel spreadsheet as the source and the SQL Server as the destination. Double-click on the Transformation task, which connects the two connections. The first step is to enter which "table" in Excel you'd like to transfer. In Excel, a sheet is the equivalent of a table, and in our example, we have one sheet named JanSales. Each Excel sheet is represented by a trailing dollar sign as shown below. Select JanSales and proceed to the Destination tab.

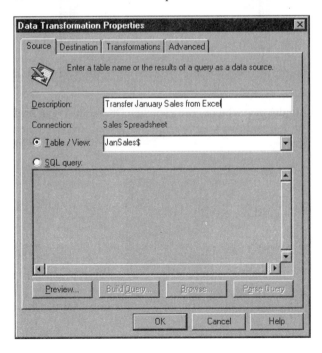

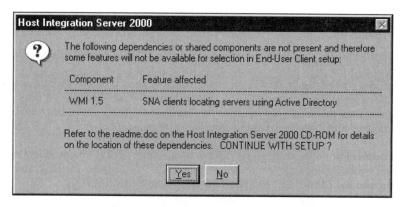

The installation is an easy one. It asks you the path and the components that you wish to install as you can see below. By default, the client installation will install the DB2 providers as well as a driver for AS/400 and VSAM, which are commonly used mainframe systems. For the purpose of this section, we will focus on using the OLE DB Provider for DB2 and connecting to a DB2 server that supports TCP/IP. Please keep in mind that the way we're explaining to do this is not the only way. You can also use methods other than TCP/IP to connect to DB2, which we'll mention briefly in a moment.

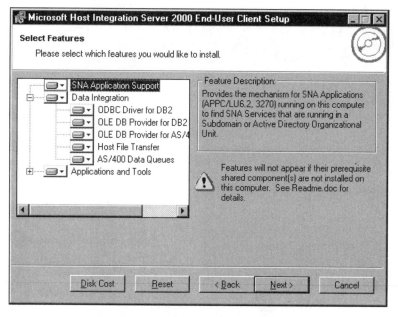

After rebooting, the installed files will be under the Microsoft Host Integration Server program group. HIS prefers using data link files (.UDL). This gives you the ability to create a data source that is actually a tiny file, which can be placed on a disk and carried from computer to computer to install. This is especially handy if you're not familiar with the provider, because it alleviates the risk of mis-typing a parameter. It also allows you to configure it once, and install it many times.

To create a new .UDL file, go to the OLE DB Data Sources under the Host Integration Services | Data Integration program group. You actually will begin in the Connection tab, with the Microsoft OLE DB Provider for DB2 as the default provider. You can go back to the Provider tab to see what provider you are using, as you can see below. You can create a data link file though to any provider:

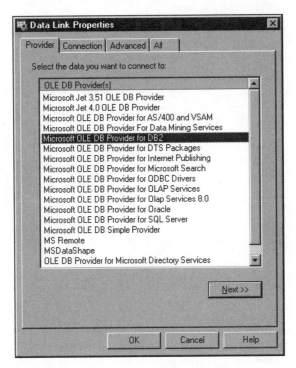

The Connection tab screen below is one of the most complex screens in the process. For some of these options, it heavily depends on what system you're running DB2 on, and it is recommended that you ask a DB2 administrator to help you. We could spend an entire book explaining the details of these settings, so this section is meant to help you ask the administrator the right questions. This is where you setup/configure the actual connection. The Data source name can be any logical name that you'll recognize later. For Network, if your DB2 server is listening on TCP/IP, then you can select it from the drop-down box. Then, click "..." to type the IP address and port of the destination DB2 Server.

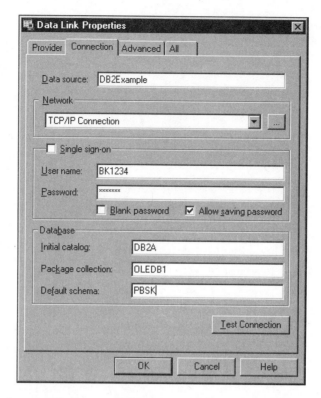

The **Single sign-on** button will gray out the user name and password options and will enable the HIS option to pass your Windows 2000 user name and password to DB2. If you don't want to use this option, you can specify a **User name** and **Password**. By default, the provider will prompt you for a password each time you try to establish a connection to the host. The **Allow saving passwords** will save the password and stop the provider from this prompting.

It's very hard to relate some of the next options to the client-server database world. The most confusing required setting is the **Initial catalog** setting, because it can mean several things, based on the DB2 system you're connecting to. The **Initial catalog** setting in DB2 (MVS, OS/390) refers to the LOCATION. This can be located in the SYSIBM.LOCATIONS table, which lists all the locations. To find out what this setting should be for a MVS or OS/390 system, ask your administrator to look up the TSO Clist DSNTINST under the DDF definitions. On OS/400 systems, this is known as the RDBNAM. This can be found by using the WRKRDBDIRE command. In DB2 Universal Database (UDB), this setting is referred to as the DATABASE, and finally SQL/DS (DB2/VM or DB2/VSE) systems refer to this as DBNAME.

The **Package collection** setting refers to the place where you'd like the Microsoft OLE DB Provider for DB2 to store its packages. We will explore creating the packages in a moment for DB2. The default schema should be fine for this setting.

The last setting is the **Default schema**. This important setting is optional and is similar to the catalog setting in SQL Server's OLE DB Provider. The reason it is so important is that if you select the wrong default schema, you will not see the tables you want in the table selection drop-down box when you transform the data. This setting in DB2 is the target owner for the tables. For DB2 on OS/400 systems, this the target COLLECTION name. Finally, in UDB, this is referred to as the SCHEMA name. If nothing is provided here, then the provider uses the user name provided earlier.

After typing the connection information, you can click Test Connection to see if your connectivity works. If it does you'll receive this message:

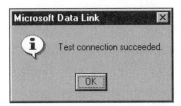

Otherwise, you'll receive a detailed error message. Usually, the errors fall into three categories when connecting through TCP/IP. The first category is when you type the wrong IP address or port. This results in the error shown below:

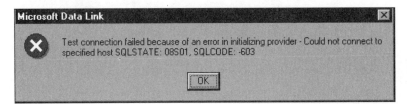

The next category is typically when your user name and password doesn't have rights to the system you're trying to connect to:

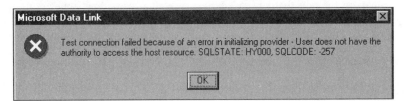

The last typical error you'll see is when you type a wrong initial catalog. These errors could vary depending on the system you're connecting to. A common error though is the following:

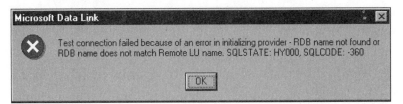

The Advanced tab of the Data Link Properties screen allows you to set the code page for the remote and local machines. Most of these settings should be left as default. The one that you may want to adjust is the Distributed transactions button. This allows you to perform two-phase commits using Microsoft Distributed Transaction Coordinator on the server side. Two-phase commits allow you to begin a transaction across multiple database systems and, if one part of the transaction fails, roll-back the entire transaction across all systems.

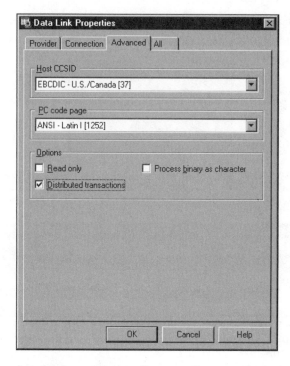

The All tab summarizes the tabs that you saw earlier, as well as providing some additional options that should really be left as the default:

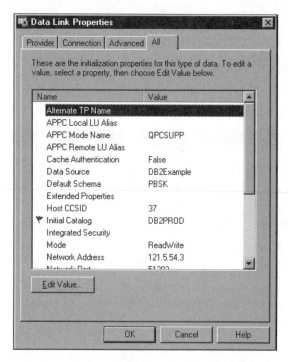

You are now complete with the data link file. You can find the data link file for later editing or transportation under your C:\Program Files\Common Files\system\ole db\data links folder. The drive where this folder is located will vary based on where your system drive is.

The next step before you are fully ready to go is to bind the DB2 packages. Although DB2 provides a utility to do this, HIS also ships with one that can perform the task just as easily. The program is found under the Host Integration Services program group | Data Integration | Packages for DB2 and is called Create Packages for DB2, as shown below. The program is going to create five sets of packages:

- ❑ AUTOCOMMIT package, (MSNC001)
- ❑ READ_UNCOMMITTED package, (MSUR001)
- ❑ REPEATABLE_READ package, (MSRR001)
- ❑ READ_COMMITTED package, (MSCS001)
- ❑ SERIALIZABLE or REPEATABLE_READ package, (MSRS001)

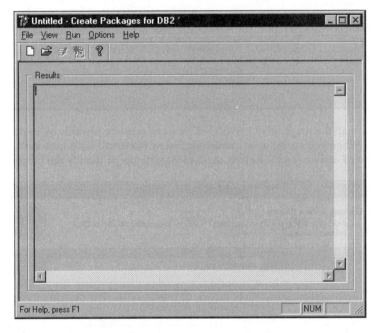

Select the Load icon, select the .UDL file that you created a few seconds ago and click on Open. Again, the default location is \Program Files\Common Files\SYSTEM\ole db\data links. The name of the files will be the name of the data source with a .UDL extension. After you have opened the .UDL file, you can select Create packages under the Run menu. As shown below, the program will create the packages and allow anyone the rights to execute them.

Handling Foreign and Primary Keys

Primary and foreign keys are two ways of keeping your data integrity good. Primary keys are one way of insuring that you can't duplicate your records, while foreign keys make sure that you can't insert an order for a customer that doesn't exist. The common issue we keep bringing up in these chapters is the lack of DTS support for primary and foreign keys. There are several ways of handling this. Some enterprise systems like Oracle and DB2 allow you to reverse engineer a database, then apply the scripts on the destination to create the keys. You can also use design tools like Erwin to script out this process.

There is also a manual process, which in some cases may be easier if the number of tables is small. You can create a SQL Server diagram to click-and-drag the foreign keys in place. To create a new diagram, open **Enterprise Manager** and drill-down to the database you'd like to create a diagram in. Then click your right mouse button on **Diagrams** and select **New Database Diagram**.

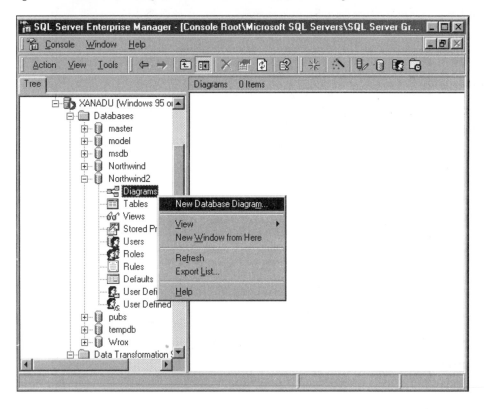

Next, select the tables you'd like to add to the diagram and click **Add**. SQL Server will expose the system tables as well, so make sure you only select the tables you need, as shown below:

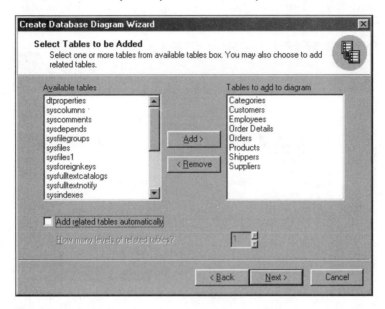

The diagramming tool will then generate a diagram for you. As you will be able to see below, there are no relationships between any of the tables, nor any primary keys. In the screenshot below, we've zoomed into two tables that need to have a foreign and primary key.

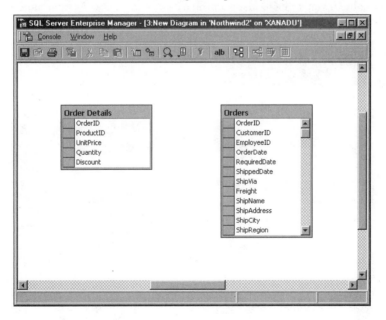

We first must change the view from the **Column Names** view to **Standard** view. You can do this by drawing a box around the tables you'd like to have this view, then selecting **Standard** from the drop-down box, as shown below. This is not required, but it gives you more information about the table before you make modifications to it.

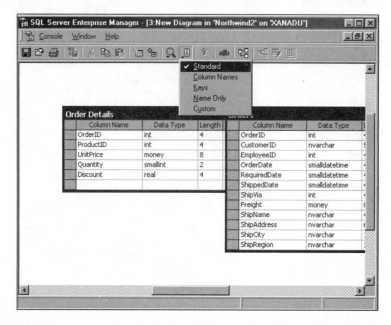

Next, select the column you'd like to make a primary key and click your right mouse button on it, selecting **Set Primary Key**.

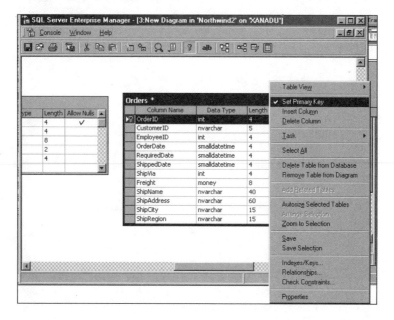

You can then click on the OrderID in the Order Details table and drag it onto the Orders table. The screen below will display to confirm that you'd like to create a relationship between the tables. Click OK to confirm.

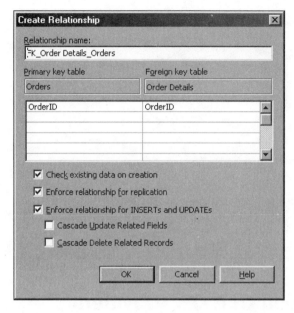

You now have a foreign key between the Order Details table and the Orders table. For an OrderID in the Order Details table, there must also be a parent record in the Orders table. Clicking on the save icon completes the process.

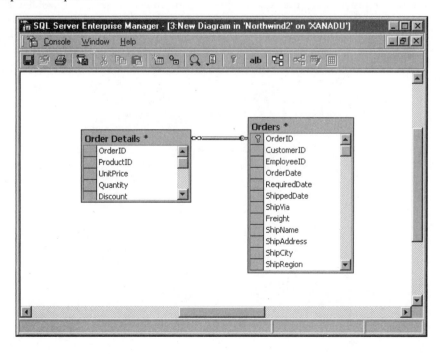

After clicking Save, SQL Server will prompt you to confirm changes to the Orders and Order Details tables. Once you click Yes, then the changes are saved to the production tables. You can also save the changes to a text file for later execution.

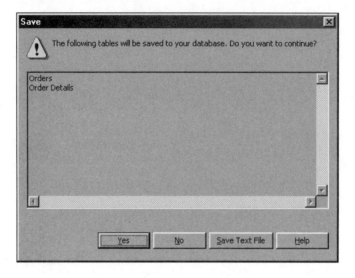

Single Threaded OLE DB Providers

An important note to consider when configuring your package is that OLE DB providers that are single threaded can cause Access Violations (AV) at run time. This is because as DTS allows steps to use other threads, the OLE DB provider can't handle the new thread. You can correct this problem by forcing anything that uses the connection to use the main thread. This can be done by selecting the step workflow properties and selecting Execute on main package thread under the Options tab:

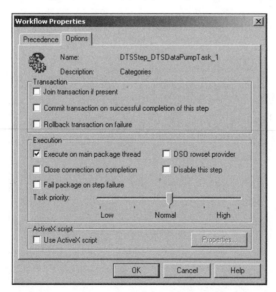

Summary

Microsoft provides DTS partly as a tool to upgrade your current database system to SQL Server. Although the data may upgrade relatively easily, in most cases your queries will not. In migrating your Access application, you will have to go through a rigorous process to upgrade your non-SQL Server queries to views, stored procedures, or Transact SQL queries. The same may hold true as you reinstate your relationships (foreign keys).

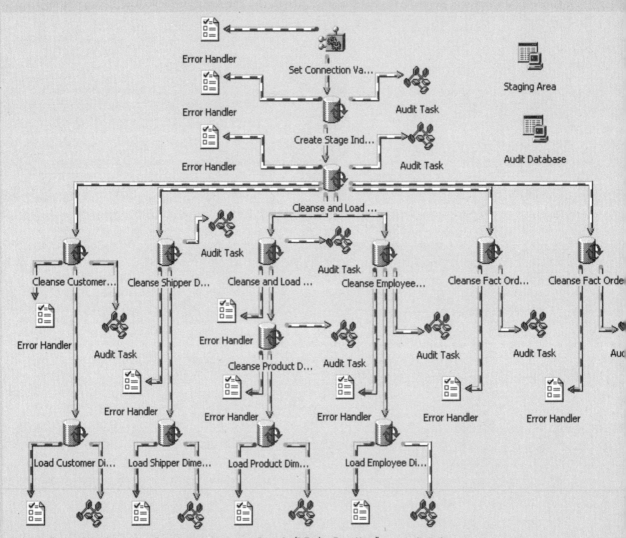

Error Handler

Set Connection Va...

Audit Task

Staging Area

Error Handler

Create Stage Ind...

Audit Task

Audit Database

Error Handler

Cleanse and Load ...

Audit Task

Cleanse Customer...

Cleanse Shipper D...

Audit Task

Cleanse and Load ...

Cleanse Employee...

Cleanse Fact Ord...

Cleanse Fact Orde...

Error Handler

Audit Task

Error Handler

Cleanse Product D...

Audit Task

Audit Task

Audit Task

Aud...

Error Handler

Error Handler

Error Handler

Error Handler

Error Handler

Error Handler

Load Customer Di...

Load Shipper Dime...

Load Product Dim...

Load Employee Di...

Error Handler   Audit Task Error Handler   Audit Task Error Handler   Audit Task   Error Handler   Audit Task

ActiveX Script Task Fundamentals

By now, you should have a basic understanding of Data Transformation Services. The rest of the book is dedicated to looking under the DTS hood, and programming lean applications to wrap around DTS. This cannot be done without an understanding of the **ActiveX Script task**. Once you have an understanding of the ActiveX Script task, you will be able to expand the functionality of DTS to perform almost any transformation task.

In this chapter we will:

❑ Give you an introduction to the ActiveX Script task

❑ Explain what languages can be used with the ActiveX Script task

❑ Provide an introduction to scripting in VBScript

❑ Explain how to develop modular code around DTS

In the next chapter we'll see in detail how we can use the ActiveX Script task. First though, we'll concentrate on some basics.

The Role of ActiveX Scripts in DTS

The ActiveX Script task allows you to use nearly any interpreted scripting language to perform an action by a script. This chapter will focus on some of the basic functions that you can do with this task. Since you can use any scripting language for this task, we could dedicate an entire book to this topic alone, but we'll focus on scenarios that you'll probably face in DTS using the **VBScript** language. In this chapter, and the rest of the book, we'll be concentrating on VBScript, so all the examples you see here will be VBScript.

We can use ActiveX scripts to do the following:

❏   Customize data transformation

❏   Dynamically set properties on tasks, connections, or global variables

❏   Move, copy, or read files

❏   Manipulate COM objects

We'll see examples of some of these in later chapters.

Starting with SQL Server 7.0, this task was widely used for dynamically setting properties in a package. For example, you would create an ActiveX script before a Bulk Insert task to dynamically set the import file after scanning a directory:

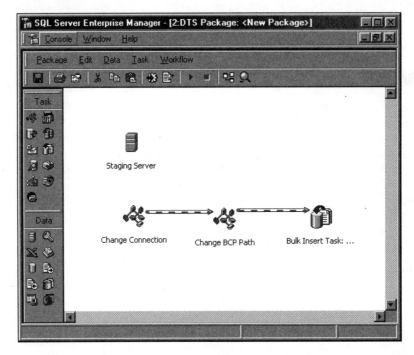

In general, you would use this scenario if you didn't know the exact file name you would be receiving.

Using the ActiveX Script Task

For the purpose of this chapter, create a New Package from Enterprise Manager, and select Task | ActiveX Script Task from the Designer menu. The ActiveX Script Task Properties screen will be displayed automatically. Here's an example of an ActiveX Script task:

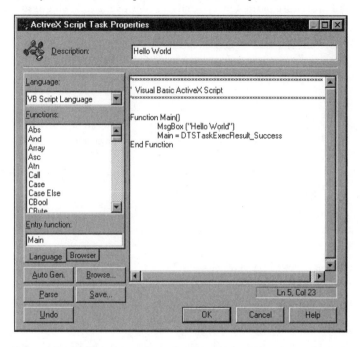

You can also access the ActiveX Script Task Properties screen at any time by right-clicking the task and selecting Properties from the context menu, or simply by double-clicking the task. Otherwise, you can left-click the task, and select Package | Properties.

Let's look at what each part of this dialog does in detail.

First, it's always advisable to choose a meaningful Description for your task, especially when scripting – having a task named the default ActiveX Script task: undefined isn't particularly useful. Usually it's a good idea to name your tasks based on the action that they perform. For example, the task in the above example is named Hello World, because it displays a message box with that statement.

The Language option allows you to set the interpreted scripting language you are going to use. VBScript and JScript (Microsoft's version of JavaScript) are both installed by default when you install Internet Explorer 5 or later, which is a prerequisite before installing SQL Server. You can also use any other ActiveX scripting engine to script in, like PerlScript, if needed. If you program in a language like PerlScript, you will need to ensure that any system that executes your DTS package also has this language installed. The XML scripting language XMLScript is also installed by default on any SQL Server 2000 servers.

Once you select a scripting language, a list of functions specific to the chosen language will populate the Functions box. Each language has its own library. In some scripting languages, it is not unusual to see this list unpopulated.

You can find out which ActiveX Scripting engines are installed by running the extended stored procedure xp_enum_activescriptengines, which is located in the master database:

```
EXEC MASTER..XP_ENUM_ACTIVESCRIPTENGINES
```

Executing the stored procedure in the Query Analyzer returns the following results on my machine:

	Program ID	Description
1	XML	XML Script Engine
2	VBS	VB Script Language
3	VBScript.Encode	VBScript Language Encoding
4	ECMAScript	JScript Language
5	JScript.Encode	JScript Language Encoding
6	PerlScript	PerlScript Language

The results displayed on your system may vary from what is shown above depending on which scripting engines you have installed.

The **Auto Gen** button will create a functional shell script appropriate for the specified language. This shell simply creates the Main function with a valid return value. In VBScript, what you get is:

```
Function Main()
    Main = DTSTaskExecResult_Success
End Function
```

We'll look at functions in detail later in the chapter – for now, just realize that the code within the Function Main() ... End Function delimiters is what is executed at startup in our examples.

The main routine for the script doesn't have to be named Main. The **Entry Function** option tells the ActiveX Script which function will be called first when the task is executed. SQL Server uses the Main function by default. However, any function can be used as the entry point, as long as the **Entry Function** field references the appropriate name.

The **Properties** dialog always defaults to the last language that was used, so if you change the language, you will need to use **Auto Gen** to generate the correct syntax for the new language.

The **Parse** button will check the syntax of your script. It is the first tier of debugging that can be performed before you execute the script. It's only reliable for finding syntax errors – it won't find errors like invalid object calls or logic errors.

The **Save** button will save your script to a transportable file with an extension appropriate for the specified language (for example, .BAS or .VBS for VBScript, .JS for JavaScript). The **Browse** button in turn can open one of these files.

Finally, the script memo area is where you actually write the script. In the example above, the window contains the following VBScript, which will create a dialog box that says **Hello World**:

```
Function Main()
    MsgBox ("Hello World")
    Main = DTSTaskExecResult_Success
End Function
```

Don't worry about the details of this code for the moment – by the end of the chapter you'll see that this script is quite trivial. Most of this script is just the shell that is created automatically when you first launch the Properties dialog (or use the Auto Gen button). You only need to add the shaded line.

After adding this script and clicking OK, you can execute it by selecting Package | Execute from within the Designer:

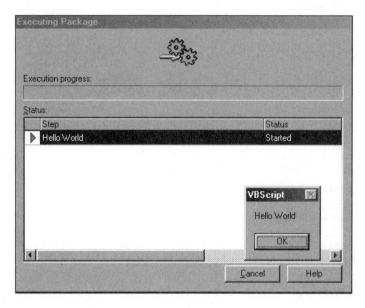

In this example, the task will not show a status of Complete until you click OK in the dialog box. We'll see why when we look at message boxes shortly.

Scripting Language Performance

VBScript and JavaScript are both **interpreted**, meaning that they are not compiled until run time. One advantage of interpreted code is that you can change a piece of your VBScript without having to recompile it. The disadvantage to interpreted code is the time needed to interpret the code before execution. This slowdown will occur with any ActiveX Scripting language that you use.

In DTS, VBScript performs more efficiently than JavaScript, which in turn is faster than PerlScript. It is for this reason that a majority of the examples in this book will be in VBScript. Be very wary of using third party scripting languages. ActiveX scripts have only been fully tested with the pre-installed VBScript and JScript languages. Introducing a new scripting language into DTS could yield unpredictable results.

Basic Programming Terminology in DTS

Every programming language has similar features, whether you're using JavaScript, VBScript, or PerlScript. The differences lie in their syntax and how they process the code after it is created. Once you learn one language though, you can switch between languages easily by learning a few of the core features of the new language.

Most programming languages hold the following in common:

- Variables
- Branching
- Loops

Let's take a look at how these are implemented in VBScript.

Variables

The most fundamental concept of programming is the use of **variables.** Variables are temporary memory locations that allow us to store information that a script needs while it is executing. Variables help us make code dynamic and flexible.

For example, you could use a variable to designate a directory path. Rather than having to hard-code the path into each statement, you can designate the variable once and call it as many times as is needed. When the path changes, rather than having to change the many hard-coded paths, you just change the variable once.

Prior to using a variable, it's good practice to **declare** it. By declaring a variable, we are telling the system to memorize the variable name, and reserve a chunk of memory for the variable's value. To declare a variable you need to dimension it, as shown below:

```
Dim FirstName
```

> Note: you don't generally have to declare variables before you use them. However, it is possible to require variables to be declared by adding the code `Option Explicit` to the top of your script. Then, if a variable is encountered at run time that has not been declared, an error will be displayed.

One great benefit of using Option Explicit in your code is that it can help reduce the number of logic errors or typos in your script.

After we've declared a variable, we should **initialize** it. Simply put, initializing a variable means that we assign a value to it:

```
Dim FirstName
Dim CustomerAge
'Initialize the string value
FirstName = "Brian"
'Initialize the numeric value
CustomerAge = 32
```

As you can see, to initialize a variable that has a string value, we need to place quotes around the value. Numeric values do not require the quotes – in fact, if you put quotes around a numeric value it will be treated as a string. If you don't explicitly initialize a variable, VBScript will implicitly initialize it as an empty string.

You might have noticed some **comments** in the code above. The VBScript method of commenting code is with a single quote ('). VBScript will ignore these lines of code when executing the script. Commenting, of course, is an important element to any script that you write. Just ask any programmer who's taken over someone else's project. Or for that matter, try picking up code you wrote yourself six months ago – you may well wish you had commented it better.

You can also set a variable to be equal to a value that is returned by a function or another variable. A **function** is a routine, or piece of code, that executes and returns a value. So far, we've only seen one function: Main. In our earlier ActiveX Script task, we set the return value of the Main function with the following line:

```
Main = DTSTaskExecResult_Success
```

This just tells DTS that our task has been successfully completed.

VBScript has lots of built in functions that you can utilize in your code. For example, you can set a variable to the function Date to log the current system date while running the script:

```
Dim TodayDate
TodayDate = Date
```

There is a group of internal functions associated with almost every scripting language.

This leads to some interesting predicaments, where we must watch what names we used for variables. There are **reserved words** that each scripting engine uses, such as the word Date in VBScript, which would cause a conflict in your code if used as a variable name. A complete list of VBScript system functions and reserved words can be found in Appendix C.

Message Boxes

The basic concept of raising a dialog box is useful in DTS for debugging more complex code. For example, if we're trying to see whether an external application is passing the correct variables to our ActiveX script, then we can have the task use a **message box** to manually confirm the variables.

To raise a simple dialog box in VBScript, we use the following syntax:

```
MsgBox "Hello World!"
```

We can also raise a dialog box by passing a variable to the Msgbox function. Try placing the following code in an ActiveX Script:

```
Function Main()
    Dim CurrentTime
    CurrentTime = Time
    MsgBox CurrentTime
    Main = DTSTaskExecResult_Success
End Function
```

We create a variable `CurrentTime`, and assign the current time to it using the VBScript `Time` function. We then display the value of `CurrentTime` in a message box.

Executing this task results in the following:

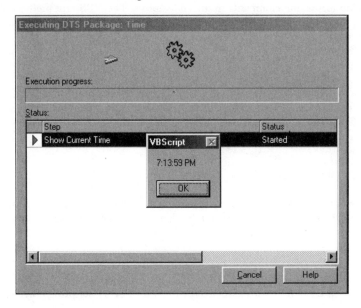

Notice in the above example the lack of quotes around the variable when it is called. If the variable had quotes around it, it would display the literal value CurrentTime.

Once a package is put into production, you shouldn't keep dialog boxes like these in your code. Dialog boxes are typically used in DTS solely to debug code. Most packages are run remotely or on a scheduled basis. The last thing you would want is to have your data transformation freeze indefinitely because of a dialog box waiting for someone to click OK. More advanced debugging techniques will be discussed in a later chapter.

Concatenating Variables

An important concept to learn in scripting is how to concatenate data. **Concatenation** is when we combine or string together multiple data elements. We can do this by using the ampersand (&) symbol.

The code below demonstrates concatenating text with the variable `CurrentTime`:

```
Function Main()
    Dim CurrentTime
    CurrentTime = Time
    MsgBox "The time is " & CurrentTime & "."
    Main = DTSTaskExecResult_Success
End Function
```

If you run our concatenation example in an ActiveX Script task, it should look like the following:

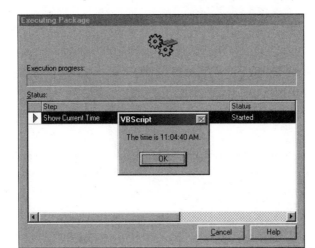

The ampersand symbol is an **operator**. You've been using operators without even knowing it during this chapter. An operator is a symbol that allows us to set a value. Other operators include mathematical operators such as +, −, * and /. There are also operators such as the equal sign, used regularly in code to set values, and bitwise operators (which are used to compare binary data).

The + operator can also be used for concatenation, but care needs to be taken to prevent possible errors. For example, changing the & operator to the + operator in the example above would generate an error at run time. This is because of the underlying data type of the CurrentTime variable – it can't be treated as a string. In order to use the + operator, it would be necessary to make a minor modification to the code:

```
Function Main()
    Dim CurrentTime
    CurrentTime = Time
    MsgBox "The time is " + CStr(CurrentTime) + "."
    Main = DTSTaskExecResult_Success
End Function
```

Here, we're using VBScript's CStr function to explicitly convert CurrentTime to a string.

Keep in mind that if you attempt to concatenate two numeric variables with the + operator, the scripting engine will perform addition instead of concatenation. In order to correctly concatenate numeric values, use the & operator as shown below:

```
Function Main()
    Dim Num1
    Dim Num2

    Num1 = 5
    Num2 = 10

    MsgBox "Using + gives " & Num1 + Num2
    MsgBox "Using & gives " & Num1 & Num2
    Main = DTSTaskExecResult_Success
End Function
```

This gives us the following two messages in sequence:

Branching

Branching is the first sign of logic in any scripting language. Simply put, branching looks for a certain condition to be met, and then performs an action when it is. Branching is done through conditional statements such as If, Else, and ElseIf.

If ... Else

To begin our example let's take an old example and modify it slightly:

```
Function Main()
    Dim CurrentDate
    CurrentDate = InputBox("What is the Current Date?")
    MsgBox "The date is " & CurrentDate & "."
    Main = DTSTaskExecResult_Success
End Function
```

As you can see above, we are now using the function InputBox to replace the Date function. The InputBox procedure will pop up a box and wait for input from a user. It gives a script a level of interactivity that most packages will not need in our development. When the above script is executed the output should look like this:

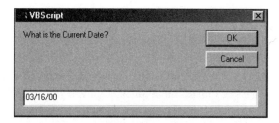

After entering the date you should receive the output shown below:

In this script, we wait for the user to input a value in the input box. Once the user clicks OK, the script will assign that value to the CurrentDate variable. This is great in a perfect world, but you can never predict what users are going to type into a dialog box that you present them with. That's where branching comes in handy.

In this next example, branching can be used to add a level of error handling to make sure the user is inputting the type of value that is acceptable. You can modify the code to include error code by changing the code to the following:

```
Function Main()
    Dim CurrentDate
    CurrentDate = InputBox ("What is the Current Date?")
    If Not IsDate(CurrentDate) Then
        MsgBox "You didn't enter a date"
        Main = DTSTaskExecResult_Failure
    Else
        MsgBox "The date is " & Replace(CurrentDate,"-","/") & "."
        Main = DTSTaskExecResult_Success
    End If
End Function
```

Note how we indent the code within the If and Else blocks – this is standard coding practice to make code more readable. It can also help reduce errors when coding – you're less likely to miss out an End If statement if you structure the code like this.

In the above example, we have added a pretty large chunk of code to do a small layer of error checking. First, we will detect if the user entered a valid date value for the variable CurrentDate. We do this by using the If...Then statement and the IsDate function. The fundamental rule to If...Then statements is that every If statement must be accompanied by a Then statement and an End If to close the branch.

If the script detects an empty string or an invalid date value for the variable CurrentDate, the code opens a dialog box that warns the user that they did not enter a date. The ActiveX Script task will then raise an error, and the code resumes at the point of the End If statement. The line:

```
Main = DTSTaskExecResult_Failure
```

tells the package that the Main function failed, and to quit the entire task because of this failure. As we've seen, to report a task as succeeding, change this line to say Success rather than Failure:

```
Main = DTSTaskExecResult_Success
```

So, execute the script and don't enter a value in the dialog box, then click OK. You will then receive the popup box:

When a task fails execution, it will be noted in the package status dialog:

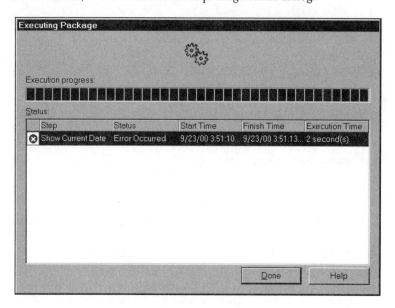

If you double-click on the failed error to get details, DTS will report the following:

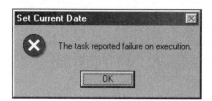

Unfortunately, this error message just reports the failure and nothing more. We have dedicated an entire chapter to proper error handling later in the book.

Now, back to the code. The `Else` statement simply says, "If the other criteria are not met then do this". In this code there are only two branches to worry about: the user enters a value, or the user doesn't enter a value. If the user enters a value, we display a dialog box that reports their input and report to the package that the task has successfully executed.

There is one more twist that we have thrown into this code:

```
MsgBox "The date is " & Replace(CurrentDate,"-","/") & "."
```

Here, we use a function called Replace(), so when the user enters a date like 3-13-1990, we replace it with the string 3/13/1990. The `Replace` function is often used to scrub data.

In this example, we use the `Replace` function with a variable. You can also replace literal text by using something like the following:

```
Replace("03/16-1990","-","/")
```

Now, execute the package again, but this time, enter the value as 03-13-1999.

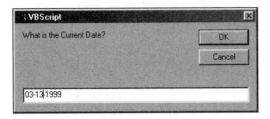

This will output the date as:

ElseIf

Branching can also become quite detailed by using ElseIf. ElseIf helps you build a more structured logic than just using Else. Modify your code as shown below:

```
Function Main()
    Dim CurrentDate
    CurrentDate = InputBox ("What is the Current Date?")
    If CurrentDate = "" Then
        MsgBox "You didn't enter a date"
        Main = DTSTaskExecResult_Failure
    ElseIf CurrentDate = "Why" Then
        MsgBox "Because I need it for this example!"
        Main = DTSTaskExecResult_Failure
    Else
        MsgBox "The date is " & Replace(CurrentDate,"-","/") & "."
        Main = DTSTaskExecResult_Success
    End If
End Function
```

If the first If isn't met, then we go to the ElseIf. If this isn't met either, we go to the Else.

The above code will first verify that the user entered any input at all. As before, if we didn't enter anything, we display the You didn't enter a date dialog and raise the Failure, then pass to the End If without executing any more of the code.

If we did answer something, the code passes on to the ElseIf condition. Enter Why and the code will open the following dialog box:

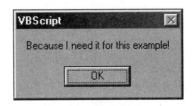

However, note what happens if you input the value why:

This shows the case-sensitivity of the values in the variable: in our example, why and Why are two different values. The same applies when dealing with global variables, as we'll see in the next chapter. When we enter the value why, the ElseIf condition is not met, so the code for the Else condition is executed.

To correct the problem of case-sensitivity, we can modify our script to force the case of the text the user enters. Modify the example as shown below to use all upper case values when comparing text:

```
Function Main()
   Dim CurrentDate
   CurrentDate = InputBox ("What is the Current Date?")
   If CurrentDate = "" Then
      MsgBox "You didn't enter a date"
      Main = DTSTaskExecResult_Failure
   ElseIf UCase(CurrentDate) = "WHY" Then
      MsgBox "Because I need it for this example!"
      Main = DTSTaskExecResult_Failure
   Else
      MsgBox "The date is " & Replace(CurrentDate,"-","/") & "."
      Main = DTSTaskExecResult_Success
   End If
End Function
```

Now, regardless of whether the user enters Why or why the ElseIf condition will be met. Of course, a better alternative would be to follow the first example and use the IsDate function to ensure that a valid date value was entered.

Nested Conditions

To add the final layer of logic, we can use a **nested** condition. Nested conditions allow you to place an If condition inside another If condition. In the example below, we've modified the code to add an extra layer, to make sure the date that was entered was the real current date:

```
Function Main()
   Dim CurrentDate

   CurrentDate = InputBox ("What is the Current Date?")

   If CurrentDate = "" Then
      MsgBox "You didn't enter a date"
      Main = DTSTaskExecResult_Failure
   ElseIf CurrentDate = "Why" Then
      MsgBox "Because I need it for this example!"
      Main = DTSTaskExecResult_Failure
```

```
    ElseIf IsDate(CurrentDate) Then

    If CDate(CurrentDate) = Date Then
        MsgBox "You have the correct date of " & _
                    Replace(CDate(CurrentDate),"-","/") & "."
        Main = DTSTaskExecResult_Success
    Else
        MsgBox "You did not enter today's date"
        Main = DTSTaskExecResult_Failure
    End If

    Else
        MsgBox "You did not enter a valid date."
        Main = DTSTaskExecResult_Failure
    End If

End Function
```

In the above code, after we've done our regular checks, we check to see if the date entered is a valid date using the `IsDate` function. If it is a valid date, the code checks to see if it matches the current date. We used the function `CDate`, which converts the string value into a date in the form 3/8/00. We'll come back to these functions in just a moment. Finally, if it doesn't meet any of our previous conditions, then we know the user didn't enter something that was a valid date, so we send a `Failure` message to DTS.

Now execute the package, entering today's date as a value. You should receive something like the following output after you click **OK**:

Note that the code we use to display this message box is split over two lines. In order do this, we need to use a line continuation character (_) at the end of the first line, to indicate that the next line is actually just a continuation of the first:

```
MsgBox "You have the correct date of " & _
            Replace(CDate(CurrentDate),"-","/") & "."
```

This can help make code more readable when we have very long and complex statements.

In DTS, you will rarely use the `InputBox` function, since most of your tasks will be running unattended and the script will halt indefinitely awaiting user input. The only reason to use this function would be if you wanted to add interactivity between the package and the user, but this is probably best kept to a minimum. However, the input box is especially handy for setting global variables and connection string information for a user who does not understand DTS. We'll use this function extensively throughout this book to demonstrate a few more vital points.

Types of Variables

There is only one type of variable in VBScript: the **Variant**. The Variant however, has many different subtypes, which change automatically based on the value stored in it. The subtype can also be manually changed with the use of a conversion function, such as `CDate`. Without the `CDate` conversion functions, we couldn't have compared the variable like this:

```
If CDate(CurrentDate) = Date Then
```

Even if the user had entered a valid date, such as 02-14-2000, the script would not have been able to properly compare the date entered with the current system date, because it would be in the wrong format.

You can also test a variable for its type. We've already seen `IsDate` in action, and there are also test functions called `IsNumeric` and `IsObject`, among others. For example, to test a date in order to validate that it really is a date, we'd use the code below:

```
Function Main()

    Dim CurrentDate
    CurrentDate = InputBox("Enter a date")
    If IsDate(CurrentDate) Then
        MsgBox "The CurrentDate Variable is a Date"
    Else
        Main = DTSTaskExecResult_Failure
        Exit Function
    End If
    Main = DTSTaskExecResult_Success

End Function
```

When executing the above script, the dialog box should read:

If `CurrentDate` had been an incorrect date, like 03/166/2000 the `Else` statements would have executed. Note that in addition to setting the return code for the routine to `DTSTaskExecResult_False`, we have also instructed the code to exit the function. If we don't do this, the code will continue executing and will return `DTSTaskResult_Success` erroneously.

The table below shows the valid data types, how to convert them manually, and how to test them:

Data Type	Storage Needed (bytes)	Conversion Function	Test Function
Byte	1	CByte() .	IsNumeric()
Integer	2	CInt()	IsNumeric()
Long	4	CLng()	IsNumeric()
Single	4	CSng()	IsNumeric()
Double	8	CDbl()	IsNumeric()
Currency	8	CCur() ()	IsNumeric()
Decimal	14	N/A	IsNumeric()
Boolean	2	CBool()	N/A
String	10+ Length of String	CStr()	N/A
Date	8	CDate()	IsDate()
Variant	16 or 22	CVar()	N/A
Object	4	N/A	IsObject()

The test functions `IsNumeric`, `IsDate`, `IsObject`, and others are discussed in further detail in Appendix C.

In addition to the various test functions, the `VarType` function can also be used to determine the underlying subtype of a variable. When you pass `VarType` the variable you want to check, it returns a numeric value that identifies the subtype. Appendix C provides the values that the `VarType` function returns.

For example, this code demonstrates the use of `VarType` to determine that the underlying subtype of the variable `MyStr` is a string data type:

```
Function Main()
    Dim MyStr
    MyStr = "SQL Server DTS"
    MsgBox VarType(MyStr)
    Main = DTSTaskExecResult_Success
End Function
```

This code should display the following simple message box:

Looping

As well as branching, we can also loop through a piece of code until a condition is met. In DTS, this is especially helpful when you are collecting data about your tasks.

Do Loops

Below is a sample loop that will prompt the user for the current date, and continue to prompt them until they enter the correct date:

```
Function Main()
    Dim CurrentDate
    Dim TryOver

    TryOver = "No"
    Do
        CurrentDate = InputBox("Please enter the current date")
        If VarType(CurrentDate) =0 or CurrentDate = "" Then
          Exit Do
        Else
          CurrentDate = CDate(CurrentDate)
        End If

        If Not CurrentDate = Date Then
            MsgBox "That is not the current date. Please try again."
            TryOver = "Yes"
        Else
            MsgBox "That is the current date."
            TryOver = "No"
        End If

    Loop While TryOver = "Yes"

    Main = DTSTaskExecResult_Success
End Function
```

We begin our loop with the Do statement, and end it with the Loop statement. We start by initializing the variable TryOver. If we don't initialize this variable properly, we could have an infinite loop, where the loop's condition is never met. The loop's condition in our code is for the variable TryOver to be equal to Yes, as you can see in the Loop While line.

In this scenario, our If statement is looking for the results to be not equal to the current date. We do this with the Not operator. We could also use the following:

```
If CurrentDate <> Date Then
```

If the date that was entered is not the current date, then a dialog box will appear and ask you to retry. Let's go ahead and execute the package, entering an incorrect date:

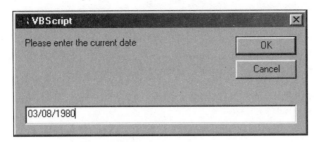

Now, you will receive the warning:

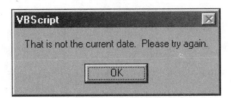

Enter the correct date the next time around, and you'll receive the result below:

For...Next Loop

Let's add to the complexity a little with a For...Next loop. When the correct date is entered, the code below will take the current date and add four days to it, displaying a dialog box each time.

```
Function Main()
    Dim CurrentDate
    Dim TryOver
    Dim LoopCtr

    TryOver = "No"
    Do
        CurrentDate = InputBox("Please enter the current date")
        If VarType(CurrentDate) =0 or CurrentDate = "" Then
          Main = DTSTaskExecResult_Failure
          Exit Do
        Else
          CurrentDate = CDate(CurrentDate)
        End If

        If Not  CurrentDate = Date Then
           MsgBox "That is not the current date. Please try again."
           TryOver = "Yes"
```

283

```
        Else
            MsgBox "That is the current date."
            TryOver = "No"
            For LoopCtr  = 1 to 5
                MsgBox CurrentDate
                CurrentDate = CurrentDate + 1
            Next
            Main = DTSTaskExecResult_Success
        End If

    Loop While TryOver = "Yes"

End Function
```

When executing the script you should see the following (with your own dates of course):

The most vital part of the code above is the line:

```
        For LoopCtr  = 1 to 5
```

This is where our code tells the engine that we want to perform the code between the `For` and the `Next` lines as many times as can be counted between 1 and 5. In real life code, you will most likely see a variable in the place of the numbers 1 and 5. This is also an example of how to nest a loop inside another loop.

More Useful Loops

You may be wondering what practical purpose these loops can serve. Now that you know the basics, let's try an example that will be a little more useful. In this example, we will manually set the variable `strFullFileName` to be equal to a fully qualified file name. We will then create a loop to scan the variable to find the actual file name. The loop will read the variable character by character, from right to left, looking for the character \. Once found, anything to the right of that is assumed to be the file's name, and it is displayed. This is all done with the following code:

```
Function Main()
    Dim strFullFileName
    Dim strShortFileName
    Dim lngIndex
    Dim lngStrLen

    strFullFileName = "C:\Logs\Log.txt"
    lngStrLen = Len(strFullFileName)
```

```
    For lngIndex = lngStrLen to 1 Step -1
        If Mid(strFullFileName, lngIndex, 1) = "\" Then
            strShortFileName = Right(strFullFileName, lngStrLen - lngIndex)
            Exit For
        End If
    Next
    MsgBox strShortFileName

    Main = DTSTaskExecResult_Success
End Function
```

When executing the code, you should see the output below:

After we declare and initialize the `strFullFileName` variable, we set the `intStrLen` variable to the length of the `strFullFileName` variable, which is 15. This variable is set using the `Len` function, which can determine the length of any string.

> *Notice the way we name our variables here – the strings start with* `str` *and the numbers with* `int`. *This is a standard way of naming variables known as Hungarian notation. You're under no obligation to use this convention, but it can help make your code more readable. For more on naming conventions, see Appendix D.*

We then begin a `For...Next` loop that will loop from the index of 15 to 1 working backwards. As you can see, to make a loop count backwards, we can use the `Step` keyword, and a negative value. Step can take other values too – for example, we could have the loop skip every other value moving forwards by specifying `Step 2`.

The next line uses the `Mid` function, which will capture the 1 character to the right of the `intIndex` variable. If the value is a \, then it performs an action. For example, the first time the loop passes, the value of `lngIndex` is 15 so the string will read:

```
If Mid("C:\Logs\Log.txt", 15, 1) = "\" Then
```

Since the fifteenth value is a `t`, the condition is not met, and the loop then proceeds again until the eighth value. At that point, the line of code will read:

```
If Mid("C:\Logs\Log.txt", 8, 1) = "\" Then
```

The eighth value is a \ so the condition is met. The code then moves to the condition statement that can be translated to:

```
strShortFileName = Right("C:\Logs\Log.txt", 15 - 8)
Exit For
```

The Right function will take the seven characters from the right (15 – 8) and set the strShortFileName variable to that piece of data. This scenario will set the strShortFileName variable to Log.txt. We then use the Exit For keyword to exit the loop. This especially handy because it gives us two conditions that can end the loop:

❑ The loop goes through all 15 characters and doesn't find a \ character

❑ The loop goes through and finds the first \

However, this brings us to another problem. If the \ character is never found, we end up with no file name, although we could safely assume that the whole string is actually the file name. To handle the case that the \ character is never found, we could provide some additional code that would assume the value provided was only the filename without any path information. The example could be modified as follows:

```
Function Main()
    Dim strFullFileName
    Dim strShortFileName
    Dim intIndex
    Dim intStrLen

    strFullFileName = "MoreLog.txt"
    intStrLen = Len(strFullFileName)

    For intIndex = intStrLen to 1 Step -1
        If Mid(strFullFileName, intIndex, 1) = "\" Then
            strShortFileName = Right(strFullFileName, intStrLen - intIndex)
            Exit For
        End If
    Next
    If strShortFileName = "" Then
        strShortFileName = strFullFileName
    End If
    MsgBox strShortFileName

    Main = DTSTaskExecResult_Success
End Function
```

> *For more information on the Mid and Right functions, and the parameters associated with them, as well as many other intrinsic functions of VBScript, please consult Appendix C.*

In Chapter 9, we will make this process automated with the FileSystem object. The FileSystem object is the main way you can have DTS interact with the OS from the scripting level.

These examples have been pretty simplistic by loop standards. We will use the fundamentals demonstrated in these examples to move forward in the next couple of chapters, where the code becomes a bit more complex.

Functions and Subprocedures

As you can see in the previous examples, as we add logic and complexity to our code, the code becomes harder and harder to read. Functions and subprocedures are a way to compartmentalize your code.

Functions

Functions allow you to execute individual pieces of your code, and allow the chunks of code in a single ActiveX task to communicate with each other.

We've already used several functions. An example of a **system function** is `Right` in the previous example. With the `Right ()` function, you pass in some text and receive modified text in return.

Let's look at a familiar piece of code that has been converted to a function:

```
Function GetCurrentDate()
    Dim CurrentDate
    Dim TryOver

    TryOver = "No"
    Do
        CurrentDate = InputBox("Please enter the current date")
        If VarType(CurrentDate) =0 or CurrentDate = "" Then
          Exit Do
        Else
          CurrentDate = CDate(CurrentDate)
        End If

        If Not CurrentDate = Date Then
          MsgBox "That is not the current date. Please try again."
          TryOver = "Yes"
        Else
          GetCurrentDate = CurrentDate
          TryOver = "No"
        End If

    Loop While TryOver = "Yes"

End Function
```

As you can see above, we have taken out one of the `MsgBox` procedures replacing it with the line assigning the value that the function will return as `CurrentDate`. We've also taken out the `DTSTaskExecResult_Success` statement. This is because the code above is now only a component of the entire code set. It is now standalone, and can be called multiple times from other functions in the same ActiveX Script task. This code would never execute unless it was called by the `Main` function (or some other function that is, in some way, called by the `Main` function).

So let's now our code to call the `GetCurrentDate` function:

```
Function Main()
    Dim ReturnedDate

    ReturnedDate =  GetCurrentDate
    MsgBox ReturnedDate
    Main = DTSTaskExecResult_Success
End Function
```

287

After declaring our variables, we set the `ReturnedDate` variable to the result of running the `GetCurrentDate` function. Then we create a dialog box that will display our familiar results. Notice here that the line

```
Main = DTSTaskExecResult_Success
```

is still in the `Main` function, but most of the other code has been moved out. We leave this line in `Main` because the task is not considered successful until it has fully run through the `Main` function.

The entire script in the task will look like this:

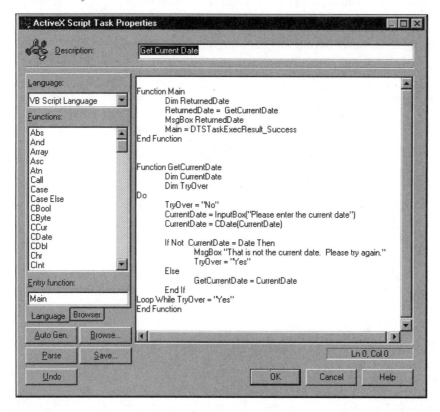

Subprocedures

Another type of routine exists that does not return a value. This type of routine is called a **subprocedure**. There may be instances where it is not particularly necessary to have a return value.

In the following example, we use both functions and subprocedures:

```
Option Explicit

Function Main()
    Dim Result
    Result = GetSomeResult
    DisplayResult Result
```

```
    Main = DTSTaskExecResult_Success
End Function

Function GetSomeResult
    GetSomeResult = "Hello, World!"
End Function

Sub DisplayResult(AVariable)
    MsgBox AVariable
End Sub
```

Entry Functions

Remember that the **Entry Function** tells the DTS engine where to begin your code. In the example above, if we wanted `GetCurrentDate` to be the first routine in the script to execute, we could have entered `GetCurrentDate` in the **Entry Function** field. One point to note, however, is that code placed outside any routine will be executed prior to the specified entry function. To understand what we mean by this, consider the following example:

```
Option Explicit
    Dim MyVar 'Script-level variable
    MyVar = "SQL 2000"
    MsgBox MyVar

Function Main()
    Dim MyVar 'Procedure-level variable
    MyVar = "Is Cool"
    MsgBox MyVar
    ShowVar
    Main = DTSTaskExecResult_Success
End Function

Sub ShowVar
    MsgBox MyVar 'Script-level variable
End Sub
```

In this code, the message box stating **SQL 2000** will be displayed prior to the `Main` function executing.

Variable Scope

There's something else we should discuss about this example. It demonstrates the various types of localized variables we can have.

These include **script-level** variables, which can only be used by the current running script (or in DTS's case, the current ActiveX task). These variables can be referenced anywhere within the current script. For example, here we reference the script-level variable `MyVar` at in the `ShowVar` subprocedure.

There are also **procedure-level** variables, which can only be referenced within the procedure in which they are declared. In our function Main, we declare a procedure level variable MyVar. This takes precedence over the script-level MyVar value so long as we're within the function Main. So the message box statement in the Main function produces the message:

However, this value is invisible outside of the Main function. Even when we call ShowVar from within the Main function, the ShowVar subprocedure only recognizes the script-level variable. So the message box within ShowVar displays:

As we've seen earlier in the book, there are also variables that can be shared between scripts, called **global variables**. Global variables can be used to pass information from one task to another, or from package to package. In Chapter 9, we'll discuss global variables in greater detail.

Passing Variables Into and Out of Functions

We've already learned how to receive a variable from a function. We can also pass a function variables or **parameters** – we've already done this with the CDate() function and others. You pass a function parameters by declaring the parameter list within the function definition, and passing them as part of the function call.

Let's modify our example again:

```
Function Main()
    Dim dtmReturnedDate
    Dim intNumDays

    intNumDays = InputBox("Enter the number of days you'd like to add.")
    dtmReturnedDate = GetCurrentDate(intNumDays)
    MsgBox dtmReturnedDate
    Main = DTSTaskExecResult_Success
End Function
```

The GetCurrentDate function will also change slightly. We need to prepare the function for the variable it will receive by adding the variable's name to the opening of the function:

```
Function GetCurrentDate(NumDays)
    Dim CurrentDate
    Dim TryOver
```

```
    TryOver = "No"
    Do
        CurrentDate = InputBox("Please enter the current date")
        If VarType(CurrentDate) = 0 or CurrentDate = "" Then
          Exit Do
        Else
          CurrentDate = CDate(CurrentDate)
        End If

        If Not CurrentDate = Date Then
            MsgBox "That is not the current date. Please try again."
            TryOver = "Yes"
        Else
            GetCurrentDate = CurrentDate + NumDays
            TryOver = "No"
        End If
    Loop While TryOver = "Yes"
End Function
```

NumDays is the single parameter accepted by the modified GetCurrentDate routine – but note that we don't need to call the variable by the same name in the call and function.

As we said earlier, the plus sign in the GetCurrentDate function is an arithmetic operator. You can use any mathematical sign to add, subtract, multiply, or divide numeric variables. However, remember that for non-numeric types, + is also a concatenation operator.

When executing the code you should see this output. Type 3 into the box:

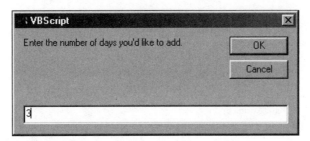

Enter today's date:

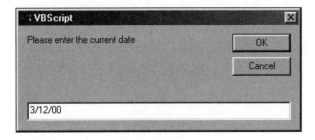

And you will then see today's date plus three.

By Reference and By Value

There are two ways to pass variables to functions and procedures. VBScript allows you to pass parameters either **by reference**, the default, or **by value**.

By reference means that the memory address of the variable is passed as the parameter. The benefit to this, if used wisely, is that the actual data contained within the specified memory address can be modified. Thus it can also be used as an output parameter. To specify this, we use the `ByRef` keyword. However, since `ByRef` is the default, we don't even have to specify it.

If we pass a parameter by value, we are only passing a copy of the data. The routine that is receiving the copy can manipulate the value however it chooses, but when the routine is exited, the original value of the parameter in the calling code is intact. We specify this type of parameter with the `ByVal` keyword.

Let's clarify this with a simple example:

```
Function Main()
    Dim Num1
    Dim Num2
    Dim Result

    Num1 = 5
    Num2 = 5
    MsgBox "Number 1: " & Num1 & vbCr & "Number 2: " & Num2
    ShowParamTypes Num1, Num2
    MsgBox "Number 1: " & Num1 & vbCr & "Number 2: " & Num2
    Main = DTSTaskExecResult_Success
End Function

Sub ShowParamTypes (ByVal FirstNum, ByRef SecondNum)
    FirstNum = 10
    SecondNum = 10
End Sub
```

When the first message box is displayed, both numbers have their original values:

Our code then calls a subprocedure which changes the number values. However, when we see the second message box, while the second number is different, the first number is unchanged:

This is because the first number was sent by value. Although the ShowParamTypes procedure modified the value, it was only modifying a local copy of that value. The SecondNum parameter, on the other hand, was passed by reference. Since we passed the actual memory location, when ShowParamTypes modified the value, we modified the original value, not a copy.

Passing variables in and out of functions adds an extra layer of maintainability to your code. Ideally, when a change is needed to your code, you can just change the function rather than have to search through thousands of lines of code for the piece you need.

Summary

We have learned in this chapter how to declare variables and use them in code. We've also learned how to control the flow of your code by using If...Then statements and looping. Some of the important points that you'll need to remember are:

❑   You can expand the functionality of DTS by importing your own scripting languages, such as PerlScript

❑   VBScript is the fastest way to program the ActiveX Script task in DTS

❑   There is only one type of variable in VBScript – the Variant – with many subtypes

❑   You can make your code more manageable by using functions

❑   FunctionName = DTSTaskExecResult_Success or FunctionName = DTSTaskExecResult_Failure will signal to DTS that a task has successfully executed or failed

Most of the remainder of the book will focus on scripting and programming with DTS.

If you need a further reference on scripting with VBScript consider reading VBScript Programmer's Reference, *ISBN 1-861002-71-8, from Wrox Press.*

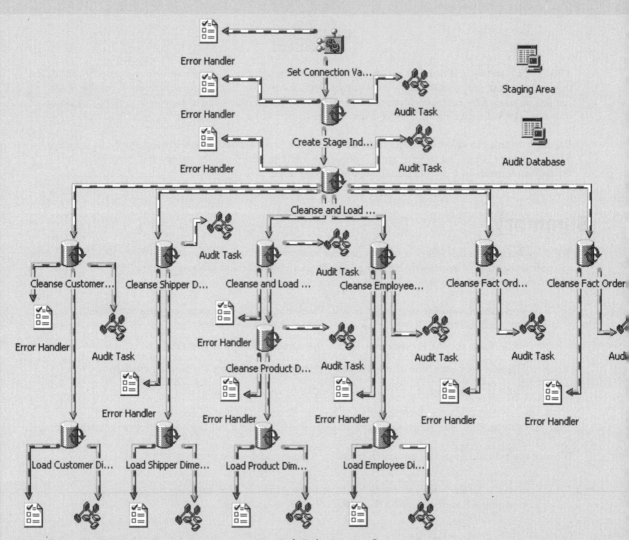

Error Handler

Set Connection Va...

Audit Task

Staging Area

Error Handler

Create Stage Ind...

Audit Task

Audit Database

Error Handler

Audit Task

Cleanse and Load ...

Audit Task

Cleanse Customer...   Cleanse Shipper D...   Cleanse and Load ...   Cleanse Employee...   Cleanse Fact Ord...   Cleanse Fact Order...

Error Handler   Audit Task   Error Handler   Audit Task   Audit Task   Audi...

Error Handler   Cleanse Product D...   Audit Task   Error Handler   Error Handler

Error Handler   Error Handler   Error Handler

Load Customer Di...   Load Shipper Dime...   Load Product Dim...   Load Employee Di...

Error Handler   Audit Task   Error Handler   Audit Task   Error Handler   Audit Task   Error Handler   Audit Task

8
Dynamic Configuration of Package Objects

By this stage in the book, you should have gained good experience in using several aspects of DTS and packages. Many, but not all, of the examples will have used some sort of dynamic information within them. The aim of this chapter is to demonstrate how to dynamically configure packages using differing methods, from VBScript through to Visual Basic. You will want to ensure that when you develop your package, you do not have to keep altering the information every time the package runs.

This chapter assumes that you have read the previous chapter on ActiveX Script tasks, and that you have little or no knowledge of using object models; also, that you have limited experience of Visual Basic. To enable you to achieve this functionality, in some instances, it will be necessary to be familiar with the DTS Object Model. That's the first area that we'll be addressing in this chapter.

The DTS object model will be fully detailed in Appendix A at the end of this book.

By the end of this chapter you will know how to:

❑ Find your way around the basics of the DTS Object Model

❑ Develop solutions using the object model

❑ Add tasks and steps at run time

❑ Use the object model within Visual Basic

❑ Dynamically configure a package using the Dynamic Properties task

The DTS Object Model, to a developer, is known as a **COM object**. COM actually stands for **Component Object Model**. COM is a method that allows any software vendor (in this case Microsoft with SQL Server DTS) to expose the many aspects of the object to a developer, in order to allow flexible solutions that can be manipulated at run time.

In this case, the DTS Object Model will allow run time solutions to be developed that can dynamically configure the DTS package, depending on events that occur during the life time of the package. Before we create an example with the DTS Object Model, let's take a minute to go through the figure of the model above.

Commencing at the very top of the graphic, the **Package2 object** is what is termed the **root level object**.

The `Package2` object is the SQL 2000 version of the `Package` object that shipped with SQL Server 7. The main difference that `Package2` offers is the extension of the functionality of the `Package` object. However, although full backward compatibility is maintained, if you wish to have a task "listen" for events from packages, the `Package2` object does not implicitly handle events. You will have to define the object with the `WithEvents` command.

Much of the new extensibility found within `Package2` that you will find useful surrounds the saving of packages created at run time, which we cover later in the chapter, and how error handling is dealt with.

You still define variables using the `Package` object, which you will see shortly; however, if you use any of the `Package2` extensibility, then be warned that the package will not run on SQL Server 7.

It is from the `Package2` object level that, by moving through the structure, you can access the rest of the model. Once the root level is defined in your solution, moving to the next level of the object model is a very straightforward process. In the case of DTS, the next level would be any tasks, connections, steps, or global variables that have been defined in the package. Very shortly we'll go through several different ways of completing this.

Firstly, there's a pretty important question we should answer.

What is an Object?

At this point of the chapter, you might be wondering what an object actually is, and what is held in an object. A COM object provides an interface to a developer, to the object that it is representing. In this case, DTS is itself an object, just as a car is an object, or a house, or even this book, and the DTS object model is providing that interface. The interface provides access to the properties and methods of the object and so allows that object to be manipulated programmatically.

> **An object is basically a container holding information about itself.**

To give an example, a car is an object. Notice we don't say Ford or Rolls Royce here, just a plain car. There are attributes of a car that every car has. These would be tyres, steering wheel, seats, and so on. These are called **properties** and, for example, you would set tyres to 4, steering wheel to "classic", seats to 2, 4, or the number of seats within the car. You can make every car accelerate, brake, turn, start, stop, and so on. These are called **methods**. Finally, we have **events**. A car's events, for example, would be starting engine (which would occur when the key is turned in the ignition), gas consumption (which would occur with engine revolution), and engine temperature (which would occur with engine usage and may be called from different types of usage or external events, like outside air temperature). So, when you turn the car, you would then get sent back a change in direction of movement. When you tell the car to accelerate, you would find that gas consumption increases. So an event is something that is fed back to you, and not something that you tell the car to do.

If we now move on to look at DTS and the sub-objects within, and if we look at the actual DTS package object, which is the main object we will be dealing with, we can say it has properties such as **Name, Description, LogFileName**, and methods which include **Execute**, and **SaveAs**. However, we won't list everything here, as you can find a comprehensive list in Appendix A at the back of the book. Also, DTS contains other objects, or sub-objects, within itself. Checking back to the object model, these sub objects are:

- **Tasks** –units of work to be performed

- **Connections** –OLE DB connections to data sources

- **Steps** – the glue which informs the package how to run the tasks

- **Global Variables** –used for passing information between tasks within a package

However, they are still part of the DTS Object Model and can only be accessed through the DTS Object Model.

Now that you know what an object is, you're probably wondering how to use this new found information. We can use any of:

- A task such as an ActiveX Script task within a DTS package

- Visual Basic for Applications (VBA)

- Visual Basic (VB)

- Any other development tool that allows you access to the DTS COM Object Model

to develop solutions to dynamically configure your package, or even create a new DTS package at run time. Powerful stuff! Let's move on now and see how we can use the DTS Object Model in a developed solution.

Developing with the Object Model

As I mentioned above, you can use any number of different development environments to use the DTS Object Model. However, we will concentrate initially on using VBScript within the ActiveX Script task. Later on we will demonstrate how your code will differ in Visual Basic. Don't worry if you don't have Visual Basic or know Visual Basic, things will be kept very simple.

If you want to move in to any of the other environments, in essence the same techniques can be applied. We'll start with a very simple example.

Enumerating Steps

We'll assume that you have SQL Server started, so navigate to **Data Transformation Services**, select **Local Packages**, right mouse click, and select **New Package**. Once the new package is created, then select **Task | ActiveX Script Task**:

This should open up an empty ActiveX Script development environment, as we saw in the previous chapter. Now let's add some code. First of all, define a variable to hold the package object model within it:

```
'*************************************************************************
'   Visual Basic ActiveX Script
'*************************************************************************

Function Main()

    ' Define a variable to hold this package's details
    Dim oPackage
```

As you can see, this is just a straight `Dim` statement with the name of the variable. There is no code after this determining what the variable is, like a string, or an integer. Reflect back to earlier in the book, where we said that all variables within VBScript are defined **variant**. You have seen no different within the book so far, and are probably wondering why I am mentioning this. Basically, the definition of variables changes when we reach the Visual Basic section, where we do have to define what data type is being used. The next section of code places the current package into the variable:

```
    ' Now place this active package in to that variable
    Set oPackage = DTSGlobalVariables.Parent
```

As you can see, this isn't as straightforward a process as you might expect. It is not possible to get to the actual DTS package directly. What the code above is actually doing is cheating a bit. In an ActiveX Script task within DTS, you have to move to the next level down in the object model, and then reference the `Parent` property. What this does is put a reference to the current package into the variable you wish to assign.

Now that there is a variable defined with the current package, the whole object model of DTS is available to you. If you look at the object model diagram, you will see that one of the next levels down is the `Steps` collection, so let's access that now:

```
' Display the number of steps in the package
MsgBox oPackage.Steps.Count
```

If you check back to the object model diagram, you will see that the `Steps` object sits directly underneath the `Package2` object. Therefore this line of code is specifically telling VBScript to check the DTS package, then the `Steps` collection of the package, and finally, tell the `MsgBox`, and ultimately the user, the contents of the `Count` property, or, in other words, how many items are contained within the `Steps` collection.

The only step created in the package is the ActiveX Script task that we are currently developing. So when we look at the `Steps` collection, there will only be one step included. The `Count` property, which gives us the number of `Steps` in the collection, will therefore return the value 1.

> **A collection is a group of related items and is common to Object Models. In a package, each step is its own item within the package. However, they are all part of the one package, but collected together. If the package had five steps, you would say that the package had a `Steps` collection containing five items.**

Let's finish off this introductory example with the remainder of the code. As we saw in the last chapter, all that is happening is that we are returning a success:

```
' Send back a success results
Main = DTSTaskExecResult_Success

End Function
```

Save the step in the package, and then run the step. Don't worry about naming the step at this point as we are just demonstrating the `Steps` collection:

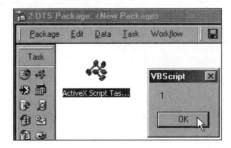

As we were expecting, the message box is displaying the number 1.

Now, add another ActiveX Script task, with nothing in it, and save it in the package. Run the first package, and this time, as you might expect, the number 2 is displayed, demonstrating that the package has 2 steps included:

It is also possible to add tasks during run time. You could do this based on a set of criteria, like when a particular condition is met. This is an unusual scenario, and you probably wouldn't want to do this too often. One thing about DTS packages is that as a developer, you will know in the main what is happening with your developed solution. However, it is important to know how to add a task – which is why we'll look at it here.

> If you add a task programmatically, be warned that it is not displayed in your DTS package designer until you complete an explicit refresh (if you are using a Beta version, you have to leave SQL Server and then return for it to display).

Adding Tasks and Steps at Run Time

In this next example, we're going to expand our knowledge of the DTS Object model into the arena of `Task` and `Step` objects. We'll add a Send Mail task at run time, and demonstrate how you would then access the properties and methods of that task. In essence, the next example can be easily modified to be a custom task, an Execute SQL task, a Data Pump task, or a Transfer Objects task.

The following example is a bit more complex than the previous one, but we'll go through it step by step. We'll discuss and explain the object model, and refer back to the object model diagram we saw earlier in the chapter to help you understand what's going on.

Earlier in the chapter, we added a second, but empty, ActiveX script task. Open up this task and place the following code into it.

First of all, define the function we're creating, and the variables that will be used within the example. The first variable is the `oPackage` variable. As in the previous example, this will hold a reference to the package we're currently in. This is the root level of the package object model:

```
'********************************************************************
'  Visual Basic ActiveX Script
'********************************************************************

Function Main()

    ' Define a variable to hold this package's details
    Dim oPackage
```

The aim of this example is to send a mail to a recipient each time this step is run. We will ignore any possibility of other tasks within the package, and assume that this task is the only task within the package.

If you look back at the object model diagram, you will notice that there is a "level" of functionality between the `Tasks` object level and the `SendMail` object level. This is the `CustomTask` object level. Therefore, to get to the `SendMail` task level, we need to access this through the `CustomTask` object level. The following variable will hold that anchor point:

```
    Dim oMailTask
```

The next variable actually holds the `SendMail` task object, and will allow access to all the methods and properties within a `SendMail` object:

```
    Dim oMail
```

Remember, to find a full list of properties and methods for this or any other object, refer to Appendix A at the end of this book.

Finally, a variable is required to hold the Step that is being created within the package, which we will execute:

```
    Dim oStep
```

> **Don't get confused between tasks and steps. A task is defining the actual unit of work to be performed at a defined stage within a package. A step is associated with a task and is defined to execute a task that has been created. A task cannot execute without a step. So when using the DTS Object Model, when you create a `Task`, you must also create a `Step`.**

As in the previous example, we retrieve an anchor on the DTS package we are developing within. From this anchor, we can ensure that we're working with the right package:

```
    ' Now place this active package in to that variable
    Set oPackage = DTSGlobalVariables.Parent
```

To ensure that we have only the two ActiveX Script tasks in the package at this time – and unlike David Copperfield, there is nothing up my sleeve – we'll display the number of tasks there are within this package:

```
' Display the number of tasks in the package
MsgBox oPackage.Tasks.Count
```

Of course, this will display a message box as before, informing us that there are only two steps. Again this is making good use of the object model, as we are using a property from the `Tasks` object level.

Now that we've confirmed that there are only two tasks, the example moves on to the next stage of processing. The next section of code is a very clear demonstration of how to use the `Tasks` and `Steps` collections, and inspect each task or step one at a time. Note that there is a variable defined as `oTask`. However, you will not find this variable, which will hold each task found within the `Tasks` collection, and is set by the `For Each` command. This demonstrates that in VBScript, there is no real need to define variables. However, it can be seen as bad programming practice, so you should really define this variable before using it:

```
' ensure that the task being added below,
' doesnt already exist from a previous run
For Each oTask in oPackage.Tasks
    If oTask.Name = "DTSSendMail_Added_At_Runtime" Then
        oPackage.Tasks.Remove ("DTSSendMail_Added_At_Runtime")
    End If
Next
```

You notice that there is a `For Each...Next` loop, which you might not have seen before. This is similar to the `For...Next` loop we saw in the previous chapter. For example, we could say:

```
For iLoop = 3 to 10
```

This means that the loop is keeping a count of the number of times that it has been performed, in a variable called, iLoop and it will loop from the number 3 to the number 10, in other words, 8 times. Simple and straightforward, exactly what every developer loves. A `For Each` loop is quite similar. However, it doesn't know how many times it has to perform. It is looping around a collection of objects, from the first object in the collection to the last, rather than just looping around adding a count to a variable.

So, in the first section of code, we're looping round each `Task` within the `Tasks` collection of the package:

```
' ensure that the task being added below,
' doesnt already exist from a previous run
For Each oTask in oPackage.Tasks
```

There are at this point only 2 tasks – the message box above told us so. It could easily have been 10, or even 1 task – it really doesn't matter. However, for each task we do find, the section of code between the `For` statement and the `Next` statement will be executed. If you think back to the object model, the `Tasks` collection is directly beneath the `Package` level.

Now that we are finding each task in turn, we need to check to see what tasks have been defined. Later on in the example, we'll add a task called `DTSSendMail_Added_At_Runtime`.

> **If you ever create a package that contains a task that programmatically creates a new step within the package, it will not be visible within the package design. Therefore it is important to place a label within the package, informing any other developers that there is a task which does this.**

If the task `DTSSendMail_Added_At_Runtime` is found, then we want to remove it, as it should only exist from our addition within this ActiveX Script task:

```
If oTask.Name = "DTSSendMail_Added_At_Runtime" Then
    oPackage.Tasks.Remove ("DTSSendMail_Added_At_Runtime")
```

This brings us nicely on to using methods of objects within the object model. Each object has a set of properties and methods associated with it, and maybe sometimes an event. Think back to the example at the start of the chapter, where we described what all of these are. In the line of code above, you will see that the program has navigated from the `Package` level, down to the `Task` level (which is a collection of the tasks), and from there, the program calls a method to remove the task from the package. The `Remove` method has a required parameter, which is the identifier of which task to remove. In this case we are using the objects name – straightforward and simple.

The next two lines of code just close off the `If` statement, and the `For` statement:

```
    End If
Next
```

Just as we did with the `Task`, we must do the same with the step that will be added in a few moments. The logic is exactly the same, but in this instance, we're removing the step.

```
' ensure that the step being added below,
' doesnt already exist from a previous run
For Each oStep in oPackage.Steps
    If oStep.Name =  "AutoMailSend" Then
        oPackage.Steps.Remove ( "AutoMailSend")
    End If
Next
```

This code also proves a very important point with the DTS and all other object models. Different objects will share similar, if not exactly the same, methods, properties, and events, and will behave in a similar or the same fashion. To give an example, Steps and Tasks both have the `Remove` method, and both work in exactly the same fashion, in that they remove a specific Step or Task from their respective collections. The only difference in our first and second `For` loops is that we are using a `Step`. Two totally different objects, completing a totally different unit of work, but both have a collection, both have a `Remove` method, and both have a `Name` property. Of course, there are other items the same, which can be seen in Appendix A at the end of this book.

Now that the program is certain that the tasks we will be adding are not within the package, it is possible to start the process of inserting them.

First of all, you must create a new step to place the task into. A step is a generic item that any task can be placed into. Also, don't forget that a step has to be associated with a task to get that task to execute. Therefore, it is best for the step to be created first. It isn't essential, but it is easier to code this way as we know that a step has been created.

The New method of the Steps collection doesn't require any parameters. Keep this in mind for the next few seconds until when we discuss the next section of code. The New method doesn't actually add the Step to the package – it's just preparing the step for the addition to the package. This occurs later in the code. This line of code is actually performing quite a powerful instruction. What has happened is that the oStep variable is now instantiated with an object. After this line of code, you can access any property or method of the object via the oStep variable. This is also adding a new Step object to the Steps collection of objects. Now enter the next section of code and let's move on:

```
' You must NEW and then Add the step and task
Set oStep = oPackage.Steps.New
```

The next piece of code is creating the task we want to use. In this case, we want to create a Send Mail task:

```
Set oMailTask = oPackage.Tasks.New ("DTSSendMailTask")
```

As you can see, this time a parameter is required for the New method. This is where you have to be careful when using object models. Although you'll see in Appendix A that these two collections each have a New method, you just have to check if any extra information is required to use them. Familiarity can breed contempt, and so just take that extra moment to ensure that you're not missing anything.

Notice that the task type is a literal within quotes. This is how you must define the different tasks to add. It could easily have been any one of the remaining tasks, for example, "DTSExecutePackageTask" or perhaps "DTSDataPumpTask".

The ActiveX Script task now has the new task and step. A reference to these has been placed in their respective variables. These variables, unlike other variables that you will be used to, will actually hold the respective object. If this is the first time you have put an object into a variable, it may seem a bit hard to picture. These variables are in fact holding several pieces of information in one place, as you will see as we continue through this example. The easiest way to think of this is that the variable is a container and a fast way to reference the object created.

The task level object exposes very little as it is the generic container for all tasks. A requirement though, is that the task must be given a name. The logic behind this is as you have seen above – this provides a method of identifying a task for such times as you need it, like the removal of the task:

```
' You must set at least a name
oMailTask.Name = "DTSSendMail_Added_At_Runtime"
```

Now that the generic task details have been set, again by checking the object model, you will see that the SendMailTask is, in fact, at the next level down. Therefore, we set another variable to this level. It is not mandatory to complete this step. However, you will see in a few moments how this reduces the amount of typing on each line. In the mean time, set the oMail variable to the CustomTask level:

```
' Get to the SendMail level
Set oMail = oMailTask.CustomTask
```

Let's just take a moment to prove that there is in fact, a new step created:

```
' Display the NEW number of tasks in the package
MsgBox oPackage.Tasks.Count
```

You will recall that earlier the Tasks count was displayed in a message box as 2. When you run this script, in a few moments after all the code is entered, you will now see the number 3 be displayed. There has been no outside interference in the package except through this script, so this line is proof that you have achieved your goal of adding a new task at run time. Of course, you could alter this or duplicate these message box lines of code to demonstrate the number of steps.

> **MsgBox** statements are very dangerous lines of code within DTS. They are great for debugging; however, if they ever make it to production, it is usually the case that the SQL Server is on a remote server, and so no-one may see the message and reply to it, thus causing the package to hang and not complete. Double check your package before going live for any interactive statements, such as **MsgBox**.

It is now time to complete the details of the mail you wish to send. To keep things very simple, global variables have not been used, but it would be easy to use the Package object variable, oPackage, to get to the GlobalVariables to set up the necessary details.

```
' complete the email details
oMail.MessageText = "This is a test mail from a runtime send mail task"
oMail.ToLine = "testing@stable_computers.co.uk"
oMail.Subject = "Test Mail"
```

Of course, do change the ToLine otherwise I will be inundated with hundreds of mails – thanks!

As we said a few moments ago, the oMail variable holds the CustomTask object. It would have been just as simple not to have set this variable, and instead of you seeing oMail, you would have seen oMailTask.CustomTask as the prefix. A great deal more typing!

At this juncture, we have added a new step, and a new task, but there has been nothing linking the two together. If this was a complex example, and several tasks and several steps were added at run time, then you would need some method of joining the two. The next line of code does just that. By informing the step of the associated Task Name, not forgetting that the name of each task must be unique, a direct one-to-one reference can be created:

```
' Complete the details on the step
oStep.TaskName = oMail.Name
```

Let's now give the step its own name. We've placed this here to demonstrate that it doesn't matter where you name the object, as long as it is named before we make the final code that makes the physical addition to the package:

```
oStep.Name = "AutoMailSend"
```

We are now complete, and ready to physically add the step and the task to the package. We have to add the actual step and task objects, and this is done by passing in as parameters the variables holding the respective objects:

```
' Add the step and the task to the package
oPackage.Steps.Add oStep
oPackage.Tasks.Add oMailTask
```

For some readers, the next line of code may have to be entered, for those that have to log on to an Exchange Server for example. For others, like those who have Microsoft Outlook used on a dial up account, then the following line should be ignored. Exchange needs to know what Exchange profile has to be used when sending the mail message.

```
oMail.Profile "Microsoft Outlook"
```

If you don't know what your MAPI profile is, a simple solution is to hand. Shortly, you will create through Visual Basic a new package, which will have a Send Mail task within it. Once you have run this, or if you know how to create a Send Mail task already, and once you have added this task to a package, you can get to the properties of the task, and you will see that one of the properties, is the "Profile". Just copy what has been entered there into your code. Nothing could be simpler.

Now that the task and step are added and you have set up the profile, if required, it is possible to execute the step, which will run the SendMailTask. If you have Outlook, start it up, and you will see the mail in your Outbox. Notice how the code uses the name of the step to find which step to execute. This could just as easily be any other step within the package:

```
' Execute the step
oPackage.Steps("AutoMailSend").Execute
```

Now that the step has executed, we must tidy up behind ourselves and remove the task and step:

```
' Remove the task and step from the package
oPackage.Tasks.Remove ("DTSSendMail_Added_At_Runtime")
oPackage.Steps.Remove ("AutoMailSend")
```

Then send back to the package that this task has run successfully:

```
' Send back a success results
Main = DTSTaskExecResult_Success

End Function
```

> If you ever do find the need to create a step or task at run time, then it is important to create a label within your package denoting that fact. Otherwise, other developers may miss the step or task if you leave it in. You should also remove all programmatically created steps and packages at the end of your task.

This example has shown you how to look at the DTS Object Model, traverse through its structure, and implement a solution creating code that uses the object model correctly. We have also successfully built a solution that has created objects at the correct level of the object model, and then found the exposed methods and properties and used them in the correct manner and at the correct time. Now that we can create objects inside an existing package, what if we actually wanted to use the object model to create a new package at run time from within an existing package?

Creating Packages at Run Time

It's quite simple to create a new package at run time. From this new package, new steps and tasks can be created. Therefore, one package can create and control a second. The following section demonstrates how simple it is to create this package and work with it. This example takes the previous example, so that you can see the differences between running within an existing package and using a new package. The section subsequent to this will then take this current example and demonstrate how to achieve this in Visual Basic. These three sections will clearly demonstrate the object model being used in three different ways.

First of all create an empty package and give this a name of "Chapter8-Example2". Add in two ActiveX Script tasks: one will be used to place our code into, and the other just to give the package we are running in two tasks (to distinguish it from the package we're creating, which will have just one task – that way we can prove that we are in fact using a new package).

Let's dive straight in to the code. This example has a new variable called oNewPackage. This will hold the package that we are creating. The original oPackage will still be used just to prove the difference between the two packages, which will be used within MsgBox functions to prove that there are two separate packages:

```
'*********************************************************************
'   Visual Basic ActiveX Script
'*********************************************************************

Function Main()

    ' Define a variable to hold this package's details
    Dim oPackage
    Dim oNewPackage
    Dim oMailTask
    Dim oMail
    Dim oStep
    Set oPackage = DTSGlobalVariables.Parent
```

The next line of code is new to you from the last example. Using the CreateObject function creates a DTS package and assigns it to the variable. It's as simple as that. This means that the oNewPackage variable will have the full DTS Object Model available to it, just as the oPackage variable does as well. However, the oNewPackage variable has no other objects within it:

```
    ' Create a new package.
    Set oNewPackage = CreateObject("DTS.Package")
```

Just to prove the point, the script displays the number of tasks within the current package, and then the new package. Of course, the existing package will show the number of tasks, which should be 2, and the new package will display 0 tasks:

```
' Display the number of tasks in the existing package
MsgBox oPackage.Tasks.Count


' Display the number of tasks in the existing package
MsgBox oNewPackage.Tasks.Count
```

As before, we'll be removing the existing tasks and steps. However, this is an empty package, and so there is nothing to remove. Therefore, the `MsgBox` in the `For Each...Next` step will never be displayed – again, proof that the package is empty, and that the object model is still available for your use.

```
' ensure that the task being added below,
' doesnt already exist from a previous run
For Each oTask in oNewPackage.Tasks
    MsgBox "You will never see this"
    If oTask.Name = "DTSSendMail_Added_At_Runtime" Then
        oNewPackage.Tasks.Remove ("DTSSendMail_Added_At_Runtime")
    End If
Next
```

We've removed the `For Each...Next` step for the `Steps` collection. Just as before, we can add `Steps` and `Tasks`, and set up the properties within these ready to be used.

```
' You must NEW and then Add the step and task
Set oStep = oNewPackage.Steps.New
Set oMailTask = oNewPackage.Tasks.New ("DTSSendMailTask")

' You must set at least a name
oMailTask.Name = "DTSSendMail_Added_At_Runtime"

' Get to the SendMail level
Set oMail = oMailTask.CustomTask
```

Although in the code above we have used the New statement, these tasks have not been added to the package at this point: they are still in memory. Therefore the number of `Tasks` and `Steps` are still at 2, and 0, respectively. In a few moments you'll see a difference:

```
' Display the NEW number of steps in the package
MsgBox oPackage.Tasks.Count

' Display the NEW number of steps in the package
MsgBox oNewPackage.Tasks.Count
```

Continue to add the necessary values to the mail properties:

```
' complete the email details
oMail.MessageText = "This is a test mail from a runtime send mail task"
oMail.ToLine = "testing@stable-computers.co.uk"
oMail.Subject = "Test Mail"

' Complete the details on the step
oStep.TaskName = oMail.Name
oStep.Name = "AutoMailSend"
```

It is now time to specifically add the Step and Task to the package. It is at this point that the steps and tasks are available, and you will see the numbers or tasks alter:

```
' Add the step and the task to the package
oNewPackage.Steps.Add oStep
oNewPackage.Tasks.Add oMailTask

' Display the number of tasks in the existing package
MsgBox oNewPackage.Tasks.Count
```

The remainder of the code is the same with the exception, of course, that we are still working with the new package:

```
' Execute the step
oNewPackage.Steps("AutoMailSend").Execute

' Remove the task and step from the package
oNewPackage.Tasks.Remove ("DTSSendMail_Added_At_Runtime")
oNewPackage.Steps.Remove("AutoMailSend")

' Send back a success results
Main = DTSTaskExecResult_Success

End Function
```

Although very similar to the previous example, this does quickly demonstrate that creating a new package is just as easy as using an existing package, and that there is no difference in either method when it comes to checking out the object model. It's time to move on to looking at the Object Model within Visual Basic.

Using the DTS Object Model in Visual Basic

Visual Basic may be familiar to you, but a large number of you have probably only developed stored procedures before, probably within SQL Server. However, although teaching you Visual Basic itself is outside the scope of this book, it's important to know how to use the DTS Object Model from within Visual Basic. The following section will demonstrate how our Send Mail task example, from the *Adding Tasks and Steps at Run Time* section earlier, would look within **Visual Basic**.

The knowledge gained from this previous example, and your work so far with VBScript, will help you enormously in knowing what is happening within Visual Basic. The following section assumes that you have Visual Basic Version 6.0, with, at least, Service Pack 3 installed.

Before we go any further, there are a few points to make clear. What the following example is about to do, you probably will not do in a real scenario. This example is going to programmatically create a DTS package, and add tasks and steps at run time. It will be very rare that you will actually create a package within a Visual Basic project. However, as we'll see in later chapters, you may well use Visual Basic to create steps and tasks in a much more advanced way than we're presenting here. Keep in mind that the sole purpose of the following example is to demonstrate how to get to the DTS Object Model within Visual Basic.

Creating a Visual Basic Project

First of all, start up Visual Basic, which can be found at Start I Programs I Microsoft Visual Studio 6.0 I Microsoft Visual Basic 6.0. The first screen you will be presented with is the New Project window. This window allows you to select the type of project, from a number of different types. Select Standard Exe, and click Open:

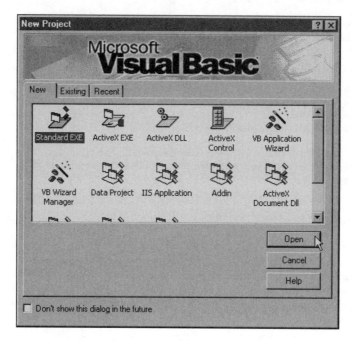

You've now created your first project in Visual Basic! There is nothing within the project, so it is totally pointless in its existence, but it is complete. Just to ensure that you are at the right place, you should now be at the screen opposite. This is the empty project and clean form.

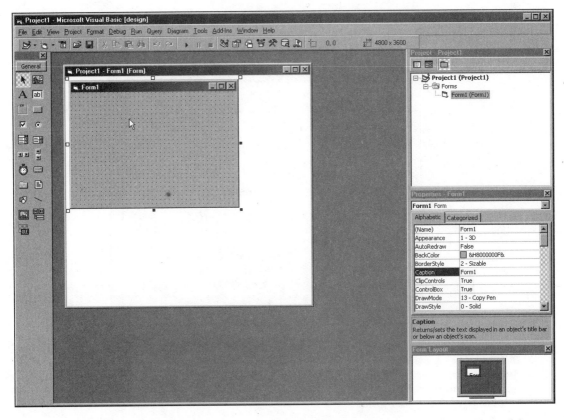

You can name the project and the form by populating the (Name) properties on the project and form, and you can also give the form a proper title by populating the caption. I have quite deliberately not done this as you will probably only copy this code into your own example.

So that you have some control of when you want to actually run the example, the form will have a command button placed on it. The following graphic shows the form with the button, and the mouse is highlighting where within the project you need to click to get the command button. Double click on the button and you will find the button automatically placed on the form for you:

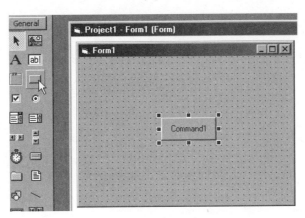

Now, from the Project menu item, select and click on the References menu option. You will be confronted with an extremely long list of items, but there is only one item in this list that we need to concern ourselves with at this point. This is the Microsoft DTSPackage Object Library:

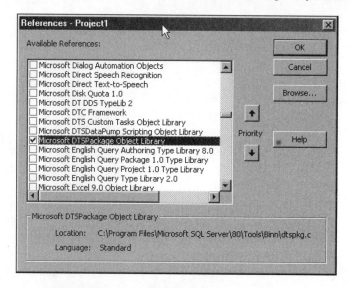

By checking this, you are informing your Visual Basic Project that you wish to include the DTS Object Model, and that you will be creating a program solution that will include the DTS Object Model within it. By making this selection, the whole DTS Object Model is available to use, just as if you were in DTS itself, using perhaps the ActiveX Script task. So, select the DTS Object Model, and click OK. This will then bring you back to your form.

Let's move on now and create some code. In the main, it's the same as our earlier example. However there are one or two differences: partly since the development languages are different, but also because of the whole solution that Visual Basic enforces.

Coding the Visual Basic Project

To start entering the code, double-click on the button on the form. This will take you into the coding window, which will initially look as follows:

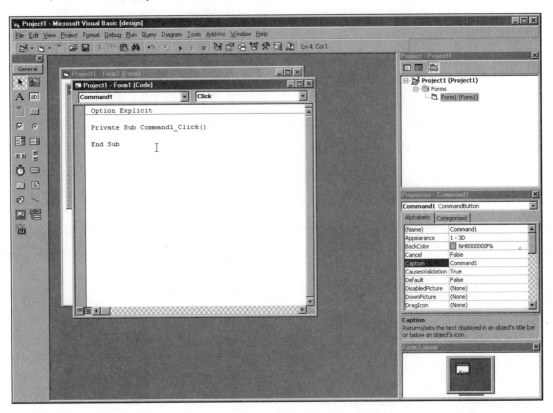

You will instantly see that there is not a great deal there. This is great news, as there is nothing that I need to explain ahead of time. The very first line of code is informing Visual Basic that all variables have to be defined, and that you can't use a variable without creating it first.

This line of code may be there when you first start up Visual Basic and enter the code window. However, if it is not, it is very simple to create rather than type in. This is an option defined for Visual Basic, along with other options. If you look at the tab overleaf, found under Tools | Options, you will see the Require Variable Declaration (second option from the top in the left-hand column). This is the option that instructs Visual Basic to place the Option Explicit line of code into the code window. At this point, I would also recommend that you set up your Visual Basic environment as you can see in the screenshot. Without going in to a great deal of depth, we will shortly be demonstrating the Auto List Members option when defining our variables. We won't cover any other options. If you are using Visual Basic more than the examples in this book, and you don't know Visual Basic already, then these options are covered in *Beginning SQL Server 2000 for VB Developers* (published by Wrox Press; *ISBN 1-861004-67-2*).

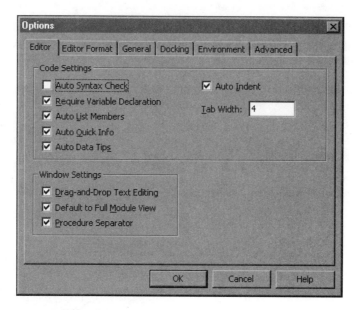

So leave this line in, or enter this line if it doesn't exist (it is placed automatically if you have the Visual Basic **Require Variable Declaration** option switched on).

```
Option Explicit
```

The next lines of code create the variables we will be using within the program. The first thing to note is our second difference between VBScript and Visual Basic, which is that we inform Visual Basic what we are expecting the variable to be. As a developer, this is a great asset, as you can tell instantly what you are expecting from that variable, and what you want it to do:

```
' Define our variables first of all
Dim oDTS As DTS.Package
Dim oStep As DTS.Step
Dim oMail As DTS.SendMailTask
Dim oTaskobj As DTS.Task
Dim oMailTask As DTS.Task
```

This code is placed outside of any subroutine or function. Without getting in to too much detail, by placing this here, the variable is then available for use anywhere within the form, which if you expand on this example, will be what you may require.

Before moving on to the remainder of the code, if you have entered the above code already, and your Visual Basic installation has the **Auto List Members** option switched on, you will have found Visual Basic giving you a list of potential options at several steps of the way. What happens is that Visual Basic uses its in-built functionality to list every possible option to you as a developer, to try to save confusion and time. The following screenshot demonstrates the creation of our all our variables. Take a close look at our final variable, oMailTask. As soon as the period is placed into the code window, next to the DTS object, the list of options of possible members appears. You can either scroll through these or reach the object called **Task** by pressing *T*:

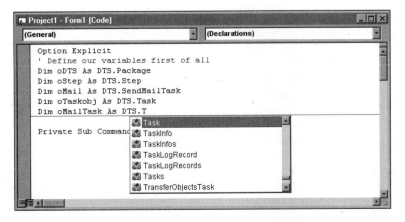

This is yet another bonus of using Visual Basic. There are times when it is worthwhile creating packages, or parts of packages within Visual Basic first, to use these utilities and extra features, to ensure that your scripting code is cleaner and consistent.

Moving on now to the actual code that creates the example, we have placed this within our command button Click event. This fires when, as you would expect, the command button on the form is clicked on during run time.

```
Private Sub Command1_Click()
```

In this instance, we have to create a package to place our tasks and steps in. The VBScript example was already in a package, and the requirement was only to get a reference to the package. This is a major difference between the two:

```
' This creates our package. This differs from our VBScript example
Set oDTS = New DTS.Package
```

This time, we want to look at the DTS topmost level of the object model, which is the package itself. Don't be surprised when you see that, just like all the other objects, it too has similar properties and methods. We will be saving this package into SQL Server at the end, and so we want to give it a name:

```
' Give the package a name that we want to see in SQL Server
oDTS.Name = "Chapter8-From-Visual-Basic"
```

To prove that this is a new package, with no objects in it, the number of Tasks within the package is displayed. Of course, this will show 0:

```
' Just to prove that there are no tasks
MsgBox oDTS.Tasks.Count
```

What follows is almost straight from the VBScript example, where we would be tidying up the existing package that we were working with. However, as we have just seen, there is nothing to tidy up, and so the MsgBox within this section – as long as you placed this somewhere within the For...Next loop – will never be displayed:

317

```
' The following section is left in to demonstrate that in fact
' there is nothing to remove
For Each oTaskobj In oDTS.Tasks
    If oTaskobj.Name = "DTSSendMail_Added_At_Runtime" Then
        MsgBox "Can never be displayed"
        oDTS.Tasks.Remove "DTSSendMail_Added_At_Runtime"
    End If
Next
```

The next section of code is exactly the same logically as the VBScript example:

```
' Create the step
Set oStep = oDTS.Steps.New

' Create the send mail task
Set oMailTask = oDTS.Tasks.New("DTSSendMailTask")

oMailTask.Name = "DTSSendMail_Added_At_Runtime"

Set oMail = oMailTask.CustomTask
```

Again to prove that the task is still not physically within the package, the code displays the number of tasks that there are. When you come to run this code, you will find that 0 is still displayed. We then move on as before to populate the necessary values of the SendMailTask object:

```
' This differs from before. This time, this displays 0
MsgBox oDTS.Tasks.Count

' complete the email details
oMail.MessageText = "This is a test mail from a runtime send mail task"
oMail.ToLine = "testing@stable-computers.co.uk"
oMail.Subject = "Test Mail"

' Complete the details on the step
oStep.TaskName = oMail.Name
oStep.Name = "AutoMailSend"
```

Once the Add method has been executed, you will find that the Step and Task objects are finally found and inserted into the package, and that the Task Count increases:

```
' Add the step and tasks
oDTS.Steps.Add oStep
oDTS.Tasks.Add oMailTask

' This will now show 1. It is not until the add that it is
' in the package
MsgBox oDTS.Tasks.Count
```

Now of course, send the mail, and after a few seconds (depending on your computer and network) you will see the mail appear either in your Outbox, or your Sent Items folder within Outlook:

```
' Send the mail
oDTS.Steps("AutoMailSend").Execute
End Sub
```

The last line of code in the above example, `oDTS.Steps`, demonstrates how to find an item within a collection, in this case the `Steps` collection, by name, rather than the specific index position. This method saves having to loop around every single item within the `Steps` collection to find the item we wish.

Now that the code has been completely entered, then we need to run this to see the following output. This is simple to do, and pressing *F5* will execute the form:

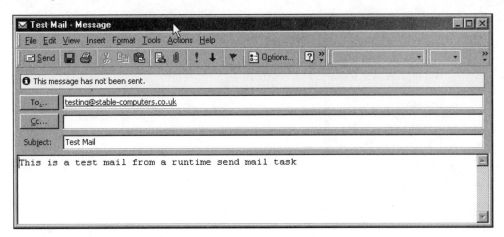

Saving the Package to SQL Server

Now that we're done, let's save the package to SQL Server DTS. Then, in a few moments, we will move into SQL Server to view what has been saved.

With the DTS package, the DTS Object Model allows different methods and places to save the package to. You can save to a file, to the repository, or in our case, directly into SQL Server: providing of course, you know the necessary IDs and passwords.

My SQL Server is running locally on my own notebook, where I have an sa user ID with no password. Once again, by checking Appendix A you will not only see the DTS options, but also the required and optional parameters for this method. It's as simple as this to save the package:

```
' Time to save the package
oDTS.SaveToSQLServer "(local)", "sa", "", DTSSQLStgFlag_Default
```

The next section of code will be new to you. Visual Basic is storing these objects in memory, therefore memory is being used. Just to tidy up and retrieve that memory, we set the variables to `Nothing`:

```
' Now tidy up
Set oTaskobj = Nothing
Set oMail = Nothing
Set oMailTask = Nothing
Set oStep = Nothing
Set oDTS = Nothing
End Sub
```

You can close the form now, by clicking on the **X** in the top right-hand corner. Once you've done this, switch into SQL Server, as you would probably like to check out what Visual Basic has in fact saved.

If SQL Server Enterprise Manager was running during the previous example, and you were in **Data Transformation Services**, then when you switch to SQL Server, nothing will have changed – the same packages will still be displayed. Click on the **Refresh** button, which the mouse is pointing to in the following screenshot and, as if by magic, the package created in the previous example appears:

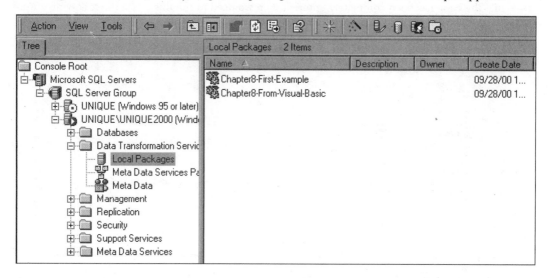

As you can see, the second package down is the package created in Visual Basic. Double-click on it to see what it contains. There is a very large and over the top icon right in the middle of the screen, showing the **SendMailTask**, just as we were expecting:

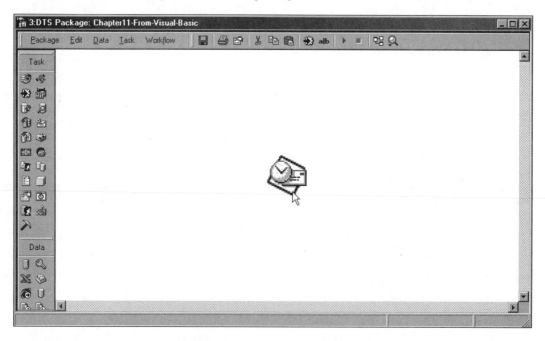

Double-clicking on the icon takes you into the Send Mail task, and as expected, the required parameters have been set out as they were populated within the Visual Basic example:

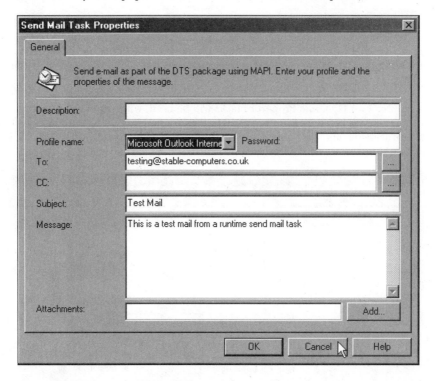

Creating and saving packages within Visual Basic, Visual Basic for Applications, or any other development tool really should be completed with great care, and avoided when possible. There are too many dangerous scenarios and situations that can occur with this process where the SQL Server DBA is not in control of the SQL Server itself. It also could expose your company to security issues. Many organizations forbid saving packages for these reasons.

Very quickly you can see that using the DTS Object Model is just as easy in Visual Basic as it is in anything else. There are no specific object model sections of code that require to be implemented in Visual Basic to make it work. It's time now to leave the Object Model behind and move on to altering properties dynamically within a package.

Using the Dynamic Properties Task

We have seen above how to develop packages by creating new tasks and steps with the DTS Object Model and the ActiveX Script task. However, don't forget that an ActiveX Script Task is not the fastest of tasks within DTS: in fact, it's one of the slowest. By using the ActiveX Script Task to alter a step's Global Variable value, or to disable a step because there has been decision made within the package to do so, is a bit like taking a sledgehammer to crack a nut. So is there another solution? Luckily there is.

Microsoft has supplied a fast and custom-built task to use in such scenarios, and the following section will demonstrate how you can configure steps and packages at run time quite easily using the **Dynamic Properties task**.

The following example will create a simple package that can be easily adapted and placed into a package of your own. The basis will be to run a simple SQL query against a table in the Northwind database. At the end, an e-mail will be sent detailing the number of records found, or that a failure has occurred.

We'll use the Dynamic Properties task to alter the mail properties depending on whether the SQL is a success or a failure. Two Dynamic Properties tasks will be used, where one task marks the other task as complete. Properties will be altered in the Send Mail task depending on which route the Execute SQL task sends the processing, and the values for these properties come from Global Variables. The following screenshot demonstrates exactly what we are trying to achieve:

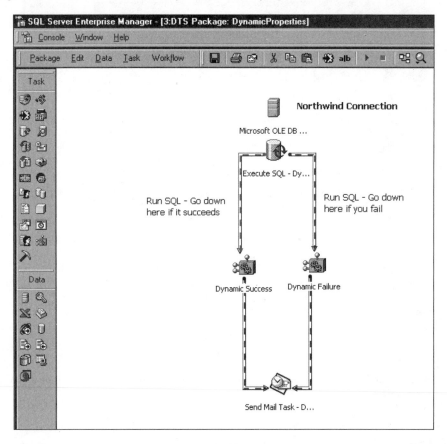

It's time to build this package, and demonstrate how to use the Dynamic Properties task to alter properties at run time.

Building the Package

Create a new an empty package in SQL Server. Once a new and empty package window is displayed, select from the Connection menu Microsoft OLE DB Provider For SQL Server. Select the server you are on, and ensure that it points to Northwind (although you can alter this to any database, as the SQL we will be running is very simple – if you feel more comfortable using another, then do so):

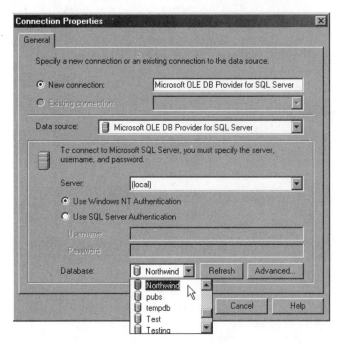

The first task that this example requires is a task to run some SQL against the Northwind database. From the Task menu, select the Execute SQL Task option, which will then open up the properties window for the task. Alter the description to something meaningful, like Execute SQL - Dynamic Properties. Then, in the SQL statement box, enter the following SQL:

```
Select COUNT(*) From Employees
```

Then parse the query by pressing the Parse Query button as shown by the cursor position in the screenshot overleaf, to make sure you haven't made any errors. Click OK once you have a successful parse, and then click OK on the Execute SQL Task Properties form:

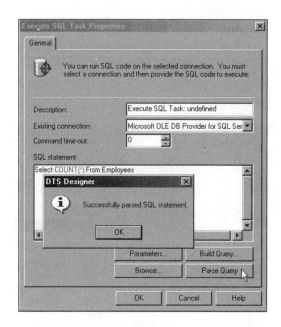

Before we move on to the Dynamic Properties task, it would be appropriate to create the Send Mail task first. The sole purpose of this task is to send an e-mail informing the recipient if the task was a success or a failure. You could just as easy have two Send Mail tasks, one for a success and one for a failure. However, with a large and complex package, that would mean having to search and alter several e-mails properties.

Select from the Task menu the Send Mail Task, which will bring up the properties dialog form. Complete the Description property with Send Mail Task: Dynamic Properties. You must provide the To property with a valid e-mail address. It doesn't matter what that address is, as the Dynamic Properties will change this to a valid address depending on what happens. I entered a@b.com which is totally fictitious; or perhaps you can enter your own e-mail address for testing. It really doesn't matter what the contents are, as the example does alter this in all scenarios. Once these are complete, click OK, which will add this task to the package:

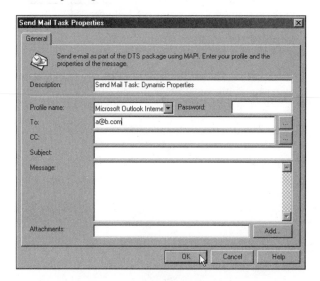

The final action before adding our Dynamic Properties task configurations is to create the Global Variables we will be using. These Global Variables will be used by the Dynamic tasks to alter what is placed within the e-mail. One of the properties comes from the SQL Statement created earlier in the Execute SQL task. So first of all, move back to the Execute SQL Task, right mouse click on it, and select **Properties**. This will then bring you back to the screen from before, where you entered the SQL Statements. You will notice a button called **Parameters**. Click on this, which brings up the **Parameter Mapping** dialog.

This form allows input parameters to be set, or output parameters to be returned. What we wish to achieve is, within the mail, to return the number of records found from the query. Perhaps in your package, you wish to return a column from a number of fields. This is where to do it. Click on the button named **Create Global Variables...** and enter the variable name as **NoOfRecords**, with a type of Int and initialized to 0:

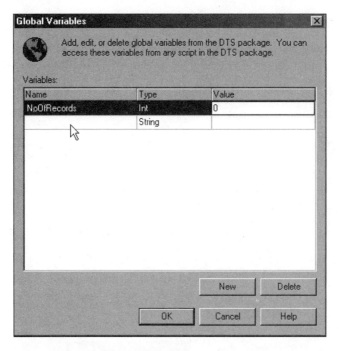

Once done, click on **OK** and the Global Variable will be created. Now you must set this new Global Variable as an **Output Parameter**. By clicking on the right-hand side of the Parameter Mapping area, you will be given the list of Global Variables created so far. In this case, there is only the one Global Variable, which is the one we have just defined:

The final set of Global Variables will be the variables used in creating the mail recipient, and the message header in the Send Mail task.

Click **OK** twice to get back to the main package screen. Ensure that no tasks are highlighted in the package and then from the **Package** menu select **Properties**. Choose the **Global Variables** tab. You will see from the screenshot below that the package requires four other Global Variables, so go ahead and create these now:

Finally, we are now ready to build the Dynamic Properties tasks. Add the first Dynamic Properties task, selecting this from the **Tasks** menu. Give this a **Description** of **Dynamic Success**. Then click the **Add** button at the base of this form. You will then find yourself in the dialog used for setting Dynamic Properties when this task takes its turn in running.

When building up your package, you would place this task in a position within the whole process where you wish to set specific properties. In our instance, this actual task will run when the SQL query runs successfully. Keep in mind that we will use an On Success workflow command; this step will set up the mail for a successful run.

The Dynamic Properties task allows the alteration of any package included properties, whether these are Global Variables, package settings (for example Logging details), or Step and Task level settings. So as you can see, this is a very powerful task. In the following screen we have expanded the Tasks level as we want to alter settings of the SendMail task, which you can see highlighted.

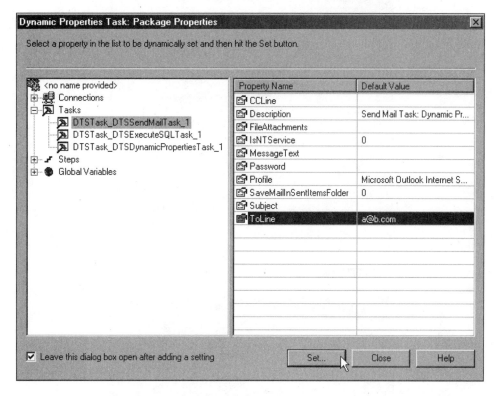

The properties of the Send Mail task that should be altered, are ToLine, Subject, and MessageText. You'll notice a check box in the bottom left hand corner labelled Leave this dialog box open after adding a setting. Check this, as we wish to alter more than one property – this reduces the amount of clicking and moving around in this whole task, as it closes this dialog after each setting otherwise.

Once you have selected the property you wish to alter, click on the Set... button. This is where you can Add/Edit Assignments. In this case we will want to set the ToLine to the ToSuccess Global Variable.

The Source can be from a number of sources from an INI File, through to a Constant. This time, select Global Variable:

This alters how the dialog appears, and you'll now only see a combobox with a list of all the Global Variables that have been created. You can of course create further Global Variables if required.

Select ToSuccess and then click OK:

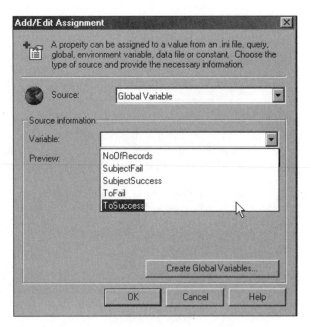

After this, select the Subject property and set this to the SubjectSuccess global variable, and finally, select MessageText and set this to NoOfRecords. Until we create the second Dynamic Task, these are all the properties we can set at the moment. However, we will be coming back to this shortly.

Let's test what we have so far. Select the Execute SQL task, and then while pressing the *Ctrl* button on your keyboard, select the Dynamic Properties task. From the Workflow menu item, select the On Success option. Ensure that the arrow is pointing from the Execute SQL task to the Dynamic Properties task. Then from the Dynamic Properties task to the Send Mail task, select an On Completion workflow, ensuring that the arrow goes from the Dynamic Properties task to the Send Mail task. The package should now look as follows:

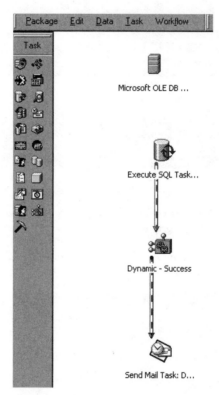

Now execute the package, and you will see either in your Outbox or Sent Items, depending on your current mail status, for example, if you are connected to your mail server at this time, a mail for the success of the SQL:

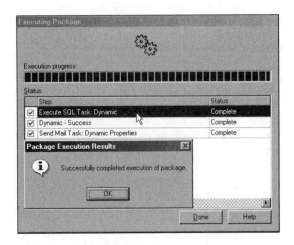

The Outbox will look similar to the following:

Perfect. Now create a second Dynamic Properties task, as we have just done, but this time, set the ToLine property and the Subject property to the Global Variables ToFail and SubjectFail respectively. The MessageText property, however, we will set as a Constant of −1. To set this, instead of selecting Global Variable in the combobox in the Add/Edit Assignment dialog, select instead Constant. Then in the text box below, enter the value −1:

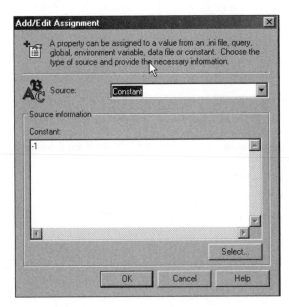

There is another setting we have to make. This is where things get a bit complex. If you think back to the original screenshot of this section, showing the full picture of the solution we are aiming for, you will see that into the Send Mail task, there are two precedences where the two dynamic tasks must complete. You will also notice that from the Execute SQL task, one leg runs if the SQL succeeds, and the other leg runs if the SQL fails. So how does the Send Mail task know that the leg not run has completed?

Simple, one Dynamic Task sets the other Dynamic Task's status as being completed. We've demonstrated below what happens without setting this property. We've set the package up as it looks in the opening screenshot of this section. This is what happens:

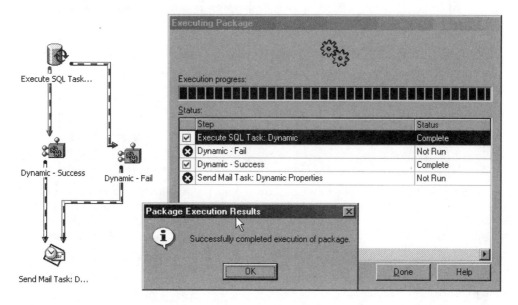

As you can see, the Execute SQL task ran successfully, as did the Dynamic Properties task. However, the Dynamic Properties task for the fail didn't run – which is exactly what we wanted – but unfortunately, neither did the Send Mail task. This is because the Fail Dynamic Property task didn't make it to a Completed status. This is where we have to use one Dynamic Properties package to set the other package as completed. This will then satisfy both precedences for the Send Mail task, and it will then run.

Ensuring that you are still in the Dynamic Task set up for the fail step, choose and expand the Steps tree option and select DTSStep_DTSDynamicPropertiesTask_1. Not the most meaningful of names, but you can ensure that this is the correct step by checking the Description, which should say Dynamic Success. Then select ExecutionStatus and press the Set... button once again:

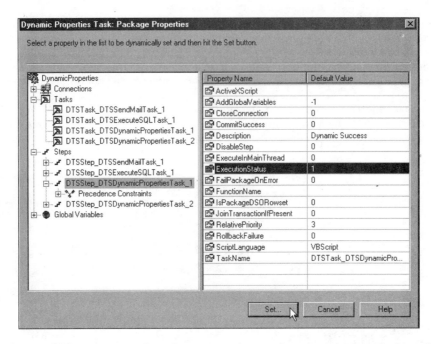

Alter the Source of the property to be a Constant and input the value of 4 into the lower box. This is the constant value for DTSExecStat_Completed. Click OK all the way back until you get to the diagram. Then select the Dynamic Success Dynamic Properties task, right mouse click and choose Properties. Then, as above, go through setting up the property but this time, the step you wish to choose is the step DTSStep_DTSDynamicPropertiesTask_2.

Now that both Dynamic Tasks set each other up as being a Success when they run, the send mail should work. Execute the package:

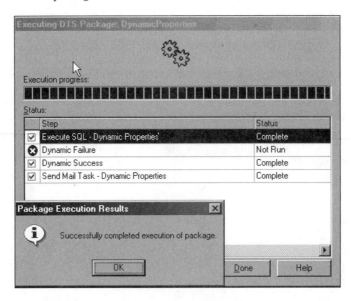

Notice that the Dynamic Failure step did not run. However, by setting the ExecutionStatus of the step, both precedences have now been set which allows the Send Mail task to run.

Although this is just one way of using the Dynamic Property task, this is a powerful and useful tool. This example demonstrates how to dynamically configure packages, steps, and tasks at run time using constants and global variables.

Altering different tasks, or using different sources for properties, is no harder than what we have covered here, and we could almost have a whole book covering each task and demonstrating how you could use the Dynamic Properties task with it – obviously highly impractical and extremely repetitive.

The one drawback of the Dynamic Properties task is that in its simplest form, it isn't the most intelligent or complex of items. There will no doubt be many times that a little bit of further decision making will be required, or a greater degree of flexibility is needed, and this is where you might use an ActiveX Script task.

Summary

This chapter has taken the DTS Object Model and discovered how to take this model, and build solutions, which can create a flexible and decisive DTS process for your SQL Server. Although similar tasks and solutions have been presented, these have been built to avoid clouding the issue of dynamically building and altering the model as each package has moved along.

The chapter started off exploring the object model, and even if you haven't used object models before, by now you should feel much more comfortable in taking the DTS Object Model apart and rebuilding this in a developed solution.

This rebuilding has been demonstrated within a package, within a new package created at run time, and even within a development language such as Visual Basic. Right from the first example, there have been demonstrations of how to dynamically alter DTS objects and properties.

Although we have limited ourselves to a couple of tasks, the requirements of each package are the same, and the methods involved in altering properties and packages are the same throughout. Therefore, by knowing how to use the object model effectively by moving through the hierarchy, and knowing which method to use, either with code or a task, then everything else is the same and straightforward. This chapter should give you the confidence and ability to complete this.

Finally, we have demonstrated how to control the flow of package steps and tasks dynamically at run time. This was completed by having one task set another task as completed, which then ensured that a task which had a precedence constraint placed on it could run and so not hinder the execution of the package as a whole.

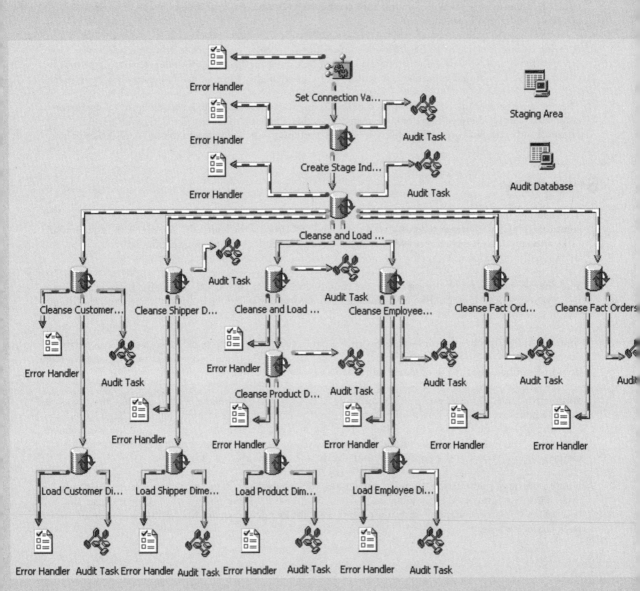

Error Handler

Set Connection Va...

Audit Task

Staging Area

Error Handler

Create Stage Ind...

Audit Task

Error Handler

Audit Database

Error Handler

Cleanse and Load ...

Audit Task

Cleanse Customer...

Cleanse Shipper D...

Cleanse and Load ...

Audit Task

Cleanse Employee...

Cleanse Fact Ord...

Cleanse Fact Orders

Error Handler

Audit Task

Error Handler

Cleanse Product D...

Audit Task

Audit Task

Audit Task

Audit

Error Handler

Error Handler

Error Handler

Error Handler

Error Handler

Load Customer Di...

Load Shipper Dime...

Load Product Dim...

Load Employee Di...

Error Handler Audit Task Error Handler Audit Task Error Handler Audit Task Error Handler Audit Task

Advanced ActiveX Scripting

You look at your design document and gasp at the programming time you're mentally projecting. The design document calls for you to receive a file from the mainframe, whose name changes daily, then move it to a client directory. At that point, you must derive from the filename the client number and the date of the extract. Then, your DTS package must magically know the extract file, and extract it to the client's SQL Server database. Well rest easy, DTS has you covered. All of this can be easily done through the ActiveX Scripting task and some creative package design.

At this point, you should have a basic understanding of DTS programming with VBScript. We've already explored the DTS Object Model. We'll now tie all that we've learned together and put it to more practical use.

In this chapter we will:

- ❏ Expand on the use of global variables
- ❏ Explain how to open a package inside another package using a script
- ❏ Learn how to use the `FileSystemObject` object model
- ❏ Explain a few other object models and how to use them in DTS

We'll start by looking at global variables.

Global Variables

As we discussed earlier, variables declared in the ActiveX Script task are considered **private**. This means that ActiveX Task B can't see a variable that you use in ActiveX Task A. The rule is lifted when you use global variables. Global variables allow you to set a variable that can be used throughout the entire package or passed to other packages.

To set a global variable, go to Properties under the Package menu and go to the Global Variables tab.

Note that if any task is highlighted, this will show the properties of the task, not the package.

Create two variables in a new package as shown below:

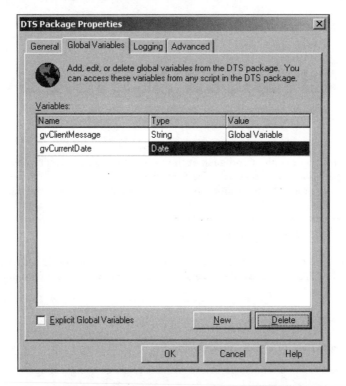

If you click OK with the screen as it is in this shot, you should see the following error:

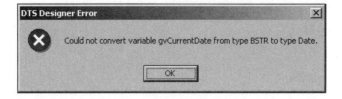

This is because we didn't enter a date value in the appropriate Value box. DTS is trying to convert the null string value to a date, which is invalid. The way around this dilemma is to enter a dummy date as the value of gvCurrentDate. At that point it will accept that value when clicking OK.

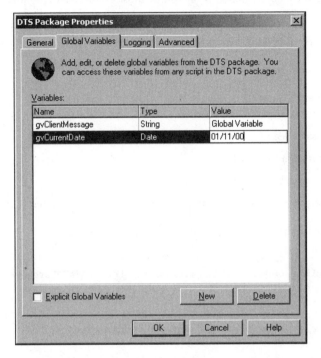

One added value you must watch is Explicit Global Variables. This option, when checked, is the equivalent of Option Explicit in Visual Basic. Checking Explicit Global Variables makes you formally declare every global variable you use. Once we have the global variables set, we can create a sample ActiveX Script Task using VBScript to display and change the global variables:

```
Function Main()
    DTSGlobalVariables("gvCurrentDate").Value = Date
    MsgBox (DTSGlobalVariables("gvClientMessage").Value & "   " & _
            DTSGlobalVariables("gvCurrentDate").Value)
    Main = DTSTaskExecResult_Success
End Function
```

This script demonstrates how to set and call a global variable with the Value property. Even though our original date was 1/11/00 for global variable gvCurrentDate, it will be overwritten here by today's date. Try executing the script, and you should see the two global variables concatenated:

Now that we've completed a simple example, let's get a little more complex.

The FileSystemObject Object

The `FileSystemObject` object model is one of the most useful object models available. Any system where the SQL Server client pieces such as Enterprise Manager are installed will have this object model pre-installed. It is also installed automatically on any servers running IIS and Internet Explorer 4.0. The object model can do the following handy things:

- Copy, move, and rename files
- Delete files
- Create, delete, and rename directories
- Detect the existence of a file
- Read a text stream from a file
- Write a text stream to a file and create a file
- Examine the properties of a file and directory, such as date created

We'll look at how to use the `FileSystemObject` in the next few sections.

> More details of the complete **`FileSystemObject`** Object Model are given in Appendix E.

We can create the `FileSystemObject` using the following syntax:

```
Dim objFSO
Set objFSO = CreateObject("Scripting.FileSystemObject")
```

We can also add an extra layer of error handling. This code will trap a problem with the creation of the object and you can add your own condition in place of the `MsgBox`. In the code below, we detect if the object had trouble creating with the `Nothing` keyword. The `Nothing` keyword is used to disassociate a variable from the object. If the object has not been created, then we exit the function and present a message to the user. This type of error handling is not required but is a nice touch. (Remember that these are just fragments of code, which will not run as they are.)

```
Dim objFSO
Set objFSO = CreateObject("Scripting.FileSystemObject")
If (objFSO Is Nothing) Then
    'Filesystemobject had problems opening
    MsgBox "The FileSystemObject could not be created."
    Main = DTSTaskExecResult_Failure
    Exit function
End If
```

> Before we begin these examples, create a directory on your C drive called **`FSOExamples`**.

Managing Drives

It's not often the case that you have to manage drives in DTS. However, it is nice to be able to detect how large a drive is before you do a large bulk insert, to make sure the drive is capable of the load. We do this because the SQL Server database in 7.0 or 2000 can automatically grow if the option is set, and it's a great way of preventing potential problems. We can also do this before we copy a large file over from a UNC path.

The example below uses the `FileSystemObject` to do half of that task. The script will go out to drive C and detect how much space you have on the drive. It also uses the `VolumeName` property to read the volume label for the drive:

```
Function Main()
    Dim objFSO, objdrive, strmsg, drvPath

    drvPath = "C"
    Set objFSO = CreateObject("Scripting.FileSystemObject")
    Set objdrive = objFSO.GetDrive(drvPath)

    strmsg = "Drive " & drvPath & " "
    strmsg = strmsg & objdrive.VolumeName & " "
    strmsg = strmsg & "Free Space: " & FormatNumber(objdrive.FreeSpace/1024, 0)
    strmsg = strmsg & " Kbytes"

    MsgBox strmsg

    Set objFSO = nothing

    Main = DTSTaskExecResult_Success
End Function
```

When executed, you should hopefully see more impressive results than my C drive below. The `MsgBox` below reports a little more than 2 GB on my C drive:

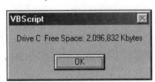

In the above example, we first set the local variable `drvPath` to C after creating the object. We then use the `VolumeName` property to add the volume name for drive C to the concatenated variable `strmsg`:

```
    strmsg = strmsg & objdrive.VolumeName & " "
```

In my case, the drive's volume name is MAIN DRIVE.

The `FreeSpace` property will return the amount of free space on the C drive. It returns this amount in bytes, however. We can use the `FormatNumber` built-in function to a convert the data to a better format with commas for thousands at the same time dividing the free space by 1024 to convert it to kilobytes. The 0 after the `FreeSpace` tells the function how many trailing numbers you'd like after the decimal.

```
    strmsg = strmsg & "Free Space: " & FormatNumber(objdrive.FreeSpace/1024, 0)
```

> **Note: Setting the object to nothing takes the object out of scope and out of memory. It's a good idea when using external objects set to variables to do this type of cleanup work.**

Let's have a little more fun with this example before moving on. To complete the requirement of failing the package if there is not enough hard drive space to transfer a file, we'll need to add some conditional statements to our old code and clean it up slightly. Pay special attention to the `FormatNumber` function. We have added it globally on any numeric field including the global variable. By doing this, every number will be in the same format when we do compare them.

```
Function Main()
  Dim objFSO, objdrive, strmsg, drvPath

  drvPath = "C"

  Set objFSO = CreateObject("Scripting.FileSystemObject")
  Set  objdrive = objFSO.GetDrive(drvPath)

  strmsg =  FormatNumber(objdrive.FreeSpace/1024,0)
  If strmsg < FormatNumber(DTSGlobalVariables("gvMinSpaceRequired").Value,0) Then
    Main = DTSTaskExecResult_Failure
    MsgBox "Not enough disk space to proceed.  Need at least " & _
            FormatNumber(DTSGlobalVariables("gvMinSpaceRequired").Value,0) & "K"
  Else
    Main = DTSTaskExecResult_Success
  End If

  Set objFSO = nothing
End Function
```

We need to also add a global variable called `gvMinSpaceRequired`. Make the value of that global variable a little more in kilobytes than the space your hard drive has available. Since we had about 2 GB on our C drive, we're setting the value to 2,500,000 kilobytes or about 2.3 GB. Also note that since the global variable is numeric, we set the type to `Integer`.

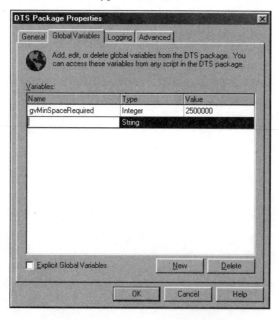

Now, when executing the package, you should see the following output if you met the condition. The task then fails:

You might use this kind of procedure to create a package like the one below. Don't actually create this package at the moment. This is just to show what you can actually do with it.

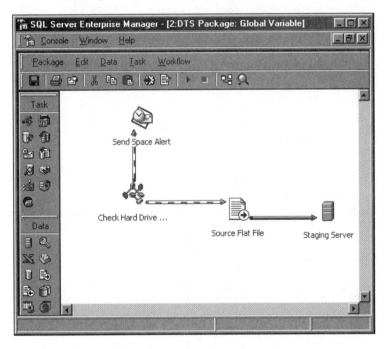

In this package, we first check the drive space. If it meets the requirements, we move on to import the flat file. If it does not meet our requirements, we send an administrative e-mail to alert the NT operator.

Managing Folders

The scenario often arises where you must load data from a source file and archive it after you're done. So what if the directory where you're going to deposit the archived files does not exist?

In this example, we'll check for the existence of a folder. If it doesn't exist, we'll create it. If you haven't already created the directory FSOExamples on your C drive, do so now.

We're going to break up this scenario into a few examples. In the first example, we are going to detect the existence of a directory based on the current date, and if it does not exist, present a pop-up box to report the fact.

First, we will need to create a global variable called `gvFilePathRoot`. Make the value of `gvFilePathRoot` `C:\FSOExamples`.

Then add the following code to an ActiveX script:

```
Function Main()

    Dim objFSO, strTodaysShortDate, strFullDir

    Set objFSO = CreateObject("Scripting.FileSystemObject")
    'Find out today's short date and strip the forward slash
    strTodaysShortDate = Replace(FormatDateTime(Date, 2),"/","")
    'Combine the root path plus today's date
    strFullDir = DTSGlobalVariables("gvFilePathRoot").Value & "\" & _
                 strTodaysShortDate

    If (objFSO.FolderExists(strFullDir)) Then
        MsgBox "The directory exists"
    Else
        MsgBox "The directory does not exist"
    End If

    Set objFSO = Nothing
    Main = DTSTaskExecResult_Success
End Function
```

Let's break this code apart. We have created a few unnecessary variables to simplify our code slightly. After creating the object and declaring the variables, we initialize the variable `strTodaysShortDate`. We do this in a rather confusing way, using a function inside another function to clean the variable.

```
strTodaysShortDate = Replace(FormatDateTime(date, 2),"/","")
```

The first function, `FormatDateTime`, is used to change the standard date output to our liking. In this case we will format it with the parameter 2, which means short date: for example, `March 15, 2000` will be converted to `3/15/00`. Appendix C has a full listing of parameters that you can use with the `FormatDateTime` function.

We then use the `Replace` function to strip the forward slashes out of the date. This would translate `3/15/00` to `31500`. For brevity, we've left out the leading zeros, but keep in mind in a production environment you'd want them. Otherwise, you'd have a directory for November 1st (`11100`) the same as January 11th (`11100`). To fix this, you can change the short date settings on the computer executing the package in the control panel, as shown in the next screenshot. This is done in the **Control Panel** under **Regional Options** and in the **Date** tab. To add the leading zeros for the month and day, you'd want to change the **Short date format** to **MM/dd/yy**.

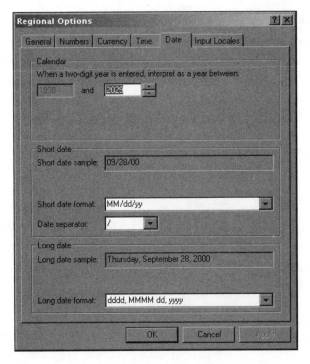

We concatenate the root path `C:\FSOExamples` with the results from the scrubbed date. That gives us `C:\FSOExamples\31500` (if, of course, you did this on March 15, 2000).

```
strFullDir = DTSGlobalVariables("gvFilePathRoot").Value & "\" & _
             strTodaysShortDate
```

The next line of code uses the `FolderExists` method to detect the existence of the folder. We pass the variable `strFullDir` for the directory name.

```
If (objFSO.FolderExists(strFullDir)) Then
```

The literal meaning of the above could be translated as:

```
If (objFSO.FolderExists("C:\FSOExamples\31500")) Then
```

But this directory shouldn't exist on our system, so we move into the `Else` clause:

```
Else
    MsgBox "The directory does not exist"
```

So if you execute the package, you should see the following output:

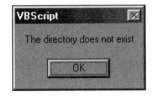

Creating a Directory

That's all very well, but what we actually want to do is create the folder if it doesn't exist. Let's take the last example a little further:

```
Function Main()

    Dim objFSO, strTodaysShortDate, strFullDir

    Set objFSO = CreateObject("Scripting.FileSystemObject")
    'Find out today's short date and strip the forward slash
    strTodaysShortDate = Replace(FormatDateTime(date, 2),"/","")
    'Combine the root path plus today's date
    strFullDir = DTSGlobalVariables("gvFilePathRoot").Value&"\" & _
                 strTodaysShortDate

    If (objFSO.FolderExists(strFullDir)) Then
        msgbox "The directory already exists"
    Else
        objFSO.CreateFolder(strFullDir)
        msgbox "Directory created"
    End If

    Set objFSO = nothing
    Main = DTSTaskExecResult_Success

End Function
```

Now, if the directory doesn't exist, we use the `CreateFolder` method with the fully qualified path to create it. Execute the package again and you should see this dialog box:

After you receive this message, you can run the package again and receive the output below:

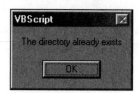

Deleting a Directory

You can also delete a directory and any contents in that directory by using the following code. Again, the variable `strFullDir` is the fully qualified directory name:

```
Function Main()

    Dim objFSO, strTodaysShortDate, strFullDir

    Set objFSO = CreateObject("Scripting.FileSystemObject")
    'Find out today's short date and strip the forward slash
    strTodaysShortDate = Replace(FormatDateTime(date, 2),"/","")
    'Combine the root path plus today's date
    strFullDir = DTSGlobalVariables("gvFilePathRoot").Value&"\" & _
                 strTodaysShortDate

    If (objFSO.FolderExists(strFullDir)) Then
        objFSO.DeleteFolder(strFullDir)
        MsgBox "The directory was deleted"
    Else
        objFSO.CreateFolder(strFullDir)
        msgbox "Directory created"
    End If

    Set objFSO = nothing
    Main = DTSTaskExecResult_Success

End Function
```

This chunk of code is handy for purging a directory where you archive old extracts.

File Management

File management is the most essential part of a dynamic extract. Generally, you don't know the file's name before receiving it. The only common variable is normally the file's extension. Before we begin with this example, create the following three text files in your `FSOExamples` directory. The files can be empty, since we'll only be using the properties, not the contents:

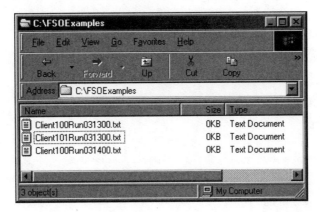

Also, all of these examples will use the global variable `gvFilePathRoot`, which needs to have the value of `C:\FSOExamples`.

Find a File

There are many ways to find a file using a `FileSystemObject` object. One of the easiest ways is to use the `FileExists` method as shown below:

```
Function Main()

   Dim objFSO, strFullNm·
   Set objFSO = CreateObject("Scripting.FileSystemObject")

   strFullNm = DTSGlobalVariables("gvFilePathRoot").Value & _
               "\Client100Run031300.txt"

   If objFSO.FileExists(strFullNm) Then
     MsgBox "The File Exists"
   Else
     MsgBox "You still need to create the file"
   End If

   Set objFSO = nothing
   Main = DTSTaskExecResult_Success
End Function
```

In the above code, we use the fully qualified filename to detect the existence of the file `Client100Run031300.txt`. This is a very direct way to detect the existence of a file if you know the exact location and name of the file. On executing the code you should see the following:

A slightly more advanced way to do it is to place all the `.TXT` files into collections. Then perform an action on each file in the collections:

```
Function Main()

    Dim objFSO, objFolder, objFile, colFiles

    Set objFSO = CreateObject("Scripting.FileSystemObject")
    Set objFolder = objFSO.GetFolder(DTSGlobalVariables("gvFilePathRoot").Value)
    Set colFiles = objFolder.Files

    If colFiles.Count > 0 Then
       For Each objFile in colFiles
           If UCase(Right(objFile, 4)) = ".TXT" Then
               MsgBox objFile.Name
           End If
       Next
    Else
       MsgBox "There are no files in this directory"
    End If

    Set objFSO = nothing
    Set objFolder = nothing
    Set colFiles =  nothing

    Main = DTSTaskExecResult_Success
End Function
```

Let's again take this code one chunk at a time. After declaring our variables and creating our `FileSystemObject`, we open a second object for the folder object. We set this object to `C:\FSOExamples`:

```
Set objFolder = objFSO.GetFolder(DTSGlobalVariables("gvFilePathRoot").Value)
```

The next step is to place all the files in that folder into a collection called `colFiles`. We have a small error-checking step that will make sure that there are files in our collection before moving on. We do this using the `Count` property:

```
Set colFiles = objFolder.Files
If colFiles.Count > 0 Then
```

We then establish a `For...Next` loop to scan through the list of files in our collection, and perform an action on each file with the `.TXT` extension. The reason we use the `UCase` function is because of case sensitivity in the VBScript; we want to make sure we're comparing the exact string. In other words, if someone named a file filename.TxT, we may miss it when we perform our comparison. You can display a file's name in collection by using the `Name` property:

```
For Each objFile in colFiles
    If UCase(Right(objFile, 4)) = ".TXT" Then
        MsgBox objFile.Name
    End If
Next
```

Lastly, we must clean up our environment by setting all the objects and collections to `Nothing`. The basic rule of thumb here is anything that you use the `Set` statement on, you must set back to `Nothing` at the end of your code. Be careful with the placement of these statements. If you place your cleanup code too soon, your code may not work because it needs the objects; too late in your code and it may never release the objects.

```
Set colFiles = nothing
Set objFolder = nothing
Set objFSO = nothing
```

Now, execute the code and you should receive the following results:

If there were no files in the directory with a `.TXT` extension, you should receive the following output. In production, you may move any files with another extension to a different directory and log their occurrence.

Move and Copying Files

In this example, we are going to read the filename and create a directory based on which client it represents. Then, we will move the file into the newly created directory:

```
Function Main()

    Dim objFSO, objFolder, objFile, colFiles, strClientID

    Set objFSO = CreateObject("Scripting.FileSystemObject")
    Set objFolder = objFSO.GetFolder(DTSGlobalVariables("gvFilePathRoot").Value)
    Set colFiles = objFolder.Files

    If colFiles.Count > 0 Then
        For Each objFile in colFiles
            If UCase (Right(objFile, 4)) = ".TXT" Then
                strClientID = mid(objFile.Name,7, 3)

                    If objFSO.FolderExists(objFolder&"\"&strClientID) then
                        objFile.Move(objFolder&"\"&strClientID&"\")
                    Else
                        objFSO.CreateFolder(objFolder&"\"&strClientID)
                        objFile.Move(objFolder&"\"&strClientID&"\")
                    End If

            End If
        Next
    Else
        MsgBox "There are no files in this directory"
    End If

    Set objFSO = nothing
    Set objFolder = nothing
    Set colFiles =  nothing
    Main = DTSTaskExecResult_Success
End Function
```

We've introduced a helpful function in this example called mid():

```
                strClientID = mid(objFile.Name,7, 3)
```

This is similar to the right() function. This lets us extract characters from the string that we specify in the first parameter, here objFile.Name. The next parameter, 7, tells the script which character to begin at, and the 3 tells the script how many characters to move to the right. We've used this to find the client number in our filename. Conveniently, the client numbers for our company are always three characters long.

We then branch our code into two directions after detecting whether the directory has been created. One branch detects that the directory exists and no creation is needed. The other sees that the client directory does not exist and needs to be created. After this logic is complete, we move our files to the appropriate directory.

```
    objFile.Move(objFolder&"\"&strClientID&"\")
```

This could have also been done with the `Copy` method.

Try to execute the task now. You should be able to go to the `FSOExamples` directory and see the following results:

Remember, moving a file takes much less time than copying a file. When moving a file, the OS simply changes the "pointer" to that file, rather than physically copying the file on the disk, if the move is on the same disk or partition. It is also worth noting that the `Move` method will fail if the target file already exists while the `Copy` method will not.

Extra File Properties

The `FileSystemObject` object model also exposes a number of other helpful properties that can be exploited in your code. One of these is the `DateLastModified` property. With this, you can tell when the file was last modified or created. This is helpful when purging your archive – you can use the `Delete` method to purge any files older than a certain date criterion.

This example will briefly demonstrate how to use this property:

```
Function Main()

   Dim objFSO, objFolder, objFile, colFiles

   Set objFSO = CreateObject("Scripting.FileSystemObject")
   Set objFolder = objFSO.GetFolder(DTSGlobalVariables("gvFilePathRoot").Value)
   Set colFiles = objFolder.Files

   If colFiles.Count > 0 Then
      For Each objFile in colFiles
         If UCase(Right(objFile, 4)) = ".TXT" Then
            MsgBox objFile.Name & " - " & objFile.DateLastModified
         End If
      Next
   Else
      MsgBox "There are no files in this directory"
   End If

   Set objFSO = nothing
   Set objFolder = nothing
   Set colFiles =  nothing

   Main = DTSTaskExecResult_Success
End Function
```

Before executing the package, move the files back to their original location. When executing this example, you should see something like the following results.

Writing Text to a File

Writing content to a text file comes in handy when you want to do some low-level error checking in a later chapter. Rather than writing to a table, you can write to a text file so that anyone without SQL experience could read it, or have it e-mailed to them through a different object (CDO), which is covered in a Chapter 14.

In the following example, we're going detect when the first step began, and log it to a text file. Again gvFilePathRoot represents the value C:\FSOExamples.

```
Function Main()

    Dim objFSO, TargetFile, objCurrentPackage, objStep

    Set objCurrentPackage = DTSGlobalVariables.Parent
    Set objStep = objCurrentPackage.Steps(1)

    Set objFSO = CreateObject("Scripting.FileSystemObject")
    Set TargetFile =
        objFSO.CreateTextFile(DTSGlobalVariables("gvFilePathRoot").Value & _
        "\newfile.txt", True)
    TargetFile.WriteLine("Step: " & objStep.Name&" Started -  " & _
                        objStep.StartTime)
    TargetFile.Close

    Set objFSO = Nothing
    Set TargetFile = Nothing

    Main = DTSTaskExecResult_Success
End Function
```

Hopefully, you remember your DTS object model from the last chapter. Before we can get to Step level in our object model, we must first define which package we're referring to. Using the Parent property as shown below can do this:

```
Set objCurrentPackage = DTSGlobalVariables.Parent
Set objStep = objCurrentPackage.Steps(1)
```

> At this point, we use the ordinal number for the current step, since there's only one step in this package. Normally, you may find it easier to use the logical name for the step – you should use this as standard, because who is to say what number the step ends up being?

We then create a text file with the Boolean parameter of True. This True specifies to overwrite any file with the current name that already exists. We then write the step's start time to the text file using the WriteLine method:

```
Set objFSO = CreateObject("Scripting.FileSystemObject")
Set TargetFile =
    objFSO.CreateTextFile(DTSGlobalVariables("gvFilePathRoot").Value & _
    "\newfile.txt", True)
TargetFile.WriteLine("Step: " & objStep.Name&" Started -  " & _
                    objStep.StartTime)
```

Cleanup work is necessary after you open a TextStream. We close the file using the close method to release any locks. After executing the package, look at the contents of newfile.txt in the FSOExamples directory. You should see the following:

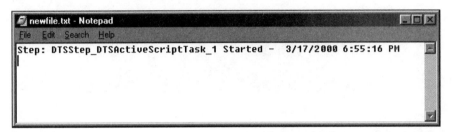

Reading Text

Reading a text file is very similar to writing to one. In this example, we'll read the file we created in the last example:

```
Function Main()

    Const ForReading = 1, ForWriting = 2, ForAppending = 8
    Dim objFSO, TargetFile

    Set objFSO = CreateObject("Scripting.FileSystemObject")
    Set TargetFile =
        objFSO.OpenTextFile(DTSGlobalVariables("gvFilePathRoot").Value & _
        "\newfile.txt", ForReading)
    ReadTextFileTest = TargetFile.Read(100)
    MsgBox ReadTextFileTest

    TargetFile.Close

    Set objFSO = nothing
    Set TargetFile = nothing
    Main = DTSTaskExecResult_Success
End Function
```

We create a constant so we don't have to memorize the parameters to read the file and the code becomes more readable. The OpenTextFile method needs a numeric value after you specify the file of 1, 2, or 8. Constants in this case make our code easier to read by allowing us to simply say ForReading instead of 1.

```
Const ForReading = 1, ForWriting = 2, ForAppending = 8

Set TargetFile =
    objFSO.OpenTextFile(DTSGlobalVariables("gvFilePathRoot").Value & _
    "\newfile.txt", ForReading)
```

We then read 100 characters of text using the Read method. If there are less characters in the text file, then it will not display extra padding. You could easily set this to a higher number, if you think your file will have more than 100 characters.

```
ReadTextFileTest = TargetFile.Read(100)
```

Now, execute the package and you should see the following output:

The Package as an Object

Combining the FileSystemObject and DTS object models allows you to go completely beyond the capabilities of pure DTS and create new functionality. This section covers a few ways to use the DTS object model to make your code more object-oriented.

Open a Package in a Package

The main way to make your code more object-driven is to separate any large packages you may have into smaller, more manageable packages. This is especially useful when you need to import an unpredictable number of files. You can load a collection with all the filenames in one package, and in the second package actually perform the transformation. Please keep in mind that you can also use the Execute Package task to perform this same function, but this is an easy way to perform the same function in your code through the package object.

Below is a simple example that demonstrates how to open a package inside a package. First you will need to create a new task with a single ActiveX Script task and call the task Hello World Child:

```
Function Main()
    MsgBox DTSGlobalVariables("gvClientMessage").Value
    Main = DTSTaskExecResult_Success
End Function
```

Designate a global variable `gvClientMessage` to have a null value. The above code will present a dialog box to the user with the value from the global variable.

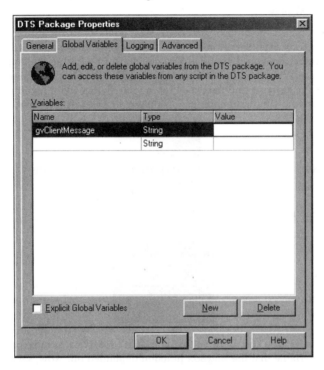

Save the first package as `Hello World`. Now, create a second package with a single ActiveX Script task with the following code:

```
Function Main()
    Dim objPackage
    Set objPackage = CreateObject("DTS.Package")

    'Load Hello World package from SQL Server
    objPackage.LoadFromSQLServer "BKNIGHT\BKNIGHT2", "validusername", _
                        "password",,,,,"Hello World"

    objPackage.Execute

    ' Cleanup
    objPackage.Uninitialize()
    Set objPackage = nothing

    Main = DTSTaskExecResult_Success
End Function
```

The only thing really different in this code is the `LoadFromSQLServer` method. There are also `LoadFromStorageFile` and `LoadFromRepository` methods available. The first parameter is the server name, followed by the login and password you're going to use – you'll obviously have to change these to run this on your own server. In the above code, we're using the server name `BKNIGHT\BKNIGHT2` with the username of `validusername` and a password of `password`. Then, you specify the package you want to execute on that server. The `Execute` method will actually execute the package:

In order to utilize the Script Debugger or the Visual InterDev debugger, you must first turn on just-in-time debugging for DTS. This is done by selecting the **Data Transformation Services** node in Enterprise Manager and selecting **Action | Properties** from the menu. This displays the DTS **Package Properties** dialog, as shown below:

Select the **Turn on just-in-time debugging** check box to enable script debugging. With this option selected, the Script Debugger can be launched either due to an error or by a forced stop. The latter is the easiest way to enter a script for debugging. This is done by placing the `stop` statement at the location in the code where you want to begin debugging. The following code places the statement at the very beginning of the script, so the entire script can be debugged:

```
stop
Function Main()
    Main = DTSTaskExecResult_Success
End Function
```

Note that the `stop` statement is placed outside the `Main()` function. This will cause the debugger to halt script execution even before our entry point is executed.

Once you have added the `stop` statement to your script, you can execute the script in the normal fashion (either by executing the package or by executing the specific task). When the scripting engine encounters the `stop` statement, the debugger will be launched (or activated if it is already running) and the script will be loaded for debugging. As you can see in the following image, the `stop` statement has done its job and the script is now being executed in the context of the Script Debugger. The current line (which is where our statement is located) is highlighted in yellow, with a yellow arrow in the gutter.

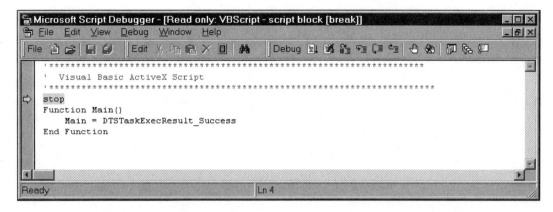

This would be a good point to discuss the capabilities that are provided by the debugger. The Script Debugger provides many of the same features as Microsoft's other integrated debuggers. One important thing to remember that is different, however, is that the Script Debugger only provides Read-Only capabilities. It is not possible to edit a file within the Script Debugger. This can be a bit annoying at times, but eventually you get used to it and accept it.

Most of the menu items provided by the Script Debugger are common Windows functions, so only those that are specific to the Script Debugger will be discussed here. The following is an active Debug toolbar. All of the buttons represented on the toolbar are also available via the Debug menu.

Let's look at the toolbar buttons from left to right, to see what they each perform:

Button	Function
Run (*F5*)	Runs the script without interaction
Stop Debugging (*Shift +F5*)	Stops the debugging process
Break at Next Statement	Causes the debugger to stop at the next executable statement
Step Into (*F8*)	Steps into a function or procedure for debugging
Step Over (*Shift+F8*)	Steps over a function or procedure to avoid stepping through additional code
Step Out (*Ctrl+Shift+F8*)	Steps out of a function or procedure that is being debugged
Toggle Breakpoint (*F9*)	Toggles a breakpoint (or stopping point) on or off
Clear All Breakpoints (*Ctrl+Shift+F9*)	Clears any breakpoints that may be set
Running Documents	Displays a dialog that lists all running documents
Call Stack	Displays the call stack
Command Window	Displays a command window that can be used to evaluate/modify script items

The importance of compartmentalizing your code into cohesive routines cannot be over emphasized. If the scripts you develop are logically broken up into functions and procedures that are responsible for specific tasks, you will find your debugging is greatly simplified. This is, of course, a common programming task, so this should not be anything new.

Let's take a look at an example that explores the debugger's capabilities. The code is shown again below for your review. Keep in mind that this is just a very simple example, and in a real-world situation the script would most likely be much more complex. The only modification we have made to this example is the addition of the stop statement to launch the debugger.

```
Function Main()
     Dim Result
     stop
     Result = GetSomeResult
     DisplayResult Result
     Main = DTSTaskExecResult_Success
End Function

Function GetSomeResult
     GetSomeResult = "Hello, World!"
End Function

Sub DisplayResult(AVariable)
     MsgBox AVariable
End Sub
```

Upon executing this script, the debugger is launched (if it is not already running) and the script is loaded. Just like in the previous screenshot above, the script will be halted at the stop statement. From this point, we can use the debug commands provided on the debug menu or toolbar. To execute the next statement, press *F8*. We can use *F8* to execute each consecutive statement within the script. Continue stepping through the script line by line, until you receive a message stating that the script was executed successfully.

To further examine the options offered by the debugger, execute the script again. After our extensive testing, we know that the GetSomeResult function has been proven to be bug-free, so we can go ahead and skip the statement that calls it. Pressing *Shift+F8* allows us to skip over a procedure that we have already tested. There's no need to take the extra time stepping through all of the code in our routines if it's already been tested, so skipping over those routines will speed up our debugging.

So far our debugging has gone fairly well, and we have managed to test everything up to the DisplayResult routine. At this point, let's set a breakpoint at the beginning of the routine (use your imagination a little here and pretend there's more than a single line!) The following screenshot shows our code in the debugger with our breakpoint set. To set the breakpoint, place the cursor on the desired statement and press *F9*. The line will be highlighted in red, and a stop sign will appear in the gutter. Pressing *F9* again will clear the specified breakpoint.

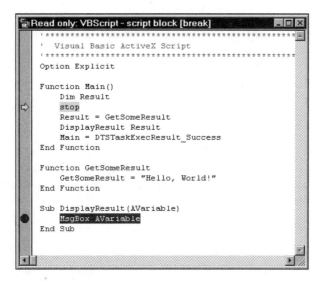

```
Read only: VBScript - script block [break]
' ********************************************************
'   Visual Basic ActiveX Script
' ********************************************************
Option Explicit

Function Main()
    Dim Result
    stop
    Result = GetSomeResult
    DisplayResult Result
    Main = DTSTaskExecResult_Success
End Function

Function GetSomeResult
    GetSomeResult = "Hello, World!"
End Function

Sub DisplayResult(AVariable)
    MsgBox AVariable
End Sub
```

Since all of the code up to this point has been tested, and we are pretty certain that the DisplayResult routine is the problem, there certainly isn't any reason to step through all of our now pristine code. Pressing *F5* will cause the script to run until it reaches a breakpoint or the end of the code, whichever comes first. Of course, we can use any number of breakpoints that we want. It is often a good idea to set breakpoints so that they create various sections within your code. As you debug each section and verify it is bug-free, you can clear the breakpoints. Unfortunately, your breakpoints will be cleared each time the script is launched.

There is one other key element to point out about the Script Debugger. Throughout this discussion you may have been asking yourself, "How do I check or change the contents of my variables?" Thanks for asking! The **Command Window** allows you to do just this task. While your code is stopped in the debugger, you can display the **Command Window** and use it to manipulate your variables. Placing the ? symbol in front of a variable name will print the variable's contents to the window after pressing the *Enter* key. Typing the variable name followed by the assignment operator (=) and a new value will modify the variable's contents. An example of this is shown below:

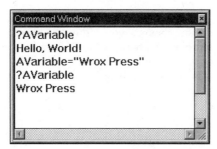

```
Command Window
?AVariable
Hello, World!
AVariable="Wrox Press"
?AVariable
Wrox Press
```

We're not quite done, yet. There is also a **Call Stack** provided that allows you to see what routines have been executed. Unfortunately, the stack does not always provide a complete execution path. Notice the example overleaf. The stack only shows two procedures, even though the GetSomeResult routine was executed. The reason for this is that when the code enters the Main() routine again, the stack is cleared.

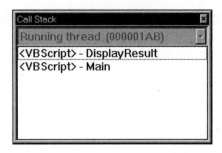

Make the following changes to our example, and step through the code from the `stop` statement to demonstrate this. Ensure that you have the `Call Stack` displayed, so you can observe the contents changing as you step through the code.

```
Option Explicit

Function Main()
    Dim Result
    stop
    Result = GetSomeResult
    DisplayResult Result
    AnotherRoutine
    Main = DTSTaskExecResult_Success
End Function

Function GetSomeResult
    GetSomeResult = "Hello, World!"
End Function

Sub DisplayResult(AVariable)
    MsgBox AVariable
End Sub

Sub AnotherRoutine
    MsgBox "AnotherRoutine"
End Sub
```

As the code is executed with the new changes, you will notice how the stack is cleared each time execution returns to `Main()`. For one final twist, we will take a look at a caveat to this. Relocate one line of code, as shown below, and notice how nested routines will be displayed properly in the order in which they were called. Of course, as soon as the execution returns to the `Main()` routine, the stack will be cleared once again.

```
Function Main()
    Dim Result
    stop
    Result = GetSomeResult
    DisplayResult Result
    Main = DTSTaskExecResult_Success
End Function
```

```
Function GetSomeResult
    GetSomeResult = "Hello, World!"
End Function

Sub DisplayResult(AVariable)
    MsgBox AVariable
    AnotherRoutine
End Sub

Sub AnotherRoutine
    MsgBox "AnotherRoutine"
End Sub
```

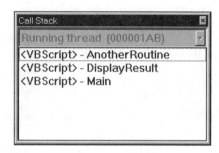

Now you should be feeling somewhat comfortable with debugging your code with the Script Debugger, instead of filling your code with message boxes that need to be removed before you place your script into production. This is not to say that message boxes don't have their place in debugging. It is to say, however, that there is often a better way. Once you have a firm understanding of how the debugger works, you should find that the time it takes to create fully functional scripts diminishes greatly.

Now that we have seen the Script Debugger, let's take a quick look at the debugger that is provided by Microsoft Visual InterDev 6.0. For the most part, the **InterDev debugger** is quite similar. Aside from the function keys that are used, there is very little difference. If you have InterDev installed and you run the scripts that we have been looking at in this section, the first thing you will notice is that you get some dialog boxes that have not been mentioned up to this point. The first dialog simply informs you that an error has occurred and asks if you would like to debug it. This dialog is shown below. Of course, since we're on the subject of debugging, we want to click the Yes button!

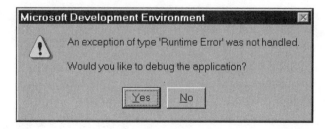

The second dialog that is displayed is shown overleaf. Since we are not interested in working with an InterDev project, we want to click No on this dialog, to move on to the debugger with only the script we are executing.

Once the InterDev debugger is active, you will notice that many things look similar to the Script Debugger. Your screen may look somewhat different depending on how you have configured your system, but it should resemble something similar to the following image:

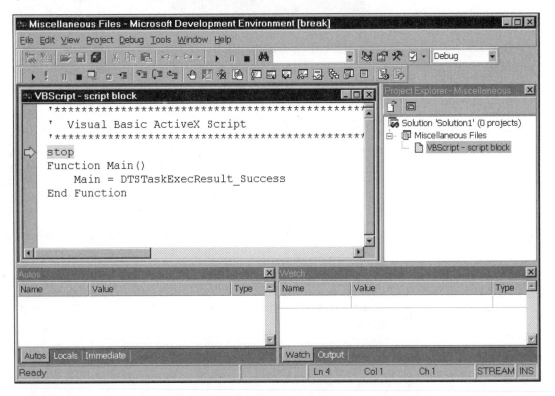

Notice that the example above is the first script we debugged in the first part of this section. Aside from a few additional windows, things are still relatively familiar. Let's take a look now at the debug toolbar, since it has changed on us.

There are several toolbar items that fall outside the scope of this context that we won't be covering here. Also, rather than explaining the same items again, we have simply provided the following table to help you cross-reference important keys between the Script Debugger and the InterDev debugger. However, we will point out some interesting things that are available to us here, which aren't available with the Script Debugger.

Option	Script Debugger	Visual InterDev
Run	*F5*	*F5*
Stop Debugging	*Shift +F5*	*Shift +F5*
Break at Next Statement		
Step Into	*F8*	*F11*
Step Over	*Shift+F8*	*F10*
Step Out	*Ctrl+Shift+F8*	*Shift+F11*
Toggle Breakpoint	*F9*	*F9*
Clear All Breakpoints	*Ctrl+Shift+F9*	*Ctrl+Shift+F9*
Running Documents		*Ctrl+Alt+R*
Call Stack		*Ctrl+Alt+C*
Command Window		
Run to Cursor		*Ctrl+F10*

Notice the last item in the table, Run to Cursor. This is a very helpful command that allows us to place the cursor at a particular location in a script, and execute every line of code between the current line and the cursor position. This is very helpful when you want to move quickly through code that you have already tested, but do not want to bother with setting breakpoints.

There are also a couple of interesting things in the extra windows provided by InterDev that might prove helpful from time to time. InterDev's debugger gives us a bit more detail concerning variables than the Script Debugger did. If the Locals window is not already visible, you can display it by selecting View | Debug Windows | Locals. This window, shown below, provides a listing of all of our local variables. The example shown here is for a script that is accessing a SQL Server database. The last variable listed contains our database connection. Note how it has been expanded to demonstrate the ability to view all of the attributes of the Connection object.

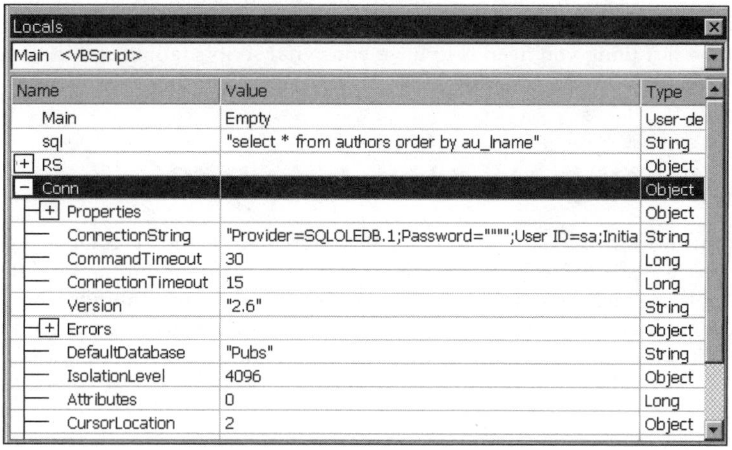

One benefit of the Locals window is that you can change data values directly in this window. However, there is also an Immediate window which is identical in behavior to the Command Window in the Script Debugger. The drop-down at the top of the window will change to match the current routine that is being executed.

The final window that will be covered is the Watch window. This window allows you to enter variables whose values you want to watch when they change. The following is an example of a watch that was placed on a local variable called sql. As the script executed, the Value column was empty. However, as soon as the value of sql changed, the new value was displayed. If the window is not visible, it may be displayed by selecting View | Debug Windows | Watch.

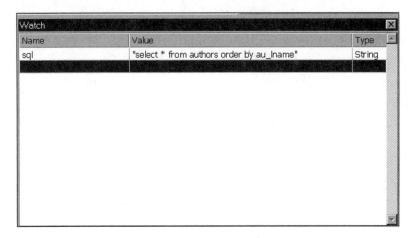

Although there are some obvious advantages that can be seen by using the InterDev debugger, it may not always be the best solution. InterDev requires a great deal more system resources than the Script Debugger, and a new instance tends to get launched each time a script executes. In addition, depending on the type of debugging you are performing, it may not be necessary to have all of the bells and whistles. Unfortunately, InterDev and the Script Debugger do not really get along too well. Each of them wants to be the default debugger, so whichever one is installed last wins. Of course, as with anything, which debugger you choose will most likely be decided by personal preference.

Hopefully this section has given you a good insight into the tools that are at your disposal for creating bug-free scripts. This is certainly an important goal, especially since your scripts are likely to be run unattended and the last thing you need is to have your vital scripts failing at 2 in the morning when you are sound asleep!

Other Helpful Objects Models in DTS

Now that you know how to call and use the FileSystemObject and DTS Object Model, why not try some others? There are some excellent components that can be found on the Web that can help solve some of your problems. Some can help you do more advanced error trapping; others can zip and unzip a file for transformation. An especially useful one is CDO, which allows you to send mail. Anything you can plug into VBScript can be also plugged into DTS using the ActiveX Script task.

Other VBScript Web Resources

Don't worry; we're not leaving you high and dry. Try some of these other web resources for more information on VBScript:

- ❑ Microsoft Scripting Homepage (http://msdn.microsoft.com/scripting) – Complete object models and documentation on VBScript and JavaScript.

- ❑ Programmer to Programmer (http://p2p.wrox.com) – A collection of message boards to help you get support from other developers.

- ❑ 15 Seconds (http://www.15seconds.com) – Downloadable components and articles on VBScript.

- ❑ Developer.com (http://www.developer.com) – Large set of tutorials and sample scripts.

Summary

In this chapter we have explored the DTS and `FileSystemObject` Object Models a little deeper. By using these two object models, you can expand the functionality of DTS beyond its native uses. Some key points to remember from this chapter are:

- ❑ The `FileExists` method detects the existence of a file

- ❑ The `Copy` and `Move` methods can transfer a file to a desired location on the same drive or network share

- ❑ The `OpenTextFile` method will open a text file for reading, writing, or appending

- ❑ Opening a package inside another package can be done with the `LoadFromSQLServer` and `Execute` methods

You're now ready to take DTS head-on.

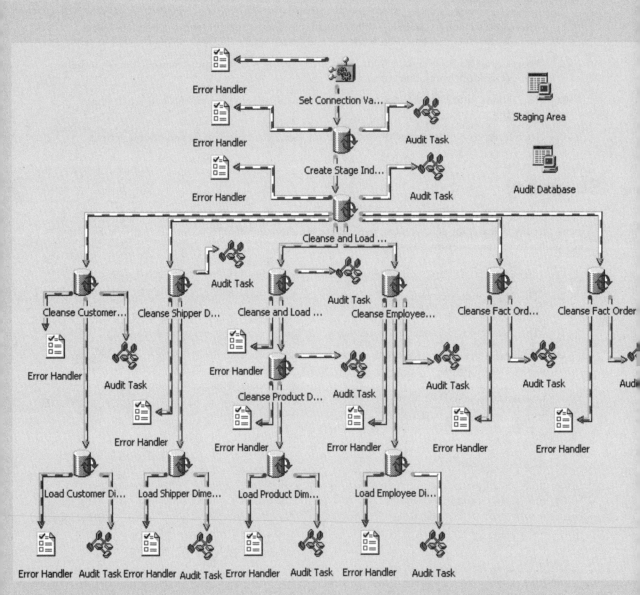

Error Handler
Set Connection Va...
Error Handler
Audit Task
Staging Area

Error Handler
Create Stage Ind...
Audit Task
Audit Database

Error Handler
Audit Task

Cleanse and Load ...

Audit Task

Cleanse Customer...
Cleanse Shipper D...
Cleanse and Load ...
Audit Task
Cleanse Employee...
Cleanse Fact Ord...
Cleanse Fact Order

Error Handler
Audit Task
Error Handler
Audit Task
Audit Task
Audit Task
Aud

Cleanse Product D...
Audit Task

Error Handler
Error Handler
Error Handler
Error Handler
Error Handler

Load Customer Di...
Load Shipper Dime...
Load Product Dim...
Load Employee Di...

Error Handler
Audit Task
Error Handler
Audit Task
Error Handler
Audit Task
Error Handler
Audit Task

10

DTS Security

In a perfect world, you wouldn't have to worry about security. But with DTS, a potential hacker has the power to do just about anything malicious not only to your database, but your server, as well as your network, with relative ease. It is imperative that enough precautions are taken to make sure your environment is as secure as possible. The goal of using security on DTS packages, and for that matter, SQL Server, is to make sure the people who need the access have it, and those who don't are denied it.

This chapter will not go over SQL Server security or Windows 95/98/NT/2000 security per se, except where it has immediate impact on securing DTS packages.

Whether you save a package locally to SQL Server or in the Meta Data Services, the package is saved in the msdb database. The tables that the package is saved on vary depending on which of the two methods you choose. We will show you how securing the msdb and its underlying tables and stored procedures can prevent unwanted access to the packages. In addition, when you save the package to the SQL Server or to a structured storage file, you have the ability to assign owner and user passwords on the package, which will encrypt the package and only allow access to those you provide a password to. Finally, if you choose to save the package to a Visual Basic file, the password in the database connection is not written to the .BAS file. You would have to provide the password in order for the Visual Basic file to work. As you can see, your security options are predominantly dependent on where you save your package, which is covered in detail in Chapter 2: *DTS Fundamentals*. Here, we will explain and compare all these options, and will also demonstrate how you can employ auditing with Microsoft Meta Data Services, and explore the issues involved when backing up your database.

With that said, in most cases when a DBA creates a new login, either using a SQL standard login or Windows Authentication, the login is granted the rights of the guest account by default. If you haven't changed anything security-wise on the server since it was installed, then the new user will have access to the following databases (if they are installed):

❑   master

❑   msdb

❑   Northwind

❑   pubs

❑   tempdb

If a user receives guest access to the msdb database, this means that anyone with a SQL Server login can create DTS packages and possibly harm your system. An instance of this could be where a user logs in and creates a package to execute a program using the Execute Process task that deletes files on your system. Even if you deny access to the msdb database, the user will still be able to create packages and execute them. Access to this is covered through stored procedures, which we will cover shortly.

During design and execution of the package, your users will also need the appropriate access required to perform the actions for their tasks and connections. For example, if you have a user who is trying to create a connection the Wrox database and doesn't have the appropriate permission, he would receive the error below. In most cases, the database roles **db_datawriter** and **db_datareader**, which allow read and write access to the database, should be sufficient. For more information on database roles and server roles, check the SQL Server Books Online, MSDN, or Robert Vieira's book.

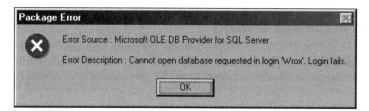

The msdb also contains the repository SQL schema, which is a mapping of information model elements to SQL schema elements. The repository engine uses data in these tables to instantiate and manage COM objects. The tables that are part of Meta Data Services are the tables whose names start with Rtbl. The stored procedures that are part of Meta Data Services have names starting with R_i. You should never modify these tables or stored procedures in any way. If you wish to make a modification, create a copy of the table or stored procedure and make your modifications to it. If you're creating applications to query these tables, use the Repository object model. That way, you don't risk falling victim to Microsoft changing the tables that you were querying directly.

The tables that DTS uses to store its packages and its logs are in the msdb as well. The main table that stores the DTS packages is sysdtspackages. Also, with SQL 2000, we have the log tables Sysdtspackagelog, Sysdtssteplog, Sysdtscategories, and Sysdtstasklog. These tables are used to store information about the package execution, if the package LogToSQLServer property has been set.

Anyone using Enterprise Manager to create and view these packages however does not use these tables directly. DTS uses two stored procedures for adding and retrieving packages, which are `sp_add_dtspackage` and `sp_get_dtspackage` respectively. If you'd like to tightly lock down users from seeing the list of packages in Enterprise Manager, simply deny them access to the `sp_enum_dtspackages` stored procedure in the `msdb` database. If you'd like to stop them from saving packages in Enterprise Manager to SQL Server, deny them access to the `sp_add_dtspackage` stored procedure in the `msdb` database. Your users will not receive an error if they try to view the Data Transformation Services tree. They just won't see any packages. If you deny them rights to `sp_enum_dtspackages`, then they won't be able to see packages that they just created in Enterprise Manager.

Scheduled Package Security

If you have ever scheduled a DTS package to run using SQL jobs, you were unknowingly using a system-stored procedure in the master called `xp_cmdshell`. In order to run DTS packages using the SQL Server Agent, it uses this system-stored procedure to execute `DTSRun` with its parameters behind the scenes. The amount of authority (or possible damage it can do) is dependant on what account SQL Server Agent is running under and the rights of the package owner. For instance, if the package is being run by someone who is a member of the `sysadmin` fixed server role, `xp_cmdshell` will be executed under the security context in which the SQL Server service is running, which is typically an administrator on the local server. When the user is not a member of the `sysadmin` group, `xp_cmdshell` will impersonate the SQL Server Agent proxy account, which is specified using `xp_sqlagent_proxy_account`. If the proxy account is not available, `xp_cmdshell` will fail. The proxy account can be configured under the SQL Server Agent properties. You can also configure a job with ActiveX Script to use the DTS object model to execute a package. We will show you how to lock both down in a moment.

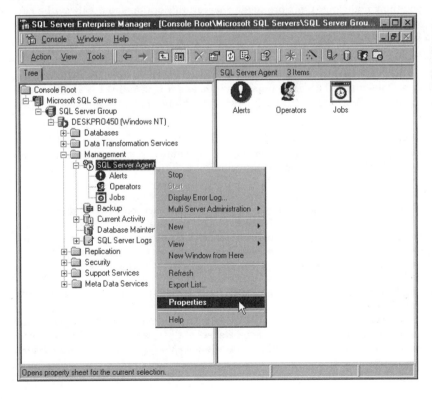

You need to click on the **Job System** tab on the resulting dialog box that appears:

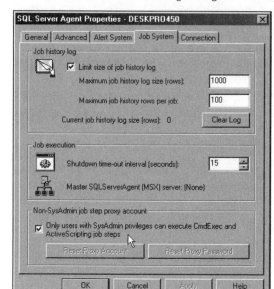

As seen here, the option group **Non-SysAdmin job step proxy account** is restricted to only allow members with SysAdmin privileges to execute job steps that have CmdExec (xp_cmdshell) and Active Scripting jobs in them. This is to prevent an untoward user from creating an Active Script task that could do something malicious. On a production server, this option should always be checked. On a development server where multiple users can be creating and executing packages, scripts and other scheduled jobs, you may need to allow non-sysadmin users to also have these privileges.

> **This is true only for Microsoft Windows NT 4 and Windows 2000. On Windows 9x or Windows Millenium, there is no impersonation and xp_cmdshell is always executed under the security context of the Windows 9x user who started SQL Server.**

This is new to SQL Server 2000, since previously it was run under the SQLAgentCmdExec account. So the bottom line is make sure that the system stored procedure xp_cmdshell is kept under wraps, and the accounts that SQL server is using have the appropriate rights for your environment.

> **As an administrator, you would much rather have someone complain that they do not have sufficient rights to a particular object, then to have that someone let you know that the table or data is no longer there. In other words, lock down your objects and allow for forgiveness rather than spend the weekend recreating a package that was maliciously deleted. In earlier versions, a user who was granted execute permissions for xp_cmdshell ran the command in the context of the MSSQLServer service's user account. SQL Server could be configured (through a configuration option) so that users who did not have sa access to SQL Server could run xp_cmdshell in the context of the SQLExecutiveCmdExec Windows NT account. In SQL Server 7.0, the account is called SQLAgentCmdExec. Users who are not members of the sysadmin fixed server role now run commands in the context of this account without specifying a configuration change.**

Since the package is executing under this proxy account, you may have ownership issues to deal with. Ownership conflicts can generate the following types of problems:

❑ File paths – File paths specified in the package may not be visible in a different security context. That is, the proxy account may not have access to the same share points as the package creator (for example, the user may not have the drive letters of the package creator mapped). To guard against this problem, use Universal Naming Convention (UNC) names rather than file paths when specifying external files.

❑ Connections – The owner of the SQL Server Agent job that runs the package must have permission to access the local paths pointed to or connections made to the local server in the package.

❑ COM – For packages that call COM components in ActiveX script tasks, the called components must exist on the same workstation on which the package is running. Also, the SQL Server Agent job account must have permission to instantiate the objects.

So how do we put together all that we learned about these tables and stored procedures to enforce security on our `msdb`? Well, for starters, access to the `msdb` should be granted by you, and not implicitly by the guest account. In addition, it is also possible to restrict users even further by only granting rights to the specific tables and stored procedures defined above.

DTS Password Protection

> Note: If you are using SQL Server 7 and you are not using an owner password on the package, there is a password vulnerability. Information about this problem and the fix are located at **http://www.microsoft.com/technet/security/bulletin/fq00-041.asp**.

When you create a DTS package, either by using the DTS Wizard, in the DTS Designer, or using Visual Basic, you have a choice of saving it in SQL Server, Meta Data Services, a structured storage file, or a Visual Basic file. In two of these cases, SQL Server and the structured storage file, you have the choice of providing your DTS packages with an additional two levels of security above and beyond the `msdb` database: **owner** and **user**. When a package is saved it can be assigned just an owner password, both an owner password and user password, or none at all. The owner password allows you to modify the existing package whereas the user password simply allows you to execute it. When saving a package into the Meta Data Services, you will lose the functionality of saving a package with owner and user passwords.

As you can see in the screenshot overleaf, the passwords are entered below the package name if desired. If you choose anything other than SQL Server or structured storage file, these boxes will be disabled.

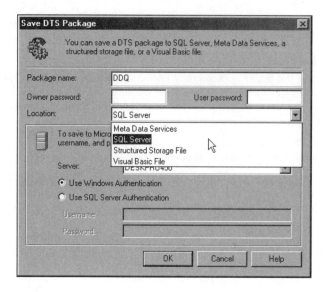

Owner Password

The owner password for the DTS package is used to protect any sensitive username and server password information in the package from unauthorized users. When an owner password has been assigned to a package, the package is stored in an encrypted format. When a DTS package or version is encrypted, all of its collections and properties are encrypted, except for the DTS package Name, Description, ID, VersionID, and CreationDate properties. Only users who know this password will be able to modify this package. All packages which access critical or sensitive data should be protected by an owner password.

If you input an incorrect password (say you typed in the User password by mistake) you will receive the following two error messages:

After clicking OK, you will then receive the next message:

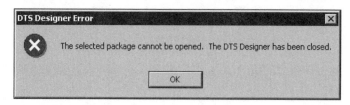

However, only this particular instance of the DTS Designer will be closed; any other packages you have open will remain as they are.

User Password

The user password for the DTS package allows a user to execute a package but not view the package in the DTS designer. You would use this to secure a package for execution, without letting the user have rights to modify the package. If you set the User password, you need to also set the Owner password. If you lose the passwords for the package, there is no way of recovering the password or information stored in the DTS package (for obvious security reasons).

Meta Data Services

So what is this Meta Data Services we keep talking about but never seem to discuss? Well, in short, Meta Data Services provide us a way to store and manage meta data. Meta data is simply information about the data that is stored. For instance, the information can include information about the data types, column lengths, objects, even the entire schema of a database. Meta Data Services act as an abstract container for all things data-related.

Meta Data Is Abstract

Meta Data contains abstract information. For instance, if we are to describe written English, it contains letters, which in turn spell words, which when placed in a proper order convey meaning. Further abstraction of any of these items could be accomplished, say for instance, the letter 'a' can be represented in numerous ways like sign language, binary, morse code. It is the grouping of these abstract layers that we are able to understand; all of these letters, words, sentences, come together to form this book.

Now with SQL Server and other development languages, we typically only see two or three layers of abstraction. For instance, when we look at the DTS object model, we have a package class, which has collections of tasks, each of which has its own properties and methods. These characteristics of this object define how all derived objects must conform.

Meta Data Has Context

When something is context sensitive it means that depending how you look at it, it can have multiple meanings. Meta data can become data in different scenarios. Let's take for example when we compare database tables. We could either look at the data contained in the tables to see if there are any differences, or we could look at the tables themselves to see if there are any differences between them. The process for comparison is the same. We would just change the context to a different type to look at it in a different way. In this manner, the standard meta data that is stored like the system catalog can become data that you can manipulate.

You can drill-down the package's lineage under the **Package** tab as shown below. As you can see, the package named Repository was executed twice by the Administrator account.

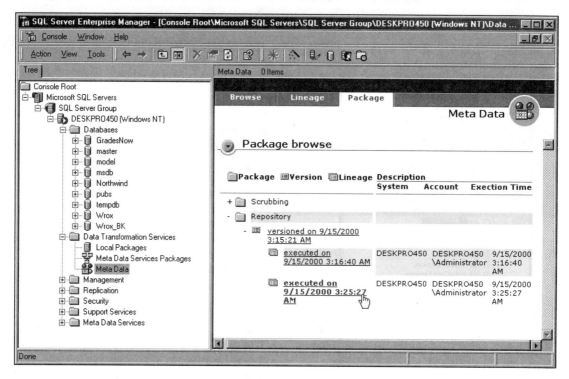

You can click on any given entry, like an execution as shown opposite, to add comments or descriptions. For example, if you're testing a package and would like to share notes about the results of your test, you could add comments here. You also have a full audit trail here of who created the package, when, and who last modified it.

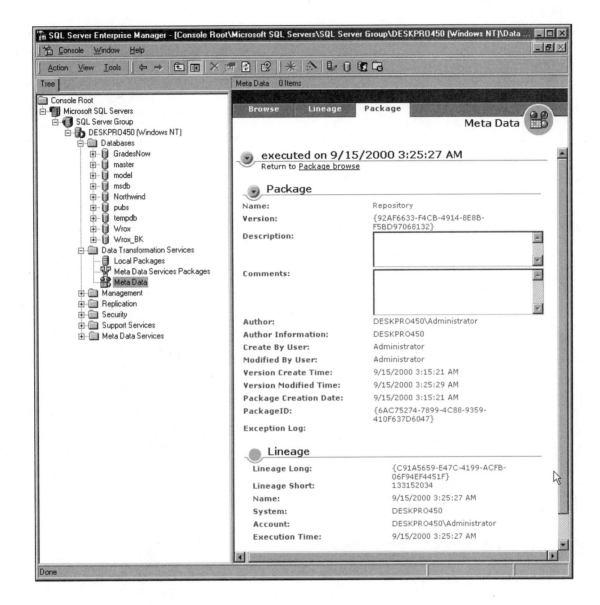

Backing Up Your Databases

In a typical environment, SQL Server runs on a server that is being backed up to some offline storage device like a tape. When the backup occurs, SQL Server is running and the files that it stores the data and logs in (.mdf and .ldf) are locked and in most cases are not backed up. A typical SQL Server backup scenario is to set up a backup schedule that backs up the databases and stores them into what is called a dump file, which then can be backed up properly by a tape system. If a restore has to occur, you can use the file located on your server, or in the case of a total disk or array failure, it can be restored off tape. This file can be used to restore the database up to the point it was backed up, and if you have the transaction logs and are using the right recovery model, right up to the point of failure.

SQL Server 2000 now has three different recovery models it uses to simplify recovery planning. These models each address different needs for performance, disk and tape space, and protection against data loss. To illustrate the three models, look at the table below:

Recovery Model	Benefits	Exposure to lost data	Recover to point in time?
Simple	Fastest. Reclaims log space. You can do bulk copy operations.	Changes since the most recent database or differential backup must be redone.	Can recover to the end of any backup. Then changes must be redone.
Bulk-Logged	Fast but does not trucate the log space. You can do bulk copy operations.	If the log is damaged, or bulk operations occured since the most recent log backup, changes since that last backup must be redone. Otherwise, no work is lost.	Can recover to the end of any backup. Then changes must be redone via log or manually.
Full (default)	No work is lost due to a lost or damaged data file. Can recover to an arbitrary point in time (for example, prior to application or user error).	Normally none. If the log is damaged, changes since the most recent log backup must be redone.	Can recover to any point in time.

Level of protection (down arrow on left) — *Speed* (up arrow on right)

The Recovery model for a database can be found by going to the properties of the database and clicking on the Options tab. As you can see above opposite, the Recovery model for the model database is Full. Since the model database is the template for any other databases you create, your new databases will also be Full unless you change it. Depending on the use of you database, you may want to change this setting. For example, if the data being loaded into the database is only done by DTS, and users have read-only access to the database, you can get away with using the Bulk_Logged model. The reasoning for this is that if you had to restore the database, it should not be a problem to re-run your DTS packages to get the database in exactly the same state it was prior to failure. Now if users *CAN* change data, you will probably want to use the Full Recovery model. In any case, it is a balance between speed and risk.

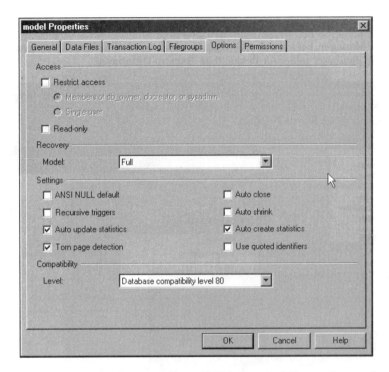

It is also recommended that you backup your files as COM-structured files, so they can be stored in a version controls system like Visual Source Safe. These .DTS files can also be taken offsite for added comfort.

Backing Up the msdb Database

Now the msdb database is important not only for DTS and the Meta Data Services, but for containing the scheduling and backup information for the server. If you already have a backup plan which is at least backing up the msdb, congratulations! Otherwise, you fall in the category of people who are running an unnecessary risk. SQL Server 2000 makes it so easy to set up a proper backup schedule that there is no excuse for not doing so.

The first option, Verify backup upon completion, enables you to make sure the backup you just completed is valid. It takes a substantial amount of extra time but it's worth it to sleep a little better at night. The backup set expiration is the amount of time SQL will wait until it reclaims the space.

If this is the first time you are using a tape or disk for backup, you can "initialize" the media for use. It simply names the media and erases the previous contents. This is equivalent to formatting a diskette regardless to the information that's on there.

Using Transact-SQL

Using Transact-SQL you can back up a database, a file or filegroup, or a log. Most people will use the GUI backup that is available in the Enterprise Manager, but I wanted to let you know about a new feature in SQL 2000 that is only available using the T-SQL commands for backup. The new feature is the ability to set a password on the media set and/or on the backup itself, so that it cannot be restored by anyone else other than someone who knows the password.

> A media set can be thought of as a folder which can contain one or more "files". These "files" are the backups themselves.

In addition the restorer would need to authenticated as a member of the sysadmin server role or the db_owner and db_backupoperator fixed database roles. For most purposes, you do not need to use this extra bit of security, since you control who is in these roles, and can also secure your server where these files are stored. However, if you have to store or send backups offsite to be archived or restored at other sites, using this password option may not be a bad idea. Remember, if someone were to get a hold of your backup file, they could restore *YOUR* database to *THIER* server.

Let's look at the syntax for backing up an entire database:

```
BACKUP DATABASE { database_name | @database_name_var }
TO < backup_device > [ ,...n ]
[ WITH
    [ BLOCKSIZE = { blocksize | @blocksize_variable } ]
    [ [ , ] DESCRIPTION = { 'text' | @text_variable } ]
    [ [ , ] DIFFERENTIAL ]
    [ [ , ] EXPIREDATE = { date | @date_var }
        | RETAINDAYS = { days | @days_var } ]
    [ [ , ] PASSWORD = { password | @password_variable } ]
    [ [ , ] FORMAT | NOFORMAT ]
    [ [ , ] { INIT | NOINIT } ]
    [ [ , ] MEDIADESCRIPTION = { 'text' | @text_variable } ]
    [ [ , ] MEDIANAME = { media_name | @media_name_variable } ]
    [ [ , ] MEDIAPASSWORD = { mediapassword | @mediapassword_variable } ]
    [ [ , ] NAME = { backup_set_name | @backup_set_name_var } ]
    [ [ , ] { NOSKIP | SKIP } ]
    [ [ , ] { NOREWIND | REWIND } ]
    [ [ , ] { NOUNLOAD | UNLOAD } ]
    [ [ , ] RESTART ]
    [ [ , ] STATS [ = percentage ] ]
]
```

So to back up the msdb database with both a media set password and backup password I would use the following command:

```
-- Create a logical backup device for the full msdb backup.
USE master

EXEC sp_addumpdevice 'disk', 'Nwind_backup',
  'd:\NWind_backup.dat'

-- Back up the full msdb database with password protection.
BACKUP DATABASE Northwind TO Nwind_backup WITH MEDIAPASSWORD = 'Test', PASSWORD =
'Password'
```

Now if I try to restore this backup using the following command:

```
RESTORE DATABASE Northwind FROM Nwind_backup
```

I get the following error message:

Server: Msg 3279, Level 16, State 6, Line 1
Access is denied due to a password failure
Server: Msg 3013, Level 16, State 1, Line 1
RESTORE DATABASE is terminating abnormally.

Once I correct the command by adding both the media and backup passwords, I get the desired results:

RESTORE DATABASE Northwind FROM Nwind_backup
WITH MEDIAPASSWORD = 'Test', PASSWORD = 'Password'

Processed 336 pages for database 'Northwind', file 'Northwind' on file 1.
Processed 1 pages for database 'Northwind', file 'Northwind_log' on file 1.
RESTORE DATABASE successfully processed 337 pages in 0.594 seconds (4.637 MB/sec).

Using a Backup Maintenance Plan

The Database Maintenance Plan Wizard can be used to help you set up the core maintenance tasks that are necessary to ensure that your database performs well, is regularly backed up in case of system failure, and is checked for inconsistencies. The Database Maintenance Plan Wizard creates a job for each of the tasks that you may assign it to do.

The maintenance tasks that can be scheduled to run automatically are:

❑ Reorganizing the data on the data and index pages by rebuilding indexes with a new fill factor

❑ Shrinking data files by removing empty database pages

❑ Updating index statistics

❑ Performing internal consistency checks of the data and data pages

❑ Backing up the database and transaction log files

❑ Transaction log shipping (Only available in Enterprise Edition)

We will show you how to do these over the next few pages.

In order to start the wizard, you can either select **Database Maintenance Planner** from the **Tools** menu, or right-click on a database, then select **All Tasks...**, then **Maintenance Plan**.

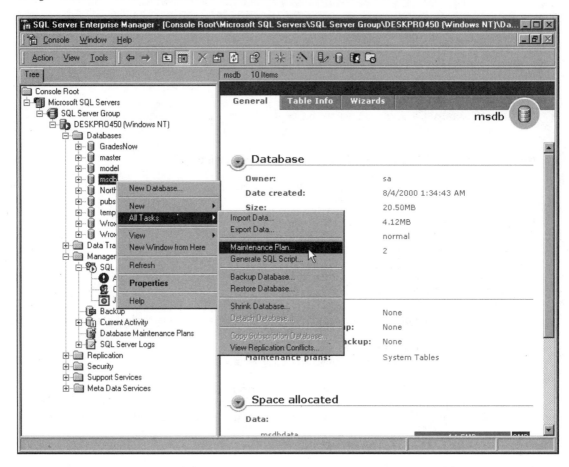

The start of the Database Maintenance Wizard describes what can be accomplished using this wizard. It will step you through each of the various tasks and it is your choice as to whether you use them or not. Each of the tasks can have its own schedule to execute. Click the **Next** button to skip the welcome screen.

Now for this example, I will be backing up my system databases and along the way, I'll be letting you know about some of the important options and what they are used for. In the screen below, I selected the All system databases option. I do this to save my system databases in a separate file from my user databases, but you can choose to select any or all of your databases. We click Next to continue.

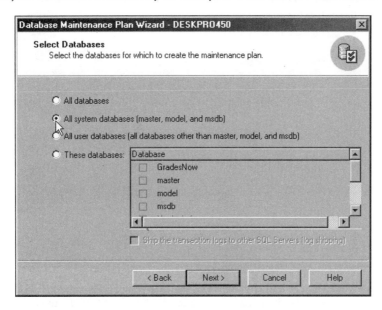

The next screen that appears allows us to reorganize our data and get rid of any excess space. The option to Reorganize data and index pages will recompile all your indexes with a specified fill factor, in this case 10%. The other option is to reorganize the data using the existing fill factor already on the indexes, by selecting Reorganize pages with the original amount of free space. Depending on the number and types of inserts you do, this value would need to be changed.

Also we see an option to Remove unused space from database files as well as its parameters. It will shrink the physical database size, if SQL server can.

In addition to the database backup, we can also set up and schedule the backup of the transaction logs. The dialog is similar to the backup database dialog. It is generally best practice to back up the transaction logs as often as, if not more often than, the database. Remember it is the duty of the transaction log to bring the SQL Server to its current state if a restore should ever have to occur.

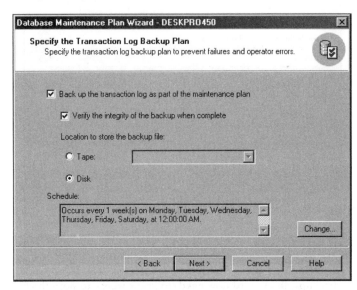

The Specify Transaction Log Backup Disk Directory dialog will only come up if you choose to back up your transaction logs. It is, again, similar to the backup disk directory dialog. You can specify the location of the file (or tape drive) and the retention of the backup.

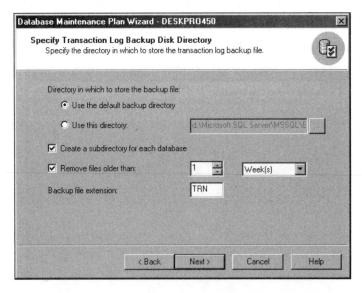

The results generated by the maintenance tasks can be written as a report to a text file and the `sysdbmaintplan_history` tables in the `msdb` database. The report can also be e-mailed to an operator. This step also has a retention, which can be set to remove any files older than the specified value.

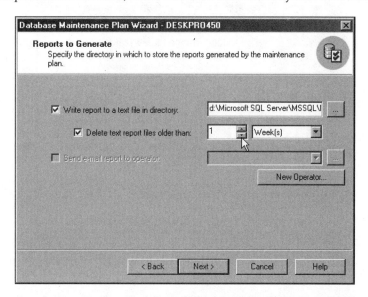

Have no fear, we're in the home stretch. One of the final dialogs is to set up the **Maintenance Plan History**. On this screen you can specify that you'd like the history of the maintenance plan's execution to be saved into the `sysdbmaintplan_history` table and how many rows you'll allow to exist on this table. You can also specify a remote server to save the logs to.

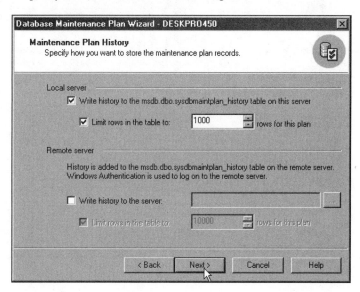

Lastly, name your maintenance plan. You may want to copy and paste the description of your maintenance plan from this screen into a report.

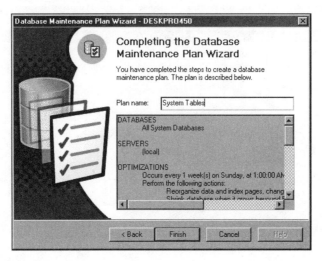

Once we have finished with the wizard, we can see the different jobs now scheduled to run in Enterprise Manager by clicking on Jobs:

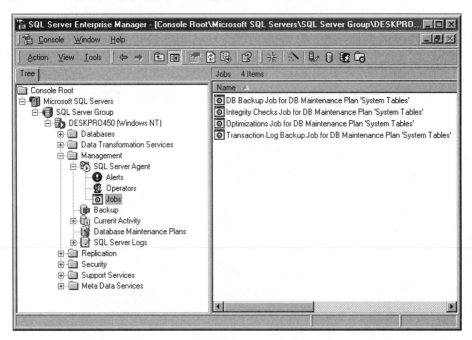

If we need to modify an existing maintenance plan, all we need to do is to go to the Database Maintenance Plans item under the Management folder. Once we click on the Database Maintenance Plans, we can see the maintenance plans we have for the server:

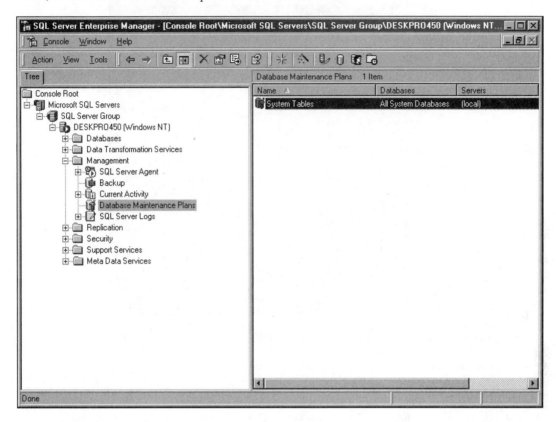

Select the maintenance plan you wish to edit in the right-hand window, and click on Action | Properties.

The next dialog appears with each of the steps that we just previously completed, although in a more compressed format:

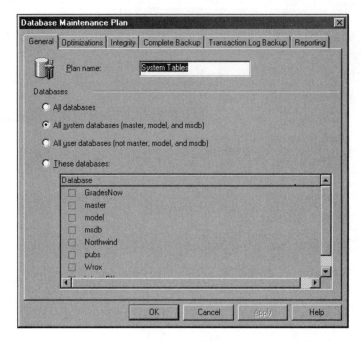

Once you make your changes, the associated jobs will be changed to reflect your new selections.

Some points to remember when working with backups:

- ❏ Maintain backups in a secure place, preferably at a site different from the site where the data resides.
- ❏ Keep older backups for a designated amount of time in case the most recent backup is damaged, destroyed, or lost.
- ❏ Establish a system for overwriting backups, reusing the oldest backups first.
- ❏ Use expiration dates on backups to prevent premature overwriting.
- ❏ Label backup media to prevent overwriting critical backups.
- ❏ Always test a restore from time to time to make sure you can!

Summary

In this chapter we briefly discussed SQL security and how it pertains to DTS. Where you store your DTS packages is typically where you need to focus your attention. For the packages you save in SQL Server and in the Repository, you need to lock down the `msdb` as much as possible; whereas with the structured storage file, your best bet is to make sure you have secured it with an `Owner` password. Since saving the file to a Visual Basic file doesn't not store the user/password information, the only information a person can garnish from it is the package design and whatever may be in the scripts. If you want to learn more about SQL Security and other concerns in programming SQL, take a look at *Professional SQL Server 2000 Programming* by Robert Viera (Wrox Press, ISBN 1-861004-48-6).

We've also learned what the Repository is and given you a brief introduction to it. Remember that with a DTS package saved in the Repository, you have a new set of options that allow you to track the package execution and the lineage of the data. If tracking this information is necessary, it's a lot easier to let the Repository track it for you, than creating your own solution.

Finally, since the `msdb` database is so critical to be up and working 100% of the time, we went over backing up an individual database, then building a backup strategy using the wizards. Make sure you check your servers to ensure you have an appropriate backup strategy for them.

In the next chapter we will cover error handling in DTS.

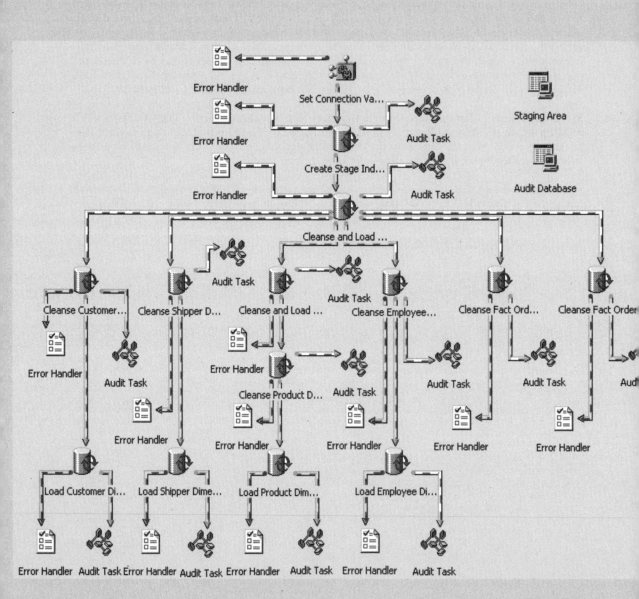

Error Handler

Set Connection Va...

Error Handler

Audit Task

Staging Area

Error Handler

Create Stage Ind...

Audit Task

Audit Database

Error Handler

Cleanse and Load ...

Audit Task

Cleanse Customer...

Cleanse Shipper D...

Audit Task

Cleanse and Load ...

Audit Task

Cleanse Employee...

Cleanse Fact Ord...

Cleanse Fact Order

Error Handler

Audit Task

Error Handler

Cleanse Product D...

Audit Task

Audit Task

Audit Task

Aud

Error Handler

Error Handler

Error Handler

Error Handler

Error Handler

Error Handler

Load Customer Di...

Load Shipper Dime...

Load Product Dim...

Load Employee Di...

Error Handler   Audit Task   Error Handler   Audit Task   Error Handler   Audit Task   Error Handler   Audit Task

11

Error Handling

When developing software, the developer is always faced with the possibility that his or her application may fail (as improbable as that seems). When using DTS, there are many opportunities for reactively or proactively handling these errors. In a mission-critical environment, such as the load procedures for a data warehouse, every error must be handled to ensure overall data integrity. This chapter will discuss several possibilities for handling errors from within DTS packages and from external applications using the DTS object model (see Appendix A, *The DTS Object Model*, for more information). It will also discuss effective methods for auditing or verifying success of DTS packages.

In this chapter we will discuss:

- ❑ DTS Designer Errors and how they are handled
- ❑ Package-Level Auditing and Error Handling
- ❑ Task Object Error Handling
- ❑ Error Handling from External Applications
- ❑ Design Considerations for Optimal Error Handling

DTS Errors

When designing packages, the developer creates objects of work in the form of DTS tasks. These objects of work represent some atomic task. Once each object or task finishes its execution, it returns a result to DTS. This result can either be success or failure, but can be handled in many ways. DTS allows the developer to decide what to do with the result. DTS will throw-up errors as they occur, from the lowest (transformation) to the highest (package) levels, depending on which level, or levels, of your package is handling errors.

DTS Designer Error Handling

As you are developing packages using the DTS Designer, DTS will automatically check for invalid connections in Data Pump objects or allow you to proactively check for typographical errors in ActiveX Script objects or improperly formed SQL in Execute SQL tasks. DTS also lets you build SQL and define column-level transformations graphically. These features assist the developer in reducing errors in package design, but only handle design-time errors.

When you begin to test or execute your packages, the DTS Designer will display run-time errors from all steps and tasks. DTS will display the result of each task in the Package Execution Status dialog. If any errors occur with any tasks, DTS will update its status.

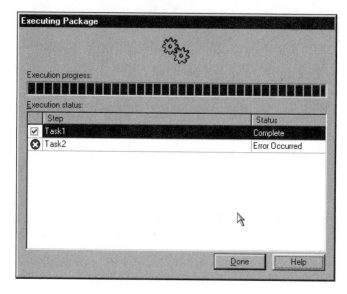

However, DTS does not display detailed error messages in this dialog. If you double-click on a step with an error, DTS will display a more detailed message, which the error settings for the called object. In the example below, DTS returned an error when attempting to execute an ActiveX Script task that contained an error.

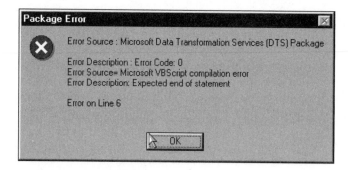

Package-Level Auditing and Error Handling

As we discuss in the *DTS Security* chapter, auditing enables you to recognize where any improper activities have occurred. This is also true within the context of error handling. Creating an audit trail for the logging of errors allows the designer to track where errors occurred in code or an administrator to quickly find and repair data issues. The audit trail can also dramatically reduce the amount of time spent debugging processes.

Enabling logging and error handling at the package level is the easiest and quickest way to implement the first level of an audit trail. You'll find package-level detailed information about the execution status of your packages and tasks. You won't be able to necessarily take definitive action, but you will be able to recognize where any improper activities have occurred. The following sections show how to implement auditing.

Package Auditing

In SQL Server 2000, DTS now has the ability to automatically log package-level events to any SQL Server of choice without saving the package to the Repository (in previous versions, this was a requirement). You can use DTS package auditing to check the success or failure of any package. You can also check which tasks within these packages executed successfully, failed or did not execute. This log information is stored in the msdb database in the sysdtspackagelog and sysdtssteplog tables. There is also a sysdtstasklog table, but this is used for custom tasks and will be examined in the Chapter 12. Each time the package is executed, a new series of records are added to the log tables so that the entire history of the package can be recorded.

To enable package-level auditing, open the package that you wish to audit, select Package from the main menu, select Properties, then choose the Logging tab when the dialog appears and check the Log package execution to SQL Server checkbox.

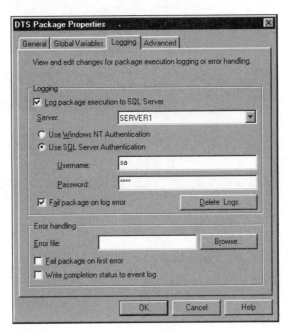

In an enterprise environment where more than one SQL Server is being used to execute DTS packages, the ability to log to a single server greatly reduces administration and auditing challenges. However, this also creates a single point of failure for auditing of each of these packages if 'Fail package on log error' is checked. This option ensures that if the package is not able to log during the course of execution, it will immediately fail and return a failure result. This means that any issue, such as network, connectivity, security, or authentication, can cause the package to fail.

Viewing Logs

In order to view package logs from Enterprise Manager, expand the Data Transformation Services node, right-click on Local Packages and choose Package Logs. Choose the package you wish to view the logs for and expand the latest version (if there is more than one). You should see a dialog like this:

Double-click on the log file for the latest execution and you'll see this information:

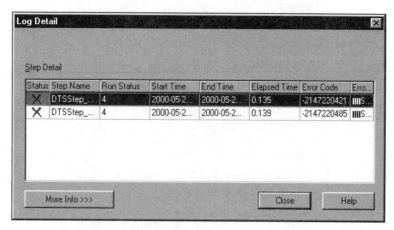

However, this interface does not show all stored information. To view all of a package's execution information using SQL, you can open Query Analyzer and run the following SQL:

```
USE msdb
go

SELECT *
FROM dbo.sysdtspackagelog
WHERE name = 'packagename'
go

-- Change 'packagename' to an existing package
```

The additional information includes version information, lineage information, and computer and user information for the machine on which the package was executed.

You can do the same from the `sysdtssteplog` table as well using the following SQL statement. This statement joins the step information with the package information to give a complete picture of the audit trail.

```
USE msdb
go

SELECT sysdtssteplog.*
FROM sysdtspackagelog INNER JOIN sysdtssteplog ON
sysdtspackagelog.lineagefull = sysdtssteplog.lineagefull
WHERE sysdtspackagelog.name = 'packagename'
ORDER BY stepexecutionid DESC

-- Change 'packagename' to an existing package
```

The format of the `sysdtspackagelog` and `sysdtssteplog` tables is contained in the following diagram:

sysdtspackagelog

Column Name	Data Type	Length	Allow Nulls
name	sysname	128	
description	nvarchar	1000	✓
id	uniqueidentifie	16	
versionid	uniqueidentifie	16	
lineagefull	uniqueidentifie	16	
lineageshort	int	4	
starttime	datetime	8	
endtime	datetime	8	✓
elapsedtime	float	8	✓
computer	sysname	128	
operator	sysname	128	
logdate	datetime	8	
errorcode	int	4	✓
errordescription	nvarchar	2000	✓

sysdtssteplog

Column Name	Data Type	Length	Allow Nulls
stepexecutionid	bigint	8	
lineagefull	uniqueidentifie	16	
stepname	sysname	128	
stepexecstatus	int	4	✓
stepexecresult	int	4	✓
starttime	datetime	8	
endtime	datetime	8	✓
elapsedtime	float	8	✓
errorcode	int	4	✓
errordescription	nvarchar	2000	✓
progresscount	bigint	8	✓

SysDTSPackageLog

The following table describes the information available in `sysdtspackagelog`. This table will comprise the bulk of package-level audit information.

Column Name	Description
name	Lists the name of the package as defined in the package properties.
description	Lists the description of the packages as defined in the package properties.
Id	Lists the globally unique identifier of the package. This is created when the package is first created.
versionid	Lists the globally unique identifier of the version of the package. This is the version of the package that was executed, not necessarily the current version.
lineagefull	If the package is saved in Microsoft Meta Data Services, this will be the unique identifier to reference the package's lineage. If not, this GUID is generated each time the package is executed.
lineageshort	The same conditions apply as the lineagefull column, but because this column is stored as an int value, it is more convenient to use for indexed columns.
starttime	Lists the date and time when the package execution started.
endtime	Lists the date and time when the package completed its execution.
elapsedtime	Lists the total execution time, in seconds, of the package
computer	Lists the computer from which the package was executed.
operator	Lists either the account of the users who executed the package from the designer or the account the SQL Server Agent executed the job under.
logdate	Lists the date and time when the log file was written to the log table.
errorcode	Lists the error code if the package failed or zero if it was successful. If more than one error occurred, this will only store the first error.
errordescription	Lists the error description if the package failed or remains blank if it was successful. If more than one error occurred, this will only store the first error.

SysDTSStepLog

The following table describes the information available in `sysdtssteplog`. This table contains all of the step-level audit information for a specific package.

Column Name	Description
stepexecutionid	Lists the sequence number for the step log record. This allows for determination of the exact order of execution.
lineagefull	If the package is saved in Microsoft Meta Data Services, this will be the unique identifier to reference the package's lineage. If not, this GUID is generated each time the package is executed.
stepname	This is the description of the step, rather than the step name.
stepexecstatus	Lists the status of the logged step execution. This value should always be 4 for DTSStepExecStat_Completed or NULL if the task is currently running.
stepexecresult	Lists the result of the task's execution. This column should be 0 (DTSStepExecResult_Success), 1 (DTSStepExecResult_Failure) or NULL if the step is still executing.
starttime	Lists the date and time when the step execution started.
endtime	Lists the date and time when the step completed its execution.
elapsedtime	Lists the total execution time, in seconds, of the step.
errorcode	Lists the error code if the step failed or zero if it was successful.
errordescription	Lists the error description if the package failed or remains blank if it was successful.
progresscount	Lists the rows (if any) that were processed during this step.

Programmatic Logging

If your design calls for programmatic control of logging, the DTS object model supports the dynamic enabling or disabling of this activity. To enable logging programmatically, you can use the DTS.Package2 properties. By setting the LogToSQLServer property to True, logging will occur and will use the LogServerName to connect to the server. Here is a list of the object model properties that control logging:

Property	Data Type	Description
LogToSQLServer	Boolean	If True, logging will occur to the specified SQL Server.
LogServerName	String	Lists the description of the packages as defined in the package properties.
LogServerUserName	String	This is the user name that DTS uses to connect to the logging server. This must be a valid user on the server or logging will fail.
LogServerPassword	String	This is the password that DTS uses to connect to the logging server.

Table continued on following page

Property	Data Type	Description
LogServerFlags	DTSSQLServer StorageFlags	Uses DTSSQLServerStorageFlags for standard (DTSSQLStgFlag_ Default) or trusted (DTSSQLStgFlag_ UseTrustedConnection) connections.
LogFileName	String	If this is specified, logging will also occur to this file.

To programmatically retrieve DTS Package, Step, and Task level log information, use either the GetPackageSQLServer or GetPackageRepository method of the Application object and specify the server and login information to return a PackageSQLServer object. The methods of the PackageSQLServer object provide server-level information about package and log information for all packages being stored or logging to there. The most useful methods are:

Method Name	Description
EnumPackageInfos	Returns a PackageInfos collection, which contains information about all of the packages stored in Meta Data Services or SQL Server storage. The PackageInfos collection contains PackageInfo objects that provide information about a package stored in the Microsoft Repository or in MSDB.
EnumPackageLogRecords	Returns a PackageLogRecords collection containing data from the package log records based in the input criteria. The PackageLogRecords collection contains one or more PackageLogRecord objects. This object contains information about a package's execution.
EnumStepLogRecords	Returns a StepLogRecords collection containing data from the step log records based in the input criteria. The StepLogRecords collection contains one or more StepLogRecord objects. This object contains information about the execution of a step in a DTS package.
EnumTaskLogRecords	Returns a TaskLogRecords collection containing data from the task log records based in the input criteria. The TaskLogRecords collection contains TaskLogRecord objects. These objects contain task information written to the DTS log by a custom task.
RemovePackage LogRecords	Removes all log records for the package based on the input criteria.
RemoveStepLogRecords	Removes all log records for the step based on the input criteria.
RemoveTaskLogRecords	Removes all log records for the task based on the input criteria.
RemoveAllLogRecords	Removes all log records for all packages. This process is not reversible and should be used with caution.

Package Error Handling

DTS has the ability to perform package-level error handling (actually, it's more like error logging). Any errors that occur during the package's execution can be logged to the operating system Application Event log or an external text file.

However, DTS does have the ability to halt execution of any package if any step error is encountered and not handled. This also means that if this option is not enabled, the package will always complete with a successful status, regardless of any error encountered. This choice should be weighed carefully before deciding on which path to choose. We will be discussing an additional option, Fail package on step failure, when we reach the workflow error handling section.

To enable package-level error handling, open the package that you wish to audit, select Package from the main menu, select Properties, choose the Logging tab when the dialog appears, and fill in your error file location (which will send the errors to an external file). You can also check the Write completion status to event log, which will send the errors to the event log. Although the dialog allows this option to be set regardless of your operating system, it will only write the status to computers running Windows NT or Windows 2000 because they are the only operating systems that have an event log.

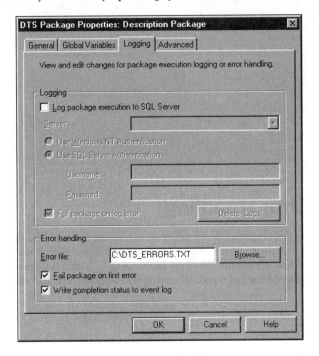

Error File

If a file name for the error file is supplied in the Error file textbox, the package will attempt to write its completion status to this file. The contents of this file are identical to the text written to the event log. However, any subsequent execution of the package appends a new status to the end of the file.

Listed below are several common and useful code snippets that can be used in DTS workflow scripts. They include:

- ❏ Restart/Retry a Workflow
- ❏ Programmatically Choose to Execute a Step
- ❏ Set Task Properties
- ❏ Implement Loops

To execute these code snippets, create an ActiveX Script task, but don't add any code to the properties. Right-click on the task to edit the workflow properties. Click on the Use ActiveX script button and paste these into the workflow properties' ActiveX script task section as shown above. The task itself doesn't have to perform any action; the purpose of these snippets is just to show the capabilities of programming the workflow.

Restart/Retry a Workflow

The following example shows how to execute a task repetitively. It uses a global variable as a counter to eventually break out of the loop. It also opens a message box that requires user input. This should not be executed on a remote server as no one will be able to respond to the message box and the task will be waiting for user input. By setting the result constant to DTSStepScriptResult_RetryLater, the DTS task will execute 3 times before asking the user if they would like to execute this task.

```
Function Main()
Dim sMsg

    If DTSGlobalVariables("retry").Value > 2 Then
        sMsg = "This is retry #" & DTSGlobalVariables("retry").Value
        sMsg = sMsg & Chr(13) & Chr(10) 'Carriage return/line feed
        sMsg = sMsg & "Would you like to execute this task?"

        ' vbQuestion, vbYesNo and vbYes are VBScript constants
        If MsgBox(sMsg, vbQuestion + vbYesNo) = vbYes Then
            Main = DTSStepScriptResult_ExecuteTask
        Else
            Main = DTSStepScriptResult_DontExecuteTask
        End If
    Else
' Increment the global variable counter by one
DTSGlobalVariables("retry").Value = _
DTSGlobalVariables("retry").Value + 1
        Main = DTSStepScriptResult_RetryLater
    End If

End Function
```

Programmatically Choose to Execute a Step

The following JScript code changes a step's properties so the step will not execute based on a global variable. This can be useful when a task should only be executed if a prior condition is met, such as the existence of a file.

```
Function Main()

    If DTSGlobalVariables("bExecuteStep").Value = True Then
        Main = DTSStepScriptResult_ExecuteTask
    Else
        Main = DTSStepScriptResult_DontExecuteTask
    End If

End Function
```

Set Task Properties

The following VBScript code sets the task, DTSStep_DTSActiveScriptTask_2, to have a status of already executed. DTS will then not execute this task. This can be used in the same scenario as above – when a prior condition is met. The difference is that this example sets another task's property, while the example above determines its own status. I would recommend using this method if you must only set one task's status. If several tasks are affected by a predetermined event, I would recommend using the above method.

```
Function Main()
Dim oPackage

    Set oPackage = DTSGlobalVariables.Parent

oPackage.Steps("DTSStep_DTSActiveScriptTask_2").ExecutionStatus = _
DTSStepExecStat_Completed

    Main = DTSStepScriptResult_ExecuteTask
End Function
```

Implement Loops

The following code will create a loop between two tasks that will execute 10 times. Task 1's name is DTSStep_DTSActiveScriptTask_1. This will allow for one or more tasks to be executed repetively, as if in a programmatic loop. It uses a global variable, nCounter, as the loop controller. By default, when a package first begins execution, every task has a status of DTSStepExecStat_Waiting. By resetting a task with this status, DTS will attempt to re-execute the task.

```
Function Main()
Dim oPackage

    DTSGlobalVariables("nCounter").Value = _
            DTSGlobalVariables("nCounter").Value + 1
```

```
    If DTSGlobalVariables("nCounter").Value <= 10 Then
       Set oPackage = DTSGlobalVariables.Parent
       oPackage.Steps("DTSStep_DTSActiveScriptTask_1").ExecutionStatus =_
                                              DTSStepExecStat_Waiting
       Main = DTSStepScriptResult_ExecuteTask
       Else
          Main = DTSStepScriptResult_ExecuteTask
       End If
End Function
```

Initialize Global Variables

The following code will initialize several global variables prior to its associated task's execution:

```
Function Main()

    DTSGlobalVariables("bVariable1").Value = True
    DTSGlobalVariables("dtCurrentDate").Value = Now()
    DTSGlobalVariables("sServer").Value = "SVRSQL"
    DTSGlobalVariables("nCounter").Value = 0

End Function
```

DTSTaskExecResult

DTSTaskExecResult constants are used when creating an ActiveX Script task. For example, as you develop code within an ActiveX Script task object, you can handle errors using the script engine's native error handling (VBScript – On Error, Jscript – try/catch) or you can allow all errors to bubble out to DTS. If you choose to handle the errors, you can decide the result of the script's execution by setting the entry function's result to either **DTSTaskExecResult_Success, DTSTaskExecResult_Failure** or **DTSTaskExecResult_RetryStep.** Depending on how the rest of your package is designed, you can fully control the direction of execution that your package takes after receiving an error. If your task doesn't return an explicit result, DTS assumes that the task failed.

```
Function Main()
Dim Variable1
Dim Variable2

    'Do something…

    'Do something else…

    If Variable1 <> Variable2 Then
       Main = DTSTaskExecResult_Success
       'Manually set the task's result to success
    Else
       Main = DTSTaskExecResult_Failure
       'Manually set the task's result to failure
    End If
End Function
```

DTSTransformStatus

DTSTransformStatus constants are used when creating an ActiveX Script transformation in a Transform Data task or a Data Driven Query ActiveX transformation. For example, the following code uses a Transform Data task to move author information from the pubs database into a new table if the author's city of residence is Oakland, CA. Instead of using the Copy Column transformation, the ActiveX Script transformation is used so that the transformation will skip the current row and move to the next row without generating an error. This functionality cannot be accomplished using only the default Copy Column transformation.

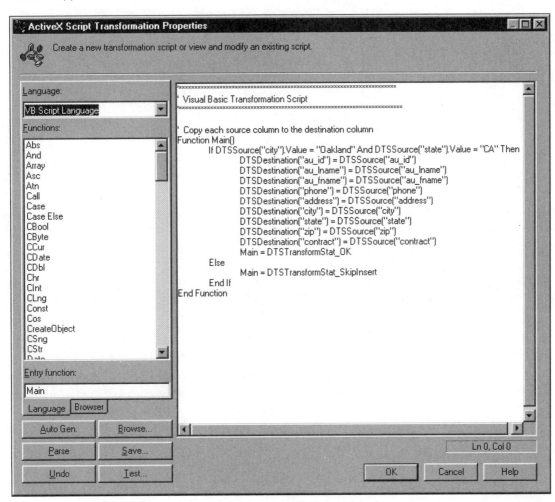

The above example, however, skips all author information where the city and state are not Oakland, CA. You may desire to export these rows to an exception file so that subsequent tasks or processes may attempt to correct any data loading issues. The following sample code will redirect these rows to an exception file:

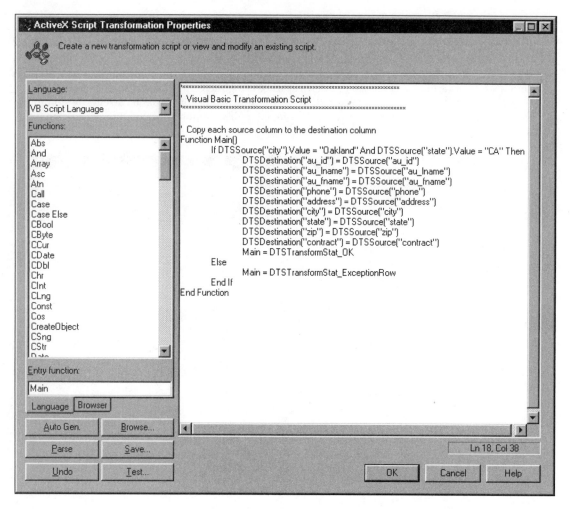

Staying with the current example, to direct these rows to an exception file, choose the Options tab from the Properties of the Transform Data task where you can specify the location and format for the exception file:

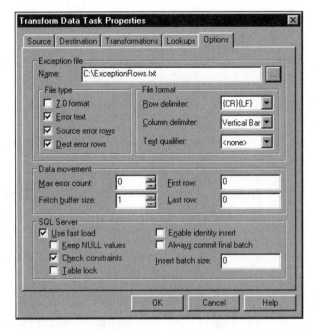

In order to log the error rows separately from the error text, you should uncheck the 7.0 format option and check the **Error text**, **Source error rows**, and **Dest error rows** check boxes. These options will log source and destination errors separately from their respective error descriptions, which will allow easier programmatic handling of the exception rows.

In the above examples, we used several of the data pump constants. The following is a list of all data pump constants that can be used to control script execution within a transformation:

Constant	Description
DTSTransformStat_OK	The current row has been transformed successfully.
DTSTransformStat_Info	The current row has been processed with additional information and the current row will be inserted into the destination. The additional information can be retrieved from OLE DB.
DTSTransformStat_OKInfo	The current row has been processed with additional information and the current row will be inserted into the destination.
DTSTransformStat_SkipRow	The current row has been processed but will not be inserted into the destination and the task's error counter will not be incremented.

Table continued on following page

Constant	Description
DTSTransformStat_ SkipRowInfo	The current row has been processed with additional information, but will not be inserted into the destination and the task's error counter will not be incremented. The additional information can be retrieved from the DTS ErrorSink.
DTSTransformStat_ SkipFetch	The current row is used again in the next pass through the transformations. For example, if you want to perform a transformation on the same row more than once, but you don't want to insert it into the destination multiple times, you can use this return value.
DTSTransformStat_ SkipInsert	The current row is not written to the destination and no error is produced.
DTSTransformStat_ DestDataNotSet	The current row is processed, but no data is inserted into the destination. This is used when doing a Write File transformation.
DTSTransformStat_ Error	The current row's processing is terminated and an error is raised. If an exception file has been specified, the error row is written there and the task's error count is incremented. Additional information is written to the DTS ErrorSink.
DTSTransformStat_ ErrorSkipRow	This current row's processing is terminated and an error is raised. However, the error row is NOT written to the exception file, even if one has been specified.
DTSTransformStat_ ExceptionRow	This current row's processing is terminated and the error row is written to the exception file. However, the task's error count is not incremented.
DTSTransformStat_ AbortPump	The current row's processing is terminated and any source rows still waiting to be processed are cancelled. The row is written to the exception file and subsequent tasks continue. The task's error count is incremented.
DTSTransformStat_ NoMoreRows	The current row's processing is terminated and any source rows still waiting to be processed are cancelled. The row is written to the exception file and subsequent tasks continue. The task's error count is not incremented.

Error Handling from External Applications

When SQL Server 2000 is installed, the DTS service provider is included in the normal installation. This DTS provider exposes its COM-based object model for applications to take advantage of. This creates the opportunity for any COM application to integrate DTS functionality directly into the application. The DTS provider also exposes some methods for error handling that are not available through the DTS designer. The following section discusses available methods for logging from external applications.

dtsrun – Command Line Execution

If your project's architecture dictates that you must start DTS packages in an automated fashion, you can use dtsrun.exe from any machine that has the server administration tools installed. Using SQL Server SQLAgent, you can schedule jobs that will execute packages on a one-time or recurring basis.

The following is an example of executing a DTS package from the command line using dtsrun and redirecting the output to a file called error.txt. The output is redirected so that the result can be used to track any issues that may occur.

```
dtsrun /F "DTSRUN Package Error.dts" > error.txt
```

If you open error.txt in a text editor, this is the text you will see:

```
DTSRun: Loading...
DTSRun: Executing...
DTSRun OnStart: DTSStep_DTSActiveScriptTask_1
DTSRun OnError: DTSStep_DTSActiveScriptTask_1, Error = -2147220482 (800403FE)
   Error string: Error Code: 0
Error Source= Microsoft VBScript runtime error
Error Description: Type mismatch: 'asdf'

Error on Line 5

   Error source: Microsoft Data Transformation Services (DTS) Package
   Help file: sqldts.hlp
   Help context: 1100

Error Detail Records:

Error: -2147220482 (800403FE); Provider Error: 0 (0)
   Error string: Error Code: 0
Error Source= Microsoft VBScript runtime error
Error Description: Type mismatch: 'asdf'

Error on Line 5

   Error source: Microsoft Data Transformation Services (DTS) Package
   Help file: sqldts.hlp
   Help context: 1100


DTSRun OnFinish: DTSStep_DTSActiveScriptTask_1
DTSRun: Package execution complete.
```

Executing from Visual Basic

If your architecture dictates that you create or execute packages programmatically, you can begin to perform active error handling. Using Visual Basic, you can open, execute, and trap any errors as they occur. You can also redesign workflow execution based on these errors. The following VB code opens and executes a DTS package. Once running, if any task or workflow errors occur, they are immediately sent to the event handler. In the event handler, you can check for the specific error type and perform alternative actions.

421

To create this project in Visual Basic, open a new project and choose a Standard EXE project:

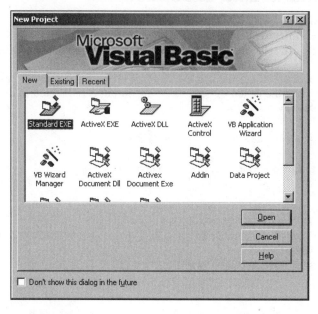

Choose Project | References and then choose the reference to Microsoft DTSPackage Object Library, as shown below:

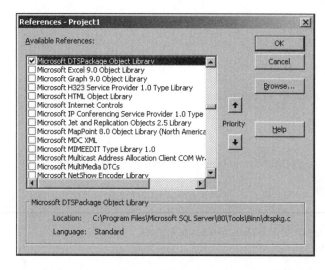

Click on OK. Add a command button to the default form and name it cmdExecutePackage.

In the following example, the DTS package, `UpdateFactTable.dts`, issues an Execute SQL task against its database. The transaction log for the database is not set to autogrow and we want to manually backup the database if we get a transaction log full error from the task. Here's the code:

```
Option Explicit
Private WithEvents objPackage As DTS.Package

Private Sub oPkg_OnError(ByVal EventSource As String, _
ByVal ErrorCode As Long, ByVal Source As String, _
ByVal Description As String, ByVal HelpFile As String, _
ByVal HelpContext As Long, ByVal IDofInterfaceWithError As String, _
                                   pbCancel As Boolean)

Dim sMessage As String

    If ErrorCode = -2147217865 Then
        Call BackupSQLDatabase()
    Else
        MsgBox "Error Occurred:" & (ErrorCode) & Description
    End If
End Sub

Private Sub BackupSQLDatabase()
' Code that backs up a database
' ...

End Sub

Private Sub cmdExecutePackage_Click()

    Set objPackage = New DTS.Package
    objPackage.LoadFromStorageFile "C:\LoadFile.dts", ""
    objPackage.Execute

End Sub
```

The code above includes some advanced concepts. The `WithEvents` keyword in Visual Basic allows a program that you write to trap or intercept an event that a COM object creates. In this case, DTS can be executing, but when it reaches a task that causes an error, instead of executing its own error handling, it will call the `OnError` subroutine and execute the included code. This can be very powerful because it allows you to create applications using COM objects as though they were your own.

Design Considerations for Optimal Error Handling

To make the packages you design more bullet proof, you must have consistent error handling that performs a series of accepted tasks or actions to audit or proactively correct any situation that may arise. Of course, in a perfect world, it would make sense to have a single piece of code that handled all errors. However, as you will see, DTS is not well suited to this.

Multiple Precedence Constraints

You can create multiple precedence constraints for any task. In the following example, Task3 has two preceding tasks, Task1 and Task2. Task3's precedents are both On Success workflows. Using this design, the execution of Task3 only occurs if Task1 and Task2 are successful.

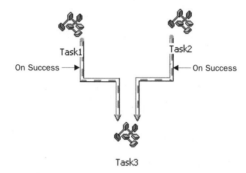

With all precedence constraints, DTS assumes a logical "AND" relationship. This works great for On Success and On Completion workflows, but not so well for On Failure workflows, if you wish to have a single point of code handle all task errors. The following example is similar to the prior example, except that the Error Handler task has both Task1 and Task2 On Error precedents.

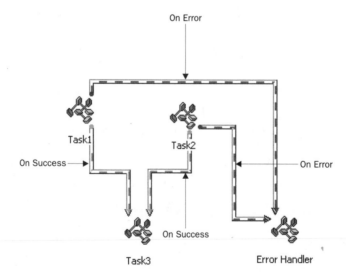

This means that both tasks, Task1 and Task2, must fail before the Error Handler task will execute. This also means that all tasks must have a single On Failure workflow to a single task to properly handle errors. The following diagram shows the proper way to handle errors:

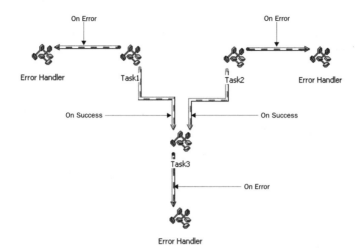

This order of execution in this example proceeds as follows:

❑ Task1 and Task2 execute simultaneously.

❑ If either Task1 or Task2 fails, Task3 does not execute and the respective Error Handler task will execute.

❑ If Task1 AND Task2 are both successful, Task3 will execute.

❑ If Task3 is successful, the package completes successfully. If not, Task3's Error Handler task will execute.

GetExecutionErrorInfo

When a step fails, the package will fail if the package's FailOnError property or the step's FailPackageOnError property is True. The error that is raised will only specify the step that failed, not the error that made the step fail. In order to programmatically use the error information when a step fails, you must use the GetExecutionErrorInfo method of the Step or Step2 object. However, this method cannot be called from script and so must be used from Visual Basic or Visual C++. To work around this problem, you can create an ActiveX DLL in Visual Basic and invoke this object from your error handling script.

To create this object, open Visual Basic and create an ActiveX DLL project. Paste the following code into the class module:

```
Public Function GetExecutionErrorInfoStub(oStep)
Dim nErrorCode As Long
Dim sErrorSource As String
Dim sErrorDescription As String

    oStep.GetExecutionErrorInfo nErrorCode, sErrorSource, _
                                       sErrorDescription

    GetExecutionErrorInfoStub = "Error Code: " & nErrorCode & ", " & _
        "Error Source: " & sErrorSource & ", Error Description: " & _
                                       sErrorDescription

End Function
```

```
    oErrorHandlerPackage.GlobalVariables.Item("gsErrorStep").Value =_
                                            oStep.Description

    '**** Execute error handler package
    oErrorHandlerPackage.Execute

    '**** Clean up
    Set oErrorHandlerPackage = Nothing
    Set oStep = Nothing
    Set oCurrPkg = Nothing
    Set oDTSHelper = Nothing

    Main = DTSTaskExecResult_Success
End Function
```

This architecture works for any type of task including Data Pump tasks.

From each Error Handler task, a second external error logging package is opened and executed. This second package can look similar to this

Error Logging Package

Main Tasks

Error Mission Control - dynamically sets the attributes of the mail task and any other task that you want executed.

Mail Error - mails notification to recipient list about the error that occurred

Error Mission Control

Mail Error

From the Error Mission Control task, you can set properties of the Mail Error task so that the administrators have the error message e-mailed to them. You can also add other dependent tasks such as creating audit records, logging to other error repositories, triggers to start other packages, sending pager alerts, interfacing with a monitoring tool such as Tivoli, or creating semaphores. Use your imagination!

Within this package, three global variables should be created:

Global Variable Name	Data Type	Description
gsErrorText	String	This value contains the error message created in the Error Handler task.
gsErrorPackage	String	This is the name of the package in which the error occurred.
gsErrorStep	String	This is the name of the step in which the error occurred.

Here's the code behind the **Error Mission Control** task:

```vb
'**********************************************************************
'  Visual Basic ActiveX Script
'**********************************************************************

Function Main()
Dim sSubject
Dim sMessageBody

Dim oCurrPkg
Dim oTask

    '**** Get Reference to the Current Package
    Set oCurrPkg = DTSGlobalVariables.Parent

    '**** Look for the sendmail task
    For Each oTask in oCurrPkg.Tasks
        If oTask.CustomTaskID = "DTSSendMailTask" Then
            Exit For
        End If
    Next

    '**** Create subject and message body strings
    sSubject = "Error in Package: " & _
                DTSGlobalVariables("gsErrorPackage").Value
    sSubject = sSubject & ", Step: " & _
                DTSGlobalVariables("gsErrorStep").Value
    sMessageBody = DTSGlobalVariables("gsErrorText").Value

    '**** Set SendMail Task Properties
    oTask.CustomTask.Subject = sSubject
    oTask.CustomTask.MessageText = sMessageBody

    Main = DTSTaskExecResult_Success
End Function
```

This creates the opportunity to standardize the process of managing errors as they occur. This is a very powerful architecture for any automated package that you create.

Summary

In this chapter we've covered many ways to handle errors internally and externally to DTS. These include:

❑ Errors in the DTS Designer

❑ Handling errors at the package level

❑ Handling errors at the task level

❑ Handling errors from Visual Basic and other applications

We also discussed the optimal method for designing your packages to handle errors with a minimum of coding. Using these examples in your own projects will ensure that if any errors do occur, they can be easily debugged with a minimum of time and effort.

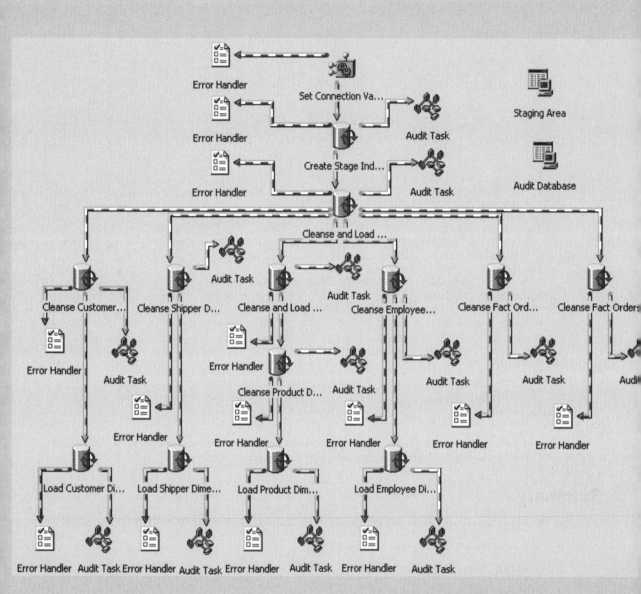

Error Handler

Set Connection Va...

Audit Task

Staging Area

Error Handler

Create Stage Ind...

Audit Task

Audit Database

Error Handler

Audit Task

Cleanse and Load ...

Audit Task

Cleanse Customer...

Cleanse Shipper D...

Cleanse and Load ...

Audit Task

Cleanse Employee...

Cleanse Fact Ord...

Cleanse Fact Orders

Error Handler

Audit Task

Error Handler

Audit Task

Audit Task

Audit Task

Audit

Error Handler

Cleanse Product D...

Audit Task

Error Handler

Error Handler

Error Handler

Error Handler

Load Customer Di...

Load Shipper Dime...

Load Product Dim...

Load Employee Di...

Error Handler   Audit Task Error Handler Audit Task Error Handler   Audit Task Error Handler   Audit Task

12

Writing Your Own Custom Tasks

As we've already seen, SQL Server 2000 DTS comes with 17 pre-built tasks that can be used for everything from moving and transforming data to executing another package. Several of Microsoft's new applications will be adding more tasks, such as the ability to process cubes (Analysis Services 2000) or import web log data (Commerce Server 2000). DTS also lets you script any task that can't be created directly. With all of these options offering a copious amount of flexibility, who could possibly want anything more?

If you find that you're one of those people who are never satisfied, then DTS Custom Tasks are for you. In this chapter we'll discuss what custom tasks are, and how you might use them. We'll also cover, in detail, the process for creating a custom task.

Creating a custom task, though, requires some detailed knowledge of Visual Basic or C++, some COM understanding and an understanding of the DTS Custom Task object model. In this chapter, we'll explain the DTS Custom Task object model and how to create a task in Visual Basic. The examples in this chapter require Visual Basic 6.0 Standard Edition or greater. If you have the need to create your task in C++, refer to the code examples included with the installation of SQL Server 2000.

In this chapter we will discuss:

- ❑ What is a Custom Task?
- ❑ Why use a Custom Task?
- ❑ How DTS uses a Custom Task
- ❑ Building a Custom Task in Visual Basic
- ❑ Debugging a Custom Task in Visual Basic

What is a Custom Task?

We already know that a **task** in DTS is defined as a unit of work to be performed within the constraints of a workflow in a DTS package. A custom task is a DLL that is written in a COM-compliant language, such as Visual Basic or C++, compiled, and registered in DTS. Custom tasks allow this unit of work to use the more powerful features of a compiled programming language. They also can hide some of the complexity of these units of work from the designer of packages. This means that you can create a very complex task, but design it in such a way that other developers can utilize it without having to know the details of how it works. This might sound familiar: the advantages of creating custom tasks are similar to the advantages of creating an object-oriented application.

Why Use a Custom Task?

You might be asking yourself, "Is it worth the trouble?" or "I can do anything from an ActiveX Script task. Why do I need to build a custom task?" There are many reasons for creating your own custom tasks. Many of the reasons are the same reasons that existed several years ago when companies were creating their own VBXs or OCXs. Here are just a few:

❑ Functionality not possible from an ActiveX Script

❑ Code maintenance/reuse

❑ Ease of use for non-programmers

❑ Encapsulation of business logic

❑ Security

❑ Performance

❑ Profit

Let's go into these in a little more detail.

Functionality Not Possible From an ActiveX Script

Scripting languages are not as flexible as compiled languages such as Visual Basic or C++. They don't perform as well and have serious limitations when manipulating COM objects, because of their loosely typed constructs. Also, you don't have any ability to create a design-time user interface in a scripting language. A design-time interface can hide many of the implementation details to allow the task to be used by inexperienced DTS programmers.

Code Maintenance/Reuse

One of the big drawbacks of DTS is that there's really no easy way to reuse code. There is no way to implement a function library or create include files without some serious coding. This means that when you write a useful function, routine, or snippet, you will find yourself cutting and pasting this code into many different ActiveX scripts. If at some point you wish to enhance or repair this code, you've now got to track every task and every transformation for this code. This can quickly become unmanageable.

Ease of Use for Non-Programmers

Not everyone who will be using DTS will be an expert coder. Complex functionality can be implemented into a nice, clean wrapper that anyone can use. Just think about some of the tasks that Microsoft included in SQL 2000 that weren't in SQL 7.0. These new tasks make life a lot more enjoyable. Using custom tasks, it's possible to write a task that meets your exact needs.

Encapsulation of Business Logic

To borrow an object-oriented design idea, encapsulation bars external access to its internal parts except through a carefully controlled interface. By creating custom tasks to encapsulate this functionality, you can prevent any incorrect redefinition of any business logic you choose.

Security

Although you may not be interested in selling your custom task, you may also not want everyone in the world to see your code. With scripting, there's no way to keep prying eyes from your code. If you create a custom task, you can compile and hide your code, which hides business logic and flow. This can be very important if you want to redistribute this task to others.

Performance

Before DTS can execute an ActiveX Script task, it must load the Microsoft Scripting Engine into memory. This process, when repeated many times, can severely affect performance. However, any custom task will have to be compiled, and any run-time objects will only be loaded the first time and kept in memory for the duration of the package.

Note that if you create your custom task in Visual Basic, DTS must set the task to run on the package's main thread. This causes these tasks to serialize and can affect performance adversely if your package is attempting to execute these tasks in parallel. We'll discuss this in much more detail in coming sections.

Profit

And finally, eventually, someone or some company will realize that not all of the desired functionality is included in DTS 2000. This will create an opportunity for third party companies to create a market for reusable DTS Custom Tasks.

The Task Object Model

Normally a DTS package contains at least one task. Some of the built-in DTS tasks require connections or other pre-existing conditions to use them, but all have the same basic characteristics; they're all created using the same object model and interface as you can use to create your own tasks.

To better understand how the CustomTask object fits into the DTS Object Model, review the fragment of the Object Model shown below:

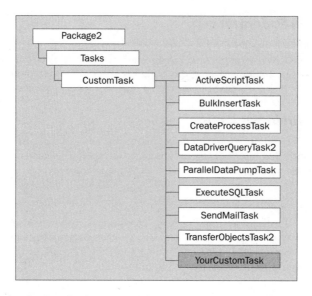

Notice that all the tasks above, whether created by Microsoft or by you, must inherit their methods from the CustomTask COM Interface. This means that all tasks must implement, at a minimum, the same methods; you can, however, still can create new methods. This is enforced so that DTS can talk to each CustomTask in the same way. Through this CustomTask interface, you can extend DTS by creating new tasks to supplement the functionality delivered out of the box.

The CustomTask Interface

The CustomTask interface is actually very simple to use. It requires implementation of only one method, one collection, and two properties to compile and function properly.

The next section covers all of the CustomTask interface elements and is followed by a simple example that can be built in Visual Basic:

Element	Description
Description property	The description of the task. DTS uses this property to label the icon when in the designer.
Name property	A DTS-assigned name, unique within the package, that DTS uses to reference the task. This should not be exposed since DTS would no longer be able to locate the task if the value changed.
Properties collection	A reference to a collection of Property objects that define each property of the Custom task. You can add additional properties by simply defining them as public in your class
Execute method	The method is where the work of the task is executed. This method is called by the DTS package when the package is being executed.

Let's look at each of these in more detail.

The Description Property

To implement the `Description` property, you must create a variable (private to the class you're implementing) to read and write from, and implement this as a class property like this:

```
' This is the variable declaration
Private msDescription As String

...

' These are both the Get and Let implementations of the Description
' property
Private Property Get CustomTask_Description() As String
    CustomTask_Description = msDescription
End Property

Private Property Let CustomTask_Description(ByVal RHS As String)
    msDescription = RHS
End Property
```

This variable will store the value of the `Description` property for all methods of the object to use. If you want to have the ability to edit this property from the DTS Designer, you must provide two implementations for this property. By default you will get the `CustomTask_Description` implementation, but you should also create a class-specific `Description` implementation and tie both of these properties together by using the same private variable like this:

```
'These methods support a public implementation of the Description property
Public Property Get Description() As String
    Description = msDescription
End Property

Public Property Let Description(ByVal RHS As String)
    msDescription = RHS
End Property
```

This is necessary to support both the `CustomTask_Description` property (which must be implemented) and the task `Description` property (which is used by DTS Designer). If you only implement the `CustomTask_Description`, none of your tasks will support descriptions in DTS Designer; you'll only see the icons.

The Name Property

The `Name` property uniquely identifies all tasks within a DTS package. It is recommended that you do not declare the `Name` property publicly, because DTS generates a unique name when the task is created. In addition, DTS also creates a `Step` object for the task at the same time. If the name changes, DTS will look for the task with the old name and will fail, thus invalidating all dependent Steps or Workflows you might have created.

The Properties Collection

The `Properties` collection contains all of a `CustomTask`'s `Property` objects. DTS can handle most of the collection management for you if you so choose. By default, DTS will manage all property persistence as long as you implement `Property Get` and `Let` code for each property (these are simply statements that declare properties). When DTS manages property persistence, it stores all of the properties of the custom task in the package's configuration so that they aren't lost the next time you open your package. If you want to manage properties yourself, we will examine this later in the chapter.

The Execute Method

The Execute method is called when the DTS package attempts to execute the custom task. This is where the work of the task must take place. From this method, we can directly control all package objects, event bubbling, logging, and task result status.

The four parameters of the Execute method are:

Parameter	Data Type	Description
pPackage	Object	This references the Package2 object where the task resides. Use this reference to retrieve global variables, workflow information, and other package information. Do not persist or save any reference to the package after the Execute method is finished.
pPackageEvents	Object	Use pPackageEvents to raise package events or perform error handling. You should ensure that pPackageEvents is not NULL or Nothing before using.
pPackageLog	Object	Use pPackageLog to write records to the server log table if logging is enabled. You should ensure that pPackageLog is not NULL before using.
pTaskResult	DTSTaskExecResult	You can set the result of the task to success or failure by setting this value to one of the DTSTaskExecResult constants: DTSTaskExecResult_Success DTSTaskExecResult_Failure DTSTaskExecResult_RetryStep

We don't need to explicitly call the Execute method from inside our task: because we implemented the CustomTask interface, DTS will call it at the appropriate time.

The best way to understand how to use this interface is to try an example: so let's do just that.

Building Your First Custom Task

Instead of jumping into a complex custom task example first, we should start with code that generates the most basic custom task possible. This task does nothing but display a message box.

Let's start by creating an ActiveX DLL project in Visual Basic. To do this, open Visual Basic and choose New Project from the File menu. Choose the ActiveX DLL project type and click OK.

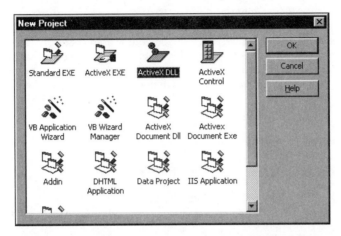

Choose References from the Project menu. Scroll down the list of Available References until you see Microsoft DTSPackage Object Library. Make sure that the check box is checked and click OK.

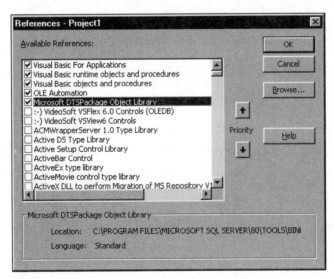

Now we're ready to insert code so that when the task is executed from a DTS package, our DLL will display a message box containing the message "CustomTask_Execute method".

To insert the code, open the class module and insert the following code. If the class module is not already open, double-click on **Class1** in the **Project Explorer** window. If the **Project Explorer** is not open, press *Ctrl+R* to open it.

```
Option Explicit
Implements DTS.CustomTask

Private msTaskName    As String
Private msDescription As String
```

Notice the `Implements DTS.CustomTask` line above. It is used to specify the `CustomTask` interface that will be implemented in the class module. This specifies that an explicit "contract" exists between the programmer and the `CustomTask` class that expects certain methods to be implemented in the project. When you type this in Visual Basic, VB will not allow your DLL to be compiled until all of the methods have been implemented.

One of the required methods is the `CustomTask_Execute` method. The `Execute` method simply displays the message box:

```
Private Sub CustomTask_Execute(ByVal pPackage As Object, _
                               ByVal pPackageEvents As Object, _
                               ByVal pPackageLog As Object, _
                               pTaskResult As DTS.DTSTaskExecResult)

    MsgBox "CustomTask_Execute method"

End Sub
```

Due to our "contract", we must also provide implementations for all of the `CustomTask` properties. The `Properties` elements is stubbed and not implemented:

```
Private Property Get CustomTask_Properties() As DTS.Properties
    Set CustomTask_Properties = Nothing
End Property
```

The code below allows for the persistent storage of the `Name` and `Description` properties by using the standard `Get` and `Let` methods:

```
Private Property Get CustomTask_Description() As String
    CustomTask_Description = msDescription
End Property

Private Property Let CustomTask_Description(ByVal RHS As String)
    msDescription = RHS
End Property

Private Property Get CustomTask_Name() As String
    CustomTask_Name = msTaskName
End Property

Private Property Let CustomTask_Name(ByVal RHS As String)
    msTaskName = RHS
End Property
```

```
Public Property Get Description() As String
    Description = msDescription
End Property
```

```
Public Property Let Description(ByVal RHS As String)
    msDescription = RHS
End Property
```

As you can see, to create the most basic custom task in Visual Basic, all you must do is create stubs for each of the required elements, and implement the setting and retrieving of the name property. This is required as there is a contract between your custom class and the SQL Server DTS Package process that requires these stubs to exist.

Registering and Using a Custom Task

Now that we've created a simple custom task, let's build and register it to see what it does. To begin with, we need to build the task in Visual Basic.

Building the DLL

These are the steps to build this custom task in Visual Basic:

1. Choose Project 1 Properties from the Project menu.

1. On the General tab, change the Project Name to SimpleCT and click OK.

2. Right-click on the Class1 class in the Project Explorer window, and choose Properties. If, for some reason, these windows are not visible, we can make them appear by selecting the View menu and selecting either Project Explorer (Ctrl+R) or Properties Window (F4). Change the name of the class module to CSimple:

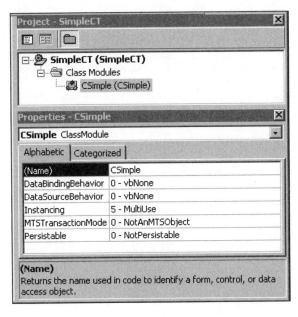

3. Build the component by choosing Make SimpleCT.dll from the File menu.

This process builds the DLL and registers the custom task in the Windows registry. If you need to move the DLL to a different machine, you will have to register it manually on that machine. You can do this by opening a command window, changing the current directory to the directory where SimpleCT.DLL exists and typing 'REGSVR32.EXE SimpleCT.DLL'. However, you still must register the task in the DTS Designer so that DTS can add the task to the task menu; it can then be used to develop packages.

Registering the Task in DTS

To register, follow these steps:

1. Open SQL Server Enterprise Manager, right-click on Data Transformation Services and choose New Package.

2. On the Task menu, choose Register Custom Task.

3. In the Register Custom Task dialog, enter the description SimpleTask. Then specify the path to the SimpleCT.DLL we just built:

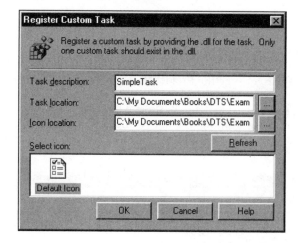

4. Finally, click OK.

The task will be added to the task menu and icon bar. Notice, that the default icon is shown because we didn't specify an icon to use.

Running the Task

Click and drag the new task to the Designer Workspace and the default property dialog appears. Since we implemented the `Description` property publicly, it can now be changed and saved from within DTS Designer.

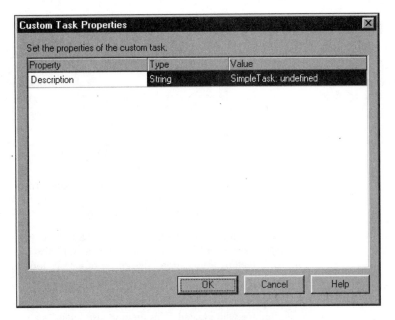

Click **OK** to get rid of the properties dialog. Now go ahead and execute the package, and you should see a message box appear (check your taskbar if it doesn't pop up – it should be a bar with SimpleCT on it):

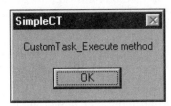

That's all there is to building and registering a custom task. Note that after you press OK you will be told that there was an error – this is because the task doesn't actually do anything, so don't worry!

Unregistering a Task

If we want to make changes to the task's code, we must first unregister the task from DTS. We can unregister the task by choosing Task | Unregister Custom Task from the menu. Pick the SimpleCT task and click OK. You must close Enterprise Manager before you can rebuild your task.

More About Custom Tasks

Now that we've seen a custom task in action, it's time to discuss adding a user interface to make property management easier.

The CustomTaskUI Interface

The CustomTaskUI interface allows you to create a dialog for design-time property maintenance of your custom task. All of the standard tasks in DTS implement this interface so a package designer can modify the tasks' properties using an intuitive user interface. Since we want to create a professional-looking custom task, we're going to implement this interface. Let's discuss the CustomTaskUI interface elements.

Element	Description
CreateCustomToolTip method	This method creates a custom tooltip window. This method draws the window for the tooltip, and returns a pointer to the handle to the calling application, usually DTS Designer. Implementing this method requires some advanced knowledge of the Windows API and is outside the scope of this book.
Delete method	This method is called when a CustomTask is removed from the design surface of DTS Designer. This method also includes a pointer to the calling application's design window as its lone parameter.
Edit method	This method is called when a task is double-clicked, or when a task's properties are to be edited. This task should display the custom user interface when called. This method also includes a pointer to the calling application's design window as its lone parameter.
GetUIInfo method	This method returns information to the calling application about the CustomTaskUI. You can implement your own custom tooltip text here if you wish.
Help method	This method is called when Help is selected from the popup menu when you right-click on the task object on the design surface.
Initialize method	This method is the first method called when the custom task is dropped onto the design surface for the first time. You can store references to the current task object here, and initialize the task's properties. This method is also called when the custom task is removed from the design surface, but it is called before the Delete and Edit methods are called.
New method	This method is called when the custom task is dropped onto the design surface. It is called after the Initialize method has been called. To provide the user with the most intuitive method of setting your custom task's properties, you should display your custom properties dialog when this method is called so that initial values can be provided.

Again, we'll look at each of these in more detail.

The CreateCustomToolTip Method

If you wish to implement your own tooltips for the task on the design surface, you can implement this method. DTS, by default, will display the description property of the task for the tooltip if this is not implemented. To implement, you must draw your own tooltip window, provide the initial location for display, and pass the handle of the tooltip window to the calling application.

The four parameters of the `CreateCustomToolTip` method are:

Parameter	Data Type	Description
hwndParent	Long	Handle of the window of the calling application in which the tooltip is to be displayed
x	Long	Horizontal coordinate of the tooltip window
y	Long	Vertical coordinate of the tooltip window
plTipWindow	Long	Handle of the window that you create in this method

Once again, the implementation of this method requires advanced understanding of the Windows API and is outside the scope of this book. It is discussed here to provide complete coverage of the CustomTaskUI interface.

The Delete Method

This method is called when the task is removed from the design surface of the calling application. You should clean up any persisted references to any objects at this point, such as any references to the current package or task, or any static files that the task may have created or have open. The calling application should pass in a handle to the window in which the `CustomTask` was displayed.

The single parameter of the `Delete` method is:

Parameter	Data Type	Description
hwndParent	Long	Handle of the window of the calling application in which the task was displayed

The Edit Method

This method is called when a user double-clicks on the custom task from the DTS Design surface, or when a user right-clicks and chooses **Properties**. This method should display the property page for the custom task when called.

The single parameter of the `Edit` method is:

Parameter	Data Type	Description
hwndParent	Long	Handle of the window of the calling application in which the property page is to be displayed

443

The GetUIInfo Method

This method returns information to the calling application about the `CustomTask`'s user interface. The four parameters of the `GetUIInfo` method are:

Parameter	Data Type	Description
pbstrToolTip	String	Custom tooltip text
pbstrDescription	String	Description of the user interface element
plVersion	Long	Reserved for future use
pFlags	DTSCustom TaskUIFlags	Value to indicate whether the `CustomTask` implements custom tooltips; possible values are: `DTSCustomTaskUIFlags_Default` and `DTSCustomTaskUIFlags_DoesCustomToolTip`

The Help Method

This method is called when a user right-clicks and chooses **Help** from the popup menu. You can create your own help file and call it from here.

The single parameter of the `Help` method is:

Parameter	Data Type	Description
hwndParent	Long	Handle of the window of the calling application in which the help is to be displayed

The Initialize Method

This method is called whenever the custom task is used in the design environment. This method can be used to supply default values for the custom user interface, or to save a reference to the current task object for any other `CustomTaskUI` methods to use.

The single parameter of the `Initialize` method is:

Parameter	Data Type	Description
pTask	DTS.Task	Task object for the current `CustomTask`

The New Method

This method is called when the custom task is first dropped onto the DTS Design surface, or the user chooses the new `CustomTask` from the **Task** menu. This method should display the property page for the custom task when called.

The single parameter of the `New` method is:

Parameter	Data Type	Description
hwndParent	Long	Handle of the window of the calling application in which the property page is to be displayed

How DTS Uses a Custom Task

DTS utilizes custom tasks in two ways: at design time and run time. `CustomTaskUI` methods are only called during design time, while the `CustomTask_Execute` method is only called at run time. Since property assignments can happen anytime, they can be called in both design and run time situations. This scenario is very similar to the way that Visual Basic uses custom controls.

Design Time

DTS creates an instance of the `CustomTask` class when the user first creates a `CustomTask` object on the design surface. This instance controls all of the user interface interaction. It is responsible for creating the custom properties dialog and tooltip window when the appropriate methods are called by DTS Designer.

Run Time

When a package that contains a custom task begins to execute, DTS automatically initializes the `CustomTask` class by instantiating an instance for each `CustomTask`. If the package contains ten `CustomTask`s, all ten tasks will be initialized at startup of execution. For performance reasons, the `Initialize` method should be kept relatively lightweight. This initialization occurs before any task or workflow executes, and happens regardless of whether or not the `CustomTask` task executes. DTS will create a run-time reference, call the `CustomTask_Execute` method, and terminate the class at the end of package execution.

Design vs. Run Time

DTS releases the design-time instance of your custom task at the start of package execution. This means that any value assignment that occurs during design time will not be persisted at execution, even if it is declared publicly. However, since DTS will automatically manage any public property that you declare within your class, you can persist values between design and run time by assigning them to a public property. Or, you may choose to persist properties by implementing a custom property bag to limit external exposure to persisted properties.

Common Situations

To understand the order in which DTS executes the `CustomTaskUI` and `CustomTask`'s events, the following common activities and the events that occur as a result are listed below.

When you drag the `CustomTask` onto the Design Surface for the first time the following events are executed:

1. `Class_Initialize`

2. `CustomTaskUI_Initialize`

3. `CustomTaskUI_New`

When you double-click or edit the properties of the `CustomTask` the following events are executed:

1. `CustomTaskUI_Initialize`

2. `CustomTaskUI_Edit`

When you right-click and choose **Help** the following events are executed:

1. `CustomTaskUI_Initialize`

2. `CustomTaskUI_Help`

When you delete the `CustomTask` from the Design Surface the following events are executed:

1. `CustomTaskUI_Initialize`

2. `CustomTaskUI_Delete`

3. `Class_Terminate`

When you execute the `CustomTask` from DTS Designer the following events are executed:

1. `Class_Terminate` (for design-time instance)

2. `Class_Initialize` (for run-time instance)

3. `CustomTask_Execute` (for run-time instance)

4. `Class_Terminate` (for run-time instance)

5. `Class_Initialize` (for design-time instance)

When you copy and paste the `CustomTask`, the following events are executed:

1. `Class_Initialize` (for the new instance)

Now that we've covered the basics of creating a custom task, we can move to something a bit more substantial.

Building a Complex Custom Task

In this section, we'll be creating a custom task that validates many of the reasons we listed at the start of the chapter for rolling your own task.

In the last chapter, we discussed the need for a standardized approach to auditing and error handling across many DTS packages. We included the sample ActiveX code for the ErrorHandler task, and the code for the ActiveX DLL to handle the COM issues with the Step object. After reviewing our earlier list of reasons to build a custom task, applying those to the ErrorHandler ActiveX Script task suggests the following:

❑ **Functionality not possible from an ActiveX Script** – the ErrorHandler script could not retrieve the Step information by using the GetExecutionErrorInfo method of the audited Step object. It requires an ActiveX DLL.

❑ **Code maintenance/reuse** – the ErrorHandler script needs to be cut and pasted into every ErrorHandler task we create. If this code requires a change, we have to update every task that uses the code.

❑ **Ease of use for non-programmers** – we want the custom task we create to require very little manual configuration by programmers using the task in a DTS package. One of the conditions for use of the ErrorHandler ActiveX script was that it required a code change for each copy of the task because each task needed to know the name of the task that immediately preceded it. One of the goals of creating this custom task is to remove this condition and let the programmer using the task set all properties, including the predecessor task, through a UI.

❑ **Encapsulation of business logic** – between projects, the ErrorHandler script was growing and evolving into something that was much more robust, but also included specific project business rules.

❑ **Security** – we don't have any security considerations for this task.

❑ **Performance** – since only one error task should be executing at one time, performance isn't the highest concern.

❑ **Profit** – Maybe, if I'm lucky, someone will send me some money for my custom task, but I'm not going to hold my breath!

We want to standardize error handling for all of our tasks and packages. This gives us the opportunity to write error handling once, share the same code with all other tasks, and handle all of our errors in the same manner. The custom task we write will still call an external error handler package that will decide how to deal with the error (log to a database, e-mail, page, etc...); the purpose of the custom task is to facilitate the passing of the error information to this external package in a standard, easily reusable way. However, we want to make the custom task as flexible as possible by adding a feature that lets each task that uses the new ErrorHandler custom task be able to handle errors in a custom manner. By default, the ErrorHandler custom task will attempt to use a global variable named ExtErrorPackage for the path information to the external error handling package. To allow for a custom external error handling package for each task, we'll add an option for the programmer to specify a path to an external error handling package.

There is one constraint we must add to our custom task. We don't want a programmer who uses our custom task to configure it improperly. Each error handler task can have only one preceding task due to the way DTS handles workflows. By default, DTS treats multiple precedence constraints with a logical AND operator (see the *Multiple Precedence Constraint* section in Chapter 11). For example, both Task1 and Task2 have On Error precedence constraints to Error Handler as shown below:

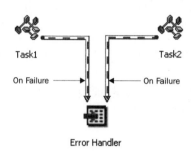

In this example, Error Handler will only execute if *both* Task1 *and* Task2 fail. This isn't the behavior we want, so we will verify that each Error Handler task has one and only one precedence constraint by including a check in the code. We'll discuss how this is done a bit later.

With all of these good reasons to build an `ErrorHandler` custom task, how can we not proceed? Let's get started.

Steps to Build

Let's start by creating a new ActiveX DLL project in Visual Basic, as we did before. Include a reference to the **Microsoft DTSPackage Object Library**, just as with the simple task. Name the project **DTSCustomTask** and the class **CErrorHandler**.

We're going to start by implementing both the `CustomTask` and the `CustomTaskUI` interfaces as we did earlier with the `CustomTask` interface. We're creating a user interface for property management so they're both necessary for this task. I'll discuss adding the UI to the project in the next section.

Open the code window for the `CErrorHandler` class you just created and add the following code:

```
Option Explicit

Implements DTS.CustomTask
Implements DTS.CustomTaskUI

Private moTask As DTS.Task

Public Enum enumSource
    Source_Global = 0
    Source_File = 1
End Enum

'Public Property declarations
Private msTaskName    As String
Private msDescription As String
Private msPredecessorName As String
Private msFileName As String
Private mnSource As enumSource
```

The above code uses the `Implements` keyword to add both `CustomTask` and `CustomTaskUI` interfaces. It also declares a private variable called `moTask` as an object of type `DTS.Task`. This variable will be used to hold a reference to the `Task` object. The reference will be used in the `CustomTaskUI` implementation. To explain further, the `CustomTaskUI` methods cannot directly reference the `CustomTask` object since they are two separate implementations. However, when you add the custom task to a DTS package, DTS instantiates the `CustomTask` object and passes that reference to the `CustomTaskUI_Initialize` method. As long as the object is part of the package, the `CustomTaskUI` methods can reference the task's properties.

The enumeration created above, `enumSource`, will be used to determine whether to use the external error handling file that's specified by the `ExtErrorHandler` global variable or to use a custom path.

The remaining declarations handle property assignments. We'll discuss these in more detail shortly.

When DTS has finished using a custom task (for example, deleting the task from a package at design-time or when execution of a package completes), the `Class_Terminate` method is automatically called because the object is destroyed. During the course of execution, the custom task could have saved a reference to the task object in a privately declared variable, `moTask`. We don't want to wait for Visual Basic to implicitly destroy any outstanding object reference; we want to clean up memory explicitly. By including the following code, we reduce the chance for memory leaks to occur.

```
Private Sub Class_Terminate()

    'Clean up Task reference
    If Not moTask Is Nothing Then
        Set moTask = Nothing
    End If

End Sub
```

CustomTaskUI Interface

We now want to begin adding code for the necessary `CustomTaskUI` interface requirements. The next subroutine declares the required method, but doesn't add any code, because we want DTS to handle the display of tool tips.

```
Private Sub CustomTaskUI_CreateCustomToolTip( _
    ByVal hwndParent As Long, _
    ByVal x As Long, _
    ByVal y As Long, _
    plTipWindow As Long)

    'We don't want to implement custom tool tips

End Sub
```

The `CustomTaskUI_Delete` method is called by DTS when the task is removed from the package at design time. We clean up our memory references for the same reasons as we did above in the `Class_Terminate` method.

```
Private Sub CustomTaskUI_Delete(ByVal hwndParent As Long)

    'Clean up Task reference
    If Not moTask Is Nothing Then
        Set moTask = Nothing
    End If

End Sub
```

This method is called by DTS when the user of the task edits the task's properties by double-clicking on the task, or right-clicking and choosing **Properties**. This method then calls the `DisplayPropertyPage` subroutine. We'll discuss this routine shortly.

```
Private Sub CustomTaskUI_Edit(ByVal hwndParent As Long)

    'Called when editing task properties
    DisplayPropertyPage
End Sub
```

This method is required because of the implementation of the `CustomTaskUI` interface. We will fulfill the requirements, but will not add any additional code.

```
Private Sub CustomTaskUI_GetUIInfo(pbstrToolTip As String, _
    pbstrDescription As String, _
    plVersion As Long, _
    pFlags As DTS.DTSCustomTaskUIFlags)

    'Not implemented

End Sub
```

If we wanted to create our own help file, we could implement the behavior to display it when a user presses *F1* when our task is selected.

```
Private Sub CustomTaskUI_Help(ByVal hwndParent As Long)

    'Not implemented

End Sub
```

We've now reached the point where we're including some substantial code. Once again, this method is called when the task is first instantiated by DTS.

```
Private Sub CustomTaskUI_Initialize(ByVal pTask As DTS.Task)
'Called when Task is dropped onto the DTS Design surface
On Error GoTo EH
Dim oPackage As DTS.Package
Dim oStep As DTS.Step
Dim colTasks As DTS.Tasks
```

```
    'Save reference to task object and get package
    'object reference
    Set moTask = pTask
    Set colTasks = moTask.Parent
    Set oPackage = colTasks.Parent
```

One of the rules we discussed earlier was that each `Error Handler` task should have one and only one precedence constraint. We verify this by iterating over the `Steps` collection in the current package and looking for a step that has our task and more than one precedence constraint. If we find one, we show the user a message box stating that fact.

```
    'Look for all steps with a TaskName of the
    'current task object and make sure that the error
    'task has only one precedence constraint
    For Each oStep In oPackage.Steps
        If oStep.TaskName = moTask.Name Then
            If oStep.PrecedenceConstraints.Count > 1 Then
                MsgBox "This task will only use the first " & _
                    "precedence constraint defined.", _
                    vbCritical, "DTSUtility"
            End If
        End If
    Next

    Set oStep = Nothing
    Set oPackage = Nothing
    Exit Sub
EH:
    MsgBox "CustomTaskUI_Initialize - Error: " & _
        Err.Description
    Exit Sub
End Sub
```

This method is called when a new instance of the task is created for the first time. The behavior we want is that the **Properties** dialog will open automatically allowing the custom task's properties to be set. This is done by calling the `DisplayPropertyPage` subroutine.

```
Private Sub CustomTaskUI_New(ByVal hwndParent As Long)

    'Show property page form
    DisplayPropertyPage

End Sub
```

We've now finished all of our required implementations for the `CustomTaskUI` interface. Let's now turn our attention to the `CustomTask` interface methods.

CustomTask Interface

The CustomTask_Execute method is only called by DTS when the package's execution reaches the custom task. There's quite a bit going on, so we'll cover the routine in pieces.

The first is the declarations section, where we define all of the variables we'll be using in this routine:

```
Private Sub CustomTask_Execute( _
    ByVal pPackage As Object, _
    ByVal pPackageEvents As Object, _
    ByVal pPackageLog As Object, _
    pTaskResult As DTS.DTSTaskExecResult)

On Error GoTo EH
Dim sPreStepName As String
Dim sErrorPackagePath As String
Dim sStepErrorText As String
Dim sPackageID As String
Dim sErrorText As String
Dim sErrorSource As String
Dim nErrorCode As Long
Dim sErrorString As String
Dim dtStartTime As Date

Dim oCurrPkg As DTS.Package
Dim oErrorHandlerPackage As DTS.Package
Dim oStep As DTS.Step
Dim oFileSystem As Object
```

We're going to implement logging for the custom task (if the user has package logging enabled). We're saving the start time to set one of the logged attributes.

```
'Save start time for logging
dtStartTime = Now
```

We save a reference to the current package so we can retrieve more information about its tasks, steps, and precedence constraints in the upcoming code.

```
Set oCurrPkg = pPackage
sPackageID = oCurrPkg.PackageID
```

During design-time configuration of the custom task, the user is required to choose which task immediately precedes the custom task. This value is saved in a variable called msPredecessorName, which we're using before it's been introduced. We'll discuss this behavior in more detail when we reach the user interface design portion of the code.

The code first looks for the Step object of the msPredecessorName task. Once we have a reference to the predecessor Step object, we can begin to collect information about the step's failure. We do this by making a call to the step method GetExecutionErrorInfo and formatting the return into an end-user friendly text string. GetExecutionErrorInfo is a method of the DTS Step object that can be called to retrieve error information programmatically. We're using the results here to create an informational error message.

```
'Find the Step Object for the Predecessor Step
For Each oStep In oCurrPkg.Steps
    If oStep.TaskName = msPredecessorName Then
        Exit For
    End If
Next

If oStep Is Nothing Or IsNull(oStep) Then
    sErrorString = "Cannot locate predecessor step, " & _
        msPredecessorName & ", in the current package."
    Err.Raise 50000, "CustomTask_Execute", sErrorString
    pTaskResult = DTSTaskExecResult_Failure
End If

'Build Error Message from GetExecutionErrorInfo
With oStep
    .GetExecutionErrorInfo nErrorCode, _
        sErrorSource, sStepErrorText

    sErrorText = "Package: " & oCurrPkg.Name _
        & vbCrLf
    sErrorText = sErrorText & _
        "Internal Step Name: " & .Name & vbCrLf
    sErrorText = sErrorText & _
        "Step Description: " & .Description & vbCrLf
    sErrorText = sErrorText & _
        "Started: " & .StartTime & vbCrLf
    sErrorText = sErrorText & _
        "Finished: " & .FinishTime & vbCrLf
    sErrorText = sErrorText & _
        "Failed with error: " & sStepErrorText
End With
```

Here's where we decide whether to use a global variable from the current package or a custom value for the path to the external error handling package. We also check to make sure the package exists before we try to open it.

```
'If the task is using a global variable to
'determine the location of the external error
'handling package, retrieve it, otherwise,
'use the custom value
If mnSource = Source_Global Then
    'Get From Package Globals for 'ExtErrorPackage'
    sErrorPackagePath = _
        oCurrPkg.GlobalVariables.Item("ExtErrorPackage").Value
    If sErrorPackagePath = "" Then
        sErrorString = "Global Variable 'ExtErrorPackage' " & _
            "not found when global variable use is " & _
            "specified. You must create this variable " & _
            "before the ErrorHandler class can be used."
        Err.Raise 50001, "CustomTask_Execute", sErrorString
        pTaskResult = DTSTaskExecResult_Failure
    End If
Else
```

```
        sErrorPackagePath = msFileName
    End If

    'Make sure that the error package exists before opening
    Set oFileSystem = CreateObject("Scripting.FileSystemObject")
    If Not oFileSystem.FileExists(sErrorPackagePath) Then
        sErrorString = "External Error Handler DTS Package not " & _
            "found at: " & sErrorPackagePath
        Err.Raise 50002, "CustomTask_Execute", sErrorString
        pTaskResult = DTSTaskExecResult_Failure
    End If

    'Open instance of error package
    Set oErrorHandlerPackage = New DTS.Package
    oErrorHandlerPackage.LoadFromStorageFile sErrorPackagePath, ""

    If oErrorHandlerPackage Is Nothing _
        Or IsEmpty(oErrorHandlerPackage) Then
        sErrorString = "Error loading External Error Handling " & _
            "Package : " & sErrorPackagePath
        Err.Raise 50003, "CustomTask_Execute", sErrorString
        pTaskResult = DTSTaskExecResult_Failure
    End If
```

Now that we have a reference to the open external error handling package, we set several of its global variables – just as if we were setting parameters on it.

```
    'Set Global Variables - gsErrorText, gsErrorPackage, gsErrorStep
    With oErrorHandlerPackage
        .GlobalVariables.Item("gsErrorText").Value = _
            sErrorText
        .GlobalVariables.Item("gsErrorPackage").Value = _
            oCurrPkg.Name
        .GlobalVariables.Item("gsErrorStep").Value = _
            oStep.Description

        '**We now also set the nErrorCode and sErrorSource values
        'from GetExecutionErrorInfo and pass to the error handling
        'package for the opportunity to deal with specific
        'errors differently
        .GlobalVariables.Item("gnErrorCode").Value = _
            nErrorCode
        .GlobalVariables.Item("gsErrorSource").Value = _
            sErrorSource
    End With
```

Now we must execute the external error handling package. Any steps defined in the package will be executed and any activity that's defined in the package will occur.

```
    'Execute the Package
    oErrorHandlerPackage.Execute
```

If the programmer using the `ErrorHandler` custom task chooses to enable package-level logging, the custom task will write its status to the log, just as all other tasks should.

```
    'Log to DTS log if applicable
    If Not pPackageLog Is Nothing Then

        pPackageLog.WriteStringToLog "Error Handling for Step: " & _
            msPredecessorName & " was successful." & vbCrLf
        pPackageLog.WriteTaskRecord 0, "Total Task Time: " & _
                    (DateDiff("s", dtStartTime, Now)) & " sec. " & _
                    vbCrLf & "Error from " & msPredecessorName & _
                    ": " & sErrorText
    End If
```

We clean up our object references explicitly to release any used memory.

```
    'Clean up references
    Set oCurrPkg = Nothing
    Set oErrorHandlerPackage = Nothing
    Set oFileSystem = Nothing
```

We MUST set the result of the task to success so that DTS will report the result correctly.

```
    pTaskResult = DTSTaskExecResult_Success

    Exit Sub
```

Here's the error handler for the `Error Handler`. If any errors occur during its execution, we can use the standard DTS events to report failure.

```
  EH:

    'Bubble any errors to the package eventsink
    If Not pPackageEvents Is Nothing Then
        pPackageEvents.OnError msTaskName & _
            " - CustomTask_Execute method", Err.Number, _
            Err.Source, Err.Description, "", 0, "", True
    End If

    'Log error to DTS log if applicable
    If Not pPackageLog Is Nothing Then
        pPackageLog.WriteTaskRecord Err.Number, _
            Err.Description
    End If

    Exit Sub
End Sub
```

The following code handles property management.

```
Private Property Get CustomTask_Properties() As DTS.Properties
    'Set to nothing - let DTS manage properties
    Set CustomTask_Properties = Nothing
End Property

Private Property Get CustomTask_Description() As String
'Implements Task.Description.
    CustomTask_Description = msDescription
End Property

Private Property Let CustomTask_Description( _
    ByVal strNewDescr As String)
'Implements Task.Description.
    msDescription = strNewDescr
End Property

Private Property Get CustomTask_Name() As String
'Implements Task.Name.
    CustomTask_Name = msTaskName
End Property

Private Property Let CustomTask_Name( _
    ByVal strNewName As String)
'Implements Task.Name.
    msTaskName = strNewName
End Property

Public Property Get Description() As String
'Implements CustTask.Description.
    Description = msDescription
End Property

Public Property Let Description(ByVal sNewDesc As String)
'Implements CustTask.Description.
    msDescription = sNewDesc
End Property
```

The following code handles public properties that we created to add more functionality to our custom task. We'll discuss what these properties are used for in the next section. These are set by the user in the properties dialog.

```
Public Property Get PredecessorName() As String
    PredecessorName = msPredecessorName
End Property

Public Property Let PredecessorName(ByVal sName As String)
    msPredecessorName = sName
End Property

Public Property Get Source() As enumSource
    Source = mnSource
End Property

Public Property Let Source(ByVal enumSource As enumSource)
    mnSource = enumSource
End Property
```

```
Public Property Get FileName() As String
    FileName = msFileName
End Property

Public Property Let FileName(sFile As String)
    msFileName = sFile
End Property
```

This subroutine initializes and displays the property page dialog. If the user makes changes to the properties in this dialog, this subroutine also updates the `CustomTask`'s persisted public properties.

The next subroutine, `DisplayPropertyPage`, manages the custom task's public properties through the use of a Visual Basic dialog that we'll be creating in the next section. For now, the purpose of the dialog is to allow the user to set the custom task's properties: the **description** of the task that DTS uses for display purposes at design time, the name of the Predecessor Task (**PredecessorName**), the **source** of the path information for the external error handling file (global or custom), and the path containing the **filename** of the custom external error handling file. To make the user's task easier, we'll be using a `ListView` control to display the name and description of the other tasks in the package. The user of the task then only has to pick the predecessor from a list.

```
Private Sub DisplayPropertyPage()
On Error GoTo EH
Dim frmExtErrorPkg As New frmExtErrorPkg

    'Fill Predecessor list box
    Dim sngLVWidth As Single
    Dim oPackage As DTS.Package
    Dim oTask As DTS.Task
    Dim colTasks As DTS.Tasks
    Dim li As ListItem
    Dim si As ListSubItem
```

`moTask` is assigned during the `CustomTaskUI_Initialize` method and we are using it here to get a reference to the current package. By examining the DTS object model, we know that every task is included in a collection of tasks, which is a property of every package.

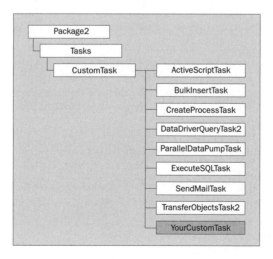

That means that by using a reference to the current task, we can determine the current package as we do in the following code. We'll be using the `oPackage` object a bit later.

```
'Save reference to task object and get package
'object reference
Set colTasks = moTask.Parent
Set oPackage = colTasks.Parent
```

We instantiated a new `frmExtErrorPkg` object earlier in the routine. We're now setting some of its properties. We're also setting the default sizing of the `ListView` control. We do this here to keep the form display logic in one place.

```
With frmExtErrorPkg
    'Task Property Assignment
    .FileName = msFileName
    .Source = mnSource
    .Description = Description

    'Add Columns
    .lvPredecessor.View = lvwReport
    sngLVWidth = .lvPredecessor.Width / 5
    .lvPredecessor.ColumnHeaders.Add _
        Text:="Task Name", Width:=(sngLVWidth * 2)
    .lvPredecessor.ColumnHeaders.Add _
        Text:="Task Description", Width:=(sngLVWidth * 3)
```

Here's where we use the reference to the current package and add all of the package's tasks (except the current `Error Handler` custom task) to the `ListView`.

```
'Look for all tasks except the current one and
'add to the ListView
For Each oTask In oPackage.Tasks
    If oTask.Name <> moTask.Name Then
        Set li = .lvPredecessor.ListItems.Add _
            (, oTask.Name, oTask.Name)
        Set si = li.ListSubItems.Add _
            (, oTask.Name, oTask.Description)
    End If
Next
```

If the user is setting the custom task's properties for the first time, the `ListView` will not have any tasks selected. If the user is changing an existing selection, we set the `ListView` to automatically select the pre-set task.

```
'Set the ListView to the previous selection
'if one has been made
If PredecessorName <> "" Then
    Set li = .lvPredecessor.FindItem(PredecessorName)
    If Not li Is Nothing Then
        Set .lvPredecessor.SelectedItem = li
        .lvPredecessor.SelectedItem.EnsureVisible
    End If
End If
```

Now set the caption of the form so the user knows which task they're setting properties for.

```
            'Set the caption of the form
            .Caption = "Set Properties for '" & _
                moTask.Description & "'"
        End With
```

Show the dialog modally. The code will wait here until the user closes the dialog. The form manages setting its public properties based on the actions taken by the user. This section of code retrieves the values of the public properties of frmExtErrorPkg.

```
        frmExtErrorPkg.Show vbModal

        If Not frmExtErrorPkg Is Nothing Then
            With frmExtErrorPkg
                'Property Assignment
                If Not .Cancelled Then
                    msFileName = .FileName
                    mnSource = .Source
                    Description = .Description
                    If Not .lvPredecessor.SelectedItem Is Nothing Then
                        PredecessorName = _
                            .lvPredecessor.SelectedItem.Key
                    Else
                        PredecessorName = ""
                    End If
                End If
            End With
```

Clean up used resources and unload the form explicitly.

```
            'Clean up references
            Set oTask = Nothing
            Set colTasks = Nothing
            Set oPackage = Nothing

            Unload frmExtErrorPkg
            Set frmExtErrorPkg = Nothing
        End If

    Exit Sub
EH:
    MsgBox "DisplayPropertyPage - Error: " & _
        Err.Description
End Sub
```

That's it for the class file. We now have to add the user interface to manage the custom task's properties.

Adding the User Interface

The `CustomTask` wouldn't be complete without the user interface for property management. The properties that need to be manipulated are the:

❑   `Description`

❑   `PredecessorName`

❑   `Source`

❑   `FileName`

Since the user may not know exactly which task is the predecessor by the internal name, the dialog needs to show both the name and the description for easy identification.

Remember that if the `CustomTaskUI` wasn't implemented, users would be forced to manually type all public properties. The dialog would look like this:

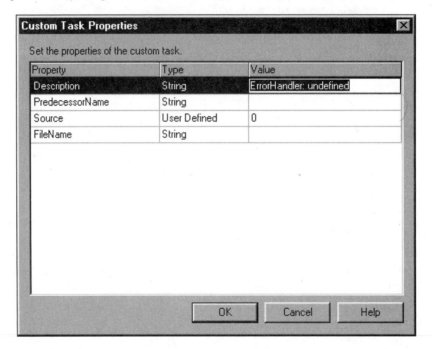

This isn't very pretty, nor is it very intuitive.

To add the `CustomTaskUI` dialog, we need to create a new Visual Basic form. To do this, choose Add Form from the Project menu. Since we're adding a new form, click on OK in the Add Form dialog.

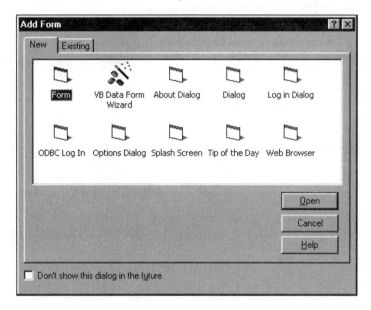

Now change the name of the form from Form1 to frmExtErrorPkg by right-clicking on Form1 in the Project Explorer window and choosing Properties. Find the (Name) property and change it to frmExtErrorPkg. Modify the Caption property of the form to be frmExtErrorPkg. Also, modify the following form properties to reflect the new value in the table listed below:

Property	New Value
BorderStyle	3 – Fixed Dialog
StartUpPosition	1 – CenterOwner

We must also add two ActiveX components to the project so we can use the `ListView` control and the `CommonDialog` control. To do this, select Components from the Project menu and scroll until you see the entry for Microsoft Common Dialog Control 6.0. Make sure that this is checked. Scroll further until you see Microsoft Windows Common Controls 6.0. Also make sure that this control is checked and click OK. (If you have installed any Visual Studio or Visual Basic service pack, you will see the name of the service pack appended to the name of the control; use the latest version available. In the screenshot below, service pack 3 has been installed).

This is the method that's called when the cmdBrowse button is clicked. The desired behavior is for an **Open File** dialog to appear that allows the user to select a file. The default filter is set to look for only files with *.DTS extensions to make searching easier. If a user picks a file, we assign the file name to the text box, txtFileName.text. If the user presses **Cancel** or closes the form without clicking **OK**, the file name text box should not be changed.

```
Private Sub cmdBrowse_Click()
On Error GoTo EH

    'Set Common Dialog defaults
    CommonDialog.Filter = "DTS Files (*.dts)|*.dts|" & _
        "All Files (*.*)|*.*"
    CommonDialog.FilterIndex = 1
    CommonDialog.DefaultExt = "*.dts"
    CommonDialog.ShowOpen
    CommonDialog.CancelError = True
    CommonDialog.Flags = cdlOFNHideReadOnly
    txtFileName.Text = CommonDialog.FileName

    Exit Sub

EH:
    'User pressed Cancel button.
    If Err.Number = cdlCancel Then
        Exit Sub
    Else
        MsgBox "cmdBrowse Error: " & Err.Description
    End If

End Sub
```

If the user decides not to set any of the task's properties by choosing **Cancel** from the dialog, we set the mbCancelled value to True. The DisplayPropertyPage subroutine that opened the form will check this value. If it is True, no custom task properties will be assigned; if it's False, any changes that were made in the properties dialog will be assigned to the custom task's persisted properties.

```
Private Sub cmdfigCancel_Click()
    mbCancelled = True
    Me.Hide
End Sub
```

If the user decides to accept the changes that might have been made in the custom task's property dialog, they will click **OK**. The following code is executed and will perform logic checking and then will assign property values to its public properties. The last property it sets is mbCancelled. When this is set to False, the calling routine knows to use the new values that have been set by the user. Reference the DisplayPropertyPage routine for clarification.

```vb
Private Sub cmdOK_Click()
On Error GoTo EH

    'Check to make sure that if the user chooses to use
    'a file name, that one has been supplied
    If optGlobal(Source_File).Value = True Then
        If Trim$(txtFileName.Text) = "" Then
            MsgBox "You must first supply a file name.", vbInformation
            Exit Sub
        End If
    End If

    'Check to ensure that a selection has been made, if there
    'are items in the ListView. There will be no items if
    'the ErrorHandler task is the first task in the package.
    If Not lvPredecessor.SelectedItem Is Nothing Then
        PredecessorName = lvPredecessor.SelectedItem.Key
    Else
        If lvPredecessor.ListItems.Count > 0 Then
            MsgBox "You must first choose a " & _
                "predecessor task.", vbInformation
            Exit Sub
        Else
            PredecessorName = ""
        End If
    End If

    'Save the Source property
    If optGlobal(Source_Global).Value = True Then
        Source = Source_Global
    Else
        Source = Source_File
    End If

    'Save the Description and FileName properties
    Description = txtDescription.Text
    FileName = txtFileName.Text
    mbCancelled = False
    Me.Hide
    Exit Sub
EH:
    MsgBox "cmdOK Error: " & Err.Description
End Sub
```

When the form is initially loaded, we want certain default values to be set to make the dialog follow standard design principles.

```vb
Private Sub Form_Load()
On Error GoTo EH

    'Set the Default values
    mbSortOrder = 0
```

```
        If Source = Source_Global Then
            txtFileName.Enabled = False
            txtFileName.BackColor = &H8000000F
            cmdBrowse.Enabled = False
        Else
            txtFileName.Enabled = True
            txtFileName.BackColor = &H80000005
            cmdBrowse.Enabled = True
        End If


        txtFileName.Text = FileName
        txtDescription.Text = Description
        optGlobal(Source).Value = True
        mbCancelled = True
        Exit Sub


EH:
        MsgBox "Form_Load Error: " & Err.Description
    End Sub
```

This adds the ability to sort the lvPredecessor ListView by name or description in ascending or descending order. This is a nice feature if the package has many tasks.

```
Private Sub lvPredecessor_ColumnClick( _
    ByVal ColumnHeader As MSComctlLib.ColumnHeader)
    'Resort the ListView depending on the column
    'that's clicked. Change order from ASC to DESC and back
    lvPredecessor.SortKey = ColumnHeader.Index - 1
    lvPredecessor.Sorted = True
    If mbSortOrder = 0 Then
        mbSortOrder = 1
    Else
        mbSortOrder = 0
    End If
    lvPredecessor.SortOrder = mbSortOrder
End Sub
```

If the user chooses to use the global variable for the external error handling file path, the dialog should automatically disable the ability to enter text into the file name text box and the ability to browse for a file. If the user chooses to use a custom file path, we re-enable both.

```
Private Sub optGlobal_Click(Index As Integer)

    If Index = Source_Global Then
        txtFileName.Enabled = False
        txtFileName.BackColor = &H8000000F
        cmdBrowse.Enabled = False
    Else
        txtFileName.Enabled = True
        txtFileName.BackColor = &H80000005
        cmdBrowse.Enabled = True
    End If

End Sub
```

The following code exposes all of the properties for public use so their values are visible to the CErrorHandler class. This is how any changes made on the Properties dialog updates the custom task's properties back in the class module.

```
'Public Property Assignments
Public Property Let Source(nSource As enumSource)
    mnSource = nSource
End Property

Public Property Get Source() As enumSource
    Source = mnSource
End Property

Public Property Let FileName(sFileName As String)
    msFileName = sFileName
End Property

Public Property Get FileName() As String
    FileName = msFileName
End Property

Public Property Let Description(sDesc As String)
    msDesc = sDesc
End Property

Public Property Get Description() As String
    Description = msDesc
End Property

Public Property Let PredecessorName(sName As String)
    msPredecessorName = sName
End Property

Public Property Get PredecessorName() As String
    PredecessorName = msPredecessorName
End Property

Public Property Get Cancelled() As Boolean
    Cancelled = mbCancelled
End Property
```

At this point, the entire project should compile. However, since it's a DLL, it won't actually do anything until it's called by an external application such as DTS. Before we do that, let's make this task a bit more professional looking by add an icon that displays in the DTS designer.

Adding the Final Touch

As we saw in the earlier simple task example, DTS, by default, will use a generic icon to represent the task when it's in the task toolbar and on the design surface:

ErrorHandler

This isn't very descriptive or very aesthetically pleasing. To add your own icon in VB, load the VB6 Resource Editor by selecting Add-In Manager from the Add-Ins menu. Select VB6 Resource Editor from the list, and check the Loaded/Unloaded check box.

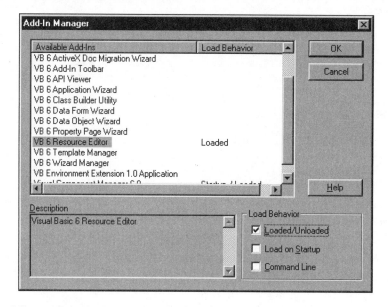

This adds the following icon to the toolbar:

Click this icon to display the VB Resource Editor window. Click the Add Icon button in this window:

and choose any icon you wish. Click on the Save icon and save the resource file as DTSCustomTask.RES. Close the VB Resource Editor and save the VB project. Now you can compile the DLL by choosing Make DTSCustomTask.DLL from the File menu. Now register the task in DTS as we did before, calling it ErrorHandler, and you've finished.

The End Result

If all went well, you should be able to drag the newly created task on to the DTS Designer surface and see this:

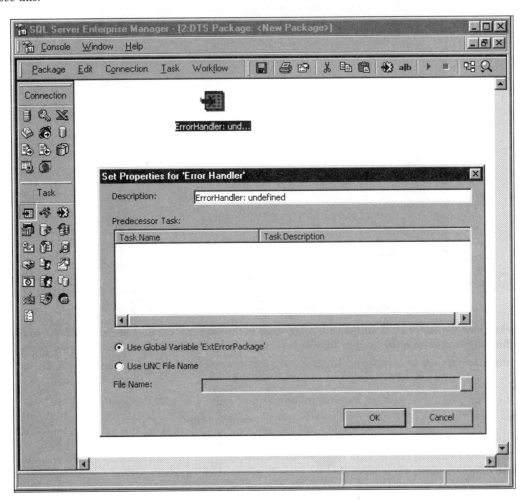

You'll see the property dialog appear, but don't set anything just yet. Press Cancel and return to editing the package.

Edit the package's Properties and add the global variable for the external error handling file, called ExtErrorPackage. Set the Type to String and the Value to the location of the external error handling package that you created in Chapter 11. If you didn't create this package, you can create an empty DTS package and save it as a COM-structured storage file. The custom task will still attempt to execute the package.

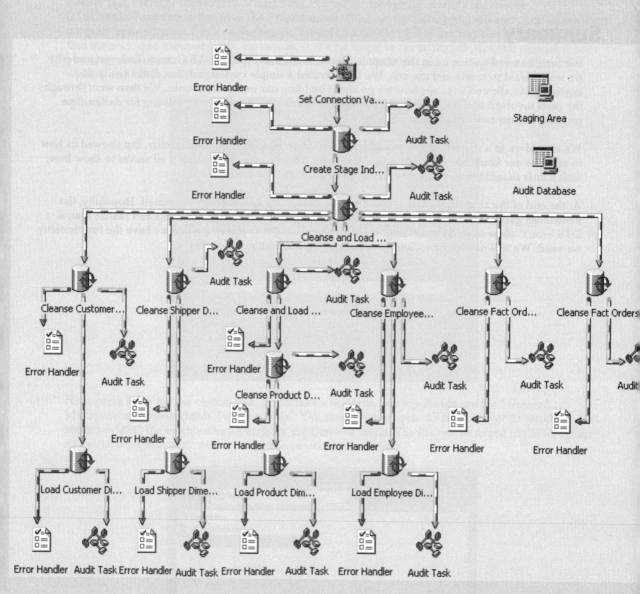

Error Handler

Set Connection Va...

Audit Task

Staging Area

Error Handler

Create Stage Ind...

Audit Task

Audit Database

Error Handler

Cleanse and Load ...

Audit Task

Cleanse Customer...   Cleanse Shipper D...   Cleanse and Load ...   Cleanse Employee...   Cleanse Fact Ord...   Cleanse Fact Orders

Error Handler   Audit Task   Error Handler   Audit Task   Audit Task   Audit Task   Audit

Cleanse Product D...

Error Handler   Error Handler   Error Handler   Error Handler   Error Handler

Load Customer Di...   Load Shipper Dime...   Load Product Dim...   Load Employee Di...

Error Handler   Audit Task   Error Handler   Audit Task   Error Handler   Audit Task   Error Handler   Audit Task

13

Data Warehouse Loading

Many steps are involved in creating a data warehouse. There are also many differing opinions as to the actual steps that should be taken and in which order. In every case, to populate a data warehouse requires an extraction, transformation, and loading process. This process will extract all pertinent information from source systems, transform and cleanse the data, and then subsequently load the data warehouse database. The range in opinions as to how this should be created is diverse. On one hand, the process can be written using the native languages of the source and target RDBMSs and tied together with batch scripts. On the other hand, expensive products can be purchased that allow much of the development to be done using a graphical user interface. Somewhere in the middle lies DTS.

In a typical data warehouse project, the Extraction, Transformation, and Loading (ETL) accounts for between 25 and 50 percent of the overall effort. Warehouse systems may source data from many different systems on many different platforms spread across a diverse geographical area. Pulling all of these data sources together can be challenging, but thankfully, DTS contains tools that can assemble this data into an organized format for staging. Many third party tools are specifically designed for moving data from place to place, but are usually very expensive and have cost structures that require payment by the data source, and don't have much in the way of extensibility. This is where DTS excels in price, performance, and flexibility since it can pull data from any OLE DB or ODBC source and allows for full customization by using built-in and custom tasks and scripts. By using DTS and following some generally accepted data warehousing design techniques, development time is shorter and on-going management has a much lower total cost of ownership. This chapter will discuss some typical steps in creating a data warehouse.

However, we can't run before we walk, so let's take some time to discuss some data warehousing basics.

In this chapter we will discuss:

- ❑   Data Warehousing Basics
- ❑   Creating a Dimensional Data Model
- ❑   Solid ETL Design
- ❑   From Source to Staging
- ❑   From Staging to the Warehouse
- ❑   Integrating Analysis Services

Data Warehousing Basics and Terminology

What is a Data Warehouse?

A data warehouse is a database that's structured to allow fast querying and analysis. It is usually separate from the transactional databases that are the sources of its data. It typically stores many months or years of transactional data representing the history of an organization, but without much of the detail that tends to conceal many of the trends that are most important to forward-looking individuals. These trends can include revenue, sales, or profits. The important concept here is to understand that a data warehouse is designed for one of three purposes: to cut costs, to increase revenue, or to have a competitive advantage.

A data warehouse usually has several characteristics:

- ❑   Data is extracted regularly from one or more existing transactional systems. It can be pulled nightly, weekly, monthly, or yearly from mainframes, web logs, accounting, or supply or demand-chain systems.

- ❑   Data is cleansed to represent a conformed view of the overall business. Each entity and attribute should have the same meaning to everyone within the organization.

- ❑   A data warehouse is usually made up of one or more integrated **data marts**, which are subject areas representing a departmental-level view of the enterprise. With proper design, these data marts can be rolled-up to an enterprise-level view.

- ❑   The data warehouse provides a historical perspective on the business on which to base trending and forecasting activities.

- ❑   The data warehouse database is dimensionally modeled to support fast and intuitive querying. Dimensional model design allows many typical queries to be fulfilled with a minimum of costly table joins. It also promotes a query structure that allows for predictive indexing. We'll discuss dimensional modeling in more detail in the next section.

Dimensional Modeling

A dimensional data model organizes and summarizes business information so that a front-end tool can quickly access data and support graphical querying. Presenting information in summarized form is useful in identifying trends. A data warehouse must be able to further explore the underlying causes of trends as quickly as possible. This section discusses the most popular design methodologies in use today.

Star Schemas

Star schemas get their name from the fact that a diagram of their structure resembles a star with one large central table and a halo of smaller tables around the larger table. Typically, the center table is called the **fact** table and the smaller tables are the **dimensions**. Each dimension is directly related to the fact table by a key column as shown in the following example:

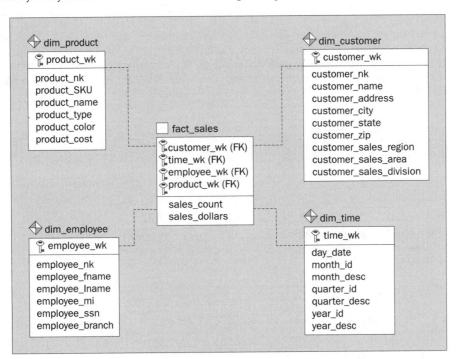

As you can see, each dimension table – dim_product, dim_customer, dim_employee, and dim_time – is related directly to the fact_sales table via a warehouse key or generalized key (product_wk, customer_wk, employee_wk, and time_wk). Generalized and warehouse keys are generally synonymous in that they have the same purpose as surrogate keys. For example, when extracting information about a company's products from several different systems, each with its own unique key, you must have a key that represents the same product to each system. Surrogate keys will be discussed in much greater detail later in the chapter.

The additional numeric attributes in the fact_sales table are called **measures** (for example, sales_count and sales_dollars). These values should, as a rule, be numeric and additive. These values can be summarized across every combination of product, customer, employee, or time. Star schema designs allow any measure to be viewed against any related dimension.

Each dimension above includes at least one hierarchy with several levels. Take for example the Time dimension – dim_time includes month, quarter, and year columns for each date row in the table. The table data looks something like this:

time _wk	day _date	month _id	month _desc	quarter _id	quarter _desc	year _id	year _desc
1	01/01/2000	1	January	1	2000 Q1	2000	2000
2	01/02/2000	1	January	1	2000 Q1	2000	2000
...							
92	04/01/2000	4	April	2	2000 Q2	2000	2000
...							

As you can see, for each day's record, you know the month, quarter, and year without requiring any date functions or calculations. Although space is wasted because of the denormalized form, it is nominal compared to the fact table, and query performance is greatly improved. If, when you query the fact table, you need fact data for the first quarter of 2000, only one table join is required and no date conversion function is necessary:

```
SELECT *
FROM fact_sales f, dim_time d
WHERE f.time_wk = d.time_wk AND
      d.quarter_desc = '2000 Q1'
```

The method of modeling dimensional hierarchies differentiates a star schema from a snowflake schema.

Snowflake

Snowflake schemas are derivatives of star schemas, in that one or more dimension hierarchies are normalized. Snowflaked dimensions require less space and are easier to manage in a traditional data warehouse design.

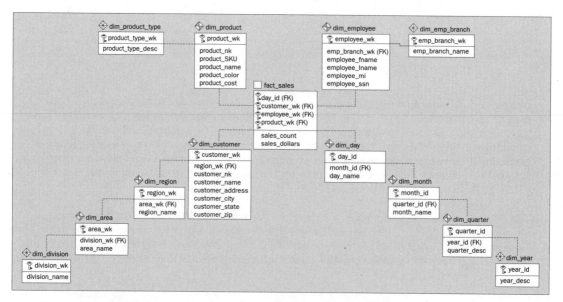

Here is an example of the SQL necessary to retrieve fact data from the first quarter of 2000, similar to the example above:

```
SELECT *
FROM fact_sales f, dim_day dd, dim_month dm, dim_quarter dq
WHERE f.day_id = dd.day_id AND
      dd.month_id = dm.month_id AND
      dm.quarter_id = dq.quarter_id AND
      dq.quarter_desc = '2000 Q1'
```

As you can see, every query that includes the date dimension must perform two additional joins each time it is run.

Star versus Snowflake

As you can see from above, there are many advantages to using a simpler star schema over a snowflake implementation. Queries are more efficient and simpler to construct. The overall number of tables to manage is decreased and dimensional browsing through SQL or a front-end tool will be more efficient.

However, if you plan to use a **Microsoft Analysis Services** multidimensional database as your reporting database, creating snowflaked dimensions will actually be more efficient during processing. Analysis Services creates its own internal representation of dimension hierarchies. Analysis Services only accesses these dimension tables when building cubes and never joins them directly to the fact table (unless your schema is not optimized). For more information about Analysis Services' optimization, refer to the SQL Server 2000 Books Online.

Hybrid Star/Snowflake Designs

If your data warehouse solution will support end-user querying of both multidimensional and relational databases, you can choose to design a hybrid approach for your dimensions. This would entail creating separate dimension tables for each hierarchy level, but also duplicating the hierarchy information in the lowest level dimension table (lowest being with the most detail, that is, Day in a Time dimension). Here is an example of this technique for the customer dimension from the previous example:

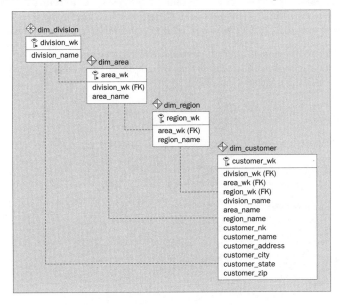

The `dim_customer` table contains not only foreign keys to all levels of hierarchy, but all non-key attributes (`division_name`, `area_name`, and `region_name`). This design can be difficult to manage administratively, but will support fast performance from both relational and multidimensional aspects. Consider using this design if your warehouse solution must meet performance goals for both relational and multidimensional queries.

OLTP versus OLAP

Online Transaction Processing (**OLTP**) systems usually represent the source systems for a data warehouse. They are usually transactional in nature and are frequently purged to improve performance. **Online Analytical Processing** (**OLAP**) is just a generalization describing data warehousing and the differences in purpose that the two systems have. OLAP and OLTP systems have different performance and resource requirements. OLAP systems typically must scan large portions of data. Successful performance means having the ability to query data at near hardware disk speed. To meet these critical throughput requirements, OLAP systems must be organized to retrieve data as quickly as possible. By denormalizing the data design, fewer joins are performed when accessing data and most queries can be heavily indexed.

OLAP systems typically take snapshots of production data at regularly spaced intervals and can represent historical data for months or years or more. The data warehouse organizes key business dimensions and measures into a format that makes decision support and historical analysis possible.

OLTP systems' performance optimizations focus on updating data and individual transaction response time rather than analytical reporting. OLTP systems are concerned with creating small atomic transactions to speed data insert events along. These smaller transactions decrease the number of I/Os necessary to fulfill a business event.

Data in OLTP systems reflects current values at any point in time. For example, a query to return current inventory levels may differ from moment to moment depending on outstanding orders. It is also impossible to determine what inventory levels were just moments, or days, or weeks ago.

When designing a transactional or OLTP system, a designer's intent is to reduce or eliminate any redundancies in data. This creates the opportunity for granular or atomic inserts to occur. Typically, the smaller the insert size, the faster the insert can be performed. However, this approach makes querying this data more complex. Database servers must join many tables together to return a complete data set. These join operations consume significant amounts of CPU and memory resources, need significant amounts of temporary workspace and require I/O between memory and disk for each table used in the query.

Take, for example, the following model of a simple invoicing system, illustrated in the diagram below. In order to generate a report for all products that were sold in Hackensack, NJ, in July of 1990, you would have to write SQL that resembled this:

```
SELECT
    a.product_desc, SUM(b.quantity)
FROM
    product a, invoice_product b, invoice c, entity d, address e
WHERE
    a.product_id = b.product_id AND
    b.invoice_id = c.invoice_id AND
    c.entity_id = d.entity_id AND
    d.address_id = e.address_id AND
    e.city_desc = 'Hackensack' AND
    e.state_desc = 'NJ' AND
    (c.invoice_date >= '07/01/1990' AND
    c.invoice_date <= '07/31/1990')
GROUP BY
    a.product_desc
```

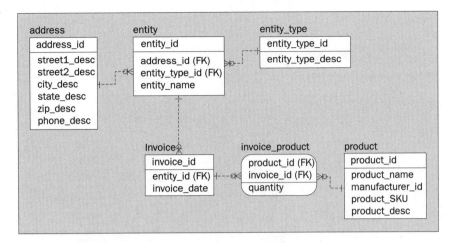

As you can see, the execution of this query will be quite expensive because four joins must be performed. As the size of these tables grow, the speed of the query will slow considerably.

Also, OLTP systems typically delete or archive much of their historical data frequently to help performance while OLAP systems typically keep history for several years. The answer to such analytical queries may not be available on the production system if this is the case. If this data is purged or archived, it makes answering questions like these and other decision support questions difficult or impossible.

If we were to model this invoicing system using an OLAP approach, we'd create a star or snowflake schema with a fact table and several dimension tables. The smallest component, or **grain**, of our fact table would be an invoiced item. We record each product sale and as much information about the sale as possible. It would look something like the figure shown below:

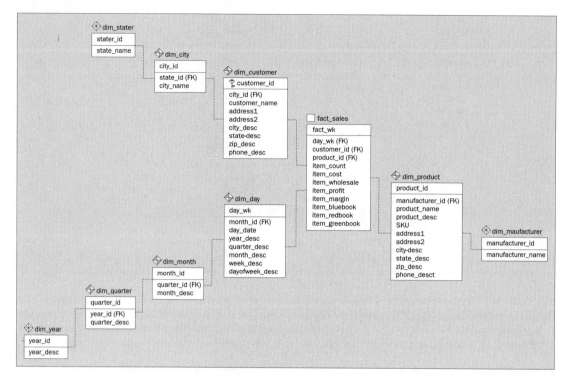

Typically, OLAP front-end systems will allow **slicing**, **dicing**, **drill-up**, and **drill-down**. They also store key values for dimensions as you slice or drill into the data. These key values are used to constrain any additional query and allow optimization by not having to join back to the dimension table. By using these key values, these front ends greatly simplify the SQL generated to fulfill queries. As a consequence of this, if you now wish to answer the same query as before, all products that were sold in Hackensack, NJ, in July of 1990, the SQL would resemble this:

```
SELECT
    b.product_name,
FROM
    fact_sales a, dim_product b
WHERE
    a.time_wk BETWEEN = 300 AND 331 AND
    a.customer_id IN (5, 14, 79, 125) AND
    a.product_id = b.product_id
```

where the time primary keys for July of 1990 fall between 300 and 331 and where customers that have offices in Hackensack are represented by primary keys of 5, 14, 79, and 125.

Data Warehouses versus Data Marts

A data warehouse is usually made up of many fact tables across many subject areas covering many areas of the enterprise. A data warehouse can be logically or physically subdivided into several data marts that share certain dimensions across multiple subject areas. These dimensions are referred to as **conformed dimensions** and can include Time, Product, Customer, and so on. Without conformed dimensions, these data marts cannot be combined into a coherent enterprise warehouse.

A data mart is usually a smaller, more manageable implementation of the enterprise data warehouse. It consists of one or a small number of fact tables with correlated data. It also contains conformed dimensions, or dimensions that mean the same thing across all subject areas, as shown in the figure below. For example, a conformed product dimension allows tracking of products across sales, orders, and RMA (Return Merchandise Authorization) areas.

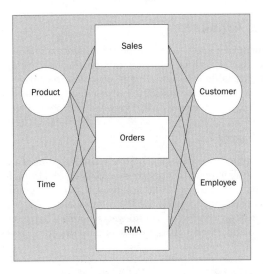

In the figure above, the circles represent the dimensions and the squares represent the facts. The important concept here is that a Customer represents the same entity to Sales, Orders, and RMAs. When designing a data warehouse or data mart, most data warehouse practitioners follow a structured architectural framework to build marts with the enterprise design in mind, rather than attempting to implement the monolithic enterprise data warehouse in a single effort. This allows designers to carve off smaller pieces of the pie. It also allows the designer to stay more focused by constantly referring back to the original strategic business questions that are driving the data mart.

Creating a Dimensional Data Model

Creating the dimensional model is the most important activity in the development of a warehouse; it is the foundation for the entire project. To ensure that your data model is complete and will lead to a successful project, it must meet several requirements:

- ❏ support queries that answer the fundamental business problems in a timely fashion
- ❏ be clearly understandable to your analysts
- ❏ have conformed dimensions across all fact groups
- ❏ have qualitative and reliable data
- ❏ have clear focus within each subject area

To help with meeting these requirements, the following section describes issues to consider or design principles to follow when creating your data model.

Issues to Consider

The following five sections cover the major issues when creating a dimensional model, but by no means have the necessary detail to guarantee success. For more information about dimensional modeling, refer to the *Suggested Reading* section later in this chapter.

Identify Clear Subject Areas

A subject area should consist of a single or a number of related fact tables that correspond to single factual entities such as purchases, orders, accounts, or web sessions. Attempting to combine these subject areas into a single fact table will result in a poor, counterintuitive design. Your analysts will have difficulty answering even the most basic questions. If you need analysis that crosses subject areas, you can use **Virtual Cubes** in Analysis Services or use views in subsequent steps.

Choose the Grain of Facts

When designing your fact tables, you must clearly state what the grain of the fact table is early in the process. **Grain** is the level at which fact records are stored. A typical grain for a fact table would be order items, purchase transactions, or phone calls, and are derived from the grain at which the transactional system stores data. Separate fact tables can be used to rollup granular tables into logical 'super units' such as order line items into orders or web page hits into web sessions where the 'super unit' or aggregate becomes a analytic entity in and of itself. This creates an unambiguous view of your facts.

Identify Dimensions

It's important to understand the relationship between the facts you identify and the possible dimensions. Start by identifying the non-additive attributes of your base-level fact, such as product name, salesman, day, shipper, customer name, and so on. However, not all of these attributes will become dimensions. In fact, many of the attributes can be combined into a single dimension. The determining factor is usually whether the attribute must be included in analysis. These attributes, when modeled properly, create the ability to slice and dice your facts.

However, in order to drill down or up, you must identify hierarchies. Identifying the hierarchies within each dimension is easier once you have defined the dimensions. Usually, within each of these dimensions, natural hierarchies will emerge, such as 'Year to Quarter to Month to Day' for Time, and 'Country to State to City to Zip Code' for Geography.

Choose the Time Context of Facts

Some subject areas can have two time contexts: transaction and snapshot. For example, a bank records debit and credit transactions on your monthly statement. This is a transaction type fact table. However, without manually adding and subtracting the debits and credits, you don't know what the account balance was on any given day. To make this possible, you can create a second fact table that takes a snapshot-in-time view of the business. This is done by recording a daily or monthly balance of every account. This type of fact table works very well for things like inventory and account balances. However, the number of snapshots you store multiplies the space required to store these fact tables. To reduce the overall storage, you can keep a rolling history of 30 or so daily balances. As you add the next day's worth of data, you can delete the 31st day.

Surrogate Keys

Surrogate keys, or generalized keys, serve several purposes in the data warehouse. Firstly, they replace natural keys as the primary keys of dimensions to reduce the overall column width of each key. In order to save space in your fact tables, you must make your foreign keys as small as possible. This serves two purposes: to reduce the amount of storage space for data and indexes on these columns and to reduce the amount of I/O necessary to retrieve these same column values.

Secondly, surrogate keys insulate changes in source system keys from the warehouse. This significantly reduces administrative tasks for the warehouse. For example, if your warehouse uses production keys for your product dimension (that is, Stock Keeping Unit or SKU), then each product must have unique SKU values. If a product is reclassified, but retains the original SKU, the dimension key can no longer represent the original product and all history will be lost.

For example, in a grocery store, products are classified by category and product SKU. If the product is Peanut Butter and the original classification had it in the 'Spreads' category, then each time a unit of Peanut Butter was sold, the Spreads category would reflect the sale. If Peanut Butter is moved into the 'Jams/Jellies' category, then the product dimension must change. If the record for Peanut Butter is **updated** to reflect the category change, then the Spreads category will appear as if no sales of Peanut Butter were ever made. If a new record for Peanut Butter were **inserted** with a new surrogate key, then two versions of Peanut Butter would exist, with the original in the Spreads category and the new record in the Jams/Jellies category. In this way, any new sales of Peanut Butter would have the sales accumulated for the Jams/Jellies category, but a historical view of Spreads would still show sales of Peanut Butter as well.

By separating the original or source system key values from the surrogate key values, you also relieve yourself the chore of creating or maintaining business rules if the key values do change.

Suggested Reading

For much more detailed explanations of designing and implementing a data warehouse, please consult either of the following titles written by Ralph Kimball:

❑ *The Data Warehouse Toolkit: Practical Techniques for Building Dimensional Data Warehouses*, Wiley & Sons, ISBN: 0-471153-37-0

❑ *The Data Warehouse Lifecycle Toolkit: Expert Methods for Designing, Developing, and Deploying Data Warehouses*, Wiley & Sons, ISBN: 0-471255-47-5

or the following book by Sakhr Youness:

❑ *Professional Data Warehousing with SQL Server 7.0 and OLAP Services,* Wrox Press, ISBN: 1-861002-81-5

Creating a Solid ETL Design

So far, we've covered the basics of dimensional modeling and data warehousing. We're now ready to cover the process that loads the data warehouse from all of your source systems.

Purpose of the ETL

The purpose of the Extraction, Transformation, and Loading (ETL) process is to move data from the many source systems into the data warehouse. There are many steps that must take place, but most fall into one of the ETL phases.

Extract

Extraction is the process of pulling data from the source system or systems into an intermediate format. This format can be flat files or a relational staging area, depending on the most efficient process of sourcing the data. If one or more systems is coming from VSAM (Virtual Storage Access Method) or mainframe databases, it may be best to extract to a set of flat files to avoid the complexities of extracting data using relational tools from mainframe databases and to avoid conversions between EBCDIC and ASCII. Once in this format, transformation can begin directly on the flat file using tools such as Perl, or the flat files can be inserted into a relational database for slower, but richer functionality.

> If possible, the source system should include a 'first added' and a 'last changed' date/time stamp. Using this to source only the information that has changed since the last cycle can drastically reduce the amount of data to extract, and thus, transform and load.

Transform

Once data is in the staging area, the ETL can begin its transformation phase. Transformation reconciles data type and format differences, resolves uniqueness issues, and ensures conformity of data before the data is loaded into the data warehouse. It also can cleanse or repair data (for example, correcting invalid zip codes by using a valid postal service database). However, the majority of the processing of the Transformation phase is usually spent formatting the staged data to resemble the warehouse data and looking up surrogate key values.

Formatting

Formatting is usually the process of ensuring conformity between all dimension and fact rows. For example, one source system may have customer name as Last name, First name. Another may have First, Last, Title or any other variation. These values must be conformed before they can be loaded into the warehouse. During this process, you may find that many customers from one system are the same as another. This requires the consolidation and tracking of both natural keys.

Surrogate Key Lookup

Warehouse dimensions should never use natural keys for uniqueness. As in the formatting example above, both customer records identify a single customer, but if the warehouse used the natural key, the records could never be consolidated.

If the source system cannot identify a date/time stamp for changes, the lookup process for dimensions must perform a lookup for each dimension record to determine whether the row should be added as a new dimension member or the dimension member should be updated. However, if the insert date and the last time the record changed can be identified, this process can update only the changed records and insert the new without performing this lookup.

> **Significant performance gains can be effected in SQL Server by pinning small dimension tables in memory using** `DBCC PINTABLE` **during the lookup process. For larger dimension tables, care must be taken not to overload the data cache for the server. See Books Online for more details.**

Load

This is the last phase in the ETL process. This phase moves the data from the staging area into the dimension and fact tables. This phase should not perform any transformation during the data load. The load phase should also be transactional and audited. The transactions can be in bulk, batch, or row-by-row with the choice allowing for more control or better performance.

Bulk Mode

Using bulk mode has the effect of blasting your data into the fact tables. This will be the most efficient method of loading data but comes with the biggest risk since transactions are not logged. If even one row fails to load, the entire process must be aborted. To avoid this, constraints can be dropped before loading, but then the reapplying of constraints can cause the ETL process to fail on this step and can invalidate the fact data, depending on the data validation that was done up to this point.

Batch Mode

Using batch mode improves control but slows performance. However, if any one batch fails, depending on your specific business rules, the load process can continue or be restarted at the point of failure once any errors have been resolved.

Single Row Mode

If commits are performed row by row, each row that fails can be pushed to an error table for processing at a later time. With this method, more control is maintained, but load times are much slower than with batch mode.

Incremental versus Full Reloads

You should always build your ETL process as if it were performing an incremental load rather than a full load. This can be accomplished by accepting begin and end dates as input parameters to the ETL. In this way, the ETL can extract only the data that falls between the input dates. Once again, this is only possible if the source system has some kind of timestamp that makes it possible to identify new records from existing records.

However, if the data warehouse loses integrity, a full reload becomes necessary. This can be accomplished by truncating the fact tables, deleting all data from the dimension tables and then calling the ETL process with start and end dates that encompass the entire history of the source system. However, this should only be used as a last resort as the transactional system may not have the entire set of data that the warehouse had contained due to purges or other activities.

Data Transformation Document

The data transformation document has the purpose of organizing the source-to-target mappings in a format that can aid the development of both the staging area and ETL. The document should include the source tables, columns, and formats, the target tables, columns, and formats, and any transformation rules that may apply for each source element. For example, a data transformation document could look like the following table. In the table below, the source system is the Suppliers table in the sample Northwind database.

Source Column	Format	Target Table	Target Column	Format	Transform Rules
Supplier ID	int	DIM_SUPPLIER	supplier_nk	int	None
Company Name	nvarchar (80)	DIM_SUPPLIER	supplier_name	nvarchar (80)	RTRIM
Contact Name	nvarchar (60)	DIM_SUPPLIER	contact_name	nvarchar (60)	RTRIM
Contact Title	nvarchar (60)	DIM_SUPPLIER	contact_title	nvarchar (60)	RTRIM
Address	nvarchar (120)	DIM_SUPPLIER	address	nvarchar (120)	RTRIM
City	nvarchar (30)	DIM_GEOGRAPHY	city	nvarchar (30)	Lookup in geography dimension
Region	nvarchar (30)	DIM_GEOGRAPHY	state_region	nvarchar (30)	Lookup in geography dimension
Postal Code	nvarchar (20)	DIM_GEOGRAPHY	poastal_code	nvarchar (20)	Lookup in geography dimension

Source Column	Format	Target Table	Target Column	Format	Transform Rules
Country	nvarchar (30)	DIM_GEOGRAPHY	country	nvarchar (30)	Lookup in geography dimension
Phone	nvarchar (48)	DIM_SUPPLIER	phone	nvarchar (48)	RTRIM
Fax	nvarchar (48)	DIM_SUPPLIER	fax	nvarchar (49)	RTRIM
HomePage	ntext	DIM_SUPPLIER	home_page	nvarchar (255)	SUBSTRING (source, 1, 255)

This document helps to identify any anomalies and ensures that all elements have been addressed. This document can also be modified to include meta data descriptions of each column or other helpful information.

From Source to Stage

In this section we will discuss the ETL process from the Source Systems to the Staging Area.

Data can be sourced from many systems simultaneously to improve performance. However, you should load only one target stage table at a time, in any order, to avoid contention issues.

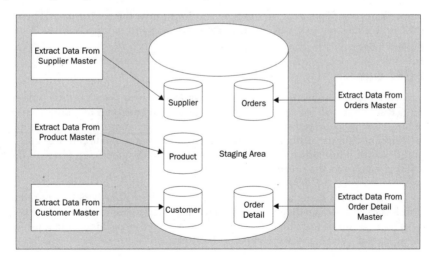

Data Acquisition

One of the reasons a data warehouse is created is to avoid overburdening the transactional system with resource intensive queries. Extracting data from the source transaction system should follow the same guidelines by extracting all of the necessary data as quickly as possible with as few table joins as feasible. This may require extracting more data than is actually needed to load to the warehouse, but the tradeoff should be evident. Once all of the data is in the staging area, the ETL process should not need to touch the source system again in this load.

Linked Servers

Creating a Linked Server reference to the source systems enables several different approaches to data extraction. It allows the ETL to address the source systems similarly without necessarily having to understand the native interface to extract data. However, the tradeoff is in performance. SQL Server issues rowset requests against the provider. This can be significantly slower than bulk extraction or native code.

Staging Area Physical Design

When designing the staging area, several questions must be considered:

- ❑ Where will the staging area physically reside?
- ❑ How should the database be created to best suit staging?
- ❑ What should the staging area look like?
- ❑ When and where should indexes be added?
- ❑ Should any transformation be performed between the source and the stage?

Several of these issues are dependent on the type and location of the source data. They may also depend on the processing window, the consistency of the data and the speed of the data warehouse and staging machines.

Get In and Get Out

One of the many possible reasons for creating a data warehouse is to decrease the resource demand on the source OLTP system by off-loading long running queries and analyses to a different machine. This includes the long-running queries used in extraction and transformation. To reduce the amount of time and resource consumed for extraction, create the staging area on a separate physical machine (usually the data warehouse) from the source OLTP system. In this way, the extraction phase of the ETL will consume as few resources on the source machine as possible.

The staging area can also reside on a completely standalone system. The benefits are reduced resource utilization and less overall storage requirements on the data warehouse machine. However, the transformation process can be considerably slower because of cross-machine table joins for dimension lookups and the cost of a staging server can be prohibitive.

> **TIP: Even though the staging area data is transitory, the data warehouse machine must have enough disk space for not only the warehouse data, but the staging area data as well if they are both on the same machine. Plan accordingly.**

Using File Groups in Staging

Using SQL Server file groups has some pretty substantial benefits in performance with few administrative drawbacks. Each file group can consist of many separate physical files. Each file can be placed on a separate drive, therefore enabling parallel reading and writing. A good rule of thumb is to create one file per physical disk in the system within each file group. Also, keep non-clustered indexes and data in separate file groups, and remember to keep your log files on separate physical disks as well.

Drop Indexes Before Loading

All indexes must be removed from the staging area before loading with data. Remember, the priority is to get the data out of the source system as quickly as possible – you don't want to have to update indexes as you insert. Also, OLE DB can use `IRowsetFastLoad` if the provider supports it. Add indexes after all of the data is loaded to increase transformation phase performance.

> **TIP: If one of the staging area sources is a large flat file or text file, make sure that it does not reside on the same physical drive as the staging area drives. SQL Server will be forced to perform serial reads and writes because of disk head contention.**

Stage Definition – Extraction

Whether you're importing from flat files or pulling directly from the source system, the staging area should resemble, as closely as possible, the flat file structure or query to extract the source data. For example, if the source system stores customer information using two tables, CUSTOMER_NAME and CUSTOMER_ADDRESS, the resulting stage table should appear as if it is the result of:

```
SELECT * FROM CUSTOMER_NAME, CUSTOMER_ADDRESS WHERE . . .
```

Of course, you don't need to source every column from both tables, but you should not be performing any transformation other than possibly casting or coercing data into specific data types. You want to make sure that all source data is captured with the smallest possibility of error. The more transformation that occurs during extract, the more likely it is that an error can occur with the process. For example, the ETL extract can decide that customer name is actually

```
customer_lastname + ', ' + customer_firstname + ' ' + customer_mi AS customer_name
```

and attempt to extract while concatenating. However, the source system may have CONCAT_NULL_YIELDS_NULL set to ON. If so, any NULL value in any of the fields will result in a NULL customer_name. However, if you've pulled the data to a system within your control, you'll have the opportunity to control the system parameters.

You can also run into problems when you expect one data type and actually get another. This is very often the case with improperly designed source systems that may mix data types within the same column. For example, a source system that contains financial information may contain a column called amount. However, the data type allows alphanumeric data. You expect all of the information to be numeric only, but someone decides that 'N/A' is appropriate for amount. This will really cause some problems.

Having a denormalized structure also makes bulk loading easier and faster. As in the customer example above, if the stage area includes a table for each of the source system tables, you may find that transforming the data can be a slow process because of the extra joins, but performing the joins in the source system will use more resources – you will have to use your best judgment here to determine the right method for your situation.

Stage Definition – Transformation

We've reached the part of the ETL where opinions differ greatly, depending on the RDBMS system, regarding the dimension transformation in the staging area. One of the primary tasks during the ETL is to resolve natural keys to surrogate keys for the dimensions that are extracted from the source system. All dimensions must have this process performed. The two possible approaches involve set-based processing and row-by-row processing. Both have merits and faults, but both must be considered as a viable approach to this task.

Row-by-Row

Row-by-row processing involves evaluating each row, one-by-one, and querying the generalized key value using the natural key. A typical process may include using the DTS Data Driven Query task or using a stored procedure to perform the work. This processing occurs for dimensions and facts if the staged data contains separate dimensions and facts (for example, customer data and sales data). However, dimension processing depends on whether or not the dimension is a slowly changing dimension like customer or product. The three options for dealing with slowly changing dimensions must be explained before continuing.

Type 1 Slowly Changing Dimensions
Type 1 slowly changing dimensions are handled by overwriting the existing dimension record with new values. This method is generally easier to handle because it involves only updating the dimension record. However, all history is lost after the update is performed. An example of this would be a correction to a product name or a consumer's name.

Type 2 Slowly Changing Dimensions
Type 2 slowly changing dimensions are handled by creating a new record for each change in the original source record. The type 2 approach is used when a fundamental change in one of the dimension attributes occurs, such as quantity in the case of a product, or zip code for a customer. If the zip code of the customer is important at the time of the purchase, and if the customer relocates, you don't want the record of this purchase to reflect a new zip code. This is handled by creating a new record for the customer. Purchases occurring prior to customer relocation associate to the old zip code and purchases occurring after the relocation associate to the new zip code.

Type 3 Slowly Changing Dimensions
Type 3 slowly changing dimensions are handled by using a slightly unorthodox approach and creating an 'old' value that represents a prior value in history. This prior value may contain the original value of the previous value, depending on the business rules. However, this only stores the most recent version and is not usually handled well by analysis tools.

Handling type 1, 2, and 3 dimensions using the row-by-row approach involves opening a cursor on the stage dimension table and querying the warehouse dimension table using the natural key of each row. However, for types 1 and 3, if the warehouse dimension record exists, an update occurs in the dimension table. For type 2 dimensions, an insert occurs only if the record values have changed.

During the fact table load, the same basic process occurs. A cursor is opened on the stage fact table and each natural key dimension value is resolved before loading the record into the warehouse fact table. During the process, each dimension record must be resolved. If the record cannot be resolved to an existing dimension record, the fact row can either be moved to an error table or the dimension value can be set to 'Unknown' or 'Invalid'. Moving the record to an error row allows an administrator to resolve the issue later. However, this can lead to data inconsistencies until the error is resolved.

As you can see, using the row-by-row approach allows a significantly higher level of control, but can be hampered by performance problems. The number of lookups that must be executed equals the product of the number of fact rows and the number of dimensions. If the amount of data to load into the fact table is large and the fact table contains several or many dimensions, the process will be terribly slow. If the amount of memory on the machine is unlimited and the dimension tables are pinned in memory, the process can be quite fast, but this is not likely.

Set-Based Processing

An alternative approach to row-by-row processing is set-based or rowset processing. This approach involves issuing single SQL commands to the dimension and fact stage tables so the data is updated in place. This approach almost always requires a table scan, but is still usually faster than row-by-row processing.

It also requires that 'placeholder' columns be created to hold temporary values. These placeholder columns are nullable columns included in the stage table design. In the case of Type 1 dimension tables, they will hold a flag as to whether the dimension record exists. For fact tables, they will hold the surrogate key value when the dimension key is looked up.

Dimensions

In the following example, a Type 1 dimension for product is being loaded into the product stage table. However, the source data includes both new products and products with changed data because of the lack of a timestamp on the source data. The products with changed data will include their original natural key, but may have a modified product name or description.

The Product Stage table is defined as follows:

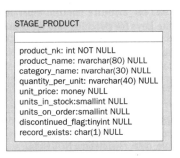

STAGE_PRODUCT

product_nk: int NOT NULL
product_name: nvarchar(80) NULL
category_name: nvarchar(30) NULL
quantity_per_unit: nvarchar(40) NULL
unit_price: money NULL
units_in_stock:smallint NULL
units_on_order:smallint NULL
discontinued_flag:tinyint NULL
record_exists: char(1) NULL

Notice the last column called 'record_exists'. This column acts as a flag when determining whether to update or insert the product dimension record. For example, the following SQL statement joins the product stage table to the warehouse dimension table and updates 'record_exists' if a match is found:

```
UPDATE STAGE_PRODUCT SET record_exists = 'Y'
FROM STAGE_PRODUCT S, DIM_PRODUCT D
WHERE S.product_nk = D.product_nk
```

Characteristic	Row-based Processing	Set-based Processing
Partial Loading	Row-based processing allows partial loading to occur.	Set-based processing does not support partial loading.
Parallel Loading	Row-based processing can process sections of stage data in parallel by dividing the data among several processes.	Set-based processing requires that the source data be physically separated to perform tasks in parallel.

From Stage to Warehouse

In this section, we will discuss the ETL process from the Staging Area to the Warehouse.

Stored Procedures versus DTS Tasks

When designing a data warehouse ETL, you will have to make a decision whether to use native procedural coding or whether certain tasks can be performed directly in DTS. This issue really matters most during the Stage to Warehouse step of the ETL (The Source to Stage will generally use some form of bulk insert or SQL queries). The choice should be made based on several inputs:

❑ Reusability

❑ Performance

❑ Suitability

Reusability

The overriding goal of most programmers when writing code is to create reusable code so that the wheel doesn't have to be reinvented for each project. Stored procedures have no means of inheriting code from another stored procedure. At best, result sets placed in to the temporary database are the only method of passing any information between one stored procedure and another. Although stored procedures can be used from several different calling points, and can be seen as reusable this way, what they do is, to quite a high degree, set in stone. Use of custom tasks within DTS can make this goal more attainable. They can be written in VB or C++ and therefore can take advantage of object-oriented characteristics that cannot be utilized in T-SQL.

Performance

In most cases, performance with native T-SQL will be much better than using VBScript, JScript, or a custom task. DTS objects will not run in the same memory context as native code would and therefore will have to marshal calls across processes. However, these performance issues should only be an issue when performing repetitive tasks.

Suitability

This is usually the biggest determining factor as to whether to use DTS or T-SQL. DTS is well suited to organizing workflow and interacting with external objects and processes. T-SQL is well suited to database-specific tasks. The rule of thumb is to decide which tools are more suited to performing certain tasks. In the case where both are equally suited, base the decision on Reusability or Performance.

Indexing

It is obvious that if you have to scan all the data to find the information you needed, there is a great deal of processing happening each time. By creating an index, or perhaps more than one, which has been carefully thought out, you can greatly enhance the performance of your application, by providing a quick way to find the information you want (in much the same way as the index of a book allows you to find the section you want without having to read the whole book). This section discusses some architectural considerations to make when determining when and where to index.

Stage

Before loading any stage table, the indexes for the table should be dropped. However, it may be appropriate to recreate indexes on the natural key columns for both dimensions and facts once the data has been loaded into the staging area. They will be utilized during the loading of the fact and dimension tables.

Dimensions

When loading dimension tables, both the natural key and surrogate key columns should be indexed as a covering index. Many lookups will be performed using the natural key and SQL Server can avoid having to read from the data pages if a covering index is in place. This just means that the entire query can be satisfied from reading the index pages.

Facts

Fact table indexes should only be dropped if the ETL is loading more than 10% or so of the total fact table rows. In most cases, though, fact data is being incrementally loaded one unit at a time. It's usually best to leave the fact table indexes in place.

Referential Integrity

Referential integrity constrains the data being inserted into dimension and fact tables based on existing relationships. However, the action of verifying referential integrity for each insert consumes resources. Referential integrity should be enforced during development and testing, but in most cases, can be dropped once the warehouse is in production. Most data warehouses are read-only, except during the ETL process, so referential integrity is not as necessary as in an OLTP database. However, be aware that data integrity could be compromised if the ETL cannot guarantee integrity during the staging process.

Integrating Analysis Services

By just completing the ETL process, we have not finished the requirement of ETL as a whole. Although we may have loaded the data, there will be many times that this data is placed into a "history" server (in other words, a server holding historical information). There will be a great deal of analysis performed on this data, as it is not being used for data entry. Therefore, it is quite important that we define the data, ready for the analysis process. This section discusses how Microsoft Analysis Services can be integrated with the ETL process. For a more complete discussion of Analysis Services, please refer to Books Online.

Analysis Services Overview

Before continuing, it might be necessary to understand the role that Microsoft Analysis Services, formerly OLAP Services, plays in data warehousing and decision support. Data warehouse systems are usually built on a relational database platform like SQL Server or Oracle. These databases consist of the traditional fact and dimension tables and require copious amounts of disk space. Performance of complex analytical queries from the relational warehouse can be poor, as relational systems are generally designed for two dimensional result sets, that is, rows and columns.

This is where Analysis Services has tremendous advantages. Analysis Services is built around the concept of a multidimensional database system. The manner in which it organizes data is drastically different from a relational database system. Without getting into too much detail, Analysis Services organizes data into a structure that can provide several orders of magnitude of performance gains over relational data warehouses. Utilizing these performance gains makes real-time, rapid analysis possible.

The following diagram shows a typical decision support system including both relational and multidimensional database systems:

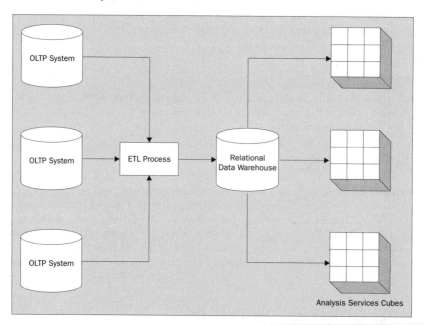

Analysis Services and OLAP technology in general are not replacements for the relational data warehouse, but rather an extension of its capabilities more suited to advanced analysis. The Analysis Services cubes cannot exist without an OLE DB data source to populate them.

Since the cubes cannot be processed until the data warehouse contains data, processing has a dependency on the successful loading of the relational data warehouse. This means that the processing can be included in a workflow as a task in the ETL created in DTS. SQL Server 2000 even includes a specific custom task for processing these Analysis Services cubes directly from DTS.

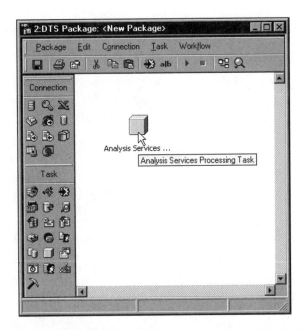

This task gives you significant control over the objects to be processed, including databases, local, linked, and virtual cubes, local and remote partitions, shared and virtual dimensions, and mining models. It also gives the programmer the option of performing a complete reprocess, refreshing the data only, or an incremental process. However, only the incremental processing interests us. Significant processing time can be saved by only refreshing subsets of data within an Analysis Services cube.

Incremental Processing

Many relational data warehouses are loaded on a recurring, time-based schedule such as daily, weekly, or monthly. Due to this, within relational fact tables there exist natural partitions for each load period. This just means that there are natural dividing lines within the data. As more data is added to the fact tables, the time necessary for performing a full process or refreshing the entire data set increases. The desirable action would be to only process the new data and add it to the existing view of the cube. This is where incremental processing comes in.

Analysis Services' cubes are really just logical representations of physical partitions, similar to the way a relational view represents a logical view of a physical table. When a cube is incrementally processed, a temporary partition is created, loaded with just the new data, and then merged back into the existing physical partition. However, the only way for Analysis Services to tell what the new data is, is by using a filter or WHERE clause to select the data. Since the relational fact table usually includes a reference to the date that the data is valid for, this can be used as the filter for new data. In the following screenshot, the warehouse 98 partition of the Warehouse cube in the FoodMart 2000 database will be processed using a filter of "inventory_fact_1998"."time_id" = 870.

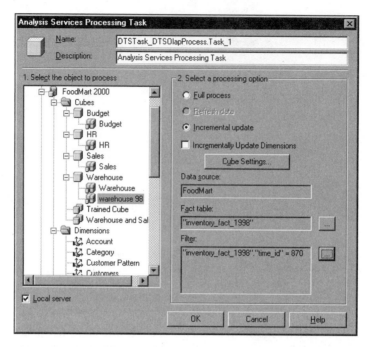

This means that when this partition is processed, it will only include data for the fact records with the `time_id` of 870. This value contains the foreign key from the "time_by_day" dimension representing the `time_id` for May 19, 1998. Examine the `foodmart 2000.mdb` Access database in the Samples directory of Analysis Services for more information.

When Analysis Services begins to process this partition, a temporary partition is created automatically. All data specified by the filter clause will be included in this temporary partition. Once the processing for this partition has been completed, it will be merged into the existing partition and the temporary partition will be deleted. If the filter value is set incorrectly by including data that already exists in the cube, no error will occur and the data for that filter value will be represented twice.

Since the filter value must change for each time period's load, you can use the Dynamic Properties task to build and set the filter statement prior to processing the new dimension. To do this, create a Dynamic Properties task that populates the filter property using a query or a global variable. You can have the query return the generalized key for the time dimension, which represents the key for the current run date of the ETL.

If the ETL process is run periodically, and if no historical data is modified and the fact data can be segmented by time, incremental updates will provide the best performance possible. If business rules allow for the changing of fact history (for example, corrections to sales transactions, etc.), or if the fact table doesn't include time variant data, you will not be able to incrementally update the cubes and must refresh all of the fact table data.

Summary

In this chapter, we discussed some general theories in data warehousing and some techniques by means of which the ETL can perform better.

We started off by examining some basic concepts to do with data warehouses, such as the different schema designs – star, snowflake, and hybrid star/snowflake – and the differences between them, as well as examining the idea of OLTP versus OLAP. We then moved on to discuss the issues we should think of and consider when we start to create a dimensional model for our data warehouse.

The next section examined the ETL process – extract, transform, and load – in detail, starting firstly with a look at each section in turn. Issues we covered here included the nature of the source system, the problems we could encounter during transformation, and the different options we can choose when loading – in bulk, in batches, or by single rows.

We then looked at how to get the data we need from the source to a staging area, and the many issues involved with this; we then looked at the next stage in the process, which is from the staging area to the warehouse. We finished off with a brief look at integrating Analysis Services.

Be aware, however, that this chapter only includes a brief discussion of data warehousing principles and should be supplemented with texts devoted to the subject, such as those books mentioned previously.

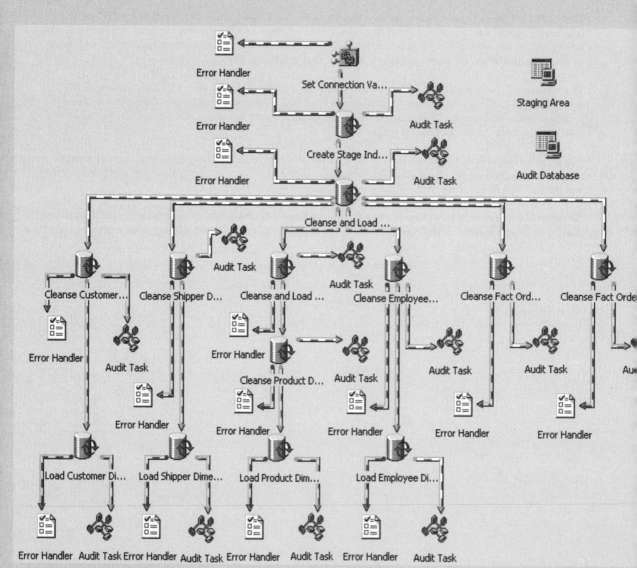

Error Handler

Set Connection Va...

Audit Task

Staging Area

Error Handler

Create Stage Ind...

Audit Task

Audit Database

Error Handler

Cleanse and Load ...

Audit Task

Cleanse Customer...

Cleanse Shipper D...

Cleanse and Load ...

Audit Task

Cleanse Employee...

Cleanse Fact Ord...

Cleanse Fact Orde

Error Handler

Audit Task

Error Handler

Audit Task

Audit Task

Audit Task

Au

Error Handler

Cleanse Product D...

Audit Task

Error Handler

Error Handler

Error Handler

Error Handler

Load Customer Di...

Load Shipper Dime...

Load Product Dim...

Load Employee Di...

Error Handler   Audit Task Error Handler   Audit Task Error Handler   Audit Task   Error Handler   Audit Task

14

Using DTS from Other Applications

The lines between a database administrator and developer are blurring. With the advent of SQL-DMO, SQL-NS, and DTS in SQL Server, database administrators can now build their own tools to help mitigate some of the administrative chores that they must contend with. Also, more developers are discovering the same SQL libraries, and have come to the aid of the DBAs.

The wonderful thing about DTS is that it can be utilized in a whole bunch of different applications. For example, we can use DTS to run packages from Active Server Pages, Excel, and Access. The Active Server Pages can be used like a menu for the available DTS packages, and allow the user to execute them any time they need to. In Excel and Access, once we have validated the data the user has input, we can call upon DTS to load it into the repository for us.

In this chapter, we'll look at a method of executing a DTS package from an Active Server Page, complete with setting global variables and monitoring the status. We will demonstrate how the various technologies that we have learned previously in this book, in addition to a few new ones that we will introduce in this chapter, can come together to offer an elegant solution to a difficult problem.

Now, you don't need to get this example working in order to benefit from it. We'll be going over many technologies that you may have never heard of before. Our goal here is to expose you to the different things that it is going to be critical for you to have an understanding of, since SQL 2000 is a big piece of the .Net architecture. When we're done, you should have a decent enough exposure to these tools and technologies to get your mind racing on what you can do with DTS, and how you can integrate it into existing and new workflows that come along.

In building this application, we will be taking a **3-tiered** approach. That means the application is broken up into three logical pieces:

- ❑ User services – responsible for the user interface (presentation)
- ❑ Business services – responsible for the implementation of business rules
- ❑ Data services – responsible for the access and maintenance of the application's data

If you're familiar with 3-tier architecture, this should be second nature; but if you're unfamiliar with these terms, we'll briefly describe them in appropriate sections below.

Application Overview

The application we'll be exploring in this chapter is the natural progression once you've built your warehouse. In most cases, as data is populated into your warehouse, there may be some package you execute on an adhoc basis, in order to populate some ancillary tables that are used for reconciliation or reporting of the new data. With this being the case, you may want to allow the users to execute this package by themselves.

It's also desirable to keep the users out of the actual package, so that they cannot make changes and start filling up your database with a hundred different versions – which can leave your database in an inconsistent state.

What Technologies Will We Be Using?

In order to build this example, we have used some technologies that you may or may not have used before. If you have, then understanding this example will be trivial. However, if you have not, we'll briefly go over these technologies, to give you a better understanding of what each one does.

SQL-DMO

The DMO in **SQL-DMO** stands for **Distributed Management Objects**. It is SQL-DMO that is the application programming interface (API) used by Enterprise Manager in SQL Server 2000. What this means is that using SQL-DMO, you can perform all functions performed by SQL Server Enterprise Manager.

SQL-DMO objects allow you to automate:

- ❑ Repetitive or commonly performed SQL Server administrative tasks
- ❑ SQL Server object creation and administration
- ❑ Creation and administration of SQL Server Agent jobs, alerts, and operators
- ❑ SQL Server replication installation and configuration

The specific piece that we will use in our example is the creation and administration of SQL Server Agent jobs. In order to create a job you must:

- ❑ Create and populate a Job object
- ❑ Add the Job object to the Jobs collection of a JobServer object
- ❑ Create and populate one or more JobStep objects
- ❑ Alter the Job object, by adding the JobStep object(s) created to the JobSteps collection

You will see these steps outlined in the example below.

If you want to know more about SQL-DMO, try Wrox's Professional SQL Server 7.0 Development Using SQL-DMO, SQL-NS & DTS, ISBN 1-861002-80-7.

COM+

COM+ is a set of services under Windows 2000 that combines COM with **Microsoft Transaction Server** (**MTS**). MTS provides the mechanism to manage a component's use. Rather than having to worry about the creation and destruction of objects for the application, COM+ has the ability to manage that for us. With the introduction of COM+, MTS has been merged into the operating system and is now called Microsoft **Component Services**. Microsoft Component Services offer new functionality over what was available in MTS, including:

- ❑ Queued Components – this combines the features of COM and **Microsoft Message Queue** Server (**MSMQ**) to be able to execute components asynchronously. Processing can occur without regard to the availability or accessibility of either the sender of the receiver.

- ❑ Object Pooling – object pooling is an automatic service provided by COM+ that enables you to have instances of a component kept active in a pool, ready to be used by any other client that requests the component. Once the application is running, COM+ manages the pool for you, handling all the details of object activation and reuse.

As well as the new features, it still offers transaction, component, and security management features.

ASP

Active Server Pages (**ASP**) is a method of creating dynamic web content. What this means is that instead of having a static HTML page, you can do processing on the server, which in turn creates HTML to be displayed in the browser. It is very similar to the code you create in an ActiveX Script task, except that it has additional objects and methods, which allow you to interact with the user via the browser interface.

In order for the file to be processed on the server, it must have an .asp extension. The .asp extension lets the server know that it needs to be processed by asp.dll. This DLL is responsible for finding and interpreting the ASP server-side code that it finds within the page.

If there is no ASP code that needs to be executed on the page, it is released to the client. When ASP receives a page that does contain server-side script code, it parses it line by line. Anything that is not server-side script, or does not require ASP, is sent back to IIS and then to the client. As each section of code is reached, it is passed to the appropriate scripting engine. The results from the scripting engine are inserted at the appropriate points into the page as it is sent back to IIS.

The common way for ASP to identify the server-side script it needs to interpret is using <% %> script delimiters:

```
<HTML>
<BODY>
<%
For i = 1 to 5
%>
<FONT SIZE=<%=i %>>The font size is <%=i %>.</FONT><BR>
```

```
<%
Next
%>
</BODY>
</HTML>
```

When this page is run, you get the following display in the browser:

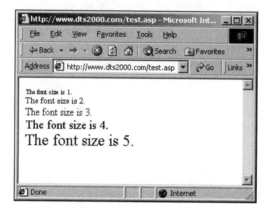

We can see how the information is interpreted and displayed in the browser. If we then look at the source of the web page by clicking on View | Source, it reveals that the variables have been replaced with the results from the server:

```
<HTML>
<BODY>

<FONT SIZE=1>The font size is 1.</FONT><BR>

<FONT SIZE=2>The font size is 2.</FONT><BR>

<FONT SIZE=3>The font size is 3.</FONT><BR>

<FONT SIZE=4>The font size is 4.</FONT><BR>

<FONT SIZE=5>The font size is 5.</FONT><BR>

</BODY>
</HTML>
```

CDO

CDO stands for **Collaboration Data Objects**. It is used to provide simple messaging services, as well as access the capabilities provided by Exchange Server. CDO is accessible from Visual Basic, C/C++, VBScript, and JScript. Over time, there have been a few versions of CDO released with different products and operating systems. The version that we will be using is CDO 2.0, more commonly known as CDO for Windows 2000.

CDONTS (**Collaboration Data Objects for NT Server**) provides a subset of the functionality of CDO. It is used to provide fast, reliable, and scalable messaging for applications that don't require the advanced calendaring and workflow capabilities that Exchange Server and CDO provide.

As an example of the simplicity of CDONTS, let's take a quick look at what's required to be able to send a mail message using the `NewMail` object. With this object, you can send an e-mail with as little as three lines of code:

```
Set objMail = CreateObject("CDONTS.NewMail")
objMail.Send "todd@toddrobinson.com", "brian@brianknight.com", _
             "Hello", "You've got mail!"
Set objMail = Nothing
```

The first line creates the object, the third line releases it, and the second line sends the e-mail using the `Send` method of the `NewMail` object, which has the following syntax:

```
objMail.Send ( [From] [,To] [, Subject] [, Body] [, Importance] )
```

We will use this object to send mail from our DTS package. This method can be used in more environments then the Send Mail task, because the Send Mail task requires a MAPI client to be installed. Not all networks have an available MAPI-compliant messaging system, and CDONTS provides a decent alternative.

What Tools Do You Need?

In order to run the examples in this chapter, you will need to have:

❑ A computer running Windows 2000 Server or Professional, and SQL 2000. In addition, the computer must be configured to use IIS and SMTP. If you want to use FrontPage (see next point) you also need Front Page Extensions.

> Note: Windows 2000 Server installation sets up the Internet services by default, but Windows 2000 Professional does not. If you do not have the services installed, you must install them by going to **Settings I Control Panel I Add/Remove Programs I Add/Remove Windows Components**, and adding the **Internet Information Services**. Click **Details** to select the particular services you want.

Creating the Package List Table

As we said earlier, we need to create a table in a database that will contain the list of the packages that the users can execute. For our example, we'll create a table called DTS_PKG in the Wrox database.

To create the table, run the following SQL in Query Analyzer, making sure you have Wrox selected as the database:

```
CREATE TABLE DTS_PKG (
    [PKG_ID] [numeric](18, 0) IDENTITY (1, 1) NOT NULL ,
    [PKG_NAME] [varchar] (64) NOT NULL ,
    [PKG_DESC] [varchar] (255) NULL ,
    [PKG_STATUS] [int] NULL
)
```

We have an identity column for the package, as well as the package name, package description, and status. This table must contain the proper name of the package to be executed from the server in PKG_NAME.

Creating the Package

For the purpose of this example, create a package called Send Mail, containing an Active Script task.

This task will do a calculation in a loop to simulate processing, and sends an e-mail upon completion. Add the following code to the task:

```
'*********************************************************************
'  Visual Basic ActiveX Script
'*********************************************************************

Function Main()

    'Simulate processing
    For i = 1 to 1000000
        dblValue = dblValue + 1 / i
    Next

    Set objMail = CreateObject("CDONTS.NewMail")

    objMail.To = DTSGlobalVariables("gvSendTo").Value
    objMail.From = "<your email address here>"
    objMail.Subject = "Web based DTS package execution"

    objMail.Body = "This email was generated by a DTS package " & _
                   "executed from the web."

    objMail.Send
    Set objMail = Nothing

    Main = DTSTaskExecResult_Success

End Function
```

> **Make sure you put your own e-mail address in the `From` property.**

The code inside the Active Script Task utilizes CDONTS (Collaboration Data Objects) in order to send the e-mail.

> *In order for this to work, the SMTP service on your server needs to be running and, if on an intranet, set up properly to interact with your existing SMTP server to send e-mail out to the outside world.*

> *The configuration of the SMTP server to work in your intranet environment is beyond the scope of the book. However, if you have an existing SMTP server on your LAN, you can configure your SMTP server to send all outbound messages to it. For more information on how to do this, refer to MSDN article Q230235.*

Next create a global variable `gvSendTo`. This will contain the e-mail address to which the e-mail is sent:

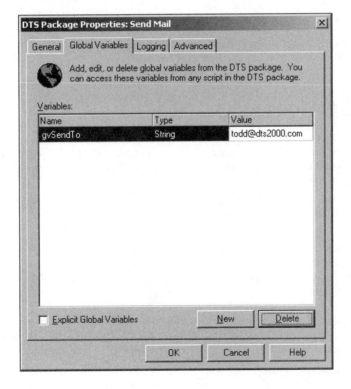

Populating the Table

Now all that's left to do is to insert a row into the DTS_PKG table. Run the following in Query Analyzer:

```
INSERT INTO DTS_PKG
    (PKG_NAME)
VALUES ('Send Mail')
```

Note that the other columns in the table allow NULLs, so we don't need to specify them here.

At this point, if there are any other packages that you would like make available to be executed via the web, simply insert the appropriate package name into the DTS_PKG table using the following syntax:

```
INSERT INTO DTS_PKG
    (PKG_NAME)
VALUES ('<Insert Package Name Here>')
```

I also inserted the package Dynamic Properties Task from Chapter 3 as well.

We've now prepared the data services for the remaining layers to be built on. Next we need to look at how we're going to access this newly created data and package.

Business Services

Let's get started with the VB COM+ object. We are going to look at the code and give you reasons as to why we did what we did. We'll see the basics of how to create a COM+ object from scratch, but we'll focus most of our attention on understanding what the code is doing.

Remember, you can download the code for this chapter, along with that for the rest of the book, from Wrox's web site at http://www.wrox.com.

What this object contains is the core piece of the application we have built to help us with the adhoc execution of DTS packages. It contains one public subroutine, two public functions (methods which you can call externally from other programs), and one private function (used only by the object itself). The public methods are as follows:

- ❑ RunPackageAsync – this public subroutine requires the package name, the authentication information required to access the package on the server, and the global variables as a recordset. It uses the private function to script a job via SQL-DMO, place it on the server, and execute it.

- ❑ GetPackageList – this function requires the authentication information for the database that contains the DTS_PKG table (which is the list of packages that you have authorized the users to execute). This function returns the list of DTS Package names from the DTS_PKG table, and reports the execution status of the package as run by the application in a recordset.

- ❑ GetGlobalVariables – this function requires the package name, and authentication information for the database where the packages are stored. It opens the package and checks for any global variables. If there are any, it takes the name and value information, and stores it in a recordset to be displayed and modified prior to package execution.

Now let's look at the private function (the one that the public ones use):

❑   GetScript – this function requires the authentication information for the database that
     contains the DTS_PKG table. It returns a string that contains the entire Active X Script needed
     for the job to execute properly.

We'll look at each of these functions in more detail shortly.

Creating the DLL

So let's get started by creating a new ActiveX DLL project. Make the project name DTSManager, the
class name Package, and set the MTSTransactionMode to 1-No Transactions as shown below:

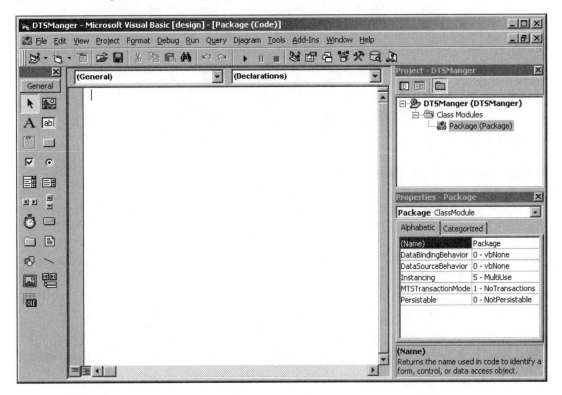

Now we need to set the references to the project. This lets the designer know which libraries to include when you compile the .dll. Select references to the objects shown below:

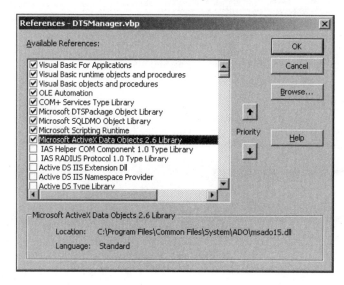

Now that we have the basic shell of this object, we can start to enter the code we're going to use.

Coding the Package Class

Start by entering the following code to the Package class:

```
Option Explicit

Const jobPrefix = "dts_"
```

We'll use Option Explicit to make sure all variables are defined. The second statement, Const jobPrefix = "dts_", sets the prefix for the jobs that will be stored on the server. For instance, for a package named SendMail, the job that will be created will be named dts_SendMail.

Next up is the COM+ specific interface, ObjectControl. This is used to define context-specific initialization and cleanup procedures for your COM+ objects, and to specify whether or not the objects can be recycled:

```
'=============================================================================
'=== COM+ Specific Interfaces
'=============================================================================
Implements ObjectControl

Private Sub ObjectControl_Activate()
End Sub

Private Sub ObjectControl_Deactivate()
End Sub

Private Function ObjectControl_CanBePooled() As Boolean
    ObjectControl_CanBePooled = True
End Function
```

We are using this interface simply to take advantage of **Object Pooling**. Object Pooling enables you to configure a component so that instances of it are kept active in a **pool**, ready to be used by any client that requests the component. This significantly increases performance for the client.

Note that even though we are only changing the CanBePooled method, we still have to define the initialization (ObjectControl_Activate) and cleanup (ObjectControl_Deactivate) methods for this interface.

The RunPackageAsync Method

The RunPackageAsync subroutine is what actually creates the job on the SQL Server and then executes it. It does this by using SQL-DMO to connect to the server and interact with the Jobs collection:

```
'==============================================================================
'=== DTS Specific Interfaces
'==============================================================================
Public Sub RunPackageAsync(ByVal oRec As ADODB.Recordset , _
                           ByVal strPkgName As String, _
                           ByVal strServer As String, _
                           ByVal strUser As String, _
                           ByVal strPassword As String)
    On Error GoTo ErrEvt
```

The first thing we do is to make sure that the recordset that is passed in (which contains the global variables if any) is a valid recordset. If not, we raise an error:

```
    If (TypeName(oRec) <> "Recordset") Then
        Err.Raise 1000, "RunPackageAsync", "Invalid input parameter oRec"
    End If
```

Once we've done our preliminary check, we build a string that contains the job name we will be looking for in the Jobs collection. We do this by concatenating the prefix, which we defined as dts_, to the package name that's specified in strPkgName:

```
    Dim strJobName As String
    strJobName = jobPrefix & strPkgName
```

Now we connect to the SQL Server, and look for a job with this specific job name:

```
    '--- Connect to the server
    Dim oSQLServer As New SQLDMO.SQLServer
    oSQLServer.Connect strServer, strUser, strPassword
```

Next, we check to see if a job with that particular name is on the server, by trying to assign the job to a local variable. If the job does not exist, we'll get an error, which will be shown. Obviously we can't run a job that doesn't exist:

```
    '--- Check if a job already exists
    Dim oChkJob As SQLDMO.Job
    On Error Resume Next
    Set oChkJob = oSQLServer.JobServer.Jobs(strJobName)
    On Error GoTo ErrEvt
```

At this point, we know whether the job exists, and that if it does, it is stored in the oChkJob variable. Next, we'll check to see if the job is idle, or if it is currently running. If it is running we don't want to disturb it, so we'll notify the user of that fact. Otherwise, we remove that job and get prepared to script the new one:

```
If (TypeName(oChkJob) <> "Nothing") Then
    If (oChkJob.CurrentRunStatus = SQLDMOJobExecution_Idle) Then
        oChkJob.Remove
    Else
        Err.Raise 1001, "RunPackageAsync", "Unable to run a job " & _
                        "because it is already running"
    End If
    Set oChkJob = Nothing
End If
```

Now we create the step necessary to execute the package with the global variables that we specified:

```
'--- Create job step
Dim oJobStep As New SQLDMO.JobStep
With oJobStep
    .Name = "step_1"
    .StepID = 1
    .SubSystem = "ActiveScripting"
    .DatabaseName = "VBScript"
    .OnFailAction = SQLDMOJobStepAction_QuitWithFailure
    .OnSuccessAction = SQLDMOJobStepAction_QuitWithSuccess
    .Command = GetScript(oRec, strPkgName, strServer, strUser, _
                         strPassword)
End With
```

As you can see, we are creating an ActiveScripting job. Also, we set the command to the return of the function GetScript. The GetScript function, as we said before, creates the ActiveX script necessary to execute our package.

Once we've created the job step, we need to add it to the Jobs collection:

```
'--- Create and add job to the server
Dim oJob As New SQLDMO.Job
oJob.Name = strJobName
oSQLServer.JobServer.Jobs.Add oJob
With oJob
    .BeginAlter
    .JobSteps.Add oJobStep
    .StartStepID = 1
    .DeleteLevel = SQLDMOComp_None
    .DoAlter
    .ApplyToTargetServer strServer
    .Start
End With
```

Finally, we close our connection and set our objects to `Nothing` to clean up after ourselves:

```
    oSQLServer.Close
    Set oSQLServer = Nothing
    Set oJob = Nothing
    Set oJobStep = Nothing

    GetObjectContext().SetComplete
    Exit Sub

ErrEvt:
    Set oSQLServer = Nothing
    Set oJob = Nothing
    Set oJobStep = Nothing
    Set oChkJob = Nothing

    GetObjectContext().SetAbort
    Err.Raise Err.Number, Err.Source, Err.Description

End Sub
```

The GetPackageList Function

The `GetPackageList` function returns a recordset that contains the names of the packages in the `DTS_PKG` table, as well as their last execution status if previously run.

The first thing it does is create an empty recordset to populate with the package and status information. Then it connects to the server and grabs the list of packages from `DTS_PKG`. Once it has this list, it checks the jobs in the `Jobs` collection one by one to see if a job exists with the package name specified. For example, if we try to execute the `Send Mail` package, we'd be looking for the `dts_Send Mail` job. Remember that the jobs are prefixed with the constant above to make sure that we can readily identify the jobs created by our application.

Start by entering the following code:

```
Public Function GetPackageList(ByVal strServer As String, _
                               ByVal strDatabase As String, _
                               ByVal strUser As String, _
                               ByVal strPassword As String) As Object
    On Error GoTo ErrEvt
```

Now we need a container to store the package information that we are going to return to the client. So what we do is create an empty recordset and define the fields that are to be returned:

```
    Dim oRec As New ADODB.Recordset
    With oRec
        Set .ActiveConnection = Nothing
        .CursorLocation = adUseClient
        .LockType = adLockBatchOptimistic
        With .Fields
            .Append "PKG_NM", adBSTR, 64
            .Append "PKG_STATUS", adInteger
            .Append "PKG_STARTED", adDBTimeStamp, , adFldIsNullable
            .Append "PKG_STOPPED", adDBTimeStamp, , adFldIsNullable
        End With
        .Open
    End With
```

Now we open our connections: one to the SQL Server using SQL-DMO, and the other using ADO:

```
'--- Connect to the server
Dim oSQLServer As New SQLDMO.SQLServer
oSQLServer.Connect strServer, strUser, strPassword

'--- Create Connection
Dim oConn As New ADODB.Connection
With oConn
    .CursorLocation = adUseClient
    .ConnectionTimeout = 15
    .ConnectionString = "provider=SQLOLEDB" & _
                    ";Data Source=" & strServer & _
                    ";User Id=" & strUser & _
                    ";Password=" & strPassword & _
                    ";Initial Catalog=" & strDatabase
    .Open
End With
```

Next, we query the DTS__PKG table in the database we specified, and return a list of package names in a recordset. Once we've obtained the information, we close our ADO connection to SQL Server:

```
'--- Create Recordset
Dim oPkgRec As New ADODB.Recordset
With oPkgRec
    Set .ActiveConnection = oConn
    .Open "select PKG_NAME from DTS_PKG", , adOpenForwardOnly, _
                                    adLockReadOnly
    Set .ActiveConnection = Nothing
End With

'--- Close connection
oConn.Close
Set oConn = Nothing
```

Now we need to loop through the list of packages that we just retrieved from the DTS_PKG table. For each of these packages, we are checking to see if a job has been created, and if so, what its status is:

```
While (Not oPkgRec.EOF)
    oRec.AddNew
    oRec("PKG_NM").Value = Trim(oPkgRec("PKG_NAME").Value)
    oRec("PKG_STATUS").Value = SQLDMOJobOutcome_Unknown
    oRec("PKG_STARTED").Value = Null
    oRec("PKG_STOPPED").Value = Null

    Dim strJobName As String
    strJobName = jobPrefix & oRec("PKG_NM").Value

    Dim oJob As SQLDMO.Job
    On Error Resume Next
    Set oJob = oSQLServer.JobServer.Jobs(strJobName)
    On Error GoTo ErrEvt
```

If we get to this section of code, it means that a job exists for the specific package in the recordset we're looking at. Now we can go into the job history to see the information about the last execution, including the start and end times:

```
If (TypeName(oJob) <> "Nothing") Then
    oRec("PKG_STATUS").Value = oJob.LastRunOutcome
    oRec("PKG_STARTED").Value = oJob.DateCreated
```

Then we check to see the job outcome:

```
If (oJob.LastRunOutcome = SQLDMOJobOutcome_Unknown) Then
    If (oJob.CurrentRunStatus <> SQLDMOJobExecution_Idle) Then
        oRec("PKG_STATUS").Value = SQLDMOJobOutcome_InProgress
    End If
Else
```

If the job LastRunOutcome is unknown, then we can look at the execution history for that particular job

In order to get the job execution start and end times, we need to look at a class in the SQL-DMO library – QueryResults. QueryResults has to be queried in a special way in order to retrieve the necessary values, as shown by the GetColumnLong() method:

```
        Dim oQueryResult As SQLDMO.QueryResults
        Set oQueryResult = oJob.EnumHistory

        If (oQueryResult.ResultSets > 0) Then
            Dim val As Long
            val = oQueryResult.GetColumnLong(1, 12)
            oRec("PKG_STOPPED").Value = DateAdd("s", val, _
                                        oRec("PKG_STARTED").Value)
        End If

        Set oQueryResult = Nothing

    End If

    Set oJob = Nothing
End If

oPkgRec.MoveNext
Wend
```

After we loop through all the packages we need to make sure we clean up.

```
oPkgRec.Close
Set oPkgRec = Nothing

oSQLServer.Close
Set oSQLServer = Nothing

If (Not oRec.BOF) Then oRec.MoveFirst
Set GetPackageList = oRec

GetObjectContext().SetComplete
Exit Function
```

Finally, we have a routine to clean up in the event of an error:

```
ErrEvt:

    If (TypeName(oPkgRec) <> "Nothing") Then
        If (oPkgRec.State = adStateOpen) Then oPkgRec.Close
        Set oPkgRec = Nothing
    End If

    If (TypeName(oConn) <> "Nothing") Then
        If (oConn.State = adStateOpen) Then oConn.Close
        Set oConn = Nothing
    End If

    Set oSQLServer = Nothing
    Set oQueryResult = Nothing
    Set oJob = Nothing
    Set oRec = Nothing
    GetObjectContext().SetAbort
    Err.Raise Err.Number, Err.Source, Err.Description

End Function
```

The GetGlobalVariables Function

The GetGlobalVariables function returns a recordset to the client, which contains the global variables for the particular package that is being prepared for execution. In order to get the global variables, all we need to do is load the package using the LoadFromSQLServer method in the DTS Package object. Once we've opened the package, it's a simple matter to go through the GlobalVariables collection and grab all of the names and values.

> If you were storing your packages in the Repository or in a structured file, you would need to make the appropriate changes to the oPkg.LoadFromSQLServer line in this function in order for it to work properly. For instance, if you keep your packages in the Repository, you would need to use oPkg.LoadFromRepository.

Enter the following:

```
Public Function GetGlobalVariables(ByVal strPkgName As String, _
                                   ByVal strServer As String, _
                                   ByVal strUser As String, _
                                   ByVal strPassword As String) As Object

    On Error GoTo ErrEvt
```

We want to create an empty recordset, which will contain the name/value pairs of all the global variables in the DTS package:

```
    Dim oRec As New ADODB.Recordset
    With oRec
        Set .ActiveConnection = Nothing
        .CursorLocation = adUseClient
        .LockType = adLockBatchOptimistic
        With .Fields
            .Append "NAME", adBSTR, 64
            .Append "VALUE", adBSTR, 64
        End With
        .Open
    End With
```

Now we need to load the package in order to determine what the global variables contain – if there are any. We do this by loading the package and looping though the GlobalVariables collection:

```
Dim oPkg As New DTS.Package
oPkg.LoadFromSQLServer strServer, strUser, strPassword, 0, , , , _
                       strPkgName

Dim oVar As DTS.GlobalVariables
Set oVar = oPkg.GlobalVariables
```

Then we loop through the collection and insert the name and value for the global variable:

```
Dim Item As DTS.GlobalVariable
For Each Item In oVar
   oRec.AddNew
   oRec("NAME").Value = Item.Name
   oRec("VALUE").Value = Item.Value
Next
If (Not oRec.BOF) Then oRec.MoveFirst
```

And finally, time for cleanup once again:

```
   oPkg.UnInitialize
   Set oPkg = Nothing
   Set oVar = Nothing

   Set GetGlobalVariables = oRec
   GetObjectContext().SetComplete
   Exit Function

ErrEvt:
   If (TypeName(oPkg) <> "Nothing") Then oPkg.UnInitialize
   Set oPkg = Nothing
   Set oVar = Nothing
   Set oRec = Nothing
   GetObjectContext().SetAbort
   Err.Raise Err.Number, Err.Source, Err.Description

End Function
```

The GetScript Function

This GetScript function builds the ActiveX Script required to execute the package, along with its global variables, if any.

> As in the previous function, if you are loading the package from something other than the SQL Server itself, you will need to change the **LoadFromSQLServer** method to the appropriate one.

Start with the following declaration:

```
'=========================================================================
'=== Private Functions
'=========================================================================
Private Function GetScript(oRec, _
                           strPkgName As String, _
                           strServer As String, _
                           strUser As String, _
                           strPassword As String) As String
```

The next few lines simply set a variable to the new line and quote characters, to make the code more readable:

```
Dim NL As String: NL = Chr$(13) & Chr$(10) '--- New line
Dim QT As String: QT = Chr$(34) '--- Quote
```

The first part of the script does not change much. It's populated with the parameters that are passed into the function – the information needed in order to access the package and execute it:

```
Dim strScript As String
strScript = _
"Dim oPkg, oGVar" & NL & _
"Set oPkg = CreateObject(" & QT & "DTS.Package" & QT & ")" & NL & _
"oPkg.LoadFromSQLServer " & QT & strServer & QT & ", " & _
                           QT & strUser & QT & ", " & _
                           QT & strPassword & QT & ", 0, , , , " & _
                           QT & strPkgName & QT & NL & _
"Set oGVar = oPkg.GlobalVariables" & NL
```

Here's where it gets interesting again. We loop thought the collection, adding the code to execute to the script recordset:

```
If (Not oRec.BOF) Then oRec.MoveFirst
While (Not oRec.EOF)
    strScript = strScript & "oGVar(" & QT & oRec("NAME") & QT & ") = " & _
                           QT & oRec("VALUE") & QT & NL

    oRec.MoveNext
Wend
```

Finally, we add the execution and uninitialization of the object variables:

```
strScript = strScript & _
"oPkg.Execute" & NL & _
"oPkg.UnInitialize" & NL & _
"Set oGVar = Nothing" & NL & _
"Set oPkg = Nothing"

GetScript = strScript
End Function
```

And that wraps up all the code we need for this component.

Compiling the Component

Now that we've typed in all that code, we need to compile it and then migrate the `DTSManager.dll` to its final destination. To compile the `.dll`, simply click on File | Make DTSManager.dll.

Now we need to copy the `.dll` file to the server that will be running this application. You might want to create a directory called `COM` on the root of your `C:` drive specifically for the components that you build. Then under that directory, create a folder for each COM+ application, and place the `.dlls` for that application there. For this example, the `DTSManager.dll` would go in the `C:\COM\DTSManager` directory.

Installing the Component in Component Services

Now that we've completed our tour of the VB component responsible for the execution of the package, we need to know how to install it on the server machine once we've compiled it, so that we can use it. As we said earlier, this is not a difficult process at all, but it does require a few steps.

Creating the COM+ Application

The first thing we need to do is go to Component Services under Administrative Tools. The MMC will come up with the Component Services in it. Expand Component Services | Computers | My Computer and highlight COM+ Applications. Select Action | New | Application:

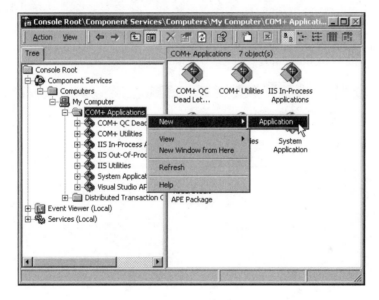

You'll be presented with a wizard, which will guide you through the creation of a COM+ application. Click Next on the first 'Welcome' screen. On the next screen, we need to select the Create an Empty Application button to create a new application:

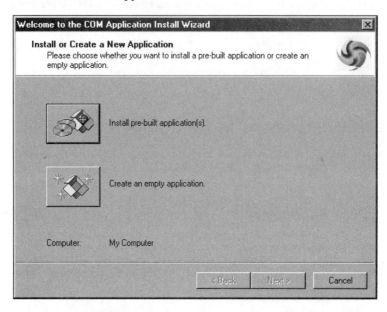

Next, we're asked to name the application, and are given a choice between a library and server application. We will name this empty package DTSManager.:

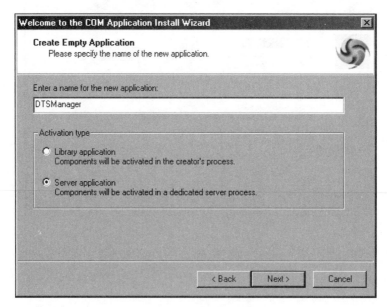

The difference between the two different types of COM+ applications is the process space in which the objects executes:

❑   A **Server application** is a COM+ application whose components run inside a dedicated process, called `dllhost.exe`. All COM+ Services are available from within a Server application.

❑   A **Library application** is a COM+ application that runs in the process space of the calling application. For an ASP application, it runs in the same thread as the page itself. Library applications tend to perform better, but do not support advanced COM+ features.

We want to be able to isolate our process from any other on the server, so choose the option for a Server application, and click Next.

Now we need to specify the account under which the object will operate:

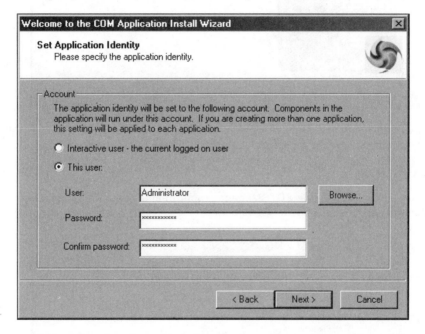

If we leave it as Interactive user, the account that the object uses to do its work on the server is that of the user who happens to be logged onto the server. The only problem with that is that when there is no one logged on to the server – which is most of the time – the object cannot be created. You should use an account on the server that has sufficient privileges, not only on the server, but also on the network, in case you are trying move or write to files on network shares. For this example, we'll be using the built in Administrator account.

> *Of course, you wouldn't want to use the Administrator account in the real world, and we're only doing it here for the purpose of simplifying the example. Elsewhere, you should create a new account and give it the specific rights it needs just for this COM+ application.*

That's it. You've created your first empty COM+ application:

Unfortunately this is only half of the job. The application is merely the container into which you place your COM+ components. Now we need to actually install the COM component.

Adding the Component

In order to do that, expand the new **DTSManager** application to get to the **Components** folder. Right-click on **Components** and select **New | Component**:

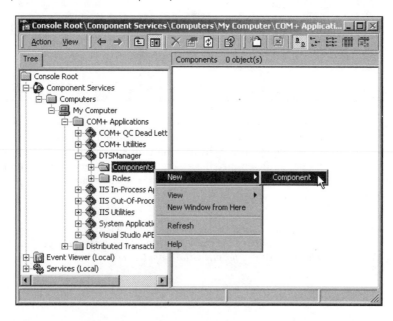

Once again, we're led by a wizard, this time to install the component. Click Next on the Welcome screen to proceed.

We want to install a new component, so click on the Install New Component(s) button:

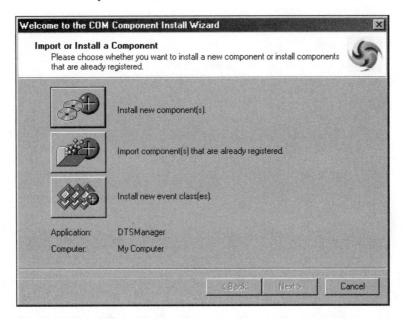

Now we need to tell COM+ where the .dll file is located, so that it can examine it and determine how it needs to instantiate it. Also, if this is the first time the component is being used on the server, it will register it. Browse to the directory where you installed DTSManager.dll, and Open it:

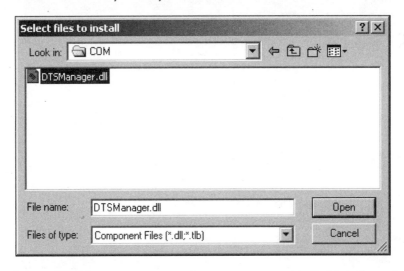

Here we see that our DTSManager component has one component in it: this is the package component, which is also a COM+ component.

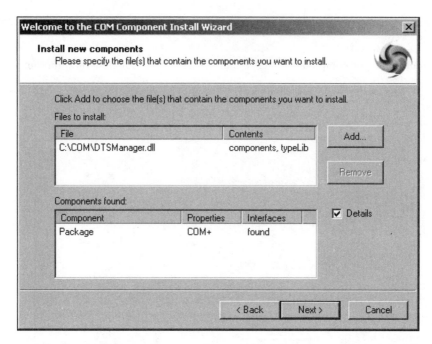

Click Next and Finish, and that's it. We've now installed the component, and can start using it on our server. If your component is installed properly under COM+, the MMC should look something like this:

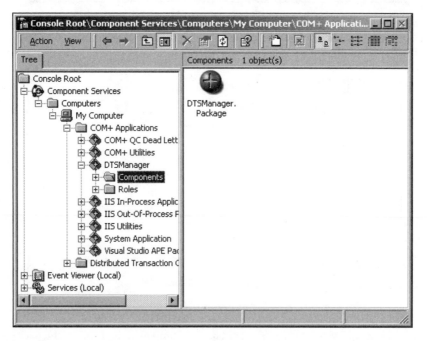

Now all that we have left to do is build the Active Server Page, which instantiates this object and displays the information to the user so that they can start using it.

User Services

As we stated earlier, you must be running IIS or PWS in order to use Active Server Pages. All we need to display the packages, edit the global variables, and execute them, is contained within one Active Server page.

Teaching you ASP is unfortunately beyond the scope of this book, so in this chapter, we'll just explain the bare minimum you need to follow what the code does. You should be able to type it in and run it without understanding every line. If you want to know more about ASP in Windows 2000, take a look at Wrox's Professional Active Server Pages 3.0, *ISBN 1-861002-61-0.*

This page uses a recursive method that occurs quite often in ASP – it calls itself, so the code in the page is interpreted again and redisplayed. When the page calls itself, it is able to supply information to the new version of the page via a **QueryString**. A QueryString is a nothing more than a list of parameter names and their values passed from one ASP to another via the URL. You'll see the QueryString appended to the URL of the page when you view it in a browser. When we parse that information, it allows us to determine which section of the page to execute.

The only code that you'll need to modify for yourself is to set the database information to your particular settings. You should save this file as `default.asp` in the default web publishing directory for IIS. This is also called the home directory, and the location provided by Setup is `\Inetpub\Wwwroot`.

Simply enter all of the following code into the `default.asp` file, in the order that we discuss it:

```
<%@ Language=VBScript %>
<%Option Explicit%>
<HTML>

<BODY>
<%
   On Error Resume Next
```

This simply specifies what scripting language we're using, along with some familiar VBScript statements. Then we open up the BODY of the HTML document.

General Declarations

First, we have the declaration section of the Active Server Page, where we can change the fonts, colors, and database information easily and in one section. This is where you will need to change the connection information to the database. You need to supply the correct values for the server name, database name, user name, and password:

```
Dim strThisPage    : strThisPage = "default.asp"
Dim fontHeader     : fontHeader = "<font face='Helv' size=1><B>"
Dim fontBody       : fontBody   = "<font face='Helv' size=1>"
Dim fontError      : fontError  = "<font face='Helv' size=1" & _
                                  "color='#ff0000'>"
Dim strServer      : strServer   = "DESKPRO450" '<Use your server name>
Dim strDatabase    : strDatabase = "Wrox"       '<Use your database name>
Dim strUser        : strUser     = "Wrox"       '<Use your user name>
Dim strPassword    : strPassword = "Wrox"       '<Use your password>
```

You can see how we are going to use our own object here. We've declared a variable, oDTS, as DTSManager.Package:

```
Dim oRec
Dim oDTS          : Set oDTS = Server.CreateObject("DTSManager.Package")
Dim command       : command  = Request.QueryString("command")
Dim strPkgName    : strPkgName = Request.QueryString("pkgname")
Dim bShowPackages : bShowPackages = True
```

Checking the QueryString

We use a parameter in the QueryString to determine what section of code to execute on the Active Server Page. For example, if we have the following URL:

http://www.dts2000.com/default.asp?command=properties&pkgname=Send+Mail

we can see that the command we should be executing is properties and the package name is Send Mail.

The following section of the ASP is executed when the QueryString has a value in it. The first time the page is executed, the QueryString will be empty, so the code in this section only applies when the page is calling itself.

We populate a recordset with values obtained from our object:

```
If( command <> "" ) Then

    Set oRec = oDTS.GetGlobalVariables(CStr(strPkgName), CStr(strServer)_
                              , CStr(strUser), CStr(strPassword))
    If( not IsEmpty(oRec) ) Then
```

And in a Case statement, we use the value of the command parameter we passed in through the QueryString to determine what to display. Our first choice is to display the global variables (if command is properties):

```
        Select Case (command)

            Case "properties"
                bShowPackages = False
                ShowProperties oRec, strPkgName
```

in which case we simply call the ShowProperties subroutine in our ASP, which we'll see more of later.

Alternatively, we can execute the package (if command is run):

```
            Case "run"
                While(Not oRec.EOF)
                    oRec("VALUE").Value = Request.Form(oRec("NAME").Value)
                    oRec.MoveNext
                Wend
                oDTS.RunPackageAsync oRec, CStr(strPkgName), CStr(strServer)_
                              , CStr(strUser), CStr(strPassword)

        End Select
    End If
End If
```

We do this by calling RunPackageAsync in our object, oDTS.

Displaying the Packages

We set the Boolean flag bShowPackages to True in our general declarations section. The only way this flag can change is in the case where command is properties that we just saw above:

```
Case "properties"
    bShowPackages = False
```

So, if we're displaying the page for the first time, or if command is run, bshowPackages is still True. In both these cases, what we want to do next is display the list of available packages:

```
    If( bShowPackages ) Then
        Set oRec = oDTS.GetPackageList(CStr(strServer), CStr(strDatabase), _
                                       CStr(strUser), CStr(strPassword))

        ShowPackages oRec
    End if

    Set oRec = Nothing
    Set oDTS = Nothing
%>
</BODY>
</HTML>
```

We first call the GetPackageList function in the object oDTS, to get the list of packages available. We then call another subroutine in our ASP – ShowPackages – to do all the work of displaying them for us.

That ends the main body of our page. We now need to add on the subroutines and functions that we've called so far.

The ShowPackages Subroutine

Let's start with the subroutine ShowPackages, which we've just seen called from the main section of code. This subroutine displays an HTML TABLE containing the packages, utilizing the recordset oRec that we populated earlier in the page. It loops through the recordset, displaying one row for each package:

```
<%
Sub ShowPackages(oRec)
    CheckErrors
%>
<TABLE BORDER=0 CELLSPACING=1 CELLPADDING=1>
    <!-- Table header -->
    <TR bgcolor="#d3d3d3" align="center">
        <TD align="left"><%=fontHeader%>
        <A HREF="<%=strThisPage%>">Refresh</A></TD>
        <TD><%=fontHeader%>Package Name</TD>
        <TD><%=fontHeader%>Status</TD>
        <TD><%=fontHeader%>Started</TD>
        <TD><%=fontHeader%>Finished</TD>
    </TR>

<!--- Packages list -->
    <%
    While(Not oRec.EOF)
```

Displaying the Properties

As we saw earlier, if we just want to display the global variables, we call the subroutine ShowProperties:

```
Case "properties"
    bShowPackages = False
    ShowProperties oRec, strPkgName
```

This – as you might guess – shows the properties section, which enumerates each of the global variables and gives you a text box to allow you to modify the value:

```
<%
Sub ShowProperties(oRec, strPkgName)
    CheckErrors
%>
    <FORM
        action="<%=strThisPage%>?command=run&pkgname=<%=strPkgName%>"
        method=POST id=form1 name=form1>
    <%=fontHeader%>Global variables for <B><%=strPkgName%></B><br>
    <TABLE BORDER=0 CELLSPACING=1 CELLPADDING=1>
        <!-- Table header -->
        <TR bgcolor="#d3d3d3" align="center">
            <TD><%=fontHeader%>Name</TD>
            <TD><%=fontHeader%>Value</TD>
        </TR>

<!--- Properties list -->
        <%
        While(not oRec.EOF)
            Dim strName : strName = DB2Str(oRec("NAME").Value)
        %>
        <TR bgcolor="#f0f0f0" align="left">
            <TD><%=fontBody%><%=DB2HTML(strName)%></TD>
            <TD><%=fontBody%>
                <INPUT type="text" id="prop" name="<%=strName%>"
                    value="<%=DB2Str(oRec("VALUE").Value)%>">
            </TD>
        </TR>
        <%
        oRec.MoveNext
        Wend
        %>
    </TABLE>
    <INPUT type="submit" value="Run" id=submit1 name=submit1>
</FORM>
<%
End Sub
%>
```

The FORM element is important here – this is how we tell the page that we want it to call itself (action="<%strThisPage%>"), and where we specify what information we want in the QueryString when we do so.

Note that we also call CheckErrors and DB2HTML from this subroutine too.

That's all there is to our ASP page, and indeed, our application. Let's see if it works.

Putting It All Together

First make sure that both your SQL Server and SQL Server Agent are running.

Then, all you need do is open up a browser and navigate to the new page we just created. If you saved `default.asp` to the root directory of your web site, just typing in the NetBIOS name of the server should get you to the correct page. So if your server name is `TESTSQL`, your URL would be http://TESTSQL. I have my default website at http://www.dts2000.com.

> If your network has a name resolution system (typically DNS), then visitors can simply type your computer name in the address bar of their browsers to reach your site. If your network does not have a name resolution system, then visitors must type the numerical IP address of your computer.

What you should see is the list of packages that we set up for this example. As you can see, the package status is Unknown. This means the package has never been executed:

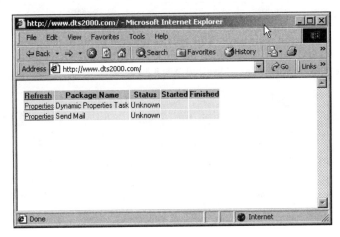

Let's click on properties to see the global variables for the Dynamic Properties task:

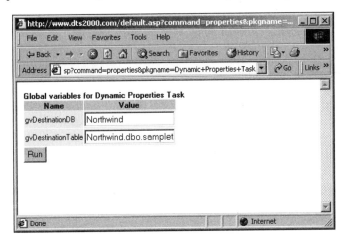

Now we can see that the package is executing. Click on **Refresh** to monitor the status of the package:

And you should see success! If everything truly worked according to our plans, when you check your mail you should find a new message from yourself:

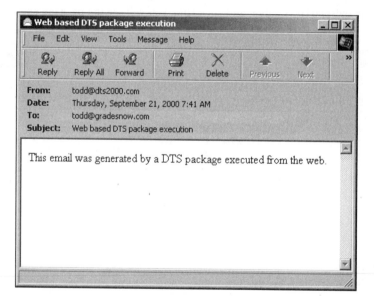

Troubleshooting

Note that after a typical installation of Microsoft SQL Server 2000, Windows Authentication is the default security mode. I connected to the database using a login, Wrox, and not Windows Authentication. If you receive an error message similar to the following:

-2147203052 Microsoft SQL-DMO (ODBC SQLState: 28000)
[Microsoft][ODBC SQL Server Driver][SQL Server]Login failed for user 'Wrox'. Reason: Not associated with a trusted SQL Server connection.

you must change the authentication mode to mixed security in order to run this example. To change the authentication mode from Windows NT Authentication Mode (only) to Mixed Mode, use the following steps:

❑ Open the Enterprise Manager

❑ Expand your server group

❑ Right-click the server name, and then click Properties

❑ Click the Security tab

❑ Under Authentication, check the SQL Server and Windows option button

❑ Click OK

Taking Things Further

This example is just the beginning – there are several ways in which you could expand it.

For example, as it stands when a job is created, it is executed immediately. You could create a similar method in the DTSPackage object – say RunPackageScheduled – which has an additional parameter containing a future date when the job will be executed.

Other possible changes include adding additional job steps to handle any kind of error notification in case the job fails. Also, don't forget about security – you would probably need to implement security measures in any live environment.

Summary

In this chapter, we managed to incorporate a myriad of technologies, all with the goal of executing DTS packages asynchronously from a web browser. We used:

❑ DTS

❑ SQL-DMO

❑ ASP

❑ COM+

❑ VB

❑ CDO

❑ IIS

We've also been exposed to a typical 3-tier design that, if you've never encountered before, you will encounter soon. Even if you do not implement the entire example, there should be sufficient material in this chapter to get you wondering what other ways you can incorporate DTS into your applications.

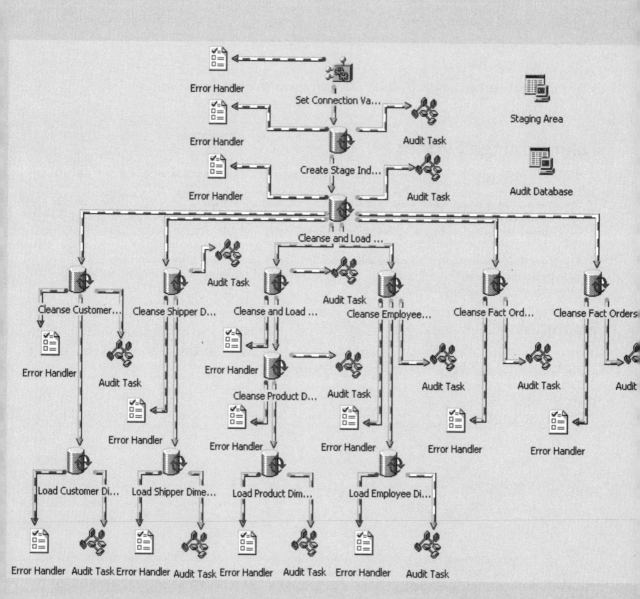

Error Handler

Set Connection Va...

Audit Task

Staging Area

Error Handler

Create Stage Ind...

Audit Task

Audit Database

Error Handler

Audit Task

Cleanse and Load ...

Audit Task

Cleanse Customer...

Cleanse Shipper D...

Cleanse and Load ...

Cleanse Employee...

Cleanse Fact Ord...

Cleanse Fact Orders

Error Handler

Audit Task

Error Handler

Cleanse Product D...

Audit Task

Audit Task

Audit Task

Audit

Error Handler

Error Handler

Error Handler

Error Handler

Error Handler

Load Customer Di...

Load Shipper Dime...

Load Product Dim...

Load Employee Di...

Error Handler   Audit Task   Error Handler   Audit Task   Error Handler   Audit Task   Error Handler   Audit Task

15

Warehouse Data Load

All of the earlier chapters in this book have attempted to prepare you to use DTS to build production quality applications that can be used in the real world. In this chapter, we will tie together many of the lessons and techniques learned, for the purpose of constructing a DTS application that performs many of the functions to load a data warehouse. However, many of the topics in this chapter require the understanding of previously covered concepts, while several sections reference code directly from Chapters 11 and 12, Error Handling and Custom Tasks, respectively. This chapter also requires some general understanding of data warehousing concepts and some familiarity with Microsoft Excel and Microsoft SQL Server 2000 Analysis Services.

There are many reasons for creating a data mart including:

❑   to combine disparate sources of information into a central repository

❑   to lower resource contention between the transactional applications creating data in an OLTP system and the analysts or report runners who must retrieve data from the same systems

❑   to support complex queries that cannot be created or performed against the source system

❑   to support historical queries that the OLTP system may purge periodically

For the purposes of this case study, we're going to create a data mart using the Northwind sample database as the source OLTP system so the Northwind Company can alleviate resource contention between analysts and the transactional system and to support historical data analysis.

> **Please note that all the code samples used in this Case Study (including the packages themselves) can be downloaded from www.wrox.com. Since many of the figures and screenshots included here are complex, and because we are unable to reproduce them in color, we have taken the liberty of providing them in `.gif` format for download along with the code.**

Extract, Transform, and Load

The purpose of an Extract, Transformation and Load (ETL) application in data warehousing is to pull data from one or more source systems, perform any transformation or consolidation of data, and load this data into a pre-defined database that supports analytical reporting. This target database is generally referred to as a data warehouse if it encompasses several subject areas and relates to many of the departments of an organization. Although the scope of this case study is much smaller and could generally be referred to as a data mart (a smaller, more focused data warehouse), it will address several of the issues that are typically found when building a data warehouse. The Northwind OLTP database supports orders, order items, customers, products, and other typical entities to support a retail business. We will construct a working ETL application with all of the bells and whistles necessary for reliable auditing, logging, and scalability. However, we would be remiss in our duties to not define the business requirements driving the creation of the data mart.

The Northwind Company has several problems with standard reporting from its transactional system: the sales team doesn't have an easy way to identify their most profitable customers, where most of the orders are going or how much discount is being applied in order to make the sale; the warehouse team can't figure out if the orders that come in are being filled in a timely manner; and the management team wants to know if the company's sales are increasing so they can take the company public.

The Northwind OLTP database is installed by default for every SQL Server 2000 installation and is modeled as shown:

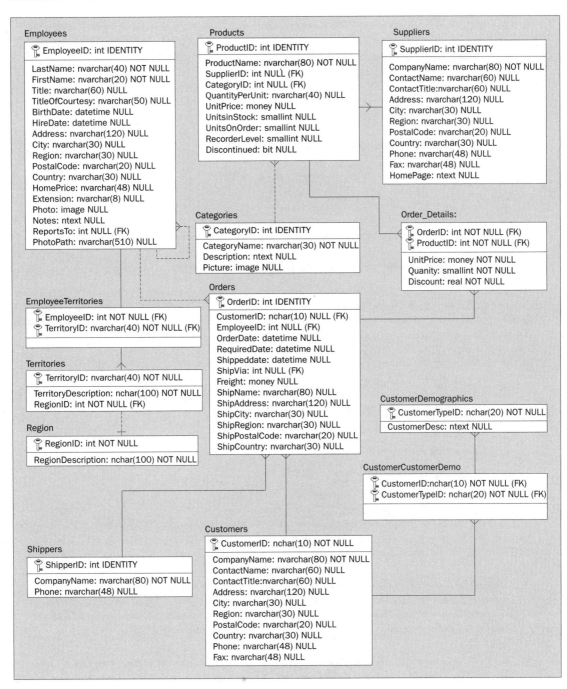

The following are just a sample of analytical questions that can be answered if Northwind creates a data mart. In order to be successful, the data mart must fulfill several business requirements to answer these questions:

1. Who are my most profitable customers based on who is ordering the most products?

2. Which regions are selling the most products?

3. How much discount is being given on each order to make a sale?

4. Which sales people are giving the most discount?

5. Which are the best and worst selling products?

6. How long is the warehouse taking to fill an order?

7. How long is it taking for the customer to receive an order?

8. How are our sales from this time last year and the previous year to this quarter?

9. How much revenue should we expect in the next quarter?

To answer these questions, we'll create a data mart with two subject areas, Orders and Order Items. In Northwind's case, these are the only two areas that are supported by the OLTP database. When building data marts or data warehouses, the source OLTP systems are generally much more complex. To build this data mart, we'll follow a plan that includes these major tasks:

- ❏ Designing the Dimensional Data Models to Support the Business Requirements
- ❏ Designing the Staging Area
- ❏ Designing the ETL Audit Tables
- ❏ Populating Default Data and Static Dimensions
- ❏ Integrating with Analysis Services
- ❏ Designing the ETL Workflow
- ❏ Verifying the Business Requirements

These tasks can be accomplished using many different tools or blending DTS with SQL Server stored procedures. However, the DBA at Northwind wants the ETL to be designed using DTS where possible and external platforms where not.

> *If you refer to the Table of Contents at the start of this book, you will see that the bullet points mentioned above reflect how we have chosen to break up this case study into manageable, logical sections. By far the biggest of these sections is "Designing the ETL Workflow", where we actually construct the four packages that will Extract, Transform, and Load our data to answer our business requirements.*

Some of you may find the ordering of these tasks to be different from what you'd expect. Our reasoning is that you cannot design the ETL Workflow until the Staging Area and Audit Areas have been defined. Also, the Verification of Business Requirements is more of a quality assurance task based on the result of the building of the ETL and warehouse.

The Northwind Dimensional Data Model

To avoid subjecting you to all aspects of dimensional modeling, several steps and processes for creating the dimensional model have been condensed. For more details about dimensional modeling, refer to Ralph Kimball's "*The Data Warehouse Lifecycle Toolkit*" (John Wiley & Sons; ISBN: 0-471255-47-5).

Also, to keep this example straightforward, we have modeled both subject areas using one-to-many relationships between the dimension and fact tables. This type of relationship will support most real-life scenarios in dimensional modeling.

Some Terms You'll Need

Although we're not providing specific details on dimensional modeling, a quick primer on some terms used is still necessary. The terms **Dimensions**, **Facts**, and **Measures** will be used throughout this chapter.

Dimensions are generally used as constraints in the detail you wish to report on, and sometimes contain hierarchical relationships. Examples of dimensions with hierarchical relationships are time and geography (Year > Quarter > Month > Day, and Country > State > City > Zip Code). These dimensions allow queries to be constrained by any one of these levels in the hierarchy.

Facts are the data elements associated with some kind of business activity such as sales or orders. The fact usually contains several attributes that represent a relationship to a dimension. An example would be a sale transaction that not only contains a numerical value for the amount of the sale, but also contains the date the sale occurred, the person making the sale, and the product that was sold.

The numeric portion of the fact is generally referred to as a **measure** since this is actually what is being measured. In the above example for fact, the measure for the sale transaction is actually the sale amount. It can be added, subtracted, or averaged with all other sales to show the overall picture of sales for all products, over all time, and by all sales persons.

Orders Dimensional Model

The first model we're going to create is for the Orders subject area. During analysis of the business requirements and through an understanding of the source system, the Orders subject area was found to have 5 dimensions and 7 measures, with several to be calculated in the multidimensional database. The dimensions are:

- **Customer** – name and location of a company purchasing from Northwind
- **Shipper** – name of the shipping company used to physically send the products to the customer
- **Time** (Order Date, Required Date, Shipped Date) – milestone dates for events that occur during the order process
- **Geography** – the geographic location of the ultimate destination of the order, which can be different from the geographic location of the customer.
- **Employee** – the employee responsible for the order and discount

The measures are:

- **Freight Dollar Amount** – the dollar amount of the shipping charge

- **Order Item Count** – the number of items included in the order

- **Order Dollar Amount** – the total dollar amount of the order

- **Order Discount Amount** – the total dollar amount of the discount on the order

- **Lead Time** (in days) – the amount of time between the date the customer places the order and when the customer requires the order

- **Internal Response Time** (in days) – the amount of time between the date the customer places the order and when the warehouse ships the order

- **External Response Time** (in days) – the amount of time between the date the order is shipped and when the customer requires the product; this measure determines if the warehouse department is shipping the product prior to the date the customer is expecting the shipment

The following entity-relationship diagram represents the Orders subject area dimensional data model. Each box represents a table and each dotted line represents a foreign key constraint. In the case of `DIM_CALENDAR`, three constraints will be created to enforce relationships for `order_date_wk`, `required_date_wk` and `shipped_date_wk`. Also, a self-referencing relationship was created for `DI_EMPLOYEE` to support a hierarchical relationship between employees and supervisors.

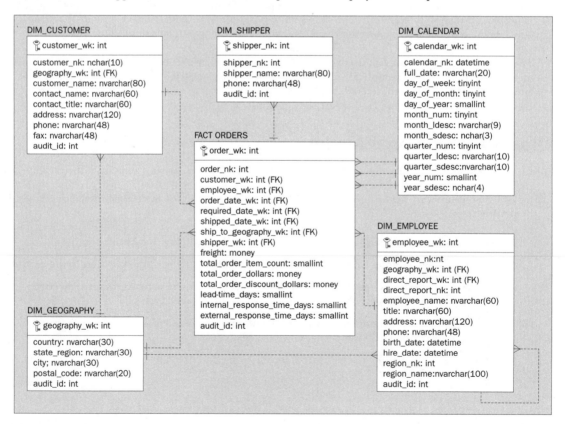

Both `Customer` and `Employee` dimensions contain geographic attributes based on their respective addresses. However, the decision was made to snowflake the `Geography` dimension because it could easily be reused in several other dimensions including customer, employee, and supplier. It could also stand alone as a separate dimension to support the ship-to location. For more information about star versus snowflaking design techniques, refer to the Dimensional Modeling section in Chapter 13.

> **Although there are many possible ways to dimensionally model this solution, the important issue to remember is that the model must foremost support the predefined business requirements. If the dimensional model cannot support these requirements, the project is sure to fail.**

Order Items Dimensional Model

The second dimensional model we're going to create is for the Order Items subject area. This subject area supports more detail for the individual line items for each order, which includes product information. The Order Items subject area also supports two additional dimensions for this level of granularity that the Orders subject area cannot, Product and Supplier, because of the one-to-many relationships between dimension and fact tables.

During analysis of the business requirements, the Order Items subject area was found to have 7 dimensions and 6 measures, with several additional measures to be calculated in the multidimensional database. The dimensions are:

- ❑ **Customer** – name and location of a company purchasing from Northwind
- ❑ **Shipper** – name of the shipping company used to physically send the products to the customer
- ❑ **Time** (Order Date, Required Date, Shipped Date) – milestone dates for events that occur during the order process
- ❑ **Geography** – the geographic location of the ultimate destination of the order
- ❑ **Employee** – the employee responsible for the order and discount
- ❑ **Product** – includes the name, description, and several attributes for products including category, quantity per unit, and others
- ❑ **Supplier** – name of the supplier company for each product. There is a direct relationship between product and supplier

The measures are:

- ❑ **Unit Price** – the dollar amount of an individual product for the line item
- ❑ **Quantity** – the number of products included in the order on the line item
- ❑ **Discount** – the total dollar amount of the discount for the line item
- ❑ **Lead Time** (in days) – the amount of time between the date the customer places the order and when the customer requires the order
- ❑ **Internal Response Time** (in days) – the amount of time between the date the customer places the order and when the warehouse ships the order
- ❑ **External Response Time** (in days) – the amount of time between the date the order is shipped and when the customer requires the product; this measure determines if the warehouse department is shipping the product prior to the date the customer is expecting the shipment

The following entity-relationship diagram represents the Order Items subject area dimensional data model. Each box represents a table and each dotted line represents a foreign key constraint.

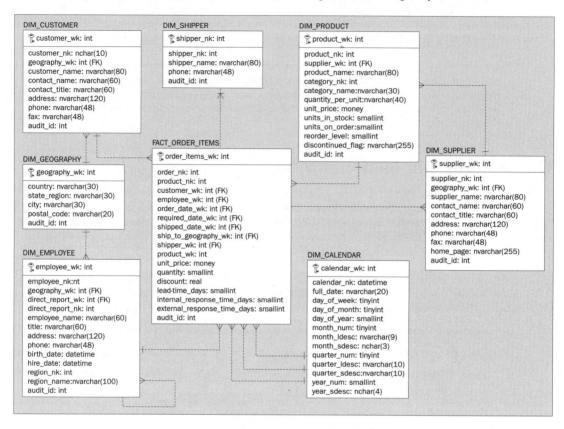

Creating the Northwind_DW Database

For the purpose of supporting the code examples in this chapter, we will create the Northwind data warehouse in a new database called **Northwind_DW**. The SQL code expects that the creator will have administrative rights within `Northwind_DW` and that security will not be a concern.

`Northwind_DW` can be created in SQL Enterprise Manager by right-clicking 'Databases' from the tree control and choosing 'New Database...', or by running the following script:

```
USE master
GO
CREATE DATABASE Northwind_DW
ON
( NAME = Northwind_DW_Data,
    FILENAME =
'C:\program files\microsoft sql server\mssql\data\NDW_Data.mdf',
    SIZE = 10,
    FILEGROWTH = 10% )
LOG ON
```

```
( NAME = 'Northwind_DW_log',
   FILENAME =
'c:\program files\microsoft sql server\mssql\data\NDW_Log.ldf',
   SIZE = 5,
   FILEGROWTH = 10% )
GO
```

This script will create the Northwind data warehouse with an initial size of 10 MB for the data and 5 MB for the transaction log. Also, the physical path must exist for this statement to work correctly.

DDL

The following DDL creates the entire set of relational tables on which the Northwind data warehouse will be built. Using these tables, we will be able to answer all of Northwind's business questions from the first section. Specifically, the following DDL will create both the Orders and Order Items subject areas and their associated dimensions, along with indexes and constraints. Several naming conventions are used here to denote which keys are surrogate keys and which are natural keys. Any column that ends with '_wk' represents a surrogate or warehouse key. Similarly, any column what ends with '_nk' represents the dimension's natural key or the OLTP system primary key. In the case of the Customer dimension, 'customer_nk' stores the 'CustomerID' column from the Northwind OLTP database. This naming convention makes it easy to identify which keys are generated from the source system and which are generated during the ETL process. For more information about surrogate and natural keys, refer to Ralph Kimball's "*The Data Warehouse Lifecycle Toolkit*" (details mentioned earlier). This book serves as an excellent reference to data warehousing techniques.

DIM_CALENDAR

The following code creates the DIM_CALENDAR table. It is the only dimension table created here that does not have an identity column as its primary key. During the loading of the table, we will use an integer value for the primary key, but it will be formatted in such a way as to make it represent the actual data (for example '19990118' will become 01/18/1999). This is done to make the task of quality assurance easier.

```
USE Northwind_DW
GO

-- Creates the Calendar dimension
CREATE TABLE DIM_CALENDAR (
        calendar_wk          int NOT NULL,
        calendar_nk          datetime NULL,
        full_date            nvarchar(20) NULL,
        day_of_week          tinyint NULL,
        day_of_month         tinyint NULL,
        day_of_year          smallint NULL,
        month_num            tinyint NULL,
        month_ldesc          nvarchar(9) NULL,
        month_sdesc          nchar(3) NULL,
        quarter_num          tinyint NULL,
        quarter_ldesc        nvarchar(10) NULL,
        quarter_sdesc        nvarchar(10) NULL,
        year_num             smallint NULL,
        year_sdesc           nchar(4) NULL
)
```

549

```
go

-- Creates a unique index on the natural key column
CREATE UNIQUE INDEX IDX_DIM_CALENDAR ON DIM_CALENDAR
(
        calendar_nk
)
go

-- Creates the Calendar dimension's primary key
ALTER TABLE DIM_CALENDAR
        ADD PRIMARY KEY (calendar_wk)
go
```

DIM_CUSTOMER

This next code segment creates the DIM_CUSTOMER table to store customer information. It also creates a unique index on the natural key and a non-unique index on geography_wk so that queries that join the two tables are faster. Also notice that for this dimension and all subsequent dimensions, we're including an 'audit_id' column. This column allows for every row that's inserted into both dimension and fact tables to have an audit trail. This audit trail stores information about the ETL processes so that the exact date and time, and whether any errors occurred, can be determined for each record. For more information, refer to Chapter 12, *Writing Your Own Custom Tasks*.

```
USE Northwind_DW
GO

-- Creates the Customer Dimension
CREATE TABLE DIM_CUSTOMER (
        customer_wk             int IDENTITY,
        customer_nk             nchar(10) NULL,
        geography_wk            int NOT NULL,
        customer_name           nvarchar(80) NOT NULL,
        contact_name            nvarchar(60) NULL,
        contact_title           nvarchar(60) NULL,
        address                 nvarchar(120) NULL,
        phone                   nvarchar(48) NULL,
        fax                     nvarchar(48) NULL,
        audit_id                int NULL
)
go

-- Creates a unique index on the customer natural key. This prevents
-- duplicate customer records from the OLTP system from creeping in.
CREATE UNIQUE INDEX IDX_DIM_CUSTOMER ON DIM_CUSTOMER
(
        customer_nk
)
go

-- Creates a non-unique index to help ETL processing times later on.
CREATE INDEX IDX_DIM_CUSTOMER_GEOGRAPHY_WK ON DIM_CUSTOMER
(
```

```
            geography_wk
)
go

-- This sets the primary key as customer_wk. This PK will be used as the
-- foreign key in all of the fact tables
ALTER TABLE DIM_CUSTOMER
        ADD PRIMARY KEY (customer_wk)
go
```

DIM_EMPLOYEE

This next section creates the Employee dimension and indexes on the natural key and the geography foreign key. It also creates an index on the `direct_report_nk` column to improve query performance.

```
USE Northwind_DW
GO

-- This creates the Employee Dimension Table.
CREATE TABLE DIM_EMPLOYEE (
        employee_wk             int IDENTITY,
        employee_nk             int NULL,
        geography_wk            int NOT NULL,
        direct_report_wk        int NOT NULL,
        direct_report_nk        int NULL,
        employee_name           nvarchar(60) NOT NULL,
        title                   nvarchar(60) NULL,
        address                 nvarchar(120) NULL,
        phone                   nvarchar(48) NULL,
        birth_date              datetime NULL,
        hire_date               datetime NULL,
        region_nk               int NULL,
        region_name             nvarchar(100) NOT NULL,
        audit_id                int NULL
)
go

-- This creates the unique index on the employee natural key
CREATE UNIQUE INDEX IDX_DIM_EMPLOYEE ON DIM_EMPLOYEE
(
        employee_nk
)
go

-- This creates a non-unique index on the geography warehouse key
CREATE INDEX IDX_DIM_EMPLOYEE_GEOGRAPHY_WK ON DIM_EMPLOYEE
(
        geography_wk
)
go

-- This creates an index on the direct_report_wk, which is used to store
-- a hierarchical relationship for the Northwind organizational structure
CREATE INDEX IDX_DIM_EMPLOYEE_DIRECT_REPORT_WK ON DIM_EMPLOYEE
(
```

```
            direct_report_wk
)
go


--  This creates the employee primary key on the employee_wk column
ALTER TABLE DIM_EMPLOYEE
        ADD PRIMARY KEY (employee_wk)
go
```

DIM_GEOGRAPHY

This section creates the geography table and a covering index because many queries will use all four columns. If a query only requires data from the columns included in an index, SQL Server will optimize the query and return results directly from the index pages rather than having to read the data pages.

```
USE Northwind_DW
GO


-- This creates the Geography dimension
CREATE TABLE DIM_GEOGRAPHY (
        geography_wk            int IDENTITY,
        country                 nvarchar(30) NULL,
        state_region            nvarchar(30) NULL,
        city                    nvarchar(30) NULL,
        postal_code             nvarchar(20) NULL,
        audit_id                int NULL
)
go


-- This creates a covering index to support many of the queries that use all
-- columns.
CREATE INDEX IDX_DIM_GEOGRAPHY ON DIM_GEOGRAPHY
(
        country,
        state_region,
        city,
        postal_code
)
go


-- This adds the primary key constraint to the geography_wk column
ALTER TABLE DIM_GEOGRAPHY
        ADD PRIMARY KEY (geography_wk)
go
```

DIM_PRODUCT

This section creates the Product dimension table, the unique index on the natural key, and the foreign key index to DIM_SUPPLIER:

```
-- This creates the Product dimension table
CREATE TABLE DIM_PRODUCT (
        product_wk              int IDENTITY,
        product_nk              int NULL,
        supplier_wk             int NOT NULL,
        product_name            nvarchar(80) NOT NULL,
        category_nk             int NULL,
        category_name           nvarchar(30) NULL,
        quantity_per_unit       nvarchar(40) NULL,
        unit_price              money NULL,
        units_in_stock          smallint NULL,
        units_on_order          smallint NULL,
        reorder_level           smallint NULL,
        discontinued_flag       nvarchar(15) NULL,
        audit_id                int NULL
)
go

-- This creates a unique index on the product natural key
CREATE UNIQUE INDEX IDX_DIM_PRODUCT ON DIM_PRODUCT
(
        product_nk
)
go

-- This creates a non-unique index to increase ETL performance
CREATE INDEX IDX_DIM_PRODUCT_SUPPLIER_WK ON DIM_PRODUCT
(
        supplier_wk
)
go


-- This adds the Product dimension primary key constraint
ALTER TABLE DIM_PRODUCT
        ADD PRIMARY KEY (product_wk)
go
```

DIM_SHIPPER

This section creates the Shipper dimension and a unique index on the natural key:

```
USE Northwind_DW
GO

-- This creates the Shipper dimension table
CREATE TABLE DIM_SHIPPER (
        shipper_wk              int IDENTITY,
        shipper_nk              int NULL,
```

```
            shipper_name        nvarchar(80) NOT NULL,
            phone               nvarchar(48) NULL,
            audit_id            int NULL
)
go


-- This creates a unique index on the Shipper dimension's natural key
CREATE UNIQUE INDEX IDX_DIM_SHIPPER ON DIM_SHIPPER
(
        shipper_nk
)
go


-- This creates the primary key constraint on the Shipper dimension table
ALTER TABLE DIM_SHIPPER
        ADD PRIMARY KEY (shipper_wk)
go
```

DIM_SUPPLIER

This section creates the Supplier dimension, and indexes on the natural key column and the foreign key to the geography dimension:

```
USE Northwind_DW
GO

-- This creates the Supplier dimension table
CREATE TABLE DIM_SUPPLIER (
        supplier_wk         int IDENTITY,
        supplier_nk         int NULL,
        geography_wk        int NOT NULL,
        supplier_name       nvarchar(80) NOT NULL,
        contact_name        nvarchar(60) NULL,
        contact_title       nvarchar(60) NULL,
        address             nvarchar(120) NULL,
        phone               nvarchar(48) NULL,
        fax                 nvarchar(48) NULL,
        home_page           nvarchar(255) NULL,
        audit_id            int NULL
)
go

-- This statement creates a unique index on the Supplier Dimension's
-- natural key
CREATE UNIQUE INDEX IDX_DIM_SUPPLIER ON DIM_SUPPLIER
(
        supplier_nk
)
go

-- This statement creates a non-unique index for the geography primary key
CREATE INDEX IDX_DIM_SUPPLIER_GEOGRAPHY_WK ON DIM_SUPPLIER
(
        geography_wk
)
```

```
go


-- This creates the Supplier dimension's primary key constraint
ALTER TABLE DIM_SUPPLIER
        ADD PRIMARY KEY (supplier_wk)
go
```

FACT_ORDER_ITEMS

This section creates the fact table for the Order Items subject area. Notice that both the order and product natural keys are included in the fact table design. This is because the source system uses a combination of these two columns for its unique constraint. We want to preserve the natural key value in the fact table to store each row's lineage, so we include both columns here. This is also the reason for creating an index on both columns. Also, each foreign key column will have an index created.

```
USE Northwind_DW
GO


-- This creates the Order Items fact table
CREATE TABLE FACT_ORDER_ITEMS (
        order_items_wk                  int IDENTITY,
        order_nk                        int NOT NULL,
        product_nk                      int NOT NULL,
        customer_wk                     int NOT NULL,
        employee_wk                     int NOT NULL,
        order_date_wk                   int NOT NULL,
        required_date_wk                int NOT NULL,
        shipped_date_wk                 int NOT NULL,
        shipto_geography_wk             int NOT NULL,
        shipper_wk                      int NOT NULL,
        product_wk                      int NOT NULL,
        unit_price                      money NOT NULL,
        quantity                        smallint NOT NULL,
        discount                        real NOT NULL,
        lead_time_days                  smallint NULL,
        internal_response_time_days     smallint NULL,
        external_response_time_days     smallint NULL,
        audit_id                        int NULL
)
go


-- Uniqueness for the Order Items fact table must be enforced by using both
-- the order number (order_nk) and the product id (product_nk) from the
-- Northwind OLTP database
CREATE UNIQUE INDEX IDX_FACT_ORDER_ITEMS ON FACT_ORDER_ITEMS
(
        order_nk,
        product_nk
)
go
```

```
-- The next several statements create non-unique indexes to improve query
-- performance on the Order Items fact table
CREATE INDEX IDX_FACT_ORDER_ITEMS_ORDER_DATE ON FACT_ORDER_ITEMS
(
        order_date_wk
)
go

CREATE INDEX IDX_FACT_ORDER_ITEMS_SHIPTO ON FACT_ORDER_ITEMS
(
        shipto_geography_wk
)
go

CREATE INDEX IDX_FACT_ORDER_ITEMS_SHIPPED ON FACT_ORDER_ITEMS
(
        shipped_date_wk
)
go

CREATE INDEX IDX_FACT_ORDER_ITEMS_REQUIRED ON FACT_ORDER_ITEMS
(
        required_date_wk
)
go

CREATE INDEX IDX_FACT_ORDER_ITEMS_SHIPPER ON FACT_ORDER_ITEMS
(
        shipper_wk
)
go

CREATE INDEX IDX_FACT_ORDER_ITEMS_PRODUCT ON FACT_ORDER_ITEMS
(
        product_wk
)
go

CREATE INDEX IDX_FACT_ORDER_ITEMS_CUSTOMER ON FACT_ORDER_ITEMS
(
        customer_wk
)
go

CREATE INDEX IDX_FACT_ORDER_ITEMS_EMPLOYEE ON FACT_ORDER_ITEMS
(
        employee_wk
)
go

-- This creates the primary key constraint on the Order Items fact table
ALTER TABLE FACT_ORDER_ITEMS
        ADD PRIMARY KEY (order_items_wk)
go
```

FACT_ORDERS

This section creates the fact table for the Orders subject area:

```
USE Northwind_DW
GO

-- This creates the Fact Orders table
CREATE TABLE FACT_ORDERS (
        order_wk                        int IDENTITY,
        order_nk                        int NOT NULL,
        customer_wk                     int NOT NULL,
        employee_wk                     int NOT NULL,
        order_date_wk                   int NOT NULL,
        required_date_wk                int NOT NULL,
        shipped_date_wk                 int NOT NULL,
        ship_to_geography_wk            int NOT NULL,
        shipper_wk                      int NOT NULL,
        freight                         money NOT NULL,
        total_order_item_count          smallint NOT NULL,
        total_order_dollars             money NOT NULL,
        total_order_discount_dollars    money NOT NULL,
        lead_time_days                  smallint NULL,
        internal_response_time_days     smallint NULL,
        external_response_time_days     smallint NULL,
        audit_id                        int NULL
)
go

-- This statement creates a unique index on the Order natural key
CREATE UNIQUE INDEX IDX_FACT_ORDERS ON FACT_ORDERS
(
        order_nk
)
go

-- The next several statements create non-unique indexes to improve query
-- performance on the Orders fact table
CREATE INDEX IDX_FACT_ORDERS_ORDER_DATE ON FACT_ORDERS
(
        order_date_wk
)
go

CREATE INDEX IDX_FACT_ORDERS_SHIPPER ON FACT_ORDERS
(
        shipper_wk
)
go

CREATE INDEX IDX_FACT_ORDERS_CUSTOMER ON FACT_ORDERS
(
        customer_wk
)
go
```

```
CREATE INDEX IDX_FACT_ORDERS_SHIP_TO ON FACT_ORDERS
(
        ship_to_geography_wk
)
go


CREATE INDEX IDX_FACT_ORDERS_EMPLOYEE ON FACT_ORDERS
(
        employee_wk
)
go


CREATE INDEX IDX_FACT_ORDERS_SHIPPED ON FACT_ORDERS
(
        shipped_date_wk
)
go


CREATE INDEX IDX_FACT_ORDERS_REQUIRED ON FACT_ORDERS
(
        required_date_wk
)
go
```

Foreign Key Constraints

The following section creates all of the foreign key constraints in the Northwind data mart. Opinions differ as to the necessity of constraints in the data warehouse. The ETL should be the only process that loads the data warehouse and constraints slow the loading process. However, if there is ANY chance of invalid data being entered, constrains should be added.

```
USE Northwind_DW
GO

-- The next several statements create all of Northwind_DW's foreign key
-- constraints. This ensures relational integrity for all tables.
ALTER TABLE FACT_ORDERS
        ADD PRIMARY KEY (order_wk)
go


ALTER TABLE DIM_CUSTOMER
        ADD FOREIGN KEY (geography_wk)
                                REFERENCES DIM_GEOGRAPHY
go


ALTER TABLE DIM_EMPLOYEE
        ADD FOREIGN KEY (geography_wk)
                                REFERENCES DIM_GEOGRAPHY
go
```

```
ALTER TABLE DIM_EMPLOYEE
      ADD FOREIGN KEY (direct_report_wk)
                            REFERENCES DIM_EMPLOYEE
go


ALTER TABLE DIM_PRODUCT
      ADD FOREIGN KEY (supplier_wk)
                            REFERENCES DIM_SUPPLIER
go


ALTER TABLE DIM_SUPPLIER
      ADD FOREIGN KEY (geography_wk)
                            REFERENCES DIM_GEOGRAPHY
go


ALTER TABLE FACT_ORDER_ITEMS
      ADD FOREIGN KEY (required_date_wk)
                            REFERENCES DIM_CALENDAR
go


ALTER TABLE FACT_ORDER_ITEMS
      ADD FOREIGN KEY (shipped_date_wk)
                            REFERENCES DIM_CALENDAR
go


ALTER TABLE FACT_ORDER_ITEMS
      ADD FOREIGN KEY (shipto_geography_wk)
                            REFERENCES DIM_GEOGRAPHY
go


ALTER TABLE FACT_ORDER_ITEMS
      ADD FOREIGN KEY (employee_wk)
                            REFERENCES DIM_EMPLOYEE
go


ALTER TABLE FACT_ORDER_ITEMS
      ADD FOREIGN KEY (customer_wk)
                            REFERENCES DIM_CUSTOMER
go


ALTER TABLE FACT_ORDER_ITEMS
      ADD FOREIGN KEY (product_wk)
                            REFERENCES DIM_PRODUCT
go
```

```
ALTER TABLE FACT_ORDER_ITEMS
      ADD FOREIGN KEY (shipper_wk)
                        REFERENCES DIM_SHIPPER
go


ALTER TABLE FACT_ORDER_ITEMS
      ADD FOREIGN KEY (order_date_wk)
                        REFERENCES DIM_CALENDAR
go


ALTER TABLE FACT_ORDERS
      ADD FOREIGN KEY (required_date_wk)
                        REFERENCES DIM_CALENDAR
go


ALTER TABLE FACT_ORDERS
      ADD FOREIGN KEY (shipped_date_wk)
                        REFERENCES DIM_CALENDAR
go


ALTER TABLE FACT_ORDERS
      ADD FOREIGN KEY (employee_wk)
                        REFERENCES DIM_EMPLOYEE
go


ALTER TABLE FACT_ORDERS
      ADD FOREIGN KEY (ship_to_geography_wk)
                        REFERENCES DIM_GEOGRAPHY
go


ALTER TABLE FACT_ORDERS
      ADD FOREIGN KEY (customer_wk)
                        REFERENCES DIM_CUSTOMER
go


ALTER TABLE FACT_ORDERS
      ADD FOREIGN KEY (shipper_wk)
                        REFERENCES DIM_SHIPPER
go


ALTER TABLE FACT_ORDERS
      ADD FOREIGN KEY (order_date_wk)
                        REFERENCES DIM_CALENDAR
go
```

This is only the first step in the ETL process. We have created the `Northwind_DW` database and have filled it with all the relational tables and data we need to answer our business requirements. However, this forms only part of getting the data into a data warehouse; now we must create a work area to stage the data before loading it into the warehouse.

The Northwind Staging Area Data Model

When extracting data from one or more source systems into a data warehouse, it frequently becomes necessary to create a temporary work area so that any intensive transformations can be run without affecting the source OLTP systems. This work area is a fundamental part of the ETL process because it also creates a common structure with which to work. By creating a staging area, two of the major segments of the ETL can be separated so that development can occur in parallel. In object-oriented parlance, this is similar to creating an object model, in which one group of developers can develop the objects and the other group can develop applications that use the objects. The same principle applies when creating a staging area.

Before beginning the design of the ETL process, we must create the staging area for the extraction and transformation of our Northwind data. The staging area will include a table for each of the dimensions and fact tables designed in the dimensional data model. The following entity-relationship diagram represents the Northwind data mart staging area. These are the tables in which the Northwind OLTP data will be stored and transformed before being loaded into the data warehouse:

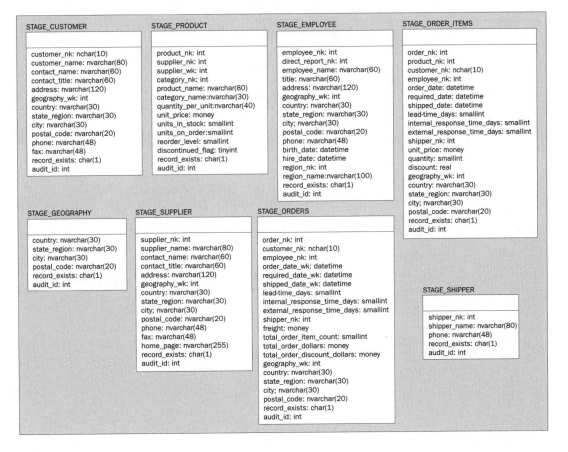

DDL

The following DDL will create both the Orders and Order Items staging areas along with all dimensions needed in the `Northwind_DW` database. It also creates indexes on the staging area tables that will help with transformation and loading performance. However, they will slow down loading the staging area in the extraction phase. Because of this, all stage indexes should be dropped prior to extraction, but can and should be added before the transformation and load phase.

STAGE_CUSTOMER

This section creates the stage table to support loading of the Customer dimension:

```
USE Northwind_DW
GO

-- This statement creates the staging area used for storing Customer data
-- before being loaded into the data warehouse
CREATE TABLE STAGE_CUSTOMER (
        customer_nk         nchar(10) NOT NULL,
        customer_name       nvarchar(80) NULL,
        contact_name        nvarchar(60) NULL,
        contact_title       nvarchar(60) NULL,
        address             nvarchar(120) NULL,
        geography_wk        int NULL,
        country             nvarchar(30) NULL,
        state_region        nvarchar(30) NULL,
        city                nvarchar(30) NULL,
        postal_code         nvarchar(20) NULL,
        phone               nvarchar(48) NULL,
        fax                 nvarchar(48) NULL,
        record_exists       char(1) NULL,
        audit_id            int NULL
)
go

-- This creates a non-unique index on the customer natural key column to
-- improve ETL performance
CREATE INDEX IDX_STAGE_CUSTOMER ON STAGE_CUSTOMER
(
        customer_nk
)
go

-- This statement creates a covering index to support queries that include
-- all four columns
CREATE INDEX IDX_STAGE_CUSTOMER_GEOGRAPHY ON STAGE_CUSTOMER
(
        country,
        state_region,
        city,
        postal_code
)
go
```

STAGE_EMPLOYEE

This section creates the stage table to support loading of the Employee dimension:

```
USE Northwind_DW
GO

-- This statement creates the staging area used for storing Employee data
-- before being loaded into the data warehouse
CREATE TABLE STAGE_EMPLOYEE (
        employee_nk             int NOT NULL,
        direct_report_nk        int NULL,
        employee_name           nvarchar(60) NULL,
        title                   nvarchar(60) NULL,
        address                 nvarchar(120) NULL,
        geography_wk            int NULL,
        country                 nvarchar(30) NULL,
        state_region            nvarchar(30) NULL,
        city                    nvarchar(30) NULL,
        postal_code             nvarchar(20) NULL,
        phone                   nvarchar(48) NULL,
        birth_date              datetime NULL,
        hire_date               datetime NULL,
        region_nk               int NULL,
        region_name             nvarchar(100) NULL,
        record_exists           char(1) NULL,
        audit_id                int NULL
)
go

-- This statement creates a non-unique index on the employee natural key
-- column to improve ETL performance
CREATE INDEX IDX_STAGE_EMPLOYEE ON STAGE_EMPLOYEE
(
        employee_nk
)
go

-- This statement creates a covering index to support queries that include
-- all four columns
CREATE INDEX IDX_STAGE_EMPLOYEE_GEOGRAPHY ON STAGE_EMPLOYEE
(
        country,
        state_region,
        city,
        postal_code
)
go
```

STAGE_GEOGRAPHY

This section creates the stage table to support loading of the Geography dimension:

```
USE Northwind_DW
GO

-- This statement creates the staging area used for storing Geography data
-- before being loaded into the data warehouse
CREATE TABLE STAGE_GEOGRAPHY (
        country                 nvarchar(30) NULL,
        state_region            nvarchar(30) NULL,
        city                    nvarchar(30) NULL,
        postal_code             nvarchar(20) NULL,
        record_exists           char(1) NULL,
        audit_id                int NULL
)
go

-- This statement creates a covering index to support queries that include
-- all four columns
CREATE INDEX IDX_STAGE_GEOGRAPHY ON STAGE_GEOGRAPHY
(
        country,
        state_region,
        city,
        postal_code
)
go
```

STAGE_ORDER_ITEMS

This section creates the stage table to support loading of the Order Items fact table:

```
USE Northwind_DW
GO

-- This statement creates the stage table to store the Order Item fact data
CREATE TABLE STAGE_ORDER_ITEMS (
        order_nk                int NOT NULL,
        product_nk              int NOT NULL,
        customer_nk             nchar(10) NULL,
        employee_nk             int NULL,
        order_date              datetime NULL,
        required_date           datetime NULL,
        shipped_date            datetime NULL,
        lead_time_days          smallint NULL,
        internal_response_time_days smallint NULL,
        external_response_time_days smallint NULL,
        shipper_nk              int NULL,
        unit_price              money NOT NULL,
        quantity                smallint NOT NULL,
        discount                real NOT NULL,
        geography_wk            int NULL,
```

```
                country                 nvarchar(30) NULL,
                state_region            nvarchar(30) NULL,
                city                    nvarchar(30) NULL,
                postal_code             nvarchar(20) NULL,
                record_exists           char(1) NULL,
                audit_id                int NULL
)
go

-- This creates a covering index on the order and product natural keys since
-- several queries will use these column during the ETL
CREATE INDEX IDX_STAGE_ORDER_ITEMS ON STAGE_ORDER_ITEMS
(
        order_nk,
        product_nk
)
go

-- This statement creates a covering index to support queries that include
-- all four columns
CREATE INDEX IDX_STAGE_ORDER_ITEMS_GEOGRAPHY ON STAGE_ORDER_ITEMS
(
        country,
        state_region,
        city,
        postal_code
)
go
```

STAGE_ORDERS

This section creates the stage table to support loading of the Orders fact table:

```
USE Northwind_DW
GO

-- This statement creates the stage table to store the Order fact data
CREATE TABLE STAGE_ORDERS (
        order_nk                int NOT NULL,
        customer_nk             nchar(10) NOT NULL,
        employee_nk             int NULL,
        order_date              datetime NULL,
        required_date           datetime NULL,
        shipped_date            datetime NULL,
        lead_time_days          smallint NULL,
        internal_response_time_days smallint NULL,
        external_response_time_days smallint NULL,
        shipper_nk              int NULL,
        freight                 money NULL,
        total_order_item_count smallint NULL,
        total_order_dollars  money NULL,
        total_order_discount_dollars money NULL,
        geography_wk            int NULL,
        country                 nvarchar(30) NULL,
```

```
                state_region              nvarchar(30) NULL,
                city                      nvarchar(30) NULL,
                postal_code               nvarchar(20) NULL,
                record_exists             char(1) NULL,
                audit_id                  int NULL
)
go

-- This statement creates a non-unique index to improve processing speed
CREATE INDEX IDX_STAGE_ORDERS ON STAGE_ORDERS
(
        order_nk
)
go

-- This statement creates a covering index to support queries that include
-- all four columns
CREATE INDEX IDX_STAGE_ORDERS_GEOGRAPHY ON STAGE_ORDERS
(
        country,
        state_region,
        city,
        postal_code
)
go
```

STAGE_PRODUCT

This section creates the stage table to support loading of the Product dimension:

```
USE Northwind_DW
GO

-- This statement creates the Product stage table
CREATE TABLE STAGE_PRODUCT (
        product_nk                int NOT NULL,
        supplier_nk               int NULL,
        supplier_wk               int NULL,
        category_nk               int NULL,
        product_name              nvarchar(80) NULL,
        category_name             nvarchar(30) NULL,
        quantity_per_unit         nvarchar(40) NULL,
        unit_price                money NULL,
        units_in_stock            smallint NULL,
        units_on_order            smallint NULL,
        reorder_level             smallint NULL,
        discontinued_flag         tinyint NULL,
        record_exists             char(1) NULL,
        audit_id                  int NULL
)
go

-- This statement creates a non-unique index to improve processing speed
CREATE INDEX IDX_STAGE_PRODUCT ON STAGE_PRODUCT
(
        product_nk
)
go
```

STAGE_SHIPPER

This section creates the stage table to support loading of the Shipper dimension:

```
USE Northwind_DW
GO

-- This statement creates the Shipper stage table
CREATE TABLE STAGE_SHIPPER (
        shipper_nk              int NOT NULL,
        shipper_name            nvarchar(80) NULL,
        phone                   nvarchar(48) NULL,
        record_exists           char(1) NULL,
        audit_id                int NULL
)
go

-- This statement creates a non-unique index to improve processing speed
CREATE INDEX IDX_STAGE_SHIPPER ON STAGE_SHIPPER
(
        shipper_nk
)
go
```

STAGE_SUPPLIER

This section creates the stage table to support loading of the Supplier dimension:

```
USE Northwind_DW
GO

-- This statement creates the Supplier stage table
CREATE TABLE STAGE_SUPPLIER (
        supplier_nk             int NOT NULL,
        supplier_name           nvarchar(80) NULL,
        contact_name            nvarchar(60) NULL,
        contact_title           nvarchar(60) NULL,
        address                 nvarchar(120) NULL,
        geography_wk            int NULL,
        country                 nvarchar(30) NULL,
        state_region            nvarchar(30) NULL,
        city                    nvarchar(30) NULL,
        postal_code             nvarchar(20) NULL,
        phone                   nvarchar(48) NULL,
        fax                     nvarchar(48) NULL,
        home_page               nvarchar(255) NULL,
        record_exists           char(1) NULL,
        audit_id                int NULL
)
go
```

```
-- This statement creates a non-unique index to improve processing speed
CREATE INDEX IDX_STAGE_SUPPLIER ON STAGE_SUPPLIER
(
        supplier_nk
)
go

-- This statement creates a covering index to support queries that include
-- all four columns
CREATE INDEX IDX_STAGE_SUPPLIER_GEOGRAPHY ON STAGE_SUPPLIER
(
        country,
        state_region,
        city,
        postal_code
)
go
```

> **Notice that indexes are created for the stage tables in this script. These indexes will be dropped before loading the stage tables and reapplied during the ETL process. They are included here to show where they can most effectively be utilized.**

The Northwind ETL Auditing Data Model

Jobs and Tasks

The following data model supports the auditing and logging requirements for the Northwind data mart. It is modeled using the notion of a single job consisting of many tasks. For each execution of the ETL process, a single job record is created in the AUDIT_JOB table. This table will store the start and end date/time of the ETL and the range of dates for which the ETL will process the OLTP system data.

Each task that is executed during the ETL logs a single record to the AUDIT_TASK table. Each task also has a start and end date/time, and includes a 'records_processed' column. This column is only updated if the task being audited actually manipulates data using either DTS's Transform Data or Data Driven Query task.

The auditing subject area looks like this:

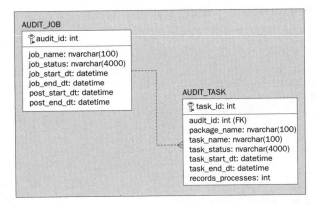

DDL

The following DDL will create the AUDIT_JOB and AUDIT_TASK tables. The job_status column in AUDIT_JOB and the task_status column in AUDIT_TASK are designed to support extremely long error messages that may be returned from any component that fails. These column sizes can be altered as desired.

AUDIT_JOB

This section creates the Job table for auditing purposes:

```
USE Northwind_DW
go

-- This statement creates the Job-level audit table
CREATE TABLE AUDIT_JOB (
        audit_id              int IDENTITY,
        job_name              nvarchar(100) NULL,
        job_status            nvarchar(2000) NULL,
        job_start_dt          datetime NULL,
        job_end_dt            datetime NULL,
        post_start_dt         datetime NULL,
        post_end_dt           datetime NULL
)
go

-- This creates a non-unique index on the job_name column
CREATE INDEX AUDIT_JOB_JOB_NAME ON AUDIT_JOB
(
        job_name
)
go

-- This creates the primary key constraint
ALTER TABLE AUDIT_JOB
        ADD PRIMARY KEY (audit_id)
go
```

AUDIT_TASK

This section creates the Task table for auditing purposes:

```
USE Northwind_DW
go


-- This creates the Task-level audit table
CREATE TABLE AUDIT_TASK (
        task_id                 int IDENTITY,
        audit_id                int NOT NULL,
        package_name            nvarchar(100) NULL,
        task_name               nvarchar(100) NULL,
        task_status             nvarchar(2000) NULL,
        task_start_dt           datetime NULL,
        task_end_dt             datetime NULL,
        records_processed       int NULL
)
go


-- This creates a non-unique index on the foreign key, audit_id
CREATE INDEX AUDIT_TASK_AUDIT_ID ON AUDIT_TASK
(
        audit_id
)
go



-- This creates the primary key constraint
ALTER TABLE AUDIT_TASK
        ADD PRIMARY KEY (task_id)
go
```

Foreign Key Constraint

This section creates the foreign key constraint on the AUDIT_TASK table:

```
USE Northwind_DW
go

-- And this creates the foreign key constraint back to AUDIT_JOB
ALTER TABLE AUDIT_TASK
        ADD FOREIGN KEY (audit_id)
                                REFERENCES AUDIT_JOB
go
```

Populating Default Values

Prior to loading the warehouse for the first time, several dimensions can be pre-loaded based on business rules and the notion that some dimensions will never change (such as time). These dimensions are generally referred to as 'static' dimensions. Also, by pre-loading these dimensions, no unnecessary processing has to occur during the ETL.

Many times, data warehouses must extract data from systems that do not have relational integrity enforced, which can lead to serious data quality issues. These data quality issues can prevent successful loading. To avoid some of these issues, each dimension can include an 'invalid' record so that all rows loaded in the fact tables can have a valid foreign key reference to a single dimension table. This row can contain a description appropriate to the business rules such as 'N/A', 'Unknown' or 'Invalid', but should exist in all dimension tables. By using these 'Invalid' records, loading of the warehouse can continue uninterrupted.

A typical scenario is a data warehouse using information extracted from several mainframe systems. These extracts include product information from one system and sales information from another, both in separate text file formats. When the extracts are processed by the ETL, it's found that the sales data includes sales records for a product that cannot be found in the product extract file. A decision must be made whether to ignore or kick-out the sales information that references a non-existent product, or to include the sale, but have the sale's product reference the 'Invalid' value. Usually, this is a business decision made by the project sponsor or an analyst.

Time Dimension

As stated before, the `Time` dimension is a static dimension; it should be loaded before the warehouse is loaded for the first time. It's always best to load a sufficient range of calendar data to support both historical and future fact data. The historical calendar data obviously supports the transactional data that occurs in the past. However, many companies wish to create forecasting data based on historical performance or create goal-based data for the future expected events, such as sales. Since we wish to create a time dimension that all fact tables can use, the range of dates should support all anticipated needs.

Also, you'll notice that much extraneous information is included with the Calendar dimension, such as month descriptions and quarter descriptions, day of week, day of month, and day of year. These columns make querying much easier for non-DBA analysts who may want to run a query that answers what the busiest day of the week is. Also, query performance is much better because many of the attributes are pre-calculated rather than being evaluated at run time. Another advantage is for companies that use a fiscal calendar: by storing the fiscal information directly, the end user doesn't have to worry about business rules regarding the Calendar dimension.

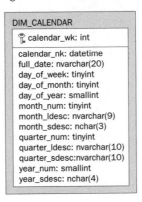

DIM_CALENDAR

🔑 calendar_wk: int

calendar_nk: datetime
full_date: nvarchar(20)
day_of_week: tinyint
day_of_month: tinyint
day_of_year: smallint
month_num: tinyint
month_ldesc: nvarchar(9)
month_sdesc: nchar(3)
quarter_num: tinyint
quarter_ldesc: nvarchar(10)
quarter_sdesc:nvarchar(10)
year_num: smallint
year_sdesc: nchar(4)

The Calendar Dimension

The SQL code listed below will populate the calendar dimension with valid date data for the years between 1995 and 2001, inclusive. Notice also that we're creating a default 'Invalid' value to handle possible invalid dates that may come from systems without relational integrity.

```
USE Northwind_DW
go

-- Insert default value
INSERT INTO DIM_CALENDAR
(calendar_wk, calendar_nk, full_date, month_ldesc,
 month_sdesc, quarter_ldesc, quarter_sdesc, year_sdesc)
VALUES
(0, NULL, 'N/A', 'N/A',
'N/A', 'N/A', 'N/A', 'N/A')

-- Begin populating dates
declare @dtStartDate datetime
declare @dtEndDate datetime
declare @dtCurrDate datetime

-- These are the default start and end dates. Change these as appropriate
-- to your business needs
SELECT @dtStartDate = '1/1/1995'
SELECT @dtEndDate = '12/31/2001'

-- Check to make sure we're not inserting
-- redundant data - we don't to get errors when inserting
SELECT @dtCurrDate = DATEADD(d, 1, MAX(calendar_nk))
FROM DIM_CALENDAR
WHERE calendar_nk IS NOT NULL

SELECT @dtCurrDate = ISNULL(@dtCurrDate, @dtStartDate)

-- Loop over this until we reach the end date
WHILE @dtCurrDate <= @dtEndDate
BEGIN
    INSERT INTO DIM_CALENDAR
    (
    calendar_wk,      -- calendar surrogate key
    calendar_nk,      -- calendar natural key
    full_date,
    day_of_week,
    day_of_month,
    day_of_year,
    month_num,
    month_ldesc,
    month_sdesc,
    quarter_num,
    quarter_ldesc,
    quarter_sdesc,
    year_num,
    year_sdesc
    )
```

```
        VALUES
          (
          -- Although this is a surrogate key, we format so that it's at
          -- least human-readable. This will format like '19950101'
          CONVERT(int, CONVERT(char(8), @dtCurrDate, 112)),
          @dtCurrDate,
          DATENAME(month, @dtCurrDate) + ' ' +
              CONVERT(nvarchar(2), DAY(@dtCurrDate)) + ', ' +
              CONVERT(char(4), YEAR(@dtCurrDate)),
          DATEPART(dw, @dtCurrDate),
          DATEPART(d, @dtCurrDate),
          DATEPART(dy, @dtCurrDate),
          DATEPART(m, @dtCurrDate),
          SUBSTRING(DATENAME(m, @dtCurrDate), 1, 3) + ' ' +
              CONVERT(char(4), YEAR(@dtCurrDate)),
          SUBSTRING(DATENAME(m, @dtCurrDate), 1, 3),
          DATEPART(qq, @dtCurrDate),
          'Q' + CONVERT(char(1), DATEPART(qq, @dtCurrDate))
              + ' ' + CONVERT(char(4), YEAR(@dtCurrDate)),
          'Q' + CONVERT(char(1), DATEPART(qq, @dtCurrDate)),
          YEAR(@dtCurrDate),
          CONVERT(char(4), YEAR(@dtCurrDate))
          )

      SELECT @dtCurrDate = DATEADD(d, 1, @dtCurrDate)
END
```

All Other Dimensions

As we discussed before, each dimension should include an 'Invalid' record for cases when fact data doesn't correlate to valid dimension data. The following SQL code will populate the remaining dimensions with a single 'Invalid' record with a primary key value of 0 by setting IDENTITY_INSERT for each table ON and insert an explicit value into the identity column. We use the standard value of zero for invalid to make ETL processing more manageable. Also, since each surrogate key is created as an identity column and the identity columns' default seed value is 1, the 'invalid' records will not get confused with a system-generated surrogate key.

DIM_GEOGRAPHY

```
USE Northwind_DW
go

-- Load Geography Dimension with default value
SET IDENTITY_INSERT DIM_GEOGRAPHY ON
INSERT INTO DIM_GEOGRAPHY
(geography_wk, country, state_region, city,
 postal_code)
VALUES
(0, 'N/A', 'N/A', 'N/A',
 'N/A')
SET IDENTITY_INSERT DIM_GEOGRAPHY OFF
```

DIM_CUSTOMER

```
USE Northwind_DW
go

-- Load Customer Dimension with default value
SET IDENTITY_INSERT DIM_CUSTOMER ON
INSERT INTO DIM_CUSTOMER
(customer_wk, customer_nk, geography_wk, customer_name)
VALUES (0, NULL, 0, 'Unknown')
SET IDENTITY_INSERT DIM_CUSTOMER OFF
```

DIM_EMPLOYEE

```
USE Northwind_DW
go

-- Load Employee Dimension with default value
SET IDENTITY_INSERT DIM_EMPLOYEE ON
INSERT INTO DIM_EMPLOYEE
(employee_wk, employee_nk, geography_wk, direct_report_wk,
 direct_report_nk, employee_name, region_nk, region_name)
VALUES
(0, NULL, 0, 0,
 NULL, 'Unknown', NULL, 'Unknown')
SET IDENTITY_INSERT DIM_EMPLOYEE OFF
```

DIM_SHIPPER

```
USE Northwind_DW
go

-- Load Shipper Dimension with default value
SET IDENTITY_INSERT DIM_SHIPPER ON
INSERT INTO DIM_SHIPPER
(shipper_wk, shipper_nk, shipper_name)
VALUES
(0, NULL, 'Unknown')
SET IDENTITY_INSERT DIM_SHIPPER OFF
```

DIM_SUPPLIER

```
USE Northwind_DW
go

-- Load Supplier Dimension with default value
SET IDENTITY_INSERT DIM_SUPPLIER ON
INSERT INTO DIM_SUPPLIER
(supplier_wk, supplier_nk, geography_wk, supplier_name)
VALUES
(0, NULL, 0, 'Unknown')
SET IDENTITY_INSERT DIM_SUPPLIER OFF
```

DIM_PRODUCT

```
USE Northwind_DW
go

-- Load Product Dimension with default value
SET IDENTITY_INSERT DIM_PRODUCT ON
INSERT INTO DIM_PRODUCT
(product_wk, product_nk, supplier_wk, product_name,
category_nk, category_name, discontinued_flag)
VALUES
(0, NULL, 0, 'Unknown',
 NULL, NULL, NULL)
SET IDENTITY_INSERT DIM_PRODUCT OFF
```

Microsoft Analysis Services

This case study has multidimensional OLAP cubes built using Analysis Services as one of its end products. The production of these cubes is an *optional* step in the building of the Northwind data mart as the original analytical questions can still be fulfilled from the relational database. To complete the steps that involve Analysis Services, several requirements must be met:

❑ Analysis Services must be installed on a computer that can access the relational data mart. AS can be installed on the same machine in this example because it is not a production environment.

❑ The Analysis Services client components must be installed on any computer that is either developing OR executing the Northwind ETL packages. The packages require the Analysis Services Processing Task, which is only installed with the Analysis Services client components.

If you choose not to include the steps that produce the Analysis Services cubes, you can disregard the steps for processing cubes in ETL 4. The ETL will still execute successfully and the relational data mart will still be loaded properly.

However, if you choose to include the Analysis Services steps and you have met the requirements above, you must restore the NorthwindDW Analysis Services database that can be found on the Wrox web site at **www.wrox.com**.

Once you've downloaded the .CAB file, you can restore it by opening Analysis Manager, expanding the **Analysis Servers** tree item and the Analysis Server you wish to restore this database to. In the example, we're using my laptop's machine name, 'LAPMCHAFFIN'.

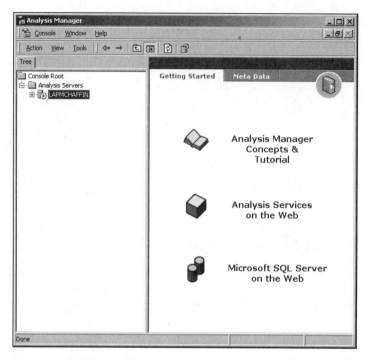

Right-click on the server and choose Restore Database... from the popup menu. Navigate to the NorthwindDW.CAB file you downloaded and select it.

Click on Open. The Restore Database dialog should appear asking for confirmation that you wish to restore this database.

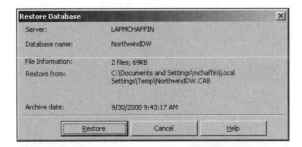

Click on **Restore**. The restore process should only take a few moments and if everything is successful, should result in this dialog:

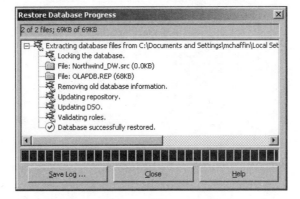

Click on **Close**.

Now we must configure the data source property of our new database. To do this, expand the server name tree item, expand the **NorthwindDW** tree item, and expand the **Data Sources** tree item.

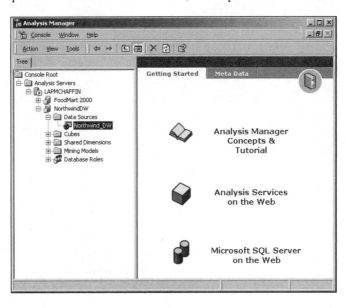

Right-click on the Northwind_DW datasource and choose Edit from the popup menu. Configure the connection information to use the Northwind_DW database we created earlier. Your configuration may look different from this:

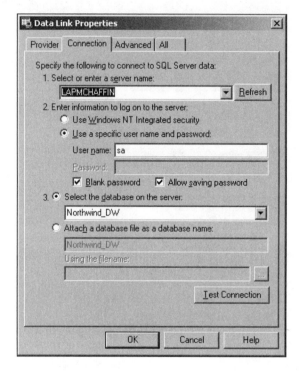

If clicking on Test Connection yields a successful connection, click on OK. Your Analysis Services database is now properly configured. We'll process it later in the ETL.

Let's continue with building the ETL.

Designing the ETL Workflow

There are several inherent features of DTS that lend themselves well to the ETL process for data warehousing. These features promote powerful, GUI-designed workflows and the ability to design tasks for parallel execution with little or no development overhead. Let's discuss how these features will let us design a powerful and flexible ETL.

One of the technical requirements for the Northwind data mart is that the ETL must finish all processing within a two-hour window each night; the backup processes for the OLTP system consume much of the available time window. As a result, the ETL must be designed to support parallel processing where possible.

Another requirement is that the ETL must be modular in design to support parallel development and object-oriented principles. This can be achieved by using a tiered approach to designing the ETL package. A master workflow package will be created that will manage the top level of workflow. Several lower-tiered packages will manage the individual task sets.

We have decided to break up our workflow into four steps – the master workflow package and three lower tiered packages. A brief summary of what each package does is as follows:

❑ The Master Workflow Package, ETL Step 1, connects to the database, then calls each lower package in turn, writing the job completion information after all the packages have executed.

❑ The first lower tier package, ETL Step 2, takes care of moving the data we want to the staging area.

❑ The second lower tier package, ETL Step 3, then cleanses and loads the dimension information from the staging area to the data warehouse.

❑ The final lower tier package, ETL Step 4, cleanses and loads the fact information from the staging area to the data warehouse.

In this way, we have broken our work up into more manageable pieces. However, to make the testing of this code easier, make sure that you have a `DTS2K_CS` folder on the root of your hard drive – this will hold the files we need to make our packages work. Let's move on by looking at the first of these packages.

ETL 1 (the Master Workflow Package)

The first step in the ETL process is to design the master workflow package. This package has to perform several tasks. These tasks are:

❑ Initiate logging for the ETL by creating a job record and setting the start date/time

❑ Execute all lower-tiered packages and pass all ETL-level variables to each package

❑ Update the job record with success or failure information and the finish date/time

Let's take a look at what the package looks like from a workflow standpoint. Its name is **ETL Step 1**, for lack of a better description. Remember that the code is available for download at **www.wrox.com**.

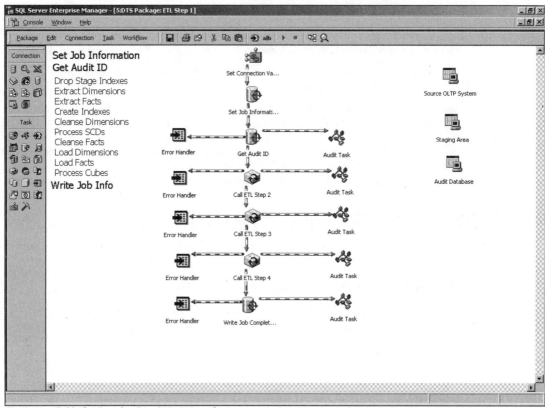

Figure available for download as CH15_01.gif

As you can see, ETL 1 is rather simple; most of the real work happens in the lower-tier packages. Also, the bold text annotations list the tasks that are performed in the current package, whereas the standard font tasks are executed in packages outside this main package. This convention is repeated in all of the packages.

To begin creating the ETL, create a new DTS package from SQL Enterprise Manager and name it **ETL Step 1**. Next, we'll create some global variables that will control many of the activities for the ETL.

Global Variables

To start, let's begin by showing the global variables that will be used in **ETL Step 1**. We define seven global variables by opening the package properties and choosing the **Global Variables** tab. Add the following variables to the package:

Global Variable	Type	Initial Value	Description
gdtPost Start	Date	1/1/1995	The earliest date for which transactional records are to be included in the sourcing of data.
gdtPostEnd	Date	1/1/2000	The latest date for which transactional records are to be included in the sourcing of data.
giAuditId	Integer	1	This value is the identity column of the audit record that's created in AUDIT_JOB. This value is updated during processing.
gsAudit DB_UDL	String	C:\DTS2K_CS\ AuditDB.udl	Path information to the UDL file that contains connection information for the audit database.
gsSource DB_UDL	String	C:\DTS2K_CS\ Source OLTP System.udl	Path information to the UDL file that contains connection information for the source OLTP database.
gsStaging AreaDB_UDL	String	C:\DTS2K_CS\ Staging Area.udl	Path information to the UDL file that contains connection information for the staging area database.
ExtError Package	String	C:\ DTS2K_CS\ ETL_ErrorHandler.dts	File system path to the error handler package.

All of these global variables will be used in the current package, ETL 1, and all of the lower-tiered packages that ETL 1 calls: ETL 2, ETL 3, and ETL 4. ETL 1 acts as a 'controller' package that allows a single point of management for the entire ETL application. ETL 1 will pass all of these global variables to the lower-tiered packages by using Outer Package Global Variables in each Execute Package task. We'll be discussing the configuration of these tasks a bit later.

Connections

In all packages used in the ETL process, the first step is always a dynamic configuration task called Set Connection Values. This task allows the entire ETL to be parameter driven, although in this case, the parameters are set using global variables; no values are hard-coded. This helps to address two issues: moving the ETL from development to testing and setting the ETL to extract from the source system based on a variable range.

The first issue can be tedious to deal with. Sometimes during development, a copy of the source OLTP source system is created to avoid interference with the production system. However, once the DTS packages are ready to be tested against the production system, all connection information must be manually updated to reflect the change. By using dynamic configuration, a single change can be propagated to all tasks without having to write any code.

The second issue is a typical data warehouse problem. A data warehouse has two different load types: initial and incremental. Typically, during the initial load, a large amount of historical data is extracted, transformed and loaded. After the initial load, incremental loading concerns only newly added data since the last load. If the ETL accepts a date range as an input, the same code can perform both types of loads.

In the case of the Northwind data warehouse, ETL 1 accepts `gdtPostStart` and `gdtPostEnd` as the date range for extraction. For an initial load, the range can encompass months or years, while an incremental load would cover only a day. Since the `Northwind` ETL handles this range, it is suitable for both types of loads.

UDL Connection Files

Notice that all of the connections for the ETL are driven from a Microsoft Universal Data Link file or UDL (a UDL is similar to a file-based DSN for ODBC except that it supports OLE DB and **requires at least MDAC 2.0 to be installed**).

To create the Audit Database UDL file, follow these steps:

For Windows NT 4.0:

- ❑ Open Windows Explorer
- ❑ Choose Microsoft Data Link from the New menu
- ❑ Create a Microsoft Data Link file
- ❑ Select the file name
- ❑ Press *F2* and change the name to `AuditDB.UDL`

For Windows 9x and Windows 2000:

- ❑ Open Windows Explorer
- ❑ Choose Text Document from the New menu (`New Text Document.txt` is created by default)
- ❑ On the Tools menu, click Folder Options. (In Windows 98, this can be found under View | Folder Options)
- ❑ On the View tab, clear the Hide file extension for known file types check box and click OK
- ❑ Select the file name
- ❑ Press *F2* and change the name to `AuditDB.UDL`
- ❑ You may receive a warning explaining that changing file extensions could cause files to become unusable. Disregard this warning.

To configure the Audit Database UDL file, follow these steps:

- ❑ Double-click on the `AuditDB.UDL` file
- ❑ Change the provider to Microsoft OLE DB Provider for SQL Server and click Next

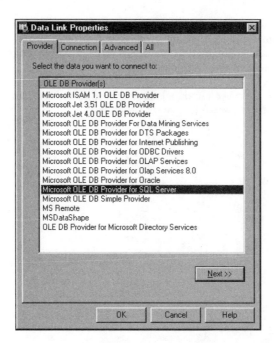

❑ Configure the Connection tab for your specific connection information

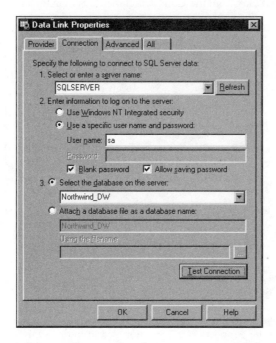

❑ Click Test Connection to make sure that the connection is valid

❑ If you receive a Test Connection Succeeded message box, click on OK

The AuditDB.UDL connection is now properly configured.

Follow the same steps for the Source OLTP database (Northwind) and the Staging database (Northwind_DW) by naming them "Source OLTP System.UDL" and "Staging Area.UDL". Once these files have been created, change global variables in ETL 1 to match the path to the respective UDL files as shown above in the Global Variables section.

Once the global variables have been updated, create three new connections in the package called Source OLTP System, Staging Area, and Audit Database.

Source OLTP System

Staging Area

Audit Database

To create the Source OLTP System connection, open the DTS package ETL 1 we've been working with and choose **Microsoft Data Link** from the **Connection** menu. Set the dialog with the following properties:

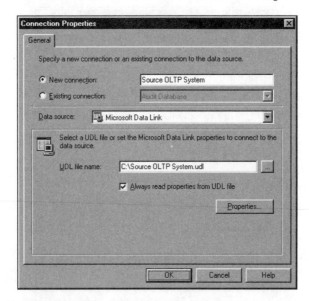

Make sure that the **Always read properties from UDL file** check box is checked. This option ensures that the package resolves the connection information stored in the UDL file at run time. However, if this value is not checked, DTS, by default, will copy connection information directly in the package and the UDL file will not be referenced again. Since these values may be updated each time the package is run, we want DTS to resolve the connections at run time. Set the other two connections in the same way, only substitute the correct UDL file reference.

Set Connection Values Task

The Dynamic Propeties task, Set Connection Values, will read three static global variables with the paths to the locations of the UDL files. The UDL files will contain the connection information that will be used in the master ETL package and all lower-tiered packages. When the time comes to move this ETL into testing or production, these UDL files can be reconfigured to connect to the production system. This change will be used by all of the ETL packages.

To set these properties, click the 'Add' button. From the following screen, expand the Connections tab, and then select which connection you want to set. Double-click on the UDLPath Property Name, and from the next screen choose Global Variable as the Source, and the appropriate setting from the lower drop down box. Either click the Add button three times to set the properties, or remember to check the 'Leave this dialog box open after adding a setting' box to keep the screen open to add all of the properties. After they have been set, close the window and return to the Properties window, which should look like the following:

Unique connections are created for the Staging Area and the Audit Database because the Audit database doesn't have to reside within the warehouse database nor even on the same machine. Other ETL processes for other data marts can share the same audit structure to make management easier.

Let's start off by taking a look at the dynamic configuration task. It reads the three global variables, gsAuditDB_UDL, gsSourceDB_UDL, and gsStagingAreaDB_UDL, and sets the UDLPath property of the UDL Connections, Audit Database, Source OLTP System, and Staging Area.

By specifying these connection parameters in one location and passing them as package parameters throughout the ETL process, all ETL packages can be moved from development to testing and then to production with few configuration changes and no re-coding. This is really taking advantage of the new dynamic configuration abilities of DTS 2000. In SQL Server 7.0, this would have required a complex ActiveX Script task to read the global variables and set the specific task properties.

Audit Information

The next two tasks in ETL Step 1, Set Job Information and Get Audit ID, handle the creation of a job record in AUDIT_JOB in the Auditing database.

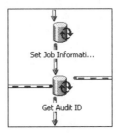

As you can see, they are both defined as Execute SQL tasks. To create these tasks, choose Execute SQL Task from the Task menu in the DTS Designer. Name the first task Set Job Information and set the Existing connection to the Audit Database connection. Add the following section to the SQL statement text window:

```
INSERT INTO AUDIT_JOB
      (job_name, job_status, job_start_dt,
      post_start_dt, post_end_dt)
VALUES
      ('Northwind DW', 'Running', GETDATE(), ?, ?)
```

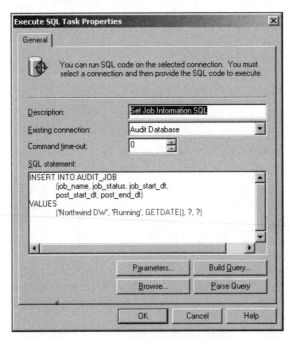

This statement uses two parameters that are supplied by the global variables, gdtPostStart and gdtPostEnd. You can set these parameters by clicking on the Parameters button from the properties dialog.

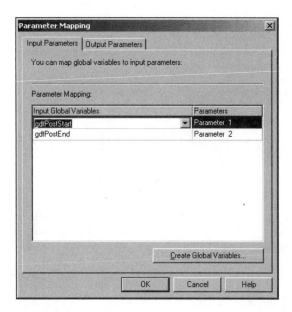

To create the next task, **Get Audit ID,** follow the same steps as above, but set the **Description** property to **Get Audit ID** and the **Existing Connection** property to the **Audit Database.** This task retrieves the newly inserted row that the Set Job Information task inserted. The following section should be added to the SQL statement text window in this task as illustrated below:

```
SELECT MAX(audit_id) AS 'audit_id'
FROM AUDIT_JOB
WHERE job_name = 'Northwind DW'
```

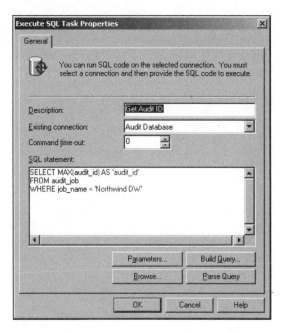

This task returns a row value that will set the `giAuditID` global variable by returning an output parameter. To configure the task to do this, click on the **Parameters** button and choose the **Output Parameters** tab. Choose the **Row Value** option button and select `giAuditID` from the **Output Global Variables** combo box as illustrated below:

The initial release of SQL Server 2000 doesn't correctly support the setting and retrieving of both Input and Output parameters in a single Execute SQL task. That's why these tasks are performed in two steps, rather than one. Once this issue has been resolved, the best method for achieving the desired result would be to perform the insert and save the return value into the global variable using **@@IDENTITY**, which would return the last inserted value.

Auditing/Error Handling

Once the job record is created, each task has associated `Error Handler` and `Audit Task` tasks created. These tasks are based on examples in Chapters 12 and 13 with few changes; both tasks log information to the `AUDIT_TASK` table.

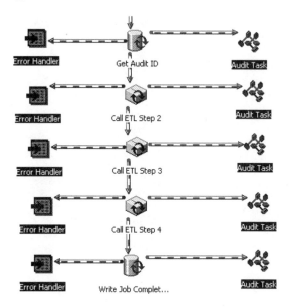

Audit Task

Every task in ETL 1, except `Set Connection Values` and `Set Job Information` has an ActiveX Script task called `Audit Task` configured to be executed on successful execution. When any of these tasks successfully completes execution, the **Audit Task** is called, in parallel with the next step in the ETL. The purpose of this configuration is to have an audit record created immediately following the successful execution of a task. That way, the information is logged immediately and in parallel. The other alternative is to batch all of the inserts together at the end of processing. However, if a catastrophic failure occurs, no audit information can be used to determine the cause of the failure.

Each **Audit Task** shares the same basic code configuration with the exception of one line in the code of each task. Currently in DTS, there is no way for a task to be able to programmatically determine which task is its immediate predecessor. This is because there is no way to determine what the currently executing task is from within an ActiveX Script task. This means that the **Audit Task** needs to be manually configured as to who its immediate predecessor is in the workflow.

To create the `Get Audit ID` task's `Audit Task`, add a new ActiveX Script task to the package and set the task's description property to **Audit Task**. Add the following code to the code window of the task and click **OK**.

```
Function Main()
Dim sStepName
Dim sTaskName
Dim nLastRow
Dim oPackage
Dim oStep
Dim oTask
Dim oProperty
Dim oConn
Dim sSQL
Dim nCntr
Dim vRecordsProcessed

'!!!!!!!!!!!!!!!!!!!!!!! Set Step Name !!!!!!!!!!!!!!!!!!!!!!!!!!!!!!!!!!
sStepName = "XXXX"

'Get Handle to Current DTS Package
Set oPackage = DTSGlobalVariables.Parent

'Find Step
For nCntr = 1 to oPackage.Steps.Count
   If oPackage.Steps(nCntr).Name = sStepName Then
       Exit For
   End If
Next
Set oStep = oPackage.Steps(nCntr)

'Set Step
sStepName = oStep.Description & " (" & oStep.Name & ")"

'Get Handle to Task
For nCntr = 1 to oPackage.Tasks.Count
   If oPackage.Tasks(nCntr).Name = oStep.TaskName Then
       Exit For
   End If
Next
Set oTask = oPackage.Tasks(nCntr)

'If the previous task processed records, we can access the
'property, otherwise set to NULL
vRecordsProcessed = "NULL"
For Each oProperty In oTask.Properties
   If oProperty.Name = "RowsComplete" Then
       vRecordsProcessed = oProperty.Value
   End If
Next

'Build SQL Statement
sSQL = "INSERT INTO AUDIT_TASK (audit_id, package_name, "
sSQL = sSQL & "task_name, task_status, task_start_dt, "
sSQL = sSQL & "task_end_dt, records_processed) VALUES ("
sSQL = sSQL & DTSGlobalVariables("giAuditId").Value & ", "
sSQL = sSQL & "'" & oPackage.Name & "', "
sSQL = sSQL & "'" & sStepName & "', 'Successful', "
sSQL = sSQL & "'" & oStep.StartTime & "', '" & oStep.FinishTime
sSQL = sSQL & "', " & vRecordsProcessed & ")"
```

```
'Insert Row
Set oConn = CreateObject("ADODB.Connection")
oConn.Open "File Name=" & _
   DTSGlobalVariables("gsAuditDB_UDL").Value
oConn.Execute sSQL

'Clean up
oConn.Close
Set oConn = Nothing

Main = DTSTaskExecResult_Success

End Function
```

In the code above, the line that begins with sStepName = "XXXX" must have XXXX replaced with the name of the preceding task, in this case Get Audit ID. To do this, right-click on the task you wish to have logged, (Get Audit ID), choose **Workflow** and then **Workflow Properties**. Then choose the **Options** tab to see this screen:

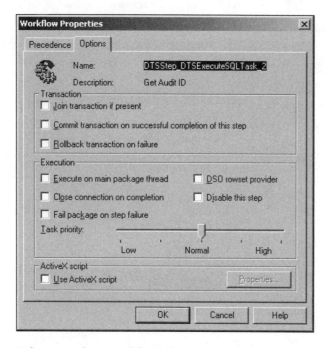

The highlighted text is the internal name of the task.

> Since DTS requires unique names for each task in a package, it will name each new task with the type of task and an incremental value. This internal name is used by DTS, but the DTS Designer shows the Description property on the design palette.

Now change XXXX to DTSStep_DTSExecuteSQLTask_2 as so:

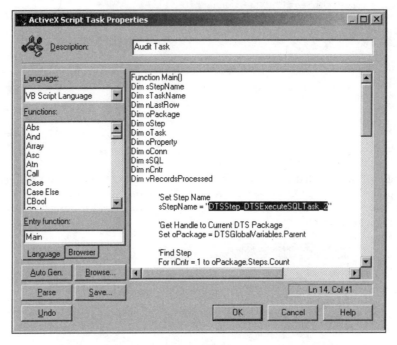

At this point, create an On Success precedence constraint, and the Audit Task for Get Audit ID is configured and ready to go. However, every other task you create should be audited. Therefore, each Audit Task that you now add to the package must be configured individually. Follow the same directions as above for all tasks you wish to have audited, but remember to change the "XXXX" to the correct task name.

Error Handler Custom Task

Error Handler

> The error handler custom task was first introduced in Chapter 12. Although it is used extensively throughout this case study, it is not necessary for successful loading of the data warehouse. If you choose to use the custom task in this case study, you must recompile the project in Visual Basic with the changes below and reregister in DTS. For more information, refer to Chapter 12.

The error handler custom task here is slightly different from the example given in Chapter 12. The layout of the properties dialog of the task and code is the same, but the CustomTask_Execute routine in the CErrorHandler class is different. Replace the CustomTask_Execute subroutine with the following code and recompile the project:

```
Private Sub CustomTask_Execute( _
    ByVal pPackage As Object, _
    ByVal pPackageEvents As Object, _
    ByVal pPackageLog As Object, _
    pTaskResult As DTS.DTSTaskExecResult)


On Error GoTo EH
Dim sPreStepName As String
Dim sErrorPackagePath As String
Dim sStepErrorText As String
Dim sPackageID As String
Dim sErrorText As String
Dim sErrorSource As String
Dim nErrorCode As Long
Dim sErrorString As String
Dim dtStartTime As Date

Dim oCurrPkg As DTS.Package
Dim oErrorHandlerPackage As DTS.Package
Dim oStep As DTS.Step
Dim oFileSystem As Object

    'Save start time for logging
    dtStartTime = Now

    Set oCurrPkg = pPackage
    sPackageID = oCurrPkg.PackageID

    'Find the Step Object for the Predecessor Step
    For Each oStep In oCurrPkg.Steps
        If oStep.TaskName = msPredecessorName Then
            Exit For
        End If
    Next

    If oStep Is Nothing Or IsNull(oStep) Then
        sErrorString = "Cannot locate predecessor step, " & _
            msPredecessorName & ", in the current package."
        Err.Raise 50000, "CustomTask_Execute", sErrorString
        pTaskResult = DTSTaskExecResult_Failure
    End If

    'Build Error Message from GetExecutionErrorInfo
    With oStep
        .GetExecutionErrorInfo nErrorCode, _
            sErrorSource, sStepErrorText
```

```
        sErrorText = "Package: " & oCurrPkg.Name & vbCrLf
        sErrorText = sErrorText & "Internal Step Name: " & .Name & vbCrLf
        sErrorText = sErrorText & "Step Description: " & .Description & vbCrLf
        sErrorText = sErrorText & "Started: " & .StartTime & vbCrLf
        sErrorText = sErrorText & "Finished: " & .FinishTime & vbCrLf
        sErrorText = sErrorText & "Failed with error: " & sStepErrorText
    End With


    'If the task is using a global variable to
    'determine the location of the external error
    'handling package, retrieve it, otherwise,
    'use the custom value
    If mnSource = Source_Global Then
        'Get From Package Globals for 'ExtErrorPackage'
        sErrorPackagePath = _
            oCurrPkg.GlobalVariables.Item("ExtErrorPackage").Value
        If sErrorPackagePath = "" Then
            sErrorString = "Global Variable 'ExtErrorPackage' " & _
                    "not found when global variable use is " & _
                "specified. You must create this variable " & _
                "before the ErrorHandler class can be used."
            Err.Raise 50001, "CustomTask_Execute", sErrorString
            pTaskResult = DTSTaskExecResult_Failure
        End If
    Else
        sErrorPackagePath = msFileName
    End If


    'Make sure that the error package exists before opening
    Set oFileSystem = CreateObject("Scripting.FileSystemObject")
    If Not oFileSystem.FileExists(sErrorPackagePath) Then
        sErrorString = "External Error Handler DTS Package not " & _
                        "found at: " & sErrorPackagePath
        Err.Raise 50002, "CustomTask_Execute", sErrorString
        pTaskResult = DTSTaskExecResult_Failure
    End If


    'Open instance of error package
    Set oErrorHandlerPackage = New DTS.Package
    oErrorHandlerPackage.LoadFromStorageFile sErrorPackagePath, ""

    If oErrorHandlerPackage Is Nothing _
        Or IsEmpty(oErrorHandlerPackage) Then
        sErrorString = "Error loading External Error Handling " & _
                        "Package : " & sErrorPackagePath
        Err.Raise 50003, "CustomTask_Execute", sErrorString
        pTaskResult = DTSTaskExecResult_Failure
    End If


    'Set Global Variables - gsErrorText, gsErrorPackage, gsErrorStep
    'and giAuditID, gdtTaskStart, gdtTaskFinish
    With oErrorHandlerPackage
        .GlobalVariables.Item("gsErrorText").Value = sErrorText
        .GlobalVariables.Item("gsErrorPackage").Value = oCurrPkg.Name
        .GlobalVariables.Item("gsErrorStep").Value = oStep.Description
```

```
            .GlobalVariables.Item("giAuditId").Value = _
                        oCurrPkg.GlobalVariables("giAuditId").Value
            .GlobalVariables.Item("gdtTaskStart").Value = oStep.StartTime
            .GlobalVariables.Item("gdtTaskFinish").Value = oStep.FinishTime

            '**We now also set the nErrorCode and sErrorSource values
            'from GetExecutionErrorInfo and pass to the error handling
            'package for the opportunity to deal with specific
            'errors differently
            .GlobalVariables.Item("gnErrorCode").Value = nErrorCode
            .GlobalVariables.Item("gsErrorSource").Value = sErrorSource
        End With

        'Execute the Package
        oErrorHandlerPackage.Execute

        'Log to DTS log if applicable
        If Not pPackageLog Is Nothing Then
            pPackageLog.WriteStringToLog "Error Handling for Step: " & _
                        msPredecessorName & " was successful." & vbCrLf
            pPackageLog.WriteTaskRecord 0, "Total Task Time: " & _
                        (DateDiff("s", dtStartTime, Now)) & " sec. " & _
                            vbCrLf & "Error from " & msPredecessorName & _
                                            ": " & sErrorText

        End If

        'Clean up references
        Set oCurrPkg = Nothing
        Set oErrorHandlerPackage = Nothing
        Set oFileSystem = Nothing

        pTaskResult = DTSTaskExecResult_Success

        Exit Sub
EH:
        'Bubble any errors to the package eventsink
        If Not pPackageEvents Is Nothing Then
            pPackageEvents.OnError msTaskName & _
                        " - CustomTask_Execute method", Err.Number, _
                        Err.Source, Err.Description, "", 0, "", True
        End If

        'Log error to DTS log if applicable
        If Not pPackageLog Is Nothing Then
            pPackageLog.WriteTaskRecord Err.Number, _
                Err.Description
        End If

        Exit Sub
End Sub
```

Error Handler Task Configuration

To configure error handling for the Get Audit ID task, add a new Error Handler task and create an On Failure Precedent as shown:

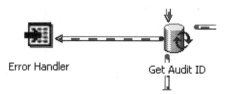

Error Handler   Get Audit ID

Double-click on the Error Handler task to edit its properties. Set the predecessor task to Get Audit ID and click OK.

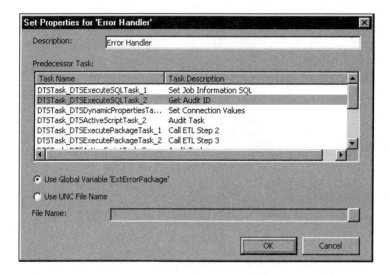

> **Follow the same steps to add error handling for all tasks that we create over the next several sections.**

Northwind Data Mart Error Handler Package

The external error handling DTS package was revised from the example in Chapter 12, to take advantage of the new logging structure. The new version looks like this:

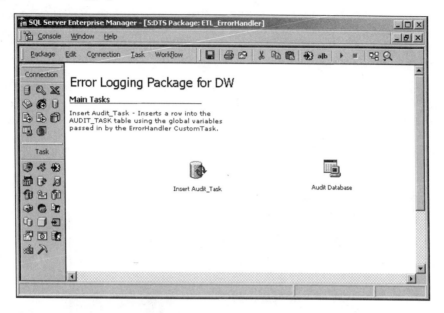

To create this package, create a new package in DTS Designer.

Any package that uses the `Error Handler` custom task must supply several values for global variables that exist in the external error handler package. Add the following global variables and configure them with the following initial values:

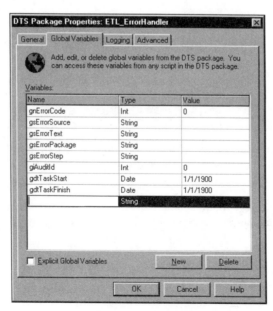

These initial values will not be used; they're just placeholders that the calling tasks will replace. By creating them as placeholders, you can now use them to set parameters in the Execute SQL task you're now ready to create.

Once the global variables have been created, add a UDL connection, called **Audit Database**, to the package and configure it to use the `AuditDB.UDL` file from the UDL section earlier. Also, add an Execute SQL task with the description of **Insert Audit_Task** and set the **Existing connection** to use the **Audit Database** connection. Add the following SQL to the SQL Statement text window:

```
INSERT INTO AUDIT_TASK
(audit_id, package_name, task_name, task_status, task_start_dt, task_end_dt)
VALUES (?, ?, ?, 'Error: ' + ?, ?, ?)
```

Since we're using six parameters in the SQL statement, we need to configure the parameters of the Execute SQL task use these parameters. Click on the **Parameters** button and set them as shown below:

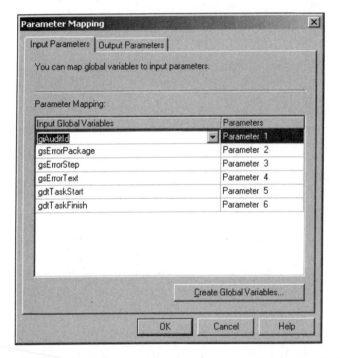

This will update the `AUDIT_TASK` table with any error and its description. It will also include the package in which the error occurred, the step, and when the task started and finished. This should allow most debugging to occur quite easily.

Now you must save the package, but it should be saved as a Structured Storage File that can be referenced from any of the other tasks. Save the package with the name of `ETL_ErrorHandler.dts`.

Executing Lower-Tier Packages

The next three steps in ETL Step 1 execute three external packages, ETL Step 2, ETL Step 3, and ETL Step 4. To create these tasks, add three new Execute Package tasks and set the description property to "Call ETL Step 2", "Call ETL Step 3" and "Call ETL Step 4", respectively. Each of the steps will connect to an external package and pass its global variables as Outer Package Parameters. However, the ETL 2, ETL 3, and ETL 4 packages do not yet exist. They'll be created during the remainder of the chapter. For now, just create the tasks and leave the parameters blank. Press Cancel to create them as empty packages. Don't worry; we will return to configure them later in the chapter.

We'll discuss each of these lower-tier packages and the output parameters in the next several sections.

Write Job Completion Info

Instead of following the execution path of the package, let's stay with ETL 1 and discuss the last step, "Write Job Completion Info". Once all of the lower-tier packages have executed, we want to update the status of the job record we created in the first two ExecuteSQL tasks. If a task failed for any reason, it will have logged an error in AUDIT_TASK. One benefit of logging status in the database is that the ETL is not responsible for passing a status variable from package to package or task to task. Another benefit is that the result of each task is persisted, and thus, not volatile and at risk from a catastrophic failure.

Since no global status variable exists, we want to write the result of the ETL as successful. We can determine its success based on the result of the individual tasks. We can then assume that if no tasks were unsuccessful, the ETL was completely successful. The "Write Job Completion Info" task uses the following SQL to set the job status based on the results of all its associated tasks:

```
declare @error_count int
declare @job_status nvarchar(15)

SELECT @error_count = 0

SELECT @error_count = COUNT(*)
FROM AUDIT_TASK
WHERE task_status <> 'Successful' AND
audit_id = ?

IF @error_count = 0
SELECT @job_status = 'Completed'
ELSE
SELECT @job_status = 'Error'

UPDATE AUDIT_JOB SET
   job_status = @job_status,
   job_end_dt = GETDATE()
WHERE audit_id = ?
```

> Unfortunately, the initial release of SQL Server 2000 doesn't allow the assignment of parameters and the declaration of variables within an ExecuteSQL statement. The only way to configure this task for the desired result is to use the Disconnected Edit feature of SQL Server 2000.

To configure this task, go ahead and insert the previous SQL into the SQL statement text window in "Write Job Completion Info". Set the Existing connection property to "Audit Database" and then click OK. We can set the parameters manually by choosing Disconnected Edit from the Package menu. Expand the Tasks tree item and find the DTSStep_DTSExecuteSQLTask_3 in the list. Make sure that the Description property is set to "Write Job Completion Info". If it's not, this isn't the correct task. You must make sure that you have the correct Execute SQL task.

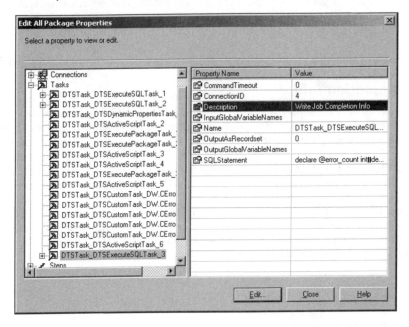

Once you've selected the correct task, select the InputGlobalVariableNames Property Name in the right window and click on Edit. Make sure the Type combo box is set to String and type the following text into the Value text box:

"giAuditId";"giAuditId"

This specifies the two global variables that are to be used as Input Global Variables.

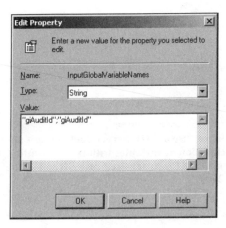

Now click **OK** to return to the Disconnected Edit dialog and then click on **Close**. The "Write Job Completion Info" task is now correctly configured.

So that's ETL 1. Once again, the purpose of separating ETL 1 from all other components is to add a "control" tier where pan-ETL issues are handled. Issues that span other tasks, like creating the audit information, can be dealt with once, rather than in each package. This simplifies both the design and execution. It also creates the opportunity for simultaneous development of several packages within the ETL.

ETL 2

The second step in the ETL process is to extract the information from the source OLTP system. This package has to perform several tasks. These tasks are:

- ❑ Drop the stage table indexes
- ❑ Extract the dimension member records
- ❑ Extract the fact records

However, these tasks aren't quite as simple as they sound. Here's what the package looks like:

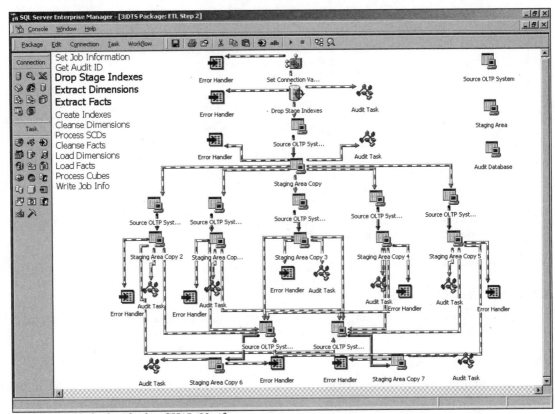

Figure available for download as CH15_02.gif

ETL 2 looks quite a bit more complex than ETL 1, but the illusion of complexity is in the parallel nature of the workflow. Don't worry. We'll step through the design in small steps that will clarify the process. Also the diagram shows the package with all of the error handling and auditing tasks already created. Here's what the package looks like without the auditing and error handling:

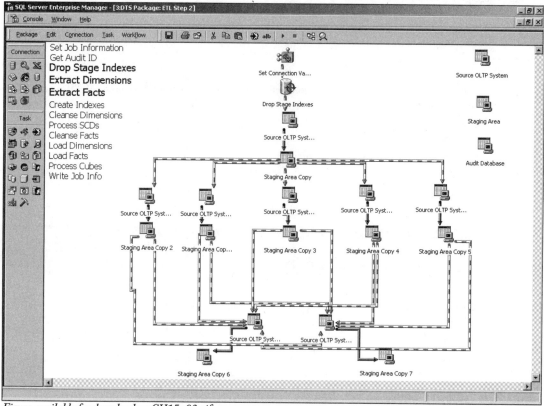

Figure available for download as CH15_03.gif

It's much less complex looking now. We definitely want to include error handling and auditing, but we'll add both once all the other tasks have been created.

Let's dive into some detail.

Creating the Package

To create the package, open a new package in SQL Server Enterprise Manager. Save the package as a Structured Storage File named ETL Step 2. Now you're ready to start configuration.

Package Properties

In ETL 2, the design necessitates that the maximum number of tasks that should be occurring in parallel is 5. Because of this, you need to change the DTS default: right-click on an empty portion of the design surface and choose Properties. Change the Limit the maximum number of tasks executed in parallel to: property to 5, as shown opposite:

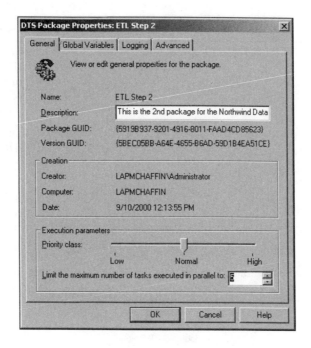

Global Variables

ETL 2 does not add any new global variables: It uses only the variables passed from ETL 1. However, for configuration purposes, create the following global variables so that subsequent tasks can be properly configured.

Global Variable	Type	Initial Value	Description
gdtPostStart	Date	1/1/1995	The earliest date for which transactional records are to be included in the sourcing of data.
gdtPostEnd	Date	1/1/2000	The latest date for which transactional records are to be included in the sourcing of data.
giAuditId	Integer	1	This value is the identity column of the audit record that's created in AUDIT_JOB. This value is updated during processing.
gsAuditDB_UDL	String	C:\ DTS2K_CS\ AuditDB.udl	Path information to the UDL file that contains connection information for the audit database.

Table continued on following page

Global Variable	Type	Initial Value	Description
gsSourceDB_UDL	String	C:\DTS2K_CS\ Source OLTP System.udl	Path information to the UDL file that contains connection information for the source OLTP database.
gsStaging AreaDB_UDL	String	C:\DTS2K_CS\ Staging Area.udl	Path information to the UDL file that contains connection information for the staging area database.
ExtError Package	String	C:\ DTS2K_CS\ ETL_ErrorHandler.dts	File system path to the error handler package.

Connections

For ETL 2, create three UDL connections, Source OLTP System, Staging Area and Audit Database:

Source OLTP System

Staging Area

Audit Database

Configure their properties to the appropriate UDL file name: C:\DTS2K_CS\Source OLTP System.udl (for Source OLTP System), C:\DTS2K_CS\Staging Area.udl (for Staging Area), and C:\DTS2K_CS\AuditDB.udl for Audit Database) – or wherever your UDL connections are located. Remember to check the Always read properties from UDL file check box.

Set Connection Values

Only three unique connections are defined in ETL 2 and all three are set via the Set Connection Values Dynamic Configuration task in the first step. However, each Transform Data task requires a new connection so they can be executed in parallel with no contention issues. Also, to make the workflow easier to read and understand, a new connection is created as a copy of the original. There is a drawback, though. The Dynamic Configuration task has to set each one of the copies, which requires extra configuration.

To do this, create a new dynamic properties task called `Set Connection Values`. Double-click on the task to edit its properties:

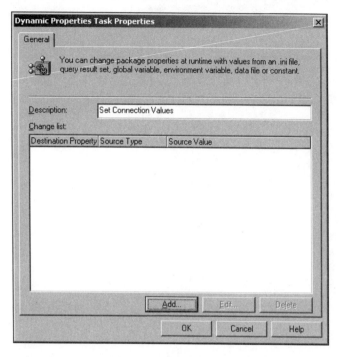

Before you change any of the properties of this task, we need to create the connections that this task will be dynamically modifying. We'll have to revisit this task to complete its configuration once all of the package's connections have been created. We'll handle this a bit later in the section entitled *Set Connection Values...Part 2*.

> **The initial release of SQL Server 2000 has an issue with UDL connections. If a UDL connection is used, but the UDL path is not valid, attempting to set properties in dynamic configuration task will cause an error. To resolve this, each UDL connection must point to an existing UDL file.**

Drop Stage Indexes

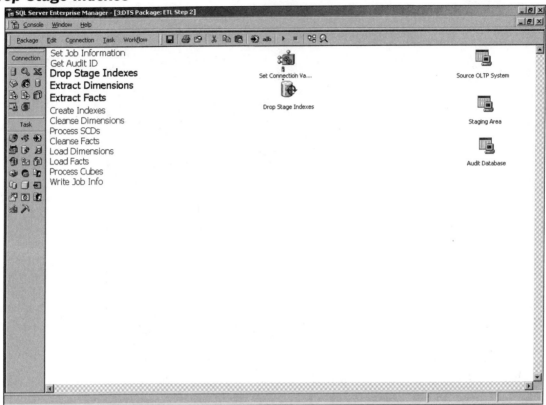

Before loading the stage tables, any indexes should be dropped so the `IRowsetFastLoad` interface can be used to bulk load the tables. This will allow the fastest loading of data since indexes would prevent SQL Server from bulk loading. Also, we truncate the stage tables to make sure that any data from a prior load is removed and will not interfere with the current load.

To add this task to ETL 2, add a new Execute SQL task, set the description to Drop Stage Indexes and set the Existing connection property to the Staging Area connection. Insert the following SQL into the SQL Statement text window (in case you'd forgotten, we'll be adding the indexes back later):

```
IF EXISTS (SELECT * FROM dbo.sysindexes WHERE NAME = 'IDX_STAGE_CUSTOMER')
DROP INDEX STAGE_CUSTOMER.IDX_STAGE_CUSTOMER
go

IF EXISTS (SELECT * FROM dbo.sysindexes WHERE NAME =
'IDX_STAGE_CUSTOMER_GEOGRAPHY')
DROP INDEX STAGE_CUSTOMER.IDX_STAGE_CUSTOMER_GEOGRAPHY
go

IF EXISTS (SELECT * FROM dbo.sysindexes WHERE NAME = 'IDX_STAGE_EMPLOYEE')
DROP INDEX STAGE_EMPLOYEE.IDX_STAGE_EMPLOYEE
go
IF EXISTS (SELECT * FROM dbo.sysindexes WHERE NAME =
'IDX_STAGE_EMPLOYEE_GEOGRAPHY')
DROP INDEX STAGE_EMPLOYEE.IDX_STAGE_EMPLOYEE_GEOGRAPHY
go
```

```
IF EXISTS (SELECT * FROM dbo.sysindexes WHERE NAME = 'IDX_STAGE_GEOGRAPHY')
DROP INDEX STAGE_GEOGRAPHY.IDX_STAGE_GEOGRAPHY
go

IF EXISTS (SELECT * FROM dbo.sysindexes WHERE NAME = 'IDX_STAGE_ORDER_ITEMS')
DROP INDEX STAGE_ORDER_ITEMS.IDX_STAGE_ORDER_ITEMS
go

IF EXISTS (SELECT * FROM dbo.sysindexes WHERE NAME =
'IDX_STAGE_ORDER_ITEMS_GEOGRAPHY')
DROP INDEX STAGE_ORDER_ITEMS.IDX_STAGE_ORDER_ITEMS_GEOGRAPHY
go

IF EXISTS (SELECT * FROM dbo.sysindexes WHERE NAME = 'IDX_STAGE_ORDERS')
DROP INDEX STAGE_ORDERS.IDX_STAGE_ORDERS
go

IF EXISTS (SELECT * FROM dbo.sysindexes WHERE NAME = 'IDX_STAGE_ORDERS_GEOGRAPHY')
DROP INDEX STAGE_ORDERS.IDX_STAGE_ORDERS_GEOGRAPHY
go

IF EXISTS (SELECT * FROM dbo.sysindexes WHERE NAME = 'IDX_STAGE_PRODUCT')
DROP INDEX STAGE_PRODUCT.IDX_STAGE_PRODUCT
go

IF EXISTS (SELECT * FROM dbo.sysindexes WHERE NAME = 'IDX_STAGE_SHIPPER')
DROP INDEX STAGE_SHIPPER.IDX_STAGE_SHIPPER
go

IF EXISTS (SELECT * FROM dbo.sysindexes WHERE NAME = 'IDX_STAGE_SUPPLIER')
DROP INDEX STAGE_SUPPLIER.IDX_STAGE_SUPPLIER
go

IF EXISTS (SELECT * FROM dbo.sysindexes WHERE NAME =
'IDX_STAGE_SUPPLIER_GEOGRAPHY')
DROP INDEX STAGE_SUPPLIER.IDX_STAGE_SUPPLIER_GEOGRAPHY
go

TRUNCATE TABLE STAGE_GEOGRAPHY
go

TRUNCATE TABLE STAGE_CUSTOMER
go

TRUNCATE TABLE STAGE_PRODUCT
go

TRUNCATE TABLE STAGE_EMPLOYEE
go
TRUNCATE TABLE STAGE_SHIPPER
go

TRUNCATE TABLE STAGE_SUPPLIER
go

TRUNCATE TABLE STAGE_ORDER_ITEMS
go

TRUNCATE TABLE STAGE_ORDERS
go
```

Extracting Dimension Information

There are several issues to consider when extracting dimension information. Most OLTP systems aren't designed with the intention of extracting information into an OLAP system. Thus, most OLTP systems do not have important attributes for their dimension information such as the creation date and last changed date. These two date/time stamps are important because they can tell you whether the dimension member was loaded in a previous ETL session. We're not lost without them, but the ETL will be more complex and take longer.

Alas, the Northwind Company did not design its OLTP system to include these timestamps and we don't want to change the source system, so we'll have to add some additional logic. That also means that we're going to extract all dimension members to the staging area so we can work with that data set there, rather than directly from the OLTP system. Remember one of the mantras of ETL design – get in and get out as quickly as possible.

Geography Dimension

The addition of the Geography Dimension Transform Data task and associated tasks and connections, makes ETL 2 look like this:

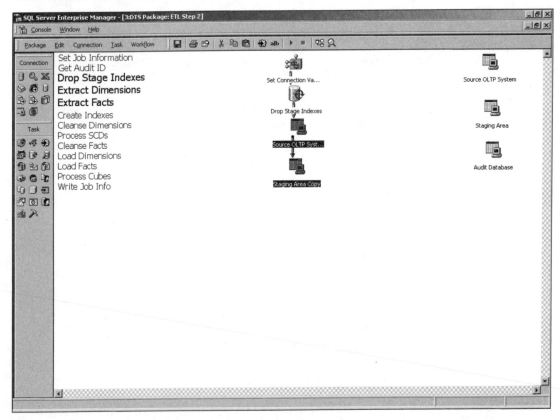

The first dimension we want to extract is actually a derived dimension. We're going to extract all of the possible combinations of `Country`, `State`, `City`, and `PostalCode` from `Customers`, `Suppliers`, `Employees`, and `Orders`. Of course, another option is to use a pre-built geography dimension sourced from the US Postal Service, but Northwind is a multi-national corporation and includes addresses from many countries.

To extract this data, we need to create a Transform Data task. The best way to do this is to create a copy of the Source OLTP system connection and a copy of the Staging Area connection (DTS will append 'Copy' to the name of any connection you copy using the Copy and Paste method). To add the Transform Data task, choose Transform Data Task from the Task menu, and choose the Source OLTP System Copy as the source and the Staging Area Copy connection as the destination. Double-click on the Transform Data Task and change the description property to Extract Geography Dimension.

> **If you look closely at the workflow, you'll see that this task occurs independent of any other activity. That way we avoid contention from this query and any other extraction query. We'll begin the parallelization in the next few tasks.**

Now you're ready to configure the task.

Source

First, change the Source tab to use a SQL query as the source of data as shown below:

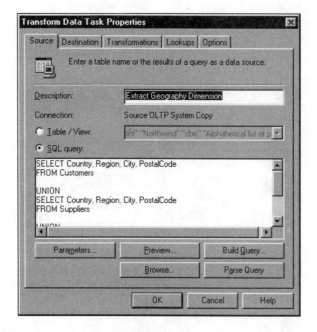

The full text of the SQL statement is listed below:

```
SELECT Country, Region, City, PostalCode
FROM Customers

UNION

SELECT Country, Region, City, PostalCode
FROM Suppliers

UNION
```

```
SELECT Country, Region, City, PostalCode
FROM Employees

UNION

SELECT ShipCountry, ShipRegion, ShipCity, ShipPostalCode
FROM Orders
```

Destination

To set the Destination properties of the Extract Geography Dimension Transform Data task, just configure the Table name to use the STAGE_GEOGRAPHY table.

Transformations

Now click on the Transformations tab and create a new transformation that uses the following source and destination columns:

Source Column	Destination Column
Country	country
Region	state_region
City	city
PostalCode	postal_code

Like this:

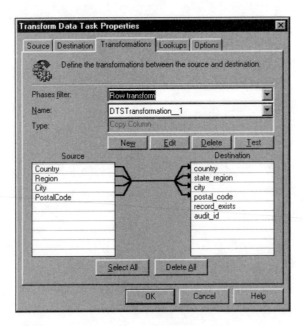

No Lookups or other Options are used in this task. Click on OK to save the task.

Customer Dimension

The addition of the Customer Dimension Transform Data task and associated tasks and connections, makes ETL 2 look like this:

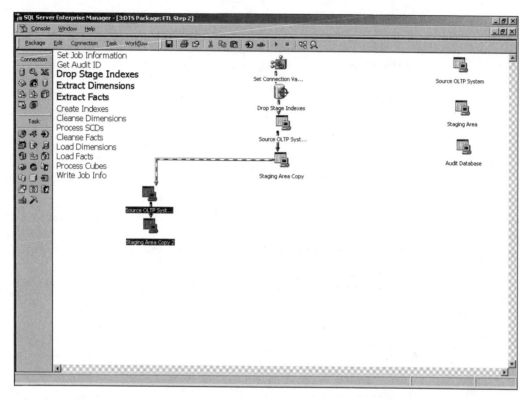

Follow the same steps to configure the extract for the Customer dimension. Use a copy of the Source OLTP System as the source and a copy of the Staging Area as the destination. Change the description of the task to **Extract Customer Dimension** and set the task's properties as follows.

Source

Use the following SQL statement as the source of the query:

```
SELECT
        CustomerID, CompanyName, ContactName, ContactTitle,
        Address, Country, Region, City, PostalCode, Phone, Fax
FROM
        Customers
```

Destination

Set the destination table to STAGE_CUSTOMER.

Transformation

Once again, we're using a simple copy column transformation. Set the source and destination columns as follows:

Source Column	Destination Column
CustomerID	customer_nk
CompanyName	customer_name
ContactName	contact_name
ContactTitle	contact_title
Address	Address
Country	Country
Region	state_region
City	city
PostalCode	postal_code
Phone	phone
Fax	fax

No other attributes need to be set for this task to function properly.

Employee Dimension

The addition of the Employee Dimension Transform Data task and associated tasks and connections, makes ETL 2 look like this:

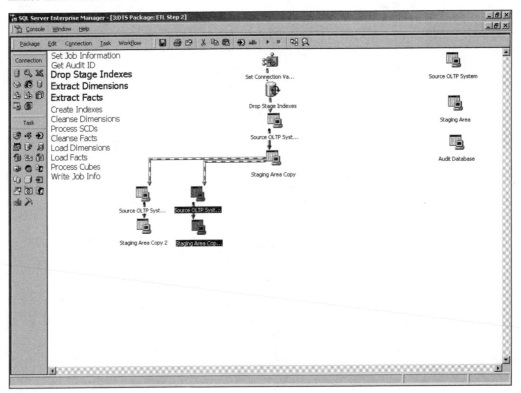

Follow the same steps as above, but set the description property of this task to **Extract Employee Dimension**.

Source

Use the following SQL statement as the source of the query:

```sql
SELECT
    E.EmployeeID, ReportsTo,
    LastName + ', ' + FirstName AS employee_name,
    Title, Address, Country, Region, City, PostalCode,
    HomePhone, BirthDate, HireDate, R.RegionID,
    R.RegionDescription
FROM
    Employees E,
    EmployeeTerritories ET,
    Territories T,
    Region R
WHERE
    E.EmployeeID = ET.EmployeeID AND
    ET.TerritoryID = T.TerritoryID AND
    T.RegionID = R.RegionID
GROUP BY
    E.EmployeeID, ReportsTo, LastName + ', ' + FirstName,
    Title, Address, Country, Region, City, PostalCode,
    HomePhone, BirthDate, HireDate, R.RegionID,
    R.RegionDescription
```

As you can see here, we're sourcing all pertinent employee information at the same time. We want to include territory and region information for each employee.

Destination

Set the destination table to the STAGE_EMPLOYEE table.

Transformation

Once again, we're using a simple copy column transformation. Set the source and destination columns as follows:

Source Column	Destination Column
EmployeeID	employee_nk
ReportsTo	direct_report_nk
employee_name*	employee_name
Title	title
Address	address
Country	country
Region	state_region
City	city
PostalCode	postal_code
HomePhone	phone
BirthDate	birth_date
HireDate	hire_date
RegionID	region_nk
RegionDescription	region_name

*This field is derived in the source query.

Product Dimension

The addition of the Product Dimension Transform Data task and associated tasks and connections, makes ETL 2 look like this:

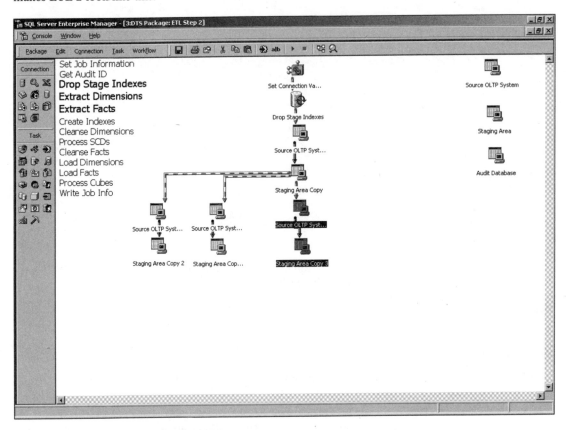

Follow the same steps as above, but set the description property to Extract Product Dimension.

Source

Use the following SQL statement as the source of the query:

```
SELECT
    ProductID, SupplierID, P.CategoryID, CategoryName, ProductName,
    QuantityPerUnit, UnitPrice, UnitsInStock, UnitsOnOrder,
    ReorderLevel, Discontinued
FROM
    Products P LEFT JOIN Categories C ON P.CategoryID = C.CategoryID
```

We're performing a left join here for precautionary reasons. We must make sure we get all products even if they don't have a designated category.

Destination

Set the destination table to STAGE_PRODUCT.

Transformation

Once again, we're using a simple copy column transformation. Set the source and destination columns as follows:

Source Column	Destination Column
ProductID	product_nk
SupplierID	supplier_nk
CategoryID	category_nk
CategoryName	category_name
ProductName	product_name
QuantityPerUnit	quantity_per_unit
UnitPrice	unit_price
UnitsInStock	units_in_stock
UnitsOnOrder	units_on_order
ReorderLevel	reorder_level
Discontinued	discontinued_flag

Supplier Dimension

The addition of the Supplier Dimension Transform Data task and associated tasks and connections, makes ETL 2 look like this:

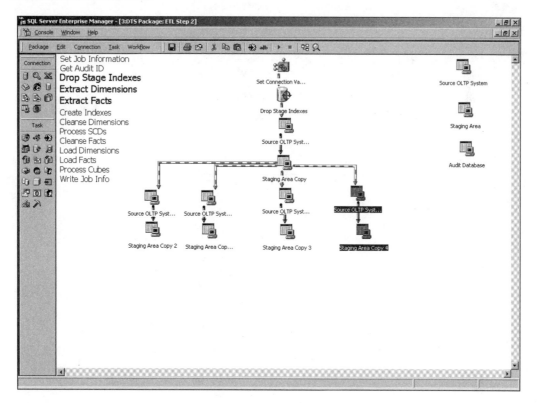

Source

```
SELECT
    SupplierID, CompanyName, ContactName, ContactTitle, Address,
    Country, Region, City, PostalCode, Phone, Fax, HomePage
FROM
    Suppliers
```

Destination

Set the destination table to STAGE_SUPPLIER.

Transformation

Once again, we're using a simple copy column transformation. Set the source and destination columns as follows:

Source Column	Destination Column
SupplierID	supplier_nk
CompanyName	supplier_name
ContactName	contact_name
ContactTitle	contact_title
Address	address
Country	country
Region	state_region
City	city
PostalCode	postal_code
Phone	phone
Fax	fax
HomePage	home_page

Shipper Dimension

The addition of the Shipper Dimension Transform Data task and associated tasks and connections, makes ETL 2 look like this:

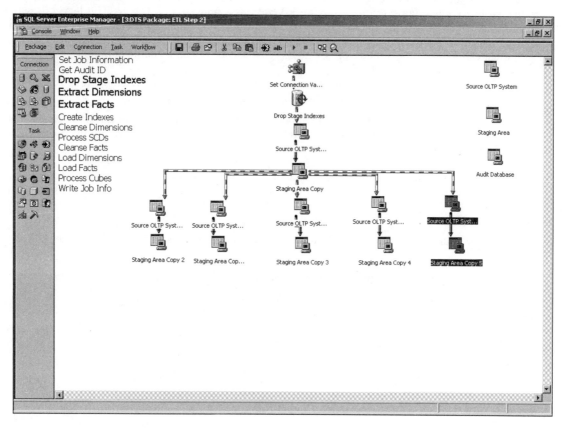

Source

```
SELECT
    ShipperID, CompanyName, Phone
FROM
    Shippers
```

Destination

Set the destination table to STAGE_SHIPPER.

Transformation

Source Column	Destination Column
ShipperID	shipper_nk
CompanyName	shipper_name
Phone	phone

Extracting Fact Information

As with the extraction of dimension information, we have several issues to consider. Fact information must be time stamped so we don't run the risk of duplicating data. The Northwind Company's Order table has three time stamps: Order Date, Required Date, and Shipped Date. This leaves us with the problem of which time stamp to use. However, the Northwind Company's business rules state that the Required Date is input at the same time as the Order Date. We also know that the record is created at the same time the order is input, Order Date. That leaves us with a couple of options.

❑   The first is to extract only orders that have Shipped Dates in the range we're looking for. However, this won't show any orders that have yet to be shipped.

❑   The second is to extract orders when both Order and Shipped Dates are in our range. This means that we'll have to update the fact table with the new Shipped Date if the record already exists. As long as this is the only update, we should be OK.

So the business rule dictates that we'll extract all of the orders that have Order Dates and Shipped Dates that occur during the time period we're looking for. The first step is to extract the information.

Orders

The addition of the Orders Transform Data task and associated tasks and connections makes ETL 2 look like this:

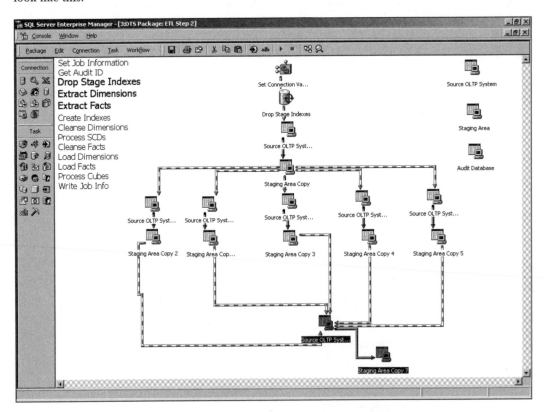

Source

```
SELECT
      O.OrderID, EmployeeID, CustomerID, ShipVia,
      OrderDate, RequiredDate, ShippedDate,
      DATEDIFF(dd, OrderDate, RequiredDate)
            AS lead_time_days,
      DATEDIFF(dd, OrderDate, ShippedDate)
            AS internal_response_time_days,
      DATEDIFF(dd, ShippedDate, RequiredDate)
            AS external_response_time_days,
      Freight,
      SUM(OD.Quantity)
            AS total_order_item_count,
      SUM((OD.Quantity * OD.UnitPrice) -
            ((OD.Quantity * OD.UnitPrice) * OD.Discount))
            AS total_order_dollars,
      SUM((OD.Quantity * OD.UnitPrice) * OD.Discount)
            AS total_order_discount_dollars,
      ShipName, ShipAddress, ShipCity, ShipRegion,
      ShipPostalCode, ShipCountry
FROM
      Orders O INNER JOIN "Order Details" OD
            ON O.OrderID = OD.OrderID
WHERE
      (O.OrderDate BETWEEN ? AND ?) OR
      (O.ShippedDate BETWEEN ? AND ?)
GROUP BY
      O.OrderID, EmployeeID, CustomerID, ShipVia,
      OrderDate, RequiredDate, ShippedDate, Freight,
      ShipName, ShipAddress, ShipCity, ShipRegion,
      ShipPostalCode, ShipCountry""
```

The parameters for this query are:

This query is a bit more complex because we're performing calculations to summarize data at the Order level. We sum the total number of ordered items, the total order amount and the total order discount. Northwind's OLTP system only stores this information at the detail level.

Destination

Set the destination table to STAGE_ORDERS.

Transformation

Source Column	Destination Column
OrderID	order_nk
EmployeeID	employee_nk
CustomerID	customer_nk
ShipVia	shipper_nk
OrderDate	order_date
RequiredDate	required_date
ShippedDate	shipped_date
lead_time_days*	lead_time_days
internal_response_time_days*	internal_response_time_days
external_response_time_days*	external_response_time_days
Freight	freight
total_order_item_count*	total_order_item_count
total_order_dollars*	total_order_dollars
total_order_discount_dollars*	total_order_discount_dollars
ShipCity	city
ShipRegion	state_region
ShipPostalCode	postal_code
ShipCountry	country

*Calculated in source query.

Order Items

The addition of the Order Items Transform Data task and associated tasks and connections, makes ETL 2 look like this:

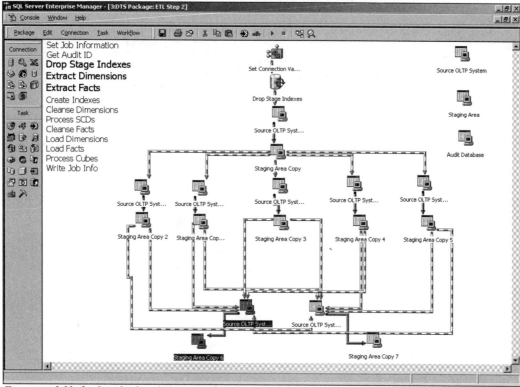

Figure available for download as CH15_03.gif

The business rules also apply here to the order items. We have the same constraints as for the order facts to extract based on the order date and shipped date. However, we must join the Orders and Order Items tables together to extract the details.

Source

```
SELECT
    OD.OrderID, CustomerID, EmployeeID, OrderDate, RequiredDate,
    ShippedDate,
    DATEDIFF(dd, OrderDate, RequiredDate)
        AS lead_time_days,
    DATEDIFF(dd, OrderDate, ShippedDate)
        AS internal_response_time_days,
    DATEDIFF(dd, ShippedDate, RequiredDate)
        AS external_response_time_days,
ShipVia, OD.ProductID, UnitPrice, Quantity, Discount, ShipCountry,
ShipRegion, ShipCity, ShipPostalCode
FROM
    "Order Details" OD FULL OUTER JOIN Orders O
        ON OD.OrderID = O.OrderID
WHERE
    (O.OrderDate BETWEEN ? AND ?) OR
    (O.ShippedDate BETWEEN ? AND ?)
```

The parameters for this query are:

Destination

Set the destination table to STAGE_ORDER_ITEMS.

Transformation

Source Column	Destination Column
OrderID	order_nk
CustomerID	customer_nk
EmployeeID	employee_nk
OrderDate	order_date
RequiredDate	required_date
ShippedDate	shipped_date
lead_time_days*	lead_time_days
internal_response_time_days*	internal_response_time_days
external_response_time_days*	external_response_time_days
ShipVia	shipper_nk
ProductID	product_nk
UnitPrice	unit_price

Source Column	Destination Column
Quantity	quantity
Discount	discount
ShipCountry	Country
ShipRegion	state_region
ShipCity	City
ShipPostalCode	postal_code

*Calculated in source query.

Set Connection Values...Part 2

Earlier in the chapter we created a dynamic configuration task called Set Connection Values. We couldn't properly configure the task until we added the connections we wanted to configure. Now we have to go back and dynamically configure all of the connections to use the global variables for the connection information. We're going to set each copy of the Source OLTP System connection to gsSourceDB_UDL, Staging Area to gsStagingAreaDB_UDL, and Audit Database to gsAuditDB_UDL. Let's configure the first several connections to show you how it's done.

Double-click on the Set Connection Values task and then the Add button. You should see a screen that looks like this:

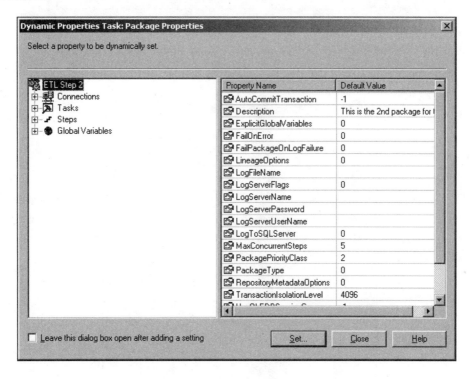

First, check the Leave this dialog box open after adding a setting check box; we're going to be making quite a few changes. Next, in the left-hand window, expand the Connections tree item to see the entire list of connections used by ETL 2. Then click on the Source OLTP System tree item in the left hand pane. You should see a screen that looks like this (your list of connection names may differ slightly):

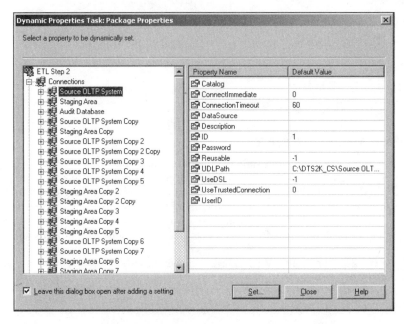

Now select the UDLPath property in the right-hand window and then click on the Set button. When the Add/Edit Assignment dialog opens, change the Source list box to Global Variable, and then choose gsSourceDB_UDL from the Variable combo box.

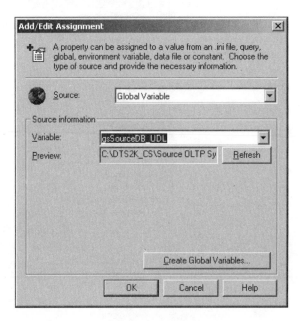

Click on **OK** to save the property assignment and to return to the previous dialog. Now you must repeat this process for all of the connections in the package. However, each copy should be set to its respective global variable (Source OLTP System Copy > gsSourceDB_UDL, Audit Database > gsAuditDB_UDL, and so on...). When you're finished, you should have 19 property assignments, one for each connection used in the package.

Auditing and Error Handling

The last step in creating ETL 2 is to add the auditing and error handling tasks. The same procedures should be followed as were described for ETL 1.

> *Be aware that when you are setting the precedence steps in this package, you must make sure that the audit tasks are referring to the relevant Data Pump tasks in their code. This is done in the same way as previously, only clicking on the transformation arrow to find the relevant information.*

After all is said and done, the end result should look like this:

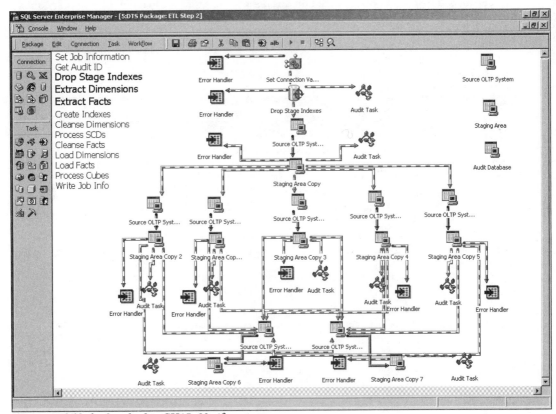

Figure available for download as CH15_02.gif

That's it! The ETL can now extract all of the data necessary to load the Northwind_DW data mart. However, all of the data is sitting the in stage tables waiting to be transformed and loaded.

ETL 3

The third step in the ETL process performs the bulk of the transformation tasks and begins to load the data mart with the dimensions. This package performs the following tasks:

❑   Create the stage table indexes for faster processing

❑   Cleanse and transform the dimension members

❑   Process the slowly changing dimensions

❑   Cleanse the facts

❑   Load the dimension members

Before we can load all of the dimensions, we need to understand some dependencies. We've chosen to snowflake the Geography dimension, which means that this dimension must be cleansed and loaded prior to any other dimension that contains a foreign key reference. These dimensions are Customer, Employee and Supplier. However, Supplier is above the Product dimension in the Product hierarchy, so it must be loaded before `Product`. Based on this design, the order for loading is Geography, then Customer, Shipper, Supplier and Employee, followed by Product. Once the dimensions are processed, the facts will be loaded. As you can see, there's complexity. Without DTS, designing the workflow would be difficult.

Here's ETL 3:

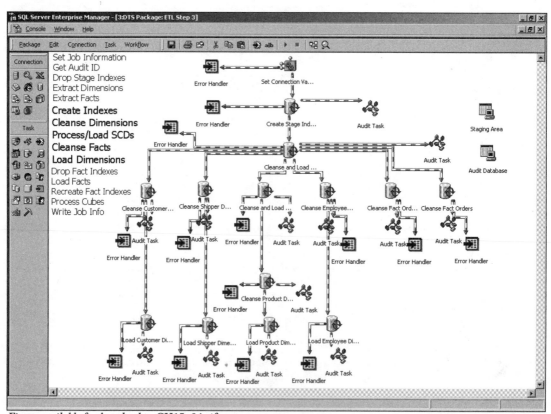

Figure available for download as CH15_04.gif

Once again, this package looks much more complex than it is because of the auditing and error handling. With these removed, the package looks like this:

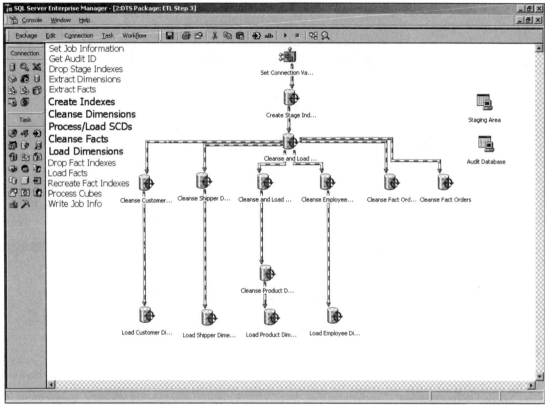

Figure available for download as CH15_05.gif

It's much less complex looking now. We definitely want to include error handling and auditing, but we'll add both once all the other tasks have been created.

Creating the Package

To create the package, open a new package in SQL Server Enterprise Manager. Save the package as a Structured Storage File named ETL Step 3. Now you're ready to start configuration.

Create Stage Indexes

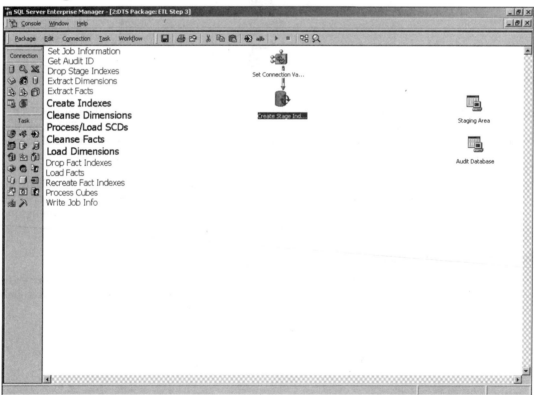

If you remember, we dropped the stage indexes back in ETL 2. We want to recreate them based on the current data so transformation and loading will go much faster. To do this, create a new Execute SQL task and set the **Description** to **Create Stage Indexes**, the **Existing Connection** property to **Staging Area** and the SQL Statement to:

```
CREATE INDEX IDX_STAGE_CUSTOMER ON STAGE_CUSTOMER
(
    customer_nk
)
go

CREATE INDEX IDX_STAGE_CUSTOMER_GEOGRAPHY ON STAGE_CUSTOMER
(
    country,
    state_region,
    city,
    postal_code
)
go

CREATE INDEX IDX_STAGE_EMPLOYEE ON STAGE_EMPLOYEE
(
    employee_nk
)
go

CREATE INDEX IDX_STAGE_EMPLOYEE_GEOGRAPHY ON STAGE_EMPLOYEE
(
    country,
    state_region,
    city,
    postal_code
)
go

CREATE INDEX IDX_STAGE_GEOGRAPHY ON STAGE_GEOGRAPHY
(
    country,
    state_region,
    city,
    postal_code
)
go

CREATE INDEX IDX_STAGE_ORDER_ITEMS ON STAGE_ORDER_ITEMS
(
    order_nk,
    product_nk
)
go
```

```
CREATE INDEX IDX_STAGE_ORDER_ITEMS_GEOGRAPHY ON STAGE_ORDER_ITEMS
(
    country,
    state_region,
    city,
    postal_code
)
go

CREATE INDEX IDX_STAGE_ORDERS ON STAGE_ORDERS
(
    order_nk
)
go

CREATE INDEX IDX_STAGE_ORDERS_GEOGRAPHY ON STAGE_ORDERS
(
    country,
    state_region,
    city,
    postal_code
)
go

CREATE INDEX IDX_STAGE_PRODUCT ON STAGE_PRODUCT
(
    product_nk
)
go

CREATE INDEX IDX_STAGE_SHIPPER ON STAGE_SHIPPER
(
    shipper_nk
)
go

CREATE INDEX IDX_STAGE_SUPPLIER ON STAGE_SUPPLIER
(
    supplier_nk
)
go

CREATE INDEX IDX_STAGE_SUPPLIER_GEOGRAPHY ON STAGE_SUPPLIER
(
    country,
    state_region,
    city,
    postal_code
)
go
```

Remember, we must drop the stage indexes prior to loading the staging tables, and recreate them to help speed dimension lookups and transformation.

Transforming and Loading Dimensions

To simplify the ETL, some dimensions can be transformed and loaded in the same step. Others can be loaded in multiple steps. This choice is up to the designer, but depends on the complexity involved.

All of the tasks that transform and load the dimensions take advantage of the fact that the staging area is in the same database as the data mart. If this is not the case, several different approaches can be used.

❑   If the staging area database resides on the same machine as the data mart, the SQL statements for each of the tasks can be updated to use a different database by fully qualifying the staging area's database, owner, and table in any statements that reference the stage table.

❑   If the staging area database doesn't reside on the same machine as the data mart, the transformations would require separate Transform Data tasks for each step in the process.

Geography

The addition of the `Cleanse and Load Geography Dimension` task makes ETL 3 look like this:

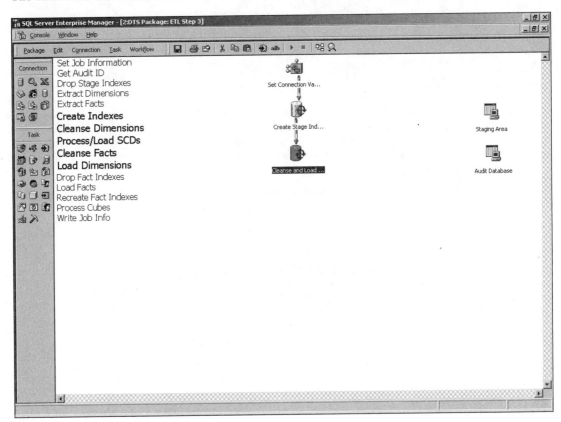

Cleanse and Load Geography Dimension

To transform and load the Geography dimensions, create a new Execute SQL task and set its Description property to Cleanse and Load Geography Dimension, its Existing connection property to Staging Area and its SQL statement to:

```
UPDATE STAGE_GEOGRAPHY SET audit_id = ?

UPDATE
    STAGE_GEOGRAPHY
SET
    record_exists = 'Y'
FROM
    STAGE_GEOGRAPHY S, DIM_GEOGRAPHY D
WHERE
    ISNULL(S.country, '') = ISNULL(D.country, '') AND
    ISNULL(S.state_region, '') = ISNULL(D.state_region, '') AND
    ISNULL(S.city, '') = ISNULL(D.city, '') AND
    ISNULL(S.postal_code, '') = ISNULL(D.postal_code, '')

INSERT INTO DIM_GEOGRAPHY
    (country, state_region, city, postal_code, audit_id)
SELECT
    country, state_region, city, postal_code, audit_id
FROM
    STAGE_GEOGRAPHY
WHERE
    record_exists IS NULL
```

Within the above UPDATE statement, stage records are being compared to dimension records to see if the stage records already exist. However, since some of the stage data's columns are NULL, we must join using the ISNULL statement to ensure the proper result. The action being performed is the setting of the record_exists flag to Y if the record is found in the data mart dimension table; otherwise the column value remains NULL.

The INSERT SQL statement inserts all records into the data mart dimension if they don't have the record_exists flag set.

Before you click OK, select the Parameters button. Set the Input Global Variable for Parameter 1 to giAuditID.

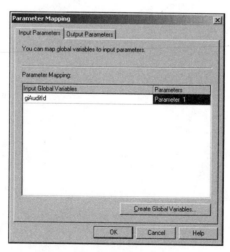

Click on OK to return to the previous dialog and then OK again to save the task's properties.

> All dimension and fact rows should include a reference to their specific audit using the `audit_id` column. This allows an administrator or analyst to track when and which version of an ETL was used to populate the row. This is very effective for identifying data quality issues.

Customers

The additions of the `Cleanse Customer Dimension` and the `Load Customer Dimension` tasks make ETL 3 look like this:

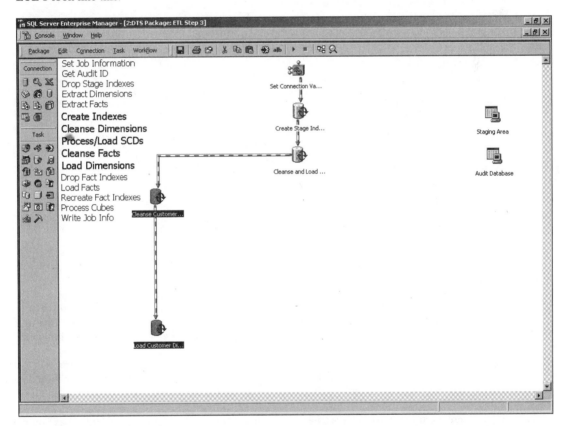

The next dimension we want to process is the Customers dimension. Technically, we're not performing any cleansing in the task, we're just performing the surrogate key lookup and checking to see if the stage record exists in the dimension table. However, this is where cleansing would occur if it was needed.

To configure this task, create a new Execute SQL task and set its Description property to Cleanse Customer Dimension, and its Existing connection property to Staging Area.

Cleanse Customer Dimension

Add the following SQL to the SQL statement text window:

```
UPDATE
    STAGE_CUSTOMER
SET
    audit_id = ?

UPDATE
    STAGE_CUSTOMER
SET
    record_exists = 'Y'
FROM
    STAGE_CUSTOMER S, DIM_CUSTOMER D
WHERE
    S.customer_nk = D.customer_nk

UPDATE
    STAGE_CUSTOMER
SET
    geography_wk = D.geography_wk
FROM
    STAGE_CUSTOMER S, DIM_GEOGRAPHY D
WHERE
    ISNULL(S.country, '') = ISNULL(D.country, '') AND
    ISNULL(S.state_region, '') = ISNULL(D.state_region, '') AND
    ISNULL(S.city, '') = ISNULL(D.city, '') AND
    ISNULL(S.postal_code, '') = ISNULL(D.postal_code, '')

UPDATE
    STAGE_CUSTOMER
SET
    geography_wk = 0
WHERE
    geography_wk IS NULL
```

As with the Geography dimension, we set the `audit_id` and the `record_exists` flag in the first few statements. The second-to-last SQL statement updates the geography warehouse key by looking up the primary key in the Geography dimension. This must happen before the `Customer` dimension can be loaded into the data mart.

The last SQL statement sets the surrogate dimension key for `Geography` to the default if the lookup doesn't find it in the data mart dimension table. This avoids any possibility of foreign key errors during loading.

The SQL statement above uses one parameter as before. Set **parameter 1** to use **giAuditID** as you did in the previous step.

Load Customer Dimension

The next task is another Execute SQL task. It will load the Customer records from the staging area into the data mart if the record doesn't already exist.

To create this task, create a new Execute SQL task and set its Description property to Load Customer Dimension, its Existing connection property to Staging Area, and its SQL statement to the following SQL:

```
INSERT INTO
    DIM_CUSTOMER
    (customer_nk, geography_wk, customer_name, contact_name,
    contact_title, address, phone, fax, audit_id)
SELECT
    customer_nk, geography_wk, customer_name, contact_name,
    contact_title, address, phone, fax, audit_id
FROM
    STAGE_CUSTOMER
WHERE
    record_exists IS NULL
go

UPDATE DIM_CUSTOMER
SET
    customer_nk = S.customer_nk,
    geography_wk = S.geography_wk,
    customer_name = S.customer_name,
    contact_name = S.contact_name,
    contact_title = S.contact_title,
    address = S.address,
    phone = S.phone,
    fax = S.fax,
    audit_id = S.audit_id
FROM
    DIM_CUSTOMER D, STAGE_CUSTOMER S
WHERE
    D.customer_nk = S.customer_nk AND
    S.record_exists = 'Y'
go
```

As you can see, the SQL to load the Customer dimension occurs in two steps: inserting and updating. If the record_exists flag is NULL, we insert; otherwise we update.

That's all there is to loading the Customer dimension. The other dimensions are handled in pretty much the same way.

Shippers Dimension

The additions of the `Cleanse Shipper Dimension` and the `Load Shipper Dimension` tasks make ETL 3 look like this:

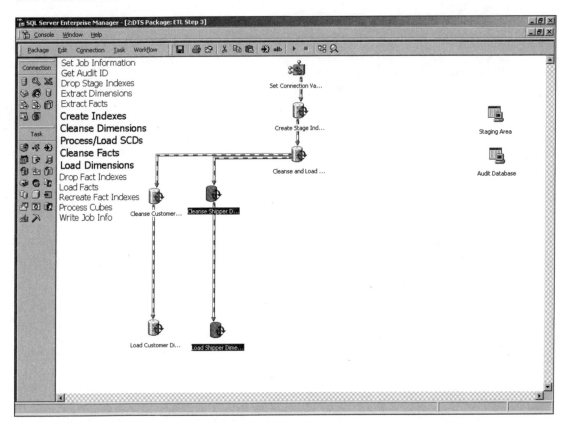

Cleanse Shipper Dimension

Create an Execute SQL task, set its Description property to Cleanse Shipper Dimension, its Existing connection property to Staging Area, and its SQL statement to the following:

```
UPDATE
    STAGE_SHIPPER
SET
    audit_id = ?
UPDATE
    STAGE_SHIPPER
SET
    record_exists = 'Y'
FROM
    STAGE_SHIPPER S, DIM_SHIPPER D
WHERE
    S.shipper_nk = D.shipper_nk
```

As before, remember to configure this query to use `giAuditID` for its parameterized value.

Load Shipper Dimension

Create an Execute SQL task, set its Description property to Load Shipper Dimension, its Existing connection property to Staging Area, and its SQL statement to the following:

```
INSERT INTO
   DIM_SHIPPER
     (shipper_nk, shipper_name, phone, audit_id)
SELECT
   shipper_nk, shipper_name, phone, audit_id
FROM
   STAGE_SHIPPER
WHERE
   record_exists IS NULL
go

UPDATE
   DIM_SHIPPER
SET
   shipper_nk = S.shipper_nk,
   shipper_name = S.shipper_name,
   phone = S.phone,
   audit_id = S.audit_id
FROM
   DIM_SHIPPER D, STAGE_SHIPPER S
WHERE
   D.shipper_nk = S.shipper_nk AND
   S.record_exists = 'Y'
go
```

Suppliers

The addition of the `Cleanse and Load Supplier Dimension` task makes ETL 3 look like this:

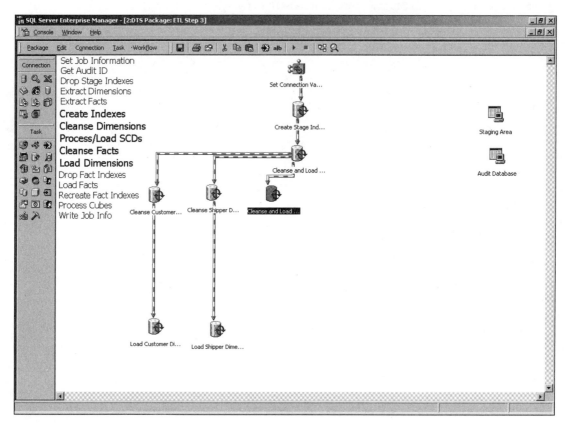

Cleanse and Load Supplier Dimension

The processing and loading for Suppliers occurs in one task, `Cleanse and Load Supplier Dimension`. The subsequent loading of the Product dimension is dependent on the successful loading of the Suppliers.

Create an Execute SQL task, set its Description property to Cleanse and Load Supplier Dimension, its Existing connection property to Staging Area, and its SQL statement to the following:

```
UPDATE
    STAGE_SUPPLIER
SET
    audit_id = ?

UPDATE
    STAGE_SUPPLIER
SET
    record_exists = 'Y'
FROM
    STAGE_SUPPLIER S, DIM_SUPPLIER D
```

```
WHERE
    S.supplier_nk = D.supplier_nk

UPDATE
    STAGE_SUPPLIER
SET
    geography_wk = D.geography_wk
FROM
    STAGE_SUPPLIER S, DIM_GEOGRAPHY D
WHERE
    ISNULL(S.country, '') = ISNULL(D.country, '') AND
    ISNULL(S.state_region, '') = ISNULL(D.state_region, '') AND
    ISNULL(S.city, '') = ISNULL(D.city, '') AND
    ISNULL(S.postal_code, '') = ISNULL(D.postal_code, '')

UPDATE
    STAGE_SUPPLIER
SET
    geography_wk = 0
WHERE
    geography_wk IS NULL

INSERT INTO
    DIM_SUPPLIER
    (supplier_nk, geography_wk, supplier_name, contact_name,
    contact_title, address, phone, fax, home_page, audit_id)
SELECT
    supplier_nk, geography_wk, supplier_name, contact_name,
    contact_title, address, phone, fax, home_page, audit_id
FROM
    STAGE_SUPPLIER
WHERE
    record_exists IS NULL

UPDATE
    DIM_SUPPLIER
SET
    geography_wk = S.geography_wk,
    supplier_name = S.supplier_name,
    contact_name = S.contact_name,
    contact_title = S.contact_title,
    address = S.address,
    phone = S.phone,
    fax = S.fax,
    home_page = S.home_page,
    audit_id = S.audit_id
FROM
    DIM_SUPPLIER D, STAGE_SUPPLIER S
WHERE
    D.supplier_nk = S.supplier_nk AND
    S.record_exists = 'Y'
```

As before, remember to configure this query to use `giAuditID` for its parameterized value.

Products

The addition of the `Cleanse Product Dimension` and the `Load Product Dimension` tasks make ETL 3 look like this:

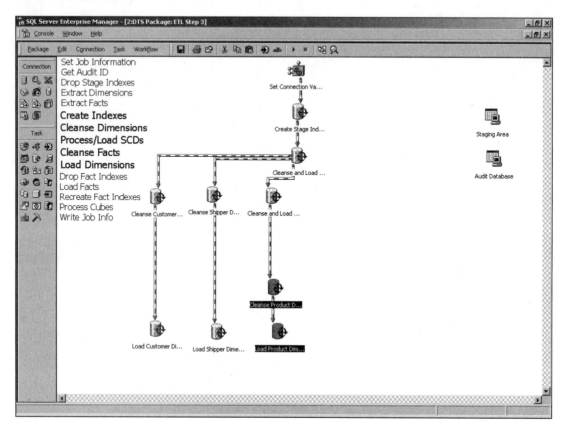

Also notice that cleansing and loading of the Product dimension requires that the Supplier dimension processing be complete. To have the ability to build this dependency graphically is what make DTS such an ideal tool for developing these types of workflows.

Cleanse Product Dimension

Since the loading of this dimension is dependent on the Suppliers dimension, it must occur after the Suppliers dimension has been successfully loaded.

Create an Execute SQL task, set its **Description** property to **Cleanse Product Dimension**, its **Existing connection** property to **Staging Area**, and its SQL statement to the following:

```
UPDATE
    STAGE_PRODUCT
SET
    audit_id = ?
```

```
UPDATE
    STAGE_PRODUCT
SET
    supplier_wk = D.supplier_wk
FROM
    STAGE_PRODUCT S, DIM_SUPPLIER D
WHERE
    S.supplier_nk = D.supplier_nk

UPDATE
    STAGE_PRODUCT
SET
    record_exists = 'Y'
FROM
    STAGE_PRODUCT S, DIM_PRODUCT D
WHERE
    S.product_nk = D.product_nk
```

As before, remember to configure this query to use `giAuditID` for its parameterized value.

Load Product Dimension

Here's the SQL:

```
INSERT INTO
    DIM_PRODUCT
    (product_nk, supplier_wk, product_name, category_nk,
    category_name, quantity_per_unit, unit_price, units_in_stock,
    units_on_order, reorder_level, discontinued_flag, audit_id)
SELECT
    product_nk, supplier_wk, product_name, category_nk,
    category_name, quantity_per_unit, unit_price, units_in_stock,
    units_on_order, reorder_level,

    CASE
        WHEN discontinued_flag = 0
        THEN 'Current'
        ELSE 'Discontinued'
    END,
    audit_id
FROM
    STAGE_PRODUCT
WHERE
    record_exists IS NULL

UPDATE
    DIM_PRODUCT
SET
    product_nk = S.product_nk,
    supplier_wk = S.supplier_wk,
    product_name = S.product_name,
    category_nk = S.category_nk,
    category_name = S.category_name,
    quantity_per_unit = S.quantity_per_unit,
    unit_price = S.unit_price,
```

643

```
    units_in_stock = S.units_in_stock,
    units_on_order = S.units_on_order,
    reorder_level = S.reorder_level,
    discontinued_flag = S.discontinued_flag,
    audit_id = S.audit_id
FROM
    DIM_PRODUCT D, STAGE_PRODUCT S
WHERE
    D.product_nk = S.product_nk AND
    S.record_exists = 'Y'
go
```

Notice the first SQL statement is using a CASE statement to transform a source system code, discontinued_flag, from its original value to an English description.

Employees

The addition of the Cleanse Employee Dimension and Load Employee Dimension tasks makes ETL 3 look like this:

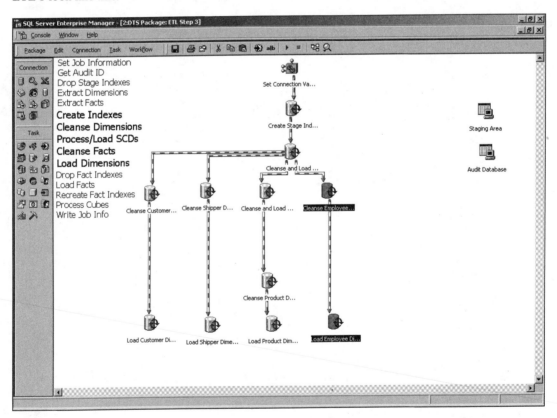

Cleanse Employee Dimension

Create an Execute SQL task, set its Description property to Cleanse Employee Dimension, its Existing connection property to Staging Area, and its SQL statement to the following:

```
UPDATE
    STAGE_EMPLOYEE
SET
    audit_id = ?

UPDATE
    STAGE_EMPLOYEE
SET
    record_exists = 'Y'
FROM
    STAGE_EMPLOYEE S, DIM_EMPLOYEE D
WHERE
    S.employee_nk = D.employee_nk

UPDATE
    STAGE_EMPLOYEE
SET
    geography_wk = D.geography_wk
FROM
    STAGE_EMPLOYEE S, DIM_GEOGRAPHY D
WHERE
    ISNULL(S.country, '') = ISNULL(D.country, '') AND
    ISNULL(S.state_region, '') = ISNULL(D.state_region, '') AND
    ISNULL(S.city, '') = ISNULL(D.city, '') AND
    ISNULL(S.postal_code, '') = ISNULL(D.postal_code, '')
```

Load Employee Dimension

Create an Execute SQL task, set its Description property to Load Employee Dimension, its Existing connection property to Staging Area, and its SQL statement to the following:

```
INSERT INTO
    DIM_EMPLOYEE
    (employee_nk, geography_wk, direct_report_wk, direct_report_nk,
    employee_name, title, address, phone, birth_date, hire_date,
    region_nk, region_name, audit_id)
SELECT
    employee_nk, geography_wk, 0, direct_report_nk,
    employee_name, title, address, phone,
    birth_date, hire_date, region_nk, region_name,
    audit_id
FROM
    STAGE_EMPLOYEE
WHERE
    record_exists IS NULL

UPDATE
    DIM_EMPLOYEE
SET
    direct_report_wk = A.employee_wk
FROM
    (SELECT employee_wk, employee_nk FROM DIM_EMPLOYEE) A
```

```
WHERE
    direct_report_nk = A.employee_nk AND
    audit_id = ?


UPDATE
    DIM_EMPLOYEE
SET
    employee_nk = S.employee_nk,
    geography_wk = S.geography_wk,
    direct_report_wk =
        ISNULL((SELECT employee_wk FROM DIM_EMPLOYEE WHERE
        employee_nk = S.direct_report_nk), 0),

    direct_report_nk = S.direct_report_nk,
    employee_name = S.employee_name,
    title = S.title,
    address = S.address,
    phone = S.phone,
    birth_date = S.birth_date,
    hire_date = S.hire_date,
    region_nk = S.region_nk,
    region_name = S.region_name,
    audit_id = S.audit_id
FROM
    DIM_EMPLOYEE D, STAGE_EMPLOYEE S
WHERE
    D.employee_nk = S.employee_nk AND
    S.record_exists = 'Y'
```

The `Employee` dimension is affectionately known as a "fish-hook" dimension. This just means that it's modeled with a self-referencing foreign key. This convention allows hierarchical relationships to be defined in a relational model. Each employee record contains a foreign key back to the `Employee` table that represents the employee's direct report.

Due to this interesting twist, the SQL to load the `Employee` dimension becomes more complex by including several sub-selects to lookup the direct report. For the new records, we use two separate statements to insert the records and then update direct report.

That's it for the dimensions. They're completely cleansed, loaded and ready for prime time. All that's left are the facts – just the facts.

Fact Cleansing

In some ETLs, fact cleansing requires a lot of processing because of the sheer number of rows. Many fact tables require processing because of non-numeric values in numeric columns, numeric columns that fall outside the bounds of normal or expected values, or because they require extensive pre-calculation. Thankfully, the Northwind Company's OLTP system doesn't require much in the way of cleansing for its facts.

Orders

The addition of the Orders task makes ETL 3 look like this:

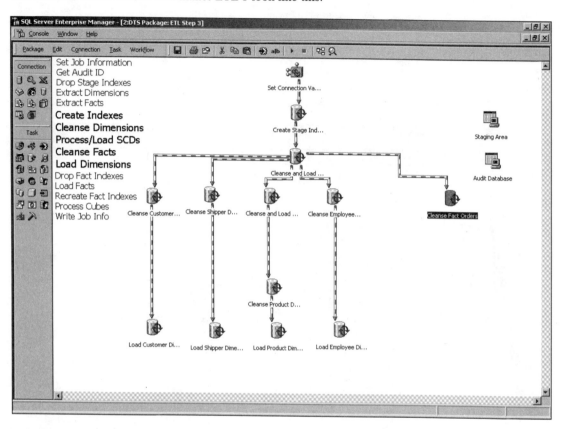

Cleanse Fact Orders

Create an Execute SQL task, set its Description property to Cleanse Fact Orders, its Existing connection property to Staging Area, and its SQL statement to the following:

```
UPDATE
    STAGE_ORDERS
SET
    audit_id = ?

UPDATE
    STAGE_ORDERS
SET
    record_exists = 'Y'
FROM
    STAGE_ORDERS S, FACT_ORDERS F
WHERE
    S.order_nk = F.order_nk
UPDATE
    STAGE_ORDERS
SET
    geography_wk = D.geography_wk
```

```
FROM
    STAGE_ORDERS S, DIM_GEOGRAPHY D
WHERE
    ISNULL(S.country, '') = ISNULL(D.country, '') AND
    ISNULL(S.state_region, '') = ISNULL(D.state_region, '') AND
    ISNULL(S.city, '') = ISNULL(D.city, '') AND
    ISNULL(S.postal_code, '') = ISNULL(D.postal_code, '')
```

Order Items

The addition of the Order Items task makes ETL 3 look like this:

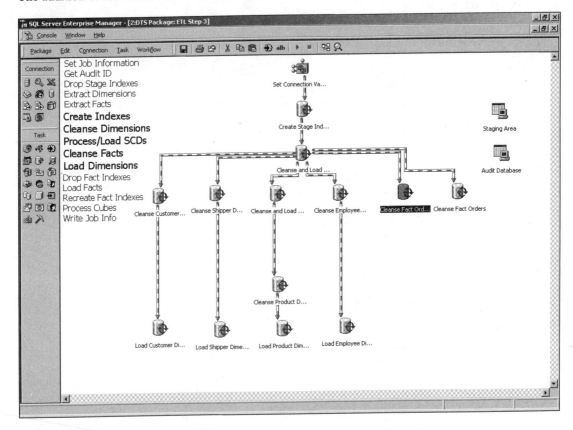

Cleanse Fact Order_Items

Create an Execute SQL task, set its Description property to Cleanse Fact Order_Items, its Existing connection property to Staging Area, and its SQL statement to the following:

```
UPDATE
    STAGE_ORDER_ITEMS
SET
    audit_id = ?

UPDATE
    STAGE_ORDER_ITEMS
```

```
SET
    record_exists = 'Y'
FROM
    STAGE_ORDER_ITEMS S, FACT_ORDER_ITEMS F
WHERE
    S.order_nk = F.order_nk AND
    S.product_nk = F.product_nk

UPDATE
    STAGE_ORDER_ITEMS
SET
    geography_wk = D.geography_wk
FROM
    STAGE_ORDER_ITEMS S, DIM_GEOGRAPHY D
WHERE
    ISNULL(S.country, '') = ISNULL(D.country, '') AND
    ISNULL(S.state_region, '') = ISNULL(D.state_region, '') AND
    ISNULL(S.city, '') = ISNULL(D.city, '') AND
    ISNULL(S.postal_code, '') = ISNULL(D.postal_code, '')
```

At this point, your package should look like this:

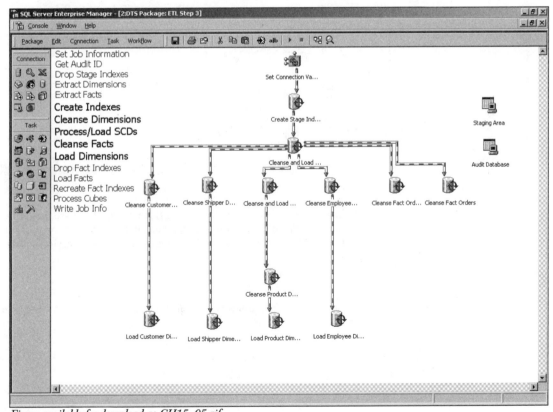

Figure available for download as CH15_05.gif

Auditing and Error Handling

The last step in configuring ETL 3 is to add the auditing and error handling tasks. The same procedures should be followed as were described for ETL 1 and ETL 2. After adding auditing and error handling, ETL 3 should look like this:

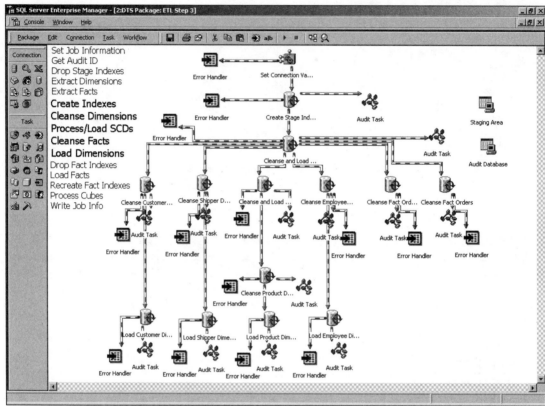

Figure available for download as CH15_04.gif

At this point, we've created the ETL that can extract data from the source `Northwind` database into our `Northwind_DW` staging area, cleanse and transform dimension and fact data, and load dimension data into the data mart. All that's left is the loading of the fact tables and the building of the Analysis Services cubes.

ETL 4

The fourth and final step in the ETL process has just a few responsibilities, but it's definitely the cleanup hitter of the group. It has the following responsibilities:

❑   Load the fact tables

❑   Create indexes that were dropped

❑   Process Analysis Services cubes

Here's ETL 4:

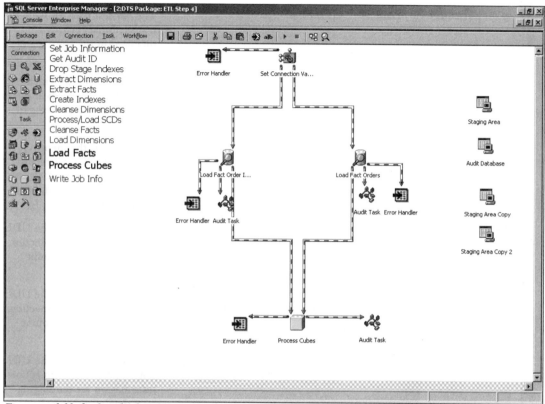

Figure available for download as CH15_06.gif

Creating the Package

To create the package, open a new package in SQL Server Enterprise Manager. Save the package as a Structured Storage File named ETL Step 4. Now you're ready to start configuration.

Package Properties

Only two primary tasks will be occurring in parallel. No modification of package properties is necessary.

Global Variables

ETL 4 does not add any new global variables. It uses only the variables passed from ETL 1. However, for configuration purposes, create the following global variables so that subsequent tasks can be properly configured.

Load Fact Orders

The addition of the Load Fact Orders task makes ETL 4 look like this:

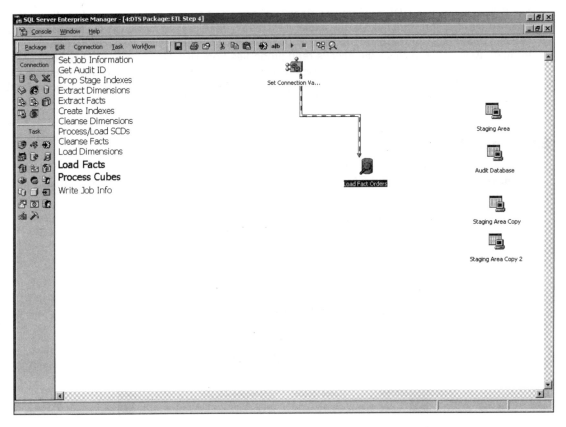

To create this task, add a Data Driven Query to the package and set its Description to Load Fact Orders. Set the Connection property to Staging Area.

Source

Set the Table/View selection on the Source tab to "Northwind_DW"."dbo"."STAGE_ORDERS".

Bindings

Click on the Bindings tab, choose Staging Area Copy in the Connection combo box and choose "Northwind_DW"."dbo"."FACT_ORDERS" in the Table Name combo box.

Transformation

Now click on the Transformations tab. The transformation for Load Fact Orders uses an ActiveX script, rather than the standard copy column transformation, because the script adds an extra level of control. This additional control is needed because we are using DTS lookups to resolve foreign key references. However, if the foreign key is not returned from the lookup, the default value, 0, is used in all cases.

To create this script, click the Delete All button, and then click the New button. Choose ActiveX Script as the new transformation type and click OK.

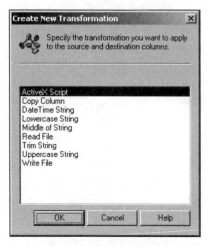

This brings you to the Transformation Options dialog. Click on the Source Columns tab and set the Selected Columns as shown below (don't worry about getting the column names in the exact order).

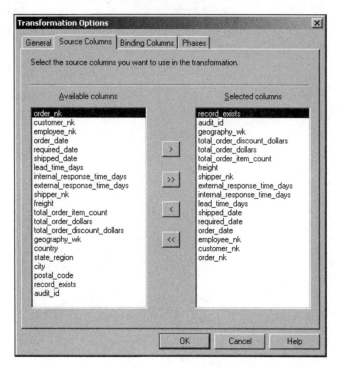

Now select the Binding Columns tab and configure the Selected columns as shown below:

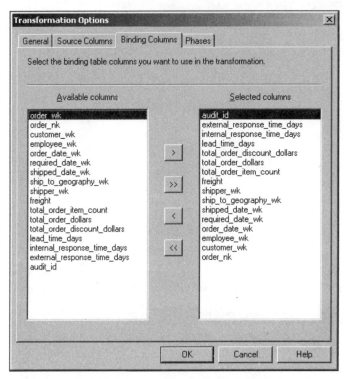

Now that you've specified which columns we're using, let's add the ActiveX Script. We're going to use VBScript as the scripting language of choice. To add this code, click on the General tab and select the Properties button:

```
'***********************************************************************
'  Visual Basic Transformation Script
'***********************************************************************

'  Copy each source column to the destination column
Function Main()

    DTSDestination("order_nk") = DTSSource("order_nk")
    DTSDestination("customer_wk") = IsNullDefault( _
        DTSLookups("customer_wk").Execute( _
        DTSSource("customer_nk")), 0)

    DTSDestination("employee_wk") = IsNullDefault( _
        DTSLookups("employee_wk").Execute( _
        DTSSource("employee_nk")), 0)

    DTSDestination("order_date_wk") = IsNullDefault( _
        DTSLookups("x_date_wk").Execute( _
        DTSSource("order_date")), 0)
```

```
     DTSDestination("required_date_wk") = IsNullDefault( _
        DTSLookups("x_date_wk").Execute( _
        DTSSource("required_date")), 0)

     DTSDestination("shipped_date_wk") = IsNullDefault( _
        DTSLookups("x_date_wk").Execute( _
        DTSSource("shipped_date")), 0)

     DTSDestination("ship_to_geography_wk") = DTSSource("geography_wk")

     DTSDestination("shipper_wk") = IsNullDefault( _
        DTSLookups("shipper_wk").Execute( _
        DTSSource("shipper_nk")), 0)

     DTSDestination("freight") = DTSSource("freight")
     DTSDestination("total_order_item_count") = _
        DTSSource("total_order_item_count")
     DTSDestination("total_order_dollars") = _
        DTSSource("total_order_dollars")
     DTSDestination("total_order_discount_dollars") = _
        DTSSource("total_order_discount_dollars")
     DTSDestination("lead_time_days") = DTSSource("lead_time_days")
     DTSDestination("internal_response_time_days") = _
        DTSSource("internal_response_time_days")
     DTSDestination("external_response_time_days") = _
        DTSSource("external_response_time_days")
     DTSDestination("audit_id") = DTSSource("audit_id")

     If DTSSource("record_exists") = "Y" Then
        Main = DTSTransformstat_UpdateQuery
     Else
        Main = DTSTransformstat_InsertQuery
     End If
End Function

Function IsNullDefault(vValue, vDefault)
     If IsNull(vValue) or IsEmpty(vValue) Then
        IsNullDefault = vDefault
     Else
        IsNullDefault = vValue
     End If
End Function
```

The code above is very straightforward; it defines column assignments to be used in the Data Driven Query.

There is an included function called IsNullDefault. This function serves two purposes. First, it replaces the functionality of the conditional if statement (IIF), which isn't supported in this version of VBScript. Second, it checks for both Null or Empty values. The script is also using several DTSLookups. These will be explained shortly.

Now click on OK to save the changes in the code window and click OK again from the Transformation Options dialog.

This will return you to the **Properties** dialog:

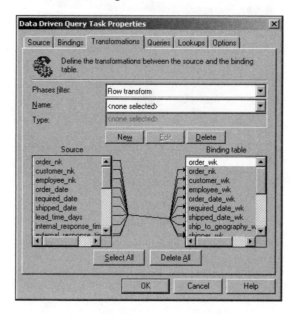

Queries

Now select the **Queries** tab. Make sure that **Query type** is set to **Insert** and insert the following SQL into the Query window:

```
INSERT INTO FACT_ORDERS
    (order_nk, customer_wk, employee_wk, order_date_wk,
    required_date_wk, shipped_date_wk, ship_to_geography_wk,
    shipper_wk, freight, total_order_item_count, total_order_dollars,
    total_order_discount_dollars, lead_time_days,
    internal_response_time_days, external_response_time_days,
    audit_id)
VALUES
    (?, ?, ?, ?, ?, ?, ?, ?, ?, ?, ?, ?, ?, ?, ?, ?)
```

so that the dialog looks like this:

Now click on the **Parse/Show Parameters** button so the SQL statement will be parsed but also so it will show the parameters that are to be used. If the SQL statement parses properly, you will receive confirmation of the fact. You now must change the parameter settings to the following:

Destination	Parameter
order_nk	Parameter 1
customer_wk	Parameter 2
employee_wk	Parameter 3
order_date_wk	Parameter 4
required_date_wk	Parameter 5
shipped_date_wk	Parameter 6
ship_to_geography_wk	Parameter 7
shipper_wk	Parameter 8
Freight	Parameter 9
total_order_item_count	Parameter 10
total_order_dollars	Parameter 11
total_order_discount_dollars	Parameter 12
Lead_time_days	Parameter 13
internal_response_time_days	Parameter 14
external_response_time_days	Parameter 15
audit_id	Parameter 16

Now, change the **Query type** to **Update** and insert the following SQL into the query window:

```
UPDATE
    FACT_ORDERS
SET
    customer_wk = ?,
    employee_wk = ?,
    order_date_wk = ?,
    required_date_wk = ?,
    shipped_date_wk = ?,
    ship_to_geography_wk = ?,
    shipper_wk = ?,
    freight = ?,
    total_order_item_count = ?,
    total_order_dollars = ?,
    total_order_discount_dollars = ?,
    lead_time_days = ?,
    internal_response_time_days = ?,
    external_response_time_days = ?,
    audit_id = ?
WHERE order_nk = ?
```

so that the dialog looks like this:

Once again, click the **Parse/Show Parameters** button. Now set the parameters for the Update query to the following:

Destination	Parameter
customer_wk	Parameter 1
employee_wk	Parameter 2
order_date_wk	Parameter 3
required_date_wk	Parameter 4
shipped_date_wk	Parameter 5
ship_to_geography_wk	Parameter 6
shipper_wk	Parameter 7
freight	Parameter 8
total_order_item_count	Parameter 9
total_order_dollars	Parameter 10
total_order_discount_dollars	Parameter 11
lead_time_days	Parameter 12
internal_response_time_days	Parameter 13
external_response_time_days	Parameter 14
audit_id	Parameter 15
order_nk	Parameter 16

Lookups

Now click on the **Lookups** tab. We've got to create the lookup queries that the ActiveX Script transformation was using for several column transformations.

You'll want to create four lookups as shown in the table below:

Lookup Name	Connection	Cache	SQL Query
customer_wk	Staging Area Copy 2	100	SELECT customer_wk FROM DIM_CUSTOMER WHERE (customer_nk = ?)
employee_wk	Staging Area Copy 2	10	SELECT employee_wk FROM DIM_EMPLOYEE WHERE (employee_nk = ?)

Table continued on following page

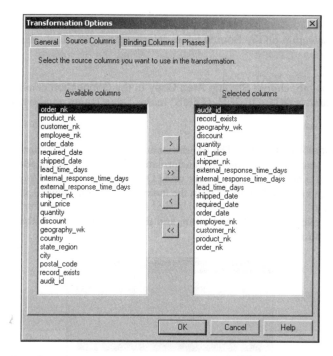

Now select the Binding Columns tab and configure the Selected columns as shown below:

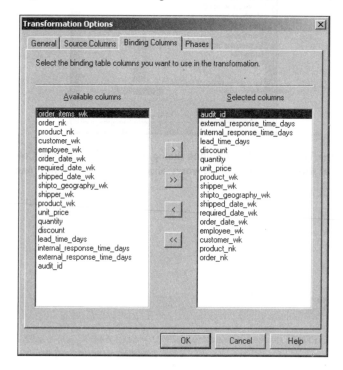

This task is using VBScript for its transformation as well. To add this code to the task, click on the **General** tab and select the **Properties** button:

```
'**********************************************************************
'  Visual Basic Transformation Script
'**********************************************************************

'  Copy each source column to the destination column
Function Main()
    DTSDestination("order_nk") = DTSSource("order_nk")
    DTSDestination("product_nk") = DTSSource("product_nk")

    DTSDestination("customer_wk") = IsNullDefault( _
        DTSLookups("customer_wk").Execute( _
        DTSSource("customer_nk")), 0)

    DTSDestination("employee_wk") = IsNullDefault( _
        DTSLookups("employee_wk").Execute( _
        DTSSource("employee_nk")), 0)

    DTSDestination("order_date_wk") = IsNullDefault( _
        DTSLookups("x_date_wk").Execute( _
        DTSSource("order_date")), 0)

    DTSDestination("required_date_wk") = IsNullDefault( _
        DTSLookups("x_date_wk").Execute( _
        DTSSource("required_date")), 0)

    DTSDestination("shipped_date_wk") = IsNullDefault( _
        DTSLookups("x_date_wk").Execute( _
        DTSSource("shipped_date")), 0)

    DTSDestination("shipto_geography_wk") = DTSSource("geography_wk")

    DTSDestination("shipper_wk") = IsNullDefault( _
        DTSLookups("shipper_wk").Execute( _
        DTSSource("shipper_nk")), 0)

    DTSDestination("product_wk") = IsNullDefault( _
        DTSLookups("product_wk").Execute( _
        DTSSource("product_nk")), 0)

    DTSDestination("unit_price") = DTSSource("unit_price")
    DTSDestination("quantity") = DTSSource("quantity")
    DTSDestination("discount") = DTSSource("discount")
    DTSDestination("lead_time_days") = DTSSource("lead_time_days")
    DTSDestination("internal_response_time_days") = _
        DTSSource("internal_response_time_days")
    DTSDestination("external_response_time_days") = _
        DTSSource("external_response_time_days")
    DTSDestination("audit_id") = DTSSource("audit_id")

    If DTSSource("record_exists") = "Y" Then
        Main = DTSTransformstat_UpdateQuery
    Else
```

```
      Main = DTSTransformstat_InsertQuery
   End If

End Function

Function IsNullDefault(vValue, vDefault)
   If IsNull(vValue) or IsEmpty(vValue) Then
      IsNullDefault = vDefault
   Else
      IsNullDefault = vValue
   End If
End Function
```

As you can see, this code is very similar to the code used to transform the Orders fact table. Let's move on by clicking OK in the code window and clicking OK again in the Transformation Options dialog.

Queries

Now select the Queries tab. Make sure that Query type is set to Insert and insert the following SQL into the Query window:

```
INSERT INTO FACT_ORDER_ITEMS
    (order_nk, product_nk, customer_wk, employee_wk, order_date_wk,
    required_date_wk, shipped_date_wk, shipto_geography_wk,
    shipper_wk, product_wk, unit_price, quantity, discount,
    lead_time_days, internal_response_time_days,
    external_response_time_days, audit_id)
VALUES
    (?, ?, ?, ?, ?, ?, ?, ?, ?, ?, ?, ?, ?, ?, ?, ?, ?)
```

so that the dialog looks like this:

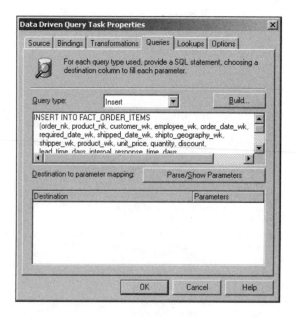

Now click on the **Parse/Show Parameters** button so the SQL statement will be parsed but also so it will show the parameters that are to be used. If the SQL statement parses properly, you will receive confirmation of the fact. You now must change the parameter settings to the following:

Destination	Parameter
order_nk	Parameter 1
product_nk	Parameter 2
customer_wk	Parameter 3
employee_wk	Parameter 4
order_date_wk	Parameter 5
required_date_wk	Parameter 6
shipped_date_wk	Parameter 7
shipto_geography_wk	Parameter 8
shipper_wk	Parameter 9
product_wk	Parameter 10
unit_price	Parameter 11
quantity	Parameter 12
discount	Parameter 13
lead_time_days	Parameter 14
internal_response_time_days	Parameter 15
external_response_time_days	Parameter 16
audit_id	Parameter 17

Now, change the **Query type** to **Update** and insert the following SQL into the query window:

```
UPDATE
    FACT_ORDER_ITEMS
SET
    customer_wk = ?,
    employee_wk = ?,
    order_date_wk = ?,
    required_date_wk = ?,
    shipped_date_wk = ?,
    shipto_geography_wk = ?,
    shipper_wk = ?,
    product_wk = ?,
    unit_price = ?,
    quantity = ?,
    discount = ?,
    lead_time_days = ?,
    internal_response_time_days = ?,
    external_response_time_days = ?,
    audit_id = ?
WHERE order_nk = ? AND product_nk = ?
```

so that the dialog looks like this:

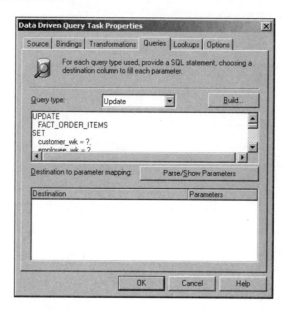

Once again, click the **Parse/Show Parameters** button. Now set the parameters for the Update query to the following:

Destination	Parameter
customer_wk	Parameter 1
employee_wk	Parameter 2
order_date_wk	Parameter 3
required_date_wk	Parameter 4
shipped_date_wk	Parameter 5
shipto_geography_wk	Parameter 6
shipper_wk	Parameter 7
product_wk	Parameter 8
unit_price	Parameter 9
quantity	Parameter 10
discount	Parameter 11
lead_time_days	Parameter 12
internal_response_time_days	Parameter 13
external_response_time_days	Parameter 14
audit_id	Parameter 15
order_nk	Parameter 16
product_nk	Parameter 17

Lookups

Now click on the **Lookups** tab. As we did for `Load Fact Order Items` a few pages ago, we've got to create the lookup queries that the ActiveX Script transformation was using for several column transformations.

You'll want to create five lookups as shown in the table below:

Lookup Name	Connection	Cache	SQL Query
customer_wk	Staging Area Copy 2	100	SELECT customer_wk FROM DIM_CUSTOMER WHERE (customer_nk = ?)
employee_wk	Staging Area Copy 2	10	SELECT employee_wk FROM DIM_EMPLOYEE WHERE (employee_nk = ?)
x_date_wk	Staging Area Copy 2	100	SELECT calendar_wk FROM DIM_CALENDAR WHERE (calendar_nk = ?)
shipper_wk	Staging Area Copy 2	5	SELECT shipper_wk FROM DIM_SHIPPER WHERE (shipper_nk = ?)
product_wk	Staging Area Copy 2	100	SELECT product_wk FROM DIM_PRODUCT WHERE (product_nk = ?)

Now click on OK.

Process Cubes

If you restored the NorthwindDW Analysis Services database as discussed earlier in the chapter, you can now configure the ETL so that processing of the database will occur after successful loading of the relational datamart. If you choose not to include the Analysis Services portion of the ETL, you can disregard this step and continue with the configuration. After adding this task, ETL 4 should look like this:

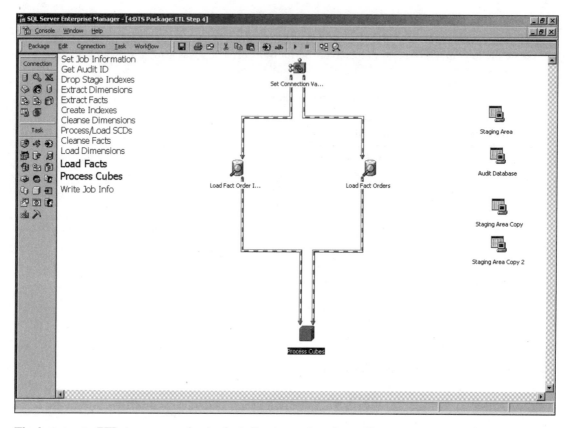

The last step in ETL 4 processes the Analysis Services cubes that will answer our original business questions. These analytics will help the Northwind Company become more efficient and (hopefully) improve sales.

Since we might be changing fact data by updating the Shipped Date, we really need to reprocess the entire multidimensional database each time the data mart is loaded. This way, both the dimensions and facts are processed in one step. This will take a bit longer, but it will ensure data consistency between the OLAP cubes and the relational data mart.

To configure this task, add an Analysis Services Processing Task to ETL 4. Double-click on the task to change its properties. Set the Description property to Process Cubes. Here are the settings:

Auditing and Error Handling

The last step in configuring ETL 4 is to add the auditing and error handling tasks. The same procedures should be followed as were described for ETL 1, ETL 2, and ETL 3. After adding auditing and error handling, ETL 4 should look like this:

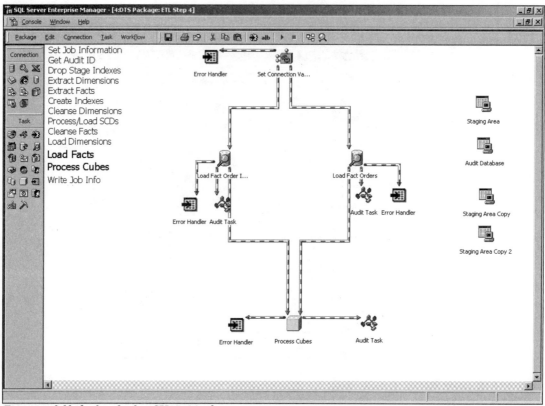

Figure available for download as CH15_06.gif

Once ETL 4 finishes executing, control is passed back to ETL 1, which writes the completion info to the AUDIT_JOB table and then ends.

ETL 1 Revisited

You might remember that we still have a couple of outstanding issues to take care of in ETL 1. We created three Execute Package tasks that we didn't do anything with. We now have to set these tasks to reference the packages we've just created. To do this, open ETL 1 and configure each task to point to its respective structured storage DTS file. Set Call ETL Step 2 to the ETL Step 2 DTS package, Call ETL Step 3 to the ETL Step 3 DTS package and Call ETL Step 4 to the ETL Step 4 DTS package.

Also, set the Outer Package Parameters for each task using the following configuration:

> The initial release of SQL Server 2000 ignores the actual returned result of the
> execution of a package and continues with the Success workflow execution. This
> means that even if ETL 2 fails, ETL 3 will still execute. This will hopefully be resolved
> in a future service pack.

Now you're ready to execute the ETL. Go ahead and run the package. If the ETL is successful, we can
continue with the last few steps.

Answering Northwind's Business Questions

At the beginning of the chapter, we listed several business questions that would help the Northwind
Company learn more about itself so processes can be improved and revenue can be increased. Using Excel
2000 and Analysis Services, we'll answer a few of these. First, let's discuss the Analysis Services database.

Northwind Analysis Services Database

Shared Dimensions

The following shared dimensions were created to support analysis:

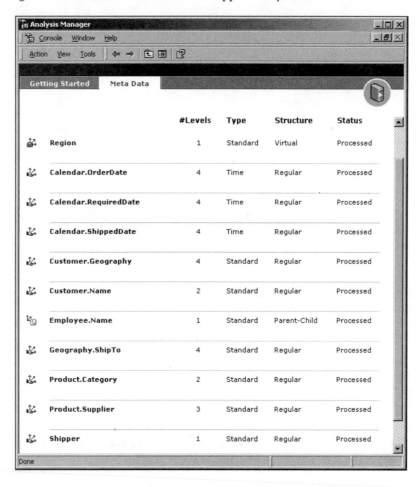

Orders Cube

The Orders cube is defined so:

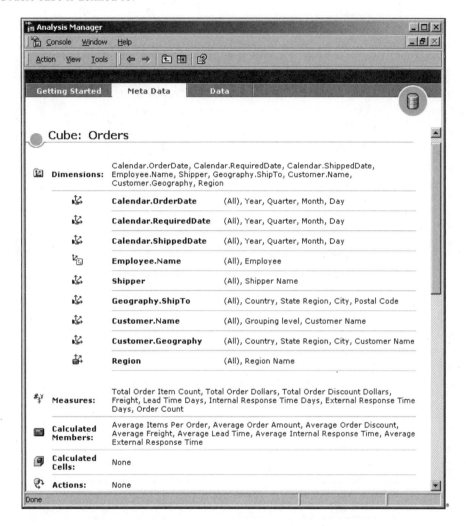

Order Items Cube

The Order Items Cube is defined as follows:

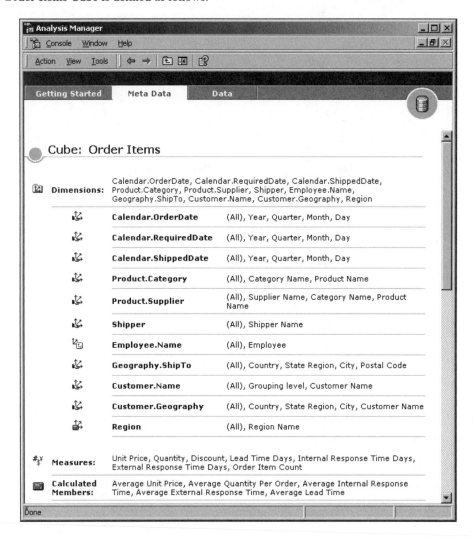

Analytical Questions

To answer the original analytical questions, we're going to use Excel 2000's Pivot Table Service and Analysis Services. We've got to configure Excel to connect to the Analysis Services database. To do this, open a new worksheet in Excel 2000. Choose PivotTable and PivotChart Report from the Data menu.

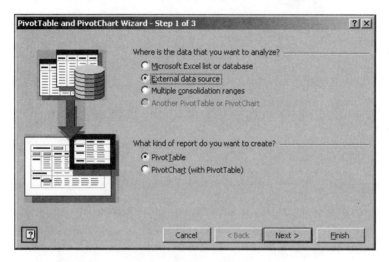

Choose External Data Source and click on Next.

Click on Get Data.

Click on the OLAP Cubes tab of the Choose Data Source dialog and choose <New Data Source> from the list of OLAP Cube sources. Click OK.

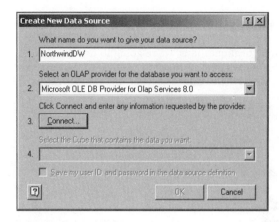

Name the new datasource, NorthwindDW and choose the Microsoft OLE DB Provider for Olap Services 8.0 provider. Click on Connect.

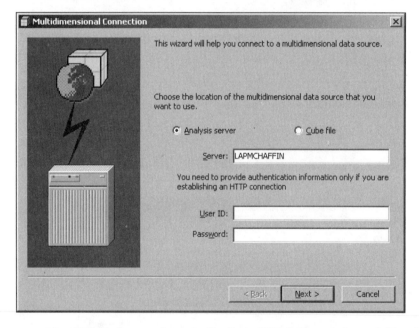

Enter the name of the Analysis Server where the NorthwindDW database is located. You do not need to complete the User ID or Password sections of this dialog. Click on Next.

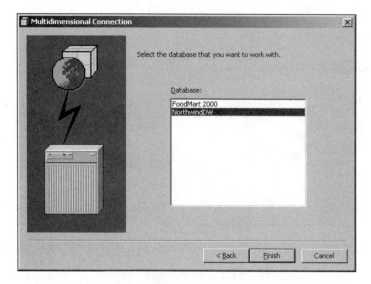

Choose the NorthwindDW database and click Finish.

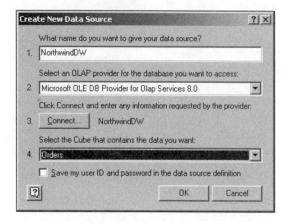

Now choose the Orders cube from the Select the Cube that contains the data you want combo box and click OK.

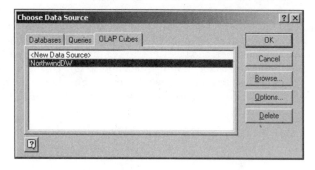

Click on OK again to return to the previous dialog.

Click on Next from Step 2 of the wizard. On Step 3, you'll need to decide which dimensions and measures to include for your pivot table.

Choose Layout to decide which dimension and measures you want to include.

You can click and drag the options from the right side onto the pivot table diagram on the left to select.

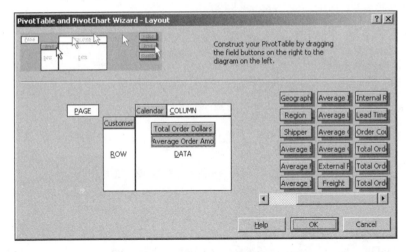

We've chosen the Customer Name dimension on the ROW axis, Calendar Order Date dimension on the COLUMN axis, and Total Order Dollars and Average Order Amount as the measures in the DATA section. You can choose any sets of dimensions or facts that you wish. Go ahead and click OK to return to the previous dialog and then click on Finish to actually return the results. The results show all customers total order and average order amounts broken down by year. You can drill down into a year by double-clicking on the year member, such as 1997, to see the order amounts by quarter. You can also drill into the Quarter dimension to see monthly data and so on. To answer the original analytical questions, you'll need to follow the same steps as we did above, but choose the dimensions and measures that will fulfill the questions. As an example, we will answer the first two of the questions posed at the beginning of this chapter.

Who Are Northwind's Most Profitable Customers?

The first question analysts at Northwind wish to answer is 'Who are my most profitable customers?' Using Excel 2000's pivot table capability, the following spreadsheet can be created to answer this question:

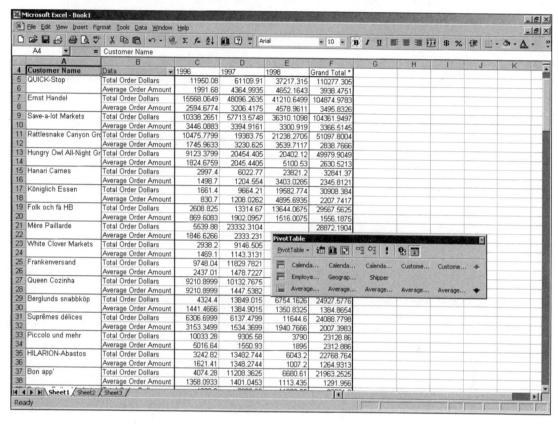

Northwind now can find out which customer has ordered the most overall for the past three years.

Which Regions Are Selling The Most Products?

Region can be an attribute of the employee dimension or part of the employee dimension hierarchy. Northwind, though, has defined region to be a virtual dimension based on the employee attribute. Using this dimension, the following spreadsheet can be created:

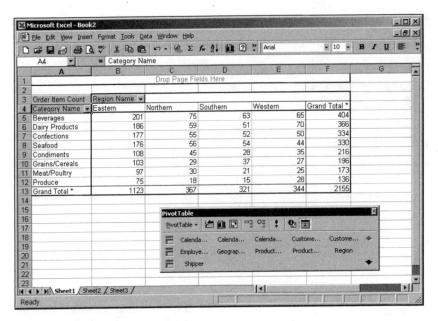

In this case, we're looking at category sales. We can expand category and hide to reveal the top selling products:

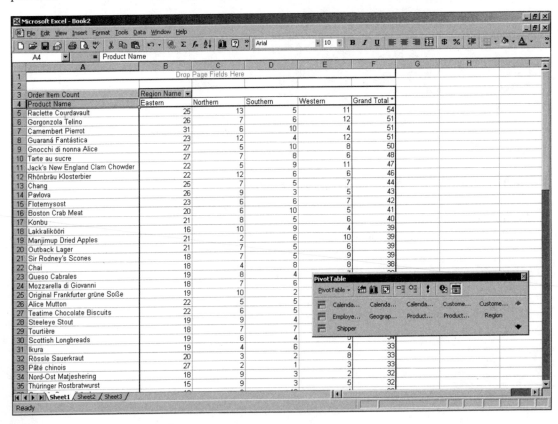

This table can be sorted and arranged any way you like to answer many other questions. The goal is that all of the original questions can be answered easily and quickly. By following this guideline for creating an ETL and associated Analysis Services cubes, a powerful analytical application can be created to support any organization's needs.

Summary

In this Case Study, we discussed the entire process of designing and building a data mart for the Northwind Company. We laid out the business reasons for creating the data mart as well as the technical steps that were required.

Hopefully, you'll find that the ETL program created here can be a good starting point for ETLs or other data moving applications of your own. Once again, this chapter doesn't define this particular architecture as the only way to create an ETL for a data mart or warehouse, but rather as one possible architecture that is flexible enough to handle change and growth relatively easily.

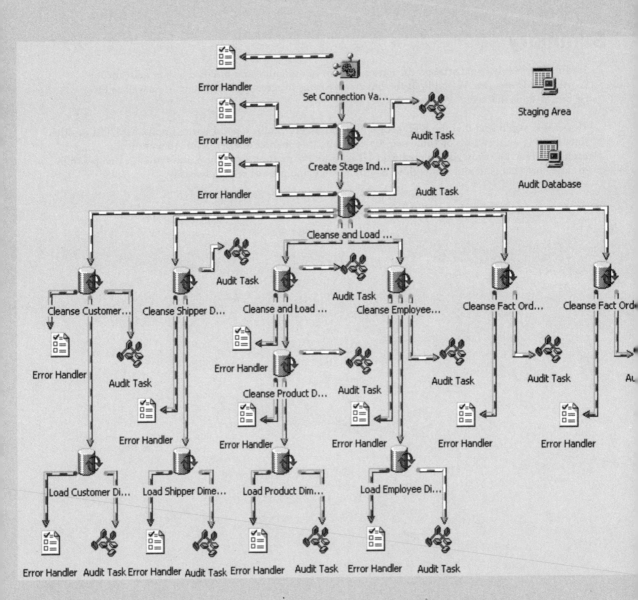

Error Handler

Set Connection Va...

Audit Task

Staging Area

Error Handler

Create Stage Ind...

Audit Task

Audit Database

Error Handler

Cleanse and Load ...

Audit Task

Cleanse Customer...

Cleanse Shipper D...

Cleanse and Load ...

Audit Task

Cleanse Employee...

Cleanse Fact Ord...

Cleanse Fact Ord...

Error Handler

Audit Task

Error Handler

Cleanse Product D...

Audit Task

Error Handler

Audit Task

Audit Task

Au...

Error Handler

Error Handler

Error Handler

Error Handler

Error Handler

Error Handler

Load Customer Di...

Load Shipper Dime...

Load Product Dim...

Load Employee Di...

Error Handler Audit Task Error Handler Audit Task Error Handler Audit Task Error Handler Audit Task

Microsoft Data Transformation Services Package Object Library Reference

The object model is shown diagrammatically overleaf. The gray boxes represent collection objects and the white boxes represent objects.

```
Package2
  ├─ Connections
  │    └─ Connection2
  │         └─ Connection Properties ─── OLE DBProperty
  │
  ├─ GlobalVariables ─── GlobalVariable2
  ├─ SavedPackageInfos ─── SavedPackageInfo
  ├─ Steps
  │    └─ Step2
  │         └─ PrecedenceConstraints ─── PrecedenceConstraints
  │
  └─ Tasks
       └─ Task
```

The hierarchy continues from the Task object as follows:

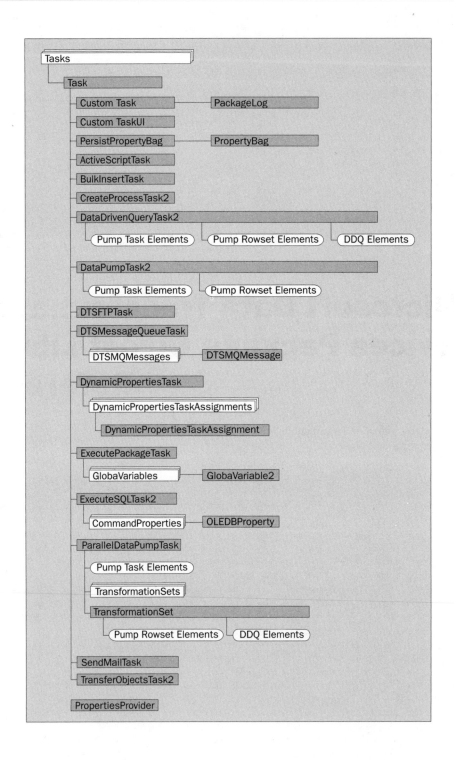

Library File Location

The source file that contains the Data Transformation Service Object library is located at `<Drive>:\MSSQL7\Binn\Resources\1033\dts.rll`.

Objects

Name	Description
ActiveScriptTask	Defines an ActiveX script task.
BulkInsertTask	Provides an interface for rapid copying of lots of data from a text file.
Column	Contains information about a source or destination column of information.
Connection	Contains information about the connection to the OLE DB service provider.
Create ProcessTask	An object that contains information about running a separate program as a task.
CustomTask	A wrapper object that encapsulates a custom DTS package task.
CustomTaskUI	Allows for the specification of specialized dialog boxes to support DTS tasks.
DataDriven QueryTask	Contains information regarding the use of individual queries rather than executing an INSERT operation at the destination.
DataPumpTask	Creates and executes an instance of the DTS data pump as a custom task.
ExecuteSQLTask	Allows the execution of a SQL statement on an open connection.
GlobalVariable	Allows the definition of global variables for sharing across scripts or tasks.
IDTSStdObject	The top level hierarchy object for the DTS Package class.
Lookup	Allows the specification of one or more query strings for custom transformation.
OleDBProperty	Used to set OLE DB session properties for the OLE DB service provider.
Package	Main object that defines DTS transformations.
PackageLog	Internal Microsoft use only.

Table continued on following page

Name	Description
Persist PropertyBag	For objects carrying out DTS custom tasks this defines an interface for persistent property storage.
Precedence Constraint	Contains information about the order that steps are executed.
Properties Provider	Defines an object supplying a DTS `Properties` collection.
Property	Defines the attributes of a DTS object.
PropertyBag	Defines an index/name container for DTS custom task implementations.
SavedPackageInfo	Contains information about a saved DTS package.
SendMailTask	Contains information that allows users to send an e-mail as a custom task.
Step	Controls the flow and execution of tasks in a DTS package.
Task	Sets a unit of work within a DTS package.
Transfer ObjectsTask	Allows the transfer of objects between a destination and source SQL Server.
Transformation	Contains information about the source, destination, and transformation of columns of data in a DTS Package.

Collections

Name	Description
Columns	Contains descriptions for columns in a data source.
Connections	Contains information about the OLE DB service providers used in a package.
DTSMQMessages	Defines the messages to be sent by the DTS Message Queue task.
DynamicProperties TaskAssignment	Defines the properties changed by a Dynamic Properties task.
GlobalVariables	A collection of `GlobalVariable` objects.
Lookups	A collection of `Lookup` objects.
OleDBProperties	A collection of `OLEDBProperty` objects.
OLEDBProvider Infos	A collection of information about available OLE DB Providers.
PackageInfos	Provides information about packages stored locally in SQL Server or in Meta Data Services.

Name	Description
PackageLineages	A collection of package lineage records from Meta Data Services.
PackageLogRecords	A collection of package log records from an instance of SQL Server.
Precedence Constraints	A collection of `PrecedenceConstraint` objects.
Properties	A collection of DTS `Property` objects.
SavedPackageInfos	A collection of `SavedPackageInfo` objects.
Scripting LanguageInfos	A collection of information about Microsoft ActiveX scripting languages available on the executing workstation.
StepLineages	A collection of step lineage records from Meta Data Services.
StepLogRecords	A collection of step log records from an instance of SQL Server.
Steps	A collection of `Step` objects.
TaskInfos	A collection of information about tasks available on the system executing the package.
TaskLogRecords	A collection of task log records from an instance of SQL Server.
Tasks	A collection of `Task` objects.
Transformation Infos	A collection of information about the DTS transformations available on the system executing the package.
Transformations	A collection of `Transformation` objects.
Transformation Sets	A collection of transformations used to process components of a hierarchical rowset.

ActiveScriptTask

Methods

Name	Returns	Description
CheckSyntax		Parses the active script for syntax errors.
Execute		Executes an `ActiveScriptTask`.

Properties

Name	Returns	Description
ActiveXScript	String	Specifies an ActiveX script.
AddGlobal Variables	Boolean	Specifies whether global variables may be used within an ActiveX script.
Description	String	A descriptive string for the ActiveScriptTask.
FunctionName	String	Identifies the function name to call within the ActiveX script.
Name	String	The name of the ActiveScriptTask.
Properties	Properties	Returns the Properties collection for the ActiveScriptTask object.
ScriptLanguage	String	Identifies the scripting language (VBScript, JScript, or PerlScript).

BulkInsertTask

Methods

Name	Returns	Description
Execute		Executes a BulkInsertTask.

Properties

Name	Returns	Description
BatchSize	Long	Sets the number of rows to load in a batch.
CheckConstraints	Boolean	Indicates whether any constraints should be checked while data is loaded.
Codepage	String	Sets code page to use while loading data. Valid values are ACP, OEM (default), RAW or a code page number (like 850).
ConnectionID	Long	Sets the ID of the Connection object.
DataFile	String	Sets the UNC path of the file to be loaded.
DataFileType	DTSBulkInsert _DataFileType	Sets the file type of the data to be inserted.

Name	Returns	Description
Description	String	The descriptive string for the BulkInsertTask.
Destination TableName	String	Specifies the name of the table that data will be inserted into.
FieldTerminator	String	Sets the column terminator value for batch inserted files.
FirstRow	Long	Sets the first source row to copy.
FormatFile	String	Specifies a bcp format file to use for load operations.
KeepIdentity	Boolean	Shows whether the data in the file should be used as values of an identity column(s).
KeepNulls	Boolean	Sets whether NULL columns should keep NULL values.
LastRow	Long	Identifies the last row to be loaded from a source file.
MaximumErrors	Long	Sets the maximum number of errors that may occur before a load operation is terminated.
Name	String	The name of the BulkInsertTask.
Properties	Properties	A list of properties for this object.
RowTerminator	String	Sets the row termination file for the source file.
SortedData	String	Sets the order of the loaded data.
TableLock	Boolean	Sets whether to perform a table lock on the destination table.

Column

Properties

Name	Returns	Description
ColumnID	Variant	Sets/Gets the ID of a source/destination column.
DataType	Long	Sets/Gets the data type of a column object.
Flags	Long	Sets/Gets the DBCOLUMNFLAGS value that describes the column.
Name	String	The name of the column object.

Table continued on following page

Name	Returns	Description
Nullable	Boolean	Specifies whether the column is or is not nullable.
NumericScale	Long	Sets/Gets the numeric scale of the column if it is a numeric or decimal value.
Ordinal	Long	Gets the ordinal position of the column within the table.
Parent	IDTSStdObject	The parent object of the Column object.
Precision	Long	Set/Gets the column precision if the column is decimal or numeric data type.
Properties	Properties	A list of properties for the object.
Size	Long	Specifies the maximum size of the column.

Columns

Methods

Name	Returns	Description
Add		Adds a DTS Column object to the collection.
AddColumn		Adds a DTS Column object to the collection by name and ordinal position.
Insert		Inserts a DTS Column object by ordinal position.
Item	Column	Retrieves a DTS Column object from the collection.
New	Column	Creates a new DTS Column object.
Remove		Removes a DTS Column object from the object.

Properties

Name	Returns	Description
Count	Long	Specifies the number of DTS Column objects in the collection.
Parent	IDTSStdObject	The parent object of the Columns object.

Connection

Methods

Name	Returns	Description
Acquire Connection		Allows the acquisition of exclusive use of the OLE DB service provider.
Release Connection		Releases ownership of the OLE DB service provider.

Properties

Name	Returns	Description
Catalog	String	Sets the name of the catalog that the Connection object will be initially established in.
Connected	Boolean	Gets the connection status of the Connection object.
Connect Immediate	Boolean	Identifies whether a package should attempt an immediate connection to the service provider upon starting.
Connection Properties	OleDB Properties	Gets the OleDBProperties object for the established connection.
Connection Timeout	Long	The number of seconds to wait while establishing a connection before generating an error.
DataSource	String	Sets the server name when an application requests an OLE DB provider for SQL Server.
Description	String	A text description of the Connection object.
ID	Long	Unique identifier for the established connection.
InTransaction	Boolean	Identifies whether the connection is involved in a distributed transaction.
InUse	Boolean	Identifies whether the connection is currently in use.
LastOwner TaskName	String	Returns the name of the last Task to utilize the connection.
Name	String	The name of the Connection object.

Table continued on following page

Name	Returns	Description
Parent	IDTSStdObject	Specifies the parent object of the Connection object.
Password	String	The password used while making the connection.
Properties	Properties	A list of properties for this object.
ProviderID	String	The ProgID of the OLE DB provider.
Reusable	Boolean	Identifies whether a connection is reusable by multiple steps within a given task.
UDLPath	String	Path of UDL (data link) file to create connection from, rather than using Connection properties.
UserID	String	The user ID utilized when making a connection.
UseTrusted Connection	Boolean	Specifies whether to use Windows NT Authentication security to establish a connection.

Connections

Methods

Name	Returns	Description
Add		Adds a Connection object to the collection.
BeginAcquire Multiple Connections		Allows the acquisition of multiple connections.
EndAcquire Mutiple Connections		Stops the acquisition of multiple connections.
Insert		Inserts a Connection object into the collection.
Item	Connection	Retrieves a Connection object from the collection.
New	Connection	Creates a new Connection object.
NewDataLink	Connection	Gets a new Connection object to populate prior to adding to this collection, using Microsoft Data Links.
Remove		Removes a Connection object from the collection.

Properties

Name	Returns	Description
Count	Long	Specifies the number of DTS Connection objects in the collection.
Parent	Object	Specifies the parent object of the Connections collection.

CreateProcessTask

Methods

Name	Returns	Description
Execute		Executes a CreateProcessTask.

Properties

Name	Returns	Description
Description	String	A text description of the CreateProcessTask.
FailPackage OnTimeout	Boolean	Identifies whether the DTS package fails within the timeout period.
Name	String	The name of the CreateProcessTask object.
Process CommandLine	String	The UNC file name of the file to execute.
Properties	Properties	A list of properties for this object.
Success ReturnCode	Long	The return code that is returned upon successful completion a task.
Terminate ProcessAfter Timeout	Boolean	Sets whether to terminate a process after a timeout period has expired.
Timeout	Long	The number of seconds in the timeout period.

CustomTask

Methods

Name	Returns	Description
Execute		Executes a `CustomTask`.

Properties

Name	Returns	Description
Description	String	A text description of the `CustomTask`.
Name	String	The name for the `CustomTask`.
Properties	Properties	A list of properties for this object.

CustomTaskUI

Methods

Name	Returns	Description
CreateCustom ToolTip		Creates a tooltip window for a custom tooltip.
Delete		Deletes a `CustomTask` object in the user interface.
Edit		Edits a `CustomTask` object in the user interface.
GetUIInfo		Returns user information about the `CustomTask`.
Help		Used to invoke help about the `CustomTask` object.
Initialize		Initializes the `CustomTaskUI` object.
New		Creates a new custom task.

DataDrivenQueryTask

Methods

Name	Returns	Description
Execute		Executes a `DataDrivenQueryTask`.

Properties

Name	Returns	Description
DeleteQuery	String	Specifies a Transact-SQL statement to delete data from a data source.
DeleteQuery Columns	Columns	Specifies columns to be placed in a parameterized `DeleteQuery`.
Description	String	A text description of the `DataDrivenQueryTask` object.
Destination ColumnDefinitions	Columns	Destination column definitions for a `DTSRowQueue` destination.
Destination CommandProperties	OleDBProperties	The OLE DB command properties for the destination data connection.
Destination ConectionID	Long	Connection object to use for destination.
Destination ObjectName	String	Sets the name of the data destination.
Destination SQLStatement	String	Specifies a SQL statement to execute at the destination.
ExceptionFile ColumnDelimiter	String	The column delimiter for the exception file.
ExceptionFileName	String	The name of the file where exception rows are written.
ExceptionFile RowDelimiter	String	The row delimiter for the data in the exception file.
FetchBufferSize	Long	Sets the number of rows to fetch during a single operation.
FirstRow	Variant	Gets the first source row.
InsertQuery	String	Sets a parameterized SQL statement to insert data at a destination.

Table continued on following page

697

Name	Returns	Description
InsertQuery Columns	Columns	Sets the column parameters for the InsertQuery parameters.
LastRow	Variant	Gets the last row from the source to copy.
Lookups	Lookups	A collection of lookup values.
MaximumErrorCount	Long	The maximum number of error rows before the data pump terminates operation.
Name	String	The name of the DataDrivenQueryTask object.
ProgressRowCount	Long	Sets the number of rows returned between notifications to the connection point during a DataDrivenQuery execution.
Properties	Properties	A list of properties for this object.
SourceCommand Properties	OleDBProperties	The OLE DB command properties for the data source connection.
Source ConnectionID	Long	The ID for the source OLE DB connection.
SourceObjectName	String	Specifies the source object name if no SQL statement is supplied.
SourceSQL Statement	String	Sets the SQL statement to be executed on the source rowset.
Transformations	Transformations	A collection of Transformation objects.
UpdateQuery	String	Sets a parameterized SQL query to update data.
UpdateQuery Columns	Columns	Specifies the column parameters for the UpdateQuery property.
UserQuery	String	Sets a parameterized user-defined SQL query.
UserQueryColumns	Columns	Specifies the column parameters for the UserQuery property.

DataDrivenQueryTask2

Extended Properties

Name	Returns	Description
Exception FileOptions	Integer	Specifies whether or not to use the SQL Server 7.0 format for exception files as well as specifying whether to keep source and destination error rows.
ExceptionFile TextQualifier	String	Specifies the text qualifier for the exception rows.
InputGlobal VariableNames	String	Specifies a list of package global variable names whose values are to be substituted for the query parameters.
RowsComplete	Integer	Specifies the number of rows that have successfully been transformed.
RowsInError	Integer	Specifies the number of rows that have errors.

DataPumpTask

Methods

Name	Returns	Description
Execute		Executes a DataPumpTask.

Properties

Name	Returns	Description
AllowIdentity Inserts	Boolean	Specifies whether the SET IDENTITY_INSERT option is ON or OFF.
Description	String	A text description of the DataPumpTask object.
Destination ColumnDefinitions	Columns	Destination column definitions for a DTSRowQueue destination.

Table continued on following page

Name	Returns	Description
Destination CommandProperties	OleDBProperties	OLE DB command properties for the destination.
Destination ConnectionID	Long	Connection object to use for destination.
Destination ObjectName	String	Sets the name of the data destination.
Destination SQLStatement	String	Specifies a SQL Statement to execute at the destination.
ExceptionFile ColumnDelimter	String	The column delimiter for the exception file.
ExceptionFileName	String	The name of the file where exception rows are written.
ExceptionFile RowDelimiter	String	The row delimiter for the data in the exception file.
FastLoadOptions	DTSFast LoadOptions	Used for the UseFastLoad property to set SQL OLE DB destination connection options.
FetchBufferSize	Long	Sets the number of rows to fetch during a single operation.
FirstRow	Variant	Gets the first source row from the source.
InsertCommitSize	Long	Number of successful InsertRows between Commits.
LastRow	Variant	Gets the last row from the source to copy.
Lookups	Lookups	A collection of lookup values.
MaximumErrorCount	Long	The maximum number of error rows before the data pump terminates operation.
Name	String	The name of the DataPumpTask object.
ProgressRowCount	Long	The number of rows returned between notifications to the connection point during a data pump execution.
Properties	Properties	A list of properties for this object.
SourceCommand Properties	OleDBProperties	OLE DB command properties for the source.
Source ConnectionID	Long	The ID for the source OLE DB connection.
SourceObjectName	String	Specifies the source object name if no SQL statement is supplied.

Name	Returns	Description
Source SQLStatement	String	Sets the SQL statement to be executed on the source rowset.
Transformations	Transformations	A collection of Transformation objects.
UseFastLoad	Boolean	Specifies whether to use the IRowsetFastLoad interface to insert rows at the data destination.

DataPumpTask2

Extended Properties

Name	Returns	Description
Exception FileOptions	Integer	Specifies whether or not to use the SQL Server 7.0 format for exception files as well as specifying whether to keep source and destination error rows.
Exception FileTextQualifier	String	Specifies the text qualifier for the exception rows.
InputGlobal VariableNames	String	Specifies a list of package global variable names whose values are to be substituted for the query parameters.
RowsComplete	Integer	Specifies the number of rows that have successfully been transformed.
RowsInError	Integer	Specifies the number of rows that have errors.

DynamicPropertiesTask

Methods

Name	Returns	Description
Execute		Executes the Dynamic Properties Task.

Properties

Name	Returns	Description
Assignments		Returns a reference to the Dynamic PropertiesTaskAssignment collection.
Description	String	Optional user-defined text label that helps define the Dynamic Properties Task.
DynamicProperties TaskAssignments	TaskAssignment	Stores the pertinent information about the source and destination properties.
Name	String	Unique user-defined text label for the task.
Properties	Properties	A list of properties for this object.

DynamicPropertiesTaskAssignment

Methods

Name	Returns	Description
Reset		Resets all targets to their defaults.

Properties

Name	Returns	Description
Destination PropertyID	String	Specifies the path through the object model to the property that has been modified.
SourceConstant Value	String	Specifies a value to a constant when the when the SourceType property is DTSDynamic PropertiesSourceType_Constant is set to.
SourceDataFile FileName	String	Specifies the data file that the dynamic property will be set to when the SourceType property is DTSDynamicPropertiesSourceType_ DataFile.

Name	Returns	Description
SourceEnvironment Variable	String	Specifies the name of the environment variable that the dynamic property will be set to if the SourceType property is DTSDynamicPropertiesSourceType_ EnvironmentVariable.
SourceGlobal Variable	String	Specifies the name of the global variable that the dynamic property will be set to if the SourceType property is DTSDynamicPropertiesSourceType_ GlobalVariable.
SourceIniFile FileName	String	Specifies the name of the INI file and path that the dynamic property will be set to if the SourceType property is DTSDynamicPropertiesSourceType_ IniFile.
SourceIniFileKey	String	Specifies the key that will be used in the INI file when the SourceType property is DTSDynamicProperties SourceType_IniFile.
SourceIniFile Section	String	Specifies the section that will be used in the INI file when the SourceType property is DTSDynamic PropertiesSourceType_IniFile.
SourceQuery ConnectionID	String	Specifies the connection ID that the SourceQuerySQL will use.
SourceQuerySQL	String	Specifies the SQL statement that will be used to derive the dynamic property will be set to if the SourceType property is DTSDynamicPropertiesSourceType_ Query.
SourceType	Long	Specifies the method in which the dynamic property will be derived.

DynamicPropertiesTaskAssignments

Methods

Name	Returns	Description
Add		Adds an object to the collection.
Item		Retrieves an object by index.
New		Creates a new object.

Properties

Name	Returns	Description
Count	Long	The number of objects in the collection.
Parent	IDTSStdObject	The parent object of the object.

ExecuteSQLTask

Methods

Name	Returns	Description
Execute		Executes an ExecuteSQLTask.

Properties

Name	Returns	Description
Command Properties	OleDB Properties	Sets the OleDBProperties object for the connection.
Command Timeout	Long	The number of seconds before the command is presumed to have failed.
ConnectionID	Long	The ID for the OLE DB connection.
Description	String	A text description of the ExecuteSQLTask object.
Name	String	The name of the ExecuteSQLTask object.
Properties	Properties	A list of properties for the object.
SQLStatement	String	The SQL statement to execute on the source rowset.

ExecuteSQLTask2

Extended Properties

Name	Returns	Description
InputGlobal VariableNames	String	Specifies a list of package global variable names whose values are to be substituted for the query parameters.
OutputAsRecordSet	Boolean	Specifies whether to output the results of the SQL task into a recordset in a global variable.
OutputGlobal VariableNames	String	Specifies whether to output the results of the SQL task into global variable(s).

GlobalVariable

Properties

Name	Returns	Description
Name	String	The name of the GlobalVariable object.
Parent	IDTSStdObject	The parent object of the GlobalVariable object.
Properties	Properties	A list of properties for the object.
Value	Variant	The value of the GlobalVariable object.

GlobalVariables

Methods

Name	Returns	Description
Add		Adds a GlobalVariable object to the collection.
AddGlobalVariable		Adds a GlobalVariable object to the collection by name.

Table continued on following page

Name	Returns	Description
Insert		Inserts an object at an ordinal position or prior to a named object.
Item	GlobalVariable	Retrieves a GlobalVariable object by index.
New	GlobalVariable	Creates a new GlobalVariable object.
Remove		Removes a GlobalVariable object from the collection.

Properties

Name	Returns	Description
Count	Long	The number of GlobalVariable objects in the collection.
Parent	IDTSStdObject	The parent object of the GlobalVariable object.

IDTSStdObject

There are no methods, events, or properties designed for this object.

Lookup

Properties

Name	Returns	Description
ConnectionId	Long	The ID for the established OLE DB connection.
MaxCacheRows	Long	The maximum number of rows to cache.
Name	String	The name of the Lookup object.
Parent	IDTSStdObject	The parent object of the Lookup object.
Properties	Properties	A list of properties for the object.
Query	String	A parameterized query to execute.

Lookups

Methods

Name	Returns	Description
Add		Adds a Lookup object to the collection.
AddLookup		Adds a Lookup object to the collection by name.
Insert		Inserts a Lookup object into the collection by index.
Item	Lookup	Retrieves a Lookup object by index.
New	Lookup	Creates a new Lookup object.
Remove		Removes a Lookup object from the collection.

Properties

Name	Returns	Description
Count	Long	The number of Lookup objects in the collection.
Parent	IDTSStdObject	The parent object of the Lookup object.

OleDBProperties

Methods

Name	Returns	Description
Item	OleDBProperty	Retrieves an OleDBProperty object by index.

Properties

Name	Returns	Description
Count	Long	The number of OleDBProperty objects in the collection.
Parent	IDTSStdObject	The parent object of the OleDBProperties object.

OleDBProperty

Properties

Name	Returns	Description
Name	String	The name of the OleDBProperty.
Parent	IDTSStdObject	The parent object of the OleDBProperty.
Properties	Properties	A list of properties for the object.
PropertyID	Long	The ID of the OleDBProperty.
PropertySet	String	The GUID of the property.
Value	Variant	The value of the OleDBProperty.

OleDBProperty2

Extended Properties

Name	Returns	Description
IsDefaultValue	Boolean	Set to False if the property has been changed from the default.

Package

Methods

Name	Returns	Description
EndPreparation ForStepsExecuting OnMainThread		Internal Microsoft use only.
Execute		Executes a Package object.
GetDTSVersionInfo		Returns the DTS object version information.
GetLastExecution Lineage	String	Returns information about the lineage of a package stored in the Microsoft Repository.

Name	Returns	Description
GetSaved PackageInfos	SavedPackage Infos	Returns a list of versions in the specified storage location.
LoadFrom Repository		Loads the DTS package from the specified Repository.
LoadFromSQLServer		Loads the DTS package from the specified SQL Server.
LoadFrom StorageFile		Loads the DTS package from the specified storage file.
RemoveFrom Repository		Removes the selected DTS package from the selected Repository.
RemoveFrom SQLServer		Removes the selected DTS package from the selected SQL Server.
SaveAs		Creates a new package ID and assigns a new name to create a new package.
SaveToRepository		Saves a package to a selected Repository.
SaveToSQLServer		Saves a package to a selected SQL Server.
SaveToStorageFile		Saves a package to a selected file.
StartPreparation forStepsExecuting OnMainThread		Internal Microsoft use only.
UnInitialize		Clears all state information and releases all objects.

Properties

Name	Returns	Description
AutoCommit Transaction	Boolean	Sets whether a specified transaction should be committed or terminated upon completion.
Connections	Connections	A collection of Connection objects.
CreationDate	Date	The package creation date.
Creator ComputerName	String	The name of the computer that created the package.
CreatorName	String	The username of the package creator.
Description	String	A descriptive text about the object.

Table continued on following page

Name	Returns	Description
FailOnError	Boolean	Sets whether to stop execution upon package error.
GlobalVariables	Global Variables	A global variable collection.
LineageOptions	DTSLineage Options	Specifies how the execution lineage should be shown.
LogFileName	String	The name of the log file.
MaxConcurrent Steps	Long	The maximum concurrent steps for the package.
Name	String	The name of the Package object.
PackageID	String	The ID value for the package (GUID).
PackagePriority Class	DTSPackage PriorityClass	The Win32 thread priority for the class.
Parent	IDTSStdObject	The parent object (IDTSStdObject) for the Package object.
PrecedenceBasis	DTSStep Precedence Basis	Indicates whether to use step status or result in PrecedenceConstraint.
Properties	Properties	Lists the properties of the object.
Repository MetadataOptions	DTSRepository Metadata Options	Specifies meta data scanning and resolution options when storing the DTS Package to a Repository.
Steps	Steps	A collection of Step objects to be executed for the package.
Tasks	Tasks	A collection of Task objects to be performed during the package execution.
Transaction IsolationLevel	DTSIsolation Level	The isolation level for the transaction for the package.
UseOLEDBService Components	Boolean	Sets whether to use OLE DB components to initialize data sources.
UseTransaction	Boolean	Sets whether the Package object should create a transaction for supporting tasks.
VersionID	String	The GUID of this version of the package.
WriteCompletionSt atusToNTEventLog	Boolean	Whether to write completion status to the Windows NT Event Log.

Events

Name	Returns	Description
OnError		Executes when error condition occurs.
OnFinish		Executes when finish condition occurs.
OnProgress		Executes during progress intervals.
OnQueryCancel		Executes on query cancel status.
OnStart		Executes on start of package.

Package2

Extended Methods

Name	Returns	Description
SaveTo RepositoryAs		Save the package and its objects to a new package in the repository, giving it a new package ID and not a new version ID.
SaveToSQL ServerAs		Saves the package and its objects to the MSDB database locally, giving it a new package ID and not a new version ID.
SaveToStorage FileAs		Saves the package and its objects to a structured storage file and assigns it a new package ID.

Properties

Name	Returns	Description
Explicit GlobalVariables	Boolean	Sets whether the package will use explicit global variables.
FailPackage OnLogFailure	Boolean	Sets or returns a value indicating whether a DTS package will fail if there is a failure during the logging of the package.
LogServerFlags	Boolean	Sets whether Windows NT Authentication is being used to login to the logging server. If this flag is set to False, then standard SQL authentication is used.
LogServerName	String	Sets the server that will hold the logs for the DTS package.

Table continued on following page

Name	Returns	Description
LogServerPassword	String	Sets the password that will be used to authenticate to the server holding the logs.
LogServerUserName	String	Sets the user name that will be used to authenticate to the server holding the logs.
LogToSQLServer	Boolean	Sets whether the logs will be written to a SQL Server's MSDB database. If set to TRUE then the logs will be written to the LogServerName server.
Nested ExecutionLevel	Long	Sets the number of levels deep that a package can call another package through the Execute Package task.
PackageType	Integer	Sets or returns a code that identifies the tool that created the package.

PackageInfo

Properties

Name	Returns	Description
CreationDate	Date	Specifies when the package's version was created.
Description	String	User-defined description for the package.
IsOwner	Boolean	True if the user logging into Package SQL Server is the owner of the package.
Name	String	User-defined name of the package.
Owner	String	Specifies the owner of the package.
PackageDataSize	Long	Specifies the size of the package data for SQL Server packages.
PackageID	String	Specifies a GUID for the package.
PackageType	DTSPackageType	Specifies the tool used to create the package.
Parent	IDTSStdObject	Hierarchical parent object
Properties	Properties	List of properties for the object.
VersionID	String	Specifies a GUID for the version.

PackageInfos

Methods

Name	Returns	Description
Next		Returns the next record in the enumeration.

Properties

Name	Returns	Description
EOF	Boolean	Specifies that the last record has been fetched in the enumeration.

PackageLineage

Properties

Name	Returns	Description
Computer	String	Specifies the server that the package executed on.
ExecutionDate	Date	Specifies the date the package was logged.
LineageFullID	String	Full GUID for the full package lineage.
LineageShortID	Long	Specifies the compressed form of the LineageFullID.
Name	String	Specifies the name of the package.
Operator	String	Specifies the individual who executed the package.
PackageID	String	Specifies the PackageID that was executed.
Parent	IDTSStdObject	Specifies the hierarchical parent object
Properties	Properties	List of properties for the object.
VersionID	String	GUID VersionID of the package that was executed.

PackageLineages

Methods

Name	Returns	Description
Next		Returns the next record in the enumeration.

Properties

Name	Returns	Description
EOF	Boolean	Specifies that the last record has been fetched in the enumeration.

PackageLog

Methods

Name	Returns	Description
WriteStringToLog	String	Writes a string to the log record that is being written for the step.
WriteTaskRecord Method	String	Writes a record to the SQL Server instances' log table for the current task that is being executed. It is formatted for the WriteStringToLog method to write.

PackageLogRecord

Properties

Name	Returns	Description
Computer	String	Specifies the server that the package executed on.
Description	String	User-defined description for the package.
ErrorCode	Long	Error code returned from the Package.Execute method.

Name	Returns	Description
Error Description	String	Full error description returned from the `Package.Execute` method.
ExecutionTime	Double	The total time it took to execute the package in seconds.
FinishTime	Date	Specifies the time at which the package finished execution.
LineageFullID	String	Full GUID for the full package lineage.
LineageShortID	Long	Specifies the compressed form of the `LineageFullID`.
LogDate	Date	Specifies the date the package was logged.
Name	String	Specifies the name of the package.
Operator	String	Specifies the user that is logged in executing the package.
PackageID	String	Specifies the `PackageID` that was executed.
Parent	IDTSStd Object	Specifies the hierarchical parent object
Properties	Properties	List of properties for the object.
StartTime	Date	Specifies the time at which the package started execution.
VersionID	String	GUID `VersionID` of the package that was executed.

PackageLogRecords

Methods

Name	Returns	Description
Next		Returns the next record in the enumeration.

Properties

Name	Returns	Description
EOF	Boolean	Specifies that the last record has been fetched in the enumeration.

PackageRepository

Methods

Name	Returns	Description
EnumPackage Infos		Enumerates the Packages that are stored in the Repository.
EnumPackage Lineages		Enumerates the Package lineages that are stored in the Repository.
EnumStep Lineages		Enumerates the Step lineages that are stored in the Repository.
RemovePackage Lineages		Removes a Package lineage from the Repository.

Properties

Name	Returns	Description
Name	String	Specifies the name of the repository the user is connected to.
Parent	IDTSStdObject	Specifies the hierarchical parent object.
Properties	Properties	List of properties for the object.

PackageSQLServer

Methods

Name	Returns	Description
EnumPackage Infos		Enumerates Packages that are stored in SQL Server.
EnumPackage LogRecords		Enumerates the Package log records that are stored in SQL Server.
EnumStepLog Records		Enumerates the Step log records that are stored in SQL Server.
EnumTaskLog Records		Enumerates the Task log records that are stored in SQL Server.

Name	Returns	Description
RemoveAllLog Records		Removes all log records that are stored in SQL Server.
RemovePackage LogRecords		Removes a Package log record that is stored in SQL Server.
RemoveStepLog Records		Removes a Step log record that is stored in SQL Server.
RemoveTaskLog Records		Removes a Task log record that is stored in SQL Server.

Properties

Name	Returns	Description
Name	String	Specifies the name of the server the user is connected to.
Parent	IDTSStd Object	Specifies the hierarchical parent object.
Properties	Properties	List of properties for the object.

ParallelDataPumpTask

Methods

Name	Returns	Description
Execute		Executes the objects in parallel while other objects in the duration of this call.

Properties

Name	Returns	Description
Description	String	A text description of the ParallelData PumpTask object.
Destination CommandProperties	OleDB Properties	OLE DB command properties for the destination.
Destination ConnectionID	Long	Connection object to use for destination.

Name	Returns	Description
Destination ObjectName	String	Sets the name of the data destination.
Destination SQLStatement	String	Specifies a SQL Statement to execute at the destination.
InputGlobal VariableNames	String	Specifies a delimited string of double-quoted Global Variables that will be passed as input parameters.
Name	String	The name of the ParallelDataPumpTask object.
Properties	Properties	A list of properties for this object.
SourceCommand Properties	OleDBProperties	OLE DB command properties for the source.
Source ConnectionID	Long	The ID for the source OLE DB connection.
Source ObjectName	String	Specifies the source object name if no SQL statement is supplied.
SourceSQL Statement	String	Sets the SQL statement to be executed on the source rowset.
Transformations SetOptions	Transformations	Specifies the sequence to copy the rowsets and the options.
Transformation Sets	Transformation Sets	Specifies the TransformationSets between each pair of rowsets in the object.

PersistPropertyBag

Methods

Name	Returns	Description
Load		Loads a custom tasks property storage.
Save		Gets a custom task to carry out property storage.

PrecedenceConstraint

Properties

Name	Returns	Description
Parent	IDTSStdObject	The parent object of the PrecedenceConstraint object.
Precedence Basis	DTSStep PrecedenceBasis	Indicates whether to use step status or result in PrecedenceConstraint.
Properties	Properties	The properties of the object.
StepName	String	The name of the Step object that will be evaluated.
Value	Variant	The value of the constraint.

PrecedenceConstraints

Methods

Name	Returns	Description
Add		Adds a PrecedenceConstraint object to the collection.
AddConstraint		Adds a PrecedenceConstraint object to the collection by name.
Insert		Inserts a PrecedenceConstraint object into the collection by index.
Item	Precedence Constraint	Retrieves a PrecedenceConstraint object by index.
New	Precedence Constraint	Creates a new PrecedenceConstraint object.
Remove		Removes a PrecedenceConstraint object from the collection.

Properties

Name	Returns	Description
Count	Long	The number of PrecedenceConstraint objects in the collection.
Parent	IDTSStdObject	The parent object of PrecedenceConstraints collection.

Properties

Methods

Name	Returns	Description
Item	Property	Returns a Property object by index value.

Properties

Name	Returns	Description
Count	Long	The number of Property objects in the collection.
Parent	IDTSStdobject	The parent object of the Properties collection.

PropertiesProvider

Methods

Name	Returns	Description
GetProperties ForObject	Properties	Gets a Properties collection for the specified automation object.

Property

Properties

Name	Returns	Description
Get	Boolean	Retrieves a property value.
Name	String	The name of the property.
Parent	IDTSStdObject	The parent object of the Property object.
Properties	Properties	The properties of the object.
Set	Boolean	Returns True when a property's value may be changed.
Type	Long	The type property specifies the value type of the Property object.
Value	Variant	The value for the Property object.

PropertyBag

Methods

Name	Returns	Description
Read		Reads a property value.
Write		Writes a property value.

SavedPackageInfo

Properties

Name	Returns	Description
Description	String	A text description of the SavedPackageInfo object.
IsVersion Encrypted	Boolean	Specifies whether this version of the package is encrypted.

Table continued on following page

Name	Returns	Description
Package CreationDate	Date	The package creation date.
PackageID	String	The GUID ID value of the package.
PackageName	String	The name of the package.
VersionID	String	The GUID version ID of the package.
VersionSaveDate	Date	The date and time the package was last saved.

SavedPackageInfos

Methods

Name	Returns	Description
Item	SavedPackageInfo	Retrieves a SavedPackageInfo object by index.

Properties

Name	Returns	Description
Count	Long	The number of SavedPackageInfo objects in the collection.

ScriptingLanguageInfo

Properties

Name	Returns	Description
ClassID	String	Specifies the identifier for the ScriptingLanguage class.
Description	String	Specifies the description of the scripting language.

Name	Returns	Description
Implementation FileName	String	Specifies the implementation file for the scripting language.
Implementation FileVersionString	String	Specifies the implementation file version for the scripting language.
Name	String	The name of the object.
Parent	IDTSStdObject	The parent object of the object.
Properties	Properties	The properties of the object.

ScriptingLanguageInfos

Methods

Name	Returns	Description
Item		Retrieves an object.
Refresh		Executes a refreshes command for the cache and collection.

Properties

Name	Returns	Description
Count	String	Number of items in the collection.
Parent	IDTSStdObject	The parent object of the Step object.
UseCache	String	Specifies whether to cache enumeration information for this collection.

SendMailTask

Methods

Name	Returns	Description
Execute		Executes a SendMailTask.
GetDefault ProfileName		Returns the default profile name.
InitializeMAPI		Initializes the MAPI provider.
Logoff		Ends a MAPI session.
Logon	String	Creates a MAPI session.
ResolveName	String	Resolves an e-mail address.
ShowAddressBook	String	Displays the address book user interface.
UnInitializeMAPI		Uninitializes the MAPI provider.

Properties

Name	Returns	Description
CCLine	String	The e-mail addresses for the CC: line.
Description	String	A text description of the SendMailTask object.
FileAttachments	String	Set the file attachments.
IsNTService	Boolean	Sets whether the caller is a Microsoft Windows NT Service.
MessageText	String	The message body of the e-mail.
Name	String	The name of the SendMailTask object.
Password	String	Specifies the password for making the MAPI connection.
Profile	String	The profile to use to send the e-mail.
Properties	Properties	The properties of the object.
SaveMailInSent ItemsFolder	Boolean	Specifies whether to move the sent e-mail to the Sent Item Folder.
Subject	String	The subject line for the e-mail.
ToLine	String	The TO: line for the e-mail.

Step

Methods

Name	Returns	Description
Execute		Executes the Step object.
GetExecution ErrorInfo		Returns the details about the execution if it fails.

Properties

Name	Returns	Description
ActiveXScript	String	The ActiveX script.
AddGlobal Variables	Boolean	Sets whether global variables may be referenced from other ActiveX scripts.
CloseConnection	Boolean	Sets whether to close a connection on step completion.
CommitSuccess	Boolean	Sets whether to commit a step if it completes successfully.
Description	String	A text description of the step.
DisableStep	Boolean	Specifies whether a step should be executed.
ExecuteIn MainThread	Boolean	Whether the step should be executed in the main thread of the package object.
ExecutionResult	DTSStepExec Result	Returns step execution results.
ExecutionStatus	DTSStepExec Status	Returns the status of the step.
ExecutionTime	Double	Specifies the total execution time in seconds.
FinishTime	Date	The date/time when the step was completed.
FunctionName	String	The name of the function from the ActiveX script.
IsPackage DSORowset	Boolean	When the package is a rowset provider, this property sets when the current step executes and returns a rowset.
JoinTransaction IfPresent	Boolean	Whether a step executes within a Package object's transaction.

Table continued on following page

Name	Returns	Description
Name	String	The name of the Step object.
Parent	IDTSStdObject	The parent object of the Step object.
Precendence Constraints	Precedence Constraints	The execution constraints for the step.
Properties	Properties	The properties of the object.
RelativePriority	DTSStepRelative Priority	The Win32 thread execution priority.
RollbackFailure	Boolean	Sets whether to roll back a step if there is a failure.
ScriptLanguage	String	The scripting language for the step (VBScript, JScript, or PerlScript).
StartTime	Date	The date/time the step began.
TaskName	String	The name of task to execute in the step.

Step2

Entended Properties

Name	Returns	Description
FailPackage OnError	Boolean	Specifies whether DTS will stop the package's execution on an error in this step.

StepLineage

Properties

Name	Returns	Description
ErrorCode	Long	Specifies the source of the error code from Step.Execute.
ErrorDescription	String	Specifies the source of the error description from Step.Execute.
ErrorHelpContext	Long	Specifies the source of the help context from Step.Execute.

Name	Returns	Description
ErrorHelpFile	String	Specifies the source of the error help file from `Step.Execute`.
ErrorSource	String	Specifies the source of the error from `Step.Execute`.
ExecutionTime	Double	Specifies the total time in fractional seconds the step took to execute.
FinishTime	Date	The date/time when the step was completed.
Name	String	The name of the `Step` object.
Parent	IDTSStd Object	The parent object of the `Step` object.
Properties	Properties	The properties of the object.
StartTime	Date	Specifies the time at which the step started.
StepExecution Result	DTSStep ExecResult	Specifies the result of the step's execution.
StepExecution Status	DTSStep ExecStatus	Specifies the status of the step.

StepLineages

Methods

Name	Returns	Description
Next		Returns the next record in the enumeration.

Properties

Name	Returns	Description
EOF	Boolean	Indicates that the last record has been fetched in the enumeration.

StepLogRecord

Properties

Name	Returns	Description
ErrorCode	Long	Specifies the source of the error code from `Step.Execute`.
ErrorDescription	String	Specifies the source of the error description from `Step.Execute`.
ExecutionTime	Double	Specifies the total time in fractional seconds the step took to execute.
FinishTime	Date	The date/time when the step was completed.
LineageFullID	String	GUID for a Package Lineage.
Name	String	The name of the `Step` object.
Parent	IDTSStdObject	The parent object of the `Step` object.
ProgressCount	Variant	Specifies a set of intervals processed by the step. For example, the number of rows that were transformed.
Properties	Properties	The properties of the object.
StartTime	Date	Specifies the time at which the step started.
StepExecutionID	Variant	Specifies the Step execution identifier.
Step ExecutionResult	DTSStep ExecResult	Specifies the result of the step's execution.
Step ExecutionStatus	DTSStep ExecStatus	Specifies the status of the step.

StepLogRecords

Methods

Name	Returns	Description
Next		Returns the next record in the enumeration.

Properties

Name	Returns	Description
EOF	Boolean	Indicates that the last record has been fetched in the enumeration.

Steps

Methods

Name	Returns	Description
Add		Adds a Step object to the collection.
Insert		Adds a Step object to the collection by index.
Item	Step	Retrieves a Step object from the collection.
New	Step	Creates a new Step object.
Remove		Removes a Step object from the collection.

Properties

Name	Returns	Description
Count	Long	The number of Step objects in the collection.
Parent	IDTSStdObject	The parent of the Steps collection.

Task

Methods

Name	Returns	Description
Execute		Executes a Task.

Properties

Name	Returns	Description
CustomTask	CustomTask	Returns the CustomTask object.
CustomTaskID	String	The ProgID or CLSID of the CustomTask object.
Description	String	A descriptive text about the Task object.
Name	String	The name of the Task object.
Parent	IDTSStdObject	The parent object of the Task object.
Properties	Properties	The properties of the object.

Tasks

Methods

Name	Returns	Description
Add		Adds a Task object to the collection.
Insert		Adds a Task object to the collection by index.
Item	Task	Retrieves a Task object from the collection.
New	Task	Creates a new Task object.
Remove		Removes a Task object from the collection.

Properties

Name	Returns	Description
Count	Long	The number of Task objects in the collection.
Parent	IDTSStdobject	The parent of the Tasks collection.

TransferObjectsTask

Methods

Name	Returns	Description
AddObject ForTransfer		Adds an object to the list of objects to be transferred.
CancelExecution		Cancels task execution.
Execute		Executes the `TransferObjectsTask`.
GetObject ForTransfer		Iterates through objects on the list.
ResetObjectsList		Clears the list of objects.

Properties

Name	Returns	Description
CopyAllObjects	Boolean	Sets whether to transfer all objects from the source database.
CopyData	DTSTransfer_ CopyDataOption	Specifies whether data should be copied, and whether existing data should be replaced or appended to.
CopySchema	Boolean	Specifies, based on the `CopyData` property, whether or not data will be copied.
Description	String	A text description of the `TransferObjectTask`.
Destination Database	String	The name of the destination database.
Destination Login	String	The login ID on a destination server.
Destination Password	String	The password for the login ID on a destination server.
Destination Server	String	The destination server name.
Destination UseTrusted Connection	Boolean	Sets whether to use a trusted connection to a destination server.
DropDestination ObjectsFirst	Boolean	Specifies whether to drop objects, if they already exist on the destination.

Table continued on following page

Name	Returns	Description
Include Dependencies	Boolean	Specifies whether dependent objects will be scripted and transferred during an object transfer operation.
IncludeLogins	Boolean	Specifies whether logins will be scripted and transferred during an object transfer operation.
IncludeUsers	Boolean	Specifies whether users will be scripted and transferred during an object transfer operation.
Name	String	The name of the `TransferObjectTask`.
Properties	Properties	The properties of the object.
ScriptFile Directory	String	The directory where the script file and log files are written.
ScriptOption	DTSTransfer_ ScriptOption	Sets the scripting option for the object.
ScriptOptionEx	DTSTransfer_ ScriptOptionEx	Sets the extended scripting option for the object.
SourceDatabase	String	The name of the source database.
SourceLogin	String	The login ID on a source server.
SourcePassword	String	The password for the login ID on a source server.
SourceServer	String	The source server name.
SourceUseTrusted Connection	Boolean	Sets whether to use a trusted connection to a source server.

TransferObjectsTask2

Extended Properties

Name	Returns	Description
DestTranslate Char	Boolean	Determines if translation will be needed for the character data on the destination server. The default setting for this is `True`.
DestUse Transaction	Boolean	Specifies whether to perform operations on the destination server within a transaction. By default, this property is set to `False`.

Name	Returns	Description
SourceTranslate Char	Boolean	Determines if translation will be needed for the character data on the source server. The default setting for this is True.
UseCollation	Boolean	Specifies whether to use column-level collation during the transfer. The default setting for this is True.

Transformation

Properties

Name	Returns	Description
Destination Columns	Columns	The collection of columns for a destination transformation.
ForceBlobs InMemory	Boolean	Specifies whether to always store each source BLOB column in a transformation as a single memory allocation.
ForceSource BlobsBuffered	DTSForceMode	Specifies whether to always buffer each source BLOB column in a transformation.
InMemoryBlob Size	Long	Specifies the size in bytes of per-column allocation for in-memory BLOBs in a transformation.
Name	String	The name of the Transformation object.
Parent	IDTSStdObject	The parent object of the Transformation object.
Properties	Properties	The properties of the object.
SourceColumns	Columns	The collection of columns for a source transformation.
TransformFlags	Long	Sets the transformation flags that indicate characteristics of a transformation.
Transform Server	Object	Contains specification of the dispatch interface of the custom COM server object for a transformation.
Transform ServerID	String	Returns the programmatic identifier (ProgID) or class identifier (CLSID) of the Transformation.

Table continued on following page

Name	Returns	Description
Transform ServerParameter	Variant	Specifies a transform server's initialization parameter.
TransformServer Properties	Properties	Specifies the collection of Automation objects available on the `TransformServer` `IDispatch` interface.

Transformation2

Extended Properties

Name	Returns	Description
TransformPhases	Long	Specifies the phase in which this transform is being called.

TransformationInfo

Properties

Name	Returns	Description
ClassID	String	Specifies the identifier for the `Transformation` class.
Description	String	Specifies the description of the `Transformation` class.
Implementation FileName	String	Specifies the implementation file for the `Transformation` class.
Implementation FileVersionString	String	Specifies the implementation file version for the `Transformation` class.
Name	String	The name of the object.
Parent	IDTSStdObject	The parent object of the object.
Properties	Properties	The properties of the object.

TransformationInfos

Methods

Name	Returns	Description
Item		Retrieves an object.
Refresh		Executes a refresh command for the cache and collection.

Properties

Name	Returns	Description
Count	String	Number of items in the collection.
Parent	IDTSStdObject	The parent object of the Step object.
UseCache	String	Specifies whether to cache enumeration information for this collection.

Transformations

Methods

Name	Returns	Description
Add		Adds a Transformation object to the collection.
Insert		Adds a Transformation object to the collection by index.
Item	Transformation	Retrieves a Transformation object from the collection.
New	Transformation	Creates a new Transformation object.
Remove		Removes a Transformation object from the collection.

Properties

Name	Returns	Description
Count	Long	The number of Transformation objects in the collection.
Parent	IDTSStdObject	The parent of the Transformations collection.

TransformationSet

Properties

Name	Returns	Description
DeleteQuery	String	Specifies the parameterized SQL statement to delete data.
DeleteQuery Columns	Columns	Specifies the column parameters for DeleteQuery.
Description	String	Description of the object.
Destination Column Definitions	Columns	Specifies the destination columns for schema definition.
Exception FileColumn Delimter	String	The column delimiter for the exception file.
Exception FileName	String	The file name where exception rows are written.
Exception FileRow Delimiter	String	The row delimiter for the data in the exception file.
FastLoad Options	DTSFast LoadOptions	Used for the UseFastLoad property to set SQL OLE DB destination connection options.
FetchBuffer Size	Long	Sets the number of rows to fetch during a single operation.
FirstRow	Variant	Gets the first source row from the source.
InsertQuery	String	Specifies the parameterized SQL statement to insert data.
InsertQuery Columns	Columns	Specifies the column parameters for InsertQuery.
LastRow	Variant	Gets the last row from the source to copy.

Name	Returns	Description
Lookups	Lookups	A collection of lookup values.
Maximum ErrorCount	Long	The maximum number of error rows before the data pump terminates operation.
Name	String	The name of the object.
ProgressRow Count	Long	Specifies the frequency at which the progress notification will happen. The default setting for this property is 1000.
Properties	Properties	A list of properties for this object.
Parent	IDTSStdObject	The parent object of the Transformation object.
Properties	Properties	The properties of the object.
Transformations	Transformations	A collection of Transformation objects.
UpdateQuery	String	Specifies the parameterized SQL statement to update data.
UpdateQuery Columns	Columns	Specifies the column parameters for UpdateQuery.
UserQuery	String	Specifies the parameterized SQL statement to user data.
UserQueryColumns	Columns	Specifies the column parameters for UserQuery.

TransformationSets

Methods

Name	Returns	Description
Add		Adds a Transformation object to the collection.
Insert		Adds a Transformation object to the collection by index.
Item	Transformation	Retrieves a Transformation object from the collection.
New	Transformation	Creates a new Transformation object.
Remove		Removes a Transformation object from the collection.

Properties

Name	Returns	Description
Count	Long	The number of Transformation objects in the collection.
Parent	IDTSStdObject	The parent of the Transformations collection.

Global Constants

For each constant enumeration described in the table below, there is a corresponding enumeration with a prefix of LP that should be used by C++ programmers (for example there is a constant enumeration called LPDTSErrorMode that corresponds to DTSErrorMode).

Name	Description
DTSBulkInsert_DataFileType	Specifies the type of data file used for bulk insert operations.
DTSCustomTaskUIFlags	Indicates the type of user interface supported by a custom task.
DTSErrorMode	Error conditions during step execution of a DTS package.
DTSFastLoadOptions	Specifies fast load options for the DataPumpTask.UseFastLoad method.
DTSForceMode	Overrides the default handling of associated properties.
DTSIsolationLevel	The isolation level of a package's transaction.
DTSLineageOptions	Specifies how package execution lineage should be presented and recorded.
DTSPackageError	Error conditions for DTS package creation and execution.
DTSPackagePriorityClass	Win32 process priority class for a DTS package.
DTSRepositoryMetadataOptions	Specifies metadata scanning and resolution options when storing the DTS package to a Repository.
DTSRepositoryStorageFlags	The Repository options when saving or loading the DTS Package.
DTSSQLObjectType	Indicates types of objects available on Microsoft SQL Server.
DTSSQLServerStorageFlags	Specifies Repository options when saving or loading the DTS package.

Name	Description
DTSStepExecResult	The execution result of a DTS Step object.
DTSStepExecStatus	The execution status of a DTS Step object.
DTSStepPrecendenceBasis	The values for a step's precedence value.
DTSStepRelativePriority	The Step object's Win32 thread relative priority.
DTSStepScriptResult	The return code from an ActiveX script step execution.
DTSTaskExecResult	The execution results of a DTS Task.
DTSTransfer_CopyDataOption	Specifies flags indicating whether data should be copied, and whether existing data should be replaced or appended to.
DTSTransfer_ScriptOption	Sets the scripting option for a DTS transfer.
DTSTransfer_ScriptOptionEx	Sets the extended scripting options for a DTS transfer.

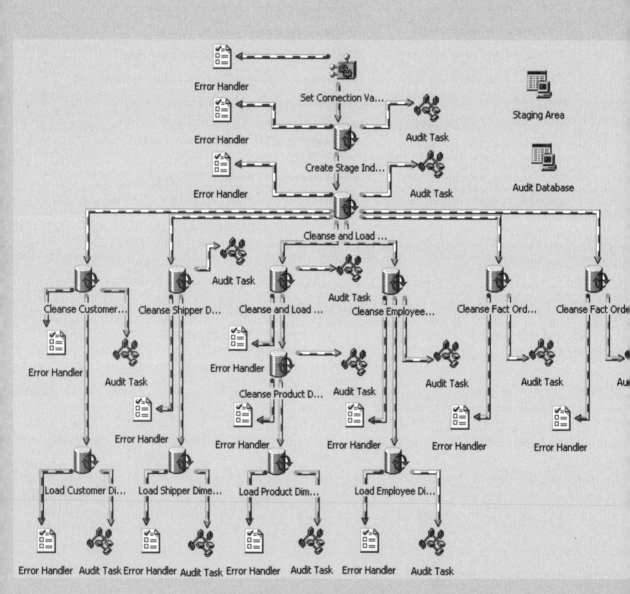

Error Handler

Error Handler

Set Connection Va...

Audit Task

Staging Area

Error Handler

Create Stage Ind...

Audit Task

Audit Database

Error Handler

Cleanse and Load ...

Audit Task

Cleanse Customer...

Audit Task

Cleanse Shipper D...

Cleanse and Load ...

Audit Task

Cleanse Employee...

Cleanse Fact Ord...

Cleanse Fact Orde

Error Handler

Audit Task

Error Handler

Audit Task

Audit Task

Audit Task

Au

Error Handler

Cleanse Product D...

Audit Task

Error Handler

Error Handler

Error Handler

Error Handler

Error Handler

Error Handler

Load Customer Di...

Load Shipper Dime...

Load Product Dim...

Load Employee Di...

Error Handler Audit Task Error Handler Audit Task Error Handler Audit Task Error Handler Audit Task

ADO Object Summary

Microsoft ActiveX Data Objects 2.6 Library Reference

Properties and methods that are new to version 2.6 are shown in **bold** in the first column.

All properties are read/write unless otherwise stated.

The Objects

The Main Objects	Description
Command	A Command object is a definition of a specific command that you intend to execute against a data source.
Connection	A Connection object represents an open connection to a data store.
Recordset	A Recordset object represents the entire set of records from: a base table; the results of an executed command; or a fabricated recordset. At any given time, the 'current record' of a Recordset object refers to a single record within the recordset.

Table continued on following page

The Main Objects	Description
Record	A Record object represents a single resource (file or directory) made available from a Document Source Provider, or a single row from a singleton query.
Stream	A Stream object is an implementation of the IStream COM interface, allowing reading and writing to blocks of memory. In conjunction with the OLE DB Provider for Internet Publishing it allows access to the contents of resources (files) made available from a Document Source Provider. It can also be used to accept the output from executed Commands.

The Other Objects	Description
Error	An Error object contains the details of a data access error pertaining to a single operation involving the provider.
Field	A Field object represents a single column of data within a common data type (Recordset or Record).
Parameter	A Parameter object represents a single parameter or argument associated with a Command object based on a parameterized query or stored procedure.
Property	A Property object represents a single dynamic characteristic of an ADO object that is defined by the provider.

The Collections	Description
Errors	The Errors collection contains all of the Error objects created in response to a single failure involving the provider.
Fields	A Fields collection contains all of the Field objects for a Recordset or Record object.
Parameters	A Parameters collection contains all the Parameter objects for a Command object.
Properties	A Properties collection contains all the Property objects for a specific instance of an ADO object.

The Command Object

Methods of the Command Object	Return Type	Description
Cancel		Cancels execution of a pending Execute or Open call.
CreateParameter	Parameter	Creates a new Parameter object.
Execute	Recordset	Executes the query, SQL statement, or stored procedure specified in the CommandText property.

Note that the **CommandStream** and **NamedParameters** properties are new to ADO 2.6.

Properties of the Command Object	Return Type	Description
ActiveConnection	Variant	Indicates to which Connection object the command currently belongs.
CommandStream	Variant	Identifies the Stream object that contains the commands to be issued against a data provider.
CommandText	String	Contains the text of a command to be issued against a data provider.
CommandTimeout	Long	Indicates how long to wait, in seconds, while executing a command before terminating the command and generating an error. Default is 30.
CommandType	CommandType Enum	Indicates the type of command specified by the Command object.
Dialect	String	A Globally Unique IDentifier (GUID) that identifies the command dialect to be used by a particular command.
Name	String	Indicates the name of the Command object.
NamedParameters	Boolean	Indicates whether or not the Parameter names are sent to the provider or whether Parameters are identified by their position in the collection.
Prepared	Boolean	Indicates whether or not to save a compiled version of a command before execution.
State	Long	Describes whether the Command object is open or closed. Read only.

Collections of the Command Object	Return Type	Description
Parameters	Parameters	Contains all of the Parameter objects for a Command object.
Properties	Properties	Contains all of the Property objects for a Command object.

The Connection Object

Methods of the Connection Object	Return Type	Description
BeginTrans	Integer	Begins a new transaction.
Cancel		Cancels the execution of a pending, asynchronous Execute or Open operation.
Close		Closes an open connection and any dependent objects.
CommitTrans		Saves any changes and ends the current transaction.
Execute	Recordset	Executes the query, SQL statement, stored procedure, or provider-specific text.
Open		Opens a connection to a data store, so that provider-specific statements (such as SQL statements) can be executed against it.
OpenSchema	Recordset	Obtains database schema information from the provider.
RollbackTrans		Cancels any changes made during the current transaction and ends the transaction.

Properties of the Connection Object	Return Type	Description
Attributes	Long	Indicates one or more characteristics of a Connection object. Default is 0.
CommandTimeout	Long	Indicates how long, in seconds, to wait while executing a command before terminating the command and generating an error. The default is 30.
ConnectionString	String	Contains the information used to establish a connection to a data source.

Properties of the Connection Object	Return Type	Description
Connection Timeout	Long	Indicates how long, in seconds, to wait while establishing a connection before terminating the attempt and generating an error. Default is 15.
CursorLocation	CursorLocation Enum	Sets or returns the location of the cursor engine.
Default Database	String	Indicates the default database for a Connection object.
IsolationLevel	IsolationLevel Enum	Indicates the level of transaction isolation for a Connection object.
Mode	ConnectMode Enum	Indicates the available permissions for modifying data in a Connection.
Provider	String	Indicates the name of the provider for a Connection object.
State	ObjectStateEnum	Describes whether the Connection object is open, closed, or currently executing a statement. Read only.
Version	String	Indicates the ADO version number. Read only.

Collections of the Connection Object	Return Type	Description
Errors	Errors	Contains all of the Error objects created in response to a single failure involving the provider.
Properties	Properties	Contains all of the Property objects for a Connection object.

Events of the Connection Object	Description
BeginTransComplete	Fired after a BeginTrans operation finishes executing.
CommitTransComplete	Fired after a CommitTrans operation finishes executing.
ConnectComplete	Fired after a connection opens.
Disconnect	Fired after a connection closes.
ExecuteComplete	Fired after a command has finished executing.
InfoMessage	Fired whenever a ConnectionEvent operation completes successfully and additional information is returned by the provider.

Table continued on following page

The Properties Collection

Methods of the Properties Collection	Return Type	Description
Refresh		Updates the Property objects in the Properties collection with the details from the provider.

Properties of the Properties Collection	Return Type	Description
Count	Long	Indicates the number of Property objects in the Properties collection. Read only.
Item	Property	Allows indexing into the Properties collection to reference a specific Property object. Read only.

The Property Object

Properties of the Property Object	Return Type	Description
Attributes	Long	Indicates one or more characteristics of a Property object.
Name	String	Indicates the name of the Property object. Read only.
Type	DataType Enum	Indicates the data type of the Property object.
Value	Variant	Indicates the value assigned to the Property object.

The Record Object

Methods of the Record Object	Return Type	Description
Cancel		Cancels any pending, asynchronous method call.
Close		Closes the currently open Record.
CopyRecord	String	Copies a file, or a directory and its contents, to a new location.
DeleteRecord		Deletes a file, or a directory and its contents.
GetChildren	Recordset	Returns a Recordset containing the child resources of the Record's underlying resource.
MoveRecord	String	Moves a resource and its contents to a new location.
Open		Opens an existing resource, or creates a new resource.

Properties of the Record Object	Return Type	Description
ActiveConnection	Variant	Identifies the connection details for the resource. Can be a connection string or a Connection object.
Mode	Connect ModeEnum	Indicates the permissions used when opening a Record.
ParentURL	String	Identifies the absolute URL of the parent of the current Record.
RecordType	Record TypeEnum	Indicates the type of the record, whether it's a directory, a simple file, or a complex file.
Source	Variant	Identifies the source of the Record. This will either be a URL or a reference to a Recordset object.
State	Object StateEnum	Indicates whether the Record is open, or closed, or a statement is currently executing.

Collections of the Record Object	Return Type	Description
Fields	Fields	Contains a Field object for each property of the resource.
Properties		Contains all of the Property objects for the current Record object.

The Recordset Object

Methods of the Recordset Object	Return Type	Description
AddNew		Creates a new record for an updateable Recordset object.
Cancel		Cancels execution of a pending asynchronous Open operation.
CancelBatch		Cancels a pending batch update.
CancelUpdate		Cancels any changes made to the current record, or to a new record, prior to calling the Update method.
Clone	Recordset	Creates a duplicate Recordset object from an existing Recordset object.
Close		Closes the Recordset object and any dependent objects, including clones.

Table continued on following page

Methods of the Recordset Object	Return Type	Description
CompareBookmarks	Compare Enum	Compares two bookmarks and returns an indication of the relative values.
Delete		Deletes the current record or group of records.
Find		Searches the Recordset for a record that matches the specified criteria.
GetRows	Variant	Retrieves multiple records of a Recordset object into an array.
GetString	String	Returns a Recordset as a string.
Move		Moves the position of the current record in a Recordset.
MoveFirst		Moves the position of the current record to the first record in the Recordset.
MoveLast		Moves the position of the current record to the last record in the Recordset.
MoveNext		Moves the position of the current record to the next record in the Recordset.
MovePrevious		Moves the position of the current record to the previous record in the Recordset.
NextRecordset	Recordset	Clears the current Recordset object and returns the next Recordset by advancing to the next in a series of commands.
Open		Opens a Recordset.
Requery		Updates the data in a Recordset object by re-executing the query on which the object is based.
Resync		Refreshes the data in the Recordset object with the current data from the underlying data store.
Save		Saves the Recordset to a file, a Stream, or any object that supports the standard COM IStream interface (such as the ASP Response object).
Seek		Searches the recordset index to locate a value.
Supports	Boolean	Determines whether a specified Recordset object supports particular functionality.
Update		Saves any changes made to the current Recordset object.
UpdateBatch		Writes all pending batch modifications (updates, inserts, and deletes) to the underlying data store.

Properties of the Recordset Object	Return Type	Description
AbsolutePage	PositionEnum	Specifies the page in which the current record resides.
AbsolutePosition	PositionEnum	Specifies the ordinal position of the Recordset object's current record.
ActiveCommand	Object	Indicates the Command object that created the associated Recordset object. Read only.
ActiveConnection	Variant	Indicates the Connection object to which the Recordset object currently belongs.
BOF	Boolean	Indicates whether the record pointer is pointing before the first record in the Recordset object. Read only.
Bookmark	Variant	Returns a bookmark that uniquely identifies the current record in the Recordset object, or sets the record pointer to point to the record identified by a valid bookmark.
CacheSize	Long	Indicates the number of records from the Recordset object that are cached locally in memory.
CursorLocation	Cursor LocationEnum	Sets or returns the location of the cursor engine.
CursorType	CursorType Enum	Indicates the type of cursor used in the Recordset object.
DataMember	String	Specifies the name of the data member to be retrieved from the object referenced by the DataSource property.
DataSource	Object	Specifies an object containing data, to be represented by the Recordset object.
EditMode	EditModeEnum	Indicates the editing status of the current record. Read only.
EOF	Boolean	Indicates whether the record pointer is pointing beyond the last record in the Recordset object. Read only.
Filter	Variant	Indicates a filter for data in the Recordset.
Index	String	Identifies the name of the index currently being used.
LockType	LockTypeEnum	Indicates the type of locks placed on records during editing.

Table continued on following page

Properties of the Recordset Object	Return Type	Description
MarshalOptions	Marshal OptionsEnum	Indicates which records are to be marshaled back to the server, or across thread or process boundaries.
MaxRecords	Long	Indicates the maximum number of records that can be returned to the Recordset object from a query. Default is zero (no limit).
PageCount	Long	Indicates how many pages of data are contained in the Recordset object (and is thus dependent on the values of PageSize and RecordCount). Read only.
PageSize	Long	Indicates how many records constitute one page in the Recordset.
RecordCount	Long	Indicates the current number of records in the Recordset object. Read only.
Sort	String	Specifies one or more field names the Recordset is sorted on, and the direction of the sort.
Source	String	Indicates the statement used to populate the data in the Recordset object.
State	Long	Indicates whether the recordset is open, closed, or is executing an asynchronous operation. Read only.
Status	Integer	Indicates the status of the current record with respect to match updates or other bulk operations. Read only.
StayInSync	Boolean	Indicates, in a hierarchical Recordset object, whether the parent row should change when the set of underlying child records changes. Read only.

Collections of the Recordset Object	Return Type	Description
Fields	Fields	Contains all of the Field objects for the Recordset object.
Properties	Properties	Contains all of the Property objects for the current Recordset object.

Events of the Recordset Object	Description
EndOfRecordset	Fired when there is an attempt to move to a row past the end of the Recordset.
FetchComplete	Fired after a Recordset has been populated with all of the rows from an asynchronous operation.
FetchProgress	Fired periodically during a lengthy asynchronous operation, to report how many rows have currently been retrieved.
FieldChangeComplete	Fired after the value of one or more Field objects has been changed.
MoveComplete	Fired after the current position in the Recordset changes.
RecordChangeComplete	Fired after one or more records change.
RecordsetChangeComplete	Fired after the Recordset has changed.
WillChangeField	Fired before a pending operation changes the value of one or more Field objects.
WillChangeRecord	Fired before one or more rows in the Recordset change.
WillChangeRecordset	Fired before a pending operation changes the Recordset.
WillMove	Fired before a pending operation changes the current position in the Recordset.

The Stream Object

Methods of the Stream Object	Return Type	Description
Cancel		Cancels any pending, asynchronous commands.
Close		Closes the current Stream.
CopyTo		Copies a number of characters or bytes into another Stream object.
Flush		Forces the contents of the buffer into the underlying object.
LoadFromFile		Loads the contents of a file into the Stream object.
Open		Opens a Stream object from a URL or a Record object.
Read	Variant	Reads a number of bytes from the Stream.
ReadText	String	Reads a number of characters from the Stream.
SaveToFile		Saves the contents of a Stream to a file.
SetEOS		Sets the position that identifies the end of the stream.

Table continued on following page

Methods of the Stream Object	Return Type	Description
SkipLine		Skips a line when reading in a text stream. Uses the LineSeparator property to identify the end of line character.
Write		Writes binary data to the stream.
WriteText		Writes text data to the stream.

Properties of the Stream Object	Return Type	Description
Charset	String	Indicates the character set to translate the Stream contents into.
EOS	Boolean	Indicates whether or not the end of the Stream has been reached.
LineSeparator	Line Separator Enum	Identifies the binary character that separates lines.
Mode	Connect ModeEnum	Identifies the permissions used when opening the Stream.
Position	Long	Identifies the current position within the Stream.
Size	Long	Indicates, in bytes, the size of the Stream.
State	Object StateEnum	Indicates whether the Stream is open or closed.
Type	Stream TypeEnum	Indicates whether the Stream contains binary or text data.

ADO Method Calls – Quick Reference

Command Object Methods

```
Command.Cancel
Parameter = Command.CreateParameter([Name As String], [Type As DataTypeEnum], _
          [Direction As ParameterDirectionEnum], [Size As Integer], _
          [Value As Variant])
Recordset = Command.Execute([RecordsAffected As Variant], _
          [Parameters As Variant], [Options As Long])
```

Connection Object Methods

```
Long = Connection.BeginTrans
Connection.Cancel
Connection.Close
Connection.CommitTrans
Recordset = Connection.Execute(CommandText As String, _
          [RecordsAffected As Variant], [Options As Long])
Connection.Open([ConnectionString As String], [UserID As String], _
          [Password As String], [Options As Long])
Recordset = Connection.OpenSchema(Schema As SchemaEnum, _
          [Restrictions As Variant], [SchemaID As Variant])
Connection.RollbackTrans
```

Errors Collection Methods

```
Errors.Clear
Errors.Refresh
```

Field Object Methods

```
Field.AppendChunk(Data As Variant)
Variant = Field.GetChunk(Length As Long)
```

Fields Collection Methods

```
Fields.Append(Name As String, Type As DataTypeEnum, [DefinedSize As Long], _
            [Attrib As FieldAttributeEnum], [FieldValue As Variant])
Fields.CancelUpdate
Fields.Delete(Index As Variant)
Fields.Refresh
Fields.Resync([ResyncValues As ResyncEnum])
Fields.Update
```

Parameter Object Methods

```
Parameter.AppendChunk(Val As Variant)
```

Parameters Collection Methods

```
Parameters.Append(Object As Object)
Parameters.Delete(Index As Variant)
Parameters.Refresh
```

Properties Collection Methods

```
Properties.Refresh
```

Record Object Methods

```
Record.Cancel
Record.Close
String = Record.CopyRecord([Source As String], [Destination As String], _
             [UserName As String], [Password As String], _
             [Options As CopyRecordOptionsEnum], [Async As Boolean])
Record.DeleteRecord([Source As String], [Async As Boolean])
Recordset = Record.GetChildren
String = Record.MoveRecord([Source As String], [Destination As String], _
             [UserName As String], [Password As String], _
             [Options As MoveRecordOptionsEnum], [Async As Boolean])
Record.Open([Source As Variant], [ActiveConnection As Variant], _
             [Mode As ConnectModeEnum], _
             [CreateOptions As RecordCreateOptionsEnum], _
             [Options as RecordOpenOptionsEnum], [UserName As String], _
             [Password As String])
```

Recordset Object Methods

```
Recordset.AddNew([FieldList As Variant], [Values As Variant])
Recordset.Cancel
Recordset.CancelBatch([AffectRecords As AffectEnum])
Recordset.CancelUpdate
Recordset = Recordset.Clone([LockType As LockTypeEnum])
Recordset.Close
CompareEnum = Recordset.CompareBookmarks(Bookmark1 As Variant, _
                Bookmark2 As Variant)
Recordset.Delete([AffectRecords As AffectEnum])
Recordset.Find(Criteria As String, [SkipRecords As Long], _
             [SearchDirection As SearchDirectionEnum], [Start As Variant])
Variant = Recordset.GetRows([Rows As Long], [Start As Variant], _
             [Fields As Variant])
String = Recordset.GetString(StringFormat As StringFormatEnum, _
             [NumRows As Long], [ColumnDelimeter As String], _
             [RowDelimeter As String], [NullExpr As String])
Recordset.Move(NumRecords As Long, [Start As Variant])
Recordset.MoveFirst
Recordset.MoveLast
Recordset.MoveNext
Recordset.MovePrevious
Recordset = Recordset.NextRecordset([RecordsAffected As Variant])
Recordset.Open([Source As Variant], [ActiveConnection As Variant], _
             [CursorType As CursorTypeEnum], [LockType As LockTypeEnum], _
             [Options As Long])
Recordset.Requery([Options As Long])
Recordset.Resync([AffectRecords As AffectEnum], [ResyncValues As ResyncEnum])
Recordset.Save([FileName As String], [PersistFormat As PersistFormatEnum])
Recordset.Seek(KeyValues As Variant, SeekOption As SeekEnum)
Boolean = Recordset.Supports(CursorOptions As CursorOptionEnum)
Recordset.Update([Fields As Variant], [Values As Variant])
Recordset.UpdateBatch([AffectRecords As AffectEnum])
```

Stream Object Methods

```
Stream.Cancel
Stream.Close
Stream.CopyTo(DestStream As Stream, [CharNumber As Long])
Stream.Flush
Stream.LoadFromFile(FileName As String)
Stream.Open([Source As Variant], [Mode As ConnectModeEnum], _
            [Options As StreamOpenOptionsEnum], [UserName As String], _
            [Password As String])
Variant = Stream.Read([NumBytes As Long])
String = Stream.ReadText([NumChars As Long])
Stream.SaveToFile(FileName As String, [Options As SaveOptionsEnum])
Stream.SetEOS
Stream.SkipLine
Stream.Write(Buffer As Variant)
Stream.WriteText(Data As String, [Options As StreamWriteEnum])
```

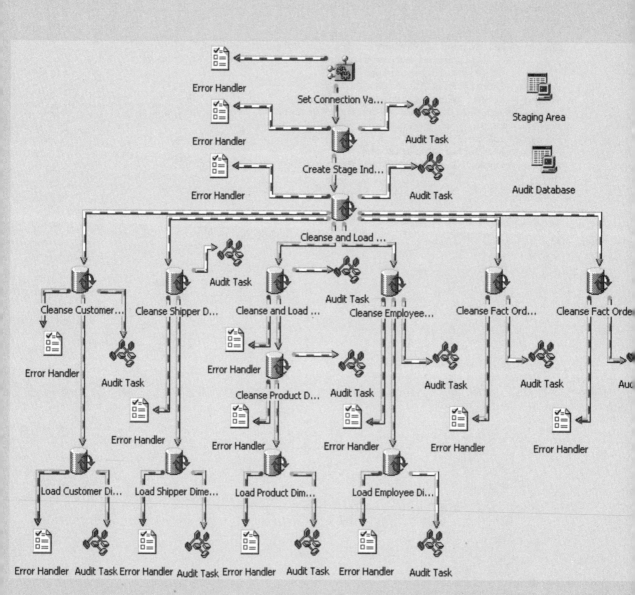

Error Handler

Set Connection Va...

Audit Task

Staging Area

Error Handler

Create Stage Ind...

Audit Task

Audit Database

Error Handler

Cleanse and Load ...

Audit Task

Audit Task

Cleanse Customer...

Cleanse Shipper D...

Cleanse and Load ...

Audit Task

Cleanse Employee...

Cleanse Fact Ord...

Cleanse Fact Order

Error Handler

Audit Task

Error Handler

Audit Task

Audit Task

Audit Task

Au

Cleanse Product D...

Audit Task

Error Handler

Error Handler

Error Handler

Error Handler

Error Handler

Load Customer Di...

Load Shipper Dime...

Load Product Dim...

Load Employee Di...

Error Handler Audit Task Error Handler Audit Task Error Handler Audit Task Error Handler Audit Task

C

Visual Basic Functions and Keywords

This appendix contains a reference of functions and keywords in VBScript. The function and keyword references are grouped in categories and they include the full syntax, an explanation, notes, sample code, and a "See also" list. The function references also include a list of named constants and their values.

Please note that there are several VB constructs that are not supported in VBScript. These include File I/O (for security reasons), the `Debug` and `Collection` objects, some conversion functions, and the complete set of financial functions. The list we provide in this appendix is only a partial list, but covers most of the functions you'll use in DTS.

Operators

An operator acts on one or more operands when comparing, assigning, concatenating, calculating, and performing logical operations.

Say you want to calculate the difference between two variables, A and B, and save the result in variable C. These variables are the operands and to find the difference you use the subtraction operator, like this:

```
C = A - B
```

Here we used the assignment operator (=) to assign the difference between A and B, which was found by using the subtraction operator (-).

Operators are one of the most important parts of any programming language. Without them, you would not be able to assign values to variables or perform calculations and comparisons! It would be a bit like a bicycle without pedals...

There are different types of operators and they each serve a specific purpose, as you will see from the following.

Assignment Operator

The assignment operator is simply used for assigning a value to a variable or property. See the **Set** keyword for an explanation of how to reference and assign objects.

=	Name	**Assignment**
	Description	Assigns the result of an expression, the value of a constant, or the value of another variable to a variable or property.
	Syntax	`Variable = value`

Arithmetic Operators

The arithmetic operators are all used to calculate a numeric value, and are normally used in conjunction with the **assignment operator** and/or one of the **comparison operators**; they are listed in order of **Operator Precedence**.

^	Name	**Exponentiation**
	Description	Raises a number to the power of an exponent.
	Syntax	`Result = number ^ exponent`
		number and *exponent* is any valid numeric expression.
	Example	`MsgBox 5 ^ 5`
		MsgBox displays *3125*, which is the result of raising the number 5 to the exponent 5.

*	Name	**Multiplication**
	Description	Multiplies two numbers.
	Syntax	`Result = number1 * number2`
	Example	*number1* and *number2* is any valid numeric expression.
		`MsgBox 5 * 5`
		MsgBox displays *25*, which is the result of multiplying the number 5 by 5.

/	Name	**Floating Point Division**
	Description	Returns a floating point result when dividing two numbers.
	Syntax	`Result = number1 / number2`
		number1 and *number2* are any valid numeric expressions.
	Example	`MsgBox 5 / 4`
		`MsgBox` displays *1.25*, which is the result of dividing the number 5 by 4.

\	Name	**Integer Division**
	Description	Returns the integer part of the result when dividing two numbers.
	Syntax	`Result = number1 \ number2`
		number1 and *number2* are any valid numeric expressions.
	Example	`MsgBox 5 \ 4`
		`MsgBox` displays *1*, which is the integer part of the result when dividing the number 5 by 4.
	Note	The numeric expressions are rounded to `Byte`, `Integer`, or `Long` subtype expressions, before the integer division is performed. They are rounded to the smallest possible subtype: a value of 255 will be rounded to a `Byte`, and 256 will be rounded to an `Integer` and so on.

Mod	Name	**Modulus Division**
	Description	Returns the remainder when dividing two numbers.
	Syntax	`Result = number1 Mod number2`
		number1 and *number2* are any valid numeric expressions.
	Example	`MsgBox 5 Mod 4`
		`MsgBox` displays *1*, which is the remainder part of the result, when dividing the number 5 by 4.
	Note	The numeric expressions are rounded to `Byte`, `Integer`, or `Long` subtype expressions, before the modulus division is performed. They are rounded to the smallest possible subtype: a value of 255 will be rounded to a `Byte`, 256 will be rounded to an `Integer` and so on.

+	Name	**Addition**
	Description	Sums two expressions.
	Syntax	`Result = expression1 + expression2`
		expression1 and *expression2* are any valid numeric expressions.
	Example	`MsgBox 5 + 5`
		MsgBox displays *10*, which is the result of adding the number 5 to 5.
	Note	If one or both expressions are numeric, the expressions will be summed, but if both expressions are strings, they will be concatenated. This is important to understand, especially if you have a Java background, in order to avoid run time errors. In general use the & operator (*see under* **Concatenation Operators**), when concatenating and the + operator when dealing with numbers.

–	Name	**Subtraction**
	Description	Subtracts one number from another or indicates the negative value of an expression.
	Syntax (1)	`Result = number1 - number2`
		number1 and *number2* are any valid numeric expressions.
	Example(1)	`MsgBox 5 - 4`
		MsgBox displays *1*, which is the result of subtracting the number 4 from 5.
	Syntax (2)	`-number`
		number is any valid numeric expression.
	Example (2	`MsgBox -(5 - 4)`
		MsgBox displays *-1*, which is the result of subtracting the number 4 from 5 and using the unary negation operator (-) to indicate a negative value.

Concatenation Operators

Concatenation operators are used for concatenating expressions; they are listed in order of **Operator Precedence**.

&	Name	**Ampersand**
	Description	Concatenates two expressions.
	Syntax	Returns the concatenated expressions:
		`Result = expression1 & expression2`
	Example	If *expression1* is "WROX " and *expression2* is " Press" then the result is "WROX Press".
	Note	The expressions are converted to a `String` subtype, if they are not already of this subtype.

+	Name	**Plus Operator**
	Description	Does the same as the & operator if both expressions are strings.
	Syntax	Returns the concatenated or summed expressions:
		`Result = expression1 + expression2`
	Example	`1 + "1" = 2`
		`"1" + "1" = "11"`
	Note	If one or both expressions are numeric, the + operator will work as an arithmetic + operator and sum the expressions. A runtime error occurs if one expression is numeric and the other a string containing no numbers. It is recommended that + should only be used for numeric addition and *never* for concatenation purposes (use & instead).

Comparison Operators

The comparison operators are used for comparing variables and expressions against other variables, constants or expressions; they are listed in order of **Operator Precedence**.

One important thing to remember when comparing strings is case sensitivity. You can use the **UCase** and **LCase** functions to make sure that the strings you compare are the same case; the **StrComp** function offers another way of dealing with case sensitivity (*see under* **String Functions**). A binary comparison is always case sensitive. If only one of the expressions is a string and the other is numeric, the numeric expression is always less than the string expression.

Null is returned if either expression is Null. If either expression is Empty, it is converted to the value 0, if the other expression is numeric and to an empty string (""), if the other expression is a string. In case both expressions are Empty, they are obviously equal.

The **Is** operator is for dealing with objects and Variants.

=	Name	**Equal to**
	Description	Returns True if *expression1* is equal to *expression2*; False otherwise.
	Syntax	`Result = expression1 = expression2`

<>	Name	**Not equal to (different from)**
	Description	Returns True if *expression1* is not equal to *expression2*; False otherwise.
	Syntax	`Result = expression1 <> expression2`

<	Name	**Less than**
	Description	Returns True if *expression1* is less than *expression2*; False otherwise.
	Syntax	`Result = expression1 < expression2`

>	Name	**Greater than**
	Description	Returns True if *expression1* is greater than *expression2*; False otherwise.
	Syntax	`Result = expression1 > expression2`

<=	Name	**Less than or equal to**
	Description	Returns True if *expression1* is less than or equal to *expression2*; False otherwise.
	Syntax	`Result = expression1 <= expression2`

>=	Name	**Greater than or equal to**
	Description	Returns True if *expression1* is greater than or equal to *expression2*; False otherwise.
	Syntax	`Result = expression1 >= expression2`

Is	Name	**Compare objects**
	Description	Returns True if *object1* and *object2* refer to the same memory location (if they are in fact the same object).
	Syntax	`Result = object1 Is object2`
	Note	Use the `Not` operator (*see under* **Logical Operators**) with the `Is` operator to get the opposite effect:
		`Result = object1 Not Is object2`
		Use the `Nothing` keyword with the `Is` operator to check if an object reference is valid. Returns True if object has been destroyed.
		`(Set object = Nothing):`
		`Result = object Is Nothing`
		Be careful, **Nothing** is NOT the same as **Empty**. **Nothing** references an invalid object reference, whereas **Empty** is used for any variable that has been assigned the value of `Empty`, or has not yet been assigned a value.

Logical Operators

The logical operators are used for performing logical operations on expressions; they are listed in order of **Operator Precedence**. All logical operators can also be used as bitwise operators (*see under* **Bitwise Operators**).

Not	Used to	Negate the expression.
	Returns	Returns the logical negation of an expression.
	Syntax	`Result = Not expression`
	Note	Result will be True if *expression* is False; and False if *expression* is True. `Null` will be returned if *expression* is `Null`.

And	Used to	Check if both expressions are True.
	Returns	Returns True if both expressions evaluate to True; otherwise, False is returned.
	Syntax	`Result = expression1 And expression2`

Or	Used to	Check if one or both expressions are True.
	Returns	Returns True if one or both expressions evaluate to True; otherwise, False is returned.
	Syntax	`Result = expression1 Or expression2`

Xor	Used to	Check if one and only one expression is True.
	Returns	`Null` will be returned if either expression is `Null`.
	Syntax	`Result = expression1 Xor expression2`
	Note	Returns True if only one of the expressions evaluates to True; otherwise, False is returned.

Eqv	Used to	Check if both expressions evaluate to the same logical value.
	Returns	Returns True if both expressions evaluate to the same value (True or False).
	Syntax	`Result = expression1 Eqv expression2`
	Note	`Null` will be returned if either expression is `Null`.

Imp	Used to	Perform a logical implication.
	Returns	Returns these values:
		`True Imp True = True`
		`False Imp True = True`
		`False Imp False = True`
		`False Imp Null = True`
		`Null Imp True = True`
		`True Imp False = False`
		`True Imp Null = Null`
		`Null Imp False = Null`
		`Null Imp Null = Null`
	Syntax	`Result = expression1 Imp expression2`

Bitwise Operators

Bitwise operators are used for comparing binary values bit-by-bit; they are listed in order of **Operator Precedence**. All bitwise operators can also be used as logical operators (*see under* **Logical** *Operators*).

Not	Used to	Invert the bit values.
	Returns	Returns 1 if bit is 0 and vice versa.
	Syntax	`Result = Not expression`
	Example	If *expression* is 101 then *Result* is 010.

And	Used to	Check if both bits are set to 1.
	Returns	Returns 1 if both bits are 1; otherwise, 0 is returned.
	Syntax	`Result = expression1 And expression2`
	Example	If *expression1* is 101 and *expression2* is 100 then *result* is 100.

Or	Used to	Check if one of the bits is set to 1.
	Returns	Returns 1 if one or both bits are 1; otherwise, 0 is returned.
	Syntax	`Result = expression1 Or expression2`
	Example	If *expression1* is 101 and *expression2* is 100 then *Result* is 101.

Xor	Used to	Check if one and only one of the bits is set to 1.
	Returns	Returns 1 if only one bit is 1; otherwise, 0 is returned.
	Syntax	`Result = expression1 Xor expression2`
	Example	If *expression1* is 101 and *expression2* is 100 then *Result* is 001.

Eqv	Used to	Check if both bits evaluate to the same value.
	Returns	Returns 1 if both bits evaluate to the same value (0 or 1).
	Syntax	`Result = expression1 Eqv expression2`
	Example	If *expression1* is 101 and *expression2* is 100 then *Result* is 110.

Imp	Used to	Perform a logical implication on two bits.
	Returns	Returns these values:
		`0 Imp 0` = 1
		`0 Imp 1` = 1
		`1 Imp 1` = 1
		`1 Imp 0` = 0
	Syntax	`Result = expression1 Imp expression2`
	Example	If *expression1* is 101 and *expression2* is 100 then *Result* is 110.

Operator Precedence

When more than one operation occurs in an expression they are normally performed from left to right. However, there are several rules.

Operators from the arithmetic group are evaluated first, then concatenation, comparison, and logical operators.

This is the complete order in which operations occur (operators in brackets have the same precedence):

```
^, -, (*, /), \, Mod, (+, -),
&,
=, <>, <, >, <=, >=, Is,
Not, And, Or, Xor, Eqv, Imp
```

This order can be overridden by using parentheses. Operations in parentheses are evaluated before operations outside the parentheses, but inside the parentheses, the normal precedence rules apply.

Math Functions

Every now and then, depending on what kind of applications you design, you will need to do some math calculations and VBScript goes a long way towards helping you here. There are a number of intrinsic functions, but it is also possible to derive many other math functions from the intrinsic ones. Math functions are especially helpful when you need to display graphics, charts etc.; the listing is in alphabetical order.

Abs	Returns the absolute value of a number, that is, its unsigned magnitude.
Syntax	`Abs(number)`
	number is any valid numeric expression.
Note	Null will be returned if *number* contains Null.
Example	`Abs(-50) ' 50` `Abs(50)  ' 50`
See Also	**Sgn**

Fix	Returns the integer part of a number.
Syntax	`Fix(number)`
Note	Fix is internationally aware, which means that the return value is based on the locale settings on the machine.
	Null is returned if *number* contains Null. The data type returned will be decided from the size of the integer part. Possible return data types in ascending order: Integer, Long, and Double.
	If *number* is negative, the first negative integer equal to or greater than *number* is returned.

Example	`Dim vntPosValue`
	
	`Dim vntNegValue`
	
	`    vntPosValue = Fix(5579.56)`
	`    vntNegValue = Fix(-5579.56)`

	vntPosValue now holds the value 5579, and vntNegValue the value -5579.
	Fix is the equivalent of Int when dealing with non-negative numbers. When you handle negative numbers, Fix returns the first negative integer, greater than, or equal to the number supplied.
See Also	**Int, Round**, and the **Conversion Functions CInt**, and **CLng**

Int	Returns the integer part of a number.
Syntax	`Int(number)` *number* is any valid numeric expression.
Note	`Int` is internationally aware, which means that the return value is based on the locale settings on the machine. `Null` is returned if *number* contains `Null`. The data type returned will be decided from the size of the integer part. Possible return data types in ascending order: `Integer`, `Long`, and `Double`. If *number* is negative, the first negative integer equal to or less than *number* is returned.

Example	<pre>Dim vntPosValue
	Dim vntNegValue
	
	    vntPosValue = Int(5579.56)
	    vntNegValue = Int(-5579.56)</pre>
	`vntPosValue` now holds the value 5579, and `vntNegValue` the value -5580.
	
	`Int` is the equivalent of `Fix` when dealing with non-negative numbers. When you handle negative numbers, `Int` returns the first negative integer, less than or equal to the number supplied.

See Also	**Fix**, **Round**, and the **Conversion Functions CInt**, and **CLng**

Randomize	Initilizes the random number generator, by giving it a new seed-value. A seed-value is an initial value used for generating "random" numbers.
Syntax	`Randomize [number]` *number* is any valid numeric expression.
Note	You can repeat a sequence of "random" numbers, by calling the `Rnd` function with a negative *number*, before using the Randomize statement with a numeric argument.

Example	<pre>Const LNG_UPPER_BOUND = 20
	Const LNG_LOWER_BOUND = 1
	
	Dim intValue
	Dim lngCounterIn
	Dim lngCounterOut
	
	    For lngCounterOut = 1 To 3
	        Rnd -1
	        Randomize 3
	
	        For lngCounterIn = 1 To 3
	            intValue = Int((LNG_UPPER_BOUND - LNG_LOWER_BOUND + 1) * _
	                        Rnd + LNG_LOWER_BOUND)
	            MsgBox intValue
	        Next
	    Next</pre>

Table continued on following page

Example	The above sample has an inner loop that generates three "random" numbers and an outer loop that calls the Rnd function with a negative number, immediately before calling Randomize with an argument. This makes sure that the "random" numbers generated in the inner loop will be the same for every loop the outer loop performs.
See Also	**Rnd**

Rnd	Returns a "random" number, less than 1 but greater than or equal to 0.
Syntax	Rnd[(number)]

number (Optional) is any valid numeric expression that determines how the random number is generated; if *number* is:

< 0 – uses same number every time,

> 0 or missing – uses next "random" number in sequence,

= 0 – uses most recently generated number. |
| Note | Use the Randomize statement, with no argument, to initialize the random-number generator with a seed based on the system timer, before calling Rnd.

The same number sequence is generated for any given initial seed, because each successive call to Rnd uses the previous number as the seed for the next number in the sequence.

Call Rnd with a negative argument immediately before using Randomize with a numeric argument, in order to repeat sequences of "random" numbers. |
| Example | ```
Const LNG_UPPER_BOUND = 20

Const LNG_LOWER_BOUND = 1

Dim intValue
Dim lngCounter

    For lngCounter = 1 To 10

        intValue = Int(_
                      (LNG_UPPER_BOUND - _
                      LNG_LOWER_BOUND + 1) * _
                      Rnd + LNG_LOWER_BOUND)

        MsgBox intValue
    Next
```

This produces 10 "random" integers in the range 1-20. |
| See Also | **Randomize** |
```

Round	Returns a number rounded to a specified number of decimal places as a Variant subtype `Double` (5).
Syntax	`Round(number, [numdecimalplaces])` *number* is any valid numeric expression. *numdecimalplaces,* (Optional) indicates how many places to the right of the decimal separator should be included in the rounding.
Note	An integer is returned if *numdecimalplaces* is missing.
Example	``` Round(10.4) ' Returns 10 Round(10.456) ' Returns 10 Round(-10.456) ' Returns -10 Round(10.4, 2) ' Returns 10.4 Round(10.456, 2) ' Returns 10.46 Round(-10.456, 2) ' Returns -10.46 ```
See Also	**Int** and **Fix**

Date and Time Functions and Statements

There are a number of ways to display and represent dates and times. These include date literals, which are valid date expressions, enclosed in number signs (#). You need to be careful when using date literals because VBScript only lets you use the US-English date format, mm/dd/yyyy. This is true even if a different locale is being used on the machine. This might lead to problems when trying to use date literals in other formats, because in most cases the date will be accepted although converted to a different date. #10/12/1997# will be interpreted as October 12, 1997, but you might in fact want December 10, 1997, because your locale settings interprets dates as dd/mm/yyyy. Date literals only accept the forward slash (/) as the date separator.

The data range for a date is January 1, 100 to December 31, 9999, both inclusive. Internally, dates are stored as part of real numbers or to be more specific as a Variant subtype `Double` (5). The digits to the left of the decimal separator represent the date and the digits to the right of the decimal separator represent the time. Negative numbers are used internally for representing dates prior to December 30, 1899.

Below is a list of functions used for converting and formatting dates and times.

CDate	Returns an expression converted to Variant subtype `Date` (7).
Syntax	`CDate(date)` *date* is any valid `date` expression.
Note	CDate is internationally aware, which means that the return value is based on the locale settings on the machine. Dates and times will be formatted with the appropriate time and date separators, and for dates the correct order of year, month and day are applied. Date and time literals are recognized.
Example	``` Dim dtmValue dtmValue = CDate(#12/10/1997#) ``` dtmValue now holds the value "10-12-97", if your locale settings use the dash (-) as the date separator and the short date format is dd/mm/yy.
See Also	**IsDate**

Date	Returns a Variant subtype `Date` (7) indicating the current system date.
Syntax	`Date`
Example	`MsgBox Date`
	Assuming that today is July 29 1999, the `MsgBox` now displays **29-07-99**, if your locale settings use the dash (–) as the date separator and the short date format is dd/mm/yy.
See Also	**Now** and **Time**
DateAdd	Adds or subtracts a time interval to a specified date and returns the new date.
Syntax	`DateAdd(interval, number, date)`
	interval can have these values:
	d Day
	h Hour
	m Month
	n Minute
	q Quarter
	s Second
	w Weekday
	ww Week of year
	y Day of year
	yyyy Year
	number is a numeric expression that must be positive if you want to add or negative if you want to subtract.
	number is rounded to the nearest whole number if it's not a `Long` value.
	date must be a Variant or `date` literal to which *interval* is added.
Note	`DateAdd` is internationally aware, which means that the return value is based on the locale settings on the machine. Dates and times will be formatted with the appropriate time and date separators, and for dates the correct order of year, month and day is applied. An error occurs if the date returned precedes the year 100.
Example	`MsgBox DateAdd("m", 3, "1-Jan-99")`
	This will add 3 months to January 1, 1999 and the `MsgBox` now displays **01-04-99**, if your locale settings use the dash (–) as the date separator and the short date format is dd/mm/yy.
See Also	**DateDiff, DatePart**

DateDiff	Returns the interval between two dates.

Syntax	`DateDiff(interval, date1, date2, [firstdayofweek],`
	`[firstweekofyear])`
	
	interval can have these values:

d	Day
h	Hour
m	Month
n	Minute
q	Quarter
s	Second
w	Weekday
ww	Week of year
y	Day of year
yyyy	Year

date1 and *date2* are date expressions.

firstdayofweek (Optional) specifies the first day of the week. Use one of the following constants:

vbUseSystemDayOfWeek   0 (National Language Support (NLS) API setting. NLS functions help Win32-based applications support the differing language- and location-specific needs of users around the world.)

vbSunday	1 (Default)
vbMonday	2
vbTuesday	3
vbWednesday	4
vbThursday	5
vbFriday	6
vbSaturday	7

firstweekofyear (Optional) specifies the first week of the year. Use one of the following constants:

vbUseSystem	0 (Use NLS API setting)
vbFirstJan1	1 (Default) Week in which January 1 occurs.
vbFirstFourDays	2 First week in the new year with at least four days.
vbFirstFullWeek	3 First full week of the new year.

Note	A negative number is returned if *date1* is later in time than *date2*.
Example	`MsgBox DateDiff("yyyy", #11-22-1967#, Now)`
	This will calculate the number of years between 11/22/1967 and now. In 1999, the `MsgBox` will display 32.
See Also	**DateAdd, DatePart**

DatePart	Returns a specified part of a date.
Syntax	`DatePart(interval, date, [firstdayofweek], [firstweekofyear])` *interval* can have these values: *d* Day *h* Hour *m* Month *n* Minute *q* Quarter *s* Second *w* Weekday *ww* Week of year *y* Day of year *yyyy* Year *date* is a date expression. *firstdayofweek* (Optional) specifies the first day of the week. Use one of the following constants: `vbUseSystemDayOfWeek` 0 (NLS API setting) `vbSunday` 1 (Default) `vbMonday` 2 `vbTuesday` 3 `vbWednesday` 4 `vbThursday` 5 `vbFriday` 6 `vbSaturday` 7 *firstweekofyear* (Optional) specifies the first week of the year. Use one of the following constants: `vbUseSystem` 0 (Use NLS API setting) `vbFirstJan1` 1 (Default) Week in which January 1 occurs. `vbFirstFourDays` 2 First week in the new year with at least four days. `vbFirstFullWeek` 3 First full week of the new year.
Example	`MsgBox DatePart("ww", Now, vbMonday, vbFirstFourDays)` This will extract the week number from the current system date. On July 29, 1999 the `MsgBox` will display **30**.
See Also	**DateAdd, DateDiff**

DateValue	Returns a Variant subtype `Date` (7).
Syntax	`DateValue(date)`
	date is an expression representing a date, a time, or both, in the range January 1, 100 – December 31, 9999.
Note	Time information in *date* is not returned, but invalid time information will result in a run-time error. `DateValue` is internationally aware and uses the locale settings on the machine, when recognizing the order of a date with only numbers and separators. If the year is omitted from *date*, it is obtained from the current system date.

Example	`DateValue("07/29/1999")`
	`DateValue("July 29, 1999")`
	`DateValue("Jul 29, 1999")`
	`DateValue("Jul 29")`

	All of the above will return the same valid date of 07/29/99 in 1999.
See Also	**Date, DateSerial, Day, Month, Now, TimeSerial, TimeValue, Weekday, and Year**

Day	Returns a number between 1 and 31 representing the day of the month.
Syntax	`Day(date)`
	date is any valid date expression.
Note	A run-time error occurs if *date* is not a valid date expression. `Null` will be returned if *date* contains `Null`.
Example	`MsgBox Day("July 29, 1999")`
	The `MsgBox` will display **29**.
See Also	**Date, Hour, Minute, Month, Now, Second, Weekday, and Year**

FormatDateTime	*See under* **String functions**

Hour	Returns an integer between 0 and 23, representing the hour of the day.
Syntax	`Hour(time)`
	time is any valid time expression.
Note	A run-time error occurs if *time* is not a valid time expression. `Null` will be returned if *time* contains `Null`.
Example	`MsgBox Hour("12:05:12")`
	The `MsgBox` will display **12**.
See Also	**Date, Day, Minute, Month, Now, Second, Weekday, and Year**

IsDate	Returns a Variant subtype `Boolean` (11) indicating whether an expression can be converted to a valid date.
Syntax	`IsDate(expression)`
	expression is any expression, you want to evaluate as a date or time.
| Example | ```
MsgBox IsDate(Now)        ' True
MsgBox IsDate("")         ' False
MsgBox IsDate(#7/29/1999#) ' True
``` |
| See Also | **CDate**, **IsArray**, **IsEmpty**, **IsNull**, **IsNumeric**, **IsObject**, and **VarType** |

Minute	Returns a number between 0 and 59, both inclusive, indicating the minute of the hour.
Syntax	`Minute(time)`
	time is any valid time expression.
Note	A run-time error occurs if *time* is not a valid time expression. `Null` will be returned if *time* contains `Null`.
| Example | ```
MsgBox Minute("12:45")
``` |
| | The `MsgBox` will display 45. |
| See Also | **Date**, **Day**, **Hour**, **Month**, **Now**, **Second**, **Weekday**, and **Year** |

Month	Returns a number between 1 and 12, both inclusive, indicating the month of the year.
Syntax	`Month(date)`
	date is any valid date expression.
Note	A runtime error occurs if *date* is not a valid date expression. `Null` will be returned if *date* contains `Null`.
| Example | ```
MsgBox Month(#7/29/1999#)
``` |
| | The `MsgBox` will display 7. |
| See Also | **Date**, **Day**, **Hour**, **Minute**, **Now**, **Second**, **Weekday**, and **Year** |

MonthName	Returns a Variant subtype `String` (8) for the specified month.
Syntax	`MonthName(month, [abbreviate])`
	month is a number between 1 and 12 for each month of the year beginning with January.
	abbreviate (Optional) is a Boolean value indicating if the month name should be abbreviated or spelled out (default).
Note	A run-time error occurs if *month* is outside the valid range (1-12). `MonthName` is internationally aware, which means that the returned strings are localized into the language specified as part of your locale settings.
| Example | ```
MsgBox MonthName(2)        ' February
MsgBox MonthName(2, True)  ' Feb
``` |
| See Also | **WeekdayName** |

Now	Returns the system's current date and time.
Syntax	`Now`
Example	```
Dim dtmValue
        dtmValue = Now
```
`dtmValue` now holds the current system date and time. |
| See Also | **Date, Day, Hour, Month, Minute, Second, Weekday**, and **Year** |

| **Second** | Returns a Variant subtype `Date` (7) indicating the number of seconds (0-59) in the specified time. |
|---|---|
| Syntax | `Second(time)`
*time* is any valid time expression. |
| Note | A runtime error occurs if *time* is not a valid time expression. `Null` will be returned if *time* contains `Null`. |
| Example | ```
MsgBox Second("12:45:56")
```
The `MsgBox` will display 56. |
| See Also | **Date, Day, Hour, Minute, Month, Now, Weekday**, and **Year** |

Time	Returns a Variant subtype `Date` (7) indicating the current system time.
Syntax	`Time`
Example	```
Dim dtmValue
        dtmValue = Time
```
`dtmValue` now holds the current system time. |
| See Also | **Date, Now** |

| **TimeValue** | Returns a Variant subtype `Date` (7) containing the time. |
|---|---|
| Syntax | `TimeValue(time)`
*time* is an expression in the range 0:00:00 – 23:59:59. |
| Note | Date information in *time* is not returned, but invalid date information will result in a run-time error. `Null` is returned if *time* contains `Null`. You can use both 24 and 12-hour representations for the *time* argument. |
| Example | ```
TimeValue("23:59")
TimeValue("11:59 PM")
```
Both will return the same valid time. |
| See Also | **Date, DateSerial, DateValue, Day, Month, Now, TimeSerial, Weekday**, and **Year** |

Weekday	Returns a number indicating the day of the week.
Syntax	`Weekday(date, [firstdayofweek])`
	date is any valid date expression.
	firstdayofweek (Optional) specifies the first day of the week. Use one of the following constants:
	`vbUseSystemDayOfWeek` 0 (Use NLS API setting)
	`vbSunday` 1 (Default)
	`vbMonday` 2
	`vbTuesday` 3
	`vbWednesday` 4
	`vbThursday` 5
	`vbFriday` 6
	`vbSaturday` 7
Note	`Null` is returned if *date* contains `Null`. A run-time occurs if *date* is invalid.
	Possible return values are:
	`vbSunday` 1
	`vbMonday` 2
	`vbTuesday` 3
	`vbWednesday` 4
	`vbThursday` 5
	`vbFriday` 6
	`vbSaturday` 7
Example	`Weekday(#July 29, 1999#)`
	Returns 5 for Thursday.
See Also	**Date, Day, Month, Now,** and **Year**

WeekdayName	Returns a Variant subtype `String` (8) for the specified weekday.
Syntax	`WeekdayName(weekday, [abbreviate], [firstdayofweek])`
	weekday is a number between 1 and 7 for each day of the week. This value depends on the *firstdayofweek* setting.
	abbreviate (Optional) is a Boolean value indicating if the weekday name should be abbreviated or spelled out (default).
	firstdayofweek (Optional) is a numeric value indicating the first day of the week. Use one of the following constants:

`vbUseSystemDayOfWeek`	0	(Use NLS API setting)
`vbSunday`	1	(Default)
`vbMonday`	2	
`vbTuesday`	3	
`vbWednesday`	4	
`vbThursday`	5	
`vbFriday`	6	
`vbSaturday`	7	

Note	A run-time error occurs if *weekday* is outside the valid range (1-7). **WeekdayName** is internationally aware, which means that the returned strings are localized into the language specified as part of your locale settings.
Example	`WeekdayName(2, , vbSunday)  ' Monday` `WeekdayName(1, , vbMonday)  ' Monday`
See Also	**MonthName**

Year	Returns a number indicating the year.
Syntax	`Year(date)`
	date is any valid date expression.
Note	A runtime error occurs if *date* is not a valid date expression. `Null` will be returned if *date* contains `Null`.
Example	`MsgBox Year(#7/29/1999#)`
	The `MsgBox` will display 1999.
See Also	**Date, Day, Month, Now, and Weekday**

Array Functions and Statements

One major difference between VB/VBA and VBScript is the way you can declare your arrays. VBScript does not support the `Option Base` statement and you cannot declare arrays that are not zero-based. Below is a list of functions and statements that you can use for array manipulation in VBScript.

Array	Returns a comma-delimited list of values as a Variant subtype `Array` (8192).
Syntax	`Array(arglist)`
	`arglist` is a comma-delimited list of values that is inserted into the one dimensional array in the order they appear in the list
Note	An array of zero length is created if `arglist` contains no arguments.
	All arrays in VBScript are zero-based, which means that the first element in the list will be element 0 in the returned array.

Example	<pre>Dim arrstrTest
	
	    ' Create an array with three elements
	        arrstrTest = Array(_
	                   "Element0", "Element1", "Element2")
	    ' Show the first list element
	    ' now in the array
	    MsgBox arrstrTest(0)
	MsgBox displays Element0</pre>

See Also	**Dim** statement

Erase	Reinitializes the elements if it is a fixed-size array and de-allocates the memory used if it is a dynamic array.
Syntax	`Erase array`
	array is the array to be reinitialized or erased.
Note	You must know if you are using a fixed-size or a dynamic array, because this statement behaves differently depending on the array type.
	As the memory is de-allocated when using `Erase` with dynamic arrays, you must re-declare the array structure with the `ReDim` statement, before you use it again.
	Fixed-size arrays are reinitialized differently depending on the contents of the elements:
	Numeric Set to 0 Strings Set to "" Objects Set to `Nothing`

Example	<pre>Dim arrstrDynamic()
	Dim arrstrFixed(3)
	
	        ' Allocate space for the
	        ' dynamic array
	        ReDim arrstrDynamic(3)
	        ' Free the memory used by
	        ' the dynamic array
	        Erase arrstrDynamic
	        ' Reinitialize the elements
	        ' in the fixed-size array
	        Erase arrstrFixed</pre>

See Also	**Dim** statement and **ReDim** statement

For Each	Performs a group of statements repeatedly for each element in a collection or an array.
Syntax	For Each element In group [statements] [Exit For] Next [element] *element* is a variable used for iterating through the elements in a collection or an array. *group* is the name of the collection or array. *statements* is one or more statements you want to execute on each item in the group.
Note	The For Each loop is only entered if there is at least one element in the collection or array. All the statements in the loop are executed for all the elements in the group. You can control this by executing the Exit For statement if a certain condition is met. This will exit the loop and start executing on the first line after the Next statement. For Each loops can be nested, but you must make sure that each loop element is unique.

Example	<pre>Dim arrstrLoop
	Dim strElement
	
	     ' Create the array
	     arrstrLoop = Array("Element0", "Element1", "Element2")
	     ' Loop through the array
	     For Each strElement In arrstrLoop
	          ' Display the element content
	          MsgBox strElement
	     Next</pre>

IsArray	Returns a Variant subtype Boolean (11) indicating if a variable is an array.
Syntax	IsArray(varname) *varname* is a variable you want to check is an array.
Note	Only returns True if *varname* is an array.

Example	<pre>Dim strName
	Dim arrstrFixed(3)
	
	     strName = "WROX rocks!"
	     MsgBox IsArray(strName) ' False
	     MsgBox IsArray(arrstrFixed) ' True</pre>

See Also	**IsDate, IsEmpty, IsNull, IsNumeric, IsObject, and VarType**

LBound	Returns the smallest possible subscript for the dimension indicated.
Syntax	`LBound(arrayname[, dimension])`
	arrayname is the name of the array variable.
	dimension is an integer indicating the dimension you want to know the smallest possible subscript for. The dimension starts with 1, which is also the default that will be used if this argument is omitted.
Note	The smallest possible subscript for any array is always 0 in VBScript. `LBound` will raise a run-time error if the array has not been initialized.

Example	`Dim arrstrFixed(3)`
	
	`        MsgBox LBound(arrstrFixed)`
	
	`MsgBox` displays 0.

See Also	**Dim** statement, **ReDim** statement, and **UBound**

ReDim	This statement is used to size or resize a dynamic array.
Syntax	`ReDim [Preserve] varname(subscripts[, varname(subscripts)]...)`
	Preserve (Optional) is used to preserve the data in an existing array, when you resize it. The overhead of using this functionality is quite high and it should only be used when necessary.
	varname is the name of the array variable.
	subscripts is the dimension of the array variable *varname*. You can declare up to 60 multiple dimensions. The syntax is: `    upper[,    upper]...` where you indicate the upper bounds of the subscript. The lower bound is always zero.
Note	A dynamic array must already have been declared without dimension subscripts, when you size or resize it. If you use the `Preserve` keyword, only the last array dimension can be resized and the number of dimensions will remain unchanged.
	Since an array can be made smaller when resizing, you should take care that you don't lose any data already in the array.

Example	`Dim arrstrDynamic()`
	
	`            ' Size the dimension to`
	`            ' contain one dimension`
	`            ' with 3 elements`
	`            ReDim arrstrDynamic(3)`
	`            ' Put data in the array`
	`            arrstrDynamic(0) = "1"`
	`            arrstrDynamic(1) = "2"`
	`            arrstrDynamic(2) = "3"`
	
	`            ' Resize the array, but`
	`            ' keep the existing data`
	`            ReDim Preserve arrstrDynamic(5)`
	`            ' Display the 3 element`
	`            MsgBox arrstrDynamic(2)`
	
	`MsgBox` displays 3.

See Also	**Dim** statement and **Set** statement

UBound	Returns the largest possible subscript for the dimension indicated.
Syntax	`UBound(arrayname[, dimension])` *arrayname* is the name of the array variable. *dimension* is an integer indicating the dimension you want to know the largest possible subscript for. The dimension starts with 1, which is also the default that will be used if this argument is omitted.
Note	**UBound** will raise a run-time error if the array has not been initialized. If the array is empty, -1 is returned.
| Example | ```
Dim arrstrFixed(3)
          MsgBox UBound(arrstrFixed)
```<br><br>`MsgBox` displays 3. |
| See Also | **Dim** statement, **UBound**, and **ReDim** statement |

String Functions and Statements

Whatever your application does, you are likely to use string manipulation. By string manipulation we mean things like extracting a name from a string, checking if a particular string is part of another string, formatting numbers as strings with delimiters, and so on. Following is a list of the various string functions in VBScript.

Some functionality is not exposed as functions, but as methods of bjects. For example, the `RegExp` object exposes regular expression support.
```

FormatCurrency	Formats an expression as a currency value with the current currency symbol. The currency symbol is defined in Regional Settings in the Control Panel.

Syntax	FormatCurrency(expression [,numdigitsafterdecimal _
	                    [,includeleadingdigit _
	                    [,useparensfornegativenumbers _
	                    [,groupdigits]]]])
	
	expression is the expression that you want formatted.
	
	numdigitsafterdecimal (Optional) is a numeric value that indicates how many places to the right of the decimal separator should be displayed. If you omit this argument, the default value (-1) will be assumed and the settings from Control Panel will be used.
	
	includeleadingdigit (Optional) indicates if a leading zero is displayed for fractional values. Use one of the following constants:

vbUseDefault	2	(Uses the settings from the Number tab in Control Panel)
vbTrue	-1	
vbFalse	0	

useparensfornegativenumbers (Optional) indicates if negative numbers are enclosed in parentheses. Use one of the following constants:

vbUseDefault	2	(Uses the settings from the Regional Settings tab in Control Panel)
vbTrue	-1	
vbFalse	0	

groupdigits (Optional) indicates if numbers are grouped using the thousand separator specified in Control Panel. Use one of the following constants:

vbUseDefault	2	(Uses the settings from the Regional Settings tab in Control Panel)
vbTrue	-1	
vbFalse	0	

Note	The way the currency symbol is placed in relation to the currency value is determined by the settings in the Regional Settings tab in Control Panel. (Is the currency symbol placed before the number, after the number, is there a space between the symbol and the number, and so on.)
| Example | ```
MsgBox FormatCurrency(7500)
MsgBox FormatCurrency(7500, , vbTrue)
MsgBox FormatCurrency(7500, 2, vbTrue)
```<br><br>If the currency symbol is a pound sign (£), the thousand separator a comma (,), and the currency symbol placed in front of the number with no spaces between, then MsgBox will display £7,500.00 in all of the above statements. |
| See Also | **FormatDateTime, FormatNumber,** and **FormatPercent** |
```

Format DateTime	Returns a string formatted as a date and/or time.
Syntax	FormatDateTime(date, [namedformat]) *date* is any valid date expression. *namedformat* (Optional) is a numeric value that indicates the date/time format used. Use one of the following constants: vbGeneralDate 0 Format date (if present) and time (if present) using the short date and long time format from the machine's locale settings. vbLongDate 1 Format date using the long date format from the machine's locale settings. vbShortDate 2 Format date using the short date format from the machine's locale settings. vbLongTime 3 Format time using the long time format from the machine's locale settings. vbShortTime 4 Format time using the short time format from the machine's locale settings.
Note	A run-time error occurs if *date* is not a valid date expression. Null will be returned if *date* contains Null.
Example	`MsgBox FormatDateTime(Now, vbShortDate)` On July 29, 1999 the MsgBox will display **07/29/99**, if the locale settings use mm/dd/yy as the short date order and the forward slash (/) as the date separator.
See Also	**FormatCurrency**, **FormatNumber**, and **FormatPercent**

FormatNumber	Returns a string formatted as a number.

Syntax	FormatNumber (expression, [, numdigitsafterdecimal _
	                           [, includeleadingdigit _
	                           [, useparensfornegativenumbers _
	                           [, groupDigits]]]])
	
	expression is the expression that you want formatted.
	
	numdigitsafterdecimal (Optional) is a numeric value that indicates how many places to the right of the decimal separator should be displayed. If you omit this argument, the default value (-1) will be assumed and the settings from Control Panel will be used.

Table continued on following page

Syntax	*includeleadingdigit* (Optional) indicates if a leading zero is displayed for fractional values. Use one of the following constants:

`vbUseDefault`	2 (Uses the settings from the Number tab in Control Panel)
`vbTrue`	-1
`vbFalse`	0

useparensfornegativenumbers (Optional) indicates if negative numbers are enclosed in parentheses. Use one of the following constants:

`vbUseDefault`	2 (Uses the settings from the Regional Settings tab in Control Panel)
`vbTrue`	-1
`vbFalse`	0

groupdigits (Optional) indicates if numbers are grouped using the thousand separator specified in Control Panel. Use one of the following constants:

`vbUseDefault`	2 (Uses the settings from the Regional Settings tab in Control Panel)
`vbTrue`	-1
`vbFalse`	0

Note	The Number tab in Regional Settings in Control Panel supplies all the information used for formatting.
| Example | ```
MsgBox FormatNumber("50000", 2, vbTrue, vbFalse, vbTrue)
MsgBox FormatNumber("50000")
``` |

The MsgBox will display 50,000.00, if the locale settings use a comma (,) as the thousand separator and a period (.) as the decimal separator.

See Also	**FormatCurrency**, **FormatDateTime**, and **FormatPercent**

FormatPercent	Returns a string formatted as a percentage, like 50%.
| Syntax | ```
FormatPercent(expression, [, numdigitsafterdecimal _
                          [, includeleadingdigit _
                          [, useparensfornegativenumbers _
                          [,groupDigits]]]])
``` |

expression is any valid expression that you want formatted.

numdigitsafterdecimal (Optional) is a numeric value that indicates how many places to the right of the decimal separator should be displayed. If you omit this argument, the default value (-1) will be assumed and the settings from Control Panel will be used.

FormatPercent	Returns a string formatted as a percentage, like 50%.
Syntax	*includeleadingdigit* (Optional) indicates if a leading zero is displayed for fractional values. Use one of the following constants:
	vbUseDefault 2 (Uses the settings from the Number tab in Control Panel)
	vbTrue -1
	vbFalse 0
	useparensfornegativenumbers (Optional) indicates if negative numbers are enclosed in parentheses. Use one of the following constants:
	vbUseDefault 2 (Uses the settings from the Regional Settings tab in Control Panel)
	vbTrue -1
	vbFalse 0
	groupdigits (Optional) indicates if numbers are grouped using the thousand separator specified in Control Panel. Use one of the following constants:
	vbUseDefault 2 (Uses the settings from the Regional Settings tab in Control Panel)
	vbTrue -1
	vbFalse 0
Note	The Number tab in Regional Settings in Control Panel supplies all the information used for formatting.

Example	`MsgBox FormatPercent(4 / 45)`
	`MsgBox FormatPercent(4 / 45, 2, vbTrue, vbTrue, vbTrue)`
	
	The MsgBox will display 8.89%, if the locale settings use a period (.) as the decimal separator.

See Also	**FormatCurrency**, **FormatDateTime**, and **FormatNumber**

InStr	Returns an integer indicating the position for the first occurrence of a substring within a string.
Syntax	`InStr([start,] string1, string2[, compare])`
	start (Optional) is any valid non-negative expression indicating the starting position for the search within *string1*. Non-integer values are rounded. This argument is required if the compare argument is specified.
	string1 is the string you want to search within.
	string2 is the substring you want to search for.
	compare (Optional) indicates the comparison method used when evaluating. Use one of the following constants:
	vbBinaryCompare 0 (Default) Performs a binary comparison, that is, a case sensitive comparison.
	vbTextCompare 1 Performs a textual comparison, that is, a non-case sensitive comparison.

Table continued on following page

Note	A run-time error will occur, if *start* contains Null. If *start* is larger than the length of *string2* (> Len(string2)) 0 will be returned.

Possible return values for different *stringx* settings:

string1	zero-length	0
string1	Null	Null
string2	zero-length	start
string2	Null	Null
string2	not found	0
string2	found	position

Example

```
Dim lngStartPos
Dim lngFoundPos
Dim strSearchWithin
Dim strSearchFor

   ' Set the start pos

lngStartPos = 1
' Initialize the strings

strSearchWithin = "This is a test string"

strSearchFor = "t"

' Find the first occurrence

lngFoundPos = InStr( lngStartPos, strSearchWithin, strSearchFor)

' Loop through the string

Do While lngFoundPos > 0

   ' Display the found position

   MsgBox lngFoundPos

   ' Set the new start pos to
             ' the char after the found position

   lngStartPos = lngFoundPos + 1

   ' Find the next occurrence

   lngFoundPos = InStr( lngStartPos, strSearchWithin, _
                    strSearchFor)
Loop
```

The above code finds all occurrences of the letter t in *string1*, at position 11, 14 and 17. Please note that we use binary comparison here, which means that the uppercase T will not be "found". If you want to perform a case-insensitive search, you will need to specify the *compare* argument as vbTextCompare.

See Also	**InStrB, InStrRev**

InStrB	Returns an integer indicating the byte position for the first occurrence of a substring within a string containing byte data.

Syntax	`InStrB([start,] string1, string2[, compare])`

start (Optional) is any valid non-negative expression indicating the starting position for the search within *string1*. Non-integer values are rounded. This argument is required, if the compare argument is specified.

string1 is the string containing byte data you want to search within.

string2 is the substring you want to search for.

compare (Optional) indicates the comparison method used when evaluating. Use one of the following constants:

`vbBinaryCompare` – 0 (Default) Performs a binary comparison, that is, a case sensitive comparison.

`vbTextCompare` – 1 Performs a textual comparison, that is, a non-case sensitive comparison.

Note	A run-time error will occur, if *start* contains `Null`. If *start* is larger than the length of *string2* (> `Len(string2)`) 0 will be returned.

Possible return values for different *stringx* settings:

string1	zero–length	0
string1	Null	Null
string2	zero–length	start
string2	Null	Null
string2	not found	0
string2	found	Position

Example	

```
Dim lngStartPos
Dim lngFoundPos
Dim strSearchWithin
Dim strSearchFor

    ' Set the start pos
    lngStartPos = 1
    ' Initialize the strings
    strSearchWithin = "This is a test string"
    strSearchFor = ChrB(0)

    ' Find the first occurrence
    lngFoundPos = InStrB( lngStartPos, strSearchWithin, strSearchFor)
    ' Loop through the string
    Do While lngFoundPos > 0
       ' Display the found position
       MsgBox lngFoundPos

       ' Set the new start pos to
             ' the char after the found position
       lngStartPos = lngFoundPos + 1

       ' Find the next occurrence
       lngFoundPos = InStrB( lngStartPos, strSearchWithin, _
                        strSearchFor)
    Loop
```

Example	The above code finds all occurrences of the byte value 0 in *string1*, at position 2, 4, 6, ...40 and 42. This is because only the first byte of the Unicode character is used for the character. If you use a double-byte character set like the Japanese, the second byte will also contain a non-zero value.
See Also	**InStr, InStrRev**

InStrRev	Returns an integer indicating the position of the first occurrence of a substring within a string starting from the end of the string. This is the reverse functionality to InStr.
Syntax	InStrRev(string1, string2[, start[, compare]])

string1 is the string you want to search within.

string2 is the substring you want to search for.

start (Optional) is any valid non-negative expression indicating the starting position for the search within *string1*; −1 is the default and it will be used if this argument is omitted.

compare (Optional) indicates the comparison method used when evaluating. Use one of the following constants:

vbBinaryCompare – 0 (Default) Performs a binary comparison, that is, a case sensitive comparison.

vbTextCompare – 1 Performs a textual comparison, that is, a non-case sensitive comparison.

Note	A run-time error will occur, if *start* contains Null. If *start* is larger than the length if *string2* (> Len(string2)) 0 will be returned.

Possible return values for different *stringx* settings:

string1	zero–length	0
string1	Null	Null
string2	zero–length	start
string2	Null	Null
string2	not found	0
string2	found	Position

InStrRev and InStr do not have same syntax!

Example	

```
Dim lngStartPos
Dim lngFoundPos
Dim strSearchWithin
Dim strSearchFor

    ' Set the start pos
    lngStartPos = -1
    ' Initialize the strings
    strSearchWithin = "This is a test string"
    strSearchFor = "t"


    ' Find the first occurrence
    lngFoundPos = InStrRev( strSearchWithin, strSearchFor, _
                            lngStartPos)

    ' Loop through the string
    Do While lngFoundPos > 0
        ' Display the found
            ' position
        MsgBox lngFoundPos

        ' Set the new start pos to
            ' the char before the found position
        lngStartPos = lngFoundPos - 1

        ' Find the next occurrence
        lngFoundPos = InStrRev( strSearchWithin, strSearchFor, _
                            lngStartPos)
    Loop
```

The above code finds all occurrences of the letter t in *string1*, at position 17, 14 and 11. Please note that we use binary comparison here, which means that the uppercase T will not be "found". If you want to perform a case-insensitive search, you will need to specify the *compare* argument as vbTextCompare.

See Also	**InStr, InStrB**

Join	Joins a number of substrings in an array to form the returned string.
Syntax	`Join(list[, delimiter])`
	list is a one dimensional array that contains all the substrings that you want to join.
	delimiter (Optional) is the character(s) used to separate the substrings. A space character " " is used as the delimiter if this argument is omitted.
Note	All the substrings are concatenated with no delimiter if a zero-length string is used as *delimiter*. If any element in the array is empty, a zero-length string will be used as the value.

Table continued on following page

| Example | ```
Dim strLights
Dim arrstrColors(3)
   ' Fill the array
   arrstrColors(0) = "Red"
            arrstrColors(1) = "Yellow"
            arrstrColors(2) = "Green"

   ' Join the array into a string
   strLights = Join( arrstrColors, ",")
strLights contains "Red,Yellow,Green".
``` |
| See Also | **Split** |

LCase	Converts all alphabetic characters in a string to lowercase.
Syntax	`LCase(string)` *string* is the string you want converted to lowercase.
Note	`Null` is returned if *string* contains `Null`. Only uppercase letters are converted.
Example	`MsgBox LCase("ThisIsLowerCase")` `MsgBox` displays thisislowercase.
See Also	**UCase**

Left	Returns *length* number of leftmost characters from *string*.
Syntax	`Left(string, length)` *string* is the string you want to extract a number of characters from. *length* is the number of characters you want to extract starting from the left. The entire *string* will be returned if *length* is equal to or greater than the total number of characters in *string*.
Note	`Null` is returned if *string* contains `Null`.
| Example | ```
Dim strExtract

        strExtract = "LeftRight"
        MsgBox Left(strExtract, 4)
```<br><br>`MsgBox` displays Left. |
| See Also | **Len, LenB, Mid, MidB**, and **Right** |

Len	Returns the number of characters in a string.
Syntax	`Len(string)`
	string is any valid string expression you want the length of.
Note	`Null` is returned if *string* contains `Null`.
| Example | ```
Dim strLength

        strLength = "1 2 3 4 5 6 7 8 9"
        MsgBox Len(strLength)
``` |
| | `MsgBox` displays 17. |
| See Also | **Left**, **LenB**, **Mid**, **MidB**, and **Right** |

LenB	Returns the number of bytes used to represent a string.
Syntax	`LenB(string)`
	string is any valid string expression you want the number of bytes for.
Note	`Null` is returned if *string* contains `Null`.
| Example | ```
Dim strLength

        strLength = "123456789"
        MsgBox LenB(strLength)
``` |
| | `MsgBox` displays 18. |
| See Also | **Left**, **Len**, **Mid**, **MidB**, and **Right** |

LTrim	Trims a string of leading spaces; " " or Chr(32).
Syntax	`LTrim(string)`
	string is any valid string expression you want to trim leading (leftmost) spaces from.
Note	`Null` is returned if *string* contains `Null`.
| Example | ```
Dim strSpaces

        strSpaces = " Hello again *"
        MsgBox LTrim(strSpaces)
``` |
| | `MsgBox` displays Hello again *. |
| See Also | **Left**, **Mid**, **Right**, **RTrim**, and **Trim** |
```

Mid	Returns a specified number of characters from any position in a string.
Syntax	`Mid(string, start[, length])` *string* is any valid string expression you want to extract characters from. *start* is the starting position for extracting the characters. A zero-length string is returned if it is greater than the number of characters in *string*. *length* (Optional) is the number of characters you want to extract. All characters from *start* to the end of the string are returned if this argument is omitted or if *length* is greater than the number of characters counting from *start*.
Note	`Null` is returned if *string* contains `Null`.

Example	```Dim strExtract
	
	        strExtract = "Find ME in here"
	        MsgBox Mid(strExtract, 6, 2)```
	
	MsgBox displays ME.

See Also	**Left, Len, LenB, LTrim, MidB, Right, RTrim**, and **Trim**

Replace	Replaces a substring within a string with another substring a specified number of times.
Syntax	`Replace(expression, find, replacewith[, start[, count[, compare]]])` *expression* is a string expression that contains the substring you want to replace. *find* is the substring you want to replace. *replacewith* is the substring you want to replace with. *start* (Optional) is the starting position within *expression* for replacing the substring. 1 (default), the first position, will be used if this argument is omitted. You must also specify the *count* argument if you want to use *start*. *count* (Optional) is the number of times you want to replace *find*. -1 (default) will be used if this argument is omitted, which means all *find* in the expression. You must also specify the *start* argument if you want to use *count*. *compare* (Optional) indicates the comparison method used when evaluating. Use one of the following constants: `vbBinaryCompare` – 0 (Default) Performs a binary comparison, that is, a case sensitive comparison. `vbTextCompare` – 1 Performs a textual comparison, that is, a non-case sensitive comparison.

Note	If *start* and *count* are specified, the return value will be the original expression, with *find* replaced *count* times with *replacewith*, from *start* to the end of the expression, and not the complete string. A zero-length string is returned if *start* is greater than the length of *expression* (`start > Len(expression)`). All occurrences of *find* will be removed if *replacewith* is a zero-length string (`""`)

Possible return values for different argument settings:

expression	zero-length	zero-length
expression	Null	Error
find	zero-length	expression
count	0	expression

Example	

```
Dim strReplace

        strReplace = Replace( "****I use binary", "I", "You", 5, 1,
vbBinaryCompare) ' You use binary
        strReplace = Replace( "****I use text", "i", "You", , ,
vbTextCompare)        ' ****You use text
```

See Also	**Left, Len, LTrim, Mid, Right, RTrim**, and **Trim**

Right	Returns *length* number of rightmost characters from *string*
Syntax	`Right(string, length)`
	string is the string you want to extract a number of characters from.
	length is the number of characters you want to extract starting from the right. The entire *string* will be returned if *length* is equal to or greater than the total number of characters in *string*.
Note	`Null` is returned if *string* contains `Null`.
Example	

```
Dim strExtract

        strExtract = "LeftRight"
        MsgBox Right(strExtract, 5)
```

MsgBox displays Right

See Also	**Left, Len, LenB, Mid**, and **MidB**

RTrim	Trims a string of trailing spaces; " " or Chr(32).
Syntax	`RTrim(string)`
	string is any valid string expression you want to trim trailing (rightmost) spaces from.
Note	`Null` is returned if *string* contains `Null`.
| Example | ```
Dim strSpaces

        strSpaces = "* Hello again    "
        MsgBox RTrim(strSpaces)
``` |
| | `MsgBox` displays * Hello again. |
| See Also | **Left, LTrim, Mid, Right,** and **Trim** |

Space	Returns a string made up of a specified number of spaces (" ").
Syntax	`Space(number)`
	number is the number of spaces you want returned.
| Example | ```
Dim strSpaces

        strSpaces = "Hello again"
        MsgBox "*" & Space(5) & strSpaces
``` |
| | `MsgBox` displays *   Hello again. |
| See Also | **String** |

Split	Returns a zero-based one-dimensional array "extracted" from the supplied string expression.
Syntax	`Split(expression[, delimiter[, count[, compare]]]))`
	expression is the string containing substrings and delimiters that you want to split up and put into a zero-based one-dimensional array.
	delimiter (Optional) is the character that separates the substrings. A space character will be used if this argument is omitted.
	count (Optional) indicates the number of substrings to return. -1 (default) means all substrings will be returned.
	compare (Optional) indicates the comparison method used when evaluating. Use one of the following constants:
	`vbBinaryCompare` – 0 (Default) Performs a binary comparison, that is, a case sensitive comparison.
	`vbTextCompare` – 1 Performs a textual comparison, that is, a non-case sensitive comparison.
Note	An empty array will be returned if *expression* is a zero-length string. The result of the `Split` function cannot be assigned to a variable of Variant subtype `Array` (8192). A run-time error occurs if you try to do so.

| Example | ```
Dim arrstrSplit
Dim strSplit

        ' Initialize the string
strSplit = "1,2,3,4,5,6,7,8,9,0"
        ' Split the string using comma as the delimiter
arrstrSplit = Split(strSplit,  ",")
``` |
|---|---|
| | The array `arrstrSplit` now holds 10 elements, 0,1,2...0. |
| See Also | **Join** |

String	Returns a string with a substring repeated a specified number of times.
Syntax	`String(number, character)`
	number indicates the length of the returned string.
	character is the character code or string expression for the character used to build the returned string. Only the first character of a string expression is used.
Note	Null is returned if *number* or *character* contains `Null`. The character code will automatically be converted to a valid character code if it is greater than 255. The formula is: `character Mod 256`.
| Example | ```
Dim strChars

        strChars = "Hello again"
        MsgBox String(5, "*") & strChars
``` |
| | `MsgBox` displays *****Hello again. |
| See Also | **Space** |

StrReverse	Returns a string with the character order reversed.
Syntax	`StrReverse(string)`
	string is the string expression you want reversed.
Note	A run-time error occurs if *string* is `Null`. If *string* is a zero-length string, a zero-length string will be returned.
	The case of the characters is not changed.
Example	`MsgBox StrReverse("Hello again")`
	`MsgBox` displays niaga olleH.

Trim	Trims a string of leading and trailing spaces; " " or Chr(20).
Syntax	`Trim(string)` *string* is any valid string expression you want to trim leading (leftmost) and trailing (rightmost) spaces from.
Note	`Null` is returned if *string* contains `Null`.
Example	```Dim strSpaces``````strSpaces = " *Hello again* "``````MsgBox Trim(strSpaces)``` `MsgBox` displays *Hello again*.
See Also	**Left, LTrim, Mid, Right,** and **RTrim**

UCase	Converts all alphabetic characters in a string to uppercase and returns the result.
Syntax	`UCase(string)` *string* is the string you want converted to uppercase.
Note	`Null` is returned if *string* contains `Null`. Only lowercase letters are converted.
Example	`MsgBox UCase("ThisIsUpperCase")` `MsgBox` displays THISISUPPERCASE.
See Also	**LCase**

String Constants

Constant	Value	Description
vbCr	Chr(13)	Carriage Return.
vbCrLf	Chr(13) & Chr(10)	A combination of Carriage Return and linefeed.
vbLf	Chr(10)	Line Feed.
vbNewLine	Chr(13) & Chr(10) or Chr(10)	New line character. This is platform-specific, meaning whatever is appropriate for the current platform.
vbNullChar	Chr(0)	Character with the value of 0.
vbNullString	String with the value of 0	This is not the same as a zero-length string (""). Mainly used for calling external procedures.
vbTab	Chr(9)	Tab (horizontal).

Conversion Functions

Normally you don't need to convert values in VBScript, because there is only one data type, the Variant.

Implicit conversion is generally applied when needed, but when you pass a value to a non-variant procedure in a COM object that needs the value passed ByRef, you will have to pass the value with the precise data subtype. This can be done by placing the argument in its own set of parentheses, which forces a temporary evaluation of the argument as an expression:

```
Dim objByRefSample
Dim intTest
    ' Initialize the variable
    intTest = "5"
    ' Create the object
    Set objByRefSample =
CreateObject("MyObject.ByRefSample")
    ' Call the method
    objByRefSample.PassIntegerByReference (intTest)
    ' Destroy the object
    Set objByRefSample = Nothing
```

The PassIntegerByReference method is a VB sub-procedure with just one argument of type integer that is passed ByRef.

What happens is that the value 5 stored in the intTest variable is actually explicitly coerced into a variable of subtype Integer, so that it conforms to the method's argument type. If you remove the parentheses, you will get a run-time error, because the implicit coercion will treat the string value as a double.

This is just one way of solving the problem. Another way is to use the **CInt** conversion function (listed below) when calling the method.

At some point, however, you might need to convert a value of one data subtype to another data subtype. This can be necessary for various reasons:

❑ You need to present a number in hexadecimal notation instead of decimal

❑ You need the corresponding character code for a character or vice versa

❑ You need to pass values to a non-variant property procedure or as a function parameter in a COM object

❑ You need to save data in a database

CBool	Returns a `Boolean` value (Variant subtype 11) corresponding to the value of an expression.
Syntax	`CBool(expression)` expression is any valid expression.
Note	A run-time error occurs if *expression* can't be evaluated to a numeric value. If *expression* evaluates to zero then False is returned; otherwise, True is returned.

Example	```
	Dim intCounter, blnValue
	        intCounter = 5
	        blnValue = CBool(intCounter)
	``
	
	blnValue now holds the value True, because `intCounter` holds a non-zero value.

See Also	**CByte, CCur, CDbl, CInt, CLng, CSng**, and **CStr**

CByte	Returns an expression converted to Variant subtype `Byte` (17).
Syntax	`CByte(expression)` *expression* is any valid numeric expression.
Note	A run-time error occurs if *expression* can't be evaluated to a numeric value or if *expression* evaluates to a value outside the acceptable range for a `Byte` (0-255). Fractional values are rounded.

Example	```
	Dim dblValue, bytValue
	        dblValue = 5.456
	        bytValue = CByte(dblValue)
	``
	
	bytValue now holds the value *5*, because `dblValue` is rounded.

See Also	**CBool, CCur, CDbl, CInt, CLng, CSng**, and **CStr**

CCur	Returns an expression converted to Variant subtype `Currency` (6).
Syntax	`CCur(expression)` *expression* is any valid expression.
Note	CCur is internationally aware, which means that the return value is based on the locale settings on the machine. Numbers will be formatted with the appropriate decimal separator and the fourth digit to the right of the separator is rounded up if the fifth digit is 5 or higher.

Example	```
	Dim dblValue, curValue
	        dblValue = 724.555789
	        curValue = CCur(dblValue)
	``
	
	curValue now holds the value 724.5558 or 724,5558, depending on the separator.

See Also	**CBool, CByte, CDbl, CInt, CLng, CSng**, and **CStr**

CDate	*See under* **Date & Time functions**

CDbl	Returns an expression converted to Variant subtype `Double` (5).
Syntax	`CDbl(expression)`
	expression is any valid expression.
Note	CDbl is internationally aware, which means that the return value is based on the locale settings on the machine. Numbers will be formatted with the appropriate decimal separator. A run-time error occurs if *expression* lies outside the range (-1.79769313486232E308 to -4.94065645841247E-324 for negative values, and 4.94065645841247E-324 to 1.79769313486232E308 for positive values) applicable to a Double.

Example	`Dim dblValue`
	
	`    dblValue = CDbl("5,579.56")`
	
	dblValue now holds the value 5579.56 or 5,57956, depending on the thousand and decimal separators in use.

See Also	**CBool, CByte, CCur, CInt, CLng, CSng**, and **CStr**

Chr	Returns the ANSI character corresponding to *charactercode*.
Syntax	`Chr(charactercode)`
	charactercode is a numeric value that indicates the character you want.
Note	Supplying a *charactercode* from 0 to 31 will return a standard non-printable ASCII character.

Example	`Dim strChar`
	
	`    strChar = Chr(89)`
	
	strChar now holds the character Y which is number 89 in the ANSI character table.

See Also	**Asc, AscB, AscW, ChrB**, and **ChrW**

ChrB	Returns the ANSI character corresponding to *charactercode*.
Syntax	`ChrB(charactercode)`
	charactercode is a numeric value that indicates the character you want.
Note	Supplying a *charactercode* from 0 to 31 will return a standard non-printable ASCII character. This function is used instead of the **Chr** (returns a two-byte character) function when you only want the first byte of the character returned.

Example	`Dim strChar`
	
	`    strChar = ChrB(89)`
	
	strChar now holds the character Y which is number 89 in the ANSI character table.

See Also	**Asc, AscB, AscW, Chr**, and **ChrW**

CInt	Returns an expression converted to Variant subtype `Integer` (2).
Syntax	`CInt(expression)` *expression* is any valid expression.
Note	CInt is internationally aware, which means that the return value is based on the locale settings on the machine. Please note that decimal values are rounded, before the fractional part is discarded. A run-time error occurs if *expression* lies outside the range (-32,768 to 32,767) applicable to an Integer.
Example	``` Dim intValue intValue = CInt("5,579.56") ``` `intValue` now holds the value 5580 or 6, depending on the thousand and decimal separators in use.
See Also	**CBool, CByte, CCur, CDbl, CLng, CSng, CStr**, and the **Math Functions Fix** and **Int**

CLng	Returns an expression converted to Variant subtype `Long` (3).
Syntax	`CLng(expression)` *expression* is any valid expression.
Note	CLng is internationally aware, which means that the return value is based on the locale settings on the machine. Please note that decimal values are rounded, before the fractional part is discarded. A run-time error occurs if *expression* lies outside the range (-2,147,483,648 to 2,147,483,647) applicable to a Long.
Example	``` Dim lngValue lngValue = CLng("5,579.56") ``` `lngValue` now holds the value 5580 or 6, depending on the thousand and decimal separators in use.
See Also	**CBool, CByte, CCur, CDbl, CInt, CSng, CStr**, and the **Math Functions Fix** and **Int**

CSng	Returns an expression converted to Variant subtype `Single` (4).
Syntax	`CSng(expression)` *expression* is any valid expression.
Note	CSng is internationally aware, which means that the return value is based on the locale settings on the machine. A run-time error occurs if *expression* lies outside the range (-3.402823E38 to -1.401298E-45 for negative values, and 1.401298E-45 to 3.402823E38 for positive values) applicable to a Single.
Example	``` Dim sngValue sngValue = CSng("5,579.56") ``` `sngValue` now holds the value 5579.56 or 5,57956, depending on the thousand and decimal separators in use.
See Also	**CBool, CByte, CCur, CDbl, CInt, CLng, CStr**, and the **Math Functions Fix** and **Int**

CStr	Returns an expression converted to Variant subtype `String` (8).
Syntax	`CStr(expression)` *expression* is any valid expression.
Note	`CStr` is internationally aware, which means that the return value is based on the locale settings on the machine. A run-time error occurs if *expression* is `Null`. `Numeric` and `Err` values are returned as numbers, Boolean values as True or False, and `Date` values as a short date.

Example	`Dim strValue`
	
	      `strValue = CStr("5,579.56")`
	
	`strValue` now holds the value 5,579.56.

See Also	**CBool, CByte, CCur, CDbl, CInt, CLng, CSng**, and the **Math Functions Fix** and **Int**

Miscellaneous Functions, Statements, and Keywords

Some functionality does not fit under any of the other categories, and so they are gathered here. Below you will find descriptions of various functions for handling objects, user input, variable checks, output on screen, etc.

CreateObject	Returns a reference to an Automation/COM/ActiveX object. The object is created using COM object creation services.
Syntax	`CreateObject(servername.typename[, location])` *servername* is the name of the application that provides the object. *typename* is the object's type or class that you want to create. *location* (Optional) is the name of the network server you want the object created on. If missing the object is created on the local machine.
Note	An Automation/COM/ActiveX object always contains at least one type or class, but usually several types or classes are contained within. *servername* and *typename* are often referred to as progID. Please note that a progID is not always a two part one, like `servername.typename`. It can have several parts, like `servername.typename.version`.

Example	<pre>Dim objRemote
	Dim objLocal
	
	        ' Create an object from class
	        ' MyClass contained in the
	        ' COM object MyApp on a
	        ' remote server named FileSrv
	        Set objRemote = CreateObject("MyApp.MyClass",
	"FileSrv")
	
	        ' Create an object from class
	        ' LocalClass contained in the
	        ' COM object LocalApp on the
	        ' local macine
	        Set objLocal = CreateObject("LocalApp.LocalClass)</pre>

See Also	**GetObject**

Dim	Declares a variable of type Variant and allocates storage space.
Syntax	`Dim varname[([subscripts])][, varname[([subscripts])]]...`
	varname is the name of the variable.
	subscripts (Optional) indicates the dimensions when you declare an array variable. You can declare up to 60 multiple dimensions using the following syntax:
	`upperbound[, upperbound]...`
	upperbound specifies the upper bound of the array. Since the lower bound of an array in VBScript is always zero, *upperbound* is one less than the number of elements in the array.
	If you declare an array with empty subscripts, you can later resize it with ReDim; this is called a dynamic array.
Note	This statement is scope specific, that is, you need to consider when and where you want to declare your variables. Variables that are only used in a specific procedure should be declared in this procedure. This will make the variable invisible and inaccessible outside the procedure. You can also declare your variables with script scope. This means that the variables will be accessible to all procedures within the script. This is one way of sharing data between different procedures.
	Dim statements should be put at the top of a procedure to make the procedure easier to read.
Example	``` ' Declare a dynamic array Dim arrstrDynamic() ' Declare a fixed size array ' with 5 elements Dim arrstrFixed(4) ' Declare a non-array variable Dim vntTest ```
See Also	**ReDim** statement and **Set** statement

Eval	Evaluates and returns the result of an expression.
Syntax	`result = Eval(expression)`
	result (Optional) is the variable you want to assign the result of the evaluation to. Although *result* is optional, you should consider using the Execute statement, if you don't want to specify it.
	expression is a string containing a valid VBScript expression.
Note	Because the assignment operator and the comparison operator is the same in VBScript, you need to be careful when using them with Eval. Eval always uses the equal sign (=) as a comparison operator, so if you need to use it as an assignment operator, you should use the Execute statement instead.

Example	```
	Dim blnResult
	Dim lngX, lngY
	
	        ' Initialize the variables
	        lngX = 15: lngY = 10
	        ' Evaluate the expression
	        blnResult = Eval("lngX = lngY")
	``

	blnResult holds the value False, because 15 is not equal to 10.
See Also	**Execute** statement

Filter	Returns an array that contains a subset of an array of strings. The array is zero-based as are all arrays in VBScript and it holds as many elements as are found in the filtering process. The subset is determined by specifying a criterion.
Syntax	`Filter(inputstrings, value[, include[, compare]])`
	inputstrings is a one dimensional string array that you want to search.
	value is the string you want to search for.
	include (Optional) is a `boolean` value indicating if you want to include (True) or exclude (False) elements in *inputstrings* that contains *value*.
	compare (Optional) indicates the comparison method used when evaluating. Use one of the following constants:
	`vbBinaryCompare` – 0 (Default) Performs a binary comparison, that is, a case sensitive comparison.
	`vbTextCompare` – 1 Performs a textual comparison, that is, a non-case sensitive comparison.
Note	An empty array is returned if no matches are found. A run-time error occurs if *inputstrings* is not a one-dimensional array or if it is `Null`.

Example	<pre>Dim arrstrColors(3)
	Dim arrstrFilteredColors
	
	        ' Fill the array
	        arrstrColors(0) = "Red"
	        arrstrColors(1) = "Green"
	        arrstrColors(2) = "Blue"
	
	        ' Filter the array
	        arrstrFilteredColors = Filter(arrstrColors, "Red")</pre>

	`arrstrFilteredColors` now holds one element (0), which has the value `Red`.
See Also	The String Function **Replace**

GetObject	Returns a reference to an Automation object.
Syntax	`GetObject([pathname][, class]])`
	pathname (Optional) is a string specifying the full path and name of the file that contains the object you want to retrieve. You need to specify *class* if you omit this argument.
	class (Optional) is a string that indicates the class of the object. You need to specify *pathname* if you omit this argument. The following syntax is used for *class*:
	`appname.objecttype`
	appname is a string indicating the application that provides the object.
	objecttype is a string specifying the type or class of the object that you want created.
Note	You can use this function to start the application associated with *pathname* and activate/return the object specified in the pathname. A new object is returned if pathname is a zero-length string ("") and the currently active object of the specified type is returned if pathname is omitted. Please note, that if the object you want returned has been compiled with Visual Basic, you cannot obtain a reference to an existing object by omitting the pathname argument. A new object will be returned instead. The opposite is True for objects that are registered as single-instance objects; the same instance will always be returned. However, you should note the above-mentioned problems with ActiveX DLL's compiled using Visual Basic.
	Some applications allow you to activate part of a file and you can do this by suffixing pathname with an exclamation mark (!) and a string that identifies the part of the object you want.
	You should only use this function when there is a current instance of the object you want to create, or when you want the object to open up a specific document. Use `CreateObject` to create a new instance of an object.
| Example | ```
Dim objAutomation

        ' Create a reference to an
        ' existing instance of an
        ' Excel application (this
        ' call will raise an error
        ' if no Excel.Application
        ' objects already exists)
        Set objAutomation = GetObject(, "Excel.Application")

        ' Create a reference to a
        ' specific workbook in a new
        ' instance of an Excel
        ' application
        Set objAutomation = GetObject( "C:\Test.xls ")
``` |
| See Also | **CreateObject** |
```

GetRef	Returns a reference to a procedure. This reference can be bound to an object event. This will let you bind a VBScript procedure to a DHTML event.
Syntax	`Set object.eventname = GetRef(procname)` *object* is the name of the object in which *eventname* is placed. *eventname* is the name of the event to which the procedure is to be bound. *procname* is the name of the procedure you want to bind to *eventname*.
Example	```Sub NewOnFocus()
        ' Do your stuff here
End Sub

        ' Bind the NewOnFocus
        ' procedure to the
        ' Window. OnFocus event
        Set Window.OnFocus = GetRef("NewOnFocus ")``` |

IsEmpty	Returns a `Boolean` value indicating if a variable has been initialized.
Syntax	`IsEmpty(expression)` *expression* is the variable you want to check has been initialized.
Note	You can use more than one variable as *expression*. If for example, you concatenate two Variants and one of them is empty, the `IsEmpty` function will return False, because the expression is not empty.
Example	```Dim strTest
Dim strInput

    strInput = "Test"

    MsgBox IsEmpty(strTest)   ' True
    MsgBox IsEmpty(strInput & strTest) ' False``` |
| See Also | **IsArray, IsDate, IsNull, IsNumeric, IsObject,** and **VarType** |

IsNull	Returns a `Boolean` value indicating if a variable contains `Null` or valid data.
	`IsNull(expression)` *expression* is any expression.
Syntax	This function returns True if the whole of *expression* evaluates to `Null`. If you have more than one variable in *expression*, all of them must be `Null` for the function to return True. Please be aware that `Null` is not the same as empty (a variable that hasn't been initialized) or a zero-length string (""). `Null` means no valid value! You should always use the `IsNull` function when checking for `Null` values, because using the normal operators will return False even if one variable is `Null`.

Table continued on following page

| Example | ```
Dim strInput

strInput = "Test"
MsgBox IsNull( strInput & Null) ' False
MsgBox IsNull(Null)             ' True
``` |
| See Also | **IsArray, IsDate, IsEmpty, IsNumeric, IsObject**, and **VarType** |

IsNumeric	Returns a `Boolean` value indicating if an expression can be evaluated as a number.
Syntax	`IsNumeric(expression)` *expression* is any expression.
Note	This function returns True if the whole expression evaluates to a number. A `Date` expression is not considered a numeric expression.
| Example | ```
MsgBox IsNumeric(55.55)            ' True
MsgBox IsNumeric("55.55")          ' True
MsgBox IsNumeric("55.55aaa")       ' False
MsgBox IsNumeric( "March 1, 1999") ' False
MsgBox IsNumeric(vbNullChar)       ' False
``` |
| See Also | **IsArray, IsDate, IsEmpty, IsNull, IsObject**, and **VarType** |

IsObject	Returns a `Boolean` value indicating if an expression is a reference to a valid Automation object.
Syntax	`IsObject(expression)` *expression* is any expression.
Note	This function returns True only if *expression* is in fact a variable of Variant subtype `Object` (9) or a user-defined object.
| Example | ```
Dim objTest

        MsgBox IsObject(objTest)                        ' False

        Set objTest = CreateObject( "Excel.Application")

        MsgBox IsObject(objTest)                        ' True
``` |
| See Also | **IsArray, IsDate, IsEmpty, IsNull, IsNumeric, Set** statement, and **VarType** |
```

MsgBox	Displays a dialog box with a custom message and a custom set of command buttons. The value of the button the user clicks is returned as the result of this function.
Syntax	`MsgBox(prompt[, buttons][, title [, helpfile, context])`

prompt is the message you want displayed in the dialog box. The string can contain up to 1024 characters, depending on the width of the characters you use. You can separate the lines using one of these VBScript constants:

> `vbCr`, `vbCrLf`, `vbLf` or `vbNewLine`

buttons (Optional) is the sum of values indicating the number and type of button(s) to display, which icon style to use, which button is the default and if the **MsgBox** is modal. The settings for this argument are:

`vbOKOnly`	**0**	Displays OK button.
`vbOKCancel`	**1**	Displays OK and Cancel buttons.
`vbAbortRetryIgnore`	**2**	Displays Abort, Retry, and Ignore buttons.
`vbYesNoCancel`	**3**	Displays Yes, No, and Cancel buttons.
`vbYesNo`	**4**	Displays Yes and No buttons.
`vbRetryCancel`	**5**	Displays Retry and Cancel buttons.
`vbCritical`	**16**	Displays critical icon.
`vbQuestion`	**32**	Displays query icon.
`vbExclamation`	**48**	Displays warning icon.
`vbInformation`	**64**	Displays information icon.
`vbDefaultButton1`	**0**	Makes the first button the default one.
`vbDefaultButton2`	**256**	Makes the second button the default one.
`vbDefaultButton3`	**512**	Makes the third button the default one.
`vbDefaultButton4`	**768**	Makes the fourth button the default one.
`vbApplicationModal`	**0**	When the `MsgBox` is application modal, the user must respond to the message box, before he/she can continue.
`vbSystemModal`	**4096**	The same effect as `vbApplicationModal`. Presumably this is a "left-over" from the good old 16-bit Windows days. The dialog box will stay on top of other windows though.

Table continued on following page

MsgBox **(cont)**	Displays a dialog box with a custom message and a custom set of command buttons. The value of the button the user clicks is returned as the result of this function.
Syntax	Please note how the values are grouped: Buttons (values 0-5) Icon (values 16, 32, 48 and 64) Default button (values 0, 256, 512 and 768) Modal (values 0 and 4096) You should only pick one value from each group when creating your MsgBox. *title* (Optional) is the text you want displayed in the dialog box title bar. The application name will be displayed if this argument is omitted. *helpfile* (Optional) is a string expression that indicates the help file to use when providing context-sensitive help for the dialog box. This argument must be used in conjunction with *context*. This is not available on 16-bit platforms. *context* (Optional) is a numeric expression that indicates the help context number that makes sure that the right help topic is displayed. This argument must be used in conjunction with *helpfile*.

Note	The following values can be returned:
	
	`vbOK (1)`
	`vbCancel.(2)`
	`vbAbort (3)`
	`vbRetry (4)`
	`vbIgnore (5)`
	`vbYes (6)`
	`vbNo (7)`
	
	The ESC key has the same effect the Cancel button. Clicking the Help or pressing *F1* will not close the MsgBox.

Example	```Dim intReturn

    intReturn = MsgBox("Exit the application?", vbYesNoCancel + vbQuestion)```

The MsgBox will display the message "Exit the application", buttons Yes, No, and Cancel and the question mark icon. This MsgBox will be application modal. |
| See Also | **InputBox** |

ScriptEngine	Returns a string indicating the scripting language being used.
Syntax	`ScriptEngine`
Note	The following scripting engine values can be returned:
	`VBScript` MS VBScript
	`JScript` MS JScript
	`VBA` MS Visual Basic for Applications
	Other third-party ActiveX Scripting Engines can also be returned, if you have installed one.
See Also	**ScriptEngineBuildVersion**, **ScriptEngineMajorVersion**, and **ScriptEngineMinorVersion**

ScriptEngine BuildVersion	Returns the build version of the script engine being used.
Syntax	`ScriptEngineBuildVersion`
Note	This function gets the information from the DLL for the current scripting language.
See Also	**ScriptEngine**, **ScriptEngineMajorVersion**, and **ScriptEngineMinorVersion**

ScriptEngine MajorVersion	Returns the major version number of the script engine being used. The major version number is the part before the decimal separator, for example 5 if the version is 5.1.
Syntax	`ScriptEngineMajorVersion`
Note	This function gets the information from the DLL for the current scripting language.
See Also	**ScriptEngine**, **ScriptEngineBuildVersion**, and **ScriptEngineMinorVersion**

ScriptEngine MinorVersion	Returns the minor version number of the script engine being used. The minor version number is the part after the decimal separator, for example 1 if the version is 5.1.
Syntax	`ScriptEngineMinorVersion`
Note	This function gets the information from the DLL for the current scripting language.
See Also	**ScriptEngine**, **ScriptEngineBuildVersion**, and **ScriptEngineMajorVersion**

Set	Returns an object reference, which must be assigned to a variable or property, or returns a procedure reference, which must be associated with an event.
Syntax	`Set objectvar = {objectexpression	New classname	Nothing}`  *objectvar* is the name of a variable or property. *objectexpression* (Optional) is the name of an existing object or another variable of the same object type. It can also be a method or function that returns either. *classname* (Optional) is the name of the class you want to create.  `Set object.eventname = GetRef(procname)` *object* is the name of the object that *eventname* is associated with. *eventname* is the name of the event you want to bind *procname* to. *procname* is the name of the procedure you want to associate with *eventname*.
Note	*objectvar* must be an empty variable or an object type consistent with *objectexpression* being assigned. `Set` is used to create a reference to an object and not a copy of it. This means that if you use the `Set` statement more than once on the same object, you will have one more reference to the same object. Any changes made to the object will be "visible" to all references. New, is only used in conjunction with *classname*, when you want to create a new instance of a class. If you use the `Nothing` keyword, you release the reference to an object, but if you have more than one reference to an object, the system resources are only released when all references have been destroyed by setting them to `Nothing` or they go out of scope.
| Example | ```vb
Dim objTest1
Dim objTest2
Dim objNewClass

    ' Create a new dictionary object
    Set objTest1 = CreateObject( "Scripting.Dictionary")
    ' Create a reference to the
    ' newly created dictionary object
    Set objTest2 = objTest1

    ' Destroy the object reference
    Set objTest1 = Nothing
    ' Although objTest2 was set
    ' to refer to objTest1, you can
    ' still refer to objTest2,
    ' because the system resources
    ' will no be released before
    ' all references have been
    ' destroyed. So let's add a key
    ' and an item
    objTest2.Add "TestKey", "Test"
    ' Destroy the object reference
    Set objTest2 = Nothing

    ' Create an instance of the
    ' class clsTest (created with
    ' the Class keyword)
    Set objNewClass = New clsTest
    ' ...
    ' Destroy the class instance
    Set objNewClass = Nothing
``` |
| See Also | **GetRef** |
```

TypeName	Returns the Variant subtype information for an expression as a Variant subtype `String` (8).
Syntax	`TypeName(expression)`
	expression is the variable or constant you want subtype information for.
Note	This function has the following return values (strings):

`Byte`	Byte
`Integer`	Integer
`Long`	Long integer
`Single`	Single-precision floating-point
`Double`	Double-precision floating-point
`Currency`	Currency
`Decimal`	Decimal
`Date`	Date and/or time
`String`	Character string
`Boolean`	True or False
`Empty`	Unitialized
`Null`	No valid data
`<object type>`	Actual type name of an object
`Object`	Generic object
`Unknown`	Unknown object type
`Nothing`	Object variable that doesn't refer to an object instance
`Error`	Error

Example

```
Dim arrstrTest(10)

         MsgBox TypeName(10)          ' Integer
         MsgBox TypeName("Test")      ' String
         MsgBox TypeName(arrstrTest)  ' Variant()
         MsgBox TypeName(Null)        ' Null
```

See Also   **IsArray, IsDate, IsEmpty, IsNull, IsNumeric, IsObject,** and **VarType**

VarType	Returns an integer indicating the subtype of a variable or constant.
Syntax	`VarType(expression)`
	expression is the variable or constant you want subtype information for.
Note	This function has the following return values:

`vbEmpty`	0	uninitialized
`vbNull`	1	no valid data
`vbInteger`	2	Integer
`vbLong`	3	Long integer
`vbSingle`	4	Single-precision floating-point number
`vbDouble`	5	Double-precision floating-point number
`vbCurrency`	6	Currency
`vbDate`	7	Date
`vbString`	8	String
`vbObject`	9	Automation object
`vbError`	10	Error
`vbBoolean`	11	Boolean
`vbVariant`	12	Variant (only used only with arrays of Variants)
`vbDataObject`	13	A data-access object
`vbByte`	17	Byte
`vbArray`	8192	Array

Example

```
Dim arrstrTest(10)

    MsgBox VarType(10)            ' 2
    MsgBox VarType("Test")        ' 8
    MsgBox VarType(arrstrTest)    ' 8204
    MsgBox VarType(Null)          ' 1
```

See Also   **IsArray, IsDate, IsEmpty, IsNull, IsNumeric, IsObject,** and **TypeName**

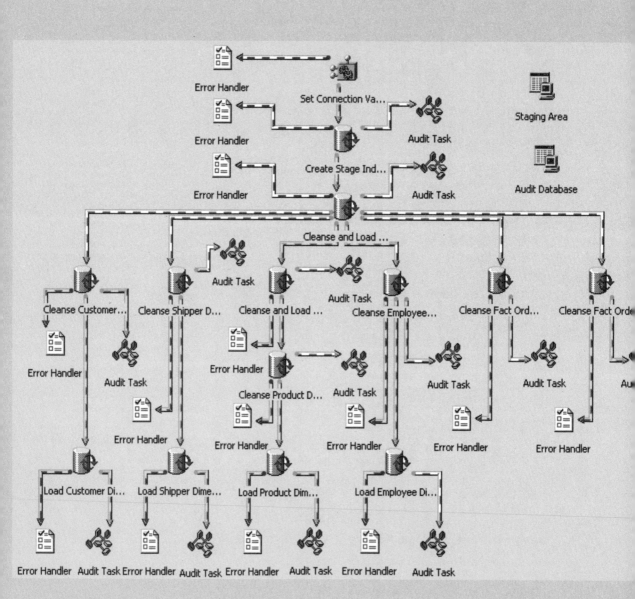

Error Handler

Set Connection Va...

Audit Task

Staging Area

Error Handler

Create Stage Ind...

Audit Task

Audit Database

Error Handler

Cleanse and Load ...

Audit Task

Cleanse Customer...

Cleanse Shipper D...

Cleanse and Load ...

Audit Task

Cleanse Employee...

Cleanse Fact Ord...

Cleanse Fact Orde

Error Handler

Audit Task

Error Handler

Cleanse Product D...

Audit Task

Audit Task

Audit Task

Au

Error Handler

Error Handler

Error Handler

Error Handler

Error Handler

Load Customer Di...

Load Shipper Dime...

Load Product Dim...

Load Employee Di...

Error Handler   Audit Task   Error Handler   Audit Task   Error Handler   Audit Task   Error Handler   Audit Task

Variable Naming and Other Code Conventions

This appendix covers coding conventions that will help us to produce code that is easily readable and understandable, minimize errors, and speed up the inevitable debugging process. Although we do not always follow these conventions in this book, as each programmer has their own preferences, we would recommend that you use at least *some* convention in your programming; the ones listed here are well recognized in the programming community.

Variable Naming Conventions

To make our variables describe themselves and their purpose, we should choose names that describe what the variable contains, for example `dailyincome` is better than `dollars` or `x`. This can be helped by the use of mixed case, and by the use of Hungarian Notation where the variable name is prefixed with a notation based on the data type that the variable is supposed to contain, for example `dblDailyIncome` is much clearer than `dailyincome`. Consistency is also important, for example if you use `Cnt` as a variable in one part of the script and `Count` in another, you're likely to introduce run-time errors by confusing the variables.

Hungarian Notation

Data Type	Hungarian Prefix	Example	VarType()
Boolean	bln (or bool)	blnValidated	11
Byte	byt	bytColor	17
Currency	cur	curAmount	6
Date or Time	dtm	dtmBirthday	7
Double	dbl	dblBalance	5
Error	err	errInvalidName	10
Integer	int	intCount	2
Long	lng	lngWidth	3
Single	sng	sngHeight	4
String	str	strName	8
Object	obj	objRS	9 or 13
Variant	var	varNumber	12

Procedure Naming

Another key to writing easy-to-read code is to descriptively name your procedures. A trick to this is to start your procedure names with a verb, for example `InitValues`, `ReadData`, `CloseWindow`, `KludgeFile`, and so on. Mixed case and consistency of use between different routines should also be used.

Indentation

The proper indentation of code is probably the greatest way of enhancing its clarity. After procedure declaration, opening loop statement, or conditional test, we indent by 2 (or 4) spaces, or use tabs; the closing statements follow the reverse indentation. By doing this, you can easily follow the flow of your program, as this example demonstrates:

```
Sub ShowIndentation()
   Dim intCount
   Dim strMessage
   For intCount = 1 to 5
       strMessage - strMessage & " " & intCount
       If strMessage = "1 2" then
         strMessage = strMessage & " -"
       End If
   Next
   MsgBox(strMessage)
End Sub
```

Commenting

Comments are an absolute must, especially when multiple people are involved in a project and you are writing functions to be used by other team members. Even if you are writing code that only you will ever see, we can guarantee that after a few months of not dealing with it (or even just certain parts of it), you will forget what it does or exactly how it works. This is where commenting comes in handy. By commenting your procedures (describing what they do, pre and post conditions, return values, etc.), important variables (ones that are changed in the procedure or passed by reference), and other parts of your code; not only will you then remember what it does six months from now, but another programmer will be able to easily follow your logic (we hope) when they take over the maintenance of your code after your big promotion!

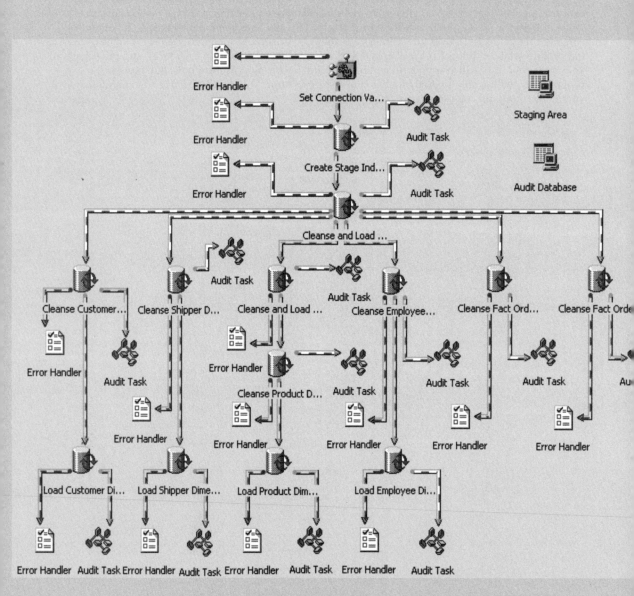

Error Handler

Error Handler

Set Connection Va...

Audit Task

Staging Area

Error Handler

Create Stage Ind...

Audit Task

Audit Database

Error Handler

Audit Task

Cleanse and Load ...

Audit Task

Cleanse Customer...

Cleanse Shipper D...

Cleanse and Load ...

Audit Task

Cleanse Employee...

Cleanse Fact Ord...

Cleanse Fact Orde

Error Handler

Audit Task

Error Handler

Audit Task

Audit Task

Audit Task

Au

Cleanse Product D...

Error Handler

Audit Task

Error Handler

Error Handler

Error Handler

Error Handler

Load Customer Di...

Load Shipper Dime...

Load Product Dim...

Load Employee Di...

Error Handler   Audit Task   Error Handler   Audit Task   Error Handler   Audit Task   Error Handler   Audit Task

Microsoft Scripting Run-time Reference

Objects

Name	Description
Dictionary	The Dictionary object allows key-based storage of general items.
Drive	The Drive object allows you to gather information about drives attached to the system.
Drives	The Drives object contains a collection of Drive objects.
File	The File object allows you to create, delete, and move files, and to query the system as to their names, paths, etc.
Files	The Files object contains a collection of File objects.
FileSystem Object	The FileSystemObject object is the main object of the Scripting group. It allows you to create, delete, and gain information about (and generally manipulate) drives, folders, and files.
Folder	The Folder object allows you to create, delete, and move folders, and to query the system as to their names, paths, etc.
Folders	The Folders object contains a collection of Folder objects.
TextStream	The TextStream object enables you to read and write text files.

The Dictionary Object

Methods

Name	Returns	Description
Add		Add a new key and item to the dictionary.
Exists	Boolean	Determine if a given key is in the dictionary.
Items	Variant	Get an array containing all items in the dictionary.
Keys	Variant	Get an array containing all keys in the dictionary.
Remove		Remove a given key from the dictionary.
RemoveAll		Remove all information from the dictionary.

Properties

Name	Returns	Description
CompareMode	CompareMethod	Set or get the string comparison method. Read/write.
Count	Integer	Get the number of key/item pairs in the dictionary. Read only
Item	Variant	Set or get the item for a given key. Read/write.
Key	Variant	Change a key to a different key. Write only.

The Drive Object

Properties

Name	Returns	Description
AvailableSpace	Variant	Get available space. Read only.
DriveLetter	String	Drive letter. Read only.
DriveType	DriveTypeConst	Drive type. Read only.
FileSystem	String	Filesystem type. Read only.
FreeSpace	Variant	Get drive free space. Read only.
IsReady	Boolean	Check if disk is available. Read only.
Path	String	Path. Read only.
RootFolder	IFolder	Root folder. Read only.

Name	Returns	Description
SerialNumber	Integer	Serial number. Read only.
ShareName	String	Share name. Read only.
TotalSize	Variant	Get total drive size. Read only.
VolumeName	String	Name of volume. Read/write.

The Drives Collection

Properties

Name	Returns	Description
Count	Integer	Number of drives. Read only.
Item	Drive	Get drive. Read only.

The File Object

Methods

Name	Returns	Description
Copy		Copy this file.
Delete		Delete this file.
Move		Move this file.
OpenAsTextStream	TextStream	Open a file as a TextStream.

Properties

Name	Returns	Description
Attributes	FileAttribute	File attributes. Read/write.
DateCreated	Date	Date file was created. Read only.
DateLastAccessed	Date	Date file was last accessed. Read only.
DateLastModified	Date	Date file was last modified. Read only.
Drive	Drive	Get drive that contains file. Read only.
Name	String	Get name of file. Read/write.
ParentFolder	Folder	Get folder that contains file. Read only.

Table continued on following page

Name	Returns	Description
Path	String	Path to the file. Read only.
ShortName	String	Short name. Read only.
ShortPath	String	Short path. Read only.
Size	Variant	File size. Read only.
Type	String	Type description. Read only.

The Files Collection

Properties

Name	Returns	Description
Count	Integer	Number of files. Read only.
Item	File	Get file. Read only.

The FileSystemObject Object

Methods

Name	Returns	Description
BuildPath	String	Generate a path from an existing path and a name.
CopyFile		Copy a file.
CopyFolder		Copy a folder.
CreateFolder	Folder	Create a folder.
CreateTextFile	TextStream	Create a file as a TextStream.
DeleteFile		Delete a file.
DeleteFolder		Delete a folder.
DriveExists	Boolean	Check if a drive or a share exists.
FileExists	Boolean	Check if a file exists.
FolderExists	Boolean	Check if a path exists.
GetAbsolutePathName	String	Return the canonical representation of the path.
GetBaseName	String	Return base name from a path.

(handwritten note on paper overlay: W)nofax // database ic s / windfax / set up ↑)

	rns	Description
	ve	Get drive or UNC share.
	g	Return drive from a path.
	g	Return extension from path.
		Get file.
	g	Return the file name from a path.
	er	Get folder.
		Return path to the parent folder.
	er	Get location of various system folders.
		Generate name that can be used to name a temporary file.
		Move a file.
		Move a folder.
	Stream	Open a file as a TextStream.

	ns	Description
	es	Get drives collection. Read only.

The Folder Object

Methods

Name	Returns	Description
Copy		Copy this folder.
CreateTextFile	TextStream	Create a file as a TextStream.
Delete		Delete this folder.
Move		Move this folder.

Properties

Name	Returns	Description
Attributes	FileAttribute	Folder attributes. Read/write.
DateCreated	Date	Date folder was created. Read only.
DateLastAccessed	Date	Date folder was last accessed. Read only.
DateLastModified	Date	Date folder was last modified. Read only.
Drive	Drive	Get drive that contains folder. Read only.
Files	Files	Get files collection. Read only.
IsRootFolder	Boolean	True if folder is root. Read only.
Name	String	Get name of folder. Read/write.
ParentFolder	Folder	Get parent folder. Read only.
Path	String	Path to folder. Read only.
ShortName	String	Short name. Read only.
ShortPath	String	Short path. Read only.
Size	Variant	Sum of files and subfolders. Read only.
SubFolders	Folders	Get folders collection. Read only.

The Folders Collection

Methods

Name	Returns	Description
Add	Folder	Create a new folder.

Properties

Name	Returns	Description
Count	Integer	Number of folders. Read only.
Item	Folder	Get folder. Read only.

The TextStream Object

Methods

Name	Returns	Description
Close		Close a text stream.
Read	String	Read a specific number of characters into a string.
ReadAll	String	Read the entire stream into a string.
ReadLine	String	Read an entire line into a string.
Skip		Skip a specific number of characters.
SkipLine		Skip a line.
Write		Write a string to the stream.
WriteBlankLines		Write a number of blank lines to the stream.
WriteLine		Write a string and an end of line to the stream.

Properties

Name	Returns	Description
AtEndOfLine	Boolean	Is the current position at the end of a line? Read only.
AtEndOfStream	Boolean	Is the current position at the end of the stream? Read only.
Column	Integer	Current column number. Read only.
Line	Integer	Current line number. Read only.

Constants

CompareMethod

Name	Value	Description
BinaryCompare	0	Binary order comparison.
DatabaseCompare	2	Database order comparison.
TextCompare	1	Text order comparison.

DriveTypeConst

Name	Value	Description
CDRom	4	Drive is a CD-ROM. No distinction is made between read only and read/write CD-ROM drives.
Fixed	2	Drive has fixed (non-removable) media.
RamDisk	5	Drive is a block of RAM on the local computer that behaves like a disk.
Remote	3	Network drives.
Removable	1	Drive has removable media.
Unknown	0	Drive type can't be determined.

FileAttribute

Name	Value	Description
Alias	64	File is an alias.
Archive	32	File has been updated since last backup.
Compressed	2048	File is compressed.
Directory	16	File is a directory.
Hidden	2	File is a hidden file.
Normal	0	File is a normal file.
ReadOnly	1	File is read only.
System	4	File is a system file.
Volume	8	File is a network volume.

IOMode

Name	Value	Description
ForAppending	8	Open a file and write to the end of the file.
ForReading	1	Open a file for reading only. You can't write to this file.
ForWriting	2	Open a file for writing. If a file with the same name exists, its previous contents are overwritten.

SpecialFolderConst

Name	Value	Description
SystemFolder	1	The System folder contains libraries, fonts, and device drivers.
TemporaryFolder	2	The Temp folder is used to store temporary files.
WindowsFolder	0	The Windows folder contains files installed by the Windows operating system.

Tristate

Name	Value	Description
TristateFalse	0	Opens the file as ASCII.
TristateTrue	-1	Opens the file as Unicode.
TristateUseDefault	-2	Opens the file using the system default.

Method Calls Quick Reference

Dictionary

Dictionary.Add(*Key As Variant, Item As Variant*)
Boolean = Dictionary.Exists(*Key As Variant*)
Variant = Dictionary.Items
Variant = Dictionary.Keys
Dictionary.Remove(*Key As Variant*)
Dictionary.RemoveAll

File

File.Copy(*Destination As String, OverWriteFiles As Boolean*)
File.Delete(*Force As Boolean*)
File.Move(*Destination As String*)
ITextStream = File.OpenAsTextStream(*IOMode As IOMode, Format As Tristate*)

FileSystemObject

*String = FileSystemObject.*BuildPath(*Path As String, Name As String*)
*FileSystemObject.*CopyFile(*Source As String, Destination As String, OverWriteFiles As Boolean*)
*FileSystemObject.*CopyFolder(*Source As String, Destination As String, OverWriteFiles As Boolean*)
*IFolder = FileSystemObject.*CreateFolder(*Path As String*)
*ITextStream = FileSystemObject.*CreateTextFile(*FileName As String, Overwrite As Boolean, Unicode As Boolean*)
*FileSystemObject.*DeleteFile(*FileSpec As String, Force As Boolean*)
*FileSystemObject.*DeleteFolder(*FolderSpec As String, Force As Boolean*)
*Boolean = FileSystemObject.*DriveExists(*DriveSpec As String*)
*Boolean = FileSystemObject.*FileExists(*FileSpec As String*)
*Boolean = FileSystemObject.*FolderExists(*FolderSpec As String*)
*String = FileSystemObject.*GetAbsolutePathName(*Path As String*)
*String = FileSystemObject.*GetBaseName(*Path As String*)
*IDrive = FileSystemObject.*GetDrive(*DriveSpec As String*)
*String = FileSystemObject.*GetDriveName(*Path As String*)
*String = FileSystemObject.*GetExtensionName(*Path As String*)
*IFile = FileSystemObject.*GetFile(*FilePath As String*)
*String = FileSystemObject.*GetFileName(*Path As String*)
*IFolder = FileSystemObject.*GetFolder(*FolderPath As String*)
*String = FileSystemObject.*GetParentFolderName(*Path As String*)
*IFolder = FileSystemObject.*GetSpecialFolder(*SpecialFolder As SpecialFolderConst*)
*String = FileSystemObject.*GetTempName
*FileSystemObject.*MoveFile(*Source As String, Destination As String*)
*FileSystemObject.*MoveFolder(*Source As String, Destination As String*)
*ITextStream = FileSystemObject.*OpenTextFile(*FileName As String, IOMode As IOMode, Create As Boolean, Format As Tristate*)

Folder

*Folder.*Copy(*Destination As String, OverWriteFiles As Boolean*)
*ITextStream = Folder.*CreateTextFile(*FileName As String, Overwrite As Boolean, Unicode As Boolean*)
*Folder.*Delete(*Force As Boolean*)
*Folder.*Move(*Destination As String*)

Folders

*IFolder = Folders.*Add(*Name As String*)

TextStream

*TextStream.*Close
*String = TextStream.*Read(*Characters As Integer*)
*String = TextStream.*ReadAll
*String = TextStream.*ReadLine
*TextStream.*Skip(*Characters As Integer*)
*TextStream.*SkipLine
*TextStream.*Write(*Text As String*)
*TextStream.*WriteBlankLines(*Lines As Integer*)
*TextStream.*WriteLine(*Text As String*)

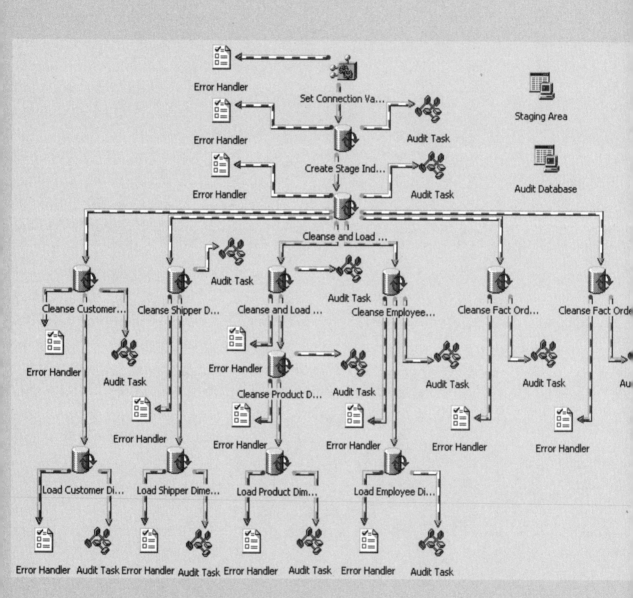

Index

A Guide to the Index

The index is arranged hierarchically, in alphabetical order, with any symbols preceding the letter A. Most second-level entries and many third-level entries also occur as first-level entries. This is to ensure that users will find the information they require however they choose to search for it.

A

Access data, convert to SQL Server example, 236
  choose destination, 237
  Column Mappings tab, 239
    Unicode data types, use of, 239
  Copy tables from source database, 237
  save package to SQL Server, 240
    view and make modifications, 240
  Select Queries, 238
Access data, migrating
  DTS will not convert
    primary keys and relationships, 236
    queries, 236
    rules or defaults, 236
  DTS, using, 236
  Upsizing Wizard
    converts data, relationships, and primary keys to SQL Server, 236
Access Queries, migrating
  SQL View
    SQL syntax, 242
  stored procedures, 241
  Transact-SQL scripts, 242
    most flexible of options, 242
  views, 241
    do not accept parameters, 241
ACID properties
  atomicity, 161
  consistency, 161
  durability, 161
  isolation, 161
Active Server Pages
  see ASP
ActiveScriptTask object
  methods and properties, 689 - 690
ActiveX Script editor, 110
  Browser tab, 111
  Language tab, 111
  Phases tab, 112
ActiveX Script Task, 49
  advanced, 335
  available in SQL Server 2000, 49
  basic programming terminology, 270
  can create and manage local or distributed transactions, 163
  can use any scripting language, 265

  customize data transformation, 266
  debugging techniques, 355
    Msgbox functions, place strategically in code, 355
  display and change global variables, 337
  dynamically set properties on tasks, connections, or global variables, 266
  Explicit Global Variables, 337
  fundamentals, 265
  Global Variables, 336
    considered private, 336
    setting, 336
  manipulate COM objects, 266
  message boxes
    useful in debugging complex code, 271
  move, copy or read files, 266
  Msgbox function, 271
  no access to DTS package transaction, 163
  open a package in a package, 352
    Hello World example, 353
    LoadFromRepository method, 353
    LoadFromSQLServer method, 353
    LoadFromStorageFile method, 353
    passing variables to other packages, 354
    useful when importing unpredictable amount of files, 352
  package as an object, 352
  role in DTS, 265
  Script Debugger, 355
    Call Stack, 359
    check and change contents of my variables, 359
    DisplayResult function, 358
    GetSomeResult function, 358
    JIT debugging for DTS, 356
    Main() function, 359
    stop statement, 356
    toolbar buttons, table, 357
  scripting language performance, 269
  SendMail Task
    create, 306
  using, 267
  VBScript, 270
    Option Explicit, 270
  VBScript, examples using, 265
ActiveX Script Task Properties dialog
  Description option, 267
  Language option, 267
    Auto Gen generates correct syntax, 268
    Functions box, 267
    Parse button, 268

ADO method calls, 757
quick reference guide, 757
ADO object model, 741
Command object, 741, 743
Connection object, 741, 744
Error object, 742, 746
Errors collection, 742, 746
Field object, 742, 747
Fields collection, 742, 748
library reference, 741
Parameter object, 742, 748
Parameters collection, 742, 749
Properties collection, 742, 750
Property object, 742, 750
Record object, 742, 750
Recordset object, 741, 751
Stream object, 742, 755
Table of Collections, 742
table of Objects, 741
Analysis Services, 575
ETL process
diagram, 498
Analysis Services 2000
process cubes, 431
application design
3-tiers, 504
business services layer, 504
data services layer, 504
user services layer, 504
business services layer, 508
COM+ object, used to get information about client
packages, 509
data services layer, 509
overview, 504
user services layer, 508
ASP, 508
Application Event Log
package error handling, 409
Arithmetic Operators, 762
Array Functions and Statements, 782
ASP
displaying packages, 531
converting empty and NULL strings, 533
displaying properrties, 534
ShowPackages method, 531
displaying packages status, 533
displaying properrties
FORM element, 534
general declaration, 529
QueryString, checking, 530
interpreted language, 508
method of creating dynamic web content, 505
sever-side script, 505
Assignment operator, 762

B

backups
points to remember, 398
BCP, 8
format files, 83
inserts data into SQL Server, 8
Bitwise Operators
see also Logical operators.
Operator Precedence, 768
branching
Else, 274

Elself, 274
If, 274
If . . . Else
current date example, 274
nested conditions, 278
Bulk Copy Program
see BCP.
Bulk Insert Task, 51, 56, 79
available in SQL Server 2000, 51
can join package transaction if right connections are
made, 163
Check constraints option, 80
column mapping option, lack of, 82
Data file type option, 80
Enable identity insert option, 80
First row option, 81
format files
create, 83
generated by internal wizard, 83
use, 83
Insert batch size option, 81
only imports data, 79
requires SQL Server connection, 79
rules, 51
Sorted data option, 80
source data must align, 79
Table lock option, 80
typical errors, 82
BulkInsertTask object
methods and properties, 690
business services layer
ActiveX DLL project
create, 513
DTSManager example, 513
VB COM+ object, 512
DTS packages, execution of, 512
GetGlobalVariables function, 512
GetPackageList function, 512
GetScript function, 513
RunPackageList method, 512

C

CDO, 506
accesses capabilities provided by Exchange Server,
506
provides simple messaging services, 506
CDONTS
provides subset of functionality of CDO, 507
simplicity, 507
choosing the destination database example
DTS Import/Export Wizard, 19
Collaboration Data Objects
see CDO.
Collaboration Data Objects for NT Server
see CDONTS.
column mappings tab
Append rows to destination table, 21
Create destination table, 21
Delete rows to destination table, 21
Drop and recreate the destination table, 22
Enable identity insert, 22
Transformations tab, 23
ActiveX logic, 23
advantages, 23
customized transformations, 23
merging fields, 23

Column object
table of properties, 691
Columns collection
methods and properties, 692
COM+
combines COM with MTS, 505
COM+ application
Component Services, 523
creating, 523
COM+ Application Install Wizard, 524
naming application, 524
Command object, 743
Cancel method, 743
collections of, 744
CreateParameter method, 743
Execute method, 743
methods, quick reference, 757
table of methods, 743
table of properties, return types, and descriptions, 743
commenting, 821
Commerce Server 2000
import web log data, 431
Comparison Operators
Operator Precedence, 765
complex custom task, 447
Component Object Model
see COM.
Component Services
Object Pooling, 505
Queued Components
combines features of COM and MSMQ, 505
COM-Structured Storage File
DTS package, saving, 65
Concatenating variables, 272
ampersand & symbol, 272
Concatenation Operators
Operator Precedence, 764
concurrency, 167
Connection object, ADO, 744
BeginTrans method, 744
Cancel method, 744
Close method, 744
collections of, 745
CommitTrans method, 744
Execute method, 744
methods, quick reference, 756
Open method, 744
OpenSchema method, 744
RollbackTrans method, 744
table of events, 745
table of methods, 744
table of properties, 744
Connection object, DTS
methods and properties, 693
Connections collection, 694
Constants
CompareMethod, 829
DriveTypeConst, 830
FileAttribute, 830
IOMode, 830
SpecialFolderConst, 831
Tristate, 831
Conversion Functions, 801

Copy Database Wizard (CDW), 36
accessing example, 36
Advanced options, 38
Modify option, 38
rules for using, 36
specifying items and executing the package example, 38
specify when package should be executed, 39
step details, 40
typical applications, 36
Copy method
FileSystemObject object
moving and copying files, 348
Copy SQL Server Objects Task, 51, 90
available in SQL Server 2000, 51
Copy Database task, compared to, 90
tasks that cannot take part in transaction, 163
transfers SQL Server objects, 90
copy tables and views option example, 20
DTS Import/Export Wizard, 20
CreateCustomToolTip method
CustomTaskUI interface, 442
CreateFolder method
FileSystemObject object
managing folders, 344
CreateProcessTask object
methods and properties, 695
current date example
branching, 274
Else statement, 276
If . . . Then statement, 275
IsDate function, 275
package status dialog
task fails execution, 276
Replace() function, 276
Custom Task object
Execute method, 438
Custom Task object model, 431
custom tasks, 431
available in SQL Server 2000, 54
building, 437
common situations, 445
copy and paste CustomTask, 446
delete CustomTask from Design Surface, 446
drag CustomTask into Design Surface for first time, 445
DLL written in COM-compliant language, 432
DLL, create, 439
DTS Designer
drag to, 441
edit properties, 446
execute CustomTask from DTS Designer, 446
Help, 446
design time, 445
reasons for use, 432
code maintenance/reuse, 432
ease of use for non-programmers, 433
encapsulation of business logic, 433
for profit, 433
functionality not possible from ActiveX Script, 432
performance, 433
security, 433
registering in DTS, 432, 440
run time, 445
running, 441
unregistering a task, 441
utilization of, 445

custom tasks message box example, 437
 ActiveX DLL project, create, 437
 Custom Task object
  Execute method, 438
 Custom Task properties
  implement, 438
 message box, 437
 persistent storage of Name and Description
 properties
  Get and Let methods, 438
 References option, 437
Customer Dimension transform data task, 611
 extracting dimension information
  Destination, 611
  Source, 611
  Transformation, 611
 illustration, 611
CustomTask interface, 434
 all tasks must inherit their methods from, 434
 Description Property, 434
 DisplayPropertyPage method, 457
 ErrorHandler custom task example, 448
 Execute method, 452
  table of parameters, 436
 Execute method element, 434
 Name Property, 434
 Properties Collection, 434
 table of elements, 434
CustomTask object
 methods and properties, 696
CustomTaskUI interface
 CreateCustomToolTip method, 442
  table of parameters, 443
 Delete method, 442, 450
  parameter, 443
 DisplayPropertyPage method, 450, 464
 Edit method, 442
  parameter, 443
 ErrorHandler custom task, 448
 GetUIInfo method, 442
  table of parameters, 444
 Help method, 442
  parameter, 444
 Initialize method, 442
  parameter, 444
 New method, 442
  parameter, 444
 table of elements, 442
CustomTaskUI object
 Methods, 696

D

data acquisition, 490
 linked servers, 490
  creating reference to source systems, 490
Data Driven Query (DDQ) Task, 52, 120
 available in SQL Server 2000, 52
 ActiveX Script transformation, 123
 Bound Table, 121
 can join package transaction if right connections are
  made, 163
 Create New Transformation dialog, 124
  Transactions table, process record by record, 124
 create queries
  inserting, 125
  updating, 125

 create tables, 121
 DDQ Queries tab
  check order of parameters, 126
  configure, 126
 DTSTransformStat_SkipRow constant
  Else condition, 125
 example, 120, 127
 final results, 127
 flexibility, 120
 insertion, updating and deletion of records, 120
 Source and Destination connections, 120
 Source information
  defining, 121
 table of constants and descriptions, 124
 target table
  defining, 122
 transformation logic, 123
  decision tree, 123
 Transformations tab, 122
  delete existing transformation, 123
Data Junction
 transfer data from any DBMS, 9
data lineage, 155
 audit on tasks, 155
 determine source of data and transformations
  performed, 155
 lineage variables as source columns, 155
 saving data to Meta Data Services, 156
  column-level data lineage, 157
  row-level data lineage, 156
 write lineage to repository, 155
data marts
 type of analytical questions that can be answered by,
  544
 data warehouses, compared to, 482
 diagram, 483
 reasons for creating, 541
Data movement options, 176, 177
 connection to sources file, 179
 create table, 178
 example, 177 - 185
 Exception file, output, 184
 Execute SQL Task, 180
 Fetch buffer size property, 177
 First and Last Row setting, 177
 Max Error Count, 176
 OLE DB Provider for SQL Server, 179
 set up package, 178
 text file containing historical data, 177
  contains error, 178
 Text File Properties
  column delimiter, 180
  First Row, 180
 Transform Data Task, 181
 Transform Data Task Properties dialog, 182
  First Row, 185
  Last Row property, 185
Data Pump Task
 see also Transform Data Task
 available in SQL Server 2000, 50
 create destination table, 59
 errors, 62
 features, 50
 naming, 62
 new features, 50
 preview data, 58

Data Pump Task (continued)
rules, 57
columns mapped for transformation, 57
destination defined, 57
source connection defined, 57
testing transformation, 61
Transformation tab
map columns and choose transformation method, 59
transformation task, opening, 57
used for transformation when data does not align, 79
data scrubbing, 188
Example
changing data, 191
Lookup tables, 188
Transform Data Task, 189
data services layer
package list table
create, 510
Send Email package example
Active Script task, 510
create, 510
data transformation document, 488
Data Transformation Services
see DTS.
data warehouses
characteristics, 476
data cleansed, 476
data extracted regularly from transactional systems, 476
dimensionally modelled to support fast, intuitive querying, 476
made up of one or more integrated data marts, 476
provides data on which to base forecasts, 476
creating, 475
data marts, compared to, 482
DTS, 475
ETL accounts for 25% to 50% of overall effort, 475
ETL application, purpose of, 542
populating default values, 571
populating static dimensions, 571
source data from systems on different platforms, 475
Database Maintainance Plan Wizard
backup maintainance plan, 389
backups, 393
Data Optimization, 392
maintaintance tasks that should be run automatically, 389
name maintenance plan, 396
reorganize data, 391
reports generated by maintainence tasks
can be saved to text file or emailed to operator, 395
save system databases in different file to user databases, 391
schedule backup of transaction logs, 394
view jobs scheduled to run, 396
Enterprise Manager, 397
Database Management System
see DBMS.
DataDrivenQueryTask object
methods and properties, 697
DataDrivenQueryTask2 object
table of extended properties, 699
DataPumpTask object
methods and properties, 699
DataPumpTask2 object
table of extended properties, 701

Date and Time Functions and Statements, 773
DB2 databases, converting, 249
Data Link Properties, 251
all tab, 254
Default schema setting, 252
error messages, 253
Initial Catalog setting, 252
Package collection setting, 252
Test Connection, 253
very complex, 251
DB2Connect, 249
Host Integration Services
AUTOCOMMMIT package, 255
bind DB2 packages, 255
Ole DB Provider, 251
READ_COMMMITED package, 255
READ_UNCOMMMITED package, 255
REPEATABLE_READ package, 255
SERIALIZABLE package, 255
Ole DB Provider, 249
Starquest's StarSQL, 249
table of compatible data type issues, 257
DBMS, 9
Delete method
CustomTaskUI interface, 442, 450
Dictionary object, 831
methods and properties, 824
dimensional data model, 483
creating, 483
requirements to be met, 483
issues to consider, 484
choose grains of facts, 484
choose time context of facts, 484
identify clear subject areas, 484
identify dimensions, 484
surrogate keys, 485
Virtual Cubes, 484
dimensional modeling, 477
snowflake schemas
diagram, 478
star schemas
center table is usually fact table, 477
diagram, 477
dimensions include art least one hierarchy with several levels, 478
measures, 477
smaller tables are dimensions, 477
star versus snowflake schemas
comparison, 479
star/snowflake schemas
hybrid designs, 479
dimensions
constraints on detail for reporting on, 545
DisplayPropertyPage method
CustomTaskUI interface, 450, 464
DisplayResult function
ActiveX Scripting Task
Script Debugger, 358
Distributed Management Objects
see DMO.
distributed queries
advantages, 208
DNS
name resolution system, 535
Do loops example, 282
prompt users until data is correct, 282

Drive object
table of properties, 824
Drives collection
table of properties, 825
DTS, 7
advanced package options, 154
advanced settings, 153
available via DTS Designer in SQL Server 2000, 153
built into SQL Server, 8
caching and control
debugging of ActiveX Scripting, 104
collection of utilities and objects, 8
Execute SQL task, 210
interact with linked servers, 210
FTP files, 8
import, export and convert data, 8
improvements with SQL Server 2000, 14
engine, 14
tasks, 14
linked servers
purge data staging area, 210
run dynamic queries, 210
update remote systems, 210
managing drives, 339
SQL Server objects, can move, 8
using from other applications, 503
requirements for examples, 507
DTS ActiveX Script editor
see Active X Script editor
DTS Designer, 47
accessing, 41
assigning priorities to Tasks, 171
Workflow Properties dialog, 172
complex logic, handles, 23
create flow of data to be transformed, 48
create, save and manage packages, 48
Disconnected Edit option, 96
DTS package
creating, 54
DTS Package Properties dialog
Advanced tab, 154
error handling, 402
graphical tool, 47
allows visual piecing together of object model, 47
integrate with Meta Data Services, 48
opening, 48
package auditing, 403
viewing logs, 404
Package Execution Status dialog, 402
does not display detailed error messages, 402
precedence constraints, 62
register and manage custom tasks, 48
SQL Server 2000
execute individual steps, 48
viewing DTS packages example, 42
Execute package, 42
DTS Import/Export Wizard
accessing, 16
advanced OLE DB connection options
accessing, 18
advanced options
column mappings tab, 21
choosing the destination database example, 19
copy tables and views option example, 20
naming and executing the package example, 26
Query Builder example, 29
saving and scheduling the package example, 24

Select Objects to Copy
advanced options, 32
Append data option, 33
Copy all objects option, 33
Copy data option, 33
Create destination objects first option, 32
Drop destination objects option, 32
Include all dependent objects option, 33
Include extended properties option, 33
Replace existing data option, 33
Script file directory, 34
Use collation option, 33
Use default option, 33
transferring data example, 16
transferring SQL objects example, 32
using queries to transfer data example, 27
DTS interoperability, 96
make standalone package, 96
SQL Server required to use DTS Designer, 96
DTS Lookup, 191
Data Driven Query Task
can be used as part of, 192
example, 192 -199
ActiveX Script, 197
add lookup definition, 192
map source and destination columns, 192
SELECT statement, 199
set connections, 192
step failure, 199
Transform Data Task, create, 192
Transform Data Task
can be used as part of, 192
used to validate data against information held in
other databases, 191
DTS Object Library Reference
ActiveScriptTask object, 689, 690
BulkInsertTask object, 690
collections, 688
Column object, 691
Columns collection, 692
Connection object, 693
Connections collection, 694
CreateProcessTask object, 695
CustomTask object, 696
CustomTaskUI object, 696
DataDrivenQueryTask object, 697
DataDrivenQueryTask2 object, 699
DataPumpTask object, 699
DataPumpTask2 object, 701
DynamicPropertiesTask object, 701 - 702
DynamicPropertiesTaskAssignment object, 702
DynamicPropertiesTaskAssignments collection, 703 -
704
ExecutesSQLTask object, 704
ExecutesSQLTask2 object, 705
Global Constants, 738
Global Variable object, 705
Global Variables collection, 705 - 706
IDTSStdObject object, 706
Lookup object, 706
Lookups collection, 707
objects, table of, 687
OleDBProperties collection, 707
OleDBProperty object, 708
OleDBProperty2 object, 708
Package object, 708 - 711
Package2 object, 711
PackageInfo object, 712

DTS Object Library Reference (continued)
PackageInfos collection, 713
PackageLineage object, 713
PackageLineages collection, 714
PackageLog object, 714
PackageLogRecord object, 714
PackageLogRecords collection, 715
PackageRepository object, 716
PackageSQLServer object, 716 - 717
ParallelDataPumpTask object, 717
PersistPropertyBag object, 718
PrecedenceConstraint object, 719
PrecedenceConstraints collection, 719 - 720
Properties collection, 720
PropertiesProvider object, 720
Property object, 721
PropertyBag object, 721
SavedPackageInfo object, 721
SavedPackageInfos collection, 722
ScriptingLanguageInfo object, 722
ScriptingLanguageInfos collection, 723
SendMailTask object, 724
Step object, 725
Step2 object, 726
StepLineage object, 726
StepLineages collection, 727
StepLogRecord object, 728
StepLogRecords collection, 728 729
Steps collection, 729
Task object, 729 - 730
Tasks collection, 730
TransferObjectsTask object, 731
TransferObjectsTask2 object, 732
Transformation object, 733
Transformation2 object, 734
TransformationInfo object, 734
TransformationInfos collection, 735
Transformations collection, 735 - 736
TransformationSet object, 736
TransformationSets collection, 737 - 738
DTS Object Model, 296
ActiveX Script Task
define functions and variables, 302
SendMail task object, 303
create package
ActiveX Tasks, add two, 309
CreateObject function
creates package and assigns it to variable, 309
creating packages at runtime, 309
CustomTask object, 433
oMail variable holds, 307
define variable to hold package object model, 300
developing with, 300
diagram, 685
DTS.Package2 properties
programmatic logging, 407
DTSSendMail_Added_At_Runtime, 305
enumerating steps, 300
every task is included in collection of tasks
property of every package, 457
Exchange Server, 308
For Each . . . Next Loop
executes code between For and Next statements, 304

illustration, 297
known as COM object, 298
methods, 299
Outlook, 308
Package2 object
backward compatibility maintained, 298
root level object, 298
programmatic logging, 407
table of object model properties that control logging, 407
properties, 299
SendMail Task
create, 306
Steps and Tasks
set properties, 310
Steps collection, 301
sub objects, 299
Connections, 299
Global Variables, 299
Steps, 299
tasks and steps
defined, 303
Tasks object level
display number of tasks in package, 304
using methods of objects, 305
VBScript variables defined as variant, 300
Visual Basic project, 311 - 318
DTS package, 10
ActiveX Script
open empty development environment, 300
contains all connection objects, 10
create, 63
Data Pump Task
inserting, 56
design considerations for optimal error handling, 423
multiple precedence constraints, 424
diagram, 13
DTS Designer
objects defined in, 10
dtsrun utility
executing using GUID
syntax, 70
dtsrunui utility, 71
execute, 65, 68
dtsrun utility, 69
loading, 67
logging, 75
logs kept in MSDB database, 75
success or failure of each step, 76
making the connections, 54
Destination Database, 55
Source Server, 54
owner password, 67
saving, 10, 65
COM-Structured Storage File, 65
Meta Data Services, 65
SQL Server, 65
table of options, 66
Visual Basic File, 65
scheduling using SQL Server Agent, 72
create job manually, 73
advanced tab, 74
Steps tab, 73
user password, 67
version control, 67
remove previous versions in COM-structured package, 68

DTS package components
connections, 10
Data Linkfiles, 11
facilitate OLE DB providers, 11
global variables, 10, 13
allow communication with other DTS tasks, 13
step object, 10
logic, 12
precedence constraints, 12
tasks, 10
built in, 12
create custom, 12
instructions, 12
precedence constraints, 12
DTS Package object
LoadFromSQLServer method, 520
DTS Package Object Library Reference, 685
DTS Package Properties dialog
Advanced tab
controlling transactions, 154
data lineage, 154
OLE DB Service Components, 154
scanning database information into Repository, 154
General tab, 169
Parallelism, 169
Task priorities, 169
Join transaction option, 164
Use transactions option, 164
DTS password protection, 373
owner and user, 373
owner password, 374
only owners can modify package, 374
packages are encrypted, 374
user password, 375
can execute but not view package in DTS Designer, 375
DTS security, 367
saving package in SQL Server or structured storage file
DTS password protection, 373
DTS service provider
error handling from external applications, 420
DTS toolbox, 15
Copy Database Wizard (CDW), 16
DTS Designer, 15
DTS Import/Export Wizards
easiest way to move data, 15
quickly create DTS packages, 15
DTS Programming Interfaces, 15
Wizards weak in terms of functionality, 15
DTS utilization of custom tasks, 445 - 446
DTS workflow scripts
implement loops, 415
programmatically choose to execute astep, 415
Restart/Retry a Workflow, 414
set task properties, 415
DTSManager example, 512
add component, 526
coding the Package class, 514
COM+ Application Install Wizard
naming application, 524
compile, 523
create, 513
GetGlobalVariables function, 520
GetPackageList function, 517
GetScript function, 521
installing in Component Services, 523
ObjectControl interface, 514

RunPackageAsync method, 515
set references to project, 514
dtsrun utility
DTS package, execute, 69
dtsrunui utility
DTRSRUN statement,write, 71
DTSStepScriptResult constants
Scripting error handling, 412
Dynamic Properties Task, 53, 127, 131, 321
alteration of any package included property, 327
available in SQL Server 2000, 53
building, 327
Bulk Insert Task properties, 132
configure steps and packages at runtime, 321
create destination connection, 132
create dynamic properties, 136
Constants, table of, 137
Data file, 138
Environmental variable, 138
Global Variables, 137
INI file, 137
Query, 138
Disconnected Edit mode
similar to, 128
ETL, 127
typical scenario, 127
Execute SQL Task, 322, 323, 329
example, 132 - 140
Execute SQL Task, 134
configure to delete data and reload, 134
Global Variables
create, 135
Send Mail Task
Add/Edit Assignment dialog, 328
alter mail properties, 322
alter properties, 327
ExecutionStatus setting, 333
one Dynamic Task sets the other Dynamic Task as completed, 331
set to fail, 330
set to success, 327
testing, 329
set up data load procedure
make dynamic, 132
Success precedence constraint, 140
tasks that cannot take part in transaction, 163
dynamically configure package objects, 295
DynamicPropertiesTask object
methods and properties, 701 - 702
DynamicPropertiesTaskAssignment object
methods and properties, 702
DynamicPropertiesTaskAssignments collection
methods and properties, 703 - 704

E

Edit method
CustomTaskUI interface, 442
ElseIf statements, 277
case-sensitivity, 278
Employee Dimension transform data task, 612
extracting dimension information
Destination, 613
Source, 613
Transformation, 613
illustration, 612

Enterprise Manager
advanced OLE DB connection options
  view, 19
Data Transformation Services
  view package logs, 404
DTS Designer, 9
linked server options
  Connection Timeout option, 221
  Query Timeout option, 221
  setting options in, 221
linked server security, 217
msdb database backing up, 384
  complete or differential backup, 385
  destination, 385
  schedule, 386
EnumPackageInfos method
PackageSQLServer object, 408
EnumPackageLogRecords method
PackageSQLServer object, 408
EnumStepLogRecords method
PackageSQLServer object, 408
EnumTaskLogRecords method
PackageSQLServer object, 408
error handling, 401
choosing an error file, 203
design considerations for optimal results, 423
FailOnError property, 204
GetExecutionErrorInfo, 425
multiple precedence constraints, 424
On Error workflow
  single method of handling task failures, 426
Scripting, 411
task object, 410
error handling from external applications
DTS service provider, 420
dtsrun - command line execution, 421
executing from VIsual Basic, 421
Error object, 746
table of properties, 746
ErrorHandler (ActiveX Script Task)
reasons for customizing task, 447
ErrorHandler custom task
add constraint, 448
adding icon in DTS Designer, 468
build, 448
compile and register, 468
CustomTask interface, 452
  define variables, 452
  determine location of external error, 453
    set its global variables, 454
  DisplayPropertyPage method
    Visual Basic dialog, 457
  error handler, 455
  execcute external error handling package, 454
  GetExecutionErrorInfo method
    Step object, 452
  implement, 448
  implement logging, 452
  property management code, 456
  public properties, 456
  set result of task to success, 455
CustomTaskUI interface, 449
  Delete method, 450
  DisplayPropertyPage method, 450, 464
  expose properties for public use, 467
  Help, implements, 450
  implement, 448
  Initialize method, 450

CustomTaskUI interface, implement
  add controls to form, 462
  adding, 460
  adding ActiveX components, 461
  adding dialog, 461
  Description Property, 460
  FileName Property, 460
  PredessorName Property, 460
  Source Property, 460
debugging, 472
each task should only have one precedence
  constraint, 451
execute on main thread, 471
filename of external error handling file, 457
ListView control, 458
  setting, 458
multiple precedence constraint, 448
On Error precedence constraints, 448
PredecessorName, 457
referencing, 449
source of path for external error handling file, 457
testing, 469
  set failure constraints, 470
user sets custom tasks properties, 457
Errors collection, 746
Clear method, 746
methods, quick reference, 757
properties, 746
Refresh method, 746
ETL Step 1, Northwinds example, 672
Execute Package Tasks
  Outer Package Parameters, 673
  reference packages, 672
ETL Step 2, Northwinds example
creating package, 602
drop stage indexes, 606
  IRowsetFastLoad interface
    bulk load tables, 606
global variables, 603
illustration of package
  without auditing and error handling, 602
set connection values, 604
UDL connections, 604
tasks
  drop stage table indexes, 601
  extract dimension member records, 601
  extract fact records, 601
  illustration of package, 601
ETL Step 3, Northwinds example
Audit Database connection, 629
auditing and error handling, 650
Cleans Employee Dimension task, 645
Cleanse and Load Geography Task, 633
Cleanse and Load Supplier Dimension, 640
Cleanse Customer Dimension task, 635, 636
Cleanse Customer Dimension task and Load, 635
Cleanse Employee Dimension task, 644
Cleanse Fact Order Items task, 648
Cleanse Fact Orders task, 647
Cleanse Product Dimension
  must occur after Suppliers has been loaded, 642
Cleanse Product Dimension task, 642
Cleanse Shipper Dimension task, 638
Cleanse Shipper Dimension task and Load, 638
create package, 627
create stage indexes, 631
Employee Dimension task illustration, 644

ETL Step 3, Northwinds example (continued)
 fact cleansing, 647
 global variables, create, 628
 illustration, 626
  without auditing and error handling, 627
 Load Customer Dimension task, 635, 636
 Load Employee Dimension task, 644, 645
 Load Employee Dimension task and Cleanse
 Load Product Dimension, 642, 643
 Load Product Dimension task and Cleanse, 642
 Load Shipper Dimension task, 638, 639
 Order Items task, 648
 Orders task, 647
 package properties, 628
 Product Dimension task illustration, 642
 set connection values, 629
 Staging Area connection, 629
 Transforming and loading dimensions, 633
ETL Step 4, Northwinds example
 Analysis Services Processing Task
  add, 669
 auditing and error handling, 671, 672
 connections, 653
  Staging Area Copy, 653
 create package, 651
 Data Driven QueryTask Properties dialog, 658
  Update query, 661
 fact table loads, 653
 global variables, 651
 illustration, 650
 Load Fact Order Items Task, 662
  Bindings, 663
  illustration, 662
  Lookups, 669
  Queries, 666
  Source, 663
  Transformation, 663
   Binding Columns, 664
  Update Query Type, 667 - 668
 Load Fact Orders Task, 654
  Bindings, 654
  illustration, 654
  Lookups, 661
  Queries, 658
   parameters, 659
  Source, 654
  Transformation, 654
  Update query
   parameters, 661
 NorthwindDW Analysis Services database
  configure after loading relational datamart, 669
 package properties, 651
 Process Cubes, 669
  illustration, 669
 set connection values, 653
 tasks, 650
 UDL connections
  Audit Database, 653
  Staging Area, 653
ETL design, 486
 data transformation document, 488
 extract, 486
 incremental versus full reloads, 488
 load, 487
  batch mode, 487
  bulk mode, 487
  single row mode, 487

 transform, 486
  formatting, 486
  surrogate key lookup, 487
ETL process
 Analysis Services
  diagram, 498
  integrating, 497
  overview, 498
 data acquisition, 490
 incremental processing, 499
 indexing, 497
  dimensions, 497
  facts, 497
  stage, 497
 referential, 497
 Source Systems to Staging Area
  diagram, 490
 Staging Area design, 490
 Staging Area to Warehouse, 496
  stored procedures versus DTS Tasks, 496
ETL workflow
 add new connections, 584
 Audit Database, connection, 598
 audit information
  creation of job record in AUDIT_JOB, 586
  Execute SQL Task, 586
  Get Audit ID, 587
  Set Job Information, 586
 auditing/error handling, 589
  Audit Task configured to be executed on successful
   execution, 589
 Dynamic Properties Task
  Set Connection Values, 585
 ETL 1
  connections, 581
 ETL 2
  package properties, 602
 Get Audit ID
  Audit Task, create, 589
 Source OLTP System connection
  create, 584
 UDL connection files, 582
 Write Job Completion Info
  sets job status based on result of its associated tasks,
   599
Excel data, converting, 243, 244
 create DTS package in DTS Designer, 244
 DTS custom package required, 243
 example, 243
 establish SQL Server connection, 244
 Query Analyzer
  validation, 248
 Transform Data Task, 245
  data type and field names, 247
Exception file, 174
 column delimiters, 176
 File format properties, 176
 logs bad rows, 174
 row delimiters, 176
 saves source and destination rows that cause errors,
  175
 values for text qualifier, 176
Exchange Server
 CDO accesses capabilities provided by, 507
Execute method
 CustomTask object, 438
 CustomTask interface, 452

Execute Package Task, 52, 140
available in SQL Server 2000, 52
bulk insert flat file into any database, 140
Bulk Insert Task, 141
can join package transaction if right connections are
made, 163
example, 140, 141
executing and debugging the task, 144
Global Variables
inner, 142
outer, 143
setting, 142
inherited transactions, 165
makes package more modular, 140
security, 141
versions of packages
saving new version, 142
Execute Process Task, 51
available in SQL Server 2000, 51
can create and manage local or distributed
transactions, 163
Description option, 85
easier task, 85
executes Win32 process or batch file
DTS package, wraps in, 85
no access to DTS package transaction, 163
Parameters option, 85
Return Code option, 85
Timeout option, 85
Win32 Process option, 85
Execute SQL Task, 51, 86
available in SQL Server 2000, 51
can join package transaction if right connections are
made, 163
Command time-out option, 88
data load procedure example, 86
Description option, 87
Existing Connection option, 87
global variables used heavily, 86
parameter mapping, 89
parameters can be passed in
receive rowsets or single values as output, 86
Properties
Parameter Mapping, 325
SQL statement
valid command for connection, 88
ExecutesSQLTask object
methods and propertes, 704
ExecutesSQLTask2 object
table of extended properties, 705
Extract, Transform and Load
see ETL

F

Facts
data elements associated with an activity, 545
Field object, 747
AppendChunk method, 747
collections, 747
GetChunk method, 747
methods, quick reference, 757
table of properties, 747
Fields collection, 748
Append method, 748
CancelUpdate method, 748

Delete method, 748
methods, quick reference, 757
properties, 748
Refresh method, 748
Resync method, 748
table of methods, 748
Update method, 748
File object, 831
methods and properties, 825
File Transfer Protocol
see FTP and FTP Task.
FileExists method
FileSystemObject object
finding file, 346
Files collection
table of properties, 826
FileSystemObject object, 338
copy, move and rename files, 338
create, 338
create, delete and rename directories, 338
DateLastModified property, 349
delete files, 338
detect existence of file, 338
DTS object model
combining to create new functionality, 352
examine properties of file or directory, 338
extra file properties, 349
file management, 345
FileExists method
finding file, 346
finding file
For . . Next loop, 347
UCASE function, 347
FoldersExists method
managing folders, 343
installed automatically with IIS, IE 4.0 and Enterprise
Manager, 338
managing drives, 339
conditional statements, add, 340
determine size of drive, 339
determines free space, 339
managing folders, 341
check for existence, 341
create a directory, 344
CreateFolder method, 344
deleting directory, 345
Folder exists method, 343
FormatDatetime function, 342
Replace function, 342
moving and copying files, 348
Copy method, 348
mid() function, 348
read text stream from file, 338
reading text, 351
table of methods, 826
table of properties, 827
write text stream to file, 338
writing text to a file, 350
WriteLine method, 351
FolderExists method
FileSystemObject object
managing folders, 343
Folder object, 831
methods and properties, 827
Folders collection, 831
table of methods, 828
For . . . . loops example
prompt users until data is correct, 283

For Each . . . Next Loop, 304
format files
  Bulk Insert Task, generates by internal wizard, 83
  can be reused in multiple packages, 84
  create, 83
FormatDatetime function
  FileSystemObject object
    managing folders, 342
FTP Task, 53, 128
  available in SQL Server 2000, 53
  configuring, 129
  FTP files, 129
  tasks that cannot take part in transaction, 163
  UNC paths, 130
    security, 130

G

Geography Dimension transform data task
  extracting dimension information
    Destination, 610
    Source, 609
    Transformations, 610
GetColumnLong() method, 519
GetExecutionErrorInfo method
  FailOnError property, 425
  FailPackageOnError step, 425
  Step object, 452
GetGlobalVariables function, 520
  create empty recordset, 520
    contain name/value pairs of all global variables in DTS
      package, 520
  LoadFromSQLServer method
    DTS Package object, 520
GetPackageList function, 517
  check for job status, 518
  check job history, 519
  create empty recordset, 517
  LastRunOutcome, 519
  querying package list table, 518
  QueryResults
    GetColumnLong() method, 519
  SQL Server
    ADO connnect with, 518
    SQL-DMO, connnect with, 518
GetScript function, 521
  ActiveXscript, builds, 521
    execute package, 521
GetSomeResult function
  ActiveX Scripting Task
    Script Debugger, 358
GetUIInfo method
  CustomTaskUI interface, 442
Global Variable object
  table of properties, 705
Global Variables collection
  methods and properties, 705 - 706
Grains
  level at which fact records are stored, 484
GROUP BY clause
  Query statement, 29

H

Help method
  CustomTaskUI interface, 442
heterogeneous data
  converting, 235
    DTS, 235
    Upsize Wizards for Access, 235
  distributed queries, 208
  handling foreign and primary keys, 258
    SQL Server diagram, 258
  legacy, largely flat database systems, 207
  merging of databases considered, 208
    DBMS, 208
  migrating Access data using DTS, 236
  pre-conversion checklist, 235
    feasibility, 236
    lessons learned, 236
    planning, 236
    testing, 236
  querying, 207
Host Integration Services, 10
  DB2 databases, converting
    AUTOCOMMMIT package, 255
    bind DB2 packages, 255
    Ole DB Provider, 251
    READ_COMMMITED package, 255
    READ_UNCOMMMITED package, 255
    REPEATABLE_READ package, 255
    SERIALIZABLE package, 255
Hungarian Notation
  variable naming conventions, 819

I

IDTSStdObject object
  no methods or properties, 706
If . . . Else
  current date example, 274
Import/Export Wizard
  see DTS Import/Export Wizard
importing data
  common errors, 201
    date and time conversion, 201
    target table has Identity, 203
  data from Excel, 202
    source fields being wrong data type, 202
    source fields NULL when destination field is not set to
      NULL, 202
  error handling, 203
incremental processing, 499
indentation of code, 820
Initialize method
  CustomTaskUI interface, 442

L

Library application (COM+)
  definition, 525
linked server options
  collation compatible option, 219, 220
    lazy schema validation option, 220
    set in T-SQL, 220
  command and connection timeout settings option,
    219
  data access option, 219
    distributed queries, 219
  Enterprise Manager
    setting options in, 221
  remote procedure calls, 220
    option, 219
**Linked Server Properties - New Linked Server dialog,
213**
  linked server security
    options, 217
  options, 213
    Catalog, 214
    Data source, 213
    Linked server, 213
    Location, 214
    Product name, 213
    Provider name, 213
    Provider string, 214
linked server security, 216
  Enterprise Manager, 217
linked servers, 207
  adding, 212
    Enterprise Manager, 212
  creating, 212
    on single server, 216
    Transact-SQL, 214
      syntax, 214
  deleting, 232
  distributed queries, 208
  establish connection dynamically, 231
    OPENROWSET command, 231
  limitations, 233
  ODBC, use, 208
  purge records from, 210
  querying, 221
    executing a stored procedure, 222
    four-part qualifier, 221
      collation compatible, 222
    join queries from two different servers, 222
  similar to linked tables in Access, 208
  Transform Data Task, 211
  viewing servers and tables, 223
LoadFromRepository method
  ActiveX Scripting Task
    open a package in a package, 353
LoadFromSQLServer method
  ActiveX Scripting Task
    open a package in a package, 353
  DTS Package object, 520
LoadFromStorageFile method
  ActiveX Scripting Task
    open a package in a package, 353
Logical Operators
  see also Bitwise Operators.
  Operator Precedence, 767
Lookup
  see also DTS Lookup

Lookup object
  table of properties, 706
Lookups collection
  methods and properties, 707
looping, 282
  Do loops example, 282
  For . . . . loops example
    prompt users until data is correct, 283
  more useful loops, 284
  scan variable looking for file name example, 284
    For . . . Next loop, 285
    Mid function, 285
    Right function, 286

M

Main() function
  ActiveX Scripting Task
    Script Debugger, 359
Math Functions, 770
MaxConcurrentSteps property
  setting, 171
Measures
  numeric portion of fact, 545
media set
  folder containing one or more files, 388
Message Queue Task, 54, 145
  add to another package, 148
  available in SQL Server 2000, 54
  can join package transaction if right connections are
    made, 163
  does not install by default, 146
  Dynamic Properties Task
    On Success precedence constraint, 149
  installing, 146
  previously MSMQ, 145
  private queues, 146
  public queues, 146
  receiving messages, 148
  uses, 146
Meta Data Services, 375
  see also Repository.
  auditing, 376
  DTS package, saving, 65
  list of options that can be configured, 377
  meta data has context, 375
  meta data is abstract, 375
  need correct permissions to msdb, 376
  scanning options, 158
  scanning package, 377
  view attributes for given column, 378
  Windows Authentication, 380
Method calls Quick Reference
  Dictionary object, 831
  FileSystemObject object, 831
  Folder object, 831
  Folders collection, 831
  TextStream object, 831
Microsoft Message Queue
  see MSMQ.
Microsoft Transaction Server
  see MTS.
mid() function
  FileSystemObject object
    moving and copying files, 348

Miscellaneous Functions, Statements and Keywords
Visual Basic functions and keywords, 805
msdb database
backing up, 383
Enterprise Manager, 384
locking down, 368
MTS
Component Services, now called, 505
merged into operating system, 505
Multiphase Data Pump
DTS Designer User Interface
enabling, 104
not exposed to by default, 104
On Batch Complete Phase, 103
On Pump Complete Phase, 103
Post Row Transform Phase, 103
Post Source Data Phase, 103
Pre Source Phase, 102
Row Transform Phase, 103
Multiphase Data Pump examples, 105
Batch Complete Phase
test, 109
data source connections, configure, 105
On Batch Complete Phase example, 118
On Pump Complete Phase example, 119
Post Row Transform Phase example, 116
Post Source Data Phase example, 118
Pre source data Phase, 110
ActiveX Script, 110
PreSourceMain function example, 113
Row Transform Phase example, 115
Transform Data Task
add, 106
configure, 106
transformation logic, 107

N

naming and executing the package example, 26
DTS Import/Export Wizard, 26
add meaningful description, 27
New method
CustomTaskUI interface, 442
Steps collection, 306
Northwind Data Mart Error Handler Package, 597
illustration, 597
Northwind dimensional data model, 545
Northwind ETL Auditing Data Model
AUDIT_JOB table
job table for auditing, 569
AUDIT_TASK table
create, 570
foreign key restraints, 570
diagram, 568
supports auditing and logging requirements for data
mart, 568
Northwind example, 544
Analysis Services
configure data source property of new database, 577
integrating, 674
requirements for example, 575
restore database, 576
Analysis Services Database
verifying business requirements, 677
Audit Database, connection, 598

auditing and error handling, ETL 2, 625
illustration, 625
create data marts with two subject areas, 544
creating the data warehouse
Northwind_DW, 548
data mart plan, 544
Dynamic Properties Task
Set Connection Values, 585
Error Handler custom task
global variables, add, 597
error handler task configuration
On Failure Precedent, create, 596
ETL Step 1
global variables, table, 580
ETL Step 3 tasks, 626
ETL Step 4, 651
ETL workflow
add new connections, 584
audit information, 586
auditing/error handling, 589
design, 578
error handler custom task, 593
create, 593
error handler task configuration, 596
ETL 2 tasks, 601
executing lower tier packages, 599
Master Workflow Package ETL 1, 579
three lower tiered packages, ETL 1, 2 & 3, 579
UDL connection files, 582
Write Job Completion Info, 599
extracting dimension information, 608
Geography Dimension transform data task
add, 608
extracting fact information, 618
must be date stamped, 618
Geography Dimension transform data task
extracting dimension information
configure, 609
Master Workflow Package
illustration, 580
tasks, 579
Northwind Data Mart Error Handler Package, 597
Order Items dimensional model, 547
Orders dimensional model, 545
populating default values, 571
Calandar dimension, 571, 572
populating with valid date data, 572
each dimension should include Invalid record, 573
static dimensions, 571
Time dimension, 571
set connection values, 623
Source OLTP System connection
create, 584
Northwind OLTP database
diagram, 543
supports orders, order items, products etc, 542
Northwind Staging Area Data Model, 561
DDL creates Orders and Order Items staging areas,
562
diagram, 561
STAGE_CUSTOMER table, 562
supports loading of Customer dimension, 562
STAGE_EMPLOYEE table
supports loading of Employee dimension, 563
STAGE_GEOGRAPHY table
supports loading of Geography dimension, 564
STAGE_ORDER_ITEMS table
supports loading of Order Items fact table, 564

Northwind Staging Area Data Model (continued)
STAGE_ORDERS table
supports loading of Orders fact table, 565
STAGE_PRODUCT table
supports loading of Product dimension, 566
STAGE_SHIPPER table
supports loading of Shipper dimension, 567
STAGE_SUPPLIER table
supports loading of Supplier dimension, 567
Northwind_DW
creating the data warehouse, 548
DDL
relational tables, create, 549
DIM_CALENDAR table, 549
DIM_CUSTOMER table, 550
load, 573
DIM_EMPLOYEE table, 551
load, 574
DIM_GEOGRAPHY table, 552
load, 573
DIM_PRODUCT table, 553
load, 575
DIM_SHIPPER table
create, 553
load, 574
DIM_SUPPLIER table, 554
load, 574
FACT_ORDER_ITEMS
fact table for Order Items subject area, 555
FACT_ORDERS
fact table for Orders subject area, 557
foreign key restraints, 558
Northwinds Analysis Services Database
Analysis Server, 678
answering analytical questions, 677
Northwinds most profitable customers, 681
which regions are selling most products, 681
Excel 2000 Pivot Table Service, 677
dimensions and measures, 680
External Data Source
OLAP Cubes, 677
Orders Cube
defined, 675
Orders Item Cube
defined, 676
shared dimensions, 674
NT Authentication Security, 43

O

ObjectControl interface
Object Pooling, 515
objects, description of, 299
events, 299
methods, 299
properties, 299
ODBC
connect using RDO, 9
OLE DB Provider, 9
communicates with systems not converted to OLE DB, 10
OLAP, 9
generalization describing data warehousing, 480
OLTP
compared to, 480
slicing, drill-up and drill-downs, 482
snapshots of production data
can represent historical data, 480
typical systems must scan large portions of data, 480
OLE DB
ADO, communicates with provider
diagram, 10
API, 9
COM APIs, exposes
ADO, communicates with provider, 9
COM applications
communicate with any data storage system, 9
communicate with legacy and relational databases, 7
distributed queries
heterogeneous data, 208
homogeneous databases, 208
extensible, 9
OLAP, 9
portability, 7
select option, 168
services made available via provider, 9
OLE DB providers, single threaded
can cause Access Violations on runtime, 262
OleDBProperties collection
methods and properties, 707
OleDBProperty object
table of properties, 708
OleDBProperty2 object
table of extended properties, 708
OLTP
data represents current values, 480
eliminate redundancies in data
granular or atomic inserts, 480
frequently purged to improve performance, 480
invoicing system example, 480
diagram, 481
modeling using OLAP approach, 481
OLAP
compared to, 480
performance optimizations
updating data and transaction response, 480
transactional in nature, 480
usually represent source systems for data
warehouse, 480
On Batch Complete Phase example, 118
On Error workflow example
Error Handler task
each shares same code as others, 426
Error Logging Package, 428
Successful Task, 426
Task That Will Fail, 426
On Pump Complete Phase example, 119
Online Analytical Processing
see OLAP.
Online Transactional Processing
see OLTP.
Open Database Connectivity
see ODBC.
Operator Precedence, 769
Operators, 761
optimistic concurrency, 167
Order Items dimensional model, 547
entity-relationship diagram, 548
list of dimensions, 547
list of measures, 547
Orders dimensional model
entity-relationship diagram, 546
list of dimensions, 545
list of measures, 546

Orders Items transform data task, 621
extracting fact information
Destination, 622
Source, 621
Transformation, 623
illustration, 621
Orders transform data task, 618
extracting fact information, 618
Destination, 620
Source, 618
Transformation, 620
illustration, 618
owner password, 67, 374
only owners can modify package, 374
packages are encrypted, 374
ownership conflicts
COM components must be on same machine as
package, 373
connections, 373
file paths, 373

P

package error handling, 409
Application Event Log, 409
error file, 409
event log, 410
package list table
populating, 512
Package object
dynamically configure, 295
table of events, 711
table of methods, 708
table of properties, 709
package transaction
commited after
package completes successfully, 165
step completes successfully, 165
diagram, 166
inherited transactions, 165
Execute Package Task, 165
no commit takes place, 166
no new package transaction initiated, 166
no rollback on package completion, 166
step joins inherited parent transaction, 166
join package transaction, 163
steps, 163
rolled back after
package fails, 165
package finishes and Commit check box is cleared,
165
step fails, 165
setting up, 162
tasks that cannot take part in transaction
Copy SQL Server Objects Task, 163
Dynamic Properties Task, 163
FTP Task, 163
Send Mail Task, 163
transaction isolation levels, 166
Package2 object
table extended methods, 711
table of properties, 711
PackageInfo object
table of properties, 712

PackageInfos collection
table of properties, 713
PackageLineage object
table of methods, 713
PackageLineages collection
methods and properties, 714
PackageLog object
table of methods, 714
PackageLogRecords collection
methods and properties, 715
PackageRepository object
methods and properties, 716
PackageSQLServer object
EnumPackageInfos method, 408
EnumPackageLogRecords method, 408
EnumStepLogRecords method, 408
EnumTaskLogRecords method, 408
RemoveAllLogRecords method, 408
RemovePackageLogRecords method, 408
RemoveStepLogRecords method, 408
RemoveTaskLogRecords method, 408
table of methods, 408, 716
table of properties, 717
ParallelDataPumpTask object
methods and properties, 717
Parallelism, 169
concurrency of data flow from source to destination,
169
precedence constraints, 170
Parameter object, 748
AppendChunk method, 748
methods, quick reference, 757
Properties collection, 749
table of properties, 748
Parameters collection, 749
Append method, 749
Delete method, 749
methods, quick reference, 757
Refresh method, 749
table of methods, 749
table of properties, 749
pass-through queries, 230
PersistPropertyBag object
table of methods, 718
pessimistic concurrency, 167
Post Row Transform Phase example
Insert Failure example, 117
Insert Success example, 117
Transform Failure example, 116
Post Source Data Phase example, 118
precedence constraints, 62
completion, 63
failure, 63
success, 63
PrecedenceConstraint object
table of properties, 719
PrecedenceConstraints collection
methods and properties, 719 - 720
PreSourceMain example
ADO connection to destination server
create, 114
DELETE statement, 114
use global variables to track state of transformation,
114

procedure naming, 820
Product Dimension transform data task, 614
  extracting dimension information
    Destination, 614
    Source, 614
    Transformation, 615
  illustration, 614
programmatic logging, 407
Properties collection, 750
  properties, 750
  methods, quick reference, 758
  Refresh method, 750
  methods and properties, 720
PropertiesProvider object
  table of methods, 720
Property object, 750
  table of properties, 721, 750
PropertyBag object
  table of methods, 721

Q

Query Analyzer
  view all of packages execution information, 405
Query Builder example
  DTS Import/Export Wizard, 29
    GROUP BY clause, 29
    translating foreign keys into their real data, 29
    WHERE clause, 30
Queued Components, 505

R

Record object, 750
  Cancel method, 750
  Close method, 750
  CopyRecord method, 750
  DeleteRecord method, 750
  GetChildren method, 750
  methods, quick reference, 758
  MoveRecord method, 750
  Open method, 750
  table of collections, 751
  table of methods, 750
  table of properties, 751
Recordset object, 751
  AddNew method, 751
  Cancel method, 751
  CancelBatch method, 751
  CancelUpdate method, 751
  Clone method, 751
  Close method, 751
  CompareBookmarks method, 752
  Delete method, 752
  Find method, 752
  GetRows method, 752
  GetString method, 752
  methods, quick reference, 758
  Move method, 752
  MoveFirst method, 752
  MoveLast method, 752
  MoveNext method, 752
  MovePrevious method, 752

NextRecordset method, 752
Open method, 752
Resync method, 752
Requery method, 752
Save method, 752
Seek method, 752
Supports method, 752
table of collections, 754
table of events, 755
table of methods, 751
table of properties, 753
Update method, 752
UpdateBatch method, 752
Remote Data Objects
  see RDO.
remote servers, 209
  SQL Server
    replication, 209
RemoveAllLogRecords method
  PackageSQLServer object, 408
RemovePackageLogRecords method
  PackageSQLServer object, 408
RemoveStepLogRecords method
  PackageSQLServer object, 408
RemoveTaskLogRecords method
  PackageSQLServer object, 408
Replace function
  FileSystemObject object
    managing folders, 342
Repository
  see Meta Data Services
Row Transform Phase
  Data Cleansing and Data Awareness, 102
  six functionally different phases, 102
  Source Data to Destination Data column, 115
  Transformation Extensibility, 102
  Transformation Restartability, 102
    ISNULL() function, 116
RunPackageAsync method, 515
  ActiveScripting job, create, 516
  checks for job name, 515
    looks for match on server, 516
  checks recordset is valid, 515
  close connection, 517
  creates job on SQL Server, 515
  execute package, 516
  SQL-DMO, uses, 515
    connects to server and interacts with Jobs collection, 515

S

SavedPackageInfo object
  table of properties, 721
SavedPackageInfos collection
  methods and properties, 722
saving and scheduling the package example, 24
  DTS Import/Export Wizard, 24
    advanced options, 25
  DTSRUN utility, 25
  replicate to other sources, 25
  transforming data, 25
Scanning Options dialog, 159
scheduled package security, 371
  SQL Server Agent, dtsrun, 371

schema validation option
only available in T-SQL, 220
Script Debugger
Call Stack, 359
check and change contents of my variables, 359
DisplayResult function, 358
GetSomeResult function, 358
JIT debugging for DTS, 356
Main() function, 359
stop statement, 356
toolbar buttons, table, 357
Visual InterDev debugger, and
table of important keys, 362
Scripting error handling, 411
data pump constants
control script execution, 419
table, 419
DTS workflow scripts, 414
DTSStepScriptResult constants, 412
DTSTaskExecResult constants, 416
DTSTransformStatus constants, 417
initialize global variables, 416
table of status and result constants for packages,
tasks and steps, 411
Scripting Runtime Reference
Constants
CompareMethod, 829
DriveTypeConst, 830
FileAttribute, 830
IOMode, 830
SpecialFolderConst, 831
Tristate, 831
Dictionary object, 824
Drive object, 824
Drives collection, 825
File object, 825
Files collection, 826
FileSystemObject object, 826 - 827
Folder object, 828
Folders collection, 828
Method calls Quick Reference, 831
Table of Objects, 823
TextStream object, 829
ScriptingLanguageInfo object
table of properties, 722
ScriptingLanguageInfos collection
methods and properties, 723
security
see also SQL Server security, scheduled package
security and DTS security, DTS password protection
and Transact-SQL
custom tasks, 433
dependant on where the package is saved, 367
DTS password protection, 373 - 375
DTS security, 367 - 373
linked server security, 217
NT Authentication, 43
owner password, 67
msdb database, locking down, 368
SQL Server security, 368 - 370
SQL Server Authentication, 369
Transact-SQL, 227
user password, 67
SELECT statement
sysdtsstep log table
view step information, 405

Send Email package example
Active Script task
CDONTS, 511
Send Mail Task, 51, 92, 324
Add/Edit Assignment dialog, 328
alter properties, 322, 327
available in SQL Server 2000, 51
configuring done by MAPI client, 92
Dynamic Properties, 324
ExecutionStatus setting, 333
Global Variables, create, 325
one Dynamic Task sets the other Dynamic Task as
completed, 331
set to fail, 330
set to success, 327
tasks that cannot take part in transaction, 163
testing, 329
SendMailTask object, 303
methods and properties, 724
Server application, (COM+)
definition, 525
Shipper Dimension transform data task, 617
extracting dimension information
Destination, 617
Source, 617
Transformation, 617
illustration, 617
ShowPackages method
CheckErrors method, 532
slowly changing dimensions
options, 492
snowflake schemas
see also dimensional modelling
diagram, 478
specifying items and executing the package example
Copy Database Wizard (CDW), 38
specify when package should be executed, 39
step details, 39
SQL Distributed Management Objects
see SQL-DMO.
SQL Server
backing up databases, 382
dump file, 382
building package in, 323
DTS package, saving, 65
linked server feature, 208
diagram, 208
recovery models
Bulk logged, 382
full, (default), 382
simple, 382
remote servers
replication, 209
used to access homogeneous data, 209
table of recovery models, 382
SQL Server 2000
advanced tasks, 101
Multiphase Data Pump, 102
SQL Server Agent
DTS package, scheduling, 72, 73
create job manually, 73, 74
advanced tab, 74
Steps tab, 73
SQL Server Agent properties
proxy account configuring, 371

SQL Server Authentication
SQL Server Out-Of-The-Box Security, 369
logins and users, 369
sa rights, 369
SQL Server database
converting DB2 database to, 7
SQL Server license
DTS Designer, 9
Oracle and Access users, 9
SQL Server options, 186
always commit final batch, 188
Check Constraints, 187
Fast Load, 186
logged bulk copy, 186
nonlogged bulk copy, 186
Identity Insert, 187
destination database, 187
Insert batch size, 188
Keep Null values, 187
Table Lock, 187
SQL Server security
Mixed Mode, 368
Windows Authentication and SQL Server Authentication, 368
msdb contains the repository SQL schema, 370
SQL Server Authentication, 369
Windows Authentication Mode, 368
most secure method offered, 368
SQL-DMO
allows automation of
SQL Server administration tasks, repetitive or commonly performed, 504
SQL Server object creation and administration, 504
SQL Server replication installation and configuring, 504
automation of
SQL Server Agent jobs, alerts and operators, creation and administration, 504
stage definition
transformations
row-by-row, 492
set-based processing, 493
Staging Area design, 490
considerations, 490
create on separate machine fromsource OLTP system, 490
drop indexes before loading, 491
stage definition
extraction, 491
transformation, 492
using file groups in staging, 491
star schemas
see also dimensional modelling
center table is usually fact table, 477
diagram, 477
dimensions include art least one hierarchy with several levels, 478
measures, 477
smaller tables are dimensions, 477
star/snowflake schemas
hybrid designs
diagram, 480
Step object
GetExecutionErrorInfo method, 452
methods and properties, 725

Step2 object
table of extended properties, 726
StepLineage object
table of properties, 726
StepLineages collection
methods and properties, 727
StepLogRecord object
table of properties, 728
StepLogRecords collection
methods and properties, 728
Steps collection
New method, 306
methods and properties, 729
stored procedures versus DTS Tasks
ETL process
performance, 496
reusability, 496
suitability, 496
Stream object, 755
Cancel method, 755
ClopyTo method, 755
Close method, 755
Flush method, 755
LoadFromFile method, 755
methods, 759
Open method, 755
Read method, 755
ReadText method, 755
SaveToFile method, 755
SetEOS method, 755
SkipLine method, 756
table of methods, 755
table of properties, 756
Write method, 756
WriteText method, 756
String Constants, 800
String Functions and Statements, 785
Supplier Dimension transform data task, 615
extracting dimension information
Destination, 616
Source, 616
Transformation, 616
illustration, 615
surrogate keys
insulate changes in source system keys from warehouse, 485
replace natural keys as primary keys of dimensions, 485
sysdtspackagelog
table of information available, 406
sysdtsstep log table
SELECT statement
view step information, 405
sysdtssteplog
table of information available, 406

T

Task object
error handling, 410
methods and properties, 729 - 730
Tasks collection
methods and properties, 730
TextStream object, 831
methods and properties, 829
transaction isolation levels
balance between concurrency and data integrity, 167
Chaos, 168
concurrency, 167
dirty read, 167
DTS Package Properties Advanced tab
setting, 167
level at which inconsistent data is accepted by
transaction, 167
nonrepeatable read, 167
optimistic concurrency, 167
pessimistic concurrency, 167
phantom, 167
Read Committed, 168
Read Uncommitted, 168
Repeatable Read, 168
Serializable, 168
transactions
ACID properties, 161
atomic unit that succeeds or fails as whole, 161
rollback, 161
supported connection types
Data Link, 164
ODBC data source, 164
OLE DB Provider for SQL Server, 164
Transact-SQL
backup of entire database
syntax, 388
gathering metadata, 224
sp_linkedservers stored procedure, 225
gathering remote column information, 226
parameters, 226
sp_columns_ex, 226
gathering remote database information, 225
gathering remote key and index information, 228
foreign keys, 228
indexes, 229
sp_indexes stored procedures, 229
primary keys, 228
gathering remote security information
sp_table_priveleges_ex, 227
gathering remote table information, 225
sp_tables_ex stored procedure, 225
linked server
provider name is important and required, 214
table of mappping between data source and provider
name, 214
linked server security, 218
stored procedures, 218
media set password and backup password, set
syntax, 389
set password on media set or backup itself, 388
Transfer Databases Task, 53, 94
available in SQL Server 2000, 53

Transfer Error Messages Task, 52, 93
available in SQL Server 2000, 52, 53
used in Copy Database Wizard, 93
Transfer Jobs Task, 53, 95
available in SQL Server 2000, 53
Transfer Logins Task, 53, 95
available in SQL Server 2000, 53
Transfer Manager, 8
functionality carried over into SQL Server 2000, 16
Transfer Master Stored Procedures Task, 53, 94
TransferObjectsTask object
methods and properties, 731
TransferObjectsTask2 object
table of extended properties, 732
transferring data example
DTS Import/Export Wizard, 16
transferring SQL objects example, 32
DTS Import/Export Wizard, 32
Select objects, 34
Transform Data Task, 50, 102
see also Data Pump Task
available in SQL Server 2000, 50
can join package transaction if right connections are
made, 163
Data Movement options, 174
Exception file can be specified, 174
move and transform data from one source to another,
173
options, 173
Row Transform Phase, 102
SQL Server options, 174
Transform Status Constants
state of transform phase, 115
table of constants and descriptions, 115
Transformation object
table of properties, 733
Transformation2 object
table of extended properties, 734
TransformationInfo object
table of properties, 734
TransformationInfos collection
methods ands properties, 735
transformations
set-based processing, 493
dimensions, 493
facts, 494
set-based processing/row-by-row
comparison, table, 495
mix and match, 495
slowly changing dimensions
options, 492
Transformations collection
methods and properties, 735 - 736
TransformationSet object
table of properties, 736
TransformationSets collection
methods and properties, 737 - 738
transforming data, 8
troubleshooting, 538

U

UCASE function
FileSystemObject object
finding file, 347
user password, 67, 375
can execute but not view packages in DTS Designer, 375
User services layer, 529
ASP
supplys information to new version of itself with QueryString, 529
uses recursive method, 529
QueryString
list of parameter names and values passed from one ASP to another via URL, 529
requirements for displaying packages
ASP, 529
using queries to transfer data example
DTS Import/Export Wizard, 27
Query Builder, 27
Parse and Browser options, 28

V

variable naming conventions, 819
Hungarian notation, 819
VBScript
commenting, 271
entry functions, 289
functions, 271, 287
compartmentalizes code, 287
global variables, 290
passing variables in and out of functions, 290
by reference and by value, 292
raise simple dialog box
syntax, 271
reserved words, 271
subprocedures, 288
does not return value, 288
table of data types, conversion functions and test functions, 281
variable scope
procedure-level variables, 290
script-level variables, 289
variables, 270
declaring, 270
initialize, 270
variants, 280
variants
changes automatically based on value stored, 280
version control
DTS package, 67
viewing DTS packages example
DTS Designer, 42
Virtual Cubes, 484
Visual Basic File
DTS package, saving, 65

Visual Basic functions and keywords
Arithmetic Operators, 762
Array Functions and Statements, 782
Assignment Operator, 762
Bitwise Operators, 768
Comparison Operators, 765
Concatenation Operators, 764
Conversion Functions, 801
Date and Time Functions and Statements, 773
Logical Operators, 767
Math Functions, 770
Miscellaneous Functions, Statements and Keywords, 805
Operator Precedence, 769
Operators, 761
String Constants, 800
String Functions and Statements, 785
Visual Basic project, 311
Auto list Members
defining variables, 315
list all options, 316
coding, 315
create new step, 318
create package, 317
creating, 312
name project and form, 313
References
DTSPackage Object Library, 314
retrieving memory
set variables to nothing, 319
save to SQL Server, 319
SendMailTask, create, 318
Step and Task objects inserted into package, 318
Visual InterDev debugger, 361
Locals Window, 363
requires more system resources than Script Debugger, 364
Run to Cursor, 363
Script Debugger
similar to, 362
Watch Window, 364
Visual InterDev debugger/Script Debugger
table of important keys, 362

W

warehouse data load example, 541
WHERE clause
DTS Import/Export Wizard, 30
Windows Authentication Mode
most secure method offered, 368
Workflow Properties dialog
MaxConcurrentSteps property
setting, 171
precedence constraints
add, modify or remove, 170
Workflow Scripts
see DTS Workflow Scripts
WriteLine method
FileSystemObject object
writing text to a file, 351

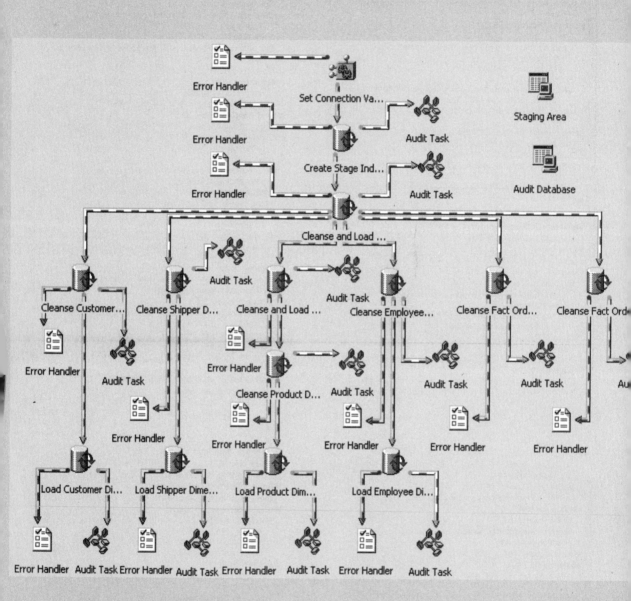